P9-ECM-750

DISCARDED

STAR GODS OF THE MAYA

THE LINDA SCHELE SERIES IN MAYA AND PRE-COLUMBIAN STUDIES

This series was made possible through the generosity of the National Endowment for the Humanities and the following donors:

Elliot M. Abrams and AnnCorinne Freter
Anthony Alofsin
Joseph W. Ball and Jennifer T. Taschek
William A. Bartlett
Elizabeth P. Benson
Boeing Gift Matching Program
William W. Bottorff
Victoria Bricker
Robert S. Carlsen
Frank N. Carroll
Roger J. Cooper
Susan Glenn
John F. Harris
Peter D. Harrison
Joan A. Holladay
Marianne J. Huber
Jānis Indrikis
The Institute for Mesoamerican Studies
Anna Lee Kahn
Rex and Daniela Koontz
Christopher and Sally Lutz

Judith M. Maxwell
Joseph Orr
The Patterson Foundation
John M. D. Pohl
Mary Anna Prentice
Philip Ray
Louise L. Saxon
David M. and Linda R. Schele
Richard Shiff
Ralph E. Smith
Barbara L. Stark
Penny J. Steinbach
Carolyn Tate
Barbara and Dennis Tedlock
Nancy Troike
Donald W. Tuff
Javier Urcid
Barbara Voorhies
E. Michael Whittington
Sally F. Wiseley, M.D.
Judson Wood, Jr.

STAR GODS
OF THE MAYA

Astronomy in Art, Folklore,
and Calendars

Susan Milbrath

University of Texas Press
Austin

Copyright © 1999 by the University of Texas Press
All rights reserved
Printed in the United States of America

First edition, 1999

Requests for permission to reproduce material from this work should be sent to
Permissions, University of Texas Press, Box 7819, Austin, TX 78713-7819.

⊚ The paper used in this publication meets the minimum requirements of American
National Standard for Information Sciences—Permanence of Paper for Printed Library
Materials, ANSI Z39.48-1984.

Library of Congress Cataloging-in-Publication Data

Milbrath, Susan.
    Star gods of the Maya : astronomy in art, folklore, and calendars / Susan Milbrath. — 1st ed.
        p.   cm. — (The Linda Schele series in Maya and pre-Columbian studies)
    Includes bibliographical references.
    ISBN 0-292-75225-3 (hardcover : alk. paper)
    ISBN 0-292-75226-1 (pbk. : alk. paper)
    1. Maya astronomy.   2. Mayas—Religion.   3. Maya calendar.   I. Title.   II. Series.
F1435.3C14   M55   1999
520′.972—ddc21
                                                                    99-6136

TO MY PARENTS, MARIANO, AND MARK

CONTENTS

4. PRECOLUMBIAN AND COLONIAL PERIOD LUNAR IMAGES AND DEITIES 105

5. VENUS AND MERCURY: THE BODY DOUBLES 157

STAR GODS OF THE MAYA

INTRODUCTION

Astronomy in ancient Mesoamerica was not an abstract science; indeed, it was an integral part of daily life, and so it remains today in the more traditional Maya communities. In Precolumbian times, astronomy played a central role in calendars and religious imagery. Art images and companion texts provide keys to understanding the thought processes of the ancient Maya. Rather than focusing on scientific accuracy, many of the best documented astronomical images seem primarily concerned with divination. Maya astronomy is really astrology (Thompson 1972:77), but not in the sense of personal horoscopes. The astrological texts in the codices often deal with cycles of illness, the fate of crops, and weather. We may dismiss them as fanciful, but there is a similar folk tradition in our *Old Farmer's Almanac.*

People today often cannot appreciate why astronomy played such an important role in ancient civilizations. For many of us, supplying our own food means cashing a paycheck and going to the grocery store. Our indoor environments insulate us from the more profound effects of the seasonal cycle. Our calendars tell us when the seasons will change, and we feel no need to watch the sun and stars as they follow their seasonal course. Indeed, it is often difficult to see the night sky. Light pollution follows electricity, dimming the spectacular beauty of the stars.

Astronomical gods form the core of the Precolumbian Maya pantheon. In the past, some Mayanists have suggested that the Maya did not worship gods; rather they believed in spiritual forces. Karl Taube (1992b:7–8) refutes this position in his study of the Maya pantheon. Stephen Houston and David Stuart (1996:295) point out that Classic period Maya rulers claimed divine status by using the names of gods as their personal names. And Patricia McAnany (1995a) shows that posthumous royal portraits depict rulers merged with gods.

As the most highly developed ancient civilization in all of the Americas, the Maya had a sophisticated astronomy that was integrated with their religion. Like the ancient Greeks, Romans, Hindus, Chinese, Mesopotamians, and Egyptians, the Maya believed that the celestial luminaries were gods who influenced human destiny and controlled events on earth. Whether Maya artworks show rulers dressed up as gods or the gods themselves is sometimes debatable, but there is no question that the star gods were invoked in Maya art for more than a thousand years. Precolumbian art, calendric cycles, and modern folklore can be integrated to tell the story of Maya astronomy, placing the Maya in their proper position as one of the great civilizations of antiquity.

The Maya live in an area bounded by the Yucatán Peninsula to the north, the state of Chiapas to the west, and the area bordering El Salvador and Honduras to the southeast (Pl. 1). Numerous Maya language groups exist today, as in times past. Yucatec, the dominant Maya language in Mexico, is spoken in the Yucatán Peninsula. The Kekchí language is found over the largest geographic area in Guatemala, but there are actually more Quiché speakers. (For an overview of the Maya, see Michael Coe's *The Maya* and Robert Sharer's *The Ancient Maya,* which both provide details about contemporary language groups, the calendar, and the geographic and chronological range of the Precolumbian Maya.)

The Maya live in the greater Mesoamerican area, a large geographical region with its northern limit at the tropic of Cancer (23½°N latitude) in central Mexico and its southern limit in western El Salvador (14°N latitude). Because the 260-day calendar was once found throughout the Mesoamerican area, there are many cognitive parallels between the Maya and other areas of Mesoamerica, especially central Mexico. The central Mexican area, where Náhuatl, Otomí, and Totonac are spoken, spans the Central Highlands and the mountains to the east, as well as the adjoining coastal plain, and has its southern limits in the Balsas Basin (Carrasco 1969). The most prominent Precolumbian cultures in central Mexico are those of the Valley of Mexico, especially Classic period Teotihuacán and the Late Postclassic Mexica, the political group that dominated Aztec society at the time of the European conquest in 1521. The southeastern section of central Mexico, the Puebla-Tlaxcala area, seems to be the site of contact with the Maya during the Classic period. This region also produced one of the greatest masterpieces of Postclassic art, the Codex Borgia, which records a core of ideas from central Mexico that may have influenced Postclassic Maya cultures to the east.

THE MESOAMERICAN CALENDAR

In Precolumbian times, the Mesoamerican area shared a 260-day calendar that was based on a repeating cycle of 260 days. The origins of the 260-day calendar can be traced back to circa 900–500 B.C.

The 260-day calendar was used to prognosticate human destiny according to the day of birth and to predict the appropriate days for the planting cycle. This ritual calendar survives today among the Quiché of Guatemala, and the daykeepers still use the calendar to prognosticate future events (Tedlock 1992b). They explain that the calendar corresponds to the human gestation period of nine lunar months (Earle and Snow 1985). In fact, the interval is very close to the length of the human gestation period, which biologists estimate to be between 255 and 266 days (Aveni 1992b:79). The 260-day period also approximates the length of the agricultural calendar in core areas of Mesoamerica (Chapter 1). Indeed, it is possible that the 260-day agricultural cycle and the cycle of human gestation were linked together at an earlier time, and that the two cycles were used to develop the unique 260-day calendar.

Over time, Mesoamerican cultures incorporated other natural cycles in the 260-day calendar. Daniel Flores (1989) notes that the 260-day calendar is well suited to recording observations of Venus. Indeed, the people of Precolumbian Mesoamerica observed both Venus and the Moon in relation to the 260-day calendar (Aveni 1992a). The cycles of Mars and other planets were also important in this calendar, because the 260-day period holds the key to correlating a number of different planetary cycles (Justeson 1989: 82). Around 1650, Jacinto de la Serna described the 260-day calendar of the Aztec as the "count of the planets," apparently referring to the seven classical planets, among which we find the Sun, the Moon, and Venus (Aveni 1991:310). Unfortunately, we do not have such direct references to astronomy in historical descriptions of the Maya 260-day calendar. Indeed, we do not even know the real name of this calendar. Although it is usually referred to as the Tzolkin (count of days), this term may be more properly applied to the almanacs used for prognostications (Justeson 1989:76).

Like other people of Mesoamerica, the Maya had a 52-year calendar called the Calendar Round. The Calendar Round was formed by an interlocking cycle of the 260-day ritual calendar and a 365-day year (the "vague" year), divided into 18 "months" of

20 days each, plus an added five-day period. The vague year only approximates the true length of the solar year (365.2422 days). The interlocking cycle of the Calendar Round repeats in the same sequence every 52 years, because the least common multiple of 260 and 365 is 18,980 days, or 52 vague years. Both forms of calendar were present by around 500 B.C. in Oaxaca and probably also appeared relatively early among the Maya, although actual documentation exists only as early as 100 B.C. (Justeson 1989:78–79). The Calendar Round may have survived into modern times, judging from a contemporary Chol term (solq'uin) that refers to a cycle of 52 years related to the sun (Aulie and Aulie 1978:106). No Mayan word for the Calendar Round is known, although Munro Edmonson (1988:14) suggests that the Precolumbian Mayan name for the Calendar Round is hunab.

Mayanists tend to follow the convention of using Haab for the 365-day vague solar year and Tun for the 360-day civil year of the Long Count, but John Justeson (1989:77) cautions that the Tun in lowland Maya probably refers to the end of a year of either 360 or 365 days. The Maya 360-day Tun was an integral part of the Long Count, a method of recording dates that allows dates to be precisely fixed in time from a starting point around 3000 B.C. Although records of contemporaneous Long Count dates begin around A.D. 250 in the lowland Maya area, the Classic Maya clearly had a sense of mythological history, for some Long Count dates on stone stelae of the Classic period refer back to events preceding the recorded epoch of the creation around 3000 B.C.

The oldest known Long Count inscription, dating to 31 B.C. at Tres Zapotes in Veracruz, is actually found outside the Maya lowlands. It belongs to the Late Preclassic period (400 B.C.–A.D. 100), when the Olmec civilization of the heartland in Veracruz and Tabasco was in decline (Milbrath 1979). At this time, early Maya centers began to flourish. On the Pacific Slope of Guatemala, dates as old as the 7th Baktun (Cycle 7) are known from Abaj Takalik and from El Baúl, where Stela 1 bears a date of 7.19.15.7.12 correlating with A.D. 36 (Graham et al. 1978; Sharer

1994:102). Elaborate glyphic writing developed beyond the Maya area during the Protoclassic period (A.D. 100–250), as seen on the La Mojarra Stela from Veracruz, which bears Mixe-Zoquean writing and Long Count dates of A.D. 143 and 156 (Justeson and Kaufman 1993; Sharer 1994, fig. 3.6).

Despite the early examples of glyphic writing outside the Maya area, the Long Count calendar saw its greatest development in the Maya lowlands, where more and more interlocking cycles were added to the calendar over time. Traditionally, the Classic Maya period (circa A.D. 250–900) is defined as the time when Long Count inscriptions were recorded in monumental art in the Maya lowlands. By around A.D. 350, the Long Count inscriptions were accompanied by lunar data of the Lunar Series (Chapter 4). Somewhat later other cycles such as the seven-day cycle and the nine-day cycle were added.

The Long Count inscriptions are invaluable in studying the chronology of sculptures, and the patterning of dates has led to major breakthroughs in our understanding of historical events (Proskouriakoff 1993). Prior to the 1960s it was believed that many of the dates had a calendric function related primarily to astronomical cycles and to a general fascination with recording long cycles of time. The historical perspective has revolutionized our understanding of the Classic Maya. Nevertheless, scholars recognize that astronomy remains important in the inscriptions, for Maya rulers were fascinated by astrology. As in the Old World, astrologer-priests correlated events in the lives of rulers with celestial events (Chapters 5 and 6).

Classic Maya Calendar Round dates apparently involve no intercalation, and they are so closely keyed to the associated Long Count inscriptions that scholars feel confident in reconstructing Long Count dates in inscriptions that include only Calendar Round dates. Such reconstructed Long Count dates are usually determined by linking the Calendar Round dates to the reign of a specific ruler. This would seem to be fairly clear-cut; any monument referring to the ruler must be dated to the 52-year Calendar Round that falls during the ruler's lifetime. But the situation becomes more uncertain if his death date is not secure, or if his life spanned more than one Calendar Round, as in the case of Pacal II of Palenque and Shield Jaguar I of Yaxchilán. Thus a certain amount of caution must be exercised when using dates derived from Calendar Round inscriptions.

Although the Maya Long Count dates indicate that there was no intercalation to keep the 365-day calendar in accord with the seasonal events during the Classic period, there does seem to be an interest in the seasonal round, for a number of scholars have detected sets of Calendar Round dates that focus on specific solar events (Chapter 3). Furthermore, the Long Count seems to be keyed to an "end" date (13.0.0.0.0 4 Ahau 3 Kankin) on the winter solstice, December 21, 2012 A.D., when the "odometer" turns over and a new cycle begins (Edmonson 1988:119).

The Long Count records dates that involve sets of days: the most basic unit being individual days (Kins), followed by 20-day periods (Uinals), 360-day periods (Tuns), Katuns (20 × 360 days), and Baktuns (20 × 20 × 360 days), a single Baktun referring to a period less than 400 years (400 years minus 2100 days [20 × 20 × 5.25 days]). Some inscriptions are to be read in simple vertical columns from top to bottom (Pl. 2); others are written in two columns to be read from left to right before moving down a row. Occasionally, inscriptions are read from left to right across horizontal rows, or more rarely from right to left in a form of "mirror writing." Usually the type of reading order can be deduced from the calendar dates.

When Long Count dates appear with an introducing element at the beginning of a text, they are known as Initial Series dates (Pl. 2). On monuments with multiple dates, the first date is usually an Initial Series inscription. Such monuments usually include a dedicatory date, often coinciding with a Katun ending or subdivision of the Katun (Satterthwaite 1965:617). With the initial dedicatory date written out in full, fixed as a "base date," the Maya used distance numbers to count forward and backward to other dates, often given as Calendar Round dates. The distance numbers formerly were thought to be the product of a calendar correction formula more accurate than our leap years (the determinant theory), but these numbers are now known to be intervals

that can be distinguished from dates by the fact that they are given in ascending order beginning with the Kins (Sharer 1994:570–571).

Most often the Classic Maya wrote dates in paired vertical columns, beginning with the Baktuns on the top, but scholars transcribe the dates horizontally with the Baktuns on the far left. A date such as 9.9.0.0.0 marks the end of a Katun, meaning all the smaller periods have flipped over on the chronological odometer so that 9 full Katuns of 20 × 360 days have been completed. This is called a period-ending date. With 9 Baktuns and 9 Katuns completed, the date corresponds to the beginning of the Late Classic Maya period (A.D. 600–800), or more precisely, to May 7, 613, in the Julian calendar (O.S. [Old Style]), or May 10, 613, in the Gregorian calendar (N.S. [New Style]) adopted by Pope Gregory in 1582 to correct for a slow slippage in the Julian calendar in use from classical antiquity. All dates given in this book are in the Julian, or O.S., calendar unless otherwise noted.

To better understand the format of the inscriptions, let us look at the Initial Series date on the Leyden Plaque, transcribed as 8.14.3.1.12 1 Eb 0 Yaxkin. It is designated with a vertical column of bar and dot numbers paired with glyphs telling the type of period (Pl. 2). The bars stand for five and the dots for one, with the largest number on the top, here referring to eight Baktuns (8 × 20 × 20 × 360 days), followed in descending order by 14, 3, 1, and 12, each with a zoomorphic glyph representing the associated time period, progressing from Katuns down to Kins or days. There follows the Tzolkin date 1 Eb (a dot with a skeletal jaw) and, three rows from the bottom, the month Yaxkin, with an implied coefficient of 0, here shown as a small torso of a seated figure representing the seating of the month in the annual cycle of 18 months, which were numbered 0 to 19. Using the 584,283 correlation, the date 8.14.3.1.12 1 Eb 0 Yaxkin is equivalent to September 14, A.D. 320 (O.S.), or September 15, 320 (N.S.), the difference between the Julian and Gregorian calendars being minimal nearer to the time the Julian calendar was introduced in Rome in 46 B.C.

The Maya calendar was by no means static, nor was it uniform throughout the lowland Maya area, although there were times during the Classic period when there was a higher degree of uniformity (Justeson 1989:87–88). During Early Classic times (A.D. 250–600), the solar year may have been especially important in calendar rituals, but by the Late Classic period, rituals began to revolve around the Katun cycle, especially at Tikal (Coggins 1980:736–737).

The Long Count coexisted for a time with the Short Count, which appears as early as 9.3.0.0.0 at Caracol (Satterthwaite 1965:626). The Short Count is not anchored to a base point, but repeats over and over, as if we noted our years in an abbreviated fashion, such as '96, without clarifying whether it is 1896 or 1996. The Short Count year was designated by the Tzolkin date on which the Katun ended, and the Katuns always ended on a day named Ahau, because of the mathematical relationship between the 20-day Uinal and the Katun of 7,200 days. Each Katun bears an Ahau date numbered two less than the preceding Katun, thus the Katun 13 Ahau is followed by 11 Ahau, and so on over the course of 256 years (13 × 7,200 days or 256.26 years).

Between A.D. 800 and 900, a number of sites stopped recording Long Count inscriptions on monuments, one symptom of the "Maya collapse," a rather sudden decline of political stability in the southern Maya lowlands brought on by a variety of factors. Endemic warfare seems to be evident throughout the Maya area during this period (Demarest 1997; Sharer 1994:346–347). Political instability and warfare may have been triggered by an extended drought (Hodell et al. 1995).

The last Long Count inscriptions were recorded on public monuments during the Terminal Classic period (A.D. 800–1000; Sharer 1994:48). In the southern Maya lowlands, monuments recording dates in the Long Count notation are found at relatively few sites during the span from A.D. 830 to 909 (10.0.0.0.0 to 10.4.0.0.0; Proskouriakoff 1993). Around A.D. 900, there is evidence of a shift toward interest in year-ending ceremonies of the Postclassic type (Justeson 1989:113–114). For example, at Machaquila and at Jimbal dates in the last month of the vague year are designated as ending the year, indicating the 365-day year was becoming more important.

By the Early Postclassic period (A.D. 900/1000–1250), the intellectual center of Maya culture had shifted from the southern lowlands to the northern area of Yucatán. Rather than being a period of intellectual decline, the Postclassic was a time when political and social changes brought calendar reform. In the Terminal Classic period, an expanded type of Short Count was introduced; the Calendar Round date was noted, as in the past, but the inscriptions added the number of the Katun and the Ahau date on which a current Katun would end (Thompson 1960:197–200, fig. 38, nos. 1–3; 1965:650). These dates lack Initial Series inscriptions, period-ending designations, and distance numbers. This type of dating is seen at Chichén Itzá in inscriptions dating between A.D. 860 and 900, but this type of inscription apparently disappeared by the time Chichén Itzá was abandoned near the end of the Early Postclassic period.

During the Early Postclassic period, the Maya still used Long Count dates to note dates of astronomical significance, but they no longer recorded historical events involving Maya rulers and city-states. The Long Count base dates in the Dresden Codex, one of the few surviving painted books from the Maya area, serve as historical reference points for astronomical cycles. The earliest recorded date is A.D. 623 (9.9.9.16.0) and the latest is A.D. 1210 (10.19.6.1.8), a date presumed to be roughly contemporary with when the codex was painted (Thompson 1972:21–22). In Long Count inscriptions of the Dresden Codex, the month glyph often appears in a separate column from the Long Count notation. Of the twenty-seven Long Count inscriptions recorded in the codex, only five appear to record the months accurately. Four appear to have mistakes in the month position, and eighteen lack references to the months entirely. It seems that the close link between the Long Count and the Calendar Round dissolves during the Early Postclassic period.

The Dresden Codex has a number of Calendar Round dates that presumably followed a pattern like that of the Classic period. The Venus pages of the Dresden Codex use Calendar Round dates to accurately note Venus events between A.D. 1100 and 1250 (Chapter 5). Apparently at this time the months still shifted through the solar year. After the epoch of the Dresden Codex, however, we cannot be sure that the Calendar Round continued in the same fashion.

In the Late Postclassic period (A.D. 1250–1550), the Yucatec Maya festival calendar may have had some form of intercalation to keep it in correspondence with the seasons. At this time, the Yucatec Maya calendar revolved around a festival cycle like that recorded by Friar Diego de Landa around 1553 (Tozzer 1941:vii, 151–167). Possibly this calendar involved an intercalation that was introduced into the area as a result of contact with central Mexico.

By the time the Aztecs founded their capital in A.D. 1325 at Tenochtitlan, the festival calendar probably was locked in with the cycle of the seasons. This calendar was widespread in the Valley of Mexico and extended beyond the Aztec realm to Tlaxcala in the east (Milbrath 1989). The monthly festivals in the Valley of Mexico described at the time of the conquest incorporate a number of seasonal events, and the festival names themselves sometimes reflect seasonal activities (Aguilera 1989; Broda 1982; Milbrath 1980a; Tena 1987:68–69). The months were not part of calendar dates inscribed on Postclassic Aztec monuments because these do not record true Calendar Round dates. Instead, Aztec inscriptions incorporate days from the 260-day calendar (Tonalpohualli) and year-bearer dates that show a specific position in the cycle of fifty-two years known as the Xiuhmolpilli (year bundle). Since the festivals (20-day "months") were not locked into these calendar dates, they could have been adjusted when they began to shift too far from the associated solar event. Indeed, the chronicles say that certain astronomical rituals could take place in one month or the next, indicating a flexibility that allowed them to shift within a 40-day period comprising two "months" or festivals. Such flexibility is also evident in the fact that specific activities from one festival often extended into the next month, and a number of festivals were paired by a specific pattern of naming, such as Tecuilhuitontli (small feast of the lords) followed by Hueytecuihuitl (great feast day of the lords), and Miccailhuitontli (small feast day of the dead) and Hueymiccailhuitl (great feast day of the dead; Milbrath 1997:196; Nicholson 1971).

The Long Count was not used in the Late Post-classic period, when the Maya recorded historical events in the Short Count. They referred to a specific Katun by noting the Ahau date that marked the Katun end in the cycle of 13 Katuns (approximately 256 years). Such inscriptions are seen in the Postclassic Paris Codex and in the Colonial period (1550–1821). The Chilam Balam books of the Colonial epoch place the events within a twenty-year period, but they usually do not furnish enough information to give precise dates, naming only the Tun in a specific Katun. These books indicate the Katun cycle was also used in prophetic history, for the texts imply that similar events would repeat in Katuns of the same name (Coe 1999:121). For example, the histories speak of the Itzá being driven from their homes repeatedly in Katuns bearing the name 8 Ahau (Roys 1967:136 n. 3).

The codices express the same interest in past, present, and future events seen in the Colonial period Chilam Balam books, but while astronomy is mentioned only obliquely in the Colonial period books, the Postclassic codices include many astronomical cycles. The codices seem to date to different periods, and they each show somewhat different forms of recording astronomical events. The Grolier Codex is a fragment that incorporates records of Venus that are quite different from those in the Dresden Codex. The Grolier Codex is probably the latest of the manuscripts, and may be Postconquest in date. It is not analyzed in this book, as it will be the subject of a separate study in the future. The opening pages of the Paris Codex, depicting the Katun cycles, pair month glyphs with Katun notations. This suggests a specific record of time that requires study in the future. As will be seen, the intervals of approximately twenty years expressed by individual Katuns may relate to astronomical events (Chapter 6). The Paris Codex apparently dates around A.D. 1450 (Love 1994:13). The Madrid Codex is slightly earlier, painted between A.D. 1350 and 1450 (Chapter 4). The Dresden Codex was probably painted between A.D. 1200 and 1250 (Chapters 4 and 5). There seems to have been a dramatic change in the calendar from the time when the Dresden Codex was painted to when the Madrid Codex was painted, for by the time the Madrid Codex was painted in the

Late Postclassic period, the Long Count was no longer used.

The latest known Long Count dates, all before the beginning of the 11th Baktun in A.D. 1225, are found in the Dresden Codex eclipse table. Presumably these dates are roughly contemporary with when the codex was painted (Chapter 4). The astronomical tables also record Long Count dates referring to events hundreds of years in the past, as well as to contemporary events. They also incorporate Calendar Round dates that follow the pattern seen in the

there was clearly no attempt to

n in the

e subor-

form of

calendar

nomical

to find

1974:90)

tary data

deciding

dic revo-

there are

n Classic

lence is a

g dates in

on 1974:

the 1930s

ade inter-

usting the

the astro-

nomical events the nificant, with little or no knowledge of the glyphs and iconography on the monuments. Today astronomical interpretations are enhanced by other lines of evidence, but still the caution must remain. If one proposes a connection between a date, an astronomical event, and specific images or glyphs, the best approach is one that investigates the calendric cycles associated with all known examples of that image or glyph. Even though studying the patterning of astronomical events in relation to dates, glyphs, and iconography provides a fruitful line of research, we must recognize that some astronomical images emphasize emblematic symbolism rather than actual astronomical

events. We cannot expect that dates on the monuments will always be useful in testing an association with a specific astronomical event, but general patterns can serve as a guide to our interpretations.

The lack of agreement on the appropriate Maya calendar correlation has been a long-standing problem in the study of calendric events. Today, the generally preferred correlation involves adding 584,283 or 584,285 days to the total number of days indicated by a Long Count inscription in order to arrive at the appropriate Julian day number in our astronomical calendar, which is then translated into a date in the Gregorian or Julian calendar. Various authors have reviewed the complex issues involved (Aveni 1980: 204–210; Satterthwaite 1965:627–630; Thompson 1960:303–310). Anthony Aveni and Lorren Hotaling (1994:S25) are convinced that the 584,283 correlation is the correct one. This is the Goodman, Martínez, Thompson correlation (GMT2), the one preferred by Thompson (1960; 1974:85) in his later work, and endorsed by Linton Satterthwaite (1965: 631) and more recently by Sharer (1994). On the other hand, Justeson (1989:120) says that the issue remains debatable, citing David Kelley's (1983) critique of current correlations. Beth Collea (1982) cautions that there may have been different correlations at different sites, or there may have been a break point between the Classic period calendar and the Colonial period records used to reconstruct the correlation point. More recently, Kelley (1989) notes that only discovery of new historical documents or a better understanding of Mesoamerican astronomy will resolve the correlation question.

I use the GMT2 (584,283) correlation throughout, but in the Classic period there are some cases in which a correlation factor placing the events two or three days later seems to work better, particularly in the case of Classic period eclipses. Except in the case of events involving the moon, shifting the recorded event by a few days will not substantially alter the interpretations. Moreover, local conditions could affect the day an event was observed. For example, the day Venus first became visible after a period of invisibility in conjunction with the Sun may have been recorded a few days later due to local weather conditions.

DECIPHERMENT OF MAYA GLYPHS

Maya dates most often appear embedded in glyphic texts that can now be read with varying degrees of accuracy. It is hoped that future study of the texts can serve as an independent test of the interpretations presented here; however, we should bear in mind that even though the text and image are complementary, they need not be identical in content.

Michael Coe's *Breaking the Maya Code* (1992) provides a good synthesis of the current state of knowledge about Maya hieroglyphic writing. After the initial phase of cataloguing the glyphs and studying the context (Thompson 1962), the first major breakthrough in Maya writing came from recognizing a relationship between text and image, most notably expressed in Tatiana Proskouriakoff's (1960) landmark study that revealed essential components of Classic Maya dynastic history. More recently, Maya glyphic workshops have sprung up across the country, modeled after one founded by Linda Schele at the University of Texas. A number of scholars today pursue decipherment using a phonetic interpretation based on work developed by Yurii Knorozov (1982). All agree that the writing system is basically logosyllabic (logograms and syllabic signs), and great progress has been made in developing a syllabary. Nonetheless, some of the readings currently accepted are bound to be revised. Indeed, Heinrich Berlin (1977:24–28) cautions that because a reading is generally accepted by a group of scholars does not mean that it is a correct reading.

The varying orthographic systems used by different scholars to transcribe Mayan languages also present a problem. Up until around 1992, many scholars followed the orthography used in Thompson's extensive publications, which was derived from Colonial Yucatec. Recently, there has been a move to revise the orthography, based on a system developed in 1989 by the Maya in Guatemala (Freidel et al. 1993:17), which is closely akin to the one developed by the linguists Robert Blair and Refugio Vermont-Salas (1965). The main innovation in the Guatemalan orthography involves a series of substitutions for certain consonants: *k* for *c; k'* for *k; p'* for *pp; q'* for *q; s* for *z; t'* for *th; tz'* for *dz;* and *w*

for *u* in situations where the sound mimics English *w.* The modern Yucatec dictionary compiled by Alfredo Barrera Vásquez (1980) follows a similar orthographic system. When referring to published works, I use the orthography of the cited source. Consequently, I often use an orthography based on Colonial sources, popularized by Thompson, because much of this book involves a synthesis of material published at a time before the new orthography was in use.

ARCHAEOASTRONOMY AND ETHNOASTRONOMY

The field of archaeoastronomy is helping to rediscover the role of astronomy in ancient societies; ethnoastronomy reveals that the changing sky still plays a central role in the cosmology of contemporary indigenous cultures throughout the world. In the last thirty years, archaeoastronomy and ethnoastronomy have developed as interdisciplinary fields. Astronomers are learning about anthropology, and anthropologists are learning about astronomy. Over the last twenty-five years, Anthony Aveni, an astronomer-turned-anthropologist, has led the way for anthropologists to understand the significance of astronomy in the patterning of culture. Calendars and architectural orientations remain central to the study of archaeoastronomy, but scholars are expanding their studies to link astronomy with the political and religious imagery, especially in studies of the Precolumbian Maya. Art historians and epigraphers are increasingly involved in such research. In a 1975 article highlighting the role of astronomy in ancient Mesoamerican cultures, Michael Coe called for ethnographers to go to the field and gather information on current beliefs about astronomy, noting that some important keys to the past are still preserved in the present. Over the last decades, ethnographers have recorded astronomical beliefs that indicate astronomy still guides the more conservative Maya communities (Tedlock 1992a, 1992b). Such fieldwork has greatly increased our understanding of contemporary Maya astronomy and has provided important clues about Precolumbian Maya astronomy.

Michael Coe's brilliant article led me to begin my study of astronomical imagery in ancient Mesoamerica. In 1979, I was awarded a Tinker Postdoctoral Fellowship to conduct research on astronomical symbols in the Aztec festival calendar. At Yale University, Michael Coe gave me access to his extensive library. Anthony Aveni at Colgate University served as my mentor. Over the course of the fellowship, I became interested in comparative data from the Maya area, and I began to explore the role of astronomy in the Postclassic Maya calendar and in calendars preserved among the Maya today.

My scope broadened considerably in 1980, when Anna Roosevelt, then curator of the Precolumbian collections at the Museum of the American Indian (now part of the Smithsonian Institution), offered me the opportunity to curate a traveling exhibit focusing on New World archaeoastronomy and ethnoastronomy. With funding we secured from the National Endowment for the Humanities, the exhibit opened at the American Museum of Natural History in 1982 and toured nationally through 1984. *Star Gods of the Ancient Americas* highlighted the celestial luminaries cross-culturally, comparing imagery of the sun, moon, stars, and planets in the Americas over many centuries. In addition, four sections of the exhibit synthesized the astronomical imagery of different areas: the U.S. Great Plains and the Southwest, the Maya area, and the Valley of Mexico, home to the Aztecs. The approach taken in the *Star Gods* exhibit has helped shape this book, but here I have the opportunity to fill out what could only be presented in fragmentary form in the exhibit. By focusing on one culture area, I am able to bring out many more patterns, and provide a more complete picture of how archaeoastronomy and ethnoastronomy can help to enhance our understanding of ancient New World cultures.

This book has also been shaped by the input from many scholars, both in published works and unpublished studies. In addition, I have benefited from discussions with Anthony Aveni, Harvey Bricker, John Carlson, Michael Coe, Clemency Coggins, Esther Pasztory, Weldon Lamb, Edward Krupp, and Andrea Stone. The time these individuals have taken to help me improve the work is greatly appreciated.

I would also like to thank Regina Cheong, Ule Crisman, and Kathryn Reed, who created the figures, and Carl Henriksen, who compiled the appendices.

OVERVIEW OF CONTENTS

When I first began this book in 1991, I intended to include comparative chapters on central Mexico, but I was not prepared for the overwhelming amount of literature on Maya astronomy generated in the last few years. Add to this the fast-breaking news from Maya epigraphers, and I began to see myself as a reporter latching on to the latest story. Furthermore, I am not sufficiently well versed in Maya writing to judge the relative merits of different readings proposed for the texts. For this reason, I have chosen to emphasize the relationship between astronomy, calendar dates, and Maya imagery. I also include a comparative study of astronomical images from Precolumbian central Mexico to strengthen the iconographic analysis. I often refer to my previously published studies on central Mexican astronomical imagery by way of comparison. The reader is also directed to *El culto a los astros entre los Mexicas* (1975), by Yólotl González Torres, an excellent overview of Postclassic central Mexican astronomy.

By synthesizing the literature on Maya astronomy, I present an overview to set the stage for presenting new interpretations. Following the trend of my past research, I link astronomical images and calendar cycles to show how the seasonal round is represented in art. In addition, I explore the astronomical attributes of Maya deities and the astronomical regalia associated with Maya rulers. Appendix 1 gives an overview of the suggested astronomical identities for different gods. Appendix 2 summarizes the Classic Maya dates and the associated astronomical events discussed in the text. Appendix 3 allows the reader to calculate intervals between Tzolkin dates.

In light of my belief that the modern Maya still hold the keys to our understanding of ancient astronomical imagery, I begin the book with what the contemporary Maya say about astronomy and the astronomical gods. In subsequent chapters, I often refer back to Chapter 1 as a touchstone to emphasize that the Maya today have provided important insights into the past through a core of knowledge preserved from Precolumbian times.

The second chapter focuses on what ancient astronomers could see with the naked eye, emphasizing what one actually sees in the sky. When reading this chapter, those unfamiliar with astronomy may want to consult H. A. Rey's *The Stars: A New Way to See Them,* an introductory book focusing on naked-eye astronomy, as well as Edward C. Krupp's *Echoes of the Ancient Skies.* Anthony Aveni's *Skywatchers of Ancient Mexico* and *Conversing with the Planets* should be companion texts for Chapter 2 and subsequent chapters, for they contain a great deal of information on the Maya calendar, architectural orientations, and the codices.

The third chapter focuses on solar themes, including the solar calendar and orientations in architecture that reflect the seasonal position of the sun. This chapter also explores how imagery of the Sun God evolved over time. It examines solar gods that express different relationships with the sun, including underworld aspects of the sun and animal deities connected with the sun, such as the macaw.

The fourth chapter investigates lunar imagery, including eclipse representations that involve death aspects of the sun and moon, and images that pair the sun and moon, such as the Paddler Twins. Animal images of the moon include the rabbit on the moon, apparently the counterpart for our "man on the moon." Other animals may embody the moon at different times of year, such as the Water-lily Jaguar associated with the rainy season and the Jaguar War God linked with the dry season. Another complex of images reflects the lunar phases, with the waxing moon represented by a youthful female and the waning moon by an aged goddess who can transform into a crone threatening the sun with solar eclipse at the time of the new moon. This chapter also explores the iconography of male lunar deities, noting that the male gender may reflect an association with the full moon.

The fifth chapter treats Venus imagery, including Postclassic Venus deities representing the seasonal cycle in the eight-year Venus Almanac. In the analysis of the Dresden Codex, we see that God L takes the role of the Morning Star in January; Lahun Chan is an aspect of the Morning Star linked with August; the howler monkey is the Morning Star of April; the central Mexican Fire God represents the Morning Star in November at the onset of the dry season; and a blindfolded god from central Mexico represents the Morning Star in June. Influence from central Mexico is also evident in imagery of the feathered serpent, Quetzalcoatl, and of Tlaloc, a central Mexican rain god who seems to be linked with the Yucatec rain god Chac. Both may be related to Venus, sharing the patterning in sets of five reflecting the Venus Almanac.

Chapter 6 explores what little we know about planetary gods, proposing that God K, one of the Triad at Palenque, represents the planet Jupiter. The Mars Beast seems specifically associated with Mars. Another planetary god is a monkey, possibly related to the Postclassic God C. Images depicting an assembly or group of gods may represent the sun, moon, and five planets.

The final chapter deals with stars, the Milky Way, and other astronomical phenomena, such as comets and meteors. A zodiac-like sequence from Yucatán reveals specific animal constellations recognized in the Postclassic period. The constellations on the sky band are linked specifically with imagery of the ecliptic crossing the Milky Way. In the Classic period, the Milky Way is depicted by the Cosmic Monster, with his two heads symbolizing the crossing points of the ecliptic. Another Milky Way image is seen in Itzamna, a god with a quadripartite nature. His four different-colored bodies find their counterpart in the Popol Vuh, a creation legend describing four different-colored roads that apparently represent two sides of the Milky Way and the two sides of the ecliptic.

Chapters 3–7 present a number of new interpretations and identifications, many of which require further testing in the future. My method has been to explore the ideas in a variety of ways, usually beginning with the sixteenth-century Colonial period. I work backward through time to trace the history of the astronomical images in the Classic period. Dates on Classic period monuments provide data for testing the interpretations. Using the historical data developed by scholars in the last decades, a new picture of Classic Maya astronomy emerges. It seems that Maya rulers manipulated celestial imagery to make themselves central to the cosmos. Different rulers or lineages claimed descent from the Sun, the Moon, and Venus. Jupiter seems to be the paramount planet of rulers in the region of Palenque and Yaxchilán. Indeed, after his death, King Pacal was transformed into a god linked with Jupiter, an apotheosis that carried the ruler to heaven. Other rulers were transformed into Venus after death. They traveled on the soul's road, the Milky Way, to reach their celestial abode. The Precolumbian Maya, like other great civilizations, believed their stars were gods, and their rulers derived power from their connection with the cosmos in life and in the afterlife.

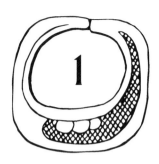

CONTEMPORARY MAYA IMAGES OF THE HEAVENS

Study of Precolumbian Maya astronomical imagery must begin with an understanding of the contemporary Maya worldview, because we cannot hope to penetrate the ancient beliefs without an understanding of what the Maya say about the heavens today. We are fortunate that many Maya groups remained isolated from the European colonists and still retain a measure of isolation today. They are able to pass down their knowledge to new generations and to scholars who find this information invaluable in the study of ancient traditions. Certainly there have been great changes in the religious system over the past five hundred years as a result of European contact, but those beliefs linked to seasonal cycles and agriculture most probably reflect ancient concepts useful in interpreting Precolumbian astronomy. Scholars studying ancient Mesoamerica see a striking continuity from the Colonial period up through modern times, especially with respect to beliefs about geography, climate, astronomy, agricultural activities, and curing practices (Broda 1989:145). Indeed, religious symbols seem to have an enduring relationship to the natural environment (Stone 1995b:12). Despite more than twenty-five different languages in the Mayan language family (Pl. 1), there is a widely shared notion that the sun and the moon control agriculture.

THE SEASONAL CYCLE

Agricultural events are a main focus of the seasonal solar calendar today, as they were at the time of the conquest in the sixteenth century. Many Maya Indians follow the practices of their ancestors, clearing the fields before the rainy season and using a digging stick to plant maize (corn), an important part of their diet. The first maize crop, considered to be the principal crop, matures at the height of the rainy season. At this time the ears are bent, which not only allows the maize to dry out, but also hastens maturity and minimizes damage from insects, fungus, and animals (Salvador 1998). The bent ears may be left in the field for harvest with the second crop at the onset of the dry season. Frequently a second maize planting takes place, interspersed with squash or beans, during the brief dry spell in late July and early August. The new tender kernels (*elotes*) appear around twelve weeks later, and the mature maize is ready to harvest around the onset of the dry season. Variations in practice relate primarily to the altitude and latitude of the fields. Although the annual rainfall varies across the Maya area, there is a rather uniform division of the year into a rainy season beginning in April or May and a dry season beginning in late November (Aveni and Hotaling 1996, fig. 1; Malmström 1997, figs. 2, 17, 32–34). In Mesoamerica, March is usually the month of least rain and September is the most rainy month (Vivó 1964:201).

It is common practice among the Maya to fix dates for sowing and harvesting by observing the two annual zenith passages of the sun (B. Tedlock 1992b: 173, 189). They use a gnomon, a vertical staff or pole, or even their own bodies to determine the solar zenith by watching for the day that the sun casts no shadow at noon (Girard 1962:147). The first solar zenith in May is very important among a number of Maya groups because it coincides with the onset of the rains, when the primary maize crop is planted in the lowlands. The date of the first solar zenith is dependent on latitude, but occurs sometime in May throughout much of the Maya area (Pl. 1; Isbell 1982, fig. 1). There may be a second planting at the second solar zenith, ranging in date from late July in Yucatán to mid August in the southernmost Maya area in western El Salvador. In some highland areas, the harvesting of valley maize begins shortly after the second solar zenith in August (B. Tedlock 1992b:189).

The Yucatec Maya, living in the northern Maya area, clear the new milpas of brush at least three months before the "burn," when the fields are set on fire to clear them and to provide fertilizing ash. The burn usually begins in March and runs through the first part of May. The date of the burn is determined by a form of divination known as *xoc kin* (Redfield and Villa Rojas 1962:44 n. 1). This usually begins in late May just before the rains or in early June just after the onset of the rains (Pérez 1942:17; 1946). They weed the fields once before the ears ripen. The early maize (*x-thup-nal*) ripens in ten to fifteen weeks, whereas late corn (*u-nuc-nal*) takes four and a half months. The ears dry on the stalks, and the harvest begins in November at the beginning of the dry season and continues through the following months. By March they finish gathering late maize before clearing the fields.

The agricultural calendar of the Kekchí in Belize begins in January when each man selects his milpa, and the milpa is consecrated with religious ceremonies (Schackt 1986:35–36). They clear the fields during February and March and set fire to the underbrush a few days before sowing. The green corn is harvested around the beginning of August; the main harvest begins in late September and lasts throughout much of October.

The Quiché of Momostenango in the department of Totonicapán, Guatemala, plant both the mountain maize and the valley maize according to a calendar that combines solar and lunar observations (B. Tedlock 1992b). The crops grow during the warm, wet season, which runs from late April or early May through October. The solar events seem to be more important in the valley, where planting is begun shortly after the first solar zenith on May 1 or 2 and harvesting is begun after the second solar zenith on August 11 or 12. At higher altitudes, they plant maize and beans in March and harvest 260 days later in December.

Among the Mam-speaking Maya of Santiago Chimaltenango in the highlands of Guatemala, the agricultural cycle begins in February, and the fields are planted in March, long before the rainy season, because the corn grows more slowly at these high altitudes (Watanabe 1992:37–41). They plant their main crop in the more temperate valley slopes below the village, where the fields are cleared in April in anticipation of rains in May. They plant beans and squash alongside the young stalks of corn during July, the time of a brief dry spell called *canicula,* a term derived from Latin that refers to the dog star, Sirius, prominent at this time of year. After canicula the rains resume, reaching their peak in September. The newly ripened corn can be picked as early as September, but the main harvest takes place in January after the corn dries on the stalk.

In 1943–1944, Miguel León-Portilla (1988:145–148) recorded a Tzeltal solar calendar at Oxchuc in highland Chiapas. The calendar of eighteen twenty-day months plus five nameless days (Haab) shows a fixed relationship to the solar year and associated agricultural activities. The Haab began in Batzul (December 26–January 14) with light agricultural activities, such as clearing the brush. By Mac (February 24–March 15), the sowing began in the cold uplands. The native religious leaders were responsible for this calendar and the church fiestas, indicating the two were linked together.

The Tzotzil of Zinacantán, Chiapas, plant highland maize in March, but in the lowlands, where the temperatures are higher, they wait until the rains begin in May (Vogt 1990:69–70). Weeding takes place in June and July. The highland harvest takes place in October. Harvesting in the lowlands begins in November and continues into December and January.

Among the Tzotzil of Chenalhó in Chiapas, the agricultural year runs from February to November (Guiteras Holmes 1961:32–35, 44–45). The agricultural cycle follows the seasonal pattern, with planting beginning around the onset of the rainy season in late May; the rains reach their first maximum in June, followed by a dry spell (canicula) in the last two weeks of July and the first week in August, then the rains resume until the next dry season begins in November (Guiteras Holmes 1961:7, 34). In September, they bend the stems of the maize ears, leaving them on the stalk; by the end of October the maize is ready for harvesting. Not all the maize is brought in at once; rather, some is left to dry so that it will not rot when it is stored. Their agricultural year is guided by the 365-day calendar and by a fixed 260-day ritual year equivalent to thirteen months beginning in Sisak and ending in Pom. In two separate field seasons in 1944 and 1955, Sisak began on February 5 and Pom ended on November 16, which suggests that the 365-day calendar remains fixed in the year. The tenth of Sisak marks the beginning of the 260-day ritual year and the agricultural cycle. Following Sisak, there are five days of carnival, the five *ch'aik'in* (uncounted days) that round out the 365-day calendar. This may be when the calendar is adjusted for leap year, for there is only a one- or two-day difference when comparing the modern calendar to a Tzotzil calendar recorded in 1688 (Berlin 1967).

The Tzotzil of Chamula in highland Chiapas divide the year into two halves, with the "right hand" direction symbolizing the rainy season and day sky, and the "left hand" direction representing the dry season and the night. Gary Gossen (1974b, fig. 2)

places the transition points at the equinoxes, even though the seasonal transition actually occurs somewhat later.

A seasonal duality is also apparent in divisions of the year among the Chortí of Guatemala. This is expressed in a fixed 360-day cycle that is divided into two halves (Girard 1962:79–80). The first solar zenith on April 25 divides the year into a light half and a dark half. The dark half is associated with the rainy season, the light half with the dry season. This division of the year forms two 180-day sets that can be divided further into periods of 9 days or 20 days, intervals that echo subdivisions in the Precolumbian Maya calendar.

The solar zenith has a complementary solar event known as the solar nadir, spaced six months from the solar zenith. The November solar nadir marks the beginning of the dry season. Barbara Tedlock's (1992b:189) work with the Quiché of Momostenango (at 15°04′N) indicates that the full moon passing overhead at midnight shows the approximate time of the two annual nadirs of the sun (early November and early February).

The Maya designate the changing length of the days and the associated seasonal changes with different terms. For example, the Tzotzil of Zinacantán say that months from January to June are called "long days," whereas the months from July to December are referred to as "short days" (Laughlin 1975:177, 249, 500). Similarly, the sharp division in the year between the rainy season and the dry is designated with appropriate seasonal names. The Tzotzil refer to the dry-season sun as *k'ak'al 'osil* (fire or sun sky) and *k'inal k'ak'al* (fire or sun days), whereas they say that the rainy season is *jo'tik*, meaning "expanse of water" or "expanse of rain" (Laughlin, personal communication 1988). The day itself is *k'ak'al*, meaning "sun or heat" (Vogt and Vogt 1980:503). The seasonal cycle of the Tzotzil solar calendar is integrated with the four directions (Gossen 1974b:33–35, fig. 2). The east is associated with the period between the winter solstice and the vernal equinox, when the days begin to grow longer. The direction of "up," rising heat, and the masculine principle are ascendant at the spring equinox. The time from the vernal equinox to the summer solstice is linked with north and the beginning of the rains and the growing season, a time of year associated with the sun's vertical path at noon. The autumn equinox symbolizes waning heat, the female principle, the west, and incipient death. The shorter days between the autumnal equinox and the winter solstice represent the end of the growing season and the south, associated with the concept of the nadir and the sun at midnight.

Often, the solstices seem to be regarded as transition points in the sun's path. The Tzotzil of Chenalhó say that the sun changes its path twice a year, and at the transition points the old men stand at dawn and command the sun "to take its proper place." On the first of Batzul (January 16), the sun moves north and the days become longer, and on the first day of 'Elech (June 30) the sun moves south and the days become shorter (Guiteras Holmes 1961:32, 36). The Quiché also refer to the winter and summer solstices as "change of path"; the most important change in direction takes place at the winter solstice when the high-altitude corn is harvested (B. Tedlock 1992b: 180). The summer solstice is more important than the winter solstice among the Chortí, but both solstices play a pivotal role as the corners in the cosmic diagram embodying the yearly cycle (Girard 1962: 245, 247, 297). Nonetheless, the Chortí say that the sun changes its path in April and May, a time linked with the first solar zenith falling on April 30 or May 1 in the Chortí area (Fought 1972:386; Girard 1962: 79, 244, 251). This is the time when the rainy season begins, the half of the year ruled by the weather god Santiago. The dry half of the year, on the other hand, is ruled by the Sun God.

A number of Maya people have a fixed 260-day agricultural calendar. The Chortí have a fixed cycle of 260 days in their agricultural calendar running from February 8 to October 24, but they apparently shift the beginning of the agricultural year to coincide with the first crescent moon (Girard 1962: 328–342). Eric Thompson (1930:41) records that the Mopan Maya of San Antonio in Belize also begin their agricultural year on February 8; this suggests that they also have a fixed agricultural cycle of 260 days. Barbara Tedlock (1992b:190) suggests that the nine-month growing period of mountain maize,

approximating the length of the human gestation period, helps account for the 260-day length of the sacred almanac.

The balance of nature depends on the sun following its course, both in the daily cycle and in the annual agricultural calendar. Today its seasonal course is reinforced by rituals and offerings, as it was in the past. The Maya people are anxious for the sun to take its proper place in the sky to open the agricultural season, but they are also concerned that there be the correct balance of sun and rain. Too much sun is most damaging to the crops, for it brings drought and then famine. The codices show us that the balance of sun and rain was also very important in Precolumbian times (Chapter 3). Similarly, there is evidence in the codices of a fixed 260-day agricultural cycle running from February to November, with special rituals relating to planting in May (Chapter 3).

THE SOLAR CALENDAR

The solar calendar used by the Maya today interfaces with the seasonal cycles. Many Maya people share a 365-day solar calendar of eighteen months of twenty days that ends with a short period of five days, a calendar derived from Precolumbian times that is known as the Haab. Although the Haab is found today in a number of communities throughout Chiapas and Guatemala (but not in Yucatán), only around thirty-four communities in northwestern Guatemala preserve both the Haab and the Tzolkin (Bricker 1981:8). These two calendars together form a cycle that repeats every fifty-two years. A name for the fifty-two-year cycle, *solq'uin*, is preserved among the Chol (Aulie and Aulie 1978:106).

The 365-day year operates separately from the 260-day divination calendar, but there is a certain coordination because only four days of the 260-day calendar fall in a position that makes them yearbearers, meaning that they are days that can begin the year. As noted in the introduction, the interlocking cycles of 365 days and 260 days forming the Calendar Round would not seem to allow for any form of intercalation. Nevertheless, in certain communities it is clear that some sort of adjustment is made to keep the festivals in accord with the seasons.

Heinrich Berlin (1967) analyzed the 365-day festival calendar preserved today among a number of different Tzotzil communities, comparing it with an early version of the Tzotzil calendar recorded by Friar Juan de Rodaz in 1688. Today, as in the past, the year begins in Batzul in early January. Berlin notes that since 1688 there has been a total shift in the Tzotzil festival calendar of only two days, and he believes this indicates that a calendar correction to account for leap years has been made, though he could not ascertain how this was done. Calixta Guiteras Holmes (1961:153) was also unable to find out how the calendar was adjusted among the Tzotzil of Chenalhó, but it clearly follows the seasons. It is likely that the Maya today link the festivals to Catholic saints' days to keep in time with the seasons (Evon Vogt, personal communication 1997).

The Tzutujil Maya of Guatemala say that the sun dies each year (Tarn and Prechtel 1986:174–178). They conduct ceremonies to bury the old year around the time of Carnival before Lent or Holy Week (the week before Easter). In preparation for the New Year ceremonies, they bury an effigy of the Mam representing the old year (Taube 1989b:375; Thompson 1970a:472). This synchronization with the Catholic calendar suggests the Tzutujil may use a combination of solar and lunar observations, for the year end must precede Easter, which occurs on the first Sunday after the full moon falling on or after the spring equinox.

The Quiché name their solar year with the day name and number combination that begins the year, known as the year-bearer (B. Tedlock 1992b:35, 91, 99–104). The new year gradually shifts in the calendar, for there is no apparent adjustment to make the new year fall at a specific time of year. Only four of the twenty day names can act as year-bearers (known as Mam), with Quej being considered the first and most important. Each of the four Mam is associated with a different mountain, and they are greeted at the beginning of the year at their respective mountain shrines at Quilaja, Tamancu, Socop, and Pipil. The five days at year end, associated with the old Mam, are considered very dangerous.

The Ixil Maya also combine the 260-day calendar and the 365-day calendar to name the year-bearers in a system that is essentially the same as that of the Quiché (Aveni 1980:43; Lincoln 1942). The new year in their solar calendar is not intercalated, but prior to the early eighteenth century, there may have been some form of correction because the month names incorporate seasonal and agricultural activities (Colby and Colby 1981:47).

Knowledge of the solar calendar is widespread among the Tzotzil of Chamula (Gossen 1974a:246; 1974b:27). The first month of the calendar usually begins in late December around the winter solstice. The people of Chamula link the seasonal cycle to the traditional Mesoamerican calendar of 365 days. However, Gossen notes that they do not allow for a leap year in their calculations. Apparently, they coordinate their festivals with the Catholic festival calendar. Ceremonies dedicated to the Sun God are sometimes fused with the Catholic festival calendar at Chamula. Christ's birthday is celebrated as the rebirth of the sun on the winter solstice, the longest night of the year (Gossen 1974b:39). Synchronizing the solar and lunar calendars also appears to be important in the Festival of Games at Chamula. Here the sun and Christ are equated with the bull killed just prior to Easter (Gossen 1986:241).

The Tzotzil of Zinacantán honor their patron saint, San Lorenzo, in a festival between August 7 and 11 (Vogt and Vogt 1980:516). This period incorporates the date of the second solar zenith at this latitude of 16°N (pl. 1). Eva Hunt (1977:226–227) notes that the Festival of San Lorenzo coincides with the position of the sun straight overhead at the latitude of Zinacantán, and she equates the saint with the summer solstice and the solar zenith, even though these two events are separated by more than a month. At the other end of the year, the Festival of San Sebastián embodies the winter solstice sun, according to Hunt (1977:226–228).

The saints' days are often used as guides for planting. The "día de San Marcos" (April 25), involving an eight-day ceremony ending on May 2, is important for timing the Chortí planting cycle (Wisdom 1940:462–463). The Day of the Holy Cross on May 3 is a rain-making ceremony that is expected to bring the first rains on the first day of the planting festival. The Chortí link this festival to the position of the zenith sun at the center of a cosmological cross marking the intersection point of the Milky Way and the ecliptic (Girard 1949:456; Milbrath 1980a:291). The "día de Santiago" (July 25) marks a temporary suspension of the rains (canicula) when the Chortí prepare the fields for a second planting (Girard 1962:251–252, table facing page 328).

Robert Redfield and Alfonso Villa Rojas (1962: 82–83) point out that the agricultural year underlies and controls aspects of the church calendar among the Yucatec Maya of Chan Kom. For example, the great emphasis placed on festival activities on the Day of the Cross in early May relates to a lull in agricultural activities at this time.

In some cases the Catholic festivals have been changed to accommodate Precolumbian Maya beliefs. In the department of Suchitepéquez, Guatemala, the Maya of San Bernardino celebrate Corpus Christi Day in July, rather than the traditional Catholic day in springtime. Jeanne Pieper (1988:28–30) points out that these festivals are thinly disguised New Year festivals similar to Precolumbian dances that took place in July in Yucatán. The Corpus Christi dance is called the Dance of the Tun. The dance maestro carries a wooden deer head, symbolizing a sacrificed deer, at the beginning of a disorderly dance on Saturday, which is followed on Sunday by a procession to the church with stops at four small chapels decorated with mirrors, colored paper, and a statue of a saint.

The Maya festival cycle links the Catholic saints' days with ancient solar rituals in a way that may seem surprising. This syncretism is just one more way the Maya have maintained core beliefs in the face of rapid change. Such syncretism is facilitated by the fact that the Catholic festivals are timed by seasonal positions of the sun and phases of the moon, the same bodies observed by the Maya in their festivals and planting cycles.

MODERN MAYA COSMIC DIAGRAMS

The cosmic directions may be associated with different colors, as among the Tzotzil of Zinacantán, who link east with red and the "upward" direction, and west with black and the "downward" direction (Vogt and Vogt 1980:504–506). At San Andrés Larraínzar, the colors of the cardinal directions are associated with different Tzotzil gods (Holland 1964:16). The east is white and is linked to the god of rain; the north is also white but is associated with the god of maize; the west is black, linked with the god of death; and the south is red, where the god of wind resides. The four corners of the heavens are intercardinal directions where the *cargadores* (bearers) reside. The Tzotzil at Chenalhó relate the north to the color white, the west to black, the south to yellow, and the east to red (Guiteras Holmes 1961:287). They link three of the colors to scarcity of maize (famine); black represents famine related to women, red famine to men, and white famine to children; but yellow is a color associated with an abundance of maize. During the Colonial period, Friar Diego de Landa recorded similar color directions associated with varying fates of maize in the four-year cycle of the year-bearers; for example, Cauac years, linked with the west and the color black, were characterized by a hot sun that would destroy the fields of maize (Tozzer 1941:148).

Just as all roads led to Rome in classical antiquity, all directions lead to the sun in Maya cosmology. A Yucatec prayer recorded in the nineteenth century refers to the sun as the "master of the east" who carries prayers to the four extremes of the sky and the four extremes of the earth (Villa Rojas 1969:272). The Maya cosmos is delimited by the sun's apparent motion. The east and west are often defined as entry and exit points for the sun (B. Tedlock 1992a:22; 1992b:173–177). Many Mayan languages reflect concepts of time and space based on the daily and annual movements of the sun (Watanabe 1983).

A quadripartite arrangement also refers to the daily course of the sun in some contexts. A Tzotzil cosmic diagram marks four principal positions of the sun in its daily course (Fig. 1.1a). At the Festival of Games in February in Chamula, the head of Sun/Christ is represented by four metal flagpole tips attached to poles (the skeletons of Sun/Christ) and banners (the body of Sun/Christ), which symbolize the four positions of Sun/Christ: rising, zenith, setting, and nadir (Gossen 1986:232). Analysis of Chamula astronomical concepts indicates that the

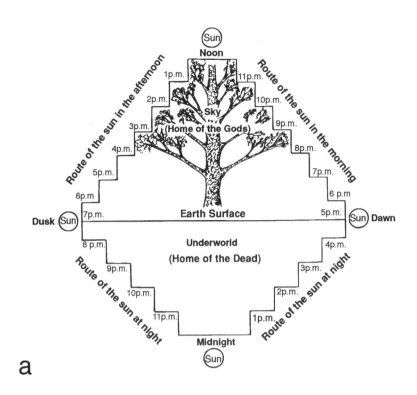

Route of the sun in the afternoon

Route of the sun in the morning

Sun
Noon

1p.m. 11p.m.

2p.m. 10p.m.

Sky
(Home of the Gods)

3p.m. 9p.m.

4p.m. 8p.m.

5p.m. 7p.m.

6p.m 6 p.m

Dusk (Sun) 7p.m. Earth Surface 5p.m. (Sun) Dawn

8 p.m. Underworld 4p.m.

(Home of the Dead)

9p.m. 3p.m.

Route of the sun at night

10p.m. 2p.m.

Route of the sun at night

11p.m. 1p.m.

Midnight

(Sun)

a

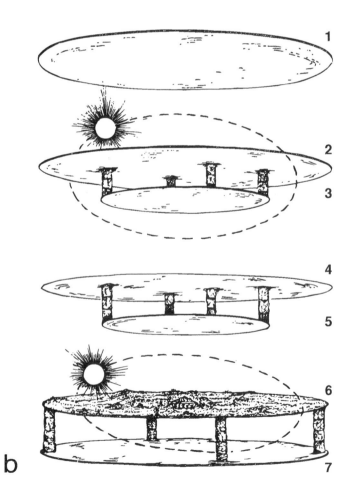

1

2

3

4

5

6

7

b

primary axis is an east-west direction based on the sun's daily path (Sosa 1986:196, table 1). Even though they recognize that the zenith position is overhead, the east is visualized as the "up" direction and the west as "down."

East and west indicate the directions where the sun rises and sets in Mayan languages, but the two other directions are not recorded in many dictionaries. When north and south are named, they are variously linked with the right and left hand of the Sun God, the direction of prevailing winds that bring rain, the topographical distinctions between highland and lowland, and the notion of above and below or zenith and nadir (B. Tedlock 1992b:176–178). Barbara Tedlock interprets the basic structure of Mayan directional symbolism as a reflection of the daily path of the sun, with north and south representing the noon and midnight positions of the sun, loosely linked with zenith and nadir. However, her data from the Quiché also suggest that north and south are the sides of heaven, with south corresponding to the left hand of the rising sun and north to the right hand, whereas east is "the sun's rising place" and west is "the sun's falling place" (Tedlock 1992a:23). Similar notions occur among the Tzotzil and Lacandón Maya, who say that north and south are sides of heaven (Köhler 1980:586).

When speaking of the cosmic directions, there is disagreement as to the location of the "corners" of the cosmos. Ulrich Köhler (1980:585–586) notes that among the Tzotzil, Lacandón, and Quiché, the sky-bearers hold up the heavens at the four intercardinal directions associated with the year-bearer days, which he links with the sun's solstice extremes. In Quintana Roo, the Yucatec Maya of X-Cacal place the great Chacs at the corners of the world associated with true cardinal directions, but an informant from the village of Tusik describes the corners of the sky as being located at the intercardinal points (Villa Rojas 1945:102 n. 12). The Maya of Yalcobá, Yucatán,

say that the corners of the cosmos are located at the intercardinal directions, whereas the cardinal directions refer to the sides of heaven (Sosa 1985:419–420, Fig. 10; 1989:132–137, Fig. 9.2). The hmèen (native priest/shaman) says that the sun reaches the corner of lak'in saman (our northeast) in June, and it moves to lak'in nohol (our southeast) by December. The beginning direction is east (lak'in), the "up" direction positioned between two of the corners of a quadrilateral cosmos defined by the annual and daily solar motion. In a like fashion, Colonial period Yucatec maps place the eastern direction at the top, indicating the "up" direction (Marcus 1992, fig. 6.16).

In some accounts, the corners of the universe are intercardinal points identified with the extreme horizon positions of the sun at the solstices (Girard 1962:40, 45, 247; Gossen 1982, fig. 2; Villa Rojas 1988:128–131). Girard points out that the cosmic cross of the Maya is often mistakenly referred to as a representation of the cardinal directions, when in fact the Chortí indicate that it marks the intercardinal horizon positions of the sun at the solstices. An idealized diagram of the Maya cosmos traces out a quincunx of five points, with the four corner points linked to the solstices, and the center point marking the equinoctial line (Villa Rojas 1988, fig. 2). In other cosmograms, the center point can be the noon position of the sun. The Yucatec Maya of Yalcobá say that the u hol gloryah (the hole in the middle of the sky) corresponds to the noon position of the sun, when there is a cosmological conduit to the sun (Sosa 1985:315, 346, 368–369, 393–395, 435; 1989:139). There is a complementary hole in the earth marking the underworld position of the sun around midnight.

Evon Vogt (1964:198) reports significant variation in the cosmological worldview from one Tzotzil town or municipio to the next, and even internal variations within municipios. In Zinacantán, the

---

FIG. 1.1. a: Contemporary Tzotzil conception of universe (after Vogt 1969, fig. 192).

b: Contemporary Lacandón conception of universe (after Rätsch and Ma'ax 1984:44–46). Layer one is heaven of Wandering Gods; layer two is heaven of Kak'och; layer three is heaven of T'uup, layer four is heaven of Hachäkyum, layer five is heaven of vultures, layer six is Earth, layer seven is underworld of Sukunkyum.

earth is a cube, and men live on top of the cube; at the lower corners of the cube are four pillars of the world, conceived of as animals or gods (Vashakmen) holding up the earth (Vogt 1969:297–298). Above the surface of the earth there is a quadrilateral space with three layers. The huts at Zinacantán have three roof joists to mirror the three-layered heavens, collectively known as Vinahel, meaning "sky" or "heavens" (Vogt 1976:58). On the other hand, the Tzotzil of San Andrés Larraínzar say that the sky is a pyramid supported by a giant ceiba, and the sun rises by six steps to the top and descends in six steps to mark the thirteen hours of daylight (Fig. 1.1a; Holland 1964:14–15; Laughlin 1969:175). The stepped aspect of the sun's course seems to have more to do with a count of hours in the day; however, the thirteenth hour is not at sunset, but instead is at noon, being equated with the thirteenth step overhead at the "heart of the sky" (Holland 1964:14–15, 17). The sun, the moon, and the Catholic saints are positioned in the thirteen levels of the sky.

Maya cosmologies report layered heavens ranging from three to fifteen. A Tzotzil cosmic model recorded in Zinacantán places the moon in the lowest layer, the stars in the middle layer, and the sun in the upper layer (Vogt 1976:58). The Maya of Chamula also visualize a three-layered heaven, with the sun moving in the highest layer. The first layer is the visible sky, the second is where the stars and moon are located, and the third is where the sun (Christ), the bright constellations, and St. Jerome are located (Gossen 1974b:21, Fig. 1). Data collected in the Yucatec Maya settlement of X-Cacal indicate that the universe has fifteen layers, seven above the earth and seven below, with a giant ceiba linking the layers together through its roots, trunk, and branches; similar traditions are known from the region of Valladolid (Roys 1972:73; Villa Rojas 1945:154; 1969:275).

Five layers are found in the Lacandón universe, according to Jon McGee (1990:61, 107–108). The first layer is the underworld; the second is the surface of the earth; the third is the sky, where Hachäkyum, Our True Lord (the creator god), and other celestial gods live; the fourth is the home of Kak'och, the creator of the gods; and the fifth layer is the most remote, the sky of Chembel K'uh, translated as "minor gods" (but see below). Gertrude Duby and Frans Blom (1969:295) record the same three sky levels, noting that the lowest is a sort of paradise where the dead go and live happily. Another Lacandón account, recorded by Christian Rätsch and K'ayum Ma'ax (1984:44–46), has seven layers, each formed by a round disk (Fig. 1.1b). The layers, numbered from top to bottom, place the *chembel k'uho'*, or "Wandering Gods" (the planets), in the highest heaven. The second layer is the abode of Kak'och, also called "two-monkey." Here is where Hachäkyum placed the sun, but this layer already contained a sun made by Kak'och to shine for Hachäkyum and the two suns together were too bright, so the sun that illuminates the earth is now in a separate layer. The third layer, suspended from the layer above, is the heaven of T'uup (the Little One), a spider monkey who is said to be lord of the sun. The fifth layer, the heaven of the vultures, hangs in a similar fashion from the fourth layer, the heaven of Hachäkyum. The sixth layer is formed by the earth, and the seventh layer, the underworld of Sukunkyum, hangs from stone columns attached to the earth.

In sum, the sun's motion defines the diagram of cosmic space. The earth often takes a quadrilateral form because its horizon is circumscribed by the motion of the sun forming an intercardinal cosmic diagram at the horizon extremes of the solstices. Another cosmic diagram marks the rising and setting points to the east and west, and the north and south are true cardinal directions apparently equated with the north and south side of the heavens or, alternatively, the above and below positions relating to the daily course of the sun. The noon sun can define both the overhead and central position, especially in constructs linking above and below with a central vertical axis. Although the noon sun is overhead, the "up position" is sometimes linked with the rising sun in the east. The cosmos may also be divided vertically by the sun's path along steps to the noon position. Another construct divides vertical space in layers. The highest layer is reserved for the planets in some accounts, but when few layers are mentioned, the sun is usually in the highest of the layers.

HOW THE SUN MOVES
AND TRANSFORMS

Because the sun seems to shift its position during the day and over the course of the seasons, it is seen as a dynamic force in the earth-centered cosmos of traditional Maya communities. The Maya use different names for the changing positions of the sun, and they visualize the sun taking a journey or transforming over the course of the days and nights of the year.

The daily movements of the sun are noted with different terms. According to the Quiché, the sun bears different names in the morning, at noon, and in the afternoon, with the noon sun identified as a two-faced god called Jakawitz (sometimes given as Cawach, Cakwitz, or Caguach; Carmack 1981:275; León 1945:45). Another source notes that the Quiché say that the sun has four faces, but it is not clear whether these express different times of day (Alvarado 1975:51). In Lacandón terms defining time, "fire base sun" describes noon, "half base sun" refers to one–two hours after sunrise, "nose base sun" to midmorning and midafternoon, and "no sun" to sunset (McGee 1990:54, table 5.4).

In the nineteenth century, Pío Pérez recorded names for the time of day in Yucatec Mayan, noting that the name for the time around midday was a contraction of *chumuc-Kin,* or "center of the day" (Sosa 1986:196). Similarly, the Tzotzil of Zinacantán say that the noon sun is the "center," "middle" or "halfway sun" (Laughlin 1975:64).

Apparently the sun ages over the course of the day, a notion in keeping with a time-space continuum in which celestial positioning equates with passage of time. The Tzotzil call the noon position the sun's maturity or aging (*syijil k'ak'al;* Laughlin 1975:385). Some names for the afternoon sun and the sun at sunset imply that the sun is old; others indicate that the sun dies after sunset (Lamb n.d.b). The aged sun evokes Precolumbian images of the aged Sun God (Chapter 3). Names for the solar designs on men's trousers among the Quiché indicate that the sun ages like a human being, for the infant sun represents the child; the young sun symbolizes the young man; and grandfather sun represents the elderly (Girard 1979:299).

The sun's nightly passage through the underworld is certainly an important event to the Maya, but there seem to be many different views on what happens to the sun at night. Some accounts involve death and rebirth, as among the Chortí, who say that the sun dies at sunset and is reborn every day at dawn (Girard 1962:723). On the other hand, the Chol say that the sun goes inside his house at night (Josserand, cited in Bassie-Sweet 1992:172). A Tzeltal term for the west is "the sleeping place of the sun," implying that the sun goes to sleep at night (B. Tedlock 1992b:176–177).

A Lacandón source says that an underworld Venus god, known as Sucunyum (Sukunkyum, or Lord Elder Brother), carries the sun on his shoulders in his journey through the underworld (Fig. 1.1b; Rätsch and Ma'ax 1984:45; Thompson 1970b:240, 303). Each day the sun grows tired; he is transformed into a skeletal form at night and at dawn he is resurrected (McGee 1990:62–65, 116). Thus the night sun is involved in both transformation and a journey to the underworld. Another Lacandón account says that the sun enters the underworld each night by climbing down the trunks of trees and through the roots (Thompson 1960:71). This echoes Precolumbian imagery showing the Sun God climbing up a tree emerging from the underworld (Fig. 3.4c).

A translation for *chik'in,* meaning "west" in Yucatec, is "eaten sun," which implies that the sun is devoured at night. Who does the devouring is not clear, but it could be the Earth Monster with a gaping cave mouth. The Yucatec Maya of Yalcobá say that the sun goes into a cave at night (Sosa 1985:423, 446–447). This image may involve water, because caves are associated with underground rivers. Yucatec terms note that the sun is diving toward water in the afternoon (Sosa 1985:426–427). A Yucatec term used for the setting sun is *t'ubul,* meaning "to sink or be submerged in water or a hollow object" (Barrera Vásquez 1980). The Chamula Maya say that the sun travels in a wide-mouthed gourd when it sets into the ocean at night (Gossen 1974b:264). Another Chamula tale says that when the sun sets it dries up the ocean, again indicating that the sun passes into the waters of the underworld (Gossen 1980:144).

In some Tzotzil accounts, the sun passes through an underworld inhabited by small people. Because the sun passes so close to them, these dwarfs must wear mud hats to protect themselves from the heat, according to Zinacantán cosmology (Vogt 1969: 298). The accounts of Chenalhó say that the helpers of the sun kneel to hand over the sun to small people waiting in the underworld to carry the sun through the underworld (Guiteras Holmes 1961:152–153, 268). The sun dries up the ocean where it enters the underworld, but the rivers replenish the waters.

When moving across the sky overhead, the sun undergoes a variety of transformations and uses many different modes of transport. The Ixil in Guatemala believe that the Sun God (Kub'aal q'ii) has twenty different manifestations and that he moves across the sky seated in a chair carried by four bearers; two other bearers carry his large headdress (Colby and Colby 1981:38). The Tzeltal of Chiapas say that the sun walks across the sky (Nash 1970: 311). On the other hand, the Quiché note that the sun is a young traveler who cannot walk in space, so an immense feathered snake known as K'ucumatz carries the sun up to its noon position (Carmack 1981:275). This same serpent also carries the sun over the ocean (León 1945:45–46). The serpent's name, K'ucumatz, may embody the two seasons of the solar year, for the dry season is identified with the serpent (*cumatz*) and the wet season with the quetzal bird (*k'uk'*; Carmack 1981:356).

The Tzotzil of Chamula say that the sun rides in a chariot or a two-wheeled cart, clearly reflecting a European mode of transport (Gossen 1974b:263–264). Another Chamula account notes that when the days are short, the sun goes in a truck so he can move rapidly across the sky, whereas when days are long, he rides a burro and moves slowly across the sky.

A more ancient Maya tradition found among the Cakchiquel says that a swift-moving deer draws the sun across the sky on the short days around the winter solstice, whereas two collared peccaries (*jabalí*) convey the sun more slowly on the long days around the summer solstice (Thompson 1967:38). These images all seem to have their counterparts in Precolumbian solar images, as will be seen in Chapter 3.

Mopan folklore about the Sun God carrying a deer or deerskin expresses a related form of solar imagery. To impress the Moon Goddess, XT'actani, the sun carries a stuffed deerskin, pretending he has just killed the deer. The skin bursts open and XT'actani laughs at him, so he changes himself into a hummingbird and continues to court her until he convinces her to elope (Thompson 1967:31–32; 1970b: 363–364).

Similarly, in a Cakchiquel tale, the sun comes to woo his lunar lover in the form of a hummingbird (Thompson 1970b:365–366). Another legend, recorded by Wirsing among the Kekchí, has the young Moon Goddess weaving when the sun visits her in the guise of a hummingbird (Thompson 1970b:370). The sun's aspect as a bird provides a natural explanation for how the sun moves through the sky.

The hummingbird's taste for flower nectar, especially from red-colored flowers, may be another reason for the connection with the sun, for flowers themselves symbolize the sun among the Tzotzil (Vogt 1976:128). Because hummingbirds are believed to hibernate during the dry season, the hummingbird's return is a seasonal metaphor for the return of the sun in spring in Tzotzil folklore (Hunt 1977:61–62, 68, 254). Hunt notes that the hummingbirds are not merely like the sun, they *are* the sun. As we shall see, the Precolumbian Maya also visualized the sun as a hummingbird (Chapter 3).

Occasionally, the solar bird is an eagle, a bird noted for its pattern of flight circling the sky and its ability to look directly at the sun. The Lacandón say that Hachäkyum created the sun out of limestone and painted a brilliant harpy eagle on his clothes, and this is why the sun is so bright (Rätsch and Ma'ax 1984:42).

Birds are not the only animal transformations symbolizing the sun flying across the sky. A butterfly in a diamond design represents the sun and the center of the cosmos for Tzotzil weavers of Magdalenas in highland Chiapas (Morris 1986:57; Morris and Foxx 1987:110).

Whereas the sun itself flies across the sky as a winged creature or is carried by an animal or a wheeled vehicle, sun beams are shot to earth as projectiles. The rays of the Lacandón solar god Äk Tet (our father) are sun arrows with flint tips (Rätsch and Ma'ax 1984:42). The Chol call the solar rays "arrowshafts of the sun" (Thompson 1960:142). The Tzotzil compare a sunbeam to a shaft, a bodkin, or a needle (Lamb n.d.b). In Mopan folklore, the sun shoots an arrow, killing his grandmother, Xkitza (Thompson 1967:23). The Sun God or a ruler impersonating the sun carries darts in Precolumbian Maya imagery (Fig. 3.5g).

In sum, an animal or a vehicle carries the sun, or the sun itself is a winged creature that can fly. Dwarfs convey the sun through the underworld in some accounts. In others, the sun travels through water or down a sacred tree. Although most of the contemporary Maya cultures have been influenced by Catholicism to varying degrees, there seem to be a number of core beliefs that reflect Precolumbian concepts, such as the sun's rays as arrows. The notion that animals carry the sun or that the sun transforms into an animal seems to have counterparts in Precolumbian times. Similarly, the sun's descent into the underworld on a tree seems to be reflected in Precolumbian imagery.

THE SUN GOD

The sun rules the cosmos for most Mayan speakers, who describe the sun as a human or godlike figure with a brilliant round face (B. Tedlock 1992b:173, 178). Generally the sun is male, but there are some instances of a female sun, as among the Chol (Iwaniszewski 1992:133). When the sun is male, he is usually identified with God or Jesus Christ in the indigenous form of Catholicism.

There is considerable variety in how the sun relates to the higher powers. A generalized link with God the Father may be expressed in the name "father sun" used by the Yucatec Maya of Quintana Roo (Villa Rojas 1969:272). Among the Tzotzil, the sun is variously identified as Our Lord Sun, Jesus Christ, the Child Jesus, God, or God the Father (Gossen 1982:29, Fig. 1; Guiteras Holmes 1961:152, 186, 313; Holland 1964:15). The Tzotzil of Chamula say that the sun is Christ, "our honorable father," who

lives with his father, San José, and carries a candle representing the Morning Star (Gossen 1974b:21, 23, Fig. 1; 1982:29, Fig. 1). The Tzotzil of San Andrés Larraínzar associate the sun with both Jesus Christ and San Salvador (Laughlin 1969:175). The Pokomchí say the Sun God admits them into the presence of God, like the saints who are also advocates with God (Mayers 1958:16). Apparently here the Sun God is not identified with God, but his role as a mediator between man and God suggests he is identified with Jesus.

In Zinacantán, the Tzotzil identify the sun with Señor Esquipulas, representing Christ on the cross; however the sun is not directly identified with Jesus Christ (Vogt 1969:360–361, 367–368). Ornamental reflecting mirrors hung on Señor Esquipulas may denote the ancient link between the sun and mirrors (Chapter 3). His image is positioned in the east of the chapel in accord with the position of the rising sun. In the year renewal rites, three silver necklaces are placed around his neck during the daylight hours, apparently to evoke sunrise (Vogt 1976:128).

Maya metaphors link the sun or Sun God with fire. The Tzeltal say that the sun carries fire from his milpa around the sky (Nash 1970:311). The Tzotzil of Chenalhó say that the sun is fire and light (Guiteras Holmes 1961:152, 292). Chamula names describing the Sun God relate him to heat and fire, and one of his names is Our Father Heat (Gossen 1974b:31). On the fourth day of the five-day Festival of Games in February, Chamula's Carnival officials run back and forth along a path of burning thatch in a fire walk that dramatizes the first ascent of the Sun/Christ into heaven (Gossen 1986:229–230, 246–247, figs. 1–2). Solar heat naturally evokes an image of solar fire, a metaphorical link also seen in Precolumbian times (Chapter 3).

Under certain conditions, the sun is associated with death. Winahel, located in the sun, is the abode of young children when they die, and of people struck by lightning or drowned as well as of women who die in childbirth, according to the Tzotzil of Chenalhó (Guiteras Holmes 1961:143, 258). Similarly, Aztec accounts record that women who died in childbirth are the companions of the sun until it reaches the western horizon.

The Sun God also influences human health. The Tzotzil pray to the sun at sunrise and sunset for good health (Thompson 1970b:238). The Yucatec Maya of Yalcobá say that when the sun is rising or at an overhead position at noon, it can send disease; the *hmèen* disposes of illness by sweeping it into a cave on the western horizon so that the sun will carry it off to the underworld at sunset (Sosa 1985:447). The Yucatec Maya of Maxcanú say that the spirits linked with death and sickness come out at noon. When the sun reaches its midnight position, it is "in the earth" and the danger of the night has passed away as the sun moves toward sunrise (Armador 1995:313). As we will see, a similar belief is recorded in Yucatec sources from the Colonial period, for in times of pestilence people made offerings to the sun at noon to prevent illness (Chapter 3). The noon sun may be connected with illness because the sun's rays are dangerously strong at this time.

Originally, the sun made by Kak'och only illuminated the upper heavens, but then the creator god made the sun Äk Tet to bring light to the earth (Bruce 1976:77). Another Lacandón solar god, Äk'inchob (cross-eyed lord), is the husband of the moon and the god of the milpa. A Tzotzil account from Chamula says that the sun gave mankind maize from his body as a hot food that came from his groin (Gossen 1974b:40). The Sun God is frequently mentioned in relation to Maya agriculture, reflecting the essential link between the sun and maize.

A Chol tale says that the moon had two children, and the younger one became the sun of our world (Cruz Guzmán 1994). Before he was transformed into the sun, the younger brother was a hunter whose older brother was lazy and jealous. He lay in his hammock when the younger brother went out to hunt birds. While hunting, the future sun found a tree filled with honey, which led to discord between the brothers. As a result, the world order was changed. The younger brother was transformed into the sun, and the world became what it is today. At this point, the sun introduced maize agriculture.

In most Maya tales that involve three brothers, the sun's relationship with one or both of his siblings is not harmonious. A Tzotzil tale from Chenalhó has Jesus Christ in the role of the sun, and his mother,

the Virgin, is the moon. Tired of his two older brothers teasing him, he transforms them into pigs (Guiteras Holmes 1961:183–186). A Chol tale identifies the moon as the mother of three boys, and the sun is the youngest of the brothers, as in the Tzotzil legend (Whittaker and Warkentin 1965:35–42). Here the sun's older brothers are maize farmers. Because they mistreat him, the future sun kills his elder brothers, so he has to learn how to plant maize from an old man. The sun clears his field during the day, but finds that each night the brush has grown back. By staying up all night he finds out that a rabbit is causing the plants to grow back, so he captures the rabbit and gives it to his lunar mother. But he gets tired of planting and decides to climb up the beam of the house to the sky. He carries a chicken with him, and his mother follows him carrying her rabbit; then they become the sun and the moon. Here the solar bird is a domesticated one introduced from Europe, but more commonly the avian transformation of the sun is a hummingbird, a solar image that can be traced back to Precolumbian times (Chapter 3).

In a tale of three brothers from the Cakchiquel of San Antonio, the sun and the moon are elder brothers who are farmers (Thompson 1970b:357). They turn their younger brother into a monkey when he tells their grandmother they are using magical hoes to do the work. Then they kill their grandmother by throwing her into a sweat bath and then into a fire.

A Mopan tale from Belize makes the three brothers blowgun hunters who provide their grandmother with meat (Thompson 1970b:355–356). When she does not share it with them, they kill her, after turning their younger brother into a monkey because he refuses to go along with the scheme. In Thompson's (1930:60–63, 120–125) earlier versions of the tale, the eldest brother is Lord Xulab, or Nohoch Ich (Big Eye), identified as both the planet Venus and the Morning Star; the middle child is the Sun (Lord Kin), and the youngest brother is T'up, who was to become Mars or Jupiter. The three hunt with their blowguns, bringing the dead birds to their grandmother (the aged moon?), who gives the meat to her tapir lover. The elder brothers (Venus and the Sun) plot to kill her, because she gives them nothing to eat. In another Mopan account, the elder and younger brother of the Sun are both aspects of Venus, representing the Morning Star and the Evening Star (Thompson 1970b: 343). The tale of a celestial family with Sun as the middle brother is also seen in Precolumbian times (Chapter 3).

A Chol tale is very similar, but there are some interesting substitutions (Thompson 1967: 30–31). The moon had seven children by a father who died. The widowed mother sends her children to work in the milpa so that she and the sun can have intercourse. She becomes pregnant, and the son of the sun is born wearing a small red hat and red trousers, carrying a machete in hand. His jealous half-brothers kill him, but he revives and returns home carrying a peccary. The same thing repeats the next day. On the third day they take him to the forest, where Son of the Sun asks his brothers to climb up and fetch some honey from the tree, but they throw down only wax. Angered, he gets the moles to eat the tree roots, felling the tree and smashing the brothers. Later the dead brothers are converted into animals.

A Tzeltal astronomical tale describes how Yax Kahkal (Green or First Sun) chops up his brother, the youngest in the family (Thompson 1967: 28–30 n. 7). Marianna Slocum (1965a) records a similar account, translating the older brother's name as Blue Sun. The wasps and bees collect the pieces, restoring the younger brother to life. The younger brother asks Blue Sun to climb a tree and throw down some honey, but he only throws down wax. Angered, the younger brother cuts down a tree, and Blue Sun is smashed to pieces that become the animals of the forest. The grandmother tried to seize the animals, but was only able to capture the rabbit, so that is what you see today on the face of the moon.

Another Tzeltal version of the tale makes Grandmother Moon the mother of three boys. Here it is the two elder brothers who climb the tree, angering their younger brother (the future sun) because they throw down only wax, which in Tzeltal is the same as the word for excrement (Nash 1970: 198–201). The tree falls and the elder brother turns into a pig; the second brother is transformed into a wild boar (peccary). The youngest brother becomes the sun when he picks up the fire from his milpa and goes up into the sky to walk around; the moon follows

him, which is why the day walks in front and the night walks behind. This is when time began.

The sun brings order and continuity to the world. Among contemporary Yucatec Maya, each dramatic break in history is a "new sun," the current sun or world age being that initiated by the Spanish conquest (Armador 1995: 316). Similarly, the Tzotzil say that the fourth creation took place about four hundred years ago (Gossen 1974a: 221).

We can conclude that in many tales the sun is a culture hero who is accorded great respect, sometimes even assigned the role of the supreme deity. The Sun God brings maize agriculture to the world or he produces maize in a more conventional fashion. The sun is hardworking and possesses many other personality traits considered to be positive. Occasionally, the sun has negative qualities, as when it sends disease at noon, an image that warns people about the dangerous rays of the noonday sun. Some tales say that the sun kills his brothers. Sibling rivalry translates into astronomical imagery that pairs the sun with an elder brother embodying the moon or the Morning Star, rivals of a younger brother representing another planet or the Evening Star.

IMAGES OF ECLIPSES

The dependence the Maya feel on the sun is reflected in their great fear of solar eclipses. The sun is the lifeblood of the people, and even a temporary loss of light is threatening. In traditional Maya communities, the people make as much noise as possible to avert calamity during an eclipse (Redfield and Villa Rojas 1962: 206–207; B. Tedlock 1992b: 184). The noise scares off the agent of the eclipse, usually identified as some sort of animal monster devouring the sun. People abstain from all normal activity during a solar eclipse. For example, in the Yucatec community of Maxcanú, women will not make tortillas and men will not farm or hunt; the animals may change their character during an eclipse, and the implements of work (digging sticks, knives, machetes) can come to life and attack their owners unless they are marked with a cross (Armador 1995: 314).

The Maya believe that solar eclipses are more dangerous than lunar eclipses (Ilía Nájera 1995; Remington 1977:79). Some say that the world will come to an end during a solar eclipse. According to the Chortí, an eclipse of the sun that lasts more than a day will bring the end of the world, and the spirits of the dead will come to life and eat those on earth (Fought 1972:428–429). The Yucatec of X-Cacal say that Don Juan Tutul Xiu will destroy the earth on the day that the sun is covered by a black curtain (eclipsed) if the Maya do not maintain their independence from the conquerors (Villa Rojas 1945:154). The Lacandón believe that the destructions of the world in previous eras all began with an eclipse, and a total eclipse will precede the end of this world (Closs 1989:393). They say an earthquake will come with an eclipse at the end of the world, and Kisin will awake and kick the pillars of the earth, splitting the earth so that the jaguars come out and eat most of the people (Perera and Bruce 1982:114–115). The moon is also threatened, and she carries loom sticks to protect herself against the jaguars that will be let loose from the underworld when this world comes to an end (Thompson 1970b:246).

The most common explanation for eclipses among the Maya is that there is an animal devouring the sun or moon. Michael Closs (1989:390–398) notes that the agent of solar and lunar eclipses is the same in most cases. Sometimes the animal is a jaguar or a *tigre,* but more often it is an ant. Precolumbian Maya images show animals biting the symbol for solar eclipse; however, none represent ants (Chapter 4).

Accounts of lunar eclipses frequently mention a feline. The Chol describe a lunar eclipse as "red moon," when a *tigre* seizes the moon (Iwaniszewski 1992:131). The Chontal Maya say that a jaguar devours the moon during an eclipse (Villa Rojas 1969:236). The Tzotzil of Chenalhó say that Poslob eats the sun or the moon during an eclipse; he is a jaguar who appears as balls of fire (Guiteras Holmes 1961:152, 227, 292). The Yucatec Maya say that lunar eclipses are caused by a jaguar or an ant called Xulab, a name for Venus in some Maya folktales (Redfield and Villa Rojas 1962:206; Thompson 1970b:235). Xulab can be translated as "to cut," suggesting the leafcutter ant and the semicircular bite they take out of leaves, apparently evoking the image of an eclipse (Lamb, personal communication 1996). Mi-

chael Closs (1989) concludes that Venus is an eclipse agent among the Maya today, as in Precolumbian times. The Lacandón accounts say that the creator god, Hachäkyum, attacks the moon, causing a lunar eclipse; the moon defends herself with her loom, but her strength is not sufficient, and she is finally covered (Rätsch and Ma'ax 1984:43).

Terms for eclipses in Yucatec Mayan reveal specific symbolism (Barrera Vásquez 1980; Ilía Nájera 1995). The term *chi'bil* (bite) is apparently used for partial eclipses, an expression that makes sense in light of what one sees during a partial solar eclipse. For total solar eclipses the Yucatec Maya say *tupa'an* (put out the flame) and *tupa'an u wich k'in* or *tupul u wich k'in,* meaning to "blind or erase the sun." The term *tupul u wich u'* is used for a lunar eclipse, evoking parallels with Precolumbian imagery of lunar eclipses showing the Moon Goddess with her eyes shut (Chapter 4). The Tojolabal Maya of Chiapas describe a solar eclipse with the term *cha' k'ab'u,* referring to the end of the sun, implying that the sun dies (Ilía Nájera 1995:323).

Thompson (1960:11, 231) notes that the widespread Mesoamerican belief that eclipses are fights between the sun and the moon is not shared by the Maya; nevertheless, a number of Maya accounts use this explanation for eclipses. The Tzeltal, Tzutujil, and the Pokomchí believe that eclipses are caused by fights between the sun and the moon. Precolumbian Aztec images suggest that the sun and the moon are fighting during eclipses (Milbrath 1995b, 1997). Images that account for eclipses as fights suggest an understanding that the relative position of the sun and the moon causes eclipses.

Some Tojolabal accounts say that the sun and the moon come together in a sexual union at the time of an eclipse (Báez-Jorge 1988:244). Others say that the moon is furious and bites the sun during a solar eclipse, but they attribute lunar eclipses to an attack by black ants (Ilía Nájera 1995:323). Such a distinction between the causes of lunar and solar eclipses suggests observations made of the relative positions of the sun and the moon, for the new moon passing in front of the sun makes it look as if the moon takes a bite out of the sun; but because lunar eclipses occur when the sun and the moon are at opposite sides of the sky at the full moon, the Tojolabal invoke a third party as the cause of lunar eclipse.

A number of Maya communities say that the eclipsed body is ill in some respect, considerably weakened or dying. The Cakchiquel believe that the sun and the moon die during an eclipse (Remington 1977:79). The Tzotzil Maya of Zinacantán say that the moon blackens or dies during an eclipse, and similar descriptions are applied to the sun during a solar eclipse (Laughlin 1988:388). A related belief about the moon is recorded among the Tzotzil of Chenalhó (Guiteras Holmes 1961:152). On the other hand, the Chortí say that the Moon Goddess loses her powers of fecundity during a lunar eclipse (Wisdom 1940:400).

Throughout the Maya area, eclipses are believed to cause illness and death and to be particularly dangerous to pregnant women (Ilía Nájera 1995:325). The Tzotzil of Chenalhó ascribe different kinds of illness to eclipses associated with different directions and colors (Guiteras Holmes 1961:36). In Zinacantán, eclipses forecast famine and death and occur when the souls of evil people try to kill the sun or the moon (Laughlin 1975:58). The Lacandón say that if there is a solar eclipse, a man will die; if there is a lunar eclipse, a woman will die (Bruce 1979:181). Lunar eclipses are also linked with the death of Tzotzil women at San Pedro Chenalhó (Guiteras Holmes 1961:152, 292). People of this village say that great birds of prey can come down and take out your eyes during a solar eclipse (Guiteras Holmes 1961:153). This metaphor expresses the belief that solar eclipses cause blindness, no doubt a warning about the real dangers of watching a solar eclipse.

Despite fears that eclipses bring famine, illness, and death, the Lacandón and Quiché watch the reflection of eclipse events in containers of water (B. Tedlock 1992b:184). During a lunar eclipse, the Tzotzil of Zinacantán place a bowl of water outside so that the moon can "wash her face." In Precolumbian times, eclipses were probably also observed in stone basins and bowls of water, and in mirrors made of reflective stones.

The Maya fear eclipses because they are irregular events that are often linked with predictions about the end of the world. Eclipse events cannot be pre-dicted without access to sophisticated tables unknown to traditional Maya communities. The eclipse agent is an animal, sometimes the same one that will devour people at the end of the world. In some cases, fights between the sun and the moon cause eclipses, an explanation that apparently recognizes that the relative position of the sun and the moon causes eclipses. Accounts that make an ant the cause of eclipses seem to refer to Venus as the third party responsible for eclipses (see below).

THE LUNAR RHYTHMS

There are a number of different explanations for why the moon disappears during conjunction (new moon). The Chortí believe that the new moon is visiting the land of the dead (Girard 1949:467–468). The Tzotzil of Chenalhó say that the new moon is dead, and evil is rampant because the protecting light of the moon is lacking (Guiteras Holmes 1961:35). Thompson (1960:111, 238) concludes that the Yucatec Maya, past and present, share the belief that when the moon disappears in conjunction, she goes to the land of rain, the abode of the Chacs, or she goes to a lake, a well, or a cenote.

Although the Quiché of Momostenango count the lunar month from the first appearance of the crescent after conjunction, farmers and midwives prefer to count the months from full moon to full moon because of the difficulty of sighting the first crescent (B. Tedlock 1992b:182–183). Köhler (1980:593) maintains that among contemporary Maya the month is usually counted from first visibility. However, Thompson (1960:236) notes that some Tzeltal, Chol, and Tzotzil villages of Chiapas begin the month when the moon disappears in conjunction.

One persistent problem is that Maya terms for the first visible crescent seem to be counterparts for our term *new moon*, referring to the invisible moon during conjunction. This terminology has led to confusion in the literature with the English term *new moon*. For example, the Tzotzil of San Andrés Larraínzar use the term *'ach' hme'tik* (new our mother) to refer to the first visible crescent. Similarly, an Early Colonial period dictionary of the Tzotzil of Zinacantán refers to first visibility with the phrases *'ach 'u* (new moon) and *nach' 'u* (have new moon appear; Köhler 1991a:319–320).

The Quiché name *nic'aj ic'* (half moon) applies to the phase we call the first quarter, which seems appropriate because the moon is half illuminated at this time (B. Tedlock 1992b:183). The waxing gibbous moon is *chak'ajic* (maturing or ripening). According to Guillermo Sedat (1955), the waxing moon in Quiché is *sa'xca xq'uic,* a name that alludes to the goddess Blood Woman. The term for the full moon is *xoroc li po,* meaning "to make the moon round." The Quiché also say that the full moon is masculine, identifying it as the nocturnal equivalent of the sun, because its movements at this time resemble those of the sun (B. Tedlock 1992b:183).

Maya descriptions of lunar phases often imply that the moon ages over the course of the month, and the Maya sometimes refer to the first visible crescent as a baby or child. The Tzotzil of Zinacantán compare the full moon to an old person or old corn (*yih;* Laughlin 1975:74, 385). The Quiché say that the waxing moon is "our mother," and the waning moon is an old woman called "our grandmother" (B. Tedlock 1992a:31; 1992b:183–184). The Zoques, living just beyond the Maya area in Chiapas, assign age grades to the lunar phases, for they relate the new moon to people who are three years or under, whereas the waning moon is related to people who are sixty-five years or older (Báez-Jorge 1988:247). In a similar fashion, the Precolumbian Maya Moon Goddess has both a youthful and aged aspect, apparently related to lunar phases (Chapter 4).

Among the Tzutujil, the lunar months are linked with the Marías and Martíns, representing a female-male dichotomy with twelve females or twelve males, or six females and six males (Tarn and Prechtel 1986:175–176, 180–181). The festivals of female saints (Marías) dominate the dry season, whereas the Martíns are associated with the wet season. The thirteenth month is the intercalary month identified with the demonic Francisca Batz'bal.

Although the Zoques of Chiapas are not Maya, their proximity to the Maya area provides an interesting comparative dimension. They divide the lunar months into three seasons: the months with cold (December–February), the months with wind and rain (June–October), and the months with heat (March–May; Báez-Jorge 1983:388–389, 1988:247).

During the waxing moon, animals, plants, trees, and people are considered to be tender, thus the Quiché avoid butchering, harvesting, woodcutting, and sexual relations. During the waning moon, however, these activities become propitious (Tedlock 1983:66–67). This is the time that the moon is mature or hard, and she remains that way until she is "buried" (conjunction).

Cycles of illness are connected with the changing lunar phases. For example, the Tzotzil say that broken bones become painful during the waning moon (Laughlin 1975:74). In Quintana Roo, the Yucatec Maya say that the full moon induces epileptic fits and the waning moon is dangerous to those who are gravely ill (Báez-Jorge 1988:256). They say that in life-threatening disease, if the patient makes it through the period of the waning moon, there will be improvement during the waxing moon (Villa Rojas 1945:136; 1969:275). On the other hand, tumors and pustules grow larger as the moon waxes, according to the Yucatec Maya of Dzitas (Thompson 1972:50). The Tojolabal say that the waxing moon infects wounds, whereas the waning moon cures wounds (Báez-Jorge 1988:248–249). For this reason, the Moon Goddess is the patroness of medicine or disease among a number of Maya cultures, such as the Cakchiquel and Kekchí (Thompson 1970b:243; 1972:50–51). It comes as no surprise, therefore, that the Moon Goddess appears in a number of Precolumbian Maya medical almanacs (Chapter 4).

The relationship between the moon and events on earth can be seen in tides that affect fishing and salt harvesting. Even in highland communities far from the coast, there seems to be a connection between the moon and salt, as among the Tzotzil, who call the Virgin (the moon) "our lady of the salt" (Laughlin and Karasik 1988:205).

It is noteworthy that the Maya believe a number of different cycles in nature respond to the lunar phases. The strongest relationship can be noted in the cycles of plants, discussed at length in the section on lunar agriculture (see below). Other important lunar cycles are noted in beekeeping. For example, the Tojolabal say that the waning moon "conserves honey and wax," hénce they extract honey at this time (Báez-Jorge 1988:248–249).

Many agree that the moon is linked with rain, although the phase associated with rainfall differs from group to group. The Tojolabal Maya say that the new moon "brings water," whereas at the time of the full moon "rain goes away" (Báez-Jorge 1988:248). The Chortí Maya explain that the waning quarter moon is a pot tipped over that allows water to spill out, whereas the full moon is a full pot that retains water, except that a *red* full moon brings rain (Fought 1972:387; Girard 1949:466, 1962:134). Similarly, the Yucatec Maya call the full moon "full pot moon" (Redfield and Villa Rojas 1962:205). The Quiché and Cakchiquel say that the rains are most abundant during the new moon and full moon (Remington 1977:80–81). These beliefs may be based on observations of nature, for scientific evidence also suggests a link between the lunar phases and variations in rainfall. One study published in *Science* noted a peak in rainfall near the middle of the first and third weeks of the synodical month, especially on the third to fifth days after the new moon and full moon (Bradley et al. 1962).

Color is another aspect of the moon that the Maya watch with great interest. Generally, the moon is visualized as white, but changes in color are deemed significant. The Chol of Buena Vista say that the rains come when there is a "red moon," and they believe a "blackened moon" will also bring rain (Iwaniszewski 1992:131).

A number of Maya groups link changes in the position of the crescent moon to variations in rainfall. The Achí of Cubulco, who speak a Quiché dialect, describe the lunar position in different seasons by using hand gestures. They say that the moon is "upright" during the dry season, with the crescent form turned in such a way that the water is unable to get out. When it is rainy, the moon is "lying on its side" with the crescent turned sideways so the water can spill out, which they show by using their hands to imitate the crescent moon tipping over to pour water

(Neuenswander 1981). Hand gestures are also part of the terminology for phases of the moon among the Tzotzil (Köhler 1991b:238). They say that when the crescent moon is horizontal, it does not have water, but when it shifts to the right it carries water. The tipped orientation certainly indicates a rainy seasonal position. The Tzutujil say that the moon holds rainwater and slowly turns sideways as the rainy season approaches until the water spills out in the form of rain (Tarn and Prechtel 1986:176). The position of the newly emerged crescent moon is directly related to the seasons. In fact, modern astronomical charts show that the first visible crescent moon is "tipped" over from June to November, which corresponds roughly to the Mesoamerican rainy season (Ottewell 1990).

Contemporary Maya people observe the moon in relation to the solar seasons. The Achí of Cubulco in Alta Verapaz divide the year into two seasons, and they say that in the rainy season, the moon is full of water (Neuenswander 1981). They believe that the moon's water content determines the beginning and end of the rainy season.

The Quiché track the sidereal cycle of the moon through the background of stars, noting the moon's positions in relation to the day names of the 260-day calendar (B. Tedlock 1992b:191–196, fig. 37). They count off a triple set of sidereal lunar months (3 × 27.32167 days = 81.96501 days), reckoning this figure as 82 days. They visit different mountain shrines in accord with this period and a 65-day count that runs simultaneously. During these visits, they look at both the phase and sidereal position of the moon.

Our month tracks the moon's changing phases, but the Maya recognize many other lunar rhythms. They observe the position of the crescent and the color of the moon as well as the lunar phases to predict rainfall. The lunar cycles are linked to the rhythms of the seasons, especially in relation to the changing position of the first crescent moon. Lunar phases are also believed to influence cycles of illness. There is a widespread belief that the phase of lunar conjunction (new moon) involves a visit to the underworld, often linked with a watery place, such as a cave or a well. Other lunar rhythms are built into imagery of the Moon Goddess, who ages over the course of the month.

LUNAR AGRICULTURE

The moon's role in the agricultural cycle may be one reason it has such a great importance among the Maya today. Quiché farmers count from full moon to full moon (B. Tedlock 1985:84–85, 87; 1992a:30; 1992b:183, 185, 189–190). The calendar begins with clearing the fields around the full moon in February. The maize crop is named for the calendar day in the 260-day count that corresponds to the full moon in March, when sowing must be complete. They determine the date of the maize harvest by a calendar count from the full moon that follows planting. The first and second weeding must be performed at the time of the full moon. They harvest black beans and the first ears of corn at the time of the full moon. The waxing moon, when the moon is female, is the appropriate time for the annual planting of dried maize kernels and black beans (B. Tedlock 1992b: 185). The fact that most aspects of the Quiché maize cycle are timed by the full moon, which is male, may account for the imagery of the moon merged with the Maize God in Classic Maya iconography (Chapter 4).

The nine-month growing period of mountain maize among the Quiché parallels the nine-month period for human gestation (B. Tedlock 1992b: 190). Ideally, the crops will come to fruition on the same day number and name in the 260-day calendar as when they were sown. The Quiché identify the 260-day cycle as the lunar agrarian year (Alvarado 1975:76; León 1954:38). This may be linked with the fixed 260-day agricultural calendar found in a number of Maya cultures.

There is considerable variety in the beliefs about lunar agriculture among the Yucatec Maya. The full moon after the first rains is the optimum planting time for maize, according to some accounts (Pérez 1942:17–18). The people of Chan Kom say that maize can be planted during any lunar phase; vines should be planted at the new moon, and the best time for planting fruit trees and root crops is when the moon is full or three days after the moon has

been "buried" (the waxing crescent; Redfield and Villa Rojas 1962:205–206). Another account says root crops are best planted three days after full moon (Sosa 1985:456). One Yucatec Maya lunar calendar calls for maize, beans, and squash to be planted on the full moon of May or June, but all other activities that involve the crops are to take place during the waning moon (Pérez 1946:204).

The Tzotzil of Chenalhó say that seeds will not sprout if planted during the new moon, for when the moon is dead and she is walking with her son (the sun), the seed will never be returned (Guiteras Holmes 1961:35, 41, 45). They prefer to plant maize around the full moon, at the time of the "mature moon" (which lasts three days). This is also the time to plant squash and beans. The mature-moon phase can be extended to include both the waxing and waning gibbous moon, allowing for nine days of agricultural activity. The mature moon is also the preferred time for felling trees and for bending the maize stalks, although there seems to be a tendency to bend the maize stalks during the waxing phase (Guiteras Holmes 1961:35, 153). On the other hand, a Tzotzil text from Chamula recorded in 1968 notes that they wait until the full moon to double over the corn as the first phase of the harvest (Gossen 1974a:252). Similarly, the Tzotzil of Zinacantán say that harvesting of the maize must be done only when the moon is full, which is also the time to fell trees so that the wood will not be attacked by insects (Vogt 1997).

Other Maya groups show similar variations in their beliefs about lunar agriculture. Some of the Chortí say that the best time for planting is four days before lunar conjunction; others say the four days after the first appearance of the moon are the best, or they recommend planting during the waxing moon so that the seed will have the best chance of germination (Girard 1949:466; Wisdom 1940:400). A contrary notion is expressed by the Tojolabal Maya, who say that the waxing moon ruins the seeds, whereas plants grow rapidly during the waning moon, the preferred time to plant maize and beans (Báez-Jorge 1988:248–249). The Pokomchí say that maguey and yucca and all sorts of plants are best planted by the full moon, which is also the best time to cut poles for the houses (Mayers 1958:38–39). The waning moon is not good for cutting wood or planting because the produce will be wormy. On the other hand, the Chol of Buena Vista say that planting and woodcutting should be avoided during the waxing moon, and the full moon is appropriate for planting tomatoes, but most other crops do better planted during the waning moon, except for maize, which can be planted in any phase of the moon (Iwaniszewski 1992: 131–132).

We can conclude that the lunar phases best suited for different activities clearly vary from group to group. Nevertheless, all seem to share a belief that the moon and agriculture are closely linked, and observation of the phases of the moon are especially important in timing agricultural activities. The most commonly preferred time for planting maize is around the full moon, and a number of other events in the maize cycle are timed by the full moon.

THE CELESTIAL PAIR

The sun and the moon, being very close in size at the time of the full moon, form a natural sky pair. Maya legends underscore a close relationship between the sun and the moon, with the sun ruling day and the moon ruling night. The notion of a day mirror and a night mirror representing the sun and the moon respectively is seen in a Kekchí Maya tale from Belize. The legend tells us that long ago the sun placed a mirror in the center of the sky. Each day the Sun God traveled from the east to the center and retraced his path back to the east, but the mirror made it seem that he continued to the west; at night the mirror image of the moon traveled across the sky in the same manner (Thompson 1930:132). The Kekchí tale goes on to explain that the moon's light was too bright for people to sleep, so Lord Kin gouged out one of the moon's eyes. Similarly, a Mopan legend from Belize recounts that when the sun and the moon ascended into heaven to take up their duties, they were equally bright, but people complained they could not sleep, so Sun took out one of Moon's eyes so she would not shine too brightly at night (Thompson 1967:35). These legends pair the sun and the full moon, but indicate that the moon is not as bright because it has only one eye.

Other sets of oppositions involve the sun and the moon. They are often paired as husband and wife in Maya folklore; indeed, when they are married they can share the same Ahau title in some highland cultures. The moon and the sun as mother and son is another common pairing of opposite genders (Thompson 1967). An opposition of genders and qualities of temperature is seen in a Tzotzil account that says the male sun created maize, which has the quality of being hot; the female moon produced beans, which are cold (López-Austin 1994:108). The sun gave humankind maize from his groin, whereas the moon gave potatoes (her breast milk) and beans (her necklace).

Many accounts indicate that the moon existed before the sun. Often the female moon is older than the sun, as indicated by the moon's role as mother of the sun and the common titles Father Sun and Grandmother Moon. Even when the pair are husband and wife, the moon seems to have priority, for the marriage of the Moon Goddess takes place in darkness before the sun and the moon take up their celestial duties (Thompson 1960:230; Watanabe 1983:724–725).

The Quiché and Cakchiquel traditions involve brothers who are the sun and the moon, apparently an ancient tradition that can be traced back to the Popol Vuh, a narrative recorded in Quiché sometime after the conquest and translated into Spanish around 1701 (D. Tedlock 1985:28; Thompson 1967: 22). In the Popol Vuh, the sun and the moon are twin brothers, which indicates a pairing of like beings rather than paired opposites. In this case, the lunar twin may represent the full moon (Chapter 4).

We can see that when the moon and the sun are paired together in primordial times, something usually happens to the moon to darken it. The sun-moon pair establishes a series of oppositions: day-night, young-old, male-female, light-dark, and even hot-cold.

THE MOON GODDESS

The moon is often associated with motherhood, sometimes playing the role of the mother of the Maya people, as among the Chortí, who refer to the moon as "our mother" (*ka tu'*; Wisdom 1940:400 n. 30). More often the moon is the sun's mother, and sometimes her duties as a mother are specified, as seen in a tale from Chamula recounting that the moon is responsible for feeding the sun maize gruel each morning on the eastern horizon (Gossen 1974b:40).

Sometimes the moon is linked with the Virgin Mary, the archetypal mother. The Virgin has multiple aspects in Maya Catholicism ideally suited to a variety of lunar images. Seasonal festivals dedicated to the Virgin may honor the moon at different times of year. The seasonal cycle of the Virgin in Maya festivals has yet to be explored in relation to lunar imagery.

The Moon Goddess influences the female body as patroness of fertility, pregnancy, and childbirth. The Tzotzil pray to the moon, the "Holy Mother," for fertility, and they believe that a woman is most fertile at the full moon. Tzotzil women note the lunar phase when they miss their period, because they will give birth after nine lunar months (Köhler 1991b:241). According to the Quiché, the feminine moon rules over birth; it gives women their menstrual cycle and stops the flow of blood during the nine lunations of pregnancy (Earle and Snow 1985:243–244). Among the Quiché Maya, menstruation is "the blood that stems from the moon" (Furst 1986:72). And the Itzaj Maya say "her moon lowered" when a woman menstruates (Hofling, personal communication 1995). The Tzotzil say the moon menstruates at the new moon (López-Austin 1994:111). Those of Chenalhó say the moon and menstruation are related (Guiteras Holmes 1961:106). The Maya word *ú* means "moon" and "menstruation" (Barrera Vásquez 1980).

Although the moon is predominantly female, there are some instances of gender transformation. Data collected among the Quiché show that the moon is generally female, but it becomes male at the time of the full moon (B. Tedlock 1992b:183). Some images suggest that the moon is a female version of the sun, as among the Lacandón, who describe the moon as a howler monkey, specifically a female howler monkey known as "mother-sun" or "lady-sun" (*na'-k'in*; Bruce 1979:141). Among the Chol from Buena Vista in Chiapas, the female sun is

the mother of the male moon, but the moon takes on a feminine quality when identified with the Virgin (Iwaniszewski 1992:133). This gender shift is explained by beliefs that the moon's waxing period is female and its waning is male. Gender ambiguity is also a characteristic of the moon in Precolumbian times (Chapter 4).

Jaguars may be connected with the moon among the Quiché, especially the full moon (D. Tedlock 1985:368–369). The jaguar may also be a lunar image among the Tzotzil. The Sun God and his jaguar companion are lifted up toward heaven to symbolize resurrection in the Carnival festival of Chamula (Gossen 1986:244). The timing of Carnival, based on both lunar and solar observations linked with Easter, may encode a relationship between the sun and the jaguar as a representative of the moon. In a like fashion, there seems to be a link between the moon and jaguars in Precolumbian times (Chapter 4).

Often the Moon Goddess has a rabbit, or the rabbit itself is seen on the moon. A number of tales explain how the Moon Goddess acquired her rabbit. The Chol say that the sun gave the rabbit to his lunar mother when he found the rabbit making the weeds grow in his garden at night (Whittaker and Warkentin 1965:35–42). They note that even when the moon is invisible, the rabbit remains in the sky (Iwaniszewski 1992:133). The Lacandón say that the creator god Hachäkyum made Äkna' (the Moon Goddess), giving her a rabbit as a house pet and painting a rabbit on her clothes. Precolumbian Maya art often shows the moon deity with a rabbit.

According to the Lacandón, Äkna' has a weaving loom that is very bright: the loom is her light and her fire, but her fire is very cold (Rätsch and Ma'ax 1984:43). Another lunar goddess, Ixchel, is the daughter of Hachäkyum (the creator god) and the wife of the "squint-eyed lord" (the sun); she is also the goddess of childbirth, weaving, and the moon (McGee 1990:65–66). Although nowhere is this explicitly stated, Äkna' and Ixchel may represent different lunar phases because the term *t'äläkbal äkna'* refers specifically to the full moon (Bruce 1979:228).

Other ethnographic accounts from the Maya area link the moon with weaving. The Quiché goddess of embroidery is Ixchel; they say that she inspires designs in weaving that represent astronomical symbols (León 1945:43). The Tzotzil recount that the moon, the mother of the sun, is a poor woman who spins and weaves in exchange for corn (Báez-Jorge 1988:243). To revive the weaving tradition, the Tzotzil weavers in Magdalenas prayed to the lunar Virgin to teach them to weave (Morris and Foxx 1987:113). A legend recorded among the Kekchí in the Mopan area says that the young moon was weaving when the sun visited her in the guise of a hummingbird, inspiring her to brocade this bird on the cloth (Thompson 1970b:370). Among the Tzutujil, all things connected with weaving are female and are linked to Grandmother Moon (Prechtel and Carlsen 1988:123, 131). The thirteenth month represents Francisca Batz'bal, the grandmother, the thread maker, and the spindle itself. Twelve females named María, like the Virgin, represent the lunar months and the parts of the loom (Tarn and Prechtel 1986:176–178). In a similar fashion, Precolumbian Maya imagery links the Moon Goddess with weaving (Chapter 4).

The Moon Goddess is widely connected with water, including rainfall and water stored in jars traditionally carried by Maya women. The Lacandón refer to September, the most rainy month, as "much rains our Lady moon" (*hahakna'*; Bruce 1979:154). The Tzutujil say that the moon contains water that becomes rain; the moon is the "lady of the stored water," meaning the water jar, and she picks up water and pours it over her body when it rains (Tarn and Prechtel 1986:174–176). They note that the Moon Goddess wears a serpent rainbow on her head when there will be rain. Their beliefs are confirmed by meteorologists, who note that a halo around the moon is a sign of rain (Hazen 1900).

In addition to rainfall, the moon is also closely linked with bodies of water. The Tzutujil say that Lake Amatitlán was formed when some boys broke the water jars belonging to the twelve Marías, who represent the lunar months born out of the moon (Orellana 1977:194–195; Tarn and Prechtel 1986:174–176). The people of the Tzotzil community of Chenalhó say that the moon is in some way related to all lakes, and they throw clothing into the lake as an offering to the Virgin (Guiteras Holmes 1961:203, 292). The Cakchiquel say that the Moon Goddess owns Lake Amatitlán (Thompson 1960:238). At the end of the dry season, the Pokomam Maya pray at Lake Amatitlán for the Virgin Mary (the Moon Goddess) to bring rain (Berlo 1984:181). For people living in Yucatán, the Moon Goddess is connected with both the cenote (well) and the sea, associations also recorded in Colonial period documents. For example, the eighteenth-century *Ritual of the Bacabs* refers to the moon as "she in the middle of the cenote" and "lady of the sea" (Thompson 1970b:244–245).

There is also a relationship between rainfall and the Virgin in her aspect as the moon. Among the Yucatec Maya, when the *hmèen* prays to the Chacs for rain, he invokes the Moon Goddess in her guise as the Virgin Mary (D. Thompson 1954:28). The Maya of Quintana Roo say that she rides forth on horseback as one of the Chacs.

The moon's monthly union with the sun is often visualized as a marriage, but despite her condition as a married woman, the moon has a licentious nature in Maya folklore (Thompson 1970b:243). In a Mopan tale from Belize, the sun suspects his wife is having an affair with his elder brother, Xulab (the future Morning Star), and to punish the couple he feeds them a tamale filled with a mixture that makes them vomit (Thompson 1967:34–35).

A number of tales involve the sun's longing for the moon, imagery that evokes the union of the sun and the moon during conjunction. There are a variety of tales among the Kekchí, Mopan, and Cakchiquel that tell about the lovesick sun capturing the moon (Preuss 1995; Thompson 1970b:365). In a Mopan tale, the sun transforms into a hummingbird to court the Moon Goddess (XT'actani), but after he is felled by her grandfather's blowgun, he resumes his human form and persuades her to elope with him in a canoe during the night (Thompson 1967:31–32; 1970b:363–364). To escape, the sun hides the crystal or jade (the *sastun*) that allows the grandfather to sees everything and everywhere, but the old man enlists the aid of one of the Chacs, who hurls a thunderbolt at the couple. At that moment, the sun turns himself into a turtle and the moon into a crab. The sun escapes injury, but the moon is killed. She is restored to life in thirteen days after dragonflies collect her flesh and blood in thirteen hollow logs. When she comes to life again, she has no vagina, so Lord Kin calls on the deer to step on her to make an imprint that forms her vagina (Thompson 1930: 126–129). But this was not such a good idea because shortly thereafter she had an affair with his brother, the Venus god Lord Xulab!

We can conclude that the Maya believe that the moon controls fertility in plants and people, cycles of agriculture, disease, menstruation, and all forms of water, including rainfall. The Moon Goddess is often connected with water-carrying, motherhood, and weaving—female activities appropriate to the moon's female gender. The moon is predominantly female, but it can change gender, especially at the time of the full moon. Although the moon has affairs with other planets, her monthly union with the sun is often visualized as a form of marriage.

VENUS AMONG THE CONTEMPORARY MAYA

When we look at contemporary Maya terms for Venus we cannot help but be impressed by how many variants there are. No doubt these names reflect subtle differences in various aspects of the planet. For example, the Lacandón say that the Morning Star is "white earth" and the Evening Star is "white sun," located in the center of the earth (Rätsch 1985: 37–38). Alternate translations for the Morning Star's name include "white lord of the earth" or "false lord of the earth" (*äh säh kab;* Bruce et al. 1971: 15; McGee 1990: 54–55). Thompson (1970b: 250) notes that the Morning Star is Ah Ahzah Cab (awakener) in both Lacandón and Yucatec. The Evening Star is "false sun" (*äh säh k'in;* Bruce et al. 1971: 15) and *ah ocsah kin,* a Yucatec expression for "he who makes the sun enter," implying that the Evening Star is responsible for the setting sun (Stone 1983: 232).

Names for Venus often refer to its large size or brilliance. Among the Quiché of Rabinal, Venus is "great star," and a similar meaning is conveyed by the terms for Venus among the Manche Chol, Chuh, Tojolabal (Chaneabal), Mam, and Ixil (Thompson

1960: 218). The Chol name for Venus in both morning and evening aspects is *lucero* (luminary one), which can be applied to other planets if Venus is absent from the sky (Iwaniszewski 1992: 132).

Catholic saints can also be connected with Venus. Santiago, a native war chief who speaks only Quiché, is the "great star" (*nima chumil;* Cook 1986: 149). This is intriguing because among the Chortí, Santiago is the god of thunder and lightning who has flames and fire as a war shield (Girard 1962: 251). Precolumbian images also link Venus with a cult of warfare associated with Tlaloc (Chapter 5).

Venus is also linked with the scorpion in Lacandón names recorded by Blom and La Farge (1926–1927, 2: 469, 472; Carlson 1991). Another variant of the insect theme is seen in the Yucatec Maya name for Venus, *xux ek',* or "wasp star," used for both the Morning Star and the Evening Star (Barrera Vásquez 1980). Colonial period accounts from Yucatán mention Venus as the "wasp star" (Roys 1972: 96). Venus is "the great destroyer" (*nah xulaab*), a species of ant, among the Lacandón (Bruce 1979: 247; Bruce et al. 1971: 15). Yucatec Maya accounts say that evil-smelling red ants or the king of leaf-cutting ants is an eclipse agent (Closs 1989: 391, 398).

In a Mopan tale already discussed, Lord Xulab, or Nohoch Ich (Big Eye), is a bearded god who is the eldest of three brothers (Thompson 1930: 60–63, 120–125, 129; 1970b: 250, 355–356). Venus as the elder brother of the sun represents a direct link between the sun and Venus through kinship. Lord Xulab is the rival of the sun for the affections of the Moon Goddess. The Morning Star is a sort of "master of the animals" among the Kekchí and Mopan. Thompson (1970b: 250) suggests that Xulab is the "keeper of wild animals," and that he is a god of hunting linked to dawn because that is the best hunting time. Everything connected with hunting and fishing is under the care of Xulab (Villa Rojas 1969: 272).

Venus is usually assigned the role of elder brother, which presumably would give the planet a position of honor, but he is neither a model of good behavior nor of physical perfection (Thompson 1930: 119–140; 1960: 218; Villa Rojas 1969: 272). A number of folktales describe Venus as ugly or lazy. A Chol tale recounts that Venus, the elder brother of the Sun, is jealous and so aggressive that his mother (the Moon) has to protect the young Sun from him (Guzmán et al. 1986). Venus is also lazy, and he lies in his hammock all day while his younger brother goes hunting. This image probably reflects observations that the Morning Star is "up" (visible) for only a few hours in the morning, while the Sun works hard all day.

Among the Kekchí, the Morning Star (Kaacwa Cakchahim) is not lazy, but he is ugly (Schackt 1986: 59, 176–178). The Morning Star was originally the "owner" of all wild animals. Also known as Señor Lucero, the Morning Star was a very good hunter who went out every morning and did not return until late at night. Because of the hours he kept, his wife did not know how ugly he was. His face was covered with warts, and his hands and clothes were covered with blood from all the animals he hunted. He got angry when she tried to see him at night, and he threw all the animals away, and cursed women so that they could eat only chili peppers.

A number of Venus images express a relationship with the sun. The Kekchí refer to the Morning Star as a dog running ahead of the sun (Thompson 1970b:250). The Quiché say that Venus as the Morning Star is the "carrier of the day" or the "carrier of the sun," and Venus is the "sun passer" in the ancient Quiché tale of the Popol Vuh (Edmonson 1971: 170; D. Tedlock 1991). The Tzotzil Maya of Chamula describe Venus as "our lord sun/Christ's candle" (Gossen 1982:29, Fig. 1). The role as a candle of the sun suggests an image of Venus, for this planet never strays far from the sun (Chapter 2).

Some Maya accounts incorporate Venus as a Catholic saint or, more often, as the fallen angel, Lucifer. Various Tzotzil communities link Venus with Saint Thomas (Köhler 1991c:252). Venus takes the role of Lucifer, or the "devil," in a number of accounts (Closs 1989; Preuss 1995). At San Pedro Chenalhó, a Tzotzil village, Lusibel (Lucifer) seems to be related to Venus (Lamb 1995:275). He had been one of two suns a long time ago, but was replaced by the Christ child (kox) because he did not give sufficient heat (Guiteras Holmes 1961:186). The notion of Venus as a "sun" in a previous world age evokes a

link with the central Mexican image of Quetzalcoatl (quetzal-serpent), the Venus god who was the sun of a previous epoch (Codex Ríos, folio 6r).

The Tzotzil of Zinacantán visualize the Morning Star as having both female and male aspects (Laughlin 1977:253–254; Laughlin and Karasik 1988:249; Vogt 1969:316–318). They say that Venus is "he who eats the river snail," indicating a masculine gender and possibly a specific seasonal aspect. Vogt (1997) notes that they refer to Venus as "eats snails" during Lent. The Morning Star is also an ugly girl who is the "elder sister." Vogt (1969:316–317) also observes that another name for the Morning Star is the "sweeper of the path," who prepares the way for the rising sun. Although the star appears to be red, it is really a black Chamulan girl. Perhaps the gender shift has to do with comparing Venus to a woman in the role of the household sweeper. The imagery also evokes comparisons with the Venus god of the Aztecs, Ehecatl-Quetzalcoatl, who wears black body paint and is described as the "sweeper of the path of the sun" (Sahagún 1950–1982, 7:8). At Zinacantán, Ehecatl appears in the Festival of St. Sebastian, which takes place at the end of January, about one month before Carnival (Bricker 1981:138, 140, Fig. 21). He is represented with a maize cob in his beak, and details of the imagery suggest a quetzal bird, perhaps an embodiment of the fertility aspect of Venus associated with maize.

A serpent aspect of Venus is known in Chiapas. One Tzotzil source identifies a Venus serpent known as mukta ch'on (big serpent; Holland 1964:14–15). Nonetheless, Robert Laughlin (personal communication 1995) notes that in Tzotzil the plumed serpent is k'uk'ul ch'on and Venus is muk'ta k'anal or "great (big) star," and there is no apparent connection between the two. Generally, the Tzotzil seem to distinguish Venus from the feathered serpent, a counterpart for Venus in central Mexico.

Another serpent form of Venus is known from Yucatán. The term for Venus, kan ek', has a double meaning. Ek' signifies both "star" and "black," and kan means both "snake" and "four" (Barrera Vásquez 1980). This suggests a quadripartite nature, perhaps linked with the four phases of Venus (Chapter 2). The name could also mean "star snake." The Precolumbian serpent aspect of Venus in Yucatán is well known as the feathered serpent, Kukulcan.

Another possible serpent image of Venus is seen in the Chortí Chicchan serpent, which is half-feathered and half-human, and sometimes wears four horns. Charles Wisdom (1940:393–397, 410–411) suggests that the Chicchan serpent is equivalent to the ancient Maya feathered serpent. There are four sky Chicchans that produce most of the sky phenomena; each lives in one of the four world directions at the bottom of a large lake. Some say the Chicchans are actually pairs, and that at the north there is a fifth pair, the most important of the Chicchans. The northern Chicchan draws up the rains at the time of the first solar zenith (May 1 in the Chortí area), a date closely linked with the Day of the Cross, celebrated on May 3 (Girard 1949:422, 456; Milbrath 1980a:291). Similarly, Tzotzil accounts of the horned serpent link it with water and the Day of the Cross in early May (Laughlin and Karasik 1988). These serpents could refer to Venus in a guise similar to Kukulcan.

A modern Yucatec tale describes a snake boy who grew up to become Kukulcan, a feathered snake with a (rattle?) tail. Colas is a boy who was born as a snake. He kept growing larger and larger, until it became apparent that he was the feathered serpent known as Kukulcan (Burns 1983:246). Like the horned serpent of the Tzotzil, Colas causes earthquakes. Every year the snake flies out of its cave to cause an earthquake in the middle of July. Although not stated in the tale, Colas means "tails" in Spanish, and one wonders whether this plural form refers to the multiple rattles on the feathered serpent's tail seen in Precolumbian imagery. As will be seen in Chapters 5 and 7, the ancient feathered serpent is Venus, and his rattle tail seems to be the Pleiades, a constellation still known as the "rattlesnake's rattle" in Yucatán. The Pleiades disappears from the sky in May during conjunction and can be seen at dawn in June. By July the constellation is well above the horizon, at the time Colas (the Pleiades tail of the Feathered Serpent?) emerges from the cave.

Among the Lacandón, K'uk'ulcan, the feathered serpent, is a giant malevolent serpent who is the pet of Hachäkyum (McGee 1990:63). Although not explicitly connected with Venus in modern lore, it seems that the feathered serpent in Lacandón and Yucatec lore is the counterpart of Kukulcan, a Precolumbian Venus deity (Chapter 5).

The Maya sometimes refer to the dual nature of Venus, assigning different roles depending on the time of visibility. The Morning Star is mentioned more often than the Evening Star. Usually Venus is ugly, stupid, or lazy. Sometimes he has a heavy beard, a trait that is not typical of the Maya. Occasionally Venus is adulterous, a sin not to be taken lightly, given that the ancient punishment for adultery in Yucatán was disembowelment (Tozzer 1941:32). Animals associated with Venus include a dog, an ant, and a serpent. Venus is also often closely linked with the sun, a natural image based on the fact that Venus always is seen relatively close to the sun. The great variety of names applied to Venus reflect the planet's multiple aspects. As we shall see, in Precolumbian times Venus had multiple personalities related to different seasonal cycles (Chapter 5).

THE PLANETS AMONG THE CONTEMPORARY MAYA

We would expect that the planets would play a major role in the Maya legends and folk astronomy, but apart from Venus, very little is mentioned about the planets. Mercury, the planet closest to the sun, seems not to be named in ethnographic accounts, and names for Saturn also seem to be lacking. Information on Mars, the red planet, is surprisingly scanty. Mars is a blood-red star that moves in the sky and sends eye diseases, according to the Tzotzil (Hunt 1977:144). Only a few names are known for Jupiter. In some cases, it may be too late to collect the information, because as far back as 1930 Thompson had difficulty getting any information on the superior planets, those in outer orbits beyond Earth's orbit.

There are some tantalizing fragments of information about Jupiter. Some of the Tzotzil of San Pablo Chalchihuitán identify the *estrella* Domingo (St. Dominic?) with a large planet (*rominko k'anal*), possibly Jupiter (Köhler 1991c:253; Lamb 1995: 271, 276). In Zinacantán, Jupiter is known as "elder brother star" or "senior star" (Laughlin 1975: 79, 458).

A monkey appears prominently in a planetary tale. Apparently, the arboreal nature of monkeys evokes the connection with planets seen overhead. The sun's younger brother is transformed into a monkey representing a planet, identified in one Mopan account as Mars or Jupiter, but in another he is the Evening Star (Thompson 1930:120–123, 138). The youngest brother (T'up) is made to climb a tree wearing a blanket hanging down like a tail. He is told to imitate the sounds of a spider monkey, and he is transformed into a monkey who is the ancestor of all the monkeys. His name evokes a connection with T'uup, the Lacandón spider monkey who is lord of the sun (Bruce 1979:203–204). T'uup resides in the third tier of the layered cosmos described earlier (Fig. 1.1b).

Sometimes general terminology links the different planets. Among the modern Quiché, Venus or any other planet appearing as a bright star in the east before dawn is called the "sun carrier," and when any planet takes the role of Evening Star, it is called rask'äk, meaning "of the night" (B. Tedlock 1992b:180).

General terms can also refer to stars and planets. The Quiché refer to the planets as cak ch'umil, meaning "red stars" (B. Tedlock 1992b:180). The Tzotzil of Zinacantán use one term, k'anal (yellowish one), to refer to stars, planets, and constellations (Vogt 1997:112–113). They modify the term to refer to specific planets, calling Venus "elder yellowish one," while "red star" (tsahal k'anal) can refer to Mars or the star Arcturus in Bootes.

Other terms seem to distinguish the "wandering" planets from the fixed stars. The contemporary Chortí say that the planets are "watchers over the earth" that travel, whereas the fixed stars are fires that are not seen traveling (Fought 1972:428). The highest heaven of the Lacandón is reserved for the planets, the "wandering gods" (Fig. 1.1b). A similar notion is seen in a 1698 Quiché dictionary by Domingo Basseta, which includes a term that may refer to a planet as cabauil ichabera, glossed as "wandering star" (estrella vaga; Basseta 1698:71v).

It is clear that the Maya recognize planets as being different from fixed stars. Nevertheless, planetary information is scarce in published ethnographies. This leads one to suppose that the planets are not of interest, but this may be a misconception. More likely, information about planets is specialized knowledge that is still useful to religious specialists such as shamans, but it is not commonly passed down among the general populace. Modern folk tales involve planets, but the identities of specific planets have been lost. This is seen in the case of the monkey character who takes a similar role in a number of tales, but his planetary identity is given as Jupiter or Mars, or even in one case as the Evening Star.

STARS AND CONSTELLATIONS

Maya accounts link stars to lights in the night. The Chortí say "those [stars] which we do not see traveling are said to be fires, so that it does not become completely dark on earth" (Fought 1972:428). The Pokomchí say that the stars serve as aids to the travelers, for they light up the trail (Mayers 1958:42). To the Lacandón, stars symbolize funerary candles; therefore, to dream of stars prophesies death (Bruce 1979:149; McGee 1990:117). The Yucatec Maya of Yalcobá say that a number of constellations have "their fire," representing a bright or large star that defines their arrangement in the night sky (Sosa 1985:431).

When referring generally to stars, the Tzotzil use the term "the yellow ones" (k'analetik) and describe them as being located in a layer of the sky above the clouds but below the paths of the sun and the moon (Vogt and Vogt 1980:506). Their knowledge of rising stars and constellations is derived from predawn observations rather than the dusk observations common in Western astronomy (that is, derived from the Greco-Roman tradition brought over from Europe) (Vogt 1997:114).

Watching the stars is important in contemporary Maya timekeeping. Among the Quiché, different constellations take the role of "sign of the night" as they move into a position opposite to the sun and become visible for the longest period of time (B. Tedlock 1985:84). During the dry season, the sign of the night in December is Orion. Mid-January is associated with Gemini, late February with Regulus, mid-March with the Big Dipper, and early April with Acrux of the Southern Cross (B. Tedlock 1992b:182).

Regulus in Leo is quite important in the Quiché agricultural calendar. If the field is to be newly planted, men go out and fell the trees, burn the undergrowth, and begin turning the soil in February when Regulus is the sign of the night (crossing the meridian at midnight). Sowing of the mountain corn, which requires a longer season, begins in March, at the time when the waxing moon passes Regulus, then near its zenith (B. Tedlock 1985:85).

The Quiché visualize the classical constellation Aquila (the eagle) as a hawk (*xic;* B. Tedlock 1985; 1992b:187–189). They link the southward migration of the Swainson's hawk with the movements of Aquila. Near the onset of the dry season the hawks are seen in great flocks of more than two thousand birds heading south to the pampas of Argentina. In the fall, Aquila drops the "dry-season cross" (Sagittarius) into the sea, reflecting the fact that Sagittarius sets some two hours before Aquila. Near the beginning of the rainy season, the hawks migrate north over Momostenango en route to Canada, appearing just around the time of the first thunderstorms. At this time, the hawks are said to lift the "wet-season cross" (Southern Cross) out of the sea.

Maya people observe the Pleiades to regulate their agricultural calendars. The Lacandón burn the cornfields in preparation for planting when the Pleiades have reached treetop level at dawn (Thompson 1974: 93). The Chortí observe the Pleiades to predict the Sun's passage over zenith around planting time (Girard 1949:453; 1962:78). Among the Quiché, the planting season for high-altitude maize is timed by observing the evening setting of the Pleiades in March, whereas planting of the low-altitude maize is timed by the conjunction of the Pleiades with the Sun in May (D. Tedlock 1985:343). In a new field, they burn the undergrowth and turn the soil in February when the Pleiades reach the meridian shortly after sunset, and their conjunction with the Sun coincides with the zenith passage of the Sun and the onset of the rains (B. Tedlock 1992b:185, 189).

In Yucatán, the Pleiades (*tzab*) are the "rattle-snake's rattle," suggesting a cluster of rattles. They are said to rise at dawn on June 13, at the time the heavy rains begin (Redfield and Villa Rojas 1962: 206; Sosa 1985:431, 454). A similar name is recorded among the Lacandón and the Manche Chol (Bruce et al. 1971:15; Thompson 1974:93). The Quiché call both the Pleiades and the Hyades "handful" (*mots* or *motz*); the Pleiades represent a handful of maize kernels and the Hyades a handful of beans, and their setting corresponds to the time when these plants are sown (Alvarado 1975:62; B. Tedlock 1985; 1992b:181). The Tzotzil of Zinacantán describe the Pleiades as *chak shonob,* literally "high-backed ceremonial sandals" (Vogt 1997:112). A number of Tzotzil groups refer to the Pleiades as a sandal (*sonom';* Köhler 1991c:252), as do the Chol and the Tzeltal.

Few terms are recorded for the Little Dipper in Ursa Minor or its North Star (Polaris), the first star in the handle of the Little Dipper. Polaris is a large celestial candle, according to the Tzotzil of Chamula (Sosa 1986:189). However, Polaris is apparently not recognized among the Tzotzil of Zinacantán, and they simply refer to it as one of many stars in an amorphous mass of stars called *'epal k'analetik,* meaning "many stars" (Vogt 1997:112–113). Polaris is the "corner star" to the Quiché (B. Tedlock 1985:86; 1992b:181). The Lacandón say that Polaris is "the north star" (*xämän ek'*) and the Little Dipper is "the crocodile" (*el lagarto;* Bruce et al. 1971:15).

The Maya link the number seven with the Big Dipper (in Ursa Major) because of its seven bright stars. This number does not seem to be a result of European influence, but instead reflects a clear grouping of seven stars. The Yucatec Maya call the Big Dipper the "seven sacraments," and they warn that counting them will result in the death of one's spouse. The Tzotzil of Zinacantán recognize a turtle constellation that includes stars in Ursa Major, Bootes, and Leo, called *vuku-pat,* referring to the bent back of a turtle or a bent-over old man (Vogt 1997:112).

The Quiché link the Big Dipper, or Ursa Major, to a bird whose name incorporates the number seven, but the Big Dipper is also a cupped hand or a spoon (B. Tedlock 1983:65; 1992b:181; D. Tedlock

1985:360). They watch for the rising and setting of the bowl of the Big Dipper. The descending position of the Big Dipper is important in timing the hurricane season from June through October (D. Tedlock 1991:169–170).

The scorpion constellation appears to have a number of different astronomical identifications in the ethnographic literature. Among the Tzotzil of Zinacantán, Scorpius is *tsek k'anal* (scorpion constellation), and the brightest star, Antares, is the "heart of the scorpion" (Vogt 1997:112–113). In Yucatán and Quintana Roo, Scorpius is also a scorpion constellation (Grube, cited in Love 1994:97; Redfield and Villa Rojas 1962:206). On the other hand, John Sosa (1985:431) records an account identifying the Yucatec Maya term *sina'an éek* (scorpion star) as a large constellation composed of stars from Orion to Sirius. The scorpion (*tzec* and *xok*) is Ursa Major among the Tojolabal (Chaneabal) and Kekchí (Girard 1949:456; Thompson 1974:93).

Lacandón folklore mentions Orion, noting the name for a number of individual stars (Bruce et al. 1971:15; Rätsch 1985:37–38). The peccary (*puerco de la montaña* or *kitam*) is linked with three bright stars in Orion. However, the configuration does not seem to include the first-magnitude stars, for Rigel is the "little woodpecker" (*tunsel*), and Betelgeuse, a red star, is the "red dragonfly" (*chäk tulix*). Three other stars of lesser magnitude are the peccary's piglets, probably positioned close to their mother. Sirius represents the "big woodpecker" (*äh ch'uhum*), apparently the companion of the "little woodpecker" nearby.

Not surprisingly, Orion is commonly connected with the number three, because the three bright stars in Orion's Belt are easily seen, even with the full moon nearby. The Tzeltal refer to Orion's Belt as "three king[s]" (*oktu rey*), and they say Orion is the "cross star" (Slocum 1965b:169). The Tzeltal "three-star" (*oxkot-ek*) constellation may refer to Orion's Belt (Villa Rojas 1990:746). The Chortí say that the belt of Orion is formed by the "three Marías" joining with Orion's sword to form the "seven Marías." The Tzotzil of Zinacantán identify the three stars in Orion's Belt (Delta, Epsilon, and Xi) as "the trio," or the "three Marías," whereas the sword is

a "trio of robbers" or a "group of eavesdroppers" (Laughlin 1975:70; 1980:139 n. 35). Vogt (1997:112) records that Alnitak, Alnilam, and Mintaka, the three stars in the belt of Orion, are called *'osh-lot* (three together). Among the Quiché, Orion is called "dispersed fire," and Orion's Belt is the "tail of the three fire lords," serving as the sign of the night in December (B. Tedlock 1985:86; 1992b:181; D. Tedlock 1985:261). Alnitak in Orion's Belt is also grouped with Rigel and Saiph to form a sort of celestial triangle in Orion called the "three hearthstones."

Castor and Pollux in Gemini are "two stars that go together" to the Quiché, who say that they are the sign for January when they rise at sunset (Remington 1977:84). They are also the "two sparks" or "two shiny ones" (B. Tedlock 1985:84; 1992b:181, 189). They mark the northern horizon extreme of the Sun at the summer solstice, the time of the heaviest rains.

Gemini is the "turtle" and the three stars lying in a straight line in the middle are its intestines, according to the Yucatec Maya of Chan Kom (Redfield and Villa Rojas 1962:206). The Lacandón also identify Gemini as a turtle (Baer and Baer n.d.). However, Thompson (1960:111, 116) notes that one Yucatec Maya account identifies the square of Orion as a turtle constellation called *ac*.

Trees also represent constellations in the sky. Sosa (1985:432) records a Yucatec prayer that refers to a great *roble* or oak tree (*ti noh bèek*) on the white road (*sak beh*) in the sky, probably referring to a constellation representing a tree on the Milky Way. The Lacandón Maya identify the Southern Cross, at the southern end of the Milky Way, as a ceiba or cork tree (*Ochromoa lagopus;* Bruce 1979:155).

The distinctive crosslike form of the Southern Cross is expressed in a number of different names. The Yucatec of Quintana Roo say that it is the "cross star," the "cross which tops the tower of Jerusalem," or the "cross rising over Jerusalem" (Redfield and Villa Rojas 1962:206; Villa Rojas 1945:156). Among the Tzotzil of Chamula, the Southern Cross is the "Jewish cross" associated with evil (Gossen 1974b: 156–158).

The Chortí call the Southern Cross the "cross of May." They say that it signals the first solar zenith, the time for planting in May, when the intersection of the Milky Way and the ecliptic, a cosmic cross-roads in the sky, is positioned overhead (Girard 1949:456–459). The feast of the Day of the Cross (May 3) may be linked to the Southern Cross crossing the meridian in the southern sky on the evening of the festival (between 9 and 11 P.M.).

The Southern Cross, not seen in latitudes north of Mesoamerica, is visible just prior to the onset of the rains, which may be one reason it is so important to the contemporary Maya. Evon Vogt's (1997:112–113) recent research at Zinacantán indicates that the Southern Cross is *krus k'anal* (cross stars). They compare this cross to Christ's cross and they identify two star crosses on either side as "thieves' crosses," constituting the three crosses of Calvary. One of these is made up of stars in Lupus, and the other includes stars in Vela and Carina, apparently the counterpart for a star grouping known as the "false cross" in Western astronomy, frequently mistaken for the Southern Cross.

Judith Remington (1977:85–87) found evidence for three "thieves' crosses" among the Quiché in the department of Quetzaltenango and among the Cakchiquel in the department of Guatemala. One is the Southern Cross, and the second is a cross in Sagittarius with delta at its center. Remington was uncertain about the identification of the third cross. Except for the Southern Cross, the three crosses in this system seem to be different from the three star crosses recorded by Vogt (1997) at Zinacantán.

The Southern Cross is one of two Quiché constellations identified with the name "thieves' cross" (B. Tedlock 1985:83; 1992a:29, 38 n. 2). The Quiché refer to the Southern Cross, visible primarily during the rainy season, as the "rainy-season thieves' cross." The "dry-season thieves' cross" is a seven-star asterism in Sagittarius, with delta at its center. This is a bent cross that the Maya relate to a stalk with bent maize ears, signaling the maize is ready to harvest. Sagittarius may be a portal to the underworld, because it is located in the rift section of the Milky Way (*xibalba be*) that the Quiché identify as an underworld road, where the Sun crosses the Milky Way at the winter solstice, which is the longest night of the year.

The souls are transformed into stars in heaven, according to a number of contemporary Maya accounts (Thompson 1960:85). The people of Zinacantán say that the souls of dead babies change into flowers tied to a celestial cross (Laughlin 1962:126). This would certainly seem to be a star cross like the Southern Cross. Perhaps the souls of the dead among the Lacandón ascend to heaven climbing the branches of a stellar ceiba representing the Southern Cross.

In sum, the seasonal positions of certain bright constellations help to regulate the cycle of the seasons in star calendars evident among a number of Maya communities. Names for the constellations vary considerably from region to region, but there seem to be some groupings of stars that bear names implying similar concepts, such as the Southern Cross being recognized as either a sacred tree or a cross constellation. Maya people often see the stars as fires in the night, and frequently they link constellations to animals. They also recognize individual stars as animals.

THE MILKY WAY

Some Maya people see a snake in the band of stars across the sky that we know as the Milky Way. The Yucatec Maya identify the Milky Way as the deadly fer-de-lance, *tamacaz* (Coe 1975:27). The Chortí say that the Milky Way is a white serpent with its mouth to the south and its tail to the north (Girard 1948:76; 1949:458, 461). They seem to visualize the Milky Way as a path or axis intersecting with the ecliptic, the path of the Sun. Raphael Girard (1948:75) also identifies the Milky Way with a cord, because he says cords and serpents are connected among the Maya, although this is apparently an interpretation on his part rather than a Chortí account of the Milky Way.

The notion of the Milky Way as a road is quite widespread. Tzotzil terms to describe the Milky Way include "road of ice," "road of water or rain," and "mother of water or rain" (Köhler 1991c:253). The "road of water" refers to the Milky Way in the summer rainy season, whereas the "road of frost" is its name during the dry season. The section of the

Milky Way with Scorpius is associated with dryness, probably because the Tzotzil usually observe stars in the predawn hours, and Scorpius is seen to reappear on the eastern horizon at dawn in December. They also refer to the Milky Way as the "road of wind" (*be 'ik'*) when it hits a "vertical" position at the time of strong winds (Vogt 1997:113).

The Quiché call the rift side of the Milky Way the "ice road" (B. Tedlock 1985:65). The other Quiché Maya name for this side of the Milky Way is the "underworld road" (*xibalba be*), running from the vicinity of Sagittarius and Scorpius as far north as the Northern Cross (Cygnus), where the rift closes. The opposite side is the "white road" (*saki be;* B. Tedlock 1985:84; 1992a:29). The Yucatec Maya of Chan Kom also call the Milky Way "white road," the same name given to ancient roads. Other Yucatec names for the Milky Way include "the road of the small lizard" and "the small path in the forest." Among the Cakchiquel, the Milky Way is the "road of the sea turtle" (a Pacific loggerhead turtle or Atlantic green turtle; Weldon Lamb, personal communication 1997).

The Lacandón say that the Milky Way is the "white way of our true lord," Hachäkyum, who is the lord of the heaven where the Lacandón go when they die (Duby and Blom 1969:295; Rätsch 1985: 37). This implies that the Lacandón go to the Milky Way when they die. A similar link with the realm of the dead is clear in the Quiché name for the rift section of the Milky Way, *xibalba be,* an underworld road. The Yucatec Maya say that the dead travel along the Milky Way at night (Sosa 1985:432). The Day of the Dead, celebrated in early November, is widely recognized as a time when the dead can return to earth. The Milky Way is especially prominent at this time of year when it arches over the sky from east to west at dusk.

The Chortí also refer to the Milky Way as the Road of Santiago, their god of thunder and lightning, and they predict rainfall by watching the Milky Way and the Moon. The position of the Milky Way on the Día de Santiago (July 25) is a sign that the rains will temporarily abate during canicula, allowing the fields to be prepared for the second planting. Among the Quiché, the planting of valley maize at

the time of the Feast of the Holy Cross (Day of the Cross) is heralded by the reappearance in May of the dark rift of the Milky Way in the "underworld road" (B. Tedlock 1992b:181, 189).

A relationship between the Milky Way and the Moon is expressed in a number of ways. The Quiché are particularly interested in the seasonal variations in the Moon's path, noting when the Moon passes through the rift of the Milky Way and predicting rainfall accordingly (B. Tedlock 1983:66–67; 1992b: 191). A tale of ill-fated lovers collected among the Kekchí of Guatemala closely links the Moon and the Milky Way. The Sun tries to steal the Moon from her old father, covering her with a turtle shell, but the old man hits the Sun with a pellet from his blowgun, and the Sun drops the lunar maiden. She smashes to pieces in the sea. Small fish gather the pieces and patch them with their silvery scales; they form a net and lift the Moon into the sky. The fish remain behind and become the Milky Way (Thompson 1967: 33; 1970b:365). The Kekchí tale explains why the Moon disappears (the Sun drops it) during conjunction, and how the Moon rises up again (with the help of ocean creatures). The Milky Way as a net made to lift up the Moon may be represented by the netted skirt of the Moon Goddess in Precolumbian Maya imagery (Chapter 4).

The Milky Way, with its dense band of stars, most often suggests a path across the sky or the more animate form of a celestial serpent. The stars of the Milky Way are watched to predict seasonal change, and the Moon's position crossing the Milky Way seems to be of interest. Some Maya groups connect the Milky Way to the dead. The Milky Way itself may embody the road of the dead, and its countless stars may represent the souls of the dead.

OTHER CELESTIAL PHENOMENA

Comets are called "tail of the star" and are considered omens of pestilence among the Quiché (B. Tedlock 1992b:180). They are "windy tail" and "fire–ill-omened star" in Colonial Yucatec sources cited by Barbara Tedlock. Among the Tzotzil, comets are called *yol,* which can mean "arrow," "bow," or "crossbow" (Lamb n.d.b). A different image is presented by the Tzotzil of Chalchihuitán, who say that the comet is a "starbeam" (Köhler 1991a:319). Halley's comet, which was particularly bright in the early part of this century, is mentioned in a number of Maya accounts (Köhler 1989:292). It may be the comet with a "long tail" in one Yucatec account (Burns 1983:89).

The Maya watch for shooting stars, the annual fireballs in meteor showers. The Tzotzil describe a falling star as a "torch" (*ch'ob;* Lamb n.d.b; Laughlin 1975:137). Shooting stars seen in the east are the cigarette butts of the Chacs among the Yucatec Maya of Quintana Roo (Villa Rojas 1945:102). Such images seem related to cigars smoked by the Hero Twins in the Popol Vuh, according to Barbara Tedlock (1992b:180–181). However, she sees a stronger mythic tradition in the association of meteors with obsidian. She suggests that the link between meteors, obsidian, war, death, and human sacrifice relates to past use of obsidian in implements of warfare, sacrifice, and bloodletting. The Lacandón name for meteors is "arrowheads," and the Yucatec name is "arrow stars." A Colonial Quiché term for meteors is the "star that makes war." Obsidian points and blades found by the Quiché in the fields of Momostenango are said to be the remains of falling stars (B. Tedlock 1992b:180–181). The Tzotzil also describe obsidian as excrement that drops from shooting stars as they fall (Laughlin 1975:93). More commonly, the Maya describe meteors themselves as star excrement (Köhler 1989:295–296; Trenary 1987–1988, table l).

Like many other Maya groups, the Tzotzil of Zinacantán believe that shooting stars have a malevolent quality. The soul of an evil person may take the form of a falling star. A falling star seen at dusk makes the leg swell; however, when seen after midnight, a falling star marks the place where treasure is hidden (Laughlin 1975:232, 284, 513).

Mention should be made of the many sky beings associated with changing winds and weather. The Yucatec Maya believe that rain deities riding on horseback pour water from an inexhaustible calabash. The rain gods reside behind a door in the eastern sky, and they come to earth in the cenotes. The Yucatec describe five different Chacs—marking the four directions and the center—who ride across the sky with their leader, *kunku-chac,* the great rain god, under orders from St. Michael. The rain aspect of Chac is seen also in Mopan legends, where he is said to be the thunder god (Thompson 1930:128).

The Yucatec Maya say that the rainbow (*chel*) is the flatulence of the demons, rising out of dry wells representing the anus of a demon called Metal (Redfield and Villa Rojas 1962:206). An evil rainbow rises from the *xab* (sinkhole or well), where an evil, snakelike monster resides in its depths, according to the Tzotzil of Chenalhó; the snake is a companion of the rainbow because both are striped, and there is a serpent under every rainbow (Guiteras Holmes 1961:203, 235, 288). Rainbows bring an end to rain, according to Maya accounts. The Chortí identify the rainbow as the body of a Chicchan serpent stretched across the sky. Even though the Chicchan serpent of the north brings rain, the rainbow aspect of the Chicchan does not let the rain fall (Fought 1972:388; Wisdom 1940:392–395). Similarly, the Tzotzil say that rainbows across the sky signify the end of rain (Laughlin, personal communication 1995).

In sum, it seems that temporary sky phenomena, such as comets, meteor showers, storms, winds, and rainbows, are usually considered malevolent, most probably because of their unpredictable nature. The Maya still believe rainbows have a demonic quality. Contrary to the Western tradition, rainbows are considered unlucky, probably because they are believed to hold back the life-giving rain. Meteors are associated with war and obsidian. Comets seem to be distinguished from meteors, especially in accounts that describe their long tails.

CONTEMPORARY MAYA ASTRONOMY IN CULTURAL CONTEXT

There is diversity in modern Maya beliefs about astronomy, but there is also an underlying unity that can be detected when studying linguistically related groups, most notable when comparing the Lacandón and Yucatec Maya astronomical terms. A belief in the layered cosmos is widespread, but sometimes the layers seem more like steps along the sun's daily course. Other images of the layered cosmos assign the sun to a specific layer, often separate from the fixed stars. Watching the moon when planting and harvesting seems to be widespread, although the lunar phases for agricultural activities differ among various Maya groups. Assigning a masculine gender to the sun and a feminine gender to the moon seems to be the norm, but the moon may be transformed into a male in order to take a role as a farmer in some accounts, especially when the moon is visualized as a sibling of the sun. A female sun and a male moon are variations in the pattern evident among the Chol, who occupy a region at the core of the area of the Classic Maya civilization.

The planet Venus has somewhat malevolent or negative associations in a number of Maya cultures, as indicated by beliefs that the Venus deity is ugly, lazy, or adulterous. Venus is often the master of the animals, and some accounts imply that the planet causes eclipses. Information on the other planets is very scarce, but some folktales speak of a monkey planet named as the younger brother of Venus and the Sun. Mars and Jupiter seem to be the only other planets that have been documented in ethnographic accounts.

Constellation names preserved in a number of communities indicate that the principal constellations are often the star groups that are most easily seen in the sky and those that mark important seasonal transitions. The Milky Way is widely connected to a serpent or to a road or a path, sometimes specifically linked with the realm of the dead.

The weather phenomena are sometimes personified, and the beings responsible for these temporary events seem to interact or even overlap with astronomical deities. Thus in one account, the Moon Goddess is one of the Chacs, the deities responsible for rainfall and thunder. Rainbows issue from wells that are also the home of the Moon Goddess during conjunction. And the Venus serpent may overlap in some way with the Chicchan serpents responsible for rain and rainbows.

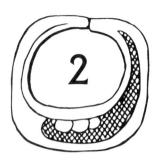

NAKED-EYE ASTRONOMY

The motions of the heavens can be mystifying to those not trained in astronomy. To understand Precolumbian astronomical imagery, we have to see the heavens from the perspective of naked-eye astronomy, quite unlike the view through a telescope. Here I describe the events from a dual perspective, both what you see from Earth and what actually happens in the sky in a Sun-centered solar system. A glossary at the end of the book will be helpful to those unfamiliar with astronomical terms. Aveni's *Skywatchers of Ancient Mexico* is an invaluable companion text to this chapter, as are H. A. Rey's *The Stars: A New Way to See Them* and E. C. Krupp's *Echoes of the Ancient Skies: The Astronomy of Lost Civilizations*.

TRACKING THE SOLAR SEASONS

From a geocentric perspective, the sun seems to be moving eastward through the background of stars over the course of the seasons. It takes a full year for the sun to "return" to the same stars along its annual path, known as the ecliptic. The earth's movement in its orbit around the sun makes the sun seem to move, and the earth spinning on its axis creates night and day.

The true length of the solar year is 365.2422 days; but our solar calendar approximates the solar year by using a period of 365 days with a day added every four years. Watching the sun over the course of several years from a fixed location, one can see the sun on the horizon at the same spot at the same time of year (Fig. 2.1a). This position can be noted in relation to a mountain or building in the distance, as in the diagram.

North of the equator, the sun reaches its northern extreme on the horizon at the summer solstice in June and the southern extreme at the winter solstice in December (see glossary). At the two solstices, the sun seems to stop moving along the horizon, just prior to turning in the opposite direction in its annual cycle (Fig. 2.1a). In

---

FIG. 2.1. *a:* Daily motion of Sun over course of year from June 21 (summer solstice) to December 22 (winter solstice), with Z marking true zenith in tropics of Mesoamerica and observer at low northern latitude (after drawing by P. Dunham, Aveni 1980, fig. 23).

b: Lunar-solar system from geocentric perspective with Sun and Moon moving around Earth; places where lunar path crosses ecliptic are nodes marked by horseshoe-shaped symbol. Angle of ecliptic relative to celestial equator is 23½°. Equinoxes occur at two places where ecliptic crosses celestial equator (after Lebeuf 1995, fig. 10).

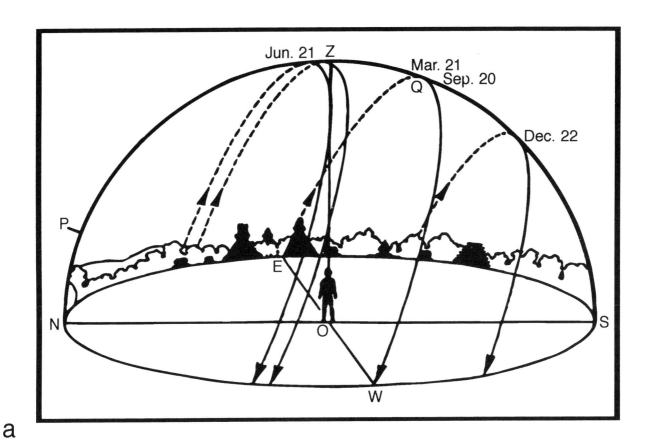

a

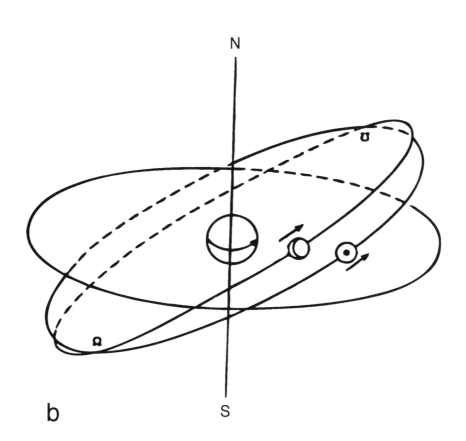

b

northern latitudes, the winter solstice occurs around December 22, when the sun is 23½° south of the equator on the longest night of the year, and the summer solstice occurs around June 21, when the sun is 23½° north of the equator on the longest day of the year. The intervals between the solstices were more even in the fifteenth century (at about 182 days) than they are today (181.77 and 183.47 days), and the midpoint between the solstices was offset from the time of the true equinox by only 2.1 days (Dearborn and White 1989:468). The tilt of the earth's axis at 23½° is what accounts for the way the sun seems to travel north and south from one horizon extreme to another. These horizon extremes are marked by the tropic of Cancer at the latitude of 23½°N and the tropic of Capricorn in the south at 23½°S, the latitudes that delimit the tropical zones on earth.

The two annual equinoxes (around September 20 and March 21) take place approximately midway between the solstices, when the viewer on earth sees the sun rise due east and set due west, and the days and nights are of equal length. As will be seen in Chapter 3, the Maya built structures oriented toward the horizon positions of the sun at the equinoxes and solstices, confirming a relationship between architecture and solar observations. The equinox orientations translate into azimuths of 90° for sunrise and 270° for sunset; you can approximate the solstice orientations by adding 23½° to the equinox azimuths for the summer solstice, and subtracting the same figure for the winter solstice. Anthony Aveni (1980, table 9) gives the precise azimuths based on different horizon elevations at the latitude of the northern extreme of the Maya area.

In the Tropics, the sun reaches a true overhead position at noon on the day of the solar zenith (Fig. 2.1a). Within tropical Mesoamerica, the sun is in the northern sky at noon on the summer solstice and reaches a zenith position twice a year on either side of the summer solstice. At the southern limit of Mesoamerica, at about 14°N latitude, the solar zeniths occur in late April and mid-August. At the tropic of Cancer, there is only one solar zenith, which takes place on the summer solstice. When the observer is north of the tropic of Cancer, the noon sun always

remains in the southern sky. In fact, the tropic of Cancer marks the northern limit of Mesoamerica at the archaeological site of Alta Vista (Aveni 1980: 226–229). A shared 260-day calendar, one of the defining characteristics of Mesoamerica, may relate to the specific geographical location of Mesoamerica. Agricultural and weather patterns tied to the latitude of the northern Tropics probably influenced the early development of the 260-day calendar still used to measure the length of the agricultural season in Mesoamerica.

Clearly the solar zenith plays a central role in unifying Mesoamerica, for this culture area does not extend north of where the sun achieves a true zenith. The zenith position of the sun can be determined by watching for the day when the sun casts no shadow at noon. The shortening length of the shadow at noon could be used to predict the zenith date. With their structured calendar and long-distance trade routes, the ancient Maya were certainly aware that the date the sun reached its zenith varied as they traveled north and south. Indeed, architectural complexes show orientations that are keyed to the local horizon position of the sun on the zenith date (Chapter 3).

The first solar zenith occurs near the onset of the rainy season throughout much of Mesoamerica. In central Mexico and the northern Maya area of Yucatán, from 19°N to 21°N latitude, the solar zenith date falls near the end of May, coinciding closely with the onset of the rains (Pl. 1). The seasonal pattern is quite extreme in Yucatán, with rainfall clustering in the period from late May through November, dividing the year into two distinct seasons (Pérez 1945:89). The first solar zenith in the central Petén, on May 8 around 17°N latitude, announces the coming rains. Rainfall in the Petén follows a similar pattern to that of Yucatán, with peak rainfall from June through October and a slight abatement during August (Aveni and Hotaling 1996:362, fig. 1). Rainfall is exceptionally low from December through April, and it is relatively dry through May, creating a six-month dry season like that of Yucatán. Rainfall patterns are more variable in Belize, but generally the entire Maya area experiences a rather long dry season.

Just as the first solar zenith is important because it coincides approximately with the onset of the rainy season in Mesoamerica, a complementary event known as the second solar nadir coincides with the beginning of the dry season (Pl. 1). For example, at the latitude of Chichén Itzá (20°41′) the sun reaches its solar nadir on November 22 and on January 21 in the Gregorian (N.S.) calendar. Further south, at 18°N latitude, the second solar nadir falls on January 30 N.S. As noted in Chapter 1, the contemporary Quiché Maya determine the date of the nadir by watching the full moon pass overhead at midnight.

LUNAR POSITIONS AND PHASES

During the twenty-nine to thirty days of the synodic lunar month (29.53059 days), the moon changes phases because it changes position relative to the earth. The moon passes in front of the sun during the new moon, a period of conjunction that lasts from two to three days (Aveni 1980:69). As the moon pulls away from the sun, you begin to see a sliver of the moon, known as the first crescent. The first visible crescent appears just above the western horizon at dusk, and it sets almost immediately thereafter. As the month progresses, the waxing moon is visible higher in the sky each night at dusk, and it is seen for a longer time before setting. At the first quarter, half of the moon can be seen overhead at dusk, and the moon sets some three hours later. Over the next days, the moon grows rounder during its gibbous stage and appears further to the east when viewed at dusk. This is because the sun illuminates more and more of the moon as it moves farther away from the sun. Around the fifteenth day of the lunar month, the moon rises opposite to the setting sun, and thus it reaches the full moon phase. During the night, the full moon moves across the sky until it sets at dawn, still in opposition to the sun. Over the next seven days, the moon is again in its gibbous stage, but now it is seen in the predawn sky. By the waning quarter, the moon is overhead at dawn. A few days later, the waning crescent moon is visible in the eastern sky in the early morning, each night closer to the eastern horizon, until it finally rises just before sunrise. On the next day, the moon

disappears in the sun's glare at the time of conjunction (the new moon), but because it drops down to the eastern horizon, it seems as if it disappears into the earth as it moves between the earth and the sun (Fig. 2.1b).

The most profound effect of the lunar phases on earth is seen in the tides, which bear a direct relationship to the moon. The moon seems to carry the tides with it. When viewed over the course of the month, the moon seems to rise fifty minutes later each night, thus the high and low tides are almost an hour later each day. The moon's path or orbit also profoundly influences the tides. The moon's orbit around the earth is elliptical, and it moves closest to the earth (perigee) every 27.55 days. When the moon is at perigee at the time of the new moon, the lowest tides of the year occur, and perigee at the full moon brings the highest tides; gravitational pull is strongest at these times (Cleere 1994:96).

Whereas the sun is relatively easy to track, serving as a model of orderly motion that defines the day and solar year, the moon has much more complex cycles because twelve lunar months do not fit exactly into the solar year (12 × 29.53059 = 354.36708). The difference each year accumulates at a rate of about eleven days a year, resulting in the need to add an extra lunar month at certain intervals in any seasonal calendar that includes lunar observations. The actual interval that it takes the full moon to return to the same date in the calendar year is the metonic cycle of nineteen years, a cycle of 235 lunations or 6,939.6 days that seems to be recorded in at least one Maya codex (Chapter 4).

The disappearance interval during conjunction varies from two to three days, with the shortest disappearance interval occurring in the spring. There is also seasonal variation in the altitude of the moon on first visibility and in the orientation of the crescent when the moon first emerges from invisibility (MacPherson 1987; Ottewell 1990). The crescent moon appears to be tipped over during the rainy-season months in Mesoamerica and lies horizontally during the dry-season months, positions noted by the modern Maya (Chapter 1).

Because the full moon rises opposite to the setting sun, it has a seasonal position opposite to the sun.

For example, in the Quiché area, the full moon's position at midnight zenith coincides with the time of the sun's nadir in November, just as the midnight zenith of the full moon in February marks the time of the second solar nadir (B. Tedlock 1992b:189). The moon at the fall equinox rises at approximately the same position as the sun at the spring equinox. The full moon at the winter solstice rises at dusk in approximately the same position as the rising sun on the summer solstice; similarly, the full moon on the summer solstice rises at dusk in the position of the winter-solstice sunrise.

The moon completes a circuit of the sky in one sidereal month (27.32166 days; Aveni 1980:69–72). Over the course of a sidereal month, the moon moves rapidly, advancing around thirteen degrees in twenty-four hours, so that it appears to jump forward each night (Fig. 2.2a). The moon passing by an individual star or star group marks the sidereal position of the moon. The full moon, which is about ½° in diameter, on some occasions actually covers stars or even clusters of stars; indeed its diameter is just large enough to cover the Pleiades. Such an occultation places the moon in a precise sidereal position and also marks an exact position along the moon's inclined orbit.

The moon's orbit is tipped by about 5° with respect to the ecliptic, so that it moves back and forth across this plane (Fig. 2.1b). The two points of intersection with the ecliptic are called the nodes. When the new or full moon crosses a node, the moon, the earth, and the sun lie on a straight line. The moon passes through a node (crosses the ecliptic) every 13.7 days. From a geocentric perspective, the node crossings represent the moon moving north and south of the sun's ecliptical path.

Each month the moon mimics the annual cycle of the sun, rising at northern and southern extremes on the horizon, but the inclined lunar orbit changes the location of the moon relative to the ecliptic. Consequently, the nodes change position (regress) along the ecliptic. Every 18.61 years the nodes return to the same position. This is also the interval between major standstills of the moon, when you will see the moon reach its maximum northern and southern positions during a month, and it will repeat these approximate positions over several months (Aveni 1997:33, 88; Krupp 1991:156).

ECLIPSES

If the moon is full when it crosses a node, there may be a lunar eclipse, but if it crosses during the new moon, a solar eclipse may occur (Aveni 1980:77–78). Since the moon continually wanders north and south, the node crossings rarely occur at the time of a full moon or new moon. Solar eclipses occur within eighteen days of a node passage, whereas lunar eclipses occur within twelve days of a node passage (V. Bricker and H. Bricker 1989:239). Lunar eclipses are spaced at least six months apart, and not every year has a lunar eclipse; on the other hand, there are at least two solar eclipses a year, and sometimes as many as five (Ortiz 1997:22). Even though solar eclipses are more common, lunar eclipses are more often seen because they are visible over the half of the earth turned toward the moon, whereas solar eclipses are seen only in a narrow band where the new moon's shadow falls on earth as the moon passes between the earth and the sun.

John Teeple (1930:90) provides a good description of solar eclipses:

The sun has its path in the sky which we call the ecliptic; the moon also has a path which is inclined about 5° to the ecliptic, hence twice a year the sun is in both the ecliptic and the moon's path where they cross, at a point which we may call the node. If a new moon occurs while the sun is at that point, or in fact within about 18 days either side of the node, then the moon will obscure some part of the sun and there will be an eclipse of the sun visible somewhere on earth. If the nodes were stationary, the sun would reach one every

---

FIG. 2.2. *a:* Moon moves 360° around sky, crossing back and forth across ecliptic over course of one month; here crossing points (lunar nodes) occur on days 7 and 21.

b: Selected positions of Venus in relation to Earth and Sun (after Closs 1979, fig. 4).

Lunar Path Relative to the Ecliptic*

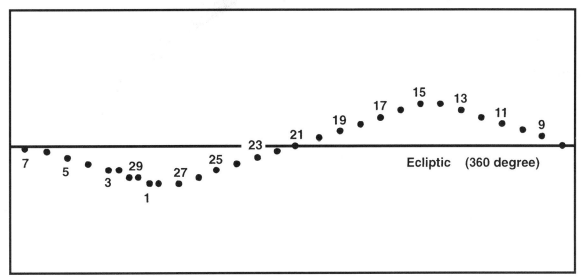

*Idealized Path over the Course of a 30-Day Month

a

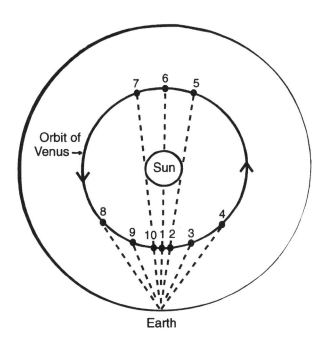

The Relation of Selected Points of the Venus Period to the Earth and the Sun:

1	Inferior Conjunction
2	Heliacal Rise after Inferior Conjunction
3	Greatest Brilliancy as Morning Star
4	Greatest Western Elongation
5	Heliacal Setting before Superior Conjunction
6	Superior Conjunction
7	Heliacal Rising after Superior Conjunction
8	Greatest Eastern Elongation
9	Greatest Brilliancy as Evening Star
10	Heliacal Setting before Inferior Conjunction

b

half year, but there is a regression of the nodes, such that the sun crosses the moon's orbit on the average of once in 173.31 days, the eclipse half year.

Solar eclipses are only visible within a limited geographic range, especially total eclipses. There are three types of solar eclipses: (1) A *partial* solar eclipse occurs when the moon covers only part of the sun because the new moon is not exactly at the node but is sufficiently close that it hides part of the sun (Rey 1976:138). (2) A *total* eclipse occurs when the new moon is crossing a node and it is also close to the earth because of its position in the elliptical orbit, so that the moon's backlit disk appears large enough to completely cover the sun, leaving only a circle of rays around the dark lunar disk. (3) An *annular* eclipse occurs if the new moon moves directly in front of the sun when it is more distant from the earth, so it does not completely cover the sun but leaves a ring of light all the way around the new moon.

Lunar eclipses can be seen in a wide geographic area; all that is required is that the eclipse occur sometime between dusk and dawn in the locale. During a lunar eclipse, the moon undergoes a dramatic transformation but does not disappear completely. As the eclipse proceeds over the course of several hours, the appearance of the moon transforms from the full moon to a crescent moon as the earth's shadow falls on the moon, until it is completely covered by a shadow that makes it look like a disk that is colored coppery red or a darker shade. It retains this color for up to an hour and forty-five minutes as the earth passes directly between the sun and the moon, preventing sunlight from illuminating the moon's surface. Then the phases repeat in reverse order, with the crescent emerging again, followed by the moon gradually filling out until it resumes its appearance as the silvery full moon. If only part of the moon passes through the earth's shadow, you see a partial lunar eclipse. The rounded shadow of the earth falling on the moon at the time of a lunar eclipse was what led Aristotle to recognize the spherical shape of the earth. A similar discovery eluded the Maya, and even today they describe the rounded shadow as a bite taken out of the moon by an eclipse monster.

THE PLANETS

Like the moon, planets are lit by reflection, distinguishing them from stars, which are actually distant suns in other solar systems. Planets are generally brighter than the stars and give off a steady light, whereas stars seem to twinkle. Mercury, however, can fool the eye and sometimes twinkles like a star when it is near the horizon. The stars represent a fixed background in the sky, like a geographic map. Although this stellar map slowly rotates, the stars remain in the same relationships, serving as signposts for the motion of the planets, called the "wanderers" in classical antiquity (Aveni 1992b:25–26).

Just as the earth's year is based on the time it takes to orbit around the sun, the sidereal cycle of a planet represents the time it takes to orbit around the sun, passing entirely around the background of stars. From a geocentric perspective, another cycle seems more pronounced, that of the synodic period—the time it takes for the planet to return to the same position relative to the earth and the sun. The synodic period has certain subsets, the most notable of which are the period of retrograde, the day of opposition, and the day of heliacal rise at dawn (see glossary).

The heliacal rise date, the day when the planet becomes visible again after being lost in the sun's glare during conjunction, is clearly the most striking and notable event in the synodic period. Predicting the heliacal rise and set dates requires considerable expertise. Calculating the timing of this event is not simply a matter of determining the degree of separation between the sun and the planet in terms of celestial longitude, because the degree of separation required for first visibility varies with the seasons (V. Bricker and H. Bricker 1986b:60). Furthermore, although modern computer programs have made it easier to determine when these events occurred in the past, these programs do not precisely re-create a past event because they cannot account for local weather conditions that could change the date the planet first became visible.

Astronomers call Venus and Mercury inferior planets because their orbits are closer to the Sun than that of Earth. They have the inside track, so to speak. They appear to be attached to the Sun, never seeming to stray far from the Sun's position. Aveni (1992b:27) points out that Mercury is never seen more than two handspans from the Sun, and Venus no more than four. They have a unique relationship with the viewer on Earth, seeming to swing back and forth, almost like a yo-yo moving toward and away from the Sun. This means that their position above the horizon is closely linked to the horizon position of the Sun (Aveni 1979, fig. 1).

Because the orbital plane of each planet is tipped slightly with respect to Earth's orbit, the planets seem to migrate north and south of the Sun's position. This motion is most noticeable with Mercury and Venus because they have the largest orbital inclination, 7° and 3°24′ respectively (Aveni 1980:92–93). Among the celestial wanderers, Mercury strays farthest from the Sun's path, rising and setting up to 7° north and south of the Sun's extreme horizon positions.

Venus and Mercury appear as celestial twins or "body doubles" because they have a similar pattern of visibility. They can only be seen in the east around dawn or in the west around dusk. This gives them a double personality. The two inferior planets are also similar because they are the only planets that have four-part synodic periods: a Morning Star phase; a phase of invisibility around superior conjunction; an Evening Star phase; and an inferior conjunction phase. When Venus and Mercury pass in front of the Sun around the time of inferior conjunction, their disappearance is relatively short. When they pass behind the Sun at the time of superior conjunction, the period of invisibility is much longer. This is because the viewing angle from Earth creates a wider arc of invisibility as the planet moves to the opposite side of the Sun (positions 5–7 in Fig. 2.2b).

Mercury's synodic period (115.9 days) is punctuated by periods of invisibility around inferior and superior conjunction, averaging five and thirty-five days respectively. As the planet closest to the Sun, Mercury is invisible for almost a third of its total synodic period. Whereas Venus reaches a maximum elongation (angular distance) from the Sun of 47°, Mercury has a maximum elongation from the Sun of no more than 26°, meaning that Mercury stays relatively close to the Sun, making it very difficult to track (Aveni 1980:85, 325 n. 14). Many ancient people in the Old World applied the term "burner" or "sparkler" to Mercury, because it seems to twinkle near the horizon (Aveni 1992b:53). Aveni reports that Mercury was characterized as a trickster, because it would elude anyone in pursuit by disappearing so frequently. For similar reasons, the Greeks said Mercury was a swift-footed messenger (Hermes) who conducted souls of the dead into the underworld (Krupp 1991:174). Mercury's speedy nature is no doubt due to its short sidereal cycle, for it takes only eighty-eight days to make a circuit around the sky.

The four-part synodic period of Venus averages 583.92 days, including two periods of invisibility that average 8 and 50 days. In practice, the disappearance intervals vary in length according to the season. The inferior conjunction interval for Venus can range from a few days around February to as many as 20 days in August (Aveni 1991:314, fig. 4; 1992b:97, table 3.2).

It is possible to see Venus move through all the constellations of the zodiac during its period of visibility in the morning or evening sky. This is because its average period as either Morning or Evening Star is 263 days, whereas the sidereal cycle of Venus is shorter, just under 225 days. The sidereal cycle may be important in the eight-year Venus cycle documented in the Dresden Codex (Chapter 5).

Venus returns to the same position in the sky at the same time of year in the same phase every eight years. This means that it returns to the same star group at the same time of year. Five synodic periods of Venus are approximately equal to eight solar years and ninety-nine lunar months, the *octaeteris* cycle (meaning eightfold) used by the Greeks (Aveni 1992b:95). The length of the five Venus synodic periods also follows a symmetrical sequence in terms of the number of days in each cycle: 587, 583, 580, 583, and 587 days, repeating at intervals of eight years. Similarly, the disappearance intervals follow a seasonal patterning over the eight-year period (Aveni and Hotaling 1994:S25).

Just as the horizon positions of Venus repeat in a cycle every eight years, Venus also seems to follow five different patterns in its motion above the horizon as Morning Star, and it displays a similar set of motions as Evening Star over the course of eight years (Aveni 1991, fig. 1). One pattern resembles a figure-eight loop, another the capital letter *D* (Fig. 2.3a). Near the vernal equinox, Venus reaches its highest position of all the five cycles. This event occurs very close to the time of maximum elongation, when the planet is positioned farthest away from the Sun. However, maximum elongation does not often coincide with highest altitude, as can be seen in plots of these two Venus events throughout the planet's cycle (H. Bricker 1996, figs. 3, 5, 6). Harvey Bricker's (1996, fig. 8) work shows that the longest interval of days between the highest altitude and maximum elongation occurs near the autumnal equinox. Although Venus at maximum elongation will usually be high in the sky, the precise elongation point cannot be seen in the sky; it must be calculated by celestial longitude. Bricker supports Aveni's (1991) conclusion that the emphasis on maximum elongations of Venus given in studies of Maya calendrics probably tells us more about what is of interest to Western astronomers than what was of interest to Precolumbian Maya observers.

Plotting the intervals of the Morning Star's ascent and descent in all its seasonal patterns indicates that Venus seems to shoot up in the sky to attain maximum altitude in approximately 80 days, but then it follows a more leisurely course in its descent, averaging about 180 days. The opposite is true in the Evening Star phase, when the descent from maximum altitude occurs relatively rapidly over 80 days.

Venus also appears to change size during its synodical cycle. It seems to be six times wider when it is nearest the horizon; this makes it especially large when it is about to disappear as Evening Star and after its first appearance as Morning Star. Although Venus seems to be very large as it is about to move in front of the Sun in inferior conjunction, it is

bright but not easily seen because it is so close to the Sun and only a thin crescent is illuminated (this shape, however, can only be seen with a telescope). Just a few weeks before it disappears as Evening Star and just a few weeks after it reappears as Morning Star more of the planet is illuminated, making it most brilliant (Fig. 2.3a; Aveni 1991:310; 1992b:32). Venus is the brightest of the planets, occasionally even visible in daylight. And in some rare instances, Venus can be seen to pass in front of the Sun during inferior conjunction. At this time, Venus is seen as a black dot moving across the face of the Sun, almost like a sunspot (Aveni 1980:85). As yet, we have no evidence that these transits of Venus were observed by the ancient Maya, but the subject has not been adequately explored.

Venus has a retrograde period that averages forty-two days, beginning just prior to inferior conjunction (Roth 1970:104–105). Its retrograde motion is different from that of the superior planets (those planets that orbit the Sun beyond Earth's orbit) because it is less obvious, for the midpoint of its retrograde period coincides with inferior conjunction when the planet is not visible. This motion does not seem to be of great interest in Classic Maya texts.

The superior planets show a different pattern of motion than the inferior planets; they are not often seen close to the sun, and when in opposition to the sun, they behave like the full moon, rising at dusk and setting at dawn. Their synodic periods involve long periods of visibility in the night sky, punctuated by a single period of invisibility during conjunction. In a single synodic period, a superior planet moves across the sky in a predictable fashion, making a single disappearance just after it reaches the western horizon at dusk. A superior planet rises earlier and earlier each day in the predawn sky, working its way across the sky until it again reaches the western horizon at dusk (Aveni 1992b:26–30, fig. 2.3).

The planets follow an eastward motion amid the background of the stars, like the sun and the moon. From time to time, as the earth passes by a planet,

---

FIG. 2.3. *a:* One of eight seasonal paths of Venus as Morning Star (after Aveni 1992b, fig. 2-4).

b: Intersecting paths of Milky Way and ecliptic from geocentric perspective.

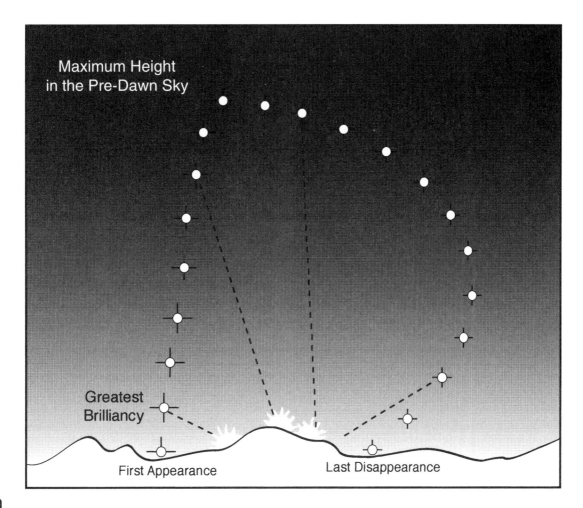

Maximum Height
in the Pre-Dawn Sky

Greatest
Brilliancy

First Appearance

Last Disappearance

a

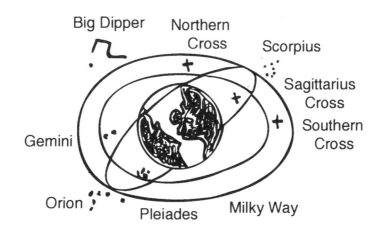

Big Dipper

Northern
Cross

Scorpius

Sagittarius
Cross

Southern
Cross

Gemini

Orion

Pleiades

Milky Way

b

the planet will appear to move backward (westward) amid the stars, a phenomenon called retrograde motion. The planet continues to orbit in the same direction as the earth, but it seems to move backward briefly as the earth passes by, just as a moving car will seem to drop back abruptly as a faster car passes it. Retrograde motion invariably occurs at a time when the superior planet is visible for a relatively long period of time over the course of the night. The approximate midpoint of retrograde motion for the superior planets coincides with opposition, when the earth is directly between the sun and the planet, which means the planet rises at sunset and sets at dawn. At the time of opposition, a superior planet is usually at its brightest and it is visible for the longest period of time during the night; the precise timing of opposition varies with the seasons.

The stationary points in retrograde motion are easily observed, although the exact duration is not readily detected. Astronomers call these stops the first stationary and second stationary, and opposition is the approximate point in time or space between the two (Aveni and Hotaling 1994:S39). As Bryant Tuckerman's (1964) tables indicate, the planets do not apply their brakes from full speed to dead stop overnight; rather, they behave more like a good driver slowing gradually to a stop. The retrograde loop is visible as an east-to-west motion in the background of stars (Aveni 1992b:26, 29–30). The entire retrograde period can last for two months in the case of Mars and over four months for Jupiter and Saturn (Aveni 1980, table 6).

In terms of the sidereal cycle, the more distant planets are exceptionally slow (Aveni 1980, table 6). The superior planets could be visualized as running a race around the Sun. Mars is on the inside track running laps around slower Jupiter and Saturn. Uranus is even slower but lies at the threshold of visibility.

Conjunction events involving all three superior planets visible with the naked eye, when Mars, Jupiter, and Saturn come together in the sky, are relatively rare, normally being separated by hundreds of years. And a great conjunction of all five planets visible with the naked eye occurs approximately every 516.33 years (Pankenier 1997:34). Such a conjunc-

tion event is expected to occur in early April of the year 2000.

The synodic periods of the planets are based on the observed relationship with the earth's motion around the sun. The time to complete a synodic revolution appears to decrease for planets more distant from the sun. Aveni (1980:88) notes that Saturn, the most distant of the planets visible with the naked eye, "scarcely moves a few degrees on its orbit around the sun before the earth has gained a lap on it." Thus its synodic period is relatively close to one year. Saturn's synodic period is 378.1 days, and the mean interval it is visible in the morning or in the evening is 353 days, with a mean disappearance interval of 25 days. Its mean retrograde period is 140 days. Saturn takes 29.45 years to make a circuit around the sky (sidereal cycle of 10,758.9 days).

Jupiter is the largest and brightest of the three superior planets. Jupiter's synodic period is 398.9 days, and its mean retrograde period is 120 days. Jupiter is gone from view for about a month (mean disappearance interval 32 days). Since Jupiter is visible approximately 367 nights, its motions can be noted in relationship to the solar year. Each successive heliacal rise would occur about a month later (399 − 365 = 34 days). This places Jupiter in a different star group every year, until it finally completes a sidereal cycle in 4,332.5 days or about twelve years (just 50.5 days short of twelve years; Aveni 1980:89, table 6).

Because of the planet's unique red color, Mars is easy to find as it moves among the stars. Mars completes its sidereal cycle in 687.1 days, a period about equal to the mean interval of its visibility (660 days). Thus Mars can be seen to move through all the constellations of the zodiac in a single synodic period, a pattern it shares with Venus.

The synodic period of Mars can vary from 770 to 800 days, but the average cycle is 780.0 days or precisely 3 × 260 days, a period that may be linked with the unique 260-day calendar of Mesoamerica. The mean retrograde period of Mars is relatively short, an average of 75 days, and the interval can fluctuate as much as 10 days from the quoted value (Aveni 1980, table 6). Retrograde follows heliacal rise after an average of 292 days (Justeson 1989:100, table 8.5).

THE STARS AND THE SEASONS 55

As with the other planets, the timing of the retrograde period of Mars varies from cycle to cycle, because it is determined by the time when Mars is in opposition to the Sun during its synodic period. The exact timing of the first stationary point is not observable because the planet is moving so slowly just before and after the precise stationary point (V. Bricker and H. Bricker 1986b:58). Mars shows the greatest variation in brightness of all the planets and occasionally can be seen to be almost as bright as Venus (Aveni 1992b:32). Its maximum brilliance occurs during retrograde motion when it is in opposition, rising around dusk and visible all night long.

Mars has the longest period of visibility in the morning or evening sky, lasting an average of 660 days before disappearing behind the Sun for approximately 120 days, notably longer than the mean disappearance interval of other planets. Heliacal rise (dawn rise) after the period of invisibility is an event of great significance in the Mars cycle; however, even using modern astronomical tables, the exact date of heliacal rise of Mars during a given synodic period cannot be predicted, especially during the spring (V. Bricker and H. Bricker 1986b:65–66). Tracking the conjunction of Mars with the Sun indicates a conjunction sequence that returns the planet at the same time of year to the same ecliptical position amid the background of stars every 205 years (Burgess 1991, fig. 1).

THE STARS AND THE SEASONS

Over the centuries, the solar seasons provide the stable framework for the yearly rhythms in the daytime sky; these seasonal cycles are echoed by stars at night that serve as seasonal markers. Unlike the sun, which meets its appointed schedule without fail year after year over the centuries, the stars lag behind the solar clock. Due to the effects of precession, a slow wobble in the tilt of the earth's axis, an individual star near the ecliptic will be seen to rise an average of five to seven days later every five hundred years, but the degree of shift varies considerably for individual stars (Aveni 1980, table 10).

The dawn, or heliacal, rise of a star is important because it marks the reappearance of a star after invisibility, just as the heliacal set (dusk set) is significant because it is the last time the star is visible before disappearing in conjunction. Over the course of several years' observation, the date of these events can be determined with some accuracy. However, predicting heliacal rise and set dates of stars with exact precision is a difficult task. Projections back through time are even more problematical. Nevertheless, astronomers are able to determine past star events with reasonable accuracy, and many computer programs are based on these calculations. Bradley Schaefer (1987) notes that calculations made by modern astronomers rely on observational data recorded by the Babylonians and the Egyptians, and on Ptolemy's method using the *arcus visionis,* a measure of the minimum vertical separation required for a planet or star to be visible. He confirms the importance of heliacal rise and set dates, but he finds that achronical rise (the last day a star is seen to rise after sunset) is unobservable if the observation took place exactly at sunset, or ill defined if the observation was made at twilight, because this time of night cannot be precisely defined.

The disappearance interval averages about a month for constellations near the ecliptic. By dividing the stars along the ecliptic, Old World astronomers developed the zodiac, the twelve constellations that serve as "signs" of the months. Western astrologers did not take precession into account, for they fixed the position of the sun at the spring equinox in Aries and then from that point they counted off twelve equal sections representing the zodiacal signs, despite the variation in size of the constellations. The zodiacal signs were determined to be of equal dimensions, each marking the position of the sun during one month, a system still used by astrologers today.

Over the course of two thousand years the relationship with the seasons has changed. Whereas Aries marked the Sun's position at the spring equinox in Greco-Roman times, for the last two thousand years, the spring equinox has been located in Pisces. Astrologers tell us that we are entering the "age of Aquarius," because the position of the Sun at the spring equinox is shifting to Aquarius, the constellation next to Pisces. The entire cycle of precession takes 26,000 years; the starry sky is expected to return to the same seasonal position it had in Greco-Roman times some 24,000 years in the future (Aveni 1980, fig. 40). Precession results from the changing position of the celestial pole as Earth wobbles like a top on its axis, currently at a 23½° tilt, but pointing to different stars in the north celestial pole. The changing position of the celestial pole does not affect the ecliptic, but it does change the position of the celestial equator and therefore the two equinox points where the ecliptic and celestial equator intersect.

The latitude of the observer determines which stars are visible and which are most prominent. In Mesoamerican latitudes, approximately 14°N to 23½°N latitude, a number of bright stars cross the meridian very close to the true zenith. Despite slight shifts in position when comparing the Precolumbian skies to those of today, generally these stars can be seen overhead in Mesoamerica today. The Pleiades crossed the zenith in central Mexico and northern Yucatán in Precolumbian times (precise zenith at 19°21′N latitude in A.D. 1507; Krupp 1982:10). In Mesoamerica, most of the circumpolar stars are seen to rise and set, except for those right around the pole star. Mesoamerican skies also display southern constellations not visible in the more northerly latitudes of Europe and the United States. Among the most important is the Southern Cross, a cross-shaped constellation that is visible for the longest period of time in April, when it is identified as the sign of the night by the Quiché (Chapter 1). The Southern Cross marks the southernmost point of the Milky Way, a dense band of stars discussed in Chapter 7.

In the Tropics of Mesoamerica, certain stars on the Milky Way serve as seasonal indicators of the alternation between the rainy and dry seasons. The most important constellations in this regard are the Pleiades, which have marked the beginning of the rainy season for thousands of years, and Scorpius, located at the opposite side of the sky, marking the onset of the dry season (Fig. 2.3b). With fine-tuning,

ancient astronomers could have focused on the same constellations from the time of the Olmecs up to the conquest, a span of over 2,500 years. For example, the dawn rise of Antares in Scorpius fell in November for over 1,500 years (Aveni 1980, table 10). The Pleiades made their dawn rise on May 7 in 500 B.C., announcing the coming rains in late May; by A.D. 1500, they rose at dawn on May 29, so that their rise coincided with the onset of the rainy season (Aveni 1980, table 10). By adjusting the observation time from a dawn rise to dusk set, this stellar clock could be used for several thousand years. Today the same star group sets at dusk on May 3 and rises at dawn on June 4, thus dusk set is seen to announce the coming rains, and the dawn rise coincides with the actual onset of the rainy season.

Other seasonal events played out across the background of stars are the annual meteor showers ("shooting stars"), generally seen after midnight. The fireballs in a meteor shower occur when the earth passes through the path of an ancient comet, and they are an annually occurring event because the earth encounters the cometary path in the same area of the sky as it orbits around the sun. These meteor showers can be quite spectacular, such as the great Leonid meteor shower of November 13, 1833. The showers can be seen in specific constellations at certain times of year. Among the most spectacular are the Aquarids visible in Aquarius around May 5 and July 29; the Perseids in Perseus between August 9 and 14; the Orionids in Orion between October 16 and 22; the Taurids in Taurus between November 1 and 7; and the Leonids in Leo between November 14 and 18. The Geminids in Gemini around December 14 is a spectacular meteor shower that produces about a hundred meteors per hour (Krupp 1993:67). Meteor showers produce intermittent displays lasting only seconds, whereas a comet may be seen to move across the sky over the course of a month or more.

Comets, which orbit in and out of our solar system, shine because they reflect sunlight and because sunlight ionizes their gases. They are of uncertain origin and have meteoric material as well as gases. Some comets have no tails; others have tails that spread over millions of miles. The tail, formed by evaporation of ice as the comet approaches the sun, appears in the opposite direction from the sun, because the solar wind pushes it away from the sun (Ortiz 1997:26). Comets, like eclipses, represent a disruption of the celestial regularity, for they do not follow a predictable seasonal course; hence they are linked to cataclysm in native cosmologies. Halley's comet's passing in 1910 was particularly dramatic, but its last appearance in 1986 was disappointing. It is hard to predict whether a comet's display will be especially dramatic, and a similar problem occurs with predictions about annual meteor showers. Nevertheless, some astronomers predict a spectacular Leonid meteor shower will be visible on November 18, 1999, in Europe and Africa (Upton 1977). This is to be followed by a rare conjunction of Mars, Jupiter, and Saturn in April 2000. With the end of the millennium approaching, there may be an added psychological jolt to this impressive sequence of events.

PRECOLUMBIAN AND COLONIAL PERIOD MAYA SOLAR IMAGES

The importance of the sun in contemporary Maya religion is a reflection of its prominent role in Precolumbian and Colonial times. Maya solar imagery features the sun as a ruler of time and space. Ancient cosmic diagrams and solar calendars evoke a direct connection with concepts that survive today. Solar orientations in Precolumbian architecture show how the Maya integrated time and space in their solar cult.

Sun worship translated into political imagery during the Classic Maya period (A.D. 250–800), when the ruler or a ruling lineage became identified with the sun. By A.D. 1000, the end of the Terminal Classic period, solar lineages faded from view, and solar worship shifted to calendar ceremonies involving the annual festival calendar. In the Postclassic period, the Sun God is one of the principal gods mentioned in the sequence of four years of the annual year-bearers' cycle of the Post-classic period, but he is surprisingly rare in the almanacs of the codices and is considered malevolent because of an association with drought.

Despite the changes over time in the role of the Sun God, Kinich Ahau (sun-faced lord), his visual imagery shows a surprising degree of continuity, for some elements can be traced from Postclassic back to Preclassic times. Hun Ahau, later known as Hunahpu in the Early Colonial period, seems to embody the underworld sun in combination with the Morning Star as far back as the Classic period. Some specialized aspects of the sun are more limited to certain areas or time periods, such as GIII of the Palenque Triad, a Late Classic manifestation of the underworld sun found primarily at this site.

Animals and plants could represent the sun in certain contexts. The sun glyph itself symbolized a flower, most probably the *Plumeria rubra*. Jaguars may be linked with the sun in some contexts. The puma, golden like the sun, represented a solar animal in central Mexican art and possibly also in parts of the Maya area. Although not actually embodying the sun, a monkey sometimes substituted for the sun during the Classic Period. A scarlet macaw embodied the noonday sun, his red color evoking the solar flames, according to Colonial period accounts. Postclassic codices show the solar macaw carrying a torch. These variations in solar imagery reflect subtle differences that conveyed specific meanings to the Precolumbian Maya.

This chapter begins with study of the seasonal cycle, the solar calendar, and solar orientations in ancient architecture. There follow sections on Precolumbian images that show how the sun moves through time and space. In subsequent sections, the

Sun God's traits are traced back from the Colonial period to the Classic period. The closing sections treat animals linked with the sun and specific deities representing underworld aspects of the sun.

THE SEASONAL CYCLE AND THE SOLAR CALENDAR

Colonial period sources make it clear that the Yucatec Maya festival calendar followed the solar seasons. The Chilam Balam of Chumayel, written in 1782 in Yucatán, mentions a number of seasonal events linked with the calendar (Roys 1967:23, 85). Xul is the time that fish spawn around early November. Yaxkin is the time that the cornstalks are bent double in late November. Zac is when the white flowers bloom in early February. Mac is when the turtles lay their eggs in late March. Muan is when there is a ring around the sun in May. Ralph Roys points out that the ring around the sun is probably caused by the smoke from the burning fields in preparation for planting at the beginning of the rainy season. The Chilam Balam text places the first of Pop on July 16 (Julian, or O.S.), as does Friar Landa's account dated to the 1560s (Tozzer 1941: 151–153 n. 15). This date corresponds to July 26 in our Gregorian (N.S.) calendar, and is the day of the second solar zenith at 19°37′, the latitude of Edzná in the state of Campeche.

The sixteenth-century Maya agricultural calendar followed the rhythm of the solar seasons, a practical necessity for all agricultural peoples. Landa observed that from the middle of January to April the Yucatec Maya collected and burned refuse in the fields (Tozzer 1941:97). Then they sowed at the beginning of the rainy season in May, making a hole in the ground with a pointed stick and dropping in five or six grains of maize. In all likelihood, the planting cycle was coordinated with the first solar zenith in May, as it is today.

Landa also recorded a 260-day count beginning in Yax (January 22–February 10 N.S.). Alfred Tozzer (1941:151–152) presumes that this statement simply refers to a new 260-day count starting during this month, but it may instead refer to the fixed 260-day count that survives today (Milbrath 1981:278).

Yax overlaps with the date that begins the count among the Chortí and Mopan (February 8) and that found among the Tzotzil (February 5). As discussed in Chapter 1, the 260-day Tzolkin calendar is well adapted to the length of the maize planting cycle in the Maya area, and it is noteworthy that any prediction made for a specific Tzolkin date would not repeat in the same agricultural cycle. Indeed, prognostications using the 260-day ritual calendar in the codices sometimes show a relationship with the solar year and the planting cycle (V. Bricker and H. Bricker 1986a; Justeson 1989:113).

The Madrid Codex, a Postclassic Yucatec Maya painted screenfold book, records a 260-day Tzolkin that probably was used to determine the best days for agricultural activities in relation to the fixed 260-day agricultural calendar (Fig. 7.3 and color cover). In my opinion, pages 13b–18b refer to a 260-day agricultural calendar beginning in Yax, the month when a new 260-day count began, according to Landa's account. The month Yax coincides with the onset of the fixed agricultural calendar in early February found today among the Maya. And counting 260 days brings the calendar to late October, coinciding with the month Xul (to end) in Landa's calendar (Milbrath 1981:276).

The dominant image of the sequence of pages 12b–18b is the Chicchan Serpent, so named because markings on its body resemble the day sign Chicchan. The snake appears with the rain god (Chac) amid a background of rainfall on page 12b. On pages 13b–18b there are five other manifestations of the serpent, all associated with falling water. This evokes a direct connection with the multiple aspects of the Chicchan serpent, a rain serpent known today among the Chortí (Chapter 1). The Pleiades may be implicated because two of the serpents wear rattle tails like the glyph for the Yucatec constellation known as the "rattlesnake's rattle" (Chapter 7).

The 260-day count begins on page 13b with the day sign Imix, the day that normally begins the Tzolkin. Since the fixed agricultural calendar could begin on any day of the 260, placing Imix as the first day shows an idealized beginning point for the fixed calendar. There are no numeral coefficients, but the numbers are implied by the positioning moving from left to right across the page. The layout shows the normal sequence of 20 days: Imix, Ix, Akbal, Kan, Chicchan, Cimi, Manik, Lamat, Muluc, Oc, Chuen, Eb, Ben, Ix, Men, Cib, Caban, Etz'nab, Cauac, and Ahau, extending over to page 15b, where a new cycle of 20 days repeats as the Chicchan serpent reverses direction. The sequence continues through page 18b, but there are only fifty-two signs on the first row. The same is true of the other three rows. The unfinished signs on the last page suggest that each row was intended to have sixty-five signs, completing a layout of 4 × 65 days to divide the 260-day calendar into quarters. Apparently, the artist did not have room to finish the last day signs, some of which are blocked out but not filled in, a very rare occurrence in a Maya codex. Perhaps the missing days are supplied on page 12b, where a black number below the Chicchan serpent indicates the appropriate interval of 13 days. The red number on the same page indicates a coefficient of 13, presumably to be linked to one of the 20 day signs that follow. According to Harvey and Victoria Bricker and Bettina Wulfing (Bricker et al. 1997:S29), page 13b shows Imix with a coefficient of one. However, instead of the expected red number, I see only a black mark, probably added inadvertently.

The pages show a narrative sequence involving a Chicchan Serpent that changes its position and appearance over the 260-day period. The overall arrangement of the Tzolkin clearly divides the 260 days in four quarters of 65 days each across the four rows, but smaller subdivisions are suggested by the way the calendar is arranged on the six pages. Since 260 days cannot be divided equally by six, it is clear that the intervals on each page must be unequal. We must try to reconstruct these intervals, since they are evidently important in understanding the narrative sequence of events shown across the six pages. Originally I proposed that the upper section of pages 14–18 provided information on the intended intervals, most representing approximately 52 days, except the last page in the sequence, representing a 27-day period (Milbrath 1980b, 1981). In addition to providing subdivisions of 52 days, the upper section of each page refers to a complete Tzolkin count repeating the same sequence of days at 52-day intervals, as seen

on page 15a, which displays a vertical column with a coefficient of four to be joined with the column of day signs to form the dates 4 Ahau, 4 Eb, 4 Kan, 4 Cib, and 4 Lamat cycling back to 4 Ahau for a total of 260 days (5 × 52 days). If the upper sections are to be read separately, as is usually the case on pages with almanacs divided in upper and lower sections, another form of calculating the appropriate subdivisions in the lower section must be found.

Counting the actual number of day signs on each page may provide the key to determining the intervals representing subdivisions of the 260-day period. The number of day signs on each page is unequal, except for pages 15b–17b, which each show a total of 40 day signs, indicating a 40-day period not unlike the contemporary count called "the feet of the year" (Miles 1965:272). Page 13b displays 32 days (4 × 8), and page 14b shows 36 days (4 × 9). Pages 15b through 17b total 120 days (3 × 4 × 10). The resulting subdivisions are not that different from those originally proposed, but they give a more convincing result in terms of the intervals between eclipses shown by winged Kin panels on pages 13b and 17b, widely recognized as eclipse glyphs (Chapter 4).

It has been suggested that Madrid Codex pages 12b–18b represent an eclipse almanac that predicts eclipses in the early tenth century, although Harvey Bricker et al. (1997) point out that none of the predicted eclipses were actually seen in the Maya area. They propose that the warning table applied to a relatively brief period of time from A.D. 924 to 926. This interpretation runs contrary to the generally accepted Late Postclassic date assigned to the Madrid Codex (Taube 1992b:3). Archaeological evidence suggests that the codex dates to around A.D. 1350, based on comparison with murals in Tancah Structure 44 (Love 1994:9). Another problem with the Brickers' analysis is that they do not explain the significance of the Chicchan serpent, the predominance of weather-related imagery, and the apparent narrative sequence of events. I am convinced that my original interpretation of pages 12b–18b remains valid, except for minor revisions in the subdivisions of the Tzolkin discussed above. As will be seen, the Madrid Codex almanac relates to the seasonal cycle of rains. It was reused each year, following the pattern of the fixed 260-day cycle in the agricultural calendar today.

The eclipse signs in the Madrid Codex probably warn of eclipses, but they seem to focus attention on eclipses at a specific time of year. Using the subdivisions of days determined for each page, the total number of days counting from page 13b to the beginning point of page 17b is 148 days (32, 36, 40 plus 40), a true eclipse interval like that recorded in the Dresden Codex (Chapter 4). Thus, the intervals represented between the two eclipse signs on pages 13b and 17b are at an appropriate distance to be an eclipse interval. And if we extend the count to include the 40 days on page 17b, then we have a total of 188 days, embracing the other eclipse interval of 177 days recorded in the Dresden Codex. Therefore, if there was an eclipse in the month that opened the fixed 260-day period shown on page 13b, another could be expected to occur around the time of the new year in Yucatán, during the 40-day period represented on page 17b.

The solar eclipse signs on page 12 are not associated with the almanac, and therefore they may float in time or be emblematic symbols announcing the eclipse sequence to follow. The latter seems likely, given that page 12b actually shows a pair of identical solar eclipse signs, which certainly could not refer to two eclipses at the same time. Indeed, the time period between two solar eclipses is often the above-mentioned eclipse interval of 148 days.

Page 12b serves as an introductory page, showing the important elements in the pages to come: eclipse glyphs, the sky band, Chac, the Chicchan Serpent, and rainfall. It may also introduce the astronomical year beginning around the winter solstice or perhaps slightly earlier on the November solar nadir in the Yucatec month Yaxkin (new sun), a name suggesting a beginning point.

The fixed 260-day count probably begins on February 8, as in the modern fixed agricultural cycle of the Chortí and coinciding with Landa's 260-day count beginning in Yax (January 22 to February 10 N.S.). Such a correlation helps us to place the solar events in relation to the sequence of pages. The start of the fixed 260-day agricultural period appears on page 13b. If the calendar begins on February 8 on

page 13b with a 32-day period, page 14b with a 36-day period coincides with the spring equinox. As I noted in previous publications, page 14b shows a male deer without horns, appropriate for March, the time of year when deer shed their horns in Yucatán (Milbrath 1980b:451; 1981:280–281). The 40 days represented on page 15b carry the calendar forward from April 17 to May 26, a period coinciding with the first solar zenith in Yucatán and the disappearance of the Pleiades, appropriate because the Chicchan serpent has lost its rattles on this page. Further support for this placement is seen in the sky band, which represents the intersection point of the Milky Way and the ecliptic, now prominently positioned above the western horizon (Chapter 7). Adding the next period of 40 days on page 16b extends the calendar from May 27 to July 5, incorporating the summer solstice. The 40-day count on page 17b begins on July 6 and ends on August 14, coinciding with the second solar zenith in Yucatán (Pl. 1). Page 18, the last page, is incomplete but would certainly incorporate the fall equinox, and the close of the calendar in late October would be supplied by a missing page or implied by the 13-day interval on page 12 (Fig. 7.3). This revised arrangement of the subdivisions of the 260-day calendar means that pages 16b to 18b are shifted earlier in time than was presented in my previous publications, but it does not substantially modify the interpretations relating to the Pleiades, for they remained invisible at dusk for the entire period represented by pages 15b–18b.

The Madrid Codex probably dates sometime from A.D. 1350 to 1450. If there was no intercalation, the months or festivals Landa recorded at the time of the conquest, more than a century after the codex was painted, would have to be adjusted. Any given festival would be around twenty-six days later in relation to the solar events around A.D. 1450, and fifty-two days around A.D. 1350. However, I am presuming that there was some form of intercalation in the Late Postclassic festival calendar, which was created after the tenth Baktun came to a close in A.D. 1224, at which point the Long Count was no longer used in the codices. I make this assumption because the imagery shown in the Madrid Codex calendar on pages 13b–18b depicts events that parallel Landa's Yucatec Maya festival calendar. And festivals described by Landa seem related to events in the solar year and the agricultural calendar.

Page 13b apparently overlaps with the month of Yax in Landa's calendar (January 12–31 O.S.), which would end on February 10 in our Gregorian calendar, around the beginning of the agricultural calendar recorded today among the Maya. An incense burner suggests a link with the incense ceremony in Yax; Chac shown with an overturned jar and a flaming bundle evokes the festival of the Chacs in Chen or Yax (Milbrath 1981:280; Tozzer 1941:161).

On page 14b, a death god holds a torch up to a deer, suggesting the sacrifice of a deer by fire in Mac, a monthly festival that ran from March 13 to April 1 O.S. (March 23 to April 11 N.S.; Milbrath 1981: 280–281). During Mac, the Maya hunted wild animals, removed their hearts and burned them, and then doused the flames with water. Tozzer (1941: 162–163) points out that the ceremony is appropriately named *tup kaak,* meaning "put out the fire." The fire ritual probably also refers to fires set in the fields to clear them in preparation for planting.

On page 15b, the merchant God M corresponds to the Muan festival honoring the merchant gods in May (Milbrath 1981:281; Tozzer 1941:164). At this time, merchants probably returned from their extended trading expeditions, for the coming rains would make long-distance trade difficult.

Page 17b coincides with the New Year ceremonies in Pop, which began on July 16 O.S. in Landa's calendar. Although there does not seem to be a specific reference to the New Year events in the imagery, the multiple Chacs on page 17b are appropriate to the repeated references to the Chacs in Landa's account of the month Pop (Tozzer 1941:151–153). Page 18b begins on August 5 (August 15 N.S.), marking a 40-day period that overlaps with the beginning of Landa's month Uo on August 6 (August 16 N.S.). Although there is no clear link with the events described for that month, the preceding page shows a frog that might be linked with Uo, for this is the Yucatec name for a variety of small frogs (Thompson 1960:108).

Landa's festival calendar, documenting the seasonal events and ceremonies in the mid-sixteenth

century, apparently survived in some form until modern times. It is clear that the months were related to seasonal activities in Landa's time and in later epochs of the Colonial period. In the nineteenth century, Pío Pérez records an association between the new year and the solar zenith in Yucatán, falling on July 16 in the Julian calendar (Aveni 1980: 42–43). Despite a clear link between the beginning of the new year in Pop and the July 16 date (July 26 N.S.) over many centuries, scholars cannot agree on whether there was a mechanism for intercalation (such as a leap year) to keep the festivals in a fixed relationship with the solar seasons. Nonetheless, as noted in Chapter 1, the Tzotzil festival calendar has remained fixed over the last three hundred years, even though no intercalation is formally acknowledged (Berlin 1967).

Daniel Flores (1995) has developed a possible solution to how the Postclassic Yucatec Maya intercalated the calendar. He proposes that Landa's four year-bearers, with their associated colors and directions, encode a way to intercalate the calendar seamlessly. He concludes that the Maya changed the time of day that the New Year ceremony was performed by rotating ahead one-quarter day every year; after four years had elapsed, a full day had been added with no real record of an intercalation.

Flores notes that in the years named Kan, associated with the south and the color yellow, the ceremony began at dawn and ran until noon. He proposes that the priest positioned himself to the south to observe the sun until it reached its noon position, symbolized by yellow for the resplendent sun overhead. In the next year, a Muluc year associated with the east and red, the ceremonies began at noon and ran until sunset. Now the priest positioned himself to the east and looked to the west to observe the setting sun, associated with the color red because of the red glow of sunset. Then followed an Ix year, symbolized by the north and black; the ceremony began at sunset and continued to midnight. At this time, the priest positioned himself to the north and focused his attention on the underworld, waiting for the sun to reach its lowest position at midnight, symbolized by the color black (however, Landa specifies the color of the Ix year-bearer as white; Tozzer 1941:

138). In the last year of the four-year sequence, a Cauac year represented by the west and white, the ceremony began at midnight and ended at dawn; the priest positioned himself to the west to observe the rising sun, associated with white because that is the usual color of the dawn sky (however, Landa specifies the color in Cauac years as black).

Although the colors Landa assigns to the north and west are different from those in the model presented by Flores, there are certain aspects of Landa's calendar that confirm the associations proposed by Flores. Landa describes Cauac New Year ceremonies as a nocturnal event, just as Flores suggests a nocturnal association for observations made in the Cauac New Year ceremony (Tozzer 1941:147–149). Furthermore, Cauac involved intoxication, which was probably restricted to nocturnal ceremonies if the Yucatec Maya followed practices like those of the Aztecs, who were prohibited from drinking intoxicating beverages before dusk. The Ix New Year ceremony, a nocturnal event according to Flores, also involved intoxication.

Flores's proposal that the Postclassic Yucatec Maya added a quarter day every year over 4 years explains how a leap day would accumulate after 4 years. Furthermore, moving the ceremonies forward by six hours each year would explain why Landa states that the Yucatec Maya have a year of 365 days and six hours (Tozzer 1941:133). However, a major problem with this interpretation remains. The New Year day is fixed on July 16 O.S., but the divination calendar (the Tzolkin) ran continuously without break. Rotating ceremonies forward one-quarter day every year would mean that 4 years hence, when the next Cauac year occurred, a full day would have accumulated. This means that the year-bearer day sign Cauac would not fall on the first day of the year, but would instead fall on the last day of the Uayeb (the five days at year end). It is possible that during the Postclassic period the months were simply shifted without regard for the Tzolkin, so that the first day of Pop and the new year always fell on July 16, and the year-bearer date was allowed to slip slowly through the year, occurring five days earlier every 20 years. After 52 years, the year-bearer would fall thirteen days before the July 16 date, which may have been the time

when an adjustment was made to realign the year-bearer. Or perhaps there was a shift to a new year-bearer set over the centuries, for different sets seem to be used in codices that presumably date to different epochs, such as the Dresden Codex and the Madrid Codex. Landa's year-bearers (Kan, Muluc, Ix, and Cauac) are like those of the Madrid Codex (34–37).

The Madrid Codex New Year pages each feature a sky band. On page 34, we find a priest-astronomer looking at the night sky in the Cauac years, indicating that the ceremony is nocturnal, as in Flores's interpretation and Landa's descriptions of the Cauac ceremony (Tozzer 1941:147–149). On page 37, we see a dog howling at a crescent moon in the Ix years, another appropriate nocturnal image if New Year ceremonies took place from dusk to midnight, as proposed by Flores (Fig. 5.1i).

There are other lines of evidence indicating an interest in the solar year in the codices. The Dresden Codex seems to refer to the stations of the Haab (365-day year), the summer solstice, meteorological events, and Yucatec Maya agricultural activities, according to Victoria and Harvey Bricker (1992). These events are positioned in relation to intervals that are subsets of the 260-day calendar, most often subdivided in five sets of 52 days or four sets of 65 days.

The most common subdivisions of the 260-day calendar in Yucatec Maya codices are groups of 52 days, and in northern Yucatán such subsets could be used in conjunction with a solar count from one solar zenith to the next. At Dzibilchaltún (21°06′ N), at the northern limits of the Maya area in Yucatán, the interval between the first solar zenith (May 25) and the second (July 17) is exactly 52 days, a period that seems to be recorded in architectural orientations (Coggins and Drucker 1988:24).

Periods of fifty-two days seem to relate to intervals in the solar cycle beyond the Maya area as well. The observatory or zenith tube at Xochicalco (18°8′ N) marks an interval of fifty-two days from when the sun first enters the chamber on April 29/30 to the summer solstice (Morante López 1995:47, 60). Rubén Morante López points out that similar configurations may be evident near the northern limit of the Maya area at Chichén Itzá (20°40′ N), where the Osario has a zenith tube that remains to be tested. In

Oaxaca, to the west of the Maya area, the subdivision of sixty-five days may be significant. At Monte Albán (17°03′ N), the zenith tube in Structure P seems to mark an interval of sixty-five days from the point that the sun first enters the tube on April 17 to the summer solstice, and another sixty-five days pass until it is last visible in the tube (Morante López 1995:55).

The intervals between the solar zeniths can also be related to the 260-day calendar. Vincent Malmström (1997:52–53, table 3, fig. 10) argues that Izapa (14°8′ N), near the southern limit of the Maya area, was the origin of the 260-day calendar because it is here that the days from the second zenith passage to the first total exactly 260. He places the origin of the 260-day almanac at 1359 B.C., when 1 Imix coincided with the August 13 zenith passage date at Izapa. However, there are no early Tzolkin records at Izapa that predate the eighth Baktun. Furthermore, Munro Edmonson (1988:119) cautions that the idea of linking the zero point of the calendar on August 13 to the zenith passage at Izapa works only if you use the 584,285 correlation. Nonetheless, he supports Malmström's conclusion that a division of the year into segments of 105/260 is evident in the placement of the zenith date at Izapa. I would add that the interval of 105 days between the two solar zeniths may also refer to the growing period of the principal maize crop, which is planted following the first solar zenith at the end of April and first matures around the second solar zenith in mid-August.

Malmström (1991:42–45; 1997, fig. 35) suggests that Edzná (19°37′ N) in Campeche was where the 365-day calendar originated because here the zenith sun coincides with July 26 (July 16 O.S.), the beginning of the year in Yucatán recorded by Landa. He concludes that the solar calendar was not intercalated, and calculates its origin date as A.D. 48, when the beginning of Pop coincided with the zenith sun. His ideas are intriguing, but we do not find very early solar calendar inscriptions at Edzná. His conclusions rest on the notion of a continuous solar calendar traced back fifteen hundred years from Landa's sixteenth-century descriptions, an unlikely situation given the calendar reforms that certainly took place throughout history. Indeed, Edmonson (1988:99, 124–127, 148) has traced a number of calendar changes in Mesoamerican history. He suggests that Edzná's calendar derives from a revised solar calendar that is first seen at Uxmal in A.D. 649.

The Tzolkin provides the framework for a calendar count tied into a 364-day computing year that may have keyed to the solstices and equinoxes. Dresden Codex pages 61–69 record intervals of 91 days, the closest integral approximation of the mean length of time between the solstices and equinoxes (V. Bricker and H. Bricker 1989:239). Such intervals are actually quite common in the Dresden Codex, sometimes forming part of a larger cycle of 1,820 days ($7 \times 260 = 20 \times 91$). The Paris Codex (23–24) also incorporates an 1,820-day cycle divided into 364-day periods (Chapter 7). Edmonson (1988:111) postulates that the earliest form of solar calendar in Mesoamerica was a year based on observations of the two solstices and the two equinoxes, calculated at 91-day intervals, yielding a calendar of 364 days.

David Kelley (1983; 1989:66–71) proposes that records of the tropical year on Classic Maya monuments allow approximate determination of the equinoxes and solstices. Linda Schele (1990a:145–146) finds tropical year anniversaries recorded at Palenque in the Classic period. Andrea Stone (1982; 1995b: 164, table 4) notes that seasonal cycles are apparent in the Classic period dates recorded for rituals in a Guatemalan cave called Naj Tunich. She points out that some dates are separated by four years minus one day, and an expression deciphered as "he arrived" (*hul-i*) coincides with dates around the winter solstice. Calendar Round dates record recurring solar events at Yaxchilán. Carolyn Tate (1992) notes that some Yaxchilán glyphic inscriptions focus on zenith passage dates, and ball-game events seem to cluster in October. A ritual involving a staff with banner (known as a "flap-staff") and a fire event are both linked with dates clustering around the summer solstice at Yaxchilán (Tate 1992, app. 2). Nikolai Grube (1992:207–208) interprets these scenes as a dance performed by a ruler in warrior costume. This suggests that the warrior dance is linked with the summer solstice, perhaps related to capture events around this time of year.

Werner Nahm (1994) notes that capture events during the Classic period are more common in the rainy season, whereas full-scale star wars—wars designated with star-glyph verbs—cluster from November through January. Few star wars took place at planting time, and none at all occurred during the harvest between mid-September and late October. Seasonal patterning of star-war dates in Classic Maya inscriptions indicates that the preferred time for warfare was between the autumn equinox and the spring equinox, according to John Justeson (1989:107), who notes that mature corn in the fields provided a food supply for the warriors at this time of year. Anthony Aveni and Lorren Hotaling (1994:S45–S46) statistically demonstrate a marked clustering of star-war events in the dry season. Hotaling (1995) records a paucity of star-war dates from June through November. Joyce Marcus (1992:430–421, table 11.1) notes that warfare events concentrated in the dry season, especially between November 13 and May 5. Seasonality also played a part in the dates selected for warfare during the Postclassic period, for the dry season was preferred for warfare by the Aztecs and the Yucatec Maya (Milbrath 1988c; Torquemada 1943, 2:299; Tozzer 1941:217). Indeed, this pattern survived into the nineteenth century, when the Maya of Yucatán abruptly abandoned their fight in the Caste War to return to their fields at the beginning of the rainy season to prepare for planting (Reed 1964:99).

The Classic Maya must have had an annual cycle of festivals, but the festivals were not closely linked with the 20-day months, which slowly shifted position relative to the solar year (tropical year) of 365.2422 days. As we have seen, tropical-year events seem to be recorded in a number of calendric inscriptions on Maya monuments at Yaxchilán, reflecting an interest in the seasonal cycle. Also, events in the lives of rulers were linked with important solar events. Accession anniversaries at Palenque follow a pattern coordinated with the solar year (Justeson 1989:113). In one case, it seems that the burial of a Copán ruler was delayed for five days to coincide with the summer solstice (Schele and Larios 1991:3–4).

Karl Taube (1988b:333–334) recognizes a spring ceremony in Classic Maya imagery showing a deer-man in a scaffold sacrifice scene. He proposes that the ceremony incorporates three distinct agricultural events: torching the victim's back represents the milpa burning in March; spearing his flesh represents the planting in May; and the blood flow symbolizes the rains of May. He correlates the ceremony with sixteenth-century descriptions of the months Mac and Pax in Landa's calendar and suggests a possible relationship with a central Mexican ceremony dedicated to Xipe Totec. It is likely that many other seasonal ceremonies appear in Classic Maya imagery, but research in this area has been scanty.

This brief survey indicates that we are only beginning to understand the importance of the seasonal cycle among the Precolumbian Maya. In the late Postclassic period, there is evidence of an intercalated 260-day agricultural calendar and an intercalated festival calendar that follows the solar seasons and agricultural events, like some of the calendars preserved among the Maya today. Seasonal ceremonies and events may be reconstructed from study of Landa's festival calendar and from specific images that seem connected with this calendar, especially those seen in the Madrid Codex. The Early Postclassic and Classic period inscriptions do not show a fixed solar calendar, but certain dates show patterns and clusters of events linked to the tropical year.

SOLAR ORIENTATIONS IN ARCHITECTURE

The Maya probably performed solar rituals in architectural complexes with alignments keyed to specific solar events. The horizon position of the sun on the equinoxes, zenith passages, and solstices was important in the alignment of Maya architecture (Aveni 1980:258–286). Anthony Aveni and Horst Hartung (1986, table 3) developed a hypothetical solar calendar for the Maya area based on orientations centered around the zenith passage dates. A number of orientations reflect an alignment toward sunset twenty days before the zenith passage. They also present a great deal of evidence documenting solstice orientations at northern Maya sites. Indeed, their sample of 113 sites shows a significant percentage with a 24°–25° solstitial orientation.

An archetypal Maya observatory is found in Group E at Uaxactún, located at 17°23′ N. From the vantage point of a Preclassic pyramid known as E-VIIsub, one sees three temples on a raised platform. The summer solstice sun rises behind the northern temple, the equinox sun rises behind the central one, and the winter solstice sun rises behind the southern temple (Aveni 1980:277–280, fig. 100). At nearby Tikal, there is a similar observatory in the Preclassic complex of the Mundo Perdido group, where the Great Pyramid (5C-54) faces a terrace supporting three temples that mark the positions of the rising sun at solstices and equinoxes (Agurcia and Valdés 1994:112–113; Fialko 1988b). Structure VI at Calakmul also seems to be part of a Preclassic observatory complex like that of Group E at Uaxactún (Folan et al. 1995, fig. 4).

Dzibilchaltún, located at 21°06′ N, has an east-west causeway (*sacbe*) aligned toward architectural groups that appear to be part of a complex of solar observatories (Aveni and Hartung 1989, table 35.3; Coggins and Drucker 1988). The eastern group resembles Group E at Uaxactún. The proposed observation point for watching the changing position of the sunrise is at Stela 3, positioned on a small platform in the center of the *sacbe*. Further to the east, the Temple of the Seven Dolls (Structure 1-sub) may provide another sight line. When viewed from Stela 3, the equinox sun rises where the tower of the temple meets the flat roof, forming a sort of "seat" for the rising sun (Coggins and Drucker 1988, figs. 3, 11). Based on a suggested seventh-century date for the construction, Clemency Coggins (1983) proposes that Dzibilchaltún's eastern group was an

equinox complex erected to honor the end Katun 9.13.0.0.0 (3/16/692 N.S.), just before the spring equinox. The Temple of the Seven Dolls itself may have been an observation point, for one of its four doors faces west at a 273°50′ azimuth, approximating the equinox sunset. Further study of this temple's orientations is required.

Equinox orientations occur at other Classic period sites in Yucatán. Recent studies of the Labyrinth (the Sanunsat) at Oxkintok (20°34′ N) indicate that a number of small openings in the west wall are oriented toward the equinox, or within a few days of the equinox (Ferrández 1990, table 1). Kabáh may also show equinox alignments (Aveni and Hartung 1989:453).

The Classic period Castillo at Chichén Itzá (20°40′ N), also known as the Pyramid of Kukulcan, expresses a relationship with the solar year in its orientations and in the four staircases with 91 steps per side, which, when added to the temple platform as the final step, total 365. At sunset on the equinoxes, shadows formed by the nine levels or stages of the pyramid create serpent markings all along the serpent balustrade on the north side of the Castillo (Aveni 1980, fig. 104; Krupp 1997:268–269). On the south side, a similar effect takes place at dawn (Morales 1990:31). My research indicates that the east-west alignment of the temple on top of the pyramid expresses a relationship with the solar zenith and solar nadir (Fig. 3.1a). The west face and doorway of the pyramid temple is aligned with a 291° azimuth toward the zenith sunset on May 25 and July 20 at the latitude of Chichén Itzá (Milbrath 1988c). The May zenith sunset orientation coincides with the beginning of the rainy season and maize planting in Yucatán. The Temple of the Warriors approximates this orientation with a 290° azimuth. The Castillo's east face and doorway is oriented in a 180° rotation

---

FIG. 3.1. *a:* Map of astronomical alignments of North Terrace Group of Chichén Itzá (after Milbrath 1988c, fig. 1).

b₁: Orientations of Caracol at Chichén Itzá; sunset last gleam; sunrise first gleam (after Aveni 1980, figs. 90–91; Aveni et al. 1975; Krupp 1983:57).

b₂: Facade of Caracol.

c: Summer solstice sunrise illuminates statue of Bird Jaguar in Late Classic Structure 33 at Yaxchilán (after Tate 1992, fig. 43b).

d: Late Postclassic figurine of aged male holding viewing device with hole in center (Mayapán, Regional Museum of Anthropology, Mérida).

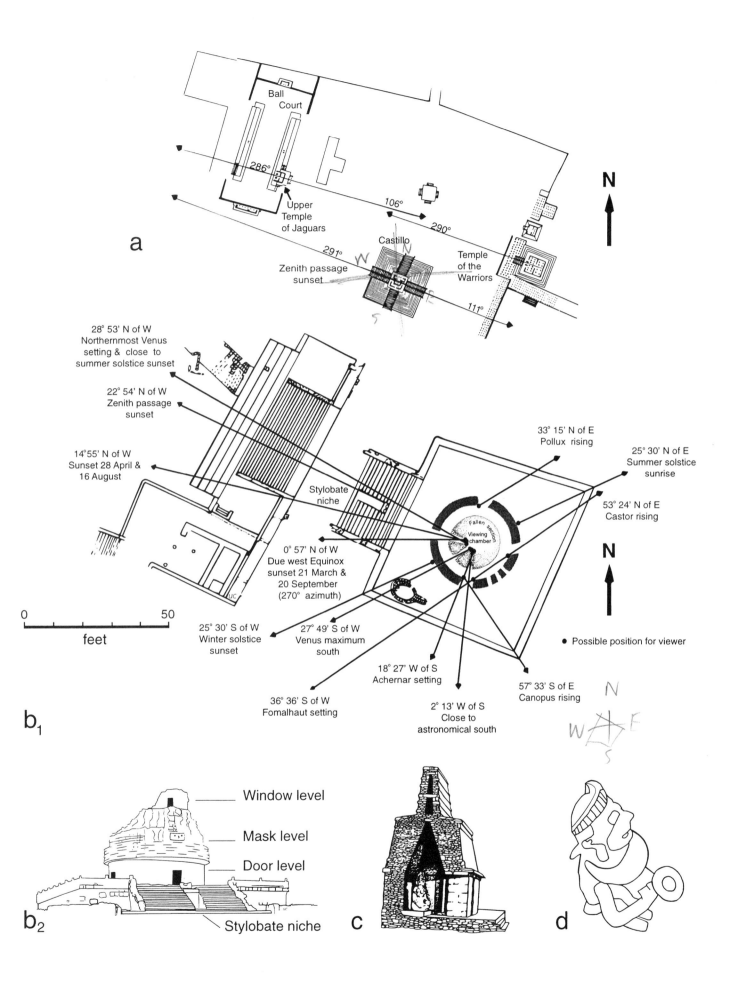

a

Ball Court

Upper Temple of Jaguars

286°

106°

290°

291°

Zenith passage sunset

Castillo

Temple of the Warriors

111°

N

b₁

28° 53' N of W
Northernmost Venus
setting & close to
summer solstice sunset

22° 54' N of W
Zenith passage
sunset

14°55' N of W
Sunset 28 April &
16 August

Stylobate
niche

33° 15' N of E
Pollux rising

25° 30' N of E
Summer solstice
sunrise

53° 24' N of E
Castor rising

Fallen section

Viewing
chamber

0° 57' N of W
Due west Equinox
sunset 21 March &
20 September
(270° azimuth)

N

• Possible position for viewer

0   50

feet

25° 30' S of W
Winter solstice
sunset

27° 49' S of W
Venus maximum
south

18° 27' W of S
Achernar setting

57° 33' S of E
Canopus rising

36° 36' S of W
Fomalhaut setting

2° 13' W of S
Close to
astronomical south

b₂

Window level

Mask level

Door level

Stylobate niche

c

d

toward the nadir sunrise on November 22 and January 21 (111° azimuth). The November solar nadir sunrise coordinates with the onset of the dry season, the beginning of the harvest, and the season of war (Milbrath 1988c:62–63).

The Caracol at Chichén Itzá, constructed toward the end of the Classic period, has several solar alignments (Fig. 3.1b; Aveni 1980, figs. 89–91; Aveni et al. 1975, table 1, fig. 5). The tower of the circular structure has a window oriented to observe the setting sun at the equinoxes, a stairway niche with one wall aligned at an azimuth of 292°54′ (22° 54′ north of west), facing the position of the setting sun on the solar zenith. The Caracol platform is irregularly shaped so that the northeast corner points toward the rising sun at the summer solstice and the southwest corner points to the winter solstice sunset.

The orientation of the Temple of the Four Lintels at Chichén Itzá reflects an azimuth of 292°47′ (22°47′ north of west), facing the setting sun on the solar zenith (Aveni 1980, table 9; Aveni, personal communication 1988). Lintel 1 on the temple features a Kin-marked bird whose wings bear markings like the day sign Etz'nab (Krochock 1988:51, 153, 231–232; 1989, fig. 4; G. Stuart 1989, fig. 3). The lintel records a ball-game event on 9 Lamat 11 Yax, a Calendar Round date reconstructed as 10.2.12.1.8 (7/7/881 O.S.; 7/11/881, N.S.). The ball game took place nine days before the second solar zenith (July 20). A date this close to the solar zenith, coupled with the zenith orientation, may confirm that the structure was somehow dedicated to rituals involving the solar zenith.

Other orientations at Chichén Itzá reflect an interest in dates about a month before and after the solar zenith (Fig. 3.1a). In the Upper Temple of the Jaguars, facing a 286° azimuth, the setting sun casts a circle of light at the center of the back wall on April 29 and August 13 (N.S.). Jesús Galindo (1994: 127) suggests that this indicates an alignment that divides the calendar into two sections of 105 days and 260 days. August 12–13 has calendric importance because it falls 52 days after the summer solstice throughout Mesoamerica, and it coincides with the second solar zenith at Teotihuacán, a site that may have influenced the development of the calendar at Chichén Itzá (Chiu and Morrison 1980:S62; Coggins 1993). Coggins (personal communication 1988) notes that the orientation of the Upper Temple of the Jaguars, like that of window 1 of the Caracol (Fig. 3.1b), is very close to the earliest orientations at Teotihuacán, which fall in the 15°5′ range facing the sunset on April 28–29 and August 12–13, the latter being the famous 4 Ahau 8 Cumku date for the foundation of the Maya calendar.

Perhaps observations of the moon were made on the two zenith dates to coordinate the lunar and solar calendars at Uxmal. Aveni and Hartung (1986, table 2; 1991, table 1) point out that at the latitude of Uxmal (20°22′ N), the solar zeniths (May 22 and July 22 N.S.) are spaced one lunar month from the summer solstice on June 21. The doorway of the lower temple of the Pyramid of the Old Woman has a zenith sunset orientation (291°58′). And the orientation of the Chenes temple (279°29′ azimuth) on the west face of the Pyramid of the Magician anticipates the first solar zenith by forty days (two Uinals). Another alignment from the pyramid crossing the Nunnery courtyard to the Platform of Stelae marks the position of the setting sun on the summer solstice.

At Tikal (17°13′ N), alignments between temples show an interest in solar events. The facade on Temple III is aligned with an azimuth of 108°16′, facing the solar nadir (antizenith) sunrise (Aveni and Hartung 1988, table 2). A line running from Temple III to Temple I has an azimuth (89°54′) oriented to the equinox sunrise. The facade of Temple I faces west (280°35′) toward sunrise 20 days before the solar zenith. Another alignment from Temple IV looking east to Temple I marks the azimuth (104°) of sunrise on February 14 and October 29, dates that approximate a division of the year into two segments of 105 and 260 days. It is noteworthy that these dates are very close to the beginning and end of the fixed 260-day agricultural calendar preserved among the Maya today.

Tikal is located at the ideal latitude for a structured calendar count of Uinals linking the zenith passages, equinoxes, and solstices (Aveni 1989:238). The spring equinox is 2 × 20 days before the first solar zenith, and the summer solstice is 2 × 20 days before the second solar zenith. The 40-day period survives today as the interval the Maya refer to as the "feet of the year." The Chilam Balam of Chumayel says that the Uinal of 20 days was created by measuring the footstep of our Lord, apparently equated with the sun in this eighteenth-century manuscript (Roys 1967:116).

The two zenith dates divide the calendar into 105/260-day intervals at the latitude of Copán (14°52′ N). Zenith orientations are not clearly evident from Aveni's (1980, app. A) measurements of Copán alignments, but a sight line running for about four miles from Copán Stela 12 to Stela 10 provides a baseline that anticipates the first solar zenith date by 20 days. When viewed from Stela 12, the sun passes behind Stela 10 on April 12, one Uinal before the first solar zenith, and again on September 1, one Uinal after the second solar zenith (Aveni 1980:240–243, fig. 78). This baseline is also seen in the window of Structure 22, which also seems to be aligned to observe Venus events (Chapter 5).

A division of the 365-day calendar into two un-equal segments of 105 and 260 days is suggested by the orientations found at a number of sites, including Palenque (17°30′ N; Anderson et al. 1981; Galindo 1994:128, 169). A T-shaped window in the tower of the Palace on the west side casts a beam of light on an oblique wall for 105 days, from April 30 to August 12, dates also seen in the alignments at Chichén Itzá and Teotihuacán, as noted earlier. The T-shaped light pattern reaches its maximum width, extending completely across the wall, on the summer solstice.

Other alignments at Palenque involve the play of light and shadow or sight lines from one building to another. The winter solstice sun sets in a line running from the Palace tower to the center of the Temple of the Inscriptions, which houses the tomb of Pacal II (Schele 1977:49). The Temple of the Sun is oriented toward the rising sun at the winter solstice so that sunlight would shine into the entrance of the temple (Aveni 1992b:66; Carlson 1976:110). Temple XIV also faces the winter solstice sunrise, and House D of the Palace faces the zenith sunset, which occurs in early May and early August at the latitude of Palenque (Aveni and Hartung 1979:173–174, fig. 1, table 1). A line from the Temple of the Cross

to the Temple of the Inscriptions marks the summer solstice sunset over the tomb. Aveni and Hartung also note that House E has an azimuth of 15°34′, like that at Teotihuacán. Perhaps the alignment allows the setting sun to illuminate Pacal's image on the Oval Tablet of Pacal. The throne below records his accession on 9.9.2.4.8 5 Lamat 1 Mol (7/27/615 N.S.), a date close to the August 12 date linked with the Teotihuacán orientation.

Solstice orientations are prominent at Yaxchilán (16°57′ N), where they occur on structures that bear dates referring to the solstices, according to Carolyn Tate (1989: 417, 425, table 32.2; 1992:111–112, fig. 43). Every temple Bird Jaguar IV built expressed a relationship with the summer and winter solstice sunrise axes. Structure 33 was oriented so that the summer solstice sunrise bathed the sculpture of Bird Jaguar IV in light (Fig. 3.1c; Tate 1989:418). Structures with orientations toward the summer solstice and the winter solstice at Yaxchilán are set slightly outside the path of the sun, allowing for only a few minutes of illumination of the interior of the building on the solstices.

The pattern of solar orientations seen in Classic architecture survives in Postclassic times at Tulum (20°12′ N). The Temple of the Diving God (Structure 5) faces the azimuth (292°4′) of the setting sun on the solar zenith (Galindo 1994:170). And a beam of light enters through the east-facing window, illuminating the area beneath the Diving God at sunrise around the winter solstice (Iwaniszewski 1987:212).

Since there is a long-standing tradition of alignments toward the solar zenith sun, we should ask how these observations were made before any architecture was set in place. The zenith sun position is determined by observing the day that the sun casts no shadow at noon. A stela, stick, or even the human body could be used to measure whether there is a shadow at noon. Another form of measurement is implied in a Colonial period account in the Codex Pérez that alludes to May 20 (around the first solar zenith) as a "good day to measure the height of the sun" (Craine and Reindorp 1979:28, 147).

At Tikal, a columnar sculpture surmounted by a stone ring could have been used to measure shadow length and as a sighting station for observations of the sun or stars on the horizon. It is usually identified as a ball-court marker, but it actually was originally positioned on Altar 48-sub, suggesting a fixed observation point like Stela 3 at Dzibilchaltún (Fialko 1988a, fig. 4a). A figurine in the Museum of Anthropology in Mérida shows an aged deity or priest holding a sighting device similar in design, but much smaller (Fig. 3.1d).

We can conclude that architecture provided the fixed vantage point for observations of specific solar positions. Some structures clearly have observing stations such as niches, windows, or vertically positioned stones, such as stelae. The featureless horizon in many areas of Yucatán would have made solar observatories essential for marking the solar calendar. In more mountainous areas to the south, however, the sun was probably observed in relation to individual mountains. Even there, solar orientations in architecture probably remained important because the Maya conducted solar rituals in these complexes. Having the sun reach its proper position during a public ritual helped to confirm the power of the ruler, showing participation in cosmic events. Furthermore, solar observations may have been the principal means of fixing festival dates during the Classic Maya period.

THE SUN IN PRECOLUMBIAN MAYA COSMIC DIAGRAMS

According to Colonial period accounts, the Sun moves through a layered heaven. The Chilam Balam of Maní, which reflects a strong element of European influence, places the Moon in the first layer or canopy of heaven, Venus in the third, the Sun and Mercury in the fourth, Mars in the fifth canopy, and Jupiter and Saturn in the sixth (Craine and Reindorp 1979:49–50). The only feature that distinguishes this account from the Ptolemaic system of crystalline spheres is that the European model places Mercury in the second layer and Saturn in the seventh.

The Chilam Balam of Kaua illustrates a layered cosmos with the Sun in the fourth layer and Venus

in the third, while the Chumayel does not position the sun, but places a god called Esperas in the sixth, no doubt the equivalent of Hesperas, a European name for Venus as the Evening Star. Ralph Roys (1967:110–111) points out that the crystalline layers recall the classical system of Ptolemaic astronomy imported from Europe in the Early Colonial period. Another section of the manuscript alludes to thirteen lay-ers of heaven, but does not position the Sun in any specific layer (Roys 1967: 99, n. 3; Villa Rojas 1969:274–275). The text describes how nine malevolent *bolontikú* seized the thirteen *oxlanhuntikú*, after which there was a great flood and the sky fell at the end of the world age; one passage implies that the *oxlanhuntikú* are layers of heaven, but another suggests that they are a count of time or days (Roys 1967:94 n. 5). The layers of heaven and the underworld may reflect the time-space continuum seen in the Sun's movement through the sky and underworld, as in modern Tzotzil accounts. Indeed, Mayan directions are not discrete cardinal or intercardinal directions; rather, they are trajectories relating to the Sun's daily course that are inseparable from the passage of time (B. Tedlock 1992b:178).

Colonial period diagrams incorporate the notion of a quadripartite time-space continuum involving the Sun. The Chilam Balam of Chumayel depicts the motion of the Sun in a diagram with a series of dots positioned in a ring around the circular earth; the outer ring has four black areas creating a cruciform design with Earth in the center (Roys 1967:87, fig. 7). In the Chilam Balam of Kaua, the Katun wheel has a round earth in the center, quartered to show the cardinal directions; diagonal lines intersect in the center and extend beyond the earth to show the horizon extremes at the solstices (Aveni 1980: 155–156, fig. 57a). The diagonals or intercardinal points end in star glyphs that may refer to Venus, suggesting a connection with both the horizon extremes of the Sun and Venus. Between the intercardinal points, the diagram notes the names of four directions, with east (*lakin*) at the top, north (*xaman*) to the right, west (*chikin*) below, and south (*nohol*) to the left; their placement suggests the cardinal points. A cardinally oriented cross accompanies the notation for east, and the Katun sequence is in a clockwise rotation (13 Ahau, 11 Ahau, etc.), with European-style faces substituting for the traditional Maya Ahau glyphs. The east is "up," conforming with some modern Maya accounts (Chapter 1).

The Postclassic Madrid Codex (75–76) shows the union of time and space with a quadripartite diagram (Fig. 3.2a). Unlike the Katun wheel, the diagram places west in the "up" position with respect to the page layout. In the Madrid Codex, the directional glyphs for east and west both incorporate a variant of the Kin glyph known as T544 in Eric Thompson's (1962) system of notation. A cupped hand is added for west (T671) and an upside-down Ahau face for east. North incorporates a simian face resembling God C, and the glyph for south is partially effaced but seems to conform to the conventional Postclassic glyph compound for south. Twenty day signs are arranged around a square enclosing the central image; but instead of following the conventional sequence, they begin with four-day intervals and rotate in a counterclockwise fashion rather than clockwise, as on the Katun wheel. Around the perimeter, the dates in the 260-day calendar also move in a counterclockwise fashion (i.e., 13 Chicchan followed by 1 Cimi to lower right of central square). Dots between the day signs represent sets of 13 days. The total design evokes the quadripartite completion sign that may be linked with the cycles of the Sun and Venus (Coggins 1980; Coggins and Drucker 1988). Footsteps marking the diagonal axes seem to chart a time-space continuum, most probably related to the course of the Sun. The footsteps suggest comparison with contemporary Maya counts of 40 days known as the "feet of the year."

The Madrid Codex diagram and the one on Codex Fejérváry-Mayer 1 both share a similar format, for they combine two different types of crosses, each enclosed by dots representing days. The diagonal cross, usually described as a St. Andrew's Cross, is positioned between the arm of a rectilinear cross referred to as a Maltese Cross (compare Figs. 3.2a and 4.4i). Aveni (1980:154–157) notes that the diagonal St. Andrew's Cross represents the horizon extremes at the solstices, and the Maltese Cross depicts the cardinal directions with the zenith at the center.

Some notable differences can be seen in the two diagrams. Whereas the Madrid Codex places God Q, a god of human sacrifice, and the Death God in the north, Codex Fejérváry-Mayer 1 shows the Maize God and Death God in the south (linked with the year sign Rabbit, symbolizing the south). In the Madrid Codex, the directional glyphs appear within the arms of a Maltese Cross. On the other hand, the Codex Fejérváry-Mayer establishes the directions at the corners of the St. Andrew's Cross, marking intercardinal directions with different year-bearer glyphs, each carried by a different bird. Like the Aztec system, these follow conventional Postclassic patterns, with the year-bearer Reed for east, Knife (flint) for north, House for west, and Rabbit for south.

Ulrich Köhler (1980:587) says that the year-bearer dates at the corners symbolize the solstice extremes at the intercardinal directions in both diagrams. However, the Madrid Codex places the directions at cardinal points, on vertical and horizontal axes. Furthermore, the Madrid Codex does not seem to treat the dates as year-bearers, because we find the date 1 Cauac on page 76 associated with the north (with God Q to the right), whereas the year-bearer 1 Cauac is linked with west, as are all Cauac dates on the New Year page 34 in the Madrid Codex. Future study should involve a more detailed comparison of the two diagrams, for although visually similar, they clearly show somewhat different constructs that may be significant in revealing variations in concepts of time and space.

Scholars agree that in Maya glyphic writing east is linked with sunrise and west with sunset, corresponding to contemporary Maya concepts, but they disagree about the glyphs referring to the other two directions. Some interpret these as north and south, referring to cardinal directions or, more generally, the sides of heaven associated with these cardinal directions. Others visualize cosmic directions in vertical space, with north and south linked with above and below or zenith and nadir. Barbara Tedlock (1992b:173) says that the directional glyphs in the Classic inscriptions and Postclassic codices can be read phonetically in Yucatec Maya as east (*lak' k'in*), west (*chik' k'in*), zenith (*yax*), and nadir (*mal*). The zenith and nadir readings can be debated, for

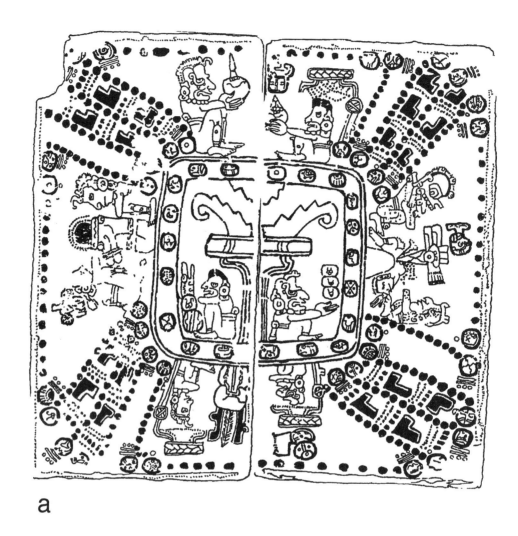

a

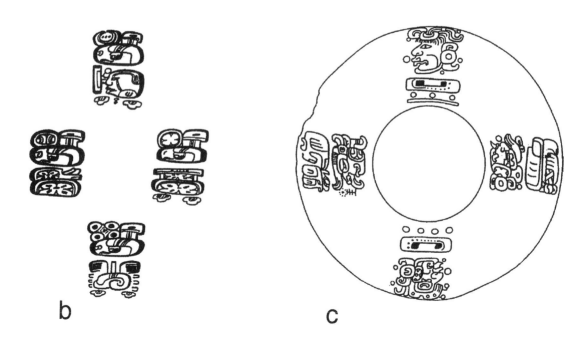

b

c

Justeson (1989:119, 126 n. 41) recognizes glyphs for six directions on Madrid Codex 77–78, noting that in addition to the four traditional glyphs, there are two that include the sign for earth (*kab*), which he interprets as zenith and nadir, and he reads *xaman* as north.

Glyphs for the four directions painted on an Early Classic period tomb at Río Azul show that east and west clearly refer to horizon positions of the sun (Fig. 3.2b). On the east wall, to the right in the figure, the superfix over Kin (the main sign) is another Kin glyph enclosed in what seems to be a bowl, a substitute for the upside-down Ahau head in the compound designating east in the Madrid Codex diagram. This bowl form is T183 or T546, a glyph interpreted as *lak'in* (east) by a number of scholars. The main sign for the west is a Kin cartouche with a hand marked with Kin as the superfix. The position of the fingers differs from the Postclassic hand representing the western direction, but both versions probably signify essentially the same expression *chik' k'in*. The head of the Maize God is the main sign on the north wall (Fig. 3.2b, top). A shell is the main sign on the south wall, perhaps the counterpart for the compound glyph for the south seen in the Madrid Codex. On all four walls of the tomb, the directions appear with a second glyph compound showing God C's head as the main sign. Each wall substitutes a different sign as the superfix over God C's brow. All the superfixes incorporate an element from the T168 glyph, most often used in expressions referring to *ahaw*, meaning "lord." The variable elements all seem to represent astronomical symbols.

The east has a Kin glyph (T544) and the west has an element from the Akbal glyph (T504), meaning "darkness" or "night," suggesting that the opposition of east and west is also the contrast of light and dark. On the north wall, we find the Moon glyph (T683), and on the south wall a Venus glyph. Victoria Bricker (1983, 1988a) concludes that these glyphs refer to the zenith and nadir, specifically marking the location of the Moon near zenith and Venus at nadir on March 6, A.D. 502, a date reconstructed from a Calendar Round record in the tomb. On the other hand, the placement of the glyphs on the walls suggests cardinal directions, with north and south representing "sides" of the sky, as in some contemporary Maya accounts. If this is the case, the Moon may be on the north side of the sky and Venus at the south side.

Four faces on a Late Preclassic earflare from Pomona evoke four directions (Fig. 3.2c). Two of the faces depict north and south or zenith and nadir, according to Norman Hammond (1987). The Sun God (Kinich Ahau) represents the east (to the right in the diagram), and west is marked by a deity head infixed with an element from the Akbal (T504) glyph, suggesting the same kind of Kin-Akbal opposition seen in the Río Azul tomb. Hammond recognizes another variant of Kinich Ahau as north (bottom of diagram). In this case, "north" could symbolize the overhead position of the sun at noon or perhaps the seasonal zenith. The Maize God represents the south, or nadir, direction (top of diagram). This contrasts with the Río Azul tomb; however, the Codex Fejérváry-Mayer 1 places the Maize

---

FIG. 3.2. *a:* Late Postclassic cosmic diagram with cardinal directions placing west in "up" position and footprint paths marking intercardinals that symbolize solstice extremes; Tzolkin day signs in center begin with four-day intervals in counterclockwise rotation. Near footprints, Tzolkin dates seem to follow counterclockwise rotation spaced at one-day and thirteen-day intervals beginning with 1 Imix in east (to left of two figures seated upside down) (Madrid Codex 75–76; after Villacorta and Villacorta 1977).

b: Early Classic Río Azul Tomb 12 mural showing four directions, with east and west marked by kin compounds; west to left, east to right; north or zenith is above; and nadir or south is below (after Bricker 1988a, fig. 1).

c: Late Preclassic earflare from Pomona showing four directions, with Akbal monkey face at west (*left*) and Sun God at east (*right*); maize god overhead may represent nadir or south; second Sun God below may symbolize zenith or north (after Hammond 1987:22).

God in the south position, indicating a possible parallel (Fig. 4.4i).

From this survey of cosmic diagrams, we see the most common forms show a quadripartite division, with the east associated with sunrise and the west with sunset. The other two directions may be generally linked with the overhead position and the underworld position, zenith and nadir, or the north and south sides of heaven associated with the cardinal directions. This same variability mirrors the lack of uniformity in contemporary Maya images of quadripartite space. Nonetheless, we can conclude that the sun defines the cosmic diagram by determining the directions east and west. Colonial period diagrams of vertical space show the sun in a layered universe, but these models clearly show elements of European influence. One Precolumbian model traces the sun's passage through time and space with footsteps along a path. There are a number of other models for how the sun moves through the cosmos.

CONCEPTS OF THE SUN'S MOTION

Sky ropes or cords in Colonial period accounts link heaven and earth, and it seems that the cord defines the sun's movement. A cord ties the womb of heaven and the womb of earth in the Popol Vuh, which records the ancient creation legend of the Quiché (Edmonson 1971:7–8). The Popol Vuh also says that the sun's motion defines the four quarters of the universe, but they actually were set in place before the sun was created, when a cord was stretched in the sky and on earth at the time of creation (D. Tedlock 1985:72). This cord seems to symbolize the four corners of the cosmos representing the extreme horizon positions of the sun at the solstices.

Another ancient tale recorded in Yucatán and Quintana Roo describes a "living cord" suspended in the sky extending from Tulum and Cobá in the east to Chichén Itzá and Uxmal in the west. Arthur Miller (1982:92–95) interprets this as a sort of cosmic umbilical cord, and he suggests a connection with a cord represented in the codices and in the Tulum murals (Fig. 3.3b). He does not, however, point out that this cord is shown as the path of the sun in the codices. Madrid Codex 19 shows a sun glyph (Kin) rolling along a sky cord, and Paris Codex 21 depicts the sun glyph suspended from a sky cord colored blue-green like a vine (Fig. 3.4a–b). In the codices, the cosmic cord seems to represent the ecliptic. A related image appears in the Yucatec Motul dictionary of the Colonial period, which notes that the sun's rays are *u tab kin,* "the cords of the sun" (Thompson 1960:142).

The ecliptical path of the Sun is represented as a cotton cord in Mixtec-Puebla art. The Codex Borgia (33) shows the Sun and the Moon traveling in the sky along a white cord representing the ecliptic (Fig. 3.3a; Milbrath 1989). The Sun and planetary gods move along a similar cord in the Mixtec murals of Mitla (Fig. 5.6h). Especially intriguing is a figure who grabs the rope as he pulls himself out of a cleft opening in the sky band. This evokes a link with a Venus god emerging from a similar cleft and descending on a cord on Codex Vindobonensis 48 (Fig. 5.4f; Milbrath 1988a). On Santa Rita Mound 1, murals on the east half of the north wall depict different astronomical gods pulling themselves along a cord (Quirarte 1982, fig. 21). These scenes represent the ecliptical cord guiding the Sun, the Moon, and the planets as they move through the sky.

In Postclassic Maya representations, the ecliptical cord can be colored white like a cotton thread, as in

FIG. 3.3. *a:* Postclassic temple with sun disk and U-shaped moon symbols positioned overhead on white cord representing ecliptic (Codex Borgia 33; after Seler 1960–1961, 4:82, fig. 61).

b: Late Postclassic Mural 1 of Tulum Structure 5 (Temple of the Diving God) showing rayed sky band, seated Moon Goddess in two aspects, Chac (God B), and Maize

God all positioned on ecliptical cord ending with serpent heads; God N in his turtle aspect is in sea below (after Miller 1982, pl. 28).

c: Late Classic ceramic vessel showing two double-headed serpents with twisted bodies serving as ecliptical cord for three astronomical gods (after Quirarte 1979, fig. 1).

a

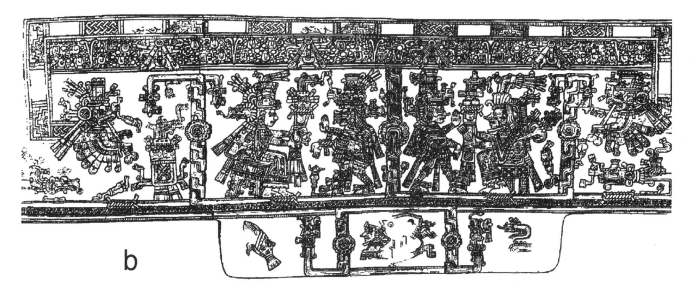

b

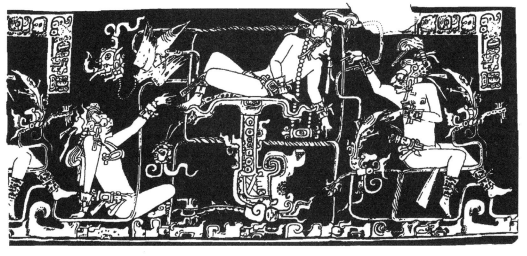

c

the Tulum murals (Fig. 3.3b), or a darker color ranging from blue-green to brownish-red, as in the codices (Fig. 3.4a–b). The cord in the Madrid Codex perforates the penises of five gods (Schele 1976:24). Consequently it is both a path for the sun and a conduit for feeding blood to the sun. Indeed, blood sacrifice is required for the sun to move, according to Aztec cosmology (Durán 1971:179; Sahagún 1950–1982, 7:8).

The ecliptical cord may also appear on a Late Classic black-background vase (Fig. 3.3c). Two double-headed serpents with twisted cord bodies serve as the path for three gods. Jacinto Quirarte (1979:103) notes that the bicephalic creature provides the ground, stage, and conveyance of the sun in its journey through the underworld.

Another way the sun moves through the underworld seems to be expressed in a Classic period vase from the American Museum of Natural History that shows a solar god (to the right) climbing a tree that rises up from the underworld (Figs. 3.4c, 4.10d). This evokes connections with Lacandón accounts of the sun passing into the underworld along the roots of a tree. A shell at the base of the tree seems to be linked with the notion of a watery underworld, also seen among the contemporary Maya. Likewise, the underworld is connected with water in Classic Maya vase painting (Hellmuth 1987). These under-

world waters emerge from caves or openings in the earth. The earth itself is visualized as a giant crocodilian floating in water, as seen in the crocodile draped with water lilies on Copán Altar T (Maudslay 1889–1902, 1, pl. 95). Tracing the imagery back to Preclassic Izapa, Stela 25 depicts a crocodile with a cosmic tree sprouting from his body (Norman 1976, pls. 41, 42). Natural history may explain this image, for crocodilians pile up earth amid water to make mounds where they lay their eggs. Trees take root in these mounds, forming miniature models of the earth.

Other Classic Maya images refer to different animals serving as modes of transport for the sun during different seasons. A modern Maya account discussed in Chapter 1 tells us that the sun travels slowly, conveyed by peccaries in the long summer days (rainy season), whereas the winter sun moves swiftly across the sky on a deer (dry season). These images of the summer and winter sun can be traced back to the Classic Maya period, and they may refer to the sun in conjunction with specific animal constellations (Chapter 7).

We can conclude that there is considerable variety in Maya imagery showing how the sun moves across the sky. A celestial cord is connected with the sun in Colonial period accounts, and Postclassic images show the sun moving along a cord. In the Classic

---

FIG. 3.4. *a:* Earth Monster devouring sun symbol surrounded by four skeletal snakes hanging from an ecliptical cord that crosses sky band at the intersection of point of Milky Way and ecliptic (Postclassic Paris Codex 21; after Villacorta and Villacorta 1977).

b: Sun glyph (Kin) moving above a rooftop along sky cord representing ecliptic (Late Postclassic Madrid Codex 19; after Villacorta and Villacorta 1977).

c: Detail from Late Classic vessel showing Sun God with spotted cheek climbing sacred tree (American Museum of Natural History vase; after Schele and Miller 1986, pl. 120).

d: Postclassic gilded copper disk with Kin glyph (Cenote of Sacrifice at Chichén Itzá; after Tozzer 1957, fig. 277b).

e: Early Classic Kin glyph (T544) with quadripartite design symbolizing both celestial flower and four directions of sun.

f: Early Classic Kin variant (T646) with cardinally oriented double lines representing flower linked with sun.

g: Ahau Kin, name of early Postclassic Sun God (Dresden Codex 5a; after Taube 1992b, fig. 22a).

h: "Sun-at-horizon" or sunrise (T561[544]:426) glyph compounds (Late Classic Piedras Negras Throne 1; after Thompson 1960, fig. 31, nos. 45–46).

i: Classic and Postclassic variants of Yaxkin, month sign variously interpreted as "new sun," "green sun," "first sun," or "dry season" (after Kurbjuhn 1989).

j: Late Classic sky band with Kin glyph in center (Sarcophagus Lid, Temple of the Inscriptions, Palenque).

k: Kin glyph forming ancestor cartouche, House A Palenque; note four skeletal snake heads, one bearing star glyph (after Tozzer 1957, fig. 267).

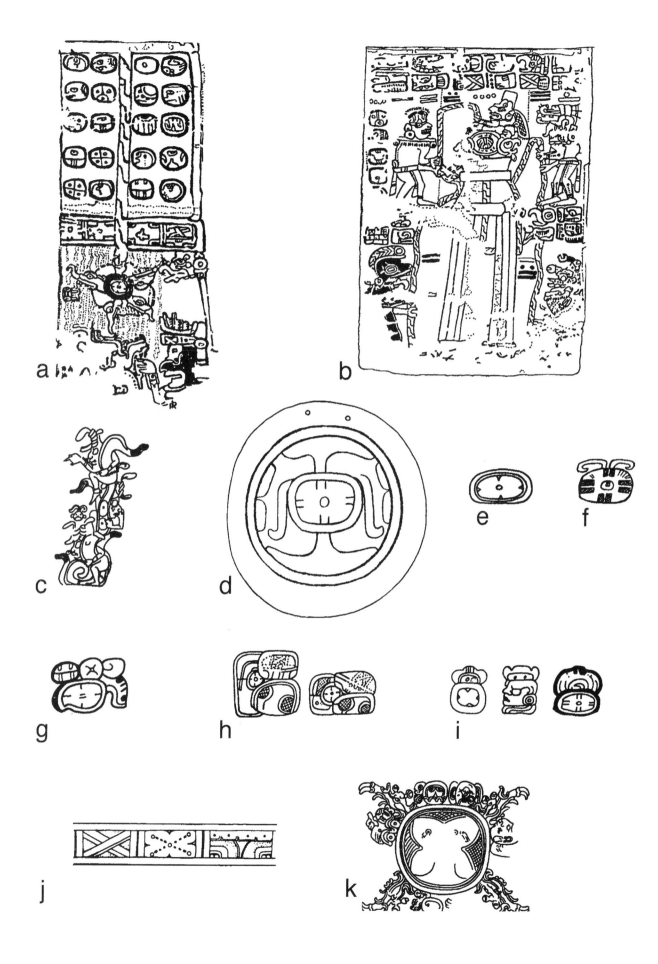

period, the cord may take on serpentine qualities, suggesting that serpents may be equated with the path of the sun in some contexts. More rarely, the Sun God climbs up a tree in his ascent from the underworld. In Chapter 4, we will see that the solar god travels in a canoe with a lunar companion, perhaps as a mode of transport through the waters of the underworld. Various animals also carry the sun, perhaps as representatives of constellations marking the seasons, an idea explored further in Chapter 7.

THE PRECOLUMBIAN KIN GLYPH

Miguel León-Portilla (1988:112) relates the sun to chronovision, "the conception of a universe in which space, living things, and mankind derive their reality from the ever-changing atmosphere of *kinh*." *K'in* means "sun," "day," or "time" in most Mayan languages (B. Tedlock 1992b:176–177; Vogt 1969:446).

The Kin glyph (T544) used as an artistic motif identifies the context as solar. Sometimes the Kin glyph represents the sun disk itself, as in Postclassic images of the sun moving along the ecliptical cord (Fig. 3.4a–b). The Postclassic variant of T544 shows a cartouche quartered by single or double lines, most often set at right angles rather than diagonally (Fig. 3.4d, g).

It is interesting to note that in the cosmic diagram of the Madrid Codex, the Postclassic Kin symbols show two different orientations (Fig. 3.2a). Radiating lines on the Kin glyph are diagonally oriented in the eastern direction, suggesting an intercardinal orientation associated with the four horizon positions of the sun at the solstices. In the west, the Kin glyph has double lines on the same axis as the directional glyphs, which seem to be placed in the cardinal directions, representing either the four sides of heaven or the four positions of the sun over the course of the day (sunrise, noon, sunset, and midnight).

In glyphic writing, Kin often names the Sun God, such as the Postclassic Sun God known as "lord sun" (Fig. 3.4g). Kin and Cauac paired with the Tun glyph and a *le* affix signifies *k'intunyaabil,* meaning "drought," as on Dresden Codex 45c (Fig. 5.9f; Thompson 1972:106). The glyphs on Dresden Co-

dex 45c predict dry conditions linked with the western direction; the image shows Chac with fire instead of rain and a deer that is dying of thirst, according to Thompson. A scene on Dresden Codex 42c, predicting drought associated with the southern direction, shows the Maize God bound up in preparation for sacrifice, perhaps indicating his death is due to drought.

The T544 Kin glyph of the Classic period places the quadripartite design on a diagonal axis with cutout areas at the cardinal positions (Fig. 3.4e). The quadripartite design of Kin glyphs evokes the cosmic diagram, but it also resembles a four-petaled flower. The T646 Kin glyph in Classic times, a closed cartouche showing cardinally oriented double lines (Fig. 3.4f), more closely resembles Postclassic Kin glyphs. It seems to be linguistically connected with flowers, for T646 is interpreted as *nicte,* meaning "flower" (Hellmuth 1988:169; Stone 1995a). An Ahau glyph (T533), the day sign that is a counterpart for the twentieth Aztec day sign "flower" (Xochitl), is found at the center of some Classic period T646 glyphs. Although Ahau (*ahaw*) means "lord," here it seems to be the center of a solar flower. The Chilam Balam of Tizimin refers to the "flower sun" (*nicte kin*) in the year 11 Ahau (Edmonson 1982b:72). In Yucatec, *nikte'*(*nicte*) is the "flor de mayo" or, more specifically, the red plumeria, *Plumeria rubra* (Barrera Vásquez 1980). The Chilam Balam of Chumayel refers to the red plumeria as the flower of east (Roys 1967:65). Although plumeria flowers have five petals, Thompson (1960:142) suggests that the Kin glyph shows a plumeria with only four petals because four is the number over which the Sun God rules.

T646 is interchangeable with T544 in a number of Classic period images, according to Nicholas Hellmuth (1988:169). However, not all the contexts are clearly solar. God H, a Venus god, sometimes has the T646 flower on his brow (Chapter 5; Taube 1992b, fig. 26b). Some T646 variants have a quatrefoil outline and a central Mexican–style star in the center, as on House E at Palenque (Robertson 1985a, pl. 30). Perhaps these are images of the night sun or some other nocturnal symbol.

The interpretation of the Kin glyph varies according to its context. Kin represents the concept of a day when used with a numeral coefficient to give a total number of days in calendar records, the most common usage in the Classic period (Thompson 1960, fig. 26, nos. 49–57). The day count also has a personified form represented by a profile head that bears the Kin glyph and the features of the Sun God (Thompson 1960, fig. 27, nos. 60, 62).

Kin is also a component of the *veintena* (month) sign Yaxkin, variously translated as "new sun," "green sun," "first sun," or "dry season" (Fig. 3.4i; Thompson 1960:110). In the Postclassic period, this month coincided with the beginning of the dry season around November. Landa represents the month Kankin with a Kin glyph (Tozzer 1941:164). Although Kin is not seen in Classic and Postclassic period glyphs for the month Kankin, Thompson (1960:113–114) interprets Kankin as "yellow sun." A yellow sun may allude to the extremely dry conditions common in Kankin, which coincides with April in Landa's calendar.

Other combinations with the Kin glyph may refer to places where the sun is located. Sometimes Kin is paired with Caban, the earth sign, probably as a reference to the sun at night beneath the earth (Madrid Codex 28c). When Kin and Caban appear with the sky glyph, the expression is interpreted as "sun at horizon" or "sunrise," when the sun "divides the earth and sky" (Fig. 3.4h; Thompson 1960:172, 174, fig. 31, nos. 41–51). Heinrich Berlin (1977:61) notes that the Petén Classic period version of this compound with a prefix of one (I.561[544]:526) indicates a difference of one day in distance numbers. Perhaps this is read as a count from one sunrise to another.

Sky bands in both the Postclassic and Classic Maya periods often depict the Kin symbol (Fig. 3.4j). Previous studies of sky bands have not shown any specific significance to the positioning of Kin glyphs relative to other astronomical symbols (Carlson 1988; Carlson and Landis 1985; Collea 1981). Nonetheless, the sky band itself does seem to allude to a specific place in the sky at the intersection of the Milky Way and the ecliptic (Chapter 7).

A Kin glyph with four radiating serpent heads on Paris Codex 21 (Fig. 3.4a) evokes links with earlier prototypes at Chichén Itzá, Tikal, Palenque, and Yaxchilán (Figs. 3.4k, 3.5i; Love 1994:81; Tate 1992:61,

fig. 23). The serpent-sun combination seems to be connected with ancestors in the Classic Maya period (see below). Taube (1994:234) suggests that sun symbols surrounded by radiating serpents are solar mirrors. In Chapter 7, I explore the possibility that this image may allude to a specific solar position.

From this survey we can see that the Kin glyph, meaning "day" or "sun," is the paramount solar symbol in Classic and Postclassic times. Whenever we see Kin, we can recognize a solar connection. The four-part Kin design evokes the sun's quadripartite cosmic diagram. When oriented diagonally, the diagram seems to refer to the solstice extremes; when aligned vertically, it seems to designate cardinal directions linked with the four sides of heaven. Kin also alludes to a solar flower (*Plumeria rubra?*), a natural connection, since many flowers turn their faces toward the sun.

THE SUN GOD IN THE COLONIAL AND POSTCLASSIC PERIODS

The Colonial period *Ritual of the Bacabs* refers to the colors of the sun in the context of curing rituals. Colors mentioned include the yellow-faced sun, the red-faced sun, and the red-ringed sun (Roys 1965: 14–15, 21). In addition, the sun is named Kin Chac Ahau ("sun red lord" or "sun great lord") and Kinich Kakmo (sun-eye fire-macaw) in this source (Roys 1965:7, 10).

Visual representations of the Sun God in the Colonial period tend to follow a European format, depicting the sun as a rayed face. On the cave walls of Dzibichén, European-style sun disks appear alongside Ahau faces emblematic of the Katun cycle (Stone 1995b:81, 84, figs. 4.73b–c). Rayed faces also represent the sun in the Chilam Balam of Chumayel (Roys 1967, figs. 8–9). Sometimes this manuscript merges a European-style sun disk with an Ahau face, as in the image of the Lord of Katun 13 Ahau (Stone 1995b, fig. 4.80).

The Postclassic Sun God has long been identified as God G in painted screenfold books (Fig. 3.5a–d). God G is represented infrequently in the codices (Schellhas 1904:27–28). In the Dresden

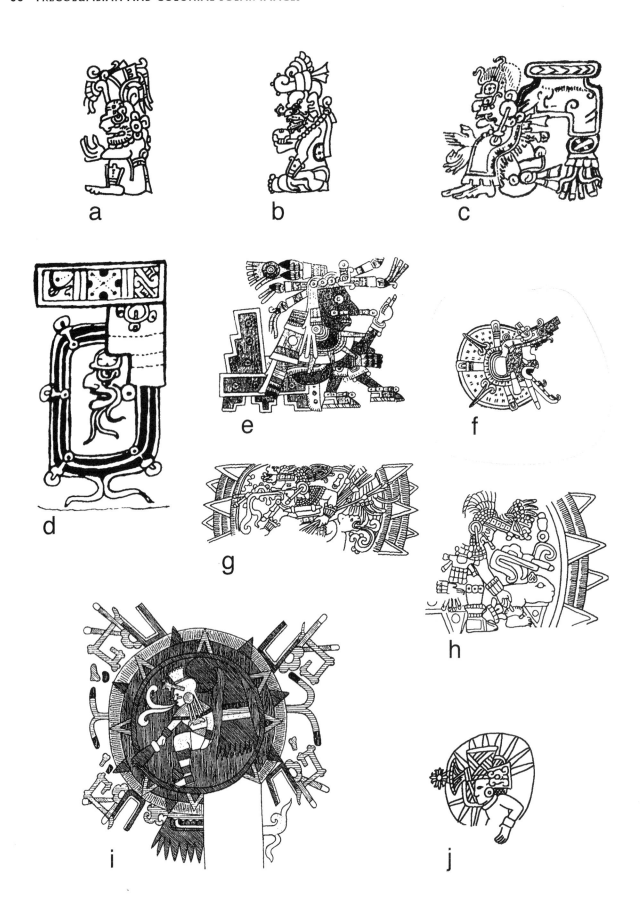

Codex, God G appears only eleven times, compared with fifty-two images of the young Moon Goddess (Thompson 1972:27). The Sun God is almost always malignant in the codices, often being associated with drought or destructive lightning and storms (Thompson 1970b:238; 1972:44, 69). Even in the imagery of God G holding T506, symbolizing maize, the associated glyphs indicate malevolence (Fig. 3.5b; Thompson 1972:61).

The Postclassic God G often wears a Kin glyph on his head, or, more rarely, it is seen on his body, as on Dresden Codex 11c and 22c (Fig. 3.5b). The Sun God's name is "lord sun" (ahaw k'in) or "sun lord" (k'inich ahaw) in both the Classic and Postclassic periods (Fig. 3.4g; Lounsbury 1973:138–139). Sometimes Kin appears paired with the head of God C in expressions that would be translated as "holy sun," according to recent interpretations of the God C glyph as ku or ch'u (Madrid Codex 36; Taube 1992b:30).

The Sun God of the codices is not a youth, for he usually shows attributes of age such as a beard or a sunken jaw with only a few teeth remaining (Fig. 3.5a–d; Taube 1992b:50, 52, 140; Thompson 1970b:237–238). In the Madrid Codex, he is a snaggletoothed old god (Fig. 3.5a). In the Dresden Codex, he seems more like a middle-aged god except in the eclipse table, which represents him as an old bearded god (Fig. 3.5d). God G's aged aspect contrasts with the youthful appearance of the central Mexican Sun God (Fig. 3.5e; Taube 1992b:140). God G's beard indicates maturity, but it also represents solar rays, which are referred to as "the beard of the sun" (mex kin) in the Motul dictionary (Thompson 1960:142).

Sometimes the Postclassic Sun God has volutes or fangs at the corners of his mouth, a trait that goes back to the Early Classic period (Figs. 3.5c, 3.7c). In the Dresden Codex, he has a pegged, up-curling volute on his nose and a similar one on his headdress, a trait sometimes seen on Classic period representations of the Sun God (Figs. 3.5b, 3.6a, 3.7a). Occasionally he has the central tooth ("egg tooth") characteristic of the Classic period Sun God (Figs. 3.5c, 3.7c). His eyes are surrounded by a beaded volute, apparently the Postclassic insignia of "god-eye."

Different aspects of the Sun God are associated with two of the four directions mentioned in Landa's descriptions of the New Year ceremonies, recorded shortly after the conquest (Tozzer 1941:144–147). The ceremonies for Muluc years of the eastern direction honor Kinich Ahau (sun-faced lord), whereas Kinich Ahau Itzamna is associated with the northern direction in Ix years.

The Sun God of the Dresden Codex appears in Postclassic New Year ceremonies associated with the north. God G is seated in the temple of the north in the Dresden Codex (26b), in a scene linked to the new year on the first of Pop in Etz'nab years (Fig. 3.5c). In front of God G there is a bowl of

---

FIG. 3.5. *a:* Late Postclassic image of aged God G with snaggletooth, beard, and Kin brow (Madrid Codex 108b; after Taube 1992b, fig. 22b).

b: Postclassic Sun God with beard, volute on nose, and Kin sign on back (Dresden Codex 22b; after Taube 1992b, fig. 22c).

c: Postclassic Sun God with Kin brow seated in Temple of North in Etz'nab years (Dresden Codex 26; after Villacorta and Villacorta 1977).

d: Postclassic bearded Sun God with aged features and Kin brow is framed by eclipse design with death eyes (Dresden Codex 55a; after Villacorta and Villacorta 1977).

e: Postclassic Tonatiuh, wearing sun-disk collar, represents central Mexican Sun God (Codex Borgia 9; after Seler 1963).

f: Sun God in solar disk (Late Postclassic mural at Santa Rita Mound 1; after Taube 1992b, fig. 77b).

g: Sun-disk figure armed with atlatl and darts seated on feline throne (Terminal Classic wooden lintel in Upper Temple of Jaguars at Chichén Itzá; after Taube 1992b, fig. 77e).

h: Sun-disk figure with serpent mask and feline throne (Terminal Classic reliefs in Lower Temple of Jaguars, Chichén Itzá; after Taube 1992b, fig. 77d).

i: Sun-disk figure framed by fret-nosed serpents (mural in Terminal Classic Upper Temple of Jaguars, Chichén Itzá; after Seler 1960–1961, 5:343, fig. 217).

j: Classic period Sun-disk figure with mat headdress (El Castillo Monument 1, Pacific Slope of Guatemala; after Taube 1992b, fig. 77a).

human hearts, probably an offering to the sun much like the hearts offered to the sun in Aztec accounts. God G is similarly associated with the northern direction in the sequence of twenty deities in the Dresden Codex Venus table (Kelley 1976, fig. 28).

From this brief survey we see that the Postclassic Sun God known as God G is rare in the codices. Many of his manifestations are aged, showing a beard and a snaggletoothed jaw. Sometimes he has fangs and a volute on his Roman nose. His eyes are usually framed by a beaded volute. When God G has a directional aspect, he is most often linked with the north. His name glyph designates him as "lord sun," a name still found among the Maya today. Colonial period imagery represents a radical transformation of the Sun God into a European image of a round rayed face, but a link with Kinich Ahau is maintained in some contexts.

THE SUN GOD AT CHICHÉN ITZÁ

Images at Chichén Itzá depict a solar deity framed by a central Mexican–style sun disk with pointed rays, like that in Mixteca-Puebla codices and murals (Fig. 3.5e–i; Thompson 1970a:473). Many of these scenes blend central Mexican elements with Maya traits typical of the Terminal Classic Maya period, from A.D. 800 to 1000. In the Upper Temple of the Jaguars, central Mexican sun disks frame solar figures armed with darts and an *atlatl,* a dart thrower common in central Mexico (Figs. 3.5g, 5.5e; Tozzer 1957:120). Taube (1992b:142; 1994:224) points out that this solar warrior has the costume and regalia of Terminal Classic Maya kings, but he also resembles Tonatiuh, the Late Postclassic Sun God of central Mexico, sharing the rayed sun disk and even the yellow hair in some cases (Figs. 3.5e, 5.5h). No doubt the yellow hair alludes to the yellow orb of the sun.

Images at Chichén Itzá pair the solar warrior with a feathered serpent (Fig. 5.5e, h). Miller (1977:220) originally identified them as historical figures, naming them Captain Sun Disk and Captain Serpent. Subsequently, Coggins (1984:160–161) identified Captain Sun Disk as a Maya ruler who met his defeat

at the hands of Captain Serpent, a star warrior who may be linked with Quetzalcoatl. This central Mexican Venus serpent is the counterpart of Kukulcan. The solar figure is a deified ruler known as Kakupacal, whose name means "fire shield." Jeff Kowalski (1987:238) notes that Kakupacal was a local ruler who led the Itzá and assumed power at Chichén Itzá by about A.D. 866 or 869. Kukulcan, presumably a foreign ruler who came to Chichén Itzá from central Mexico, is the counterpart of Quetzalcoatl (Chapter 5). In the murals, he is surrounded by rays representing the light of Venus (Fig. 5.5h, right), and the lintel shows him with a star glyph that represents Venus (Fig. 5.5e, next to the water-lily monster). Kakupacal bears a solar title that suggests the sun itself was visualized as a shield of fire. Kakupacal and Kukulcan may be ancestors or representatives of two lineages that ruled Chichén Itzá jointly in the late ninth century, one claiming descent from the Sun, the other from Venus (Milbrath 1988c).

Both celestial rulers carry darts and dart throwers. Kakupacal's darts represent solar "arrowshafts," like those representing solar rays among the Chol today (Chapter 1). And those of Kukulcan symbolize the dangerous rays Venus hurls when it first rises as the Morning Star, as described in central Mexican chronicles (Aveni 1980:150). The fact that these images of the Sun and Venus are found in a structure overlooking the Great Ball Court suggests a relationship to the ballplayers on the Great Ball Court. The ballplayers seem to represent two celestial teams. Turquoise mosaic collars and flower headbands on one team may evoke the Sun, whereas cross-sectioned conch shells (possibly symbolizing star pendants) on two members of the other team may refer to Venus as Quetzalcoatl-Kukulcan (Marquina 1964, lam. 266).

Ball-game reliefs from the Pacific Slope of Guatemala, roughly contemporary with those of the Great Ball Court complex at Chichén Itzá, show a similar interest in astronomical imagery. El Castillo Monument 1, probably dating to the Terminal Classic period, shows a ballplayer climbing up a celestial cord lined with teeth that serve as a stairway to a Sun God, surrounded by a solar disk with pointed rays, one of the earliest known examples of this type of sun disk

(Fig. 3.5j; Parsons 1969, pl. 59a; Taube 1992b:140). The ballplayer's speech scroll indicates that he prays or sings to the Sun God. The Sun God wears a flower headband, an appropriate solar motif, and a tall mat headdress. The mat probably symbolizes the sun's role as a ruler, for it is a headdress worn by a number of Maya rulers, and the mat itself is the ruler's throne among the Aztecs. To be seated upon the mat was an Aztec metaphor for accession to the throne (Heyden 1985:149–150). A mat headdress also characterizes the Sun God on Bilbao Monument 3 (Parsons 1969, pl. 32a). He is similarly positioned on high, but here his solar orb has undulating rays of fire. A ballplayer offers him a human heart, a practice reminiscent of Postclassic Aztec offerings to the Sun God.

In sum, the style of sun disk prominent in solar imagery at Chichén Itzá reflects a link with central Mexico. Connections with the Pacific Slope are seen in an association with the ball game; however, the solar images at Chichén Itzá also may be closely affiliated with politics. The solar imagery associated with Kakupacal is part of a widespread tradition in Mesoamerica linking the ruler to a solar lineage or identifying the ruler himself as a "sun king."

THE SUN KING

Solar cartouches at Tikal, Palenque, and Yaxchilán, often referred to as ancestor cartouches, resemble the sun-disk figures in the images at Chichén Itzá. In the eastern gallery of Palenque House A, thirteen blue medallions probably originally represented solar cartouches framing ancestor figures. One well-preserved example has a Kin sign surrounded by four skeletal snakes, sometimes referred to as snaggle-toothed dragons (Fig. 3.4k). This serpent-sun combination may have a specific seasonal significance (Chapter 7). Similarly, the west facade of Structure 10L-29 at Copán represents a giant Kin glyph with four radiating serpent heads (Andrews and Fash 1992, fig. 10). Tikal Stela 5 depicts a Late Classic ruler wearing a backrack that bears a solar cartouche resembling T646, but with the corners cut back to accommodate four radiating serpents with scroll snouts (Jones 1977, fig. 13).

Classic period dynastic sculptures from the Maya area frequently allude to the Sun God in some way. Sometimes the ruler holds the Sun God or variously wears his attributes. Floyd Lounsbury (1985:47–49; 1991:817) points out that many Maya rulers at Palenque carry the title *mah k'ina,* an integral part of the name for the Palenque solar god known as GIII. He suggests that this title can be read as "great sun."

Events in the lives of Palenque rulers can be connected with solar events. Pacal's birthday (3/22/603 N.S.) coincided with the spring equinox (Lounsbury 1991:818). Chan Bahlum's heir-designation event fell only a few days before the summer solstice. Another ceremony followed five days later on the summer solstice, leading Schele to suggest that the heir to the throne "became the sun" around the time of the summer solstice (Lounsbury 1989:257 n. 11; table 19.1).

A solar headdress clearly links Palenque rulers with the Sun God in House A. Chan Bahlum II, who ruled from A.D. 684 to 702, appears on Pier D wearing a blue mosaic helmet bearing a sky band and the head of the Sun God with Kin signs on his cheek and brow (Fig. 3.6a, right; Robertson 1985b:20). Another ruler, possibly Pacal, wears a similar solar headdress on Pier C (Fig. 3.6a, left).

In the Temple of the Sun at Palenque, a small figure stands on the back of a crouched god with a Roman nose, a mirror brow, a T-shaped tooth, and the crossed eyes of the Sun God (Fig. 3.6b; Schele 1974: 45). The crouching solar god supports the young ruler Chan Bahlum during his heir-designation event when he was six years old (Robertson 1991: 20–21). Apparently the young ruler draws his power from the sun.

The ruler on Copán Stela A (Fig. 3.6c, Pl. 20) is surrounded by figures of the Sun God. Claude-François Baudez (1985, 1986) points out that this ruler takes the role of a "sun king." Variously referred to as 18 Rabbit, 18 Jog, or Waxaklahun Ubah K'awil, this ruler's name glyph is actually a short-eared rodent paired with the number 18. Tatiana Proskouriakoff (1993:127–128) finds the text difficult to decipher, and identifies only the emblem glyphs, cardinal directions, the name 18 Jog, and the dates. On the other hand, Elizabeth Newsome (1991: 279–281, 330) concludes that the text makes an

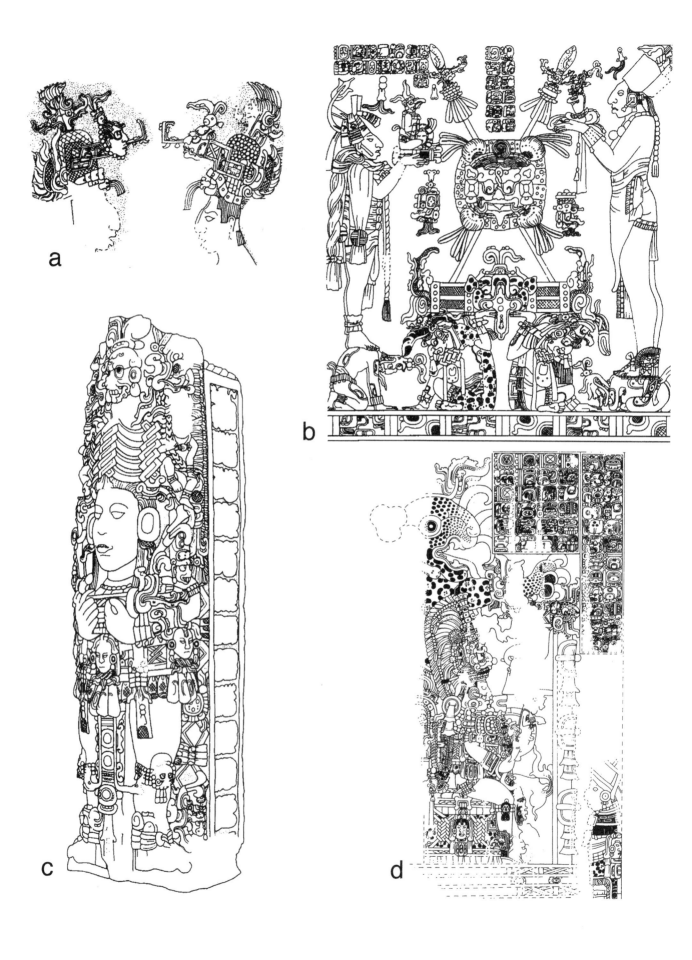

a

b

c

d

extensive reference to the apotheosis of Butz' Chan, a deceased ruler who bears the name of the Sun God in the texts. She notes that the imagery of the dead ruler's apotheosis as the Sun God recalls a solar ancestor depicted on Tikal Stela 31 (Fig. 3.7a). Perhaps the royal lineages at Copán and Tikal traced their ancestry to the sun or a solar ruler.

At Copán, the ruler Mat Head is named with a solar portrait: a conventional Sun God face with Kin cheek markings, crossed eyes, and fangs at the corners of the mouth. According to William Fash (1991, fig. 37), his name is Popol Hol K'inich, translated as "Mat Head, Fire Eye." An alternate name would be "Mat Head, Sun Eye." The links between the sun and the ruler's mat are clearly part of a metaphor for solar rulership. Another solar metaphor is seen on Stela 63, where Mat Head's title incorporates a head of the Hun Ahau Headband Twin, a god of the underworld sun and the Morning Star (see below). This title is translated as Izt'at Ahau, meaning "man of letters lord" (Fash 1991, fig. 3.7).

Early explorers named a zoomorph from Copán Altar U, but it may actually have been a solar throne (Fig. 3.7i). David Stuart (1986) interprets Altar U as a throne or pedestal, and he suggests that the texts mentioning a sun-eyed stone refer to the name of the throne itself. The text links the throne to Yax Pac's accession (Schele 1986). Apparently, his seat of power was a solar throne. The throne depicts a jawless zoomorph with Kin eyes and Ahau pupils; a raised snout bearing a row of three teeth; and an elongated, cross-hatched forehead ornament resembling bound reeds or a rolled mat, evoking the royal mat as a throne. Schele (1992b:54) notes that Altar U is literally a "sun-eyed throne-stone," a play on words linking the term *k'inich* (sun-eye) to Kin symbols in the eyes of the throne zoomorph.

A giant jaguar protector looms over a Late Classic ruler with a Sun God headdress on Lintel 3 from Temple I at Tikal (Fig. 3.6d). Temple I is the ruler's funerary monument, and it seems likely that Lintel 3 represents his apotheosis as the Sun God under the protection of the Water-lily Jaguar. Originally known as Ruler A, this ruler's name is now read as Hasaw Kan K'awil I (Coggins 1975:450–451; Schele and Mathews 1998:320).

An ancestral ruler may be apotheosized as the Sun God on the Early Classic Tikal Stela 31, which bears a dedicatory date in A.D. 445 of 9.0.10.0.0 7 Ahau 3 Yax. This monument has a very long text recording a number of dates, including the inauguration date of Curl Snout in A.D. 379. Looming above Stormy Sky (K'awil Chaan), a figure with features of the Sun God wears a headdress personifying Curl Snout (Yax Ain I), Stormy Sky's father (Fig. 3.7a–b; Coggins 1980:186; Taube 1992b:55). The floating face lacks Kin markings, but it has the Roman nose and squint eyes of the Classic Maya Sun God, as well as a sharply upturning nose ornament sometimes seen on Postclassic images of the Sun God (Fig. 3.5b). The Leyden Plaque, probably from Tikal, represents an Early Classic image of the Sun God dating to A.D. 320 (Pl. 2). It depicts a ruler known as Moon Zero Bird holding a double-headed serpent that bears Kawil (God K) and the Sun God with all his diagnostic traits, including the Kin sign.

We can conclude that solar rulers are especially common in the Classic period. At sites like Palenque and Copán, the living ruler is identified with the sun. Dead rulers were also linked with the sun, a pattern

---

FIG. 3.6. *a: Left,* Youthful Sun God on mosaic helmet worn by ruler (Pacal?) on Pier C; *right,* Chan Bahlum II on Pier D wears mosaic helmet bearing sky band that ends in monstrous head of Sun God with Kin signs on his cheek and brow (House A, Palenque Palace; after Robertson 1985b, figs. 38, 70).

b: Left, mirror-browed solar deity with spotted cheek serves as base for young Chan Bahlum; *right,* adult Chan Bahlum holds God K; *center,* Jaguar War God shield (Late Classic Temple of Sun, Palenque; after Robertson 1991, fig. 95).

c: Ruler known as 18 Rabbit carries serpent bar with figures of Sun God on Late Classic Copán Stela A (after drawing by A. Dowd in Baudez 1994, fig. 4).

d: Tikal Ruler A with Sun God headdress and Water-lily Jaguar protector (Late Classic Lintel 3, Temple I; after Jones 1977, fig. 1).

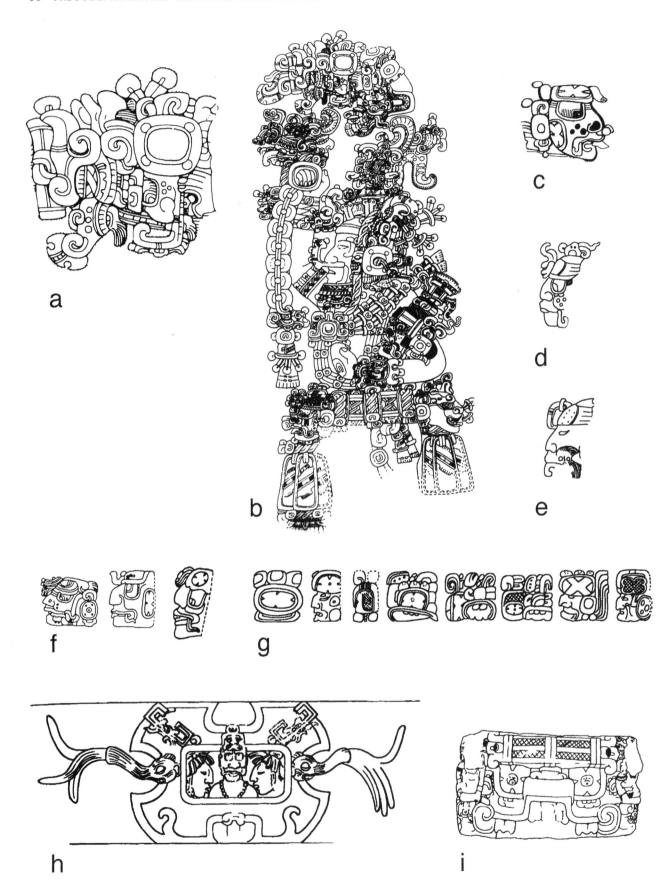

evident at Palenque, Tikal, and Yaxchilán. Clearly the Maya had lineages connected with the sun, and the king himself, living or dead, could embody the "sun king."

CLASSIC MAYA IMAGES OF THE SUN GOD AND EARLIER PROTOTYPES

In Maya imagery from the Classic period, the Sun God is characterized by a Kin glyph, a Roman nose, and a central notched or T-shaped tooth, sometimes described as an egg tooth (Fig. 3.7c; Thompson 1960:142; 1970b:236; Hammond 1987:13). The Sun God is also characterized by crossed eyes (squint eyes), a sign of beauty among the Maya (Tozzer 1941:88). The Sun God invariably wears male clothing when his full figure is shown.

The Sun God is represented with a number of traits that can be traced from the Postclassic all the way back to the Preclassic epoch, indicating continuity in both form and meaning (Taube 1992b:56). An upturned volute in the nasal area and Kin markings are seen on both early and late images of the Sun God (Figs. 3.5b, 3.6a).

The epigraphic head variants of the number four (T1010) are the clearest and most consistent representation of the Sun God in the Classic period (Taube 1992b:52). The Sun God as the personified number four often has his brow or cheek infixed with a Kin glyph or, more rarely, with a mirror (Fig. 3.7f; Thompson 1960:133). T1010 is a portrait of the Sun God used interchangeably with Kin to enumerate the number of days in Initial Series inscriptions, in the name for the month Yaxkin, and in representations of the number four (Lounsbury 1985:47–49, fig. 2). This solar-deity name is one of a number of different head forms of the Kin glyph (Thompson 1960, fig. 27).

The Sun God as the head variant of the number four on Yaxchilán Lintel 48 is especially intriguing (Fig. 3.7d). Although he lacks Kin markings, his central tooth is characteristic of the Sun God, as is his role as the god of the number four. He wears a headband with an Ahau sign and a Jester God, so named because his headdress looks like a floppy court jester's hat. The Jester God may be the counterpart of a jade mask found on the headdress of Tonatiuh, the central Mexican Sun God (Fig. 3.5e; Taube 1994:224). He has cheek spots and mouth volutes seen on a number of solar deities.

Some images of the Sun God have cheek spots grouped in sets of three, often interpreted as jaguar

---

FIG. 3.7. *a:* Ancestral ruler known as Curl Nose apotheosized as Sun God (detail of Early Classic Tikal Stela 31; after A. Miller 1986, fig. 19).

b: Stormy Sky as spotted Headband Twin with his solar ancestor overhead (Early Classic Tikal Stela 31; after A. Miller 1986, fig. 19).

c: Sun God characterized by Kin glyph, Roman nose, central notched tooth, and crossed eyes with square pupils (Early Classic mural in Río Azul Tomb 1; after Hellmuth 1987, fig. 649).

d: Death spots on cheek mark Hun Ahau (Spotted Headband Twin), who is linked with underworld Sun and Morning Star, here represented as head variant of number four (Late Classic Yaxchilán Lintel 48; after Tate 1992, fig. 62).

e: Lunar deity Yax Balam, known as Jaguar Headband Twin, has Yax sign in headdress and jaguar spots around mouth in his aspect as head variant of number nine (Late Classic Yaxchilán lintel 48; after Tate 1992, fig. 62).

f: Personified number four representing Late Classic Sun God with Kin sign or mirror brow (after Thompson 1960, fig. 24, nos. 19–20, 22).

g: Aged Sun God as G9, one of "nine lords of night," probably symbolizes sun reaching its old age at night or at year end (after Thompson 1960, fig. 34, nos. 46–53).

h: Sun God represented frontally with crossed eyes and Kin brow and flanked by a lunar figure on right who wears *po* headdress; note twin peccaries possibly alluding to sun in summer months carried by slow-moving peccaries (Late Classic panel on West Court of Palace; after Robertson 1985b, fig. 358).

i: "Sun-eyed" solar throne, probably used in Yax Pac's accession (A.D. 763), representing jawless zoomorph with Kin eyes and forehead ornament resembling rolled mat (Copán Altar U, Monument 34; after Schele 1989b:107).

spots, based on the markings characteristic of the day sign Ix, traditionally interpreted as representing the skin or ear of a jaguar (Thompson 1960:89). Cheek spots appear on the Kin-marked Sun God in an Early Classic mural from Río Azul (Fig. 3.7c). The Sun God has spotted cheeks in glyphic texts on the Early Classic Tikal ball-court marker, dating to A.D. 378 (Fialko 1988a). The Sun God climbing the world tree on a Late Classic vessel at the American Museum of Natural History also has spotted cheeks (Fig. 3.4c). The solar god representing Curl Snout on Tikal Stela 31, discussed earlier, has similar cheek spots (Fig. 3.7a).

On Yaxchilán Lintel 48, the solar god representing the head variant of the number four has spots high on his cheek, whereas his jaguar companion (Yax Balam), representing the personification of number nine, has jaguar spots around the mouth (Fig. 3.7d–e). This distinction suggests that the solar cheek spots may not be jaguar spots. In murals on the walls of the Naj Tunich cave, these spots are death markings indicating an underworld aspect. The spotted Headband Twin wears a cluster of three or four spots on the cheek, apparently replacing the single death spot more commonly seen on this deity (Fig. 3.10j; Stone 1995b:149, fig. 6.43). Three cheek spots are also seen on the monkey variant of the full-figure Kin glyph (Coe 1978a, fig. 16). These clustered death spots are not limited to the Sun God, and are also seen on a Venus god known as GI, freely substituting for a single death spot on the cheek (Fig. 5.10h–i; Chapter 5).

Having established some general traits in the imagery of the Sun God, we can now turn to representations at different sites that help to expand our understanding of his solar nature. A sculptured panel on the West Court of the Palace at Palenque depicts the Sun God, with his characteristic crossed eyes and Kin brow, in a frontal pose that clearly places him in a position of prominence, for he is flanked by two profile heads (Fig. 3.7h). One head probably represents a lunar deity wearing a *po* sign, a glyph linked to the moon (Chapter 4). Profile serpent masks at the upper corners and two peccary heads may refer to constellations (Chapter 7).

The stucco piers of House A in the Palace at Pa-

lenque may show both the youthful and aged aspects of the Sun God (Robertson 1985b:21, 49). As noted earlier, Pier D depicts a Sun God mounted on a sky band attached to a mosaic helmet crowned by twin Jester Gods (Fig. 3.6a, right). He has crossed eyes and square pupils, a Kin brow and cheek, a notched central tooth, and a volute at the corner of his mouth—all traits that resemble the aged Sun God of the codices. The Sun God on Piers C and E has the same crossed eyes and central tooth but lacks the Kin infix and monstrous features (Fig. 3.6a, left). Robertson recognizes this figure as the youthful variant of the Sun God, and the one on Pier D as the aged Sun God.

Thompson (1970b:237) also identifies the Kin-marked Sun God as aged, noting that he takes the role of Kin, whereas the youthful Sun God substitutes for Ahau. Most personified Ahau variants are now recognized as the spotted Headband Twin, the counterpart of Hunahpu in the Popol Vuh (Fig. 3.10h–i; Coe 1989). In rare instances, the T1010 Kin-marked Sun God represents the day sign Ahau (Fig. 3.8b; Lounsbury 1985). Although a number of scholars have identified the Kin-marked Sun God as aged, the only glyphic aspect of the Sun God to show obvious signs of age is the personified G9, one of the Nine Lords of the Night characterized by a sunken face with lines around the mouth (Fig. 3.7g; Thompson 1960:210, fig. 34, nos. 46–57). Thompson identifies G9 as the night sun, based on comparisons with the nine "lords of the night" in central Mexico; however, his presumed counterpart (Xochipilli) is not an aged deity. Berlin (1977:66) notes that representations of G9 are frequently associated with the end of the Tun, a period that approximates the solar year. This being the case, G9 may represent the sun growing old at year end. Alternatively, his aged features could suggest that the sun grows old each night, a belief recorded among the Aztecs (Sahagún 1950–1982, 1:82).

Some images at Palenque have been interpreted as the Sun God wearing a mirror sign like the glyph T617a (Fig. 3.8a; Schele and J. Miller 1983:20). This variant of the Sun God lacks the Kin sign but has the typical solar eye form, a mouth with a T-shaped central tooth, and volutes at the corners of the mouth.

Like the solar gods already described, the mirror-browed solar deity occasionally has spotted cheek markings, as seen on the crouching figure supporting Chan Bahlum in the Temple of the Sun (Fig. 3.6b). Mirror markings of the Sun God evoke a link with a Kekchí tale that says sunlight is the reflection of a mirror in the center of the sky (Chapter 1).

The sky band of Pier B in House A at Palenque depicts a mirror-browed head with a central tooth and crossed eyes that Robertson (1985b:16, fig. 24) identifies as the Sun God. The face lacks a lower jaw but has an element trailing from the upper jaw that Robertson identifies as a beard, which suggests links with the aged Sun God of the codices. She notes that at some time in the past the color of the mirror and beard were changed from blue to red. This is intriguing because both colors relate to solar imagery but may have had different meanings.

On Yaxchilán Stela 1, the Sun God positioned below the ruler has the classic solar features, including two notched teeth forming a T-shaped central tooth, volutes at the corners of the mouth, and crossed eyes with square pupils (Fig. 3.8c; Tate 1992:66). He has Kin body markings and a brow cartouche inscribed with a Kin glyph, not visible in the drawing published by Tate (1992). According to Stuart (1988: 181), a profile figure on the sky band above the ruler represents another Sun God. Both solar figures wear a laterally suspended pectoral with trilobe ends and crossed bands in the middle. As will be seen, this may be an insignia reserved exclusively for celestial luminaries and rulers playing the part of these deities. The god overhead is in a profile pose that shows the Roman nose and squint eyes typical of the Sun God, but he lacks Kin markings and he wears an unusual skeletal headdress and has lines around the mouth that give him an aged aspect. Perhaps the sun is shown in two different sky positions on Stela 1.

The Sun God appears on two or three different cosmic levels on the front of Copán Stela A (Fig. 3.6c, Pl. 20; Baudez 1994:23). Texts on the back of the stela refer to the sun, the full moon, and the metonic cycle, which links the lunar month to the tropical year (Chapter 4). The Sun God has typical features: a Kin glyph on his brow, crossed eyes with square pupils, and a central notched tooth. At the middle level, a ceremonial bar held by the ruler has two serpent heads at either end, each bearing the head of a Sun God. The Sun God's face is the same on both sides, but one has the markings for flint and the other bears the Akbal sign (Newsome 1991:282–283). Newsome points out that another pair of serpent heads carry underworld images of the Sun God at the ruler's feet. She notes that here one solar deity wears a headdress with a scroll-eyed deity with an Imix glyph representing a water lily, and the other wears a similar headdress with a trilobe element that links him with Uc-Zip, the god of hunting. At the top level of the monument, two figures holding skeletal serpents also appear to be solar gods with Kin glyphs decorating their brows, now destroyed but visible in an early drawing published by A. P. Maudslay (1889–1902, 1, pl. 26). The serpents on all three levels of the stela are skeletal snakes, the same creatures that frame the Kin sign in the ancestor cartouches at Palenque.

The finest image of the Sun God from Copán appears in a group of seven different celestial deities represented on a bench from Las Sepulturas, an elite residential area at Copán. The Sun God has a Roman nose, a notched central tooth, and a Kin glyph on his back and arms (Pl. 19). His domed forehead has a circular cartouche that probably represents a mirror. What makes this bench figure especially interesting is that he is a companion of other celestial deities, part of an assembly of astronomical gods that includes the Moon God and a Venus god with a scorpion tail (Chapter 6).

Early Classic solar masks, revealed in 1992 excavations on the west side of Rosalila at Copán, depict the Sun God with rectangular eyes, cross-eyed pupils, and three spots on each cheek. Although Kin signs are not apparent, the deity attributes seem to fit into the solar pattern. A date on the stairs (9.6.17.3.2) indicates that the temple was commissioned by Moon Jaguar, the tenth ruler of Copán (Agurcia and Valdés 1994:82).

Another Early Classic monumental facade at Edzná has two different images of the Sun God (Benavides 1996:30–31). Both wear large earflares that may represent Kin signs and both have crossed eyes, but the one on the northwest side has rectangular

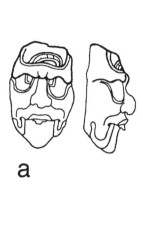

a

b

c

f

d

e

pupils and a nose ornament, whereas the one on the northeast side has circular pupils. Perhaps the two variants pertain to different seasons or directions of the sun.

Kin markings can be traced back to the Late Preclassic period. The Sun God with a Kin sign on the cheek peers down on Stela 2 in a Late Preclassic image from Abaj Takalik (Taube 1992b:55, fig. 23a). The figure wears a mat headdress like the Classic period Sun God from Bilbao, and the volute projecting from the face is also a trait seen on other solar gods. On Structure 5C-2nd at Cerros in Belize, a Preclassic Sun God has Kin signs on his cheeks, crossed eyes, and a downturned mask below his nose (Fig. 3.8e; Schele and Freidel 1990:113–114; Schele and Miller 1986:106). Although the two heads are identical, Schele and her colleagues interpret them as the rising and setting sun. Nonetheless, the cosmic diagrams analyzed earlier show that these two directions are distinguished by different images. The two heads on the upper tier of the pyramid, which Linda Schele and David Freidel (1990, fig. 3:12) identify as the Morning and Evening Star, are also identical. Each is crowned by a trefoil design interpreted as the Jester God's headband.

The Pomona Flare discussed earlier represents two Late Preclassic heads of the Sun God, one certainly symbolizing the east and the other representing either the north or the zenith (Fig. 3.2c). There are minor differences in the eye forms, ear plugs, and fangs that may be significant. Hammond (1987:13, fig. 1) says that a T60 knot in the text, associated with the Sun God of the east, refers to the birth or appearance of the sun in the east, being read as *jo:k', "to appear," here substituting for the T740 birth glyph. He notes that the head representing the north

or zenith position is associated with the number four, reinforcing the role of the Sun God as patron of the number four. This variant of the Sun God appears with a T301 footprint indicating a clockwise movement, the same footprint used with the Maize God and the number eight in the south or nadir position.

There are few known images of the Sun God on Classic Maya vase paintings. A polychrome vase shows Kinich Ahau wearing Kin body markings and a headband, a diagnostic element of a number of astronomical deities (Fig. 3.8d). The Vase of the Seven Gods depicts what seems to be a previously unrecognized representation of the Sun God (Pl. 7). The figure on the lower left is a male with a Roman nose, rectangular crossed eyes, and a central T-shaped tooth. He may originally have had a Kin glyph on the brow that was destroyed by a break in that area, visible in early photographs but not in the drawing published by Michael Coe (1973, no. 49).

A Protoclassic image of the Sun God appears on a stone vessel carved with two "swimming" figures (Coe 1973, no. 2). One of the swimmers has a sun glyph in an open hand on his headdress; his central tooth and the volute at the corner of the mouth are appropriate to a solar deity. His rectangular eye has a paw-wing design instead of the cross-eyed pupils typical of the Sun God. The paw-wing design provides a bridge to Preclassic Olmec iconography, where this form is seen on headdresses and thrones as early as 1200 B.C. (Joralemon 1971, figs. 101, 192, 194; Milbrath 1979:16, table 2, figs. 42–43).

In sum, the Classic Maya worshiped a masculine Sun God, following the predominant pattern seen among the Maya today. Continuity in solar imagery over time is evident from the fact that the Kin-

FIG. 3.8. *a:* Late Classic Sun God with mirror glyph (T617a) on brow, symbolizing sun as "day" mirror (after Schele and Miller 1983, fig. 3f).

b: Sun God with central tooth and fangs as Late Classic Ahau variant (Temple XVII, Palenque; after Lounsbury 1985, fig. 4d).

c: At base, Sun God with Kin brow holds skeletal serpent; overhead double-headed sky serpent has God K in

its jaws (Late Classic Yaxchilán Stela 1; modified after Tate 1992, fig. 124).

d: Sun God Kinich Ahau wearing Kin body markings and headband of Headband Twins (Late Classic vase; after Taube 1992b, fig. 22g).

e: Sun God with Kin signs on cheeks, crossed eyes, and downturned mouth (Preclassic Structure 5C-2nd at Cerros, Belize; after Schele and Freidel 1990, fig. 3:12).

marked body identifies the Sun God over a span of more than a thousand years. Classic and Protoclassic images of the Sun God sometimes have Kin markings and volutes at the corners of the mouth, like Postclassic images of the Sun God. Although the Kin-marked Sun God has been interpreted as aged, the only Classic period solar deity who consistently shows signs of age is the Lord of the Night (G9), representing either the old sun at dusk or the sun at year end. The Classic Maya Sun God with Kin markings has crossed eyes, a sign of beauty. Sometimes he has spots on his cheeks, often identified as jaguar markings that indicate a nocturnal aspect, but these spots may actually be death spots showing an association with the underworld, similarly indicating a nocturnal aspect. Apparently the death and rebirth of the sun take place in the darkness of the underworld. Another group of Classic period solar deities have a mirror brow, a metaphor for a shiny quality apparently expressing the solar rays.

THE MONKEY'S SUN

David Stuart (1988:201) recognizes a simian aspect of the sun, but he notes that the monkey face in Maya art never has Kin markings, and it does not substitute for the Sun God in inscriptions. The only clear substitution is seen in Kin variants representing monkeys, but these are not marked with Kin glyphs (Fig. 3.9a–c). Coe (1978a:341, fig. 16) suggests that all personified Kin variants that are not clearly the Sun God are in fact a Monkey-Man god, and he notes that some full-figure variants of this form clearly overlap with the imagery of the monkey scribes on Classic Maya vase painting (Fig. 3.9e).

A Yaxchilán Kin variant with monkey features is especially intriguing (Fig. 3.9a). Originally described as a spider monkey (*Ateles geoffroyi*) by Coe (1978a: 346), this monkey is identified as a capuchin monkey (*Cebus capucinus*) by Mary Baker (1992:219, 225), an interpretation that remains controversial because this species of monkey is not found in the Maya lowlands. Many Kin variants are especially difficult to identify in terms of species, although their simian aspect is clear (Fig. 3.9c).

It seems these Kin variants are not the sun itself, but relate to the passage of time counted by the sun. It is not known at what point the Classic Maya normally started counting a new day, but it may have been at sunrise or at midday, as among the Aztecs (Codex Telleriano-Remensis, fol. 48; Thompson 1960:177). The Kin-variant monkey may represent a count of days beginning at dusk, the time that the monkey's sun shines, according to the Tzotzil Maya. They say that when the sun disappears at sunset, there is a red glow of sunset called the "monkey's sun" (Laughlin 1977:253; Laughlin and Karasik 1988:249). This long-tailed monkey (*max*) is clearly distinguished from a howler monkey (*batz'*). It may be a spider monkey, noted for its long tail and a color that sometimes has a red quality. Another Tzotzil image of dusk is 'ik-'mach'an, meaning "black monkey's face" (Laughlin 1975:57).

Monkey scribes, an important theme in Maya

FIG. 3.9. *a:* Full-figure Kin glyph representing monkey (Late Classic Yaxchilán Lintel 48; after Tate 1992, fig. 62).

b: God of Zero holding skeletal snake alongside full-figure Kin glyph representing howler monkey with star glyph on ear (Late Classic Copán Stela D; after Coe 1978a, fig. 15).

c: Monkey Kin variants of Classic period are not characterized by Kin markings; possibly they refer to count of days initiated after sunset or before sunrise (after Coe 1978, fig. 13).

d: Throne figure with face of Sun God and lips of Lord T231 (Late Classic Tablet of Slaves at Palenque; after Schele 1991b, fig. 1).

e: Howler-monkey artists as pair (Late Classic vase; after Coe 1978b, fig. 10).

f: Late Postclassic Sun God with macaw headdress and macaw title (Madrid Codex page 89a; after Villacorta and Villacorta 1977).

g: (1)–(5): Glyphs naming GIII of Palenque Triad represent specialized form of Classic Maya Sun God (after Lounsbury 1985, figs. 2a–e). (6): GIII with attributes of Late Classic Sun God (Temple of Inscriptions glyph at E4b; after Lounsbury 1985, fig. 2f).

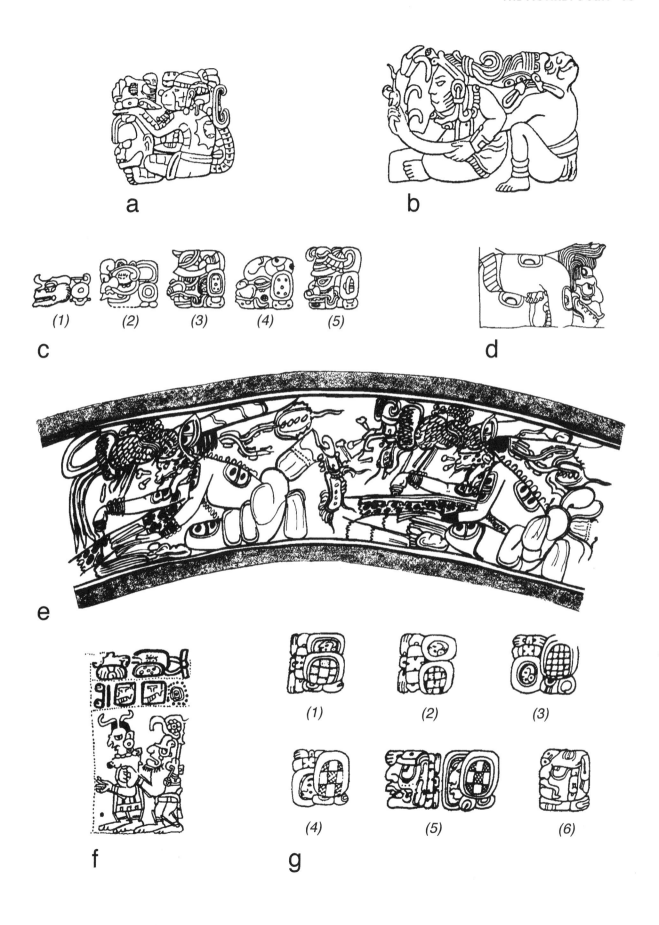

a

b

(1) (2) (3) (4) (5)

c

d

e

f

(1) (2) (3)

(4) (5) (6)

g

vase painting, are characterized by a deerlike "extra ear," and some have a cluster of three spots on the cheek, reminiscent of certain images of the Sun God and the Venus god known as GI (Figs. 3.9e, 5.10i). The monkey-man scribes may be related to the older brothers of the Hero Twins in the Popol Vuh, who were transformed into monkeys by the Hero Twins. One of the two brothers (Hun Batz) has a name linked with the howler monkey; the other (Hun Chouen) may also be a howler monkey (D. Tedlock 1985:353). Indeed, some of the monkey scribes are represented with the beards characteristic of male howlers (Fig. 3.9e, left; Coe 1978a:346). Coe (1978a: 342–345) notes that Venus is involved in the imagery because the same Monkey-Man god with an extra "deer ear" appears as one of the manifestations of the Morning Star on Dresden Codex 48b (Fig. 5.3c, center). This aspect of the Morning Star seems to be a howler monkey, characterized by a flat face, prominent teeth, and a beard.

A throne figure on the Tablet of the Slaves at Palenque may represent a howler-monkey deity with a solar aspect (Fig. 3.9d). The throne figure has the face of the Sun God and the lips of Lord T231, according to William Ringle and Thomas Smith-Stark (1996:55). In glyphic expressions, T231 is most often identified as the howler monkey (batz'; Kurbjuhn 1989:42).

As noted earlier, the Pomona Flare links a monkey with the west, the place of sunset, evoking the sunset glow of the Tzotzil "monkey's sun" embodied by a long-tailed monkey that may be a spider monkey. The Lacandón link the Sun with a spider monkey and the moon with a howler monkey (Chapter 1). In other Maya tales, the spider monkey takes the role of a planet. In Mopan Maya accounts of three celestial brothers, the Sun's youngest brother is transformed into a spider monkey, variously identified as Mars, Jupiter, or Venus (Chapter 1).

We can conclude that monkeys are connected with the sun, but they do not seem to be the sun itself. As Kin substitutes, monkeys may signal a count of nights. Howler monkeys may be connected with the Morning Star visible before dawn. Similarly, the spider monkey may take a role like the sun, but it actually seems to represent a planet, perhaps one

substituting for the sun at sunset, indicating a count begun at dusk. The monkey imagery will be analyzed further in relation to specific planets in Chapter 6.

SOLAR BIRDS AND SOLAR FIRE

The hummingbird is an avian aspect of the sun among the Maya. With their iridescent feathers, these small birds look like glints of sunlight as they dart back and forth (Benson 1997:77–78). Hummingbirds are especially attracted to flowers of red color, a color that evokes the sun. Thompson (1939; 1970a:368) first recognized that the Gann vase, a Classic period (Tepeu 2) pot from Yalloch, represents a Maya tale about the Sun God in a hummingbird disguise. Subsequently, Hammond (1985) identified a number of Classic Maya vessels that seem to show aspects of the sun's transformation into a hummingbird. Among the Aztecs, the aggressive qualities of the hummingbird apparently suggested a natural connection with the solar warrior, Huitzilopochtli (Benson 1989). Huitzilopochtli, whose name means "hummingbird of the south" (the left hand of the sun), is a solar god who is reborn each November at the beginning of the dry season, when the sun is in the southern sky (Milbrath 1980a).

The Yucatec Maya worshiped the macaw as an image of the sun called Kinich Kakmo ("sun-faced fire macaw" or "sun-eyed fire macaw"). Colonial period accounts, most notably Diego López de Cogolludo's (1954), tell us that the Sun God of Izamal (Kinich Kakmo) was a macaw who descended with the fiery rays of the sun at noon to consume the offerings made by people suffering from illness, especially pestilence. Today the Yucatec Maya pray to the sun at noon for healing, suggesting comparison with prayers to Kinich Kakmo. And the noon sun is the "fire" sun among the Lacandón, the same link we see between fire and the noonday sun in the imagery of Kinich Kakmo. The term kak (fire) or kakal (fiery), often used in contemporary Maya names for the sun, reinforces the imagery of solar fire (Thompson 1970b:236).

Macaws are certainly appropriate solar symbols, being diurnal animals that are quite noisy at daybreak. They can be seen in treetops as the sun rises overhead. At dusk they gather and fly around in circles before retiring for the night; thus their activities seem to mirror those of the sun. Tozzer (1941:n. 689, 904) identifies Kinich Kakmo as the *Ara macao* (the scarlet macaw), predominantly red in color, with yellow and blue on its wings. Red evokes the fiery rays of the sun, yellow the sun itself, and blue the daytime sky.

Kinich Kakmo, a solar bird linked with one of the founders of Izamal, is mentioned repeatedly in the Chilam Balam of Chumayel, especially in texts describing the descent of Kinich Kakmo's shield (the solar orb?) (Roys 1967:66, 82, 160, n. 2). The macaw aspect of the sun marks the arrival of the usurper of royal power in the Chilam Balam books (León-Portilla 1988:30). The divine macaw plays a beneficial role by bringing maize to humankind (Roys 1967:111–112; Thompson 1960:86). This echoes the close connection between maize and the sun among the Maya today.

The Sun God wears a macaw headdress and appears with a macaw title (*ah kak[a] mo*) in the Postclassic Madrid Codex, leading Kelley (1976:6) and other scholars to identify him as Kinich Kakmo (Fig. 3.9f; Fox and Justeson 1984:26). The solar macaw, bearing the glyphic name Kinich Kakmo, is represented on Dresden Codex 40b with torches, appropriate symbols of the scorching sun (Thompson 1960:270; 1972:100). Thompson notes that Kinich Kakmo can be traced back to the Classic period on stelae that represent the Kin glyph prefixed to the macaw head. A macaw found buried with four vultures at Tikal may represent the sun in a cosmic diagram (Benson 1997:88).

Structure 10, associated with the Classic period Ball Court A-III at Copán, originally had sixteen macaws (Fash 1991:126, pl. 80). The modern reconstruction shows the macaw with serpent-faced wings carrying an Akbal glyph surmounted by maize. The link with maize evokes the divine macaw who brought the world maize. Akbal is a nocturnal symbol, and it has been suggested that the macaw represents the sun in the underworld, a role appropriate to ball-game imagery (Kowalski and Fash 1991:65).

Thompson (1960:167) suggests that some bird variants of the Kin glyph may represent an eagle. Although common in Aztec iconography, the image of the sun as an eagle seems to be rare in Maya iconography. The connection between the eagle and the sun may be because the eagle seems to soar toward the sun and is able to look directly at the sun, a trait that was noted by Sahagún's Aztec informants (Benson 1997:79).

We can conclude that birds most commonly linked with the sun are the hummingbird and the macaw. The macaw may be a solar bird not only because of its color, which suggests solar fire, but also because it tends to fly out of its rookery around dawn and return at dusk. The macaw sun, linked with the noonday sun, can cause illness, just as the noon sun is connected with illness among the modern Maya. Another solar bird, the hummingbird, symbolizes both glinting sunlight and a connection between the sun and flowers.

THE SUN AND FELINES

The puma has a golden coat and is active primarily in the daytime, like the sun. In fact, the solar feline of central Mexico is clearly a puma. The solar puma can be seen in a puma with a crown of solar rays at Teotihuacán (Miller 1973, fig. 289). The Sun God sits with a puma on a throne in the Codex Laud (14), a codex that blends central Mexican and Mayan traits. The solar symbolism of pumas may have extended into the Maya area. Just as the sun has higher status than the moon in contemporary Maya accounts, the Tzotzil give the puma higher status than the jaguar (Braakhuis 1987:247).

A puma aspect of the sun may appear on a Classic Maya vase (Fig. 3.11c). H. E. M. Braakhuis (1987) interprets a puma head attached to a deer body as a puma disguised as a deer, evoking the deer disguise of the sun in a contemporary Maya tale about the moon's adultery with King Vulture. He points out that the vase seems to show a sequence of actions related to Landa's month Pax, the month that honors warriors and a puma god probably representing the sun as a war leader.

Feline thrones are quite common in Maya imagery, and many thrones clearly show a spotted jaguar pelt covering the throne (Fig. 3.11c, Pls. 5, 7, 17). At Palenque, the Palace Oval Tablet shows Pacal receiving his crown on a throne representing a feline with two heads (Robertson 1985a, fig. 91). Although spots are not represented, the head ornaments clearly designate the Water-lily Jaguar. In the interior of the Castillo pyramid at Chichén Itzá, archaeologists found a red feline throne with jade spots and a turquoise sun disk on its back (the turquoise mosaic was stolen in the 1960s). This suggests that other feline thrones at the site may be jaguars, such as the throne supporting the solar ruler in two temples of the Great Ball Court complex at Chichén Itzá (Fig. 3.5g–h). In these temples, however, we cannot be sure whether a puma or a jaguar is intended. And even when the throne bears jaguar skin, the significance can be lunar, as in the case of the throne marked with *po* (moon) markings that supports God D on a Late Classic Maya vase (Fig. 3.11c).

Scholars often identify the jaguar as an alter ego of the sun, but research presented here and in Chapter 4 indicates that the jaguar is more commonly an aspect of the moon. The jaguar is nocturnal and likes to swim and fish, thus it is naturally linked with the moon and the watery underworld. Thompson (1960: 11, 107, 135) developed the now widely accepted notion that the sun at night is a jaguar associated with the underworld. His strongest evidence for this association comes from the Kekchí, who say that the sun is *xbalamque* (jaguar sun), but there seems to be no mention of a link with the night or the sun in the underworld (Thompson 1967:32). Furthermore, the same name may be applied to a manifestation of the moon among the Quiché (Chapter 4; D. Tedlock 1985:368–369). Another reason for ascribing a jaguar nature to the Sun God are the spots on his cheek, interpreted as jaguar markings (see Taube 1992b). However, the discussion presented above indicates that they are probably death spots (compare Fig. 3.10e, f, j, k).

A Preclassic relief from Chalchuapa depicts the Kin-marked Sun God holding a decapitated head that may represent a jaguar (Taube 1992b, fig. 23e). Here it is the Sun God who is the decapitator and the jaguar is his victim. Rather than being a solar symbol, the decapitated jaguar head may symbolize the moon as the "jaguar sun" (Chapter 4). The Sun God decapitates the moon during a lunar eclipse in the legend of Coyolxauhqui in central Mexico (Milbrath 1995a, 1997).

We can conclude that there is some link between jaguars and solar imagery in the Maya area, but we cannot be sure the jaguar represents the sun. Indeed, Chapter 4 presents evidence that certain jaguar deities represent the moon. In some cases, the solar feline seems to be a puma. The Maya probably noted that the golden color and diurnal cycle of the puma was analogous to the sun, just as the nocturnal traits of the jaguar and its coat spotted as if by stars evoked the moon and the night.

HUNAHPU AND HUN AHAU

Hunahpu is the twin who becomes the sun at the end of the story of the Hero Twins in the Popol Vuh. He and his brother, Xbalanque, play ball with the lords of the underworld, and when the Hero Twins die, they are resurrected as the sun and the moon (D. Tedlock 1985:160). Coe (1989:180) points out that Hunahpu and Xbalanque are always mentioned in that order, and because the sun is mentioned before the moon in the description of the celestial transformation, it is reasonable to suppose that Hunahpu is the sun and Xbalanque the moon. The order of these events, with the sun transformed before the moon, is the same as in Aztec legends (Sahagún 1950–1982, 7:6). Clearly, the Hero Twins are ballplayers representing the sun and the moon in a celestial ball game. At several points in the tale, they decapitate each other in the underworld, a type of imagery that suggests eclipse cycles (Chapter 4).

Thompson (1960:77, 87–89, 219, fig. 11, nos. 17–29; 1970b:234, 237, 367, 368) suggests conflicting identities for Hunahpu. The Popol Vuh says that Hunahpu and Xbalanque were transformed into the sun and the moon, but does not say which is which. This uncertainty allows Thompson to suggest that Hunahpu was transformed into the moon, an opinion not shared by other scholars. He sees this pattern of a male moon as the result of Postclassic central Mexican influence, and he suggests that Hunahpu was originally the Morning Star in Classic Maya times. He notes that Ahau, meaning "lord" in a number of Mayan languages, is connected with the young Sun God, but when it occurs with the number one, it becomes *hun ahaw* (Hun Ahau) in the lowlands, the counterpart of *hun ahpu* among the Quiché in the highlands, a name linked with the Morning Star. Thompson is clearly inconsistent, for he also identifies Hunahpu as the youthful Sun God, noting that the personified Ahau head is almost certainly Hunahpu as the young Sun God. He bases this in part on the fact that Ahau is the counterpart for the central Mexican day sign "flower" (Xochitl), under the patronage of Xochipilli, the young Sun God. Xochipilli's role as one of the Nine Lords of the Night has been interpreted as that of the night sun, in other words, an underworld sun. Hunahpu may also play a similar role, for the major events in the Popol Vuh take place in the underworld.

The Hero Twins play a role in agricultural fertility. The twins plant maize stalks in their grandmother's house, saying that she should watch the plants as a sign of their fate in the underworld. Later, when Hunahpu's head is decapitated in the house of bats, the creators make a false head for him, which drops seeds when it is hit, permitting the plants to sprout.

The Hero Twins take the role of hunters at several points in the tale, the best known being an episode when they shoot down Vucub Caquix, a bird who wanted to be the sun. *Hun* means "one," and the *ahpu* part in Hunahpu's name means "hunter with the blowgun" or "he with the blowgun," a name for the sun, according to Thompson (1970b:234, 237). Dennis Tedlock (1985:341–342) translates Hunahpu's name as "1 Blowgunner." Most scholars identify Hunahpu with a Precolumbian god named 1 Ahau (Hun Ahau), known from both the Classic and Postclassic periods.

Prior to their transformation into the Sun and the Moon, Hunahpu and his twin brother are said to "control" the Morning Star (D. Tedlock 1985:342). Today the Morning Star is named Junajpu (Hunahpu) among the modern Quiché (B. Tedlock 1992a:28; 1992b:180). Perhaps Hunahpu symbolizes both the Sun and the Morning Star because the two are intimately linked when the Morning Star announces sunrise. Also, Venus and the Sun are often positioned together during conjunction, an event that recurs about every 260 days, the same interval for repetitions of the day sign 1 Ahau, a day apparently linked with Hunahpu.

Coe (1989) identifies Hun Ahau (1 Ahau) as the Classic and Postclassic counterpart of Hunahpu; and he sees both as closely related solar beings. Taube (1992b:115) proposes that a new designation (God S) be used for the Postclassic god with the Hun Ahau title. A Postclassic version of Hun Ahau, enthroned on page 50 of the Dresden Codex Venus pages, is covered with death spots (Fig. 3.10e; Schele and Miller 1986:51; Taube 1992b:117). Here Hun Ahau lacks the conventional spot on the cheek but has eye markings similar to the spotted Headband Twin who represents Hun Ahau in the Classic period (Taube 1992b, fig. 61d). On Dresden Codex 2a, a death-spotted god named Hun Ahau is bound as a captive and decapitated, a feature also seen on a figure of Hun Ahau on Dresden 3a (Fig. 3.10d; Coe 1989:179; Taube 1992b:115–116). This recalls imagery of the twins decapitating each other in the Popol Vuh, possibly an allusion to the eclipse cycle. The connection is strengthened by the fact that the Hun Ahau on Dresden Codex 2a wears a ball-game belt, indicating that he takes the role of a ballplayer like the Hero Twins. Taube (1992b:116–117) points out that in the Dresden Codex and in ethnohistorical accounts, Hun Ahau is strongly identified with death, sacrifice, and the underworld. Landa notes that Hun Ahau is "Lucifer, prince of all the devils" and ruler of Metnal, the Maya underworld (Tozzer 1941:132). Thus Hun Ahau is a god of the underworld, apparently representing the underworld sun, closely connected with the Morning Star as the herald of the rising sun. The same associations with death and the underworld are seen in the Classic period Hun Ahau, for he wears death spots on his cheek.

Coe (1989:167–167) identifies the Classic period Hun Ahau as the spotted Headband Twin. He bears the name Hun Ahau (1 Ahau), written with the number one and the T1000 Ahau sign (Fig. 3.10f). This T1000 variant, representing the phonetic *ahaw*, is a head with a single large death spot on the cheek (Fig. 3.10b–c). When the T1000 head is enclosed in a cartouche, it functions as a day sign, just as a

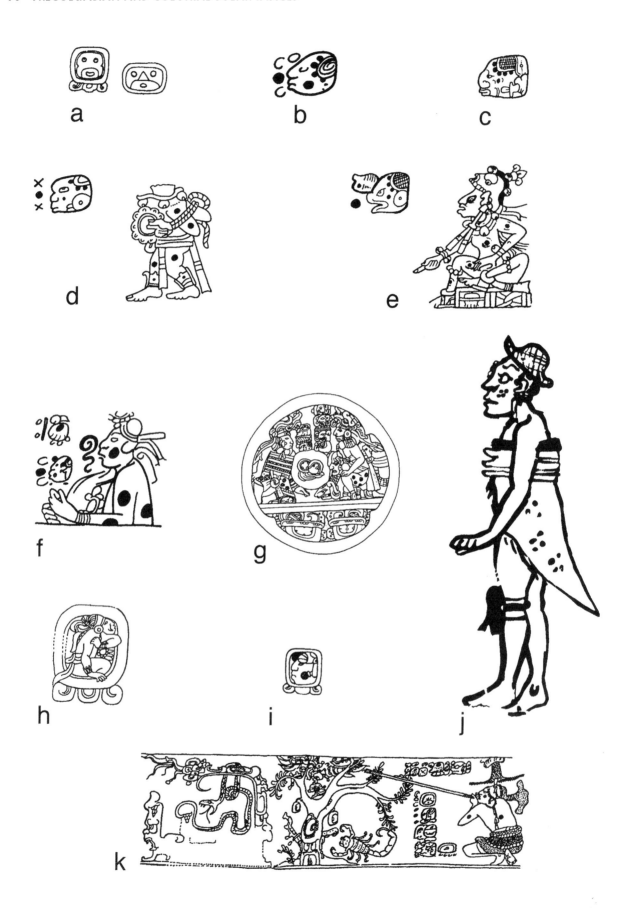

cartouche distinguishes Ahau when it is used as a day sign (Fig. 3.10a, i; Thompson 1960, fig. 11, nos. 17–29). There are also full-figure variants of the day sign Ahau with attributes of the spotted Headband Twin (Fig. 3.10h).

Monumental depictions of Hun Ahau are rare. Unlike Kinich Ahau, Hun Ahau has human features, and sometimes he wears a ball-game belt, indicating he is a ballplayer like the Hero Twins (Fig. 3.10g). On the central ball-court marker of Copán, the ballplayer on the left, named Hun Ahau, is the Classic period counterpart of Hunahpu (Schele 1987a; Schele and Miller 1986:251–252). His companion, the God of Zero, may be a lunar deity (Chapter 4).

A cave painting at Naj Tunich also represents Hun Ahau as a ballplayer (Fig. 3.10j). Stone (1995b:151, fig. 6-44) suggests that Hunahpu (Hun Ahau) plays with a ball symbolizing his brother Xbalanque, because the mural shows Hunahpu with a ball bearing the number nine, evoking Xbalanque as the personification of the number nine. Coe (1989:171) identifies the ballplayer as Hunahpu wearing death spots on his cheek and a straw hunter's hat appropriate to the role of a blowgunner. Here Hun Ahau has a cluster of four cheek spots that resemble the markings on his garment, which are usually interpreted as jaguar spots but could also represent death spots, reinforcing his role as the underworld sun, hidden in a cave. The hat is linked with Hunahpu's role as a hunter, but it also may carry a solar significance, for

the yellow straw brim could be a metaphorical image of the solar rays surrounding his face.

Tikal Stela 31 depicts the ruler Stormy Sky (K'awil Chaan) in the guise of the spotted Headband Twin, Hun Ahau, according to Taube (1992b:119), who notes that he has Hun Ahau's eye and mouth elements, and a similar death aspect seen in the crest of bones on his head (Fig. 3.7b). Andrea Stone (personal communication 1996) points out that he bears a death spot at the crook of his elbow. The fact that Curl Snout appears overhead in the guise of Kinich Ahau confirms that Hun Ahau plays a different role than the Sun God, although he appears to be closely connected with the Sun. In this image, the ruler as Hun Ahau may be an earthly aspect of the Sun closely linked with the Morning Star. Perhaps he is destined to be transformed into the Sun, like his father before him. The Initial Series date (9.0.10.0.0; 10/16/445) corresponds to a time when Venus had just completed its retrograde and was near its maximum brilliance as the Morning Star (usually reached about two weeks after the second stationary point). Perhaps Stormy Sky is compared to Venus at its greatest brilliance, second only to the Sun, paying homage to his deified solar father.

Ceramic vessels depict Hun Ahau in roles characteristic of the Hero Twins in the Popol Vuh. A scene on one pot shows Hun Ahau, wearing a straw hunter's hat, aiming his blowgun at a bird on a tree (Fig. 3.10k). Francis Robicsek and Donald Hales

---

FIG. 3.10. *a:* Classic versions of day sign Ahau (after Thompson 1960, fig. 10, nos. 51, 57).

b: Hun Ahau (1 Ahau), written with T1000 head variant of Ahau sign, representing Classic name of spotted Headband Twin (after Taube 1992b, fig. 60b).

c: T1000 Ahau head with death spot on cheek and Chicchan marking on brow (detail of Classic vase; after Taube 1992b, fig. 60c).

d: Decapitated figure of spotted Headband Twin bearing name Hun Ahau (Postclassic Dresden Codex 2a; after Taube 1992b, fig. 60d).

e: Hun Ahau covered with death spots and Chicchan variant of Ahau name glyph (Postclassic Dresden Codex 50; after Taube 1992b, fig. 60e).

f: Spotted Headband Twin with Hun Ahau name (Late Classic vase; after Taube 1992b, fig. 58d).

g: Hun Ahau as ballplayer on left; to right is God of Zero with his lunar-rabbit handstone (Classic ball-court marker at Copán; after Schele and Miller 1986, pl. 102).

h: Spotted Headband Twin (Hun Ahau) as full-figure variant of day sign Ahau (after Coe 1989, fig. 6).

i: Spotted Headband Twin (Hun Ahau) as head variant of day sign Ahau (after Coe 1989, fig. 6).

j: Hun Ahau as ballplayer (cave painting at Naj Tunich; after Stone 1995b, fig. 6-44).

k: Hun Ahau wearing straw hunter's hat and aiming his blowgun at bird on tree; tree, scorpion, and rattlesnake all represent constellations (after Coe 1989, fig. 10).

(1982:56–57, no. 20) identify the scene as a specific episode from the Popol Vuh when Hunahpu (Hun Ahau) shoots the bird Vucub Caquix in a nance tree, an interpretation that has gained wide acceptance (Coe 1989:169). Hun Ahau as a hunter may embody the early dawn hours, the optimal time for hunting, according to the Maya. Hun Ahau also wears a headband beneath his hunter's hat, the insignia of the Headband Twins. The headband itself seems to be an insignia of ballplayers (Chapter 6).

Hun Ahau, the spotted Headband Twin, is sometimes paired with his jaguar-spotted twin on painted ceramics. The Headband Twins are the Classic period counterparts of Hunahpu and Xbalanque (Coe 1973, 1978b), discussed in greater detail in Chapter 4. The Headband Twins wear the same headband knotted at the back, but they have different headdress ornaments and body markings (Fig. 3.11a–b). Death spots mark the Hun Ahau twin, and the jaguar spots appear on the jaguar twin. Sometimes even this distinction is blurred, as on the Blom plate (Coe 1989, fig. 12).

Another pot, known as Princeton 8, shows Hun Ahau aiming his blowgun at a reclining vulture (Fig. 3.11c; Coe 1978b:58–60, no. 8). Here Hun Ahau wears a headband without the straw hunter's hat. The scene has been interpreted as a representation of a folktale that tells how the Sun God retrieved his wife, the Moon Goddess, when he made King Vulture fall asleep by shooting him with a blowgun (Braakhuis 1987:246).

A pot known as Princeton 16 may represent Hun Ahau wearing a straw hunter's hat as he sits in a quatrefoil cave (Coe 1978b:108, no. 16). Although Coe does not identify the figure in the straw hat, he points out a lunar companion, the young Moon Goddess with her characteristic lunar crescent. This would seem to show the underworld sun and the moon in close proximity. The context of the cave suggests that Hun Ahau may be the sun about to emerge from the underworld.

Hun Ahau performs bloodletting in some ceramic paintings. On a pot from Huehuetenango, he is among a triad of gods shown in the act of drawing blood from the penis (Coe 1989, fig. 17). Another pot shows him enthroned on a Cauac symbol, holding a bloodletter shaped like a deity head (the Perforator God; Coe 1989:173, fig. 18).

We can conclude that Hun Ahau and his later manifestation, Hunahpu, seem to be linked with the Morning Star in the dawn sky before sunrise and with the underworld sun. Whereas Kinich Ahau is the sun up in the sky, Hun Ahau may symbolize the sun in its nightly journey or the sun prior to its transformation into the sun of this age, just as Hunahpu in the Popol Vuh became the sun only after he had passed through the underworld and had been killed by the lords of death. Hun Ahau has nocturnal and death associations, most notable in the death spots. As a ballplayer, he takes part in a celestial ball game that also involves his twin brother, the moon. Hunahpu is solar, but as the sun of a previous world age or the underworld sun, he may be merged with the Morning Star.

GIII: THE SUN AS THE MIDDLE BROTHER

The most intriguing solar deity of the Late Classic Maya is one of the three brothers referred to in seventh-century dynastic sculpture at Palenque. GIII is generally accepted as the Palenque version of the Maya Sun God. His name incorporates the Kin glyph (Fig. 3.9g; Lounsbury 1985; 1991:813). The analysis presented here confirms Kelley's (1965) initial conclusion that GIII represents the underworld sun,

---

FIG. 3.11. *a:* Headband Twins, representing sun and moon, pull Maize God up from crack in turtle shell (Late Classic vessel; after Hellmuth 1987, fig. 438).

b: Hero Twins, Hun Ahau and Yax Balam; Yax Balam, at right, pours water on Maize God (Hun Nal), who sprouts from turtle shell (Late Classic Resurrection plate; after Taube 1988a, fig. 8b).

c: Puma aspect of sun with Chac holding axe and God D on *po* ("moon") throne; second vignette shows Hun Ahau shooting vulture with blowgun (Late Classic Maya vase; after Braakhuis 1987, fig. 1).

a

b

c

a finding supported by other scholars (Robertson 1991:43). GIII is probably similar to Hunahpu of the Popol Vuh; however, being one of three siblings, he belongs to a different mythic complex than that recorded in the tale of the Hero Twins.

Scholars designate the Palenque Triad as GI, GII, and GIII because the texts often list them in this order, but their birth order is different. As the second born in the Palenque Triad, GIII parallels the role of the Sun God as the second born in the modern Mopan tale (Thompson 1930:120–123). The eldest brother in this tale is Venus, corresponding to GI. This correlation is intriguing because independent lines of evidence have led Schele and Freidel (1990:245) to conclude that GI is Venus and GIII is the Sun. The youngest brother is GII, the same birth order ascribed to a monkey character who is Mars or Jupiter in one Mopan account. The uncertain identity of the younger brother may reflect a loss of knowledge about the superior planets in modern times (Chapter 1). Apparently, the Mopan tale preserves a story of three celestial brothers that goes back to around A.D. 700 at Palenque. This triad may be known beyond Palenque, for Proskouriakoff (1978:116) notes that the "3-god indicator" appears at Caracol and at Tikal in the time of transition between the Early Classic and Late Classic periods. She suggests they represent three matrilineal clans associated with heavenly ancestors.

GIII's birthday (1.18.5.3.6 13 Cimi) corresponds to a time when a lunar eclipse could have occurred, because it coincides with the day of the full moon on 11/12/2360 B.C. (O.S.). It is possible that his birthday in November alludes to a seasonal aspect of the sun. In terms of parallel, it is intriguing that Huitzilopochtli's birthday was also celebrated around the same time of year, at the beginning of the dry season in November, and his birth may coincide with a lunar eclipse (Milbrath 1980a, 1995a, 1997).

A solar title used for GIII may refer to the underworld sun. Dennis Tedlock (1991:168 n. 6; 1992:264) proposes that GIII is the eclipsed sun or the underworld sun. Certain details of Tedlock's interpretation are questionable, such as the link he makes between GIII and Xbalanque, but it seems certain

that he is right about GIII's aspect as the underworld sun. GIII appears to be closely linked with Hunahpu through a name pattern that incorporates Hun Ahau. GIII is named *mah k'ina,* meaning "great sun" (Lounsbury 1985:49, figs. 2a–e; Schele 1992b:157). This name is followed by a T239 Ahau face with a spot on the cheek, resembling the T1000 Ahau variant representing the spotted Headband Twin, suggesting a link with the underworld sun (Fig. 3.9g). Lounsbury (1985:51) reads this compound (T239.594[:130]) as "lord sun," but Coe (1989:168) questions his reading of the woven mat sign (T594). Kelley (1976:6) interprets T239 as *xib* (youth) and T594 (a checkerboard design) as *balba* (shield), indicating that GIII's name should be read as "Lord of Xibalba." It seems therefore that GIII has an underworld connection, because this name could refer to the sun at night, an underworld sun.

A rare glyph at E4 in the texts of the Temple of the Inscriptions may represent GIII as a cross-eyed figure with a Roman nose, a T-shaped central tooth, and a mouth volute—all features that evoke the Sun God (Fig. 3.9g(6); Lounsbury 1985). In place of the Kin markings, the figure has a mirror on his brow. A face like that of the GIII portrait glyph appears at both ends of an earth band in the central panel of the Temple of the Sun at Palenque (Robertson 1991, fig. 95). This face, possibly another image of GIII, can be distinguished from the simian faces with mirror markings that alternate with Caban glyphs on the earth band itself. The crouching figure to the left, previously discussed as a solar deity with mirror markings, may also depict GIII (Fig. 3.6b). The fact that this figure is positioned on an earth band may indicate that he is an earthly or underworld sun.

We can conclude that GIII is a specialized aspect of the Sun belonging to a mythic tradition that names the Sun as the middle child in a family of three celestial brothers. Best known from Palenque, the tradition was certainly once widespread, for it survives today among the Mopan. GIII may be represented with a mirror brow in one glyphic expression of his name, but more often he is named with an Ahau variant referring to the spotted Headband Twin. The associated Kin glyph indicates a solar context, and a glyph with a checkerboard design may refer to the underworld. Such names suggest that GIII may be related to Hun Ahau as an underworld aspect of the Sun closely linked with Venus.

THE SUN IN THE PRECOLUMBIAN MAYA WORLDVIEW

Solar orientations in architecture emphasize certain seasonal positions of the sun, especially equinoxes, solstices, and solar zeniths. Orientations that anticipate these events may involve a count of Uinals or lunar months. Some orientations reflect a division of the year into segments of 105 and 260 days that probably synchronized the Tzolkin and the solar cycle.

Animal images symbolizing the sun are not all that common. In the Postclassic period, the red macaw carrying fire represents the noon sun, Kinich Kakmo, known from the Colonial period. A solar hummingbird appears in the Classic period, an image that survives in modern folktales. In some contexts, a puma may represent the golden sun crossing the daytime sky, whereas the jaguar takes the role either of the sun at night or of its close counterpart, the moon.

In Postclassic imagery, the sun travels along a cord, a metaphorical image of its ecliptical path. Other images evoke the symbolism of the solar rays and the color of the sun. The Sun God's beard suggests the rays of the sun, as described in Colonial period accounts. The Kin sign relates the sun to a flower, most probably the red plumeria (*Plumeria rubra*) mentioned in Colonial period sources. In Classic and Postclassic times, the Kin sign marks the body of the Sun God. A Classic period god with a mirror brow may be an image of the shiny aspect of the sun related to modern Maya images of the sun as a mirror.

The Classic period god of the daytime sun is Kinich Ahau or Ahau Kin, the lord of the number four, alluding to the four horizon positions of the sun traced out by the rising and setting sun at the solstices. The Sun God of the Maya is lord of time and

space, linked especially with the east and west in cosmic diagrams. The sun also takes the overhead position of the noonday sun or the seasonal zenith in certain representations, such as the Pomona Flare. Some aspects of the Sun God show him as aged, perhaps as a seasonal metaphor for the sun aging over the course of a day or the solar year. His crossed eyes reflect Maya aesthetics of beauty. Kinich Ahau, the Sun God so prevalent on monumental sculpture of the Classic Maya, is relatively rare in painted ceramics, perhaps because the ceramics are more often concerned with underworld imagery.

Classic period ceramics seem to focus especially on a death-spotted solar god known as Hun Ahau or the spotted Headband Twin. He often wears a broad-brimmed straw hat that probably depicts a corona of solar rays around his face. An underworld context is suggested by death spots and an association with caves. Hun Ahau's image on monumental sculpture is usually confined to glyphs depicting Ahau variants and to some rare representations of the Hun Ahau ballplayer. His counterpart in sculptures of Palenque may be GIII of the Palenque Triad, apparently representing the underworld sun born in mythical times into a family with astronomical siblings representing planets. The Ahau glyph in GIII's name has the face of Hun Ahau, the counterpart of Hunahpu.

In the Popol Vuh, Hunahpu plays the role of a hunter and a ballplayer in the underworld pitted against the lords of death in Xibalba. Classic Maya imagery shows Hun Ahau wearing a ball-game belt and shooting his blowgun, confirming roles seen in the Popol Vuh. A connection with the Morning Star is implied by modern Quiché accounts linking Hunahpu (Junajpu) to the Morning Star. The frequent conjunctions of the Sun and Venus, separated by approximately the same interval that separates repetitions of the day 1 Ahau (Hun Ahau), may have inspired imagery that links Hunahpu to both the Sun and the Morning Star.

Changes in solar imagery over time are notable. One clear difference is that the cult of solar ancestors seems to disappear in the Postclassic period. And although Hun Ahau is fairly common in Classic times, he seems to be quite rare in the Postclassic period, represented primarily in a deity recently identified as God S. God G, the aged Sun God, is the more prominent manifestation of the sun in the codices. God G is closely tied to seasonal ceremonies involving the year's end, indicating a focus on the 365-day calendar. Hun Ahau belongs to a different tradition, one that focuses on mythological time and the role of the sun before it emerged in the current world age. Such transformations in solar imagery over time no doubt reflects changes in religious beliefs and political systems over the centuries.

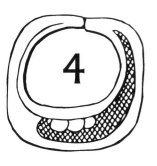

4

PRECOLUMBIAN AND COLONIAL PERIOD LUNAR IMAGES AND DEITIES

There are countless different images of the moon because the moon is constantly changing. Many of these images are expressed in a metaphorical context. The importance of metaphor in recording observations of natural history in Mesoamerica has been noted by a number of scholars. This chapter explores images of the moon that may be based on observations of the lunar season and the moon's phases, position, and motion.

Eric Thompson's (1939) seminal study concluded that a number of beliefs about the Moon Goddess were shared by the Maya and the people of central Mexico: she was a wife of the sun or the sun's mother or grandmother; she was also a patroness of weaving, divination, pregnancy, childbirth, sexual license, the earth, crops, and water. He explored these associations in subsequent publications and also determined that a youthful goddess was associated with the waxing moon, while an aging goddess represented the waning moon. The analysis presented here and in my previous publications on the Moon Goddess supports many of his interpretations and provides further elaboration through study of naming patterns and ethnographic analogy. His interpretation of the lunar complex among the Precolumbian Maya does require substantial modifications in some respects. He concluded that there was only a weak link between the Maya moon deity and water, but it is clear that the connection is in fact quite strong. Thompson also failed to explore a rather consistent relationship between the Moon Goddess and serpents. He also underplayed the role of masculine imagery in the lunar complex, suggesting that instances of a male Moon God were the result of central Mexican influence in the Maya area. In fact, male lunar imagery seems intrinsically Maya and is closely connected with ball playing and the maize complex.

The moon seems to be exceptionally important among the Precolumbian Maya, but its role is too often overlooked by scholars. This chapter draws extensively on my previous studies exploring images of lunar phases and seasonal aspects of the moon (Milbrath 1995a, 1996). In these studies, I conclude that in the Postclassic codices weaving goddesses relate to the dry season, and water-pouring goddesses to the rainy season. The youthful goddesses seem to depict the moon from first appearance through the full moon, whereas the aged goddesses represent the waning moon through the new moon, a phase sometimes represented by an eclipse monster. The cult of the aged goddesses seems most highly developed in the Postclassic period, especially at sites like Tulum, facing the sea to the east, where the waning moon disappears into the waters of the underworld. This chapter also presents new interpretations of Classic period jaguar imagery, linking a number of different jaguar deities to the moon, including the Jaguar Paddler, the Water-lily Jaguar, and possibly the Jaguar War God, also known as the Jaguar God of the Underworld.

I begin the chapter with the moon's role in the Preconquest calendar. There follows a section on eclipses and one on the moon symbol in various forms and contexts. The next sections treat animal images of the moon. The remaining sections focus on various lunar deities as manifestations of different aspects of the moon, especially those that show celestial positions, lunar phases, and seasons.

LUNAR CALENDARS

According to Landa, the Yucatec Maya had a year of 365 days and six hours "as perfect as our own," which was divided into two kinds of months, one a 20-day festival "month" and the other a true month of 30 days. Probably the latter alternated between 29 and 30 days because Landa says "they called each month V [u], which means moon, and they counted it from the time it came out new until it did not appear" (Tozzer 1941:133). Here "new" refers to the first crescent, which apparently represented the beginning of the month. As we will see, the Classic Maya may have counted the beginning of the month from different starting points at different sites.

The core of the lunar calendar is the synodic lunar month tracking the changing lunar phases. Searching the Colonial period Yucatec dictionaries, Weldon Lamb (1981:238, 246–248) found a number of different names for the lunar phases. The phrase "within the earth is the moon" commonly refers to the moon in conjunction. "Serpent-fang moon" (*dzay can u*) and "child moon" (*paal u*) refer to the first crescent moon, while "fat moon" (*nuc u*) is the name for the waxing moon. The full moon is the "old moon" or the "ear of maize moon" (*yiih* [*u*]) in the Motul dictionary.

Lunar reckonings are clearly important in the Postclassic Venus table of the Dresden Codex, which refers to intervals associated with the synodic lunar months (Chapter 5). The sidereal lunar month of 27⅓ days may also have been important in astronomical calendars, such as the one on Paris Codex 23–24 (Chapter 7).

The lunar table of the Dresden Codex (51–58) focuses on eclipse cycles involving the sun and the moon (Pl. 3). The table probably was applied primarily to eclipse prediction, as we will see in the upcoming discussion. The relationship between the Tzolkin and the lunar month was built into a cycle of approximately thirty-three years in the Dresden Codex eclipse table (11,960 days = 46 × 260 = 405 lunations). This allowed Maya astronomers to predict the new moon with an error of no more than a day, resulting in a lunar month of 29.5308642 days (Aveni 1980:169). The table also incorporates lunar intervals registered in an inscription of 19.4.19 that totals 6,939 days (235 lunations), a close approximation of nineteen tropical years, the metonic cycle that brings the solar year and lunar cycle into renewed alignment (Berlin 1977:75). For example, a full moon on the summer solstice would be seen again nineteen years later. Their use of the metonic cycle indicates that the Maya were interested in the seasonal position of eclipses.

Evidence for the metonic cycle on Copán Stela A is associated with a text naming the Sun God (T1010) and the Moon Goddess (C7–D7; Pl. 20). Pairing their names in this fashion recalls couplets in the Chilam Balam of Tizimin that say *k'inil-uil*, meaning "the period of the sun, the period of the moon" (Edmonson 1982b:264 n. 10). As noted in Chapter 1, the contemporary Maya often pair the sun and the moon. On Stela A the pairing seems to refer to the sun and the full moon, for the Initial Series date of 9.14.19.8.0 12 Ahau 18 Cumku (1/28/731) falls on the full moon, and it is followed by the date 4 Ahau 18 Muan (9.14.19.5.0; 11/29/730), also the day of the full moon (a date recorded on Stela H). The Calendar Round 4 Ahau 18 Muan at E2–F2 may refer to the metonic cycle, because it is 9.15.0 days (6,940 days) after the Katun ending 9.14.0.0.0 6 Ahau (a date not given in the text). As Heinrich Berlin (1977:75–76) notes, this interval gives a value close to the solar year (365.263 days) and the lunar month (29.532 days).

Martha Macri proposes that basic units of the

Classic Maya calendar involve counts of 13, 9, and 7 days that combine to produce a lunar count (Macri and Beattie 1996). The 13-day period of the waxing moon is linked with the personified numbers one through thirteen, including many that represent lunar deities (Macri 1982). Adding 7 days takes the count through the waning quarter and completes the cycle of twenty personified numbers; adding the 9-day cycle (Glyphs G1–G9) brings the lunar month to a close at the time of the new moon. These intervals are found on monuments with Initial Series inscriptions that record a repeating cycle of thirteen numbers in the Tzolkin dates and the Supplementary Series cycle of 7 days and another of 9 days, similar to the nine lords of the night in central Mexico (Justeson 1989:77–79; Thompson 1960:208–212; 1978:17–18). In rare instances, the three cycles are combined in an 819-day cycle that reflects the least common multiple of the numbers seven, nine, and thirteen. The cycle of 9 days, a standard feature of the Supplementary Series, also forms a long cycle that does not repeat for 468 years (9 × 52), when combined with the 52-year Calendar Round.

In 1915, Sylvanus Morley published the first extensive study of the Supplementary Series, designating letters to identify different glyphs in the series (Glyphs A–G, and X, Y, and Z; cited in Aveni 1980: 161–171). When referring only to the lunar data, scholars tend to use the term Lunar Series (Berlin 1977:69). John Teeple (1930:51, 63) first recognized that Glyph A of the Lunar Series gives the length of the current lunar month, and he also realized that Glyphs D and E record the age of the moon. Glyph A with a coefficient of nine or ten indicates whether the month is counted as twenty-nine or thirty days long (Fig. 4.1k, right). It usually is a moon sign with a dot in the center (T683a), but sometimes a moon face or another variable element may take its place, and the number ten can be represented by a skeletal face (Fig. 4.1d). Glyph D has a numeral coefficient of up to nineteen to show the actual age of the moon when it is less that twenty days old. It is usually represented by T683a, sometimes combined with a hand pointing a finger (Fig. 4.1f, right); an amphibian face may be substituted for T683a or, more rarely, a simian face (Fig. 4.1f, left). Possibly this pattern of substitution indicates months counted from different starting points. Glyph E, a T683a moon sign sometimes stylized as a human face, represents the moon age when it is twenty days or more, the number of days being indicated by coefficients of zero to nine (Fig. 4.1g). When paired with Glyph E, Glyph D does not carry a numerical coefficient. Glyph D accompanies Glyph E in a Piedras Negras inscription that shows Glyph E with the number seven, indicating the twenty-seventh day of the month, and Glyph A with the number nine to indicate that the month is counted as twenty-nine nine days long (Fig. 4.1k). Anthony Aveni (1980:163) notes that when Glyph E and Glyph D are seen together without coefficients, a new moon is implied. Some variants of Glyph D are almost identical to Glyph E, and this presents a problem in distinguishing the two, as can be seen when comparing Glyph D, representing a moon age of nine days (9D), and Glyph E, representing a moon age of twenty-six days (6E; Fig. 4.1f–g).

The Lunar Series also includes Glyph C, which counts the number of a specific lunation in a cycle of six moons (177 days) known as a "lunar semester." Glyph C is a compound with a flat hand and a moon sign with three dots in the center (the T683b glyph) combined with a third element, a deity portrait head that has three variants, indicating three different lunar semesters in an eighteen-month cycle used to predict eclipses (Fig. 4.1e; Justeson 1989:87–88, 91; Linden 1996). John Justeson points out that from A.D. 350 to about A.D. 687 (9.12.15.0.0) at least five different systems of counting the lunations were used, including two different notations for numbering the moons in a set of six lunations. Most centers used a relatively simple system of moon numbers, with the majority following the pattern of enumerating current months seen at Tikal; but around the Usumacinta area, the Maya chose to count elapsed months, resulting in numbers smaller by one than those of Tikal. The so-called period of uniformity is actually not a single period, but involves several different periods and different core areas with variant numbering systems for Glyph C. The best-known uniform number system is the one Teeple identified in the period from around 9.12.15.0.0 to 9.16.5.0.0

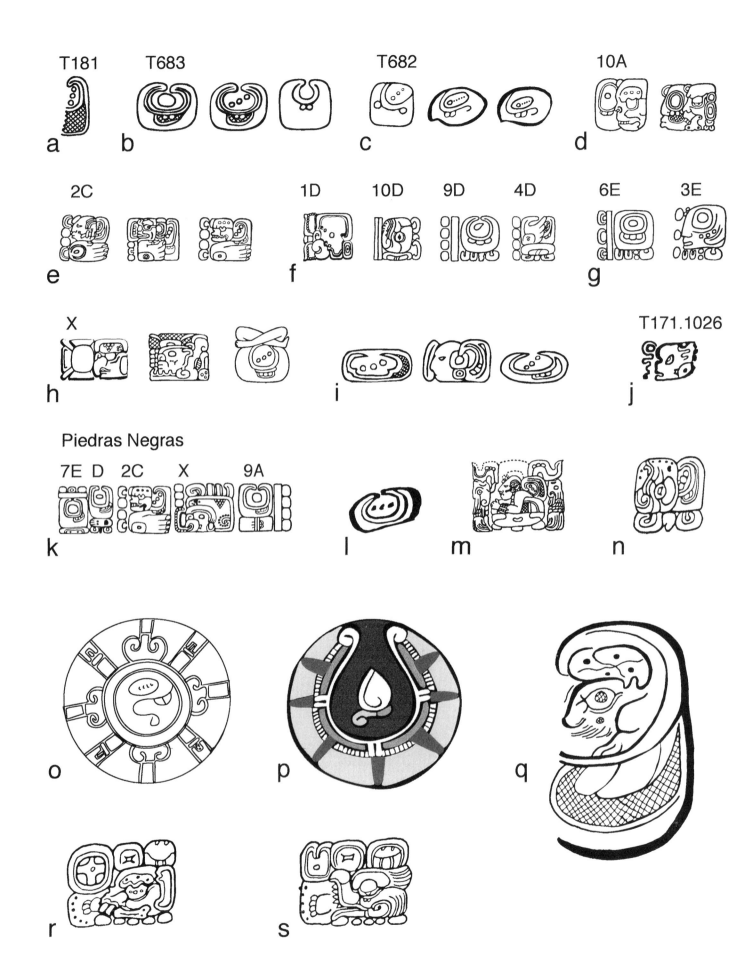

T181 T683 T682 10A

a b c d

2C 1D 10D 9D 4D 6E 3E

e f g

X T171.1026

h i j

Piedras Negras

7E D 2C X 9A

k l m n

o p q

r s

(A.D. 756), when Copán introduced an occasional five-month cycle (148 days) in the Lunar Series (Aveni 1980:163–164, 169–170). Between A.D. 687 and 756, Maya cities used the same group of six lunations, so that across the region a date of 9.15.5.0.0 has the inscription 2C. Heinrich Berlin (1977:70) extends the period of uniformity to 9.16.10.0.0, noting that this date is associated with an inscription of 1C throughout the Maya area. This seems significant because it is the date of the new moon in the 584,283 correlation, and Glyph C is now known to be part of a cycle used for tracking eclipses.

Some of the more enigmatic Lunar Series glyphs may be connected with the lunar calendar. Glyph X, also part of the Lunar Series, is part of an eighteen-month lunar calendar linked with Glyph C, which records the semesters in an eighteen-month eclipse cycle (Fig. 4.1h; Linden 1986, 1996). When a five-month semester was used, the cycle was apparently reduced to seventeen months (Justeson 1989:90–91). The twelve different forms of Glyph X may function as month names, since they lack numeral coefficients. For example, Copán Stela A has a variant of Glyph X featuring a Kan cross at A8 (Pl. 20).

FIG. 4.1. *a:* T181 as postfix, variously interpreted as phonetic sign or indicator of past tense or passive voice, clearly refers to moon in Lunar Series Glyph C (see Fig. 4.1e).

b: Classic moon glyphs in three variants: T683a (*left*) used for number 20, T683b (*center*) used phonetically and as symbol for moon, and T683c (*right*) of unknown meaning.

c: Postclassic moon symbol (T682), commonly used for number 20 but also in lunar-eclipse imagery.

d: Lunar Glyph A (T683a) symbolizing number 20 with coefficient of ten (here personified as skeletal face), indicating month is counted as thirty days; moon face replaces T683a in Glyph A on right.

e: Three deity-head variants of Glyph C record different six-month semesters (177 days) in sequence of eighteen months used for eclipse prediction; each has coefficient of two, indicating second month in their respective semesters (after Thompson 1960; fig. 36).

f: Glyph D variants of moon age, each bearing different numeral coefficient showing age of moon during first twenty days; variants of main sign may show lunar month was counted from different starting points (after Thompson 1960, figs. 36–37).

g: Two variants of Glyph E, with T683a moon sign on left and moon face on right, representing moon age when it is twenty days or older with added numeral coefficient giving number of days beyond twenty: 6E equals 26 days and 3E equals 23 days (after Thompson 1960, figs. 36–37).

h: Variants of Glyph X are keyed to eighteen-month numbering cycle expressed by Glyph C (after Thompson 1960, fig. 36).

i: Lunar glyphs as Classic Initial Series introductory glyphs for month Chen (after Thompson 1960, fig. 22, nos. 44–46).

j: Postclassic T1026 "moon lady" prefixed by T171, which may mean "moon," adding emphasis to her lunar quality.

k: Late Classic lunar inscription from Piedras Negras Stela 3 showing twenty-seventh day of lunar month (7E and D), second lunar month of six-month semester in eighteen-month cycle (2C and X), and month counted at twenty-nine days (9 A) (Piedras Negras Stela 3; after Thompson 1960, fig. 36, nos. 25–28).

l: Early Classic variant of T683b associated with northern direction in Río Azul Tomb 12 (after Bricker 1988a, fig. 1).

m: Moon Goddess with her moon symbol and fish in Late Classic Initial Series introductory glyph for month Chen (Copán Stela D; after Thompson 1960, fig. 23, no. 37).

n: Classic Maya glyph compound for birth is T740 with lunar postfix (T181).

o: Moon face (T682) appears on tin disk in Early Postclassic offering (Cenote of Sacrifice at Chichén Itzá; after Tozzer 1957, fig. 277a).

p: Rayed moon disk with shell framed by horseshoe-shaped lunar symbol (Postclassic Codex Nuttall 19).

q: Rabbit in center of T181 lunar glyph, possibly referring to rabbit on surface of moon (Late Classic Tablet of 96 Glyphs, Palenque; after Schele and Miller 1983, fig. 18a).

r: Late Classic variant of Palenque emblem glyph incorporating skeletal rabbit head (T1045) as lunar symbol (after Schele 1977, fig. 4.5c).

s: Late Classic variant of Palenque emblem glyph depicting heron (T793a), also used in name for ancestral Moon Goddess at Palenque (after Schele 1977, fig. 4.5b).

Justeson notes that any given form of Glyph X only occurs with two moon numbers, and with any given moon number associated with Glyph C, only two possible variants of Glyph X occur (Teeple 1930:61–62). Glyph X must be studied on a site-by-site basis because there is so much variability in the moon number system at different centers.

The meanings of some glyphs in the Supplementary Series are not as well understood. Previous research had suggested that Glyphs Y and Z represented dawn and the night (Aveni 1980:165). More recent studies suggest that these glyphs may be linked with the 819-day count (Justeson 1989:78, 103–104). Glyph Y, which has T739 as its main sign, is a rare and enigmatic glyph in the Supplementary Series that involves coefficients numbering two through six (A6; Pl. 20). Justeson points out that if the 819-day count was used to record the behavior of planets, Glyph Y may hold the key to understanding how they tracked the planets. Glyph Z, formerly identified as a separate glyph, is now understood to be simply a numeral coefficient of Glyph Y, essentially an elaborate spelling of the numeral five (Justeson 1989:103; Linden 1996).

Glyph F of the Supplementary Series, another enigmatic glyph, is never used without Glyph G, which records the cycle of nine days (Thompson 1960:212, fig. 34). Glyph F has symbolic forms that resemble a tied knot or a jaguar skin, and a head form that shows considerable variety.

Inscriptions recorded on Classic period monuments indicate that the Maya were able to calculate the length of the month with considerable accuracy. Based on research by Teeple, it has been understood that dates recorded at Palenque give an interval of 81 synodic lunar months (6.11.12), indicating an average lunar month of 29.53086 days, very close to the true length of the month (29.53059 days; Aveni 1980:169). However, you will not actually find the interval 6.11.12 recorded at Palenque; as Berlin (1977:71–72) points out, the number 6.11.12 is implied in the recorded interval of 1.13.4.0, or 11,960 days, equaling 405 lunations (5 × 6.11.12). Teeple also suggests that a formula of 12.4.0, or 149 synodic months of 29.53020 days, was used during the period of uniformity at Copán, but Berlin cautions that

he derived this by inventing a date (7.1.13.15.0) for Altar I.

Regional differences in the beginning point of the lunar month are clearly evident. There is a spread of about seven days in the calculated age of the moon in different Maya inscriptions. Linton Satterthwaite (1967:142, 152) concluded that variant systems were in place at different centers, with Yaxchilán and Piedras Negras using a different zero date than Quiriguá. The 584,283 correlation adopted by Thompson (1960:236, 310) in his later work would indicate that usually the Maya reckoned their months from the disappearance of the old moon or conjunction. Thompson seems to favor a count from the disappearance of the moon, the method of counting that is still current in some Tzeltal, Chol, and Tzotzil villages of Chiapas. Perhaps there were different lunar glyphs used to designate different starting points for counting the lunar month. David Kelley (1976:35) suggests that the Glyph D variant with a hand and T181 should be counted from last visibility, whereas the variant with an amphibian face known as the "upended frog" (T740) marks a count beginning with the first visible crescent (4D and 10D in Fig. 4.1f).

The Classic Maya may have timed dynastic rituals by lunar observations made in conjunction with the solar calendar. For example, Floyd Lounsbury (1989) notes that Chan Bahlum's heir-designation date at Palenque falls on the new moon just prior to the summer solstice. Only the 584,285 correlation provides this link with the astronomical new moon; shifting to the 584,283 correlation would indicate an observation of the last crescent before the summer solstice. Since the last crescent may be the beginning of the lunar month, it still could be astronomically significant. As we will see, there are many other astronomical events that correlate with the heir-designation dates (Chapters 6 and 7).

We have only scratched the surface of the lunar calendar among the Precolumbian Maya. It is clear that a number of different lunar counts existed simultaneously, and some lunar cycles can be traced back to the Preclassic period (Justeson 1989:79, 87). By the Classic period, the Lunar Series included information about the current lunar phase (Glyphs D and E), the length of the current or previous lunar month (Glyph A), and the position of the lunar month in the lunar half-year or semester (Glyph C). The length of the lunar month was calculated with precision, as seen in sets of five and six months used in eclipse predictions. In both Classic and Postclassic times, the Maya recorded cycles of 405 months, and probably also understood the metonic cycle of 235 lunations.

COLONIAL AND POSTCLASSIC ECLIPSE IMAGERY

Eclipse prediction was especially important in the Early Postclassic period (A.D. 900/1000–1250), but by the Late Postclassic and Colonial periods this knowledge may have been lost. Some Colonial period accounts of eclipses seem to show an understanding that the position of the moon relative to the sun is what causes eclipses, but the majority speak of a monster devouring the sun or the moon. Eclipse demons in the *Ritual of the Bacabs* include a snake, a lizard, and a scorpion (Roys 1965:31, 134; Lamb n.d.a). The Chilam Balam of Chumayel describes an eclipse in Katun 8 Ahau as follows: "Then the face of the sun was eaten; then the face of the sun was darkened; then its face was extinguished" (Roys 1967:76). The Vienna dictionary names an eclipse god as a supreme deity called Colup-u-uich-kin (snatcher of the eye of the sun; Roys 1965:xvii). In the *Ritual of the Bacabs,* this being is the agent of solar eclipses, just as Colup-u-uich-akab (snatcher of the eye of the night) is the agent of lunar eclipses (Roys 1965:xvii, 17, 145). Michael Closs (1989:399) believes that these two are not distinct eclipse deities, but contrasting aspects of the same deity.

Accounts of the Colonial period often attribute eclipses to animals eating the sun and the moon, and usually the agent of eclipse is an ant or a feline (Closs 1989). The chronicler Diego López de Cogolludo (1954) describes accounts of ants called *xibal* who attack the sun and eat it, noting that the Yucatec Maya made noise to scare them away. Contemporary Yucatec Maya descriptions say the sun is being bitten during an eclipse (Barrera Vás-

quez 1980; Closs 1989:390; Redfield and Villa Rojas 1962:206).

Closs (1989:396–398) concludes that Venus was the agent of eclipses among the Maya in Precolumbian times, based on ethnographic accounts identifying Xulab, a god described as Venus in some accounts, as the cause of eclipses. He also notes that this connection is indicated by the prominence of Venus in the Dresden Codex eclipse table on page 58a (Fig. 5.1a; Pl. 3). Here there is a descending figure whose head is replaced by a Lamat glyph often linked with Venus (Chapter 5). Closs (1989) notes that this is an eclipse monster representing Venus.

A skeletal figure on page 53a of the Dresden Codex eclipse table may be Venus as another form of eclipse monster (Pl. 3). The glyphic passage overhead, immediately preceding the name of the Death God, records the name *ah tzul ahaw,* a name for Venus as the Evening Star (Closs 1989:409, fig. 31.5a). This may indicate that the Death God bears a Venus title in his role as an eclipse monster. A similar name appears on Dresden Codex 47 (Fig. 5.7r). Closs suggests that this names Lahun Chan, but it may more generally refer to the scorpion aspect of Venus. The diving figure on 58b is clearly an eclipse monster representing Venus with the same *ah tzul ahaw* name (Fig. 5.1a).

Serpents devouring eclipse signs on pages 56b and 57b may refer to another aspect of Venus as an eclipse monster (Pl. 3). The remaining pictures in the eclipse tables depict the eclipsed sun or moon.

Five of the ten pictures in the Dresden Codex eclipse table include "winged" Kin glyphs that refer to eclipses (Pl. 3). The last picture includes both a winged Kin and a winged T682 lunar glyph. The last picture is also distinguished from the others by a chronological glyph recording 13 Tuns (4,680 days) at the top of the last glyph column. This gives the picture and text a larger scope referring to longer cycles of time, namely, the eclipse half-year ($173.3333 \times 27 = 4,680$ days) and eight Venus cycles ($8 \times 584 + 8 = 4,680$ days). This reinforces the connection between Venus and eclipses seen in the associated eclipse monster.

The winged Kin is usually interpreted as a solar-eclipse symbol. There are interesting variations in the black and white winged eclipse glyphs. On page 56b, the winged Kin has a crossed design formed by two eyeballs with veins attached. The extruded eyeballs recall Colonial period accounts describing how the eclipse monster is the "snatcher of the eye of the sun." Page 55a shows the bearded face of the aged Sun God (God G) surrounded by extruded eyes, an apt image for a solar eclipse that may also carry the underworld connotation of "death eyes" (Fig. 3.5d).

A goddess with her eyes closed and her neck strangled by a cord on page 53b represents the eclipsed moon (Fig. 4.7c; Pl. 3; Thompson 1970b: 301). This is a total eclipse of the moon, according to Lounsbury (1978:797–798), who notes that the strangled Moon Goddess is shown with glyphs overhead that refer to the death and darkening of the moon. Charles Hofling and Thomas O'Neil (1992: 103) point out that her closed eyes evoke contemporary Yucatec Maya descriptions of the eclipsed sun or moon with its eye blinded. This follows a general pattern seen elsewhere in the Dresden Codex, with lunar eclipses represented by a death aspect of the young Moon Goddess with closed eyes.

A glyphic reference to a solar eclipse may appear in the Dresden Codex on pages 54b (last column) and 55b (first column). A glyph compound pairs Kin with a net glyph *pa* (T586) and T568, read as *lu* by a number of scholars but also a logographic reference to piercing with a weapon (Kurbjuhn 1989:76). Victoria Bricker and Harvey Bricker (1995:97) interpret the first part of the compound as *paal,* the adjectival form of the verb *pa* 'to break.' They read the glyphs as *paal u kin,* or "the sun was broken," a graphic description of what happens to the sun during an eclipse.

In the Paris Codex (23–24), the eclipse signs are Kin glyphs framed by winged panels, one colored black, the other red (Fig. 7.2a). Bruce Love (1994: 93) describes these as symbols of the sun's position between the night sky and day sky, denying any connection with eclipses. He interprets the animals biting these solar symbols as constellations influencing the sun rather than eclipse images. Nevertheless, the devouring act suggests a different interpretation. Harvey and Victoria Bricker (1992:174) propose that animals biting the solar-eclipse symbols refer to

the sun being devoured during an eclipse, with the animal representing the constellation in which an eclipse might take place. The notion that a constellation devours the sun during an eclipse probably resulted from the fact that constellations near the sun become visible during solar eclipses.

A concern with the seasonal position of eclipses amidst the background of stars seems to be evident in the 260-day agricultural almanac on Madrid Codex 12b–18b (Fig. 7.3). A pair of identical solar-eclipse glyphs appear on page 12b of the Madrid Codex, a configuration that suggests an emblematic grouping rather than real eclipse events. Eclipse intervals are evident if you count the actual number of days represented on pages 13b–16b, as discussed in Chapter 3. The solar-eclipse sign on page 13b is separated by an interval of 148 days from the solar-eclipse sign on page 17b the same eclipse interval recorded in the Dresden Codex before most of the eclipse pictures (Pl. 3). And if you include the 40-day period on page 17b, the interval is extended to 188 days, which would include the six-month eclipse intervals of 177 and 178 days recorded in the Dresden Codex eclipse tables (Pl. 3). Since the almanac clearly was designed to be reused, the eclipse symbols warned that if there was an eclipse near the beginning of the fixed agricultural calendar in early February, there could be another around the new year in late July (Chapter 3).

Solar-eclipse glyphs often appear alone in the Dresden Codex, but lunar-eclipse symbols are invariably paired with a solar-eclipse sign (45b, 56a, 58b, 66a). Although the aged face in the lunar-eclipse glyph is of uncertain gender, it probably refers to the moon with an honorific title like "Grandmother Moon," a name found among the contemporary Maya. Clearly, solar eclipses are more prominent than lunar eclipses in the imagery and glyphs of the eclipse table.

There are a number of images that may refer to lunar eclipses in Dresden Codex almanacs that focus on the Moon Goddess. Lunar eclipses have a much wider range of visibility, thus they are seen more often than solar eclipses. This may be why there are so many images of the dead Moon Goddess in the Dresden Codex lunar almanacs. The almanacs on

Dresden Codex 16–23 show a number of different death aspects of the Moon Goddess. Often she has closed eyes or death spots, an aspect of the moon in accord with contemporary imagery of the moon "dying" during a lunar eclipse (Chapter 1). Because these death aspects of the Moon Goddess are spaced at intervals appropriate to eclipses, Hofling and O'Neil (1992) link them with a sequence of lunar eclipses, even though a lunar-eclipse glyph is lacking. Another possible lunar-eclipse image appears on Dresden Codex 61, where the lunar rabbit is devoured by a serpent.

We can conclude that the eclipse monsters described in Colonial period accounts are also evident in the Postclassic period. Venus seems to be one of the eclipse monsters. Postclassic lunar and solar eclipses are represented similarly with winged panels and death imagery. The lunar-eclipse symbol usually depicts an aged face, probably representing Grandmother Moon. Personified lunar eclipses, especially common in the lunar almanacs, usually depict a death aspect of the youthful Moon Goddess, representing her with closed eyes and death spots. Solar eclipses seem to be of greater interest in the Dresden Codex eclipse table, since there is only one pictorial image of the eclipsed moon and the only lunar-eclipse glyphs are those paired with solar-eclipse symbols.

THE DRESDEN CODEX ECLIPSE TABLE

The eclipse table in the Dresden Codex (51–58) shows eclipse glyphs and intervals during which an eclipse could occur somewhere, generally referred to as eclipse windows (Pl. 3). After an associated Long Count date in red (10.19.6.1.8, first column 51a), there follows a set of multiples of 1.13.4.0 (11,960 days) in seven columns on 51a–52a with an opening inscription of 1.9.18.0.0 that is 18 × 11,960 days. The interval of 11,960 days equals 46 Tzolkins and is very close to 405 synodic months. A period of 1,820 days, equaling five computing years (5 × 364) and seven Tzolkins (7 × 260), appears on page 52a in a Uinal-Tun notation.

Black numbers at the top of pages 53a–58b of the table show cumulative totals that carry forward a count of lunar synodic months over a period of 11,958 days, equaling approximately thirty-three years (Aveni 1980:177, table 17). This part of the table uses an average lunar month of 29.52592 days, only seven minutes away from the modern value (Aveni 1980:183). The Tzolkin dates (almanac days) below the cumulative totals indicate the dates ending five- or six-month periods over the course of 405 lunar months or 11,959 days (Lounsbury 1978: table 2). The long cycle was developed so that astronomers could reuse the canonical 12 Lamat base date, or *lub*, because 46 × 260 equals 11,960 days, which is very close to the 11,958-day period indicated in the cumulative totals and the 11,959-day period in the Tzolkin dates. The true length of 405 lunar months is 11,959.88814 days (a month equals 29.530588 days).

The table is read across the top from pages 51a to 58a, and then across the bottom beginning with page 51b. Intervals are recorded with red numbers for the 20-day periods (Uinals) and black numbers for the individual days (Kins), an unusual format because red numbers are usually reserved for coefficients for Tzolkin dates (red numbers are outlined and the black are solid on Pl. 3).

Pages 53a–58a of the table alternates counts of 177 days (six months) and 148 days (five months). Intervals of 148 days (recorded as 7.8 in vertical columns) precede all the eclipse pictures except on pages 57a and 58b, where the number is 8.17 (177 days, below Tzolkin date). The cumulative total in black over the Tzolkin date on 57a shows that the number should be 7.8. In other columns, the cumulative totals show errors of no more than 20 days, except for 5.10.16 on 54a, which should be 5.14.16 (2,096 days). Discrepancies also occur in the intervals and the cumulative totals. For example, an interval of 8.18 (178 days) appears on 57a (column A, below Tzolkin date), but the cumulative total above (11.1.6) indicates 177 days. Adding all the intervals together yields 11,959 days, a figure in accord with the Tzolkin dates.

Dates from the sacred almanac appear as sets of three consecutive Tzolkin dates (read from top to bottom) placed above the recorded intervals. The consecutive dates allowed a shift in days to account for the discrepancy between 405 lunations and 46

Almanacs. Moving from one column to the next results in the interval seen at the bottom of the column (i.e., 1 Imix to 6 Muluc equals 148 days on 53a, columns B–C). There is only one error in the Tzolkin notations (Lounsbury 1978:793). The Tzolkin dates mark potential eclipse positions. Thompson (1972) points out that glyphs referring to death and crop failure in the eclipse table indicate that eclipses could bring disaster.

As Teeple (1930:87–90) pointed out long ago, the Tzolkin itself is suited to recording the eclipse half-year, because the sum of two periods of 260 days (520) is almost equal to three eclipse half-years ($3 \times 173.31 = 519.93$). Nevertheless, the eclipse half-year cannot be made to fit precisely in the intervals that make up the groups of five and six synodic months recorded by the Tzolkin dates and associated intervals (Martin 1993).

Most scholars agree that the table deals with predictions, because there was no series of nine or ten eclipses visible in Yucatán that corresponds to the recorded intervals (Aveni 1992b:77; Kelley 1976:43). There has been debate about whether the table focuses on lunar or solar events. Thompson (1972:71–77, 108; 1974:88–90) concludes that rather than being a record of actual solar eclipses, the table was used to predict solar eclipses. He implies that the table also indicates an interest in lunar eclipses because a picture was included after each group of five lunations to indicate that when two solar eclipses occurred at intervals of 148 days, they were followed by a lunar eclipse (however, only one of the pictures seems to show a lunar eclipse). A number of scholars concur with Thompson that solar eclipses are emphasized in the table, although they note evidence that lunar eclipses are also represented (H. Bricker and V. Bricker 1983; Lounsbury 1978:789, 798–799). On the other hand, Frederick Martin (1993) argues that the table could be an actual record of eclipses referring to pairs of solar and lunar eclipses.

Aveni (1980:80–81, 173–183, tables 18–19) points out that a number recorded in column D on 52b gives the cumulative total of 18.5.5 (6,585) days, which is the Saros cycle of 223 lunations, resulting in a cycle of solar eclipses that recurs after a period of 6,585.32 days (18.03 years). After four repetitions of

the Saros cycle, a sequence of solar eclipses returns to the same place in the tropical year. Aveni (1980: 180) emphasizes the importance of lunar eclipses in the table. Justeson (1989:81–85) also favors linking the table with lunar eclipses. Both scholars point out that only twenty to thirty years of observations would produce a system of successful lunar prediction, whereas it would take hundreds of years to structure a solar-eclipse table; and the success rate for predicting solar eclipses would be only about 6 percent. Nonetheless, the table seems to emphasize glyphs and representations referring to solar eclipses, and both solar and lunar eclipses were apparently important in the recorded intervals (Aveni 1997:111–114, 200).

Even though the table is not a record of observed eclipses, it is important to determine the historical context of the table. Lounsbury (1978:775, 811) notes that the initial epoch of the system in the Dresden Codex dates to around A.D. 755, but the arrangement of the table must date to some three hundred years later. He maintains that a calculation involving a ring number suggests a record of eclipses going back to A.D. 683. The Brickers (1983:18, 21) say that the table covers a thirty-three-year period in the second half of the eighth century; however, its predictive powers extended into the fourteenth century and even beyond. In my opinion, the table was created in the thirteenth century, but it incorporates historical reference points that go back to the Classic period.

Thompson (1972:71) suggests that the first column (A) on page 51a refers to 13.0.0.0.0 4 Ahau 8 Cumku as a starting point, to which eight days are added to reach 12 Lamat (13.0.0.0.8), and then the Long Reckoning (LR) distance number of 9.16.4.10.0, shown in black (with the Baktun incorrectly noted as 8), is added to reach the Long Count date of 9.16.4.10.8 12 Lamat, which is a black number alternating or "interwritten" with a red number in the last column on 52a (column F). All the Long Count dates appear in alternating colors of the "interwritten" style. As Thompson notes, interwritten between the black LR in the first column of page 51 is a red Long Count inscription that records a date of 10.19.6.1.8 12 Lamat (the number one over time has shifted to black). Thompson identifies three more Long Count dates that can be derived from the alternating black and red numbers interwritten in the last two columns of page 52. These are 9.16.4.11.3 1 Akbal (column F in red); 9.16.4.11.18 3 Etz'nab (column E in black, mistakenly recorded with 10 Uinals); and 9.19.8.7.8 7 Lamat (column E in red), which is an inaccurate date according to Thompson (1972:71).

The Long Count dates in the table seem to span more than four hundred years. The black date in column F of page 52a (9.16.4.10.8 12 Lamat) corresponds to the last visibility of the waning moon in the 584,283 correlation, followed 17 days later by a lunar eclipse on 11/23/755 (Oppolzer 1962). The interval between this 12 Lamat date in the eighth century (11/6/755) and the thirteenth-century date (10.19.6.1.8) in red on page 51a is a lunar interval. The date 10.19.6.1.8 12 Lamat (9/18/1210) is one day before the new moon, virtually replicating the events of 9.16.4.10.8 12 Lamat (11/6/755). Both dates could relate to the last visible crescent before the new moon (Goldstine 1973). A focus on the last crescent would help to confirm Thompson's (1960:310) theory that the ancient Maya counted from the last visible crescent moon. The date in A.D. 1210 may also involve Venus events, for Venus was in conjunction with Jupiter just above the western horizon at dusk at that time.

In sum, the Dresden Codex eclipse table is concerned with predicting solar eclipses and lunar eclipses. The purpose of the table seems to be divinatory, to correlate the eclipse events with the sacred Tzolkin. The Long Count dates mark a period from A.D. 755 to A.D. 1210, recording historical observations from the Classic Maya period along with current observations made around the time the codex was painted in the thirteenth century. The way the table is structured also allows for future predictions over long periods of time.

CLASSIC PERIOD ECLIPSE IMAGERY AND EVENTS

The imagery of solar and lunar eclipses in the Classic period remains elusive. Santa Elena Poco Uinic Stela 3 has the only known example (at B7) of an eclipse glyph of the type common in the Postclassic period. The associated date (9.17.19.13.16) coincides with a total eclipse on 7/16/790, but only if you use the 584,286 correlation (Kelley 1976:38; Lounsbury 1978:815–816). Clearly, this single inscription seems aberrant, and there must have been other ways of recording eclipses. Victoria and Harvey Bricker (1995:97, fig. 2) note that a Classic period lintel from the Nunnery Annex at Chichén Itzá records a Kin glyph following a T1023 face that may be read as *paal u kin* (the sun was broken), a form of eclipse record also seen in the Dresden Codex eclipse table.

On Classic period monuments, eclipse intervals are commonly recorded in the Lunar Series, which can refer to both lunar and solar eclipses (Aveni 1980:163–164). On the Hauberg Stela, dating to the second century A.D., Glyph C at A5 bears a coefficient of 17, providing the earliest known evidence of the eighteen-month lunar synodic period (Fig. 6.4c; Justeson 1989:87). John Linden's (1996) analysis of the Lunar Series indicates that three deity head variants of Glyph C record different six-month semesters (Fig. 4.1e). These deity head variants form a sequence of three semesters of six synodic months each (totaling eighteen synodic lunar months), a calendar useful in keeping track of eclipses. Linden points out that the period of 177 days (six synodic months) inherent in the Classic period Glyph C is very close to the eclipse half-year of 173.31 days, which explains why Glyph C was recorded in cycles of six months in the Classic period.

Eclipse intervals were also recorded in dynastic history. For example, Kelley (1989:72–83) notes that Chan Bahlum I's birth and death dates are spaced at an interval of 21,320 days, commensurate with an eclipse interval (11,960 days plus 9,360 days).

Actual eclipse records seem to be very rare. Kelley (1977a, fig. 1) notes that a solar eclipse corresponds to a 9.17.0.0.0 date associated with a star glyph and a "split" sun and moon glyph at B20 on Stela E at Quiriguá (Monument 5). The eclipse was barely visible at Quiriguá, because there was only a 4.7 percent obscuration beginning at 13:28 and ending at 15:14 on 1/20/771. Despite the fact that the eclipse was barely visible, Linda Schele and Matthew Looper (1994) maintain that the monument records the eclipse because it coincided with the Katun ending, and a lunar eclipse fifteen days later would have confirmed 9.17.0.0.0 as an eclipse station. Using the 584,283 correlation, Anthony Aveni and Lorren Hotaling (1994, table 1, n. 58) note the date is three days before a visible solar eclipse and eighteen days before a lunar eclipse.

Linda Schele and Nikolai Grube (1995:39–40) recognize a number of war events on Lintel 3 of Tikal Temple IV, some of which may be connected with eclipses, although no conventional eclipse glyphs are represented (Pl. 15). Using the 584,285 correlation, they link a solar eclipse on 7/25/743 with the day of a star-war event (at B4) on 11 Ik 15 Chen (9.15.12.2.2; 7/26/743) recorded at B3–C4. The star war occurred one day after a visible solar eclipse. The star-war event, recorded as a star-over-shell glyph, is interpreted as a symbol of a war against the settlement of Yaxha. Schele and Grube conclude that generally the eclipse events at Tikal seem to precede the war events, and they suggest that the war events may have been stimulated by eclipses. It is noteworthy that the 11 Ik 15 Chen war event falls in the rainy season, not the normal time of year for warfare (Chapter 3). Astrological portents may have prompted the Maya to go to war at a time of year normally reserved for agricultural activities.

Aveni and Hotaling's (1994:S43) chi-square analysis of Classic period dates recorded with astronomical glyphs or "tags" did not reveal a high correspondence with eclipse events using the 584,283 correlation, but they note this does not mean that some of the dates were not intended to record eclipses. Indeed, they were the first to point out that the 9.15.12.2.2 date on Lintel 3 follows shortly after a visible total eclipse.

Decapitation may also be part of Classic period eclipse imagery. A jaguar is the agent of solar and lunar eclipses in a number of Colonial period and contemporary accounts (Closs 1989), but in Classic period imagery, the jaguar seems to be the victim of decapitation, suggesting that he is the eclipsed body. The link between jaguars and the moon is discussed at length later in the text, but here it is important to point out that imagery of decapitated jaguars sometimes may be linked with the date of a lunar eclipse, as on a Yaxchilán lintel discussed later. (Fig. 4.2b).

Architectural orientations may encode actual observations of lunar standstills, which could be useful in predicting eclipses. The moon rises in the same position once every 18.61 years (6,797 days; Aveni 1997:33,88). This interval is close to the Saros eclipse cycle, a cycle of similar eclipses that recurs after about 18.03 years (6,585.32 days; Aveni 1980: 100). Arnold Lebeuf (1995:260–261) points out that the northern and southern limits in the moon's monthly lunar motion are directly related to the ecliptical longitude of the nodes, positions useful in predicting eclipses. In the Maya area, Paalmul and Edzná both have architectural orientations toward lunar extremes. The oval pyramid at Paalmul faces to the northwest, closely aligned with the northern standstill that marks the northern extreme of the moon setting (300°48′ azimuth; Aveni 1980:270; Galindo 1994:143). At Edzná, the sanctuary of the five-storied pyramid has a similar orientation (Galindo 1994:168–169; Malmström 1991:45). This horizon position is marked by the Northwest Pyramid (La Vieja), which in turn serves as an observation post to watch the southern standstill over the five-storied pyramid known as Cinco Pisos. The pairing of structures to observe the horizon extremes is significant, because when the moon reaches a horizon extreme in a given month, in the next month it will reach the opposite extreme.

Other forms of construction may have been used to predict eclipses. An artificial cave with a zenith tube in the Osario at Chichén Itzá is intriguing, not only for its potential for solar observations but also because lunar observations through such a tube could help to predict eclipses, as at Xochicalco, a central Mexican site of the Classic period that shows clear evidence of Maya influence (Lebeuf 1995; Morante 1995).

We can conclude that during the Classic period the Maya had architectural orientations that indicate an understanding of the Saros cycle. They could predict when there was the potential for an eclipse, but it is not clear whether they could actually predict whether an eclipse would be visible in their area. Raids may have followed shortly after visible solar eclipses, especially at Tikal. The nature of imagery and glyphs that symbolize Classic period eclipses remains enigmatic, but there is some evidence that jaguar decapitation may represent lunar eclipses. Surprisingly few secure eclipse records are preserved on Classic Maya monuments, but this may be because we do not fully understand the types of glyphs used to designate eclipses.

MAYA MOON GLYPHS AND SYMBOLS

The glyph for "moon" and the number twenty in the Postclassic period is T682 (Fig. 4.1c; Justeson 1984: 351). The T682 glyph bears a certain resemblance to some Postclassic variants of the Yucatec day sign Men, which depicts an aged face with an eye marked by dots and a pair of teeth covering the lower lip (Thompson 1960:89, fig. 9, no. 45). Thompson suggests that Men represents the aged Moon Goddess. If T682 symbolizes the aged goddess and the number twenty, it may be because twenty days after the month begins the moon is "old." The twentieth day of the month could correspond to the full moon in a count starting with the last day of visibility, or to the waning moon in a lunar month beginning at the new moon or first crescent. In terms of the phase represented by T682, it can be noted that an eclipse panel on Dresden Codex 58b frames T682, which signals a lunar eclipse at the full moon (Pl. 3). Although William Ringle and Thomas Smith-Stark (1996) have reclassified T682 as a variant of T181, I think this may be premature in light of its role in lunar eclipse glyphs.

The T682 moon face appears on a tin disk in a Postclassic offering from the Cenote of Sacrifice at Chichén Itzá (Fig. 4.1o). Another metal offering of approximately the same size represents the sun as a gilded copper disk embossed with the Kin glyph (Fig. 3.4d). The moon disk is darker and less shiny than the sun disk, evoking Aztec accounts that explain why the moon is not as bright as the sun (Sahagún 1950–1982, 7:7).

Another lunar glyph common in the Postclassic period is the T171 curl, representing the phonetic sound u (moon) in Friar Landa's syllabary, usually interpreted as the word for "moon" (Fig. 4.1j, left; Justeson 1984:328; Kurbjuhn 1989:32). As we will see, T171 is used in the name of the Moon Goddess, and it has secondary associations with the earth and honey, both connected with the moon. The T171 lunar glyph can be traced back to the Classic period in the name Jaguar Moon Lord (Fig. 4.5g).

The Postclassic Maya moon symbol is only rarely represented as a crescent form. The lunar crescent is wrapped around the Moon Goddess on Dresden Codex 49a (Fig. 4.7i). A different form of lunar crescent appears on the New Year pages of the Madrid Codex (37a) in a scene of a dog howling at the moon (Fig. 5.1i).

The crescent moon appears on war shields in the architecture of Chichén Itzá during the Late Classic and Terminal Classic periods. Shields decorated with crescent moons appear in reliefs from the Nunnery (Bolles 1977:232). In the murals of the Upper Temple of the Jaguars, a chief standing with a feathered serpent carries a shield with multiple crescents, and some of the enemy warriors carry shields with a single crescent moon (Coggins 1984, fig. 205; Tozzer 1957, fig. 60). The same temple's cornice reliefs depict shields with lunar crescents, perhaps representing a political group claiming affiliation with the moon (Fig. 5.5i; Milbrath 1988b:35).

Shields with lunar symbols also appear on Classic Maya images. An Early Classic double vessel depicts a bird (a vulture or a quetzal-macaw?) with a T683 shield on its back; one wing bears a Kin glyph and the other a trefoil design, perhaps symbolizing the Jester God (Coe 1989, fig. 14). At Copán, an Early Classic relief on the Margarita building, constructed by Copán's second ruler, depicts a T683a glyph on a shield beneath a macaw intertwined with a quetzal, forming a logograph for the name of the founder, K'inich Yax K'uk' Mo' (G. Stuart 1997: 384–85). The T683a glyph has the number nine alongside, together suggesting a reference to the lunar month of twenty-nine days like Glyph A of the

Lunar Series (Fig. 4.1k, right). At Copán, however, the design is not part of a glyphic text, and it is accompanied by a pair of footprints, a glyphic symbol that goes back to Olmec times. The context is clearly astronomical because a sky band frames the scene and the Cosmic Monster wraps around the side. The macaw is a solar bird and the quetzal is linked with Venus; when joined with the lunar symbol, a triad of astronomical symbols is represented.

The lunar crescent appears in a number of contexts that are clearly astronomical. A T683 lunar crescent flanks a jawless god on an astronomical frieze at Xunantunich dating to the Late Classic period (MacKie 1985, pl. 6). A Late Preclassic monument from Kaminaljuyú (Stela 25) depicts a celestial deity riding on a lunar crescent above the open jaws of an earth monster, a composition not unlike Izapa Stela 3 (Norman 1976, fig. 3.4; Parsons 1988:18, fig. 1.6).

In the Classic period, a lunar crescent with a single dot in the center (T683a) is read as k'al, meaning "twenty," and it symbolizes the number twenty in Glyph A and Glyph E of the Lunar Series (Fig. 4.1b, left, 4.1g; Justeson 1984:351). The role as the number twenty suggests links with the Postclassic T682, a glyph that also symbolizes the moon in a number of contexts (Fig. 4.1c). Despite this parallel, most scholars do not attribute a lunar significance to any of the variants of T683 (Kurbjuhn 1989). This seems illogical, in my opinion.

T683b, a lunar crescent with multiple dots in the center, is usually read as the phonetic sign for ah (Fig. 4.1b, center; Justeson 1984:351). It often symbolizes the moon in sky bands. In Río Azul Tomb 12, T683b represents the moon in the north or overhead direction (Fig. 3.2b). T683b also can substitute for the Moon Goddess in her role as patroness of the month Chen (cenote) in Initial Series inscriptions (Fig. 4.1i). It obviously represents the moon in pictorial contexts, but oddly enough, the T683b glyph is not generally identified as a logograph for "moon."

The simple crescent form (T683c) has an undetermined meaning, and may not be the same glyph as the other two variants, according to Justeson (1984: 351). Ringle and Smith-Stark (1996), however, do not record a separate T683c variant. Thompson (1962:285) lists only a few examples of T683c, all from Yaxchilán and all with a T109 affix ("red" or "great"). Carolyn Tate (1992, app. 3) reads these as part of a title (he of twenty captives) used by Bird Jaguar IV. The glyph for "captives" may have some lunar connection, for Peter Mathews (1990:96) notes that the word "Bak," used to designate captives, can also mean "bone" or "heron," and it also appears in the name of the mythical Moon Mother known as Zac Bak at Palenque (Fig. 4.10e).

T181 is used as a postfix attached to the main glyph in verbs and in the Lunar Series Glyphs C and D (Fig. 4.1a, e, f, right). The T181 postfix also appears in various names and titles and in the "birth" glyph compound (Fig. 4.1n). Stephen Houston (1997:292–293) proposes a phonetic reading of ja (ha), regardless of position, revising earlier phonetic readings of both ah and ha. Kathryn Josserand (1995:293) interprets T181 as usually indicating passive voice in hieroglyphic texts.

A doughnut-shaped glyph (T687a) means "moon" (po) in Kekchí, Pokomchí, and Pokomam (Justeson 1984:352; Taube 1992b:67–68). T687a appears in emblem glyphs and in the term "lord" (ah-po), where it possibly also has a lunar significance (Fig. 4.1r–s). The Moon God on the Pearlman Trumpet sits on a throne marked with the glyph po (Fig. 4.5g). Hun Ahau and his lunar twin visit an underworld palace framed by mirrors marked with po glyphs, an image that has been described as the "House of Mirrors" (Taube 1992a:58, fig. 3). The po-marked mirrors may symbolize a lunar mirror like the one described in ethnographic accounts (Chapter 1).

In sum, the crescent design is one of the most prominent lunar symbols in the Classic period. Best known in the glyphs T181 and T683, the crescent form was used to represent the moon in art images and in glyphic writing and calendars. The T687 glyph is linked with po, meaning "moon" in several highland Maya languages; it may be a special variant referring to the moon in connection with rulership, for it frequently appears on thrones and in the expression "lord." In the Postclassic period, T171 represents the word for "moon" in Yucatec Maya, and an aged face (T682) apparently replaces variants of the Classic period T683 lunar crescent as a symbol for the moon and the number twenty.

LUNAR SYMBOLISM OF FISH, FROGS, TOADS, AND SHELLS

Fish, mollusks, toads, frogs, and water birds are all connected with the moon, because the moon controls tides and all bodies of water on earth (Chapter 1). Croaking frogs signal rain, which is under the control of the moon. One of the titles of the moon in Yucatec is Virgin Rain Frog (Edmonson 1982a: 181). Thompson (1960:47–48) notes that the moon, frogs, and toads all bear the name *po,* a lunar name in highland Mayan languages. There seems to be a natural connection between water, birth, and frogs and toads, because these animals give birth in a watery environment. In light of the fact that the Moon Goddess oversees childbirth, according to contemporary Maya accounts, it is noteworthy that the glyph for birth (T740) in the Classic Maya has been interpreted as a frog with a T181 postfix, a linguistic marker for the passive voice, but its role in this compound is unclear (Fig. 4.1n). The "upended frog" birth glyph may actually represent a salamander-like animal with teeth and gills (two attributes seen on the glyphic head), an amphibian that lives in water sources in caves (Josserand and Hopkins 1993:41). In any case, the watery world of amphibians such as salamanders and frogs was probably closely related to the moon.

The Yucatec Maya say that the moon disappears into a well during conjunction, implying that it disappears into a watery underworld. In the Initial Series introductory glyph, the Moon Goddess appears as the patroness of the month Chen, which means "cave" or "cenote" (Fig. 4.1i, center; Thompson 1960:111). Another variant of this glyph shows fish framing the Moon Goddess and her moon symbol (Fig. 4.1m).

Sometimes the youthful Moon Goddess offers fish, a food resource especially associated with the tides controlled by the moon (Fig. 4.7e). Fish-eating birds may also be lunar symbols. A heron (T793) appears in the name for the ancestral Moon Goddess at Palenque (Fig. 4.10e). A similar bird, a variant of T793, oddly represented with teeth, substitutes for the lunar rabbit in the Palenque emblem glyph (Fig. 4.1s; Schele 1977:52). The T793 glyph is usually interpreted as a heron (Kurbjuhn 1989).

Thompson (1960:49, 133–134, 173) notes that the conch symbolizes the Moon Goddess, night, darkness, water, and the earth or underworld, but he points out that the shell is a generative symbol relating to birth rather than death. The shell evokes a connection with the underworld, the place where the moon dies and is reborn. The Mixtec Codex Nuttall depicts the rayed moon disk with a shell in the center framed by the horseshoe-shaped lunar symbol (Fig. 4.1p). The central Mexican Codex Telleriano-Remensis (folio 19r) tells us that a shell associated with a lunar deity symbolizes the womb that gives birth. Marine shells bring to mind the sea and tides controlled by the moon. The Moon Goddess framed by a lunar crescent on Dresden 49a pours seawater from a conch shell, linking the moon with the tides and the sea. This scene recalls the Great Goddess of Teotihuacán, with her lunar crescent issuing seawater (Milbrath 1995a, 1996).

This brief survey indicates that the Maya linked the moon with watery creatures, most notably toads, frogs, mollusks, fish, and fish-eating birds. The Moon Goddess controls the tides by pouring water from her conch shell in one Postclassic image. Another shows her offering fish from her watery domain. The moon and frogs are closely linked in Classic period glyphs, and metaphorical images allude to the moon's control over childbirth and rainfall. The Moon Goddess herself is patron of the month Chen, associated with the watery world of caves and cenotes.

THE MOON AND RABBITS

Precolumbian Maya people visualized the rabbit as an alter ego of the moon, an association that survives today among the Maya people, who see the image of a rabbit on the face of the moon. When the moon is full, it is possible to see the dark shape of a rabbit (Schele and Miller 1983, fig. 18d). The silvery color of rabbits evokes the moon. Rabbits are more active around dawn and dusk, and in hot weather they forage primarily at night, behavioral characteristics related to the nocturnal world of the moon. The prodigious fertility of rabbits indicates a lunar connection because of the moon's association with fertility. Their gestation period of about a month may also indicate a correlation with the moon. Furthermore, rabbits hop just like the moon, which jumps forward each night as it moves through the background of stars at the rate of about 13 degrees a day (Chapter 2).

The lunar rabbit is rare in Postclassic Maya codices. The Postclassic Maya Moon Goddess does not appear with a lunar rabbit, which seems surprising in light of contemporary Maya accounts that say the rabbit is the pet of the Moon Goddess. An image of the lunar rabbit may appear on Dresden Codex 61, where a serpent biting a rabbit may allude to a lunar eclipse at the full moon. The rabbit is seen in a lunar crescent in Postclassic images depicting the central Mexican Moon Goddess, Tlazolteotl (Fig. 4.9c).

Although Thompson (1967:38) suggests that the rabbit on the moon was a central Mexican concept introduced among the Maya during the Colonial period, there is ample evidence that the lunar rabbit goes back to Classic Maya times. The lunar crescent frames a lunar rabbit on Bonampak Altar 2 (Fig. 4.6a; Schele and Miller 1983:46). The Las Sepulturas bench depicts a group of astronomical deities, among which we find a lunar deity holding a rabbit (Pl. 19). Jaina-style figurines show the Moon Goddess holding a rabbit (Miller 1975, fig. 9). On a vessel from the American Museum of Natural History, the Moon Goddess holds her lunar rabbit, and nearby a mirror-marked lunar rabbit with a bound hank of hair blows a shell trumpet (Fig. 4.10d; Schele and Miller 1986:308).

The lunar rabbit is especially prominent at Palenque. A skeletal rabbit at the entry of Temple XII has led to its being designated as the "Temple of the Dying Moon" (Robertson 1991:65). A variant of the Palenque emblem glyph with a skeletal rabbit head may be read as the "place of the dead moon" (Fig. 4.1r; Schele 1977:55–56). On the Tablet of the 96 Glyphs from Palenque, a rabbit appears in the center of a lunar glyph, T181, in a compound that

may function logographically to describe a rabbit on the surface of the moon (Fig. 4.1q; Schele and J. Miller 1983:46). Here the lunar rabbit has ears that bear the Etz'nab (Knife) sign, a detail repeated on Maya vase painting (Coe 1978b, no. 1). In Classic Maya representations, the metaphor could have a double meaning referring both to the rabbit's ears as knife-shaped and to a "knife-shaped" moon, perhaps describing the gibbous moon. The gibbous moon could also be represented by a knife-moon in the central Mexican Codex Borgia (50).

In sum, the characteristics metaphorically linking the rabbit to the moon include its silver color, crepuscular activity, and proverbial fertility. It is not clear whether there was a specific phase associated with the lunar rabbit, but its image is most easily seen on the full moon. The rabbit often appears in the arms of a lunar deity, acting as a sort of alter ego. The lunar rabbit is best known from the Classic period. Although the Postclassic Maya codices do not show clear evidence of the lunar rabbit, the tradition must have lived on, given contemporary Maya accounts of the lunar rabbit.

THE WATER-LILY JAGUAR

In the Chilam Balam of Tizimin from Colonial period Yucatán, the moon is called "jaguar head" (Edmonson 1982b:187–188). In the Quiché area to the south, *El Título de Totonicapán* (7v) identifies the jaguar twin, Xbalanquej, as the moon (Carmack and Mondloch 1983:21). Among the major jaguar deities of the Precolumbian Maya, the Water-lily Jaguar, identified by his water-lily head ornament, seems to express the moon's connection with water (Fig. 4.2a, d, e). A good swimmer, the jaguar often stalks its prey along waterways (Benson 1997:46). Its eyes glow in the darkness at night, and by day it sleeps in caves or crevices, seeming to hide from the light. The jaguar's nocturnal nature suggests a natural connection with the moon, and jaguar spots suggest the stars of the night sky.

On page 8a of the Postclassic Dresden Codex, the Water-lily Jaguar appears with a jaguar name glyph, prefixed by T109, the glyph for "red" or "great" (Fig. 4.2a; Thompson 1972:35). On page 47 of the

Venus pages, a wounded feline bears a vegetal head ornament and a name glyph identifying him as the Water-lily Jaguar in the spearing phrase above the Venus god (Column E; Fig. 5.3b). Although this feline has a brown body, it clearly bears the same name as the Water-lily Jaguar on Dresden 8a (Fig. 4.2a). In the layout of the Venus pages discussed in Chapter 5, the jaguar on page 47 represents the full moon speared by the newly risen Morning Star on 8/26/1222 during the rainy season. As we will see, imagery of the Water-lily Jaguar is associated with the rainy season, when water lilies flower.

Only a small number of Classic period monuments represent the Water-lily Jaguar, but each is worth investigating to study the pattern of seasonal imagery. Among the most impressive images is Lintel 3 of Temple I at Tikal (Fig. 3.6d). The jaguar's name at D2 follows the date 12 Etz'nab 11 Zac (9/12/695), indicating that this jaguar was invoked during the rainy season, when the water lilies bloomed.

Lintels 6 and 43 at Yaxchilán depict a Yaxchilán ruler wearing a Water-lily Jaguar headdress, and the headdress on Lintel 6 clearly has an astronomical aspect because it has a star eye (Tate 1992, fig. 44). The scene on both is a dance involving the display of God K on a basket staff. Both Lintels 6 and 43 bear a single date in mid-October, coinciding with the rainy season (Tate 1992, app. 2).

Yaxchilán Lintel 26 shows the head of the Water-lily Jaguar, representing either a headdress or a decapitated jaguar head (Fig. 4.2b). Shield Jaguar I holds a knife in his right hand, suggesting that he cut off the jaguar head to use it in a ritual or for a headdress. Most of the dates on Lintel 26 fall in the rainy season, suggesting the Water-lily Jaguar head may symbolize the moon at the time of the rains. A fragmentary Initial Series date, which Tate (1992:208) reconstructs as 9.14.14.13.16, corresponds to the summer solstice in the 584,285 correlation, but using the preferred 584,283 correlation, it coincides with a lunar eclipse that occurred on 6/19/726 (Oppolzer 1962). Thus the decapitated jaguar may refer to a lunar eclipse, correlating with other images of decapitation linked with lunar eclipses in central Mexico (Milbrath 1995b, 1997).

A circular relief from La Esperanza (Chinkultic),

Chiapas, depicts a ballplayer with a headdress bearing a water lily, a shell, and a jaguar tail (Fig. 4.2c). He also has a bound hank of hair and a headband, suggesting to Jeff Kowalski (1989:16–17) that he is linked with the Headband Twins (Fig. 4.5b), the Classic period counterparts of the Hero Twins in the Popol Vuh. Kowalski also notes that the ballplayer plays with a ball inscribed with a Chicchan variant of the Ahau glyph (compare Fig. 3.10c). He interprets this as a reference to Hunahpu (Hun Ahau), suggesting parallels with the episode in the Popol Vuh when Xbalanque uses Hunahpu's head as a ball. The widespread "rolling head" myth, describing a decapitated head that moves around by rolling, links decapitation to the ball game and to the periodicity of the sun and the moon (Gillespie 1991:330). Decapitation imagery in the context of a ball court may allude to eclipses in Aztec iconography, especially to those occurring at times of seasonal change (Milbrath 1995b, 1997). An Initial Series inscription of 9.7.17.12.14 on the border of the La Esperanza relief corresponds to 5/17/591, near the end of the dry season. Although this is not an eclipse date, it is linked with seasonal transition.

Some images of the Water-lily Jaguar in ceramic arts show a distinct relationship with the Hero Twins, who embody the sun and the moon. A plate from Burial 190 at Tikal depicts an anthropomorphic Water-lily Jaguar wearing a headband like the one worn by the Headband Twins (Coggins 1975, fig. 102; Valdés et al. 1994:69). Ceramic paintings clearly show the jaguar as the victim of decapitation, a theme seen in legends of the Hero Twins. Some pots show a decapitated Water-lily Jaguar head (Valdés et al. 1994:69). On one vessel, his head is attached to a jaguar-skin pillow (Coe 1973, no. 13).

The celestial nature of the Water-lily Jaguar is seen in Classic period ceramics depicting the jaguar surrounded by stars (Pl. 4). Other pots link the Water-lily Jaguar with sky bands. The pot known as Princeton 14 depicts the jaguar as one of three celestial creatures in sky-band backracks worn by dancing figures called the Holmul Dancers, alluding to similar themes on vessels from the site of Holmul (Coe 1978b, no. 14). All the dancers are identical; only the enthroned figure in the sky band differs.

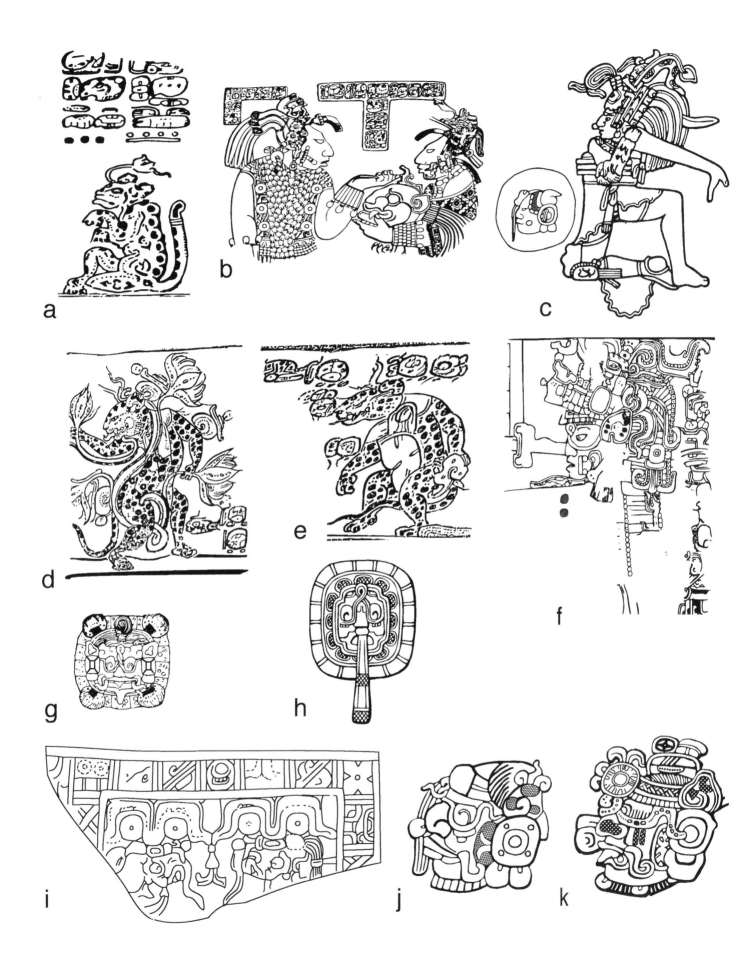

a

b

c

d

e

f

g

h

i

j

k

The hieroglyphic name of the enthroned jaguar as Ix Balam; the other two are 6 Sky and a monkey supernatural called 10 Chuen (Reents-Budet 1991:220–221, figs. 1, 7). This assembly of gods is discussed further in Chapter 6.

Ceramic vessels sometimes show the Water-lily Jaguar wrapped in water lilies (Fig. 4.2d). More often he is identified only by a hornlike appendage that seems to be the leaf and stem of a water-lily plant (Fig. 4.2e). Usually he wears a peculiar neck scarf described as the sacrificial scarf because it is sometimes associated with scenes of sacrifice (Coe 1973:28). In one such scene, the Water-lily Jaguar faces a death god who is decapitating himself (Pl. 4). Here a boa wraps around the jaguar in a fashion almost identical to images of the Moon Goddess discussed later. Another Water-lily Jaguar wearing the sacrificial scarf is unusual because he bears a Kin sign on his chest as he marches ahead of a snake (Fig. 4.2e; Coe 1973, no. 3). Images such as this one have led scholars to identify the Water-lily Jaguar as the sun (Schele and Miller 1986:51). His name glyph (T832) on this vessel is a decapitated jaguar, a glyph sometimes interpreted as a reference to an eclipse (Kurbjuhn 1989:122). The combination of solar and lunar imagery could suggest a lunar eclipse or lunar conjunction.

Alternatively, the Kin-Jaguar image may allude to the "jaguar sun," a name for the moon in the Popol Vuh (D. Tedlock 1985:368–369).

Dennis Tedlock suggests the jaguar is linked with the full moon, but in my opinion, the jaguar can refer to the moon in all phases. A preliminary study of the decapitated jaguar glyph (T832) indicates that it is not consistently associated with dates that coincide with specific lunar phases or with eclipses (full moon or new moon) in either of the two correlations. For example, on Yaxchilán Stela 18, T832 appears with a date (7/8/729) falling around the first quarter.

Images of jaguars with a rope around the neck, found beyond the central Maya area, may represent a concept similar to the jaguars wearing the scarf of sacrifice, all part of a lunar cult linked with jaguar sacrifice. Censers depicting jaguars with a knotted rope around the neck, found in the waters of Lake Amatitlán, may symbolize the connection between water, jaguars, and the moon (Berlo 1984, pls. 213–215). This link is also apparent at Cacaxtla, a Classic period site in Tlaxcala that combines central Mexican and Mayan traits. Here murals depict two jaguar men wearing ropes around their necks and pouring water that cascades in droplets like rain (McVicker 1985, figs. 3–4).

FIG. 4.2. *a:* Water-lily Jaguar probably representing rainy-season moon (Dresden 8a; after Villacorta and Villacorta 1977).

b: Water-lily Jaguar representing either headdress or decapitated jaguar head on Yaxchilán Lintel 26 (after Tate 1992b, fig. 18).

c: Lunar ballplayer with headdress bearing water lily, shell, and jaguar tail on relief from La Esperanza (Chinkultic), Chiapas (after Tozzer 1957, fig. 486).

d: Water-lily Jaguar wrapped in water lilies and wearing scarf associated with sacrifice (after Robicsek and Hales 1981, vessel 30).

e: Water-lily Jaguar with Kin sign on his belly, probably alluding to lunar eclipse or full moon as "jaguar sun" (after Coe 1973b, no. 3).

f: Jaguar War God, also known as Jaguar God of Number Seven, probably representing dry-season moon (Lintel 2 of Temple IV at Tikal; after Jones 1977, fig. 12).

g: War shield representing Jaguar War God, also known as Jaguar God of Underworld (Late Classic Temple of the Sun, Palenque [see Fig. 3.6b]; after Robertson 1991, fig. 95).

h: Jaguar War God shield, war equipment of Smoking Squirrel (Naranjo Stela 21; after Proskouriakoff 1950, fig. 32l).

i: Two Jaguar War God heads are attached to star glyphs suspended from sky band (Yaxchilán Stela 4; after Tate 1992, fig. 24c).

j: Day sign Cib represented as Jaguar War God with nocturnal Akbal cheek marking and headband of Headband Twins (Late Classic Yaxchilán Lintel 48; after Tate 1992, fig. 62).

k: Sun God with Kin cheek and T646 solar flower on headband also has traits of Jaguar War God, including jaguar ear and cruller; two gods may be merged together as symbol of new moon (Tikal Stela 31; after Hellmuth 1987, fig. 650).

We can conclude that jaguars embody the moon in a number of contexts, and one of the clearest expressions of the relationship is seen in the Water-lily Jaguar of Classic and Postclassic times. He often is associated with sacrifice by decapitation. Although the Classic monuments provide only a limited sample of dates useful in interpreting imagery of the Water-lily Jaguar, most of the dates coincide with the rainy season, which explains why the Water-lily Jaguar is crowned by rainy season vegetation.

THE JAGUAR WAR GOD

A jaguar god, known only from the Classic period, seems to embody a more warlike deity frequently represented on war shields. He has the Roman nose and egg tooth (the central notched or filed tooth) of the Sun God, but he can be distinguished by his "cruller" nose ornament, scroll eye, and jaguar ears; often he also has a bound hank of hair (Fig. 4.2g; Coe 1973: 83). Thompson (1960:11, 107, 134) originally named this deity the Jaguar God of the Underworld (JGU), the sun in the underworld or the night sun, designating him as a deity of "night, darkness, and the interior of the earth." This jaguar god is connected with the day sign Akbal, meaning "night," according to Thompson (1960:74, table 4). Many scholars have supported Thompson's interpretations. Nevertheless, in a number of contexts this jaguar god appears in the sky overhead rather than in the underworld. Mary Miller (1988:175 n. 29) notes that his associations with the underworld are no stronger than for any other deity, and in fact he is more closely connected with war. In this light, it may be more appropriate to call him the Jaguar War God. His lunar character is apparent in his role as a manifestation of the moon in Glyph C of the Lunar Series (Fig. 4.1e, center).

On Yaxchilán Lintel 48, the Jaguar War God stands for the day sign Cib, his nocturnal aspect noted with an Akbal cheek marking, and his headband evokes a connection with the Jaguar Hero Twin represented on Classic period ceramics (Fig. 4.2j; Tate 1992, fig. 62). The Jaguar War God may also appear as the patron of the month Uo, a month name that Thompson (1960:107–108) notes is the same as the name for a small black frog that burrows into the earth. Here the lunar connection may be through the world of frogs. He is also the patron of the number seven and sometimes appears with that number inscribed on his cheek (Fig. 4.2f).

Linda Schele and Mary Miller (1986:50–51) point out that the cruller-nosed jaguar god (JGU) sometimes has the same Roman nose, scalloped eyebrows, square eyes, and pointed front tooth as GI of the Palenque Triad, who apparently represents Venus (Chapter 5). The only difference they note is that the jaguar's scroll-eye form extends upward from the lower lid rather than downward, as on GI. The Jaguar War God may embody a conceptual pairing between the Moon and Venus, often seen together in the sky. He appears with star glyphs that may represent Venus in the East Court at Copán and on Stela 4 at Yaxchilán (Fig. 4.2i; Miller 1988:175). Although Venus may be significant in the imagery of the Jaguar War God, preliminary study does not reveal a consistent pattern of specific kinds of Venus events. There is, however, a notable clustering of the dates in the dry season.

Aguateca Stela 2, prominently depicting a Jaguar War God shield, bears the date 8 Kan 17 Muan (9.15.4.6.4; 11/27/735; Houston 1993, fig. 4-20). This date is linked with a star-war event coinciding with the heliacal rise of the Evening Star (Aveni and Hotaling 1994, table 2).

A sky band with seven Jaguar War God faces appears on Yaxchilán Stela 10, a monument bearing a date tentatively reconstructed as 10 Chen 18 Pop (9.16.15.0.0; 2/13/766; Tate 1992:233, fig. 130c). On this date, the Morning Star and the Moon were about to disappear in conjunction.

Naranjo Stela 21 represents Smoking Squirrel dressed with the nose cruller and shield of the Jaguar War God (Maler 1908, pl. 35; Proskouriakoff 1993: 73–74). The monument bears a dry season date (9.13.14.4.2 8 Ik 0 Zip; 3/22/706). This date, just following the spring equinox, marks a time when Venus was in conjunction with Mars and the waxing crescent Moon was in conjunction with Saturn, thus Venus and the Moon were engaged in similar events. Another dry-season date (9.13.15.0.0; 12/25/706) on the monument coincides with the last visibility of the Morning Star just following the winter solstice.

On Yaxchilán Stela 4, two Jaguar War God heads are attached to star glyphs that hang from a sky band (Figs. 4.2i, 4.10b). The monument bears a Calendar Round date of 6 Ahau 13 Kayab (9.17.5.0.0; 12/23/775) that falls in the dry season, and Venus may be represented because the Evening Star has just emerged. On top of the sky band, another bearded Jaguar War God appears between two ancestors, one a female framed in a lunar symbol, the other a male in a mirror cartouche that probably represents the sun disk.

A dry-season association is also seen in the Initial Series date on Stela 1 at Yaxchilán, a monument that depicts two faces of the Jaguar War God hanging from a sky band (Fig. 3.8d; Tate 1992, app. 2). This period-ending date, 9.16.10.0.0 1 Ahau 3 Zip (3/11/761), falls in a very dry time of year. It is also the day of the new moon, but the lunar phase does not seem to be significant in the imagery of Jaguar War Gods. Generally there is no consistent pattern linking the Jaguar War God with a specific lunar phase.

The Jaguar War God is represented on war shields with some frequency on monuments bearing dry-season dates. Aguateca Stela 2, Bonampak Stela 1, Naranjo Stela 21, Yaxchilán Lintel 3 and Stela 11, and the Palenque Temple of the Sun all record dry-season dates (Fig. 4.2g–h; Mathews 1980, fig. 3; Proskouriakoff 1950, figs. 32, k, l, p, r). Three of these also note rainy-season dates, but the Jaguar War God's association with the dry season is made clear in the Temple of the Sun. Here, the dry-season date (8 Oc 3 Kayab; 1/5/684) is positioned just above the jaguar shield (Fig. 3.6b). Indeed, among all the monuments tested with similar shields, all but one (Calakmul Stela 89) bears a dry-season date.

The Jaguar War God embodies the number seven in the full-figure glyphs used at some sites, and sometimes the god himself is inscribed with the number seven. Lintel 2 of Temple IV at Tikal depicts an anthropomorphic Jaguar God of the Number Seven, with the number inscribed on his cheek (Fig. 4.2f; Jones 1977, fig. 12, table 1). Schele and Grube (1995: 42–43) read a glyph compound at B12—a jaguar head paired with the sun glyph—as K'in Balam or "sun jaguar," referring to the jaguar protector. The text on Lintel 2 has four Calendar Round dates, but the one at B8 associated with a star-war event on 7 Ben 1 Pop (9.15.12.11.13; 2/2/744) seems to be linked with the jaguar name. The Jaguar War God is the patron of dry-season warfare. This date is also the day of the full moon, a phase that is linked with the jaguar, according to a contemporary Quiché Maya account (Chapter 1; D. Tedlock 1985:369).

In the crook of his arm, Stormy Sky (K'awil Chaan) holds a head with traits of the Jaguar War God on Tikal Stela 31 (Fig. 3.7b). A Tikal emblem glyph on the jaguar head indicates that this deity is especially important to the lineage of Tikal. Its jaguar ear and headband point to a link with the Jaguar Headband Twin; however, the cruller nose is that of the Jaguar War God. Linda Schele and David Freidel (1990:211) identify the head as the jaguar god of the Hero Twins. The jaguar head on Stela 31 has also been identified as the severed head of an ancestor (A. Miller 1986:46). It may actually represent a severed jaguar head, part of the complex of decapitated jaguar imagery linked with the moon. Stela 31's Initial Series date (9.0.10.0.0; 10/16/445) correlates with the new moon, when the moon disappeared in conjunction. In central Mexico, decapitation can symbolize the moon losing its head during conjunction or during a lunar eclipse (Milbrath 1995b, 1997).

Another head on Stormy Sky's belt ornament represents the Sun God with traits of the Jaguar War God (Fig. 4.2k). Attributes of the Sun God include a Kin-flower (T646) headband, rectangular crossed eyes, and the Kin sign on the cheek. It also has a cruller nose and jaguar ears like the Jaguar War God. This head has been interpreted as the sun in the underworld (A. Miller 1986:46; Schele and Miller 1986:50, fig. 35). Nicholas Hellmuth (1987:369, fig. 650) identifies the head as a conflation of Ah Kin, patron of the number four, and the Jaguar War God, patron of the number seven. Here the sun may appear with the traits of a lunar god because the two bodies are in conjunction, as indicated by the Initial Series date.

The Jaguar War God is also represented on Early Classic architecture. Tikal Structure 5D-22-3rd depicts a cruller-nosed mask that resembles the Jaguar War God. Arthur Miller (1986:39, 49, fig. 11) identifies this as Kinich Ahau, but it is clearly an Early

Classic form of the Jaguar War God. A lunar connection is reinforced by the T683 moon glyph below the head.

In the realm of the ceramic arts, the Jaguar War God is especially popular in the Late Classic period. At Palenque, incense-burner stands represent anthropomorphic, fleshed zoomorphic, or skeletal zoomorphic forms of the god (Freidel and Schele 1988: 63–64). These flanged stands are usually found discarded at the rear of temples, cached in the terraces of temple substructures, or placed in regional caves. Perhaps they were used in fire ceremonies performed annually or at the end of important calendar cycles such as Katuns and Calendar Rounds.

A Jaina figurine depicts the Jaguar War God seated on the earth monster represented by a crocodilian, flanked by two Venus glyphs (Miller 1975). This image may represent the crescent Moon and Venus positioned together on the horizon, a pairing that can commonly be seen around dawn or dusk.

On the Vase of the Seven Gods, the Jaguar War God is at the head of two rows of gods paying homage to God L, who is seated on a jaguar-skin throne (Pl. 7). The Jaguar War God gestures in submission with one arm and rests the other on the earth-star bundle. His name glyph, mentioned last in the text, has a jaguar ear, the distinctive cruller nose, and an Akbal (night) marking on the cheek (Coe 1973: 108–109, no. 49). As we will see, he is part of an assembly of gods representing the Sun, the Moon, and five naked-eye planets (Chapters 5 and 6).

The Jaguar War God appears in other astronomical scenes on painted ceramics. A vase depicting a ball game represents a black Jaguar War God standing on the head of Hunahpu, a scene that surely has astronomical symbolism (Coe 1982: 32, no. 10). On another pot, two identical figures of the Jaguar War God tip jars over (Coe 1982: 40, no. 14). Instead of containing water, the jars seem to issue volutes of smoke, perhaps indicating the empty water jars of the dry season. The two are distinguished only by their thrones, one a Cauac throne and the other a throne with crossed bands, possibly designating two different positions in the sky.

The Jaguar War God is a decapitated head held in the beak of the Muan bird on a painted vase (Coe

1982: 42, no. 15). Perhaps this image depicts a lunar eclipse or the new moon. Michael Coe (1978b: 34, no. 4) identifies a reclining jaguar baby on the Metropolitan Museum vase as the Jaguar God of the Underworld, the counterpart of our Jaguar War God (Pl. 8). A 7 Muluc 7 Kayab date on the vessel may be of astronomical significance, according to Coe. This Calendar Round date correlates with a dry-season date throughout the Classic period, and if the pot dates near the beginning of the Late Classic, the Calendar Round coincides with the new moon (1/23/627), when the moon "lost its head" as it joined the sun in conjunction. This may be why the jaguar has some solar traits, such as the squint eyes of the Sun God.

In sum, the Jaguar War God is associated with the dry season, the epoch of warfare. His lunar aspect appears on Glyph C of the Lunar Series. His image often appears on war shields in the central Maya area, perhaps the counterpart for lunar crescents on war shields in the northern Maya lowlands. Dates on monuments with the Jaguar War God do not consistently correlate with a specific lunar phase, but the majority coincide with the dry season. Monuments depicting the Jaguar War God often bear dates that coincide with Venus events, but there is no clear patterning in this respect. Perhaps the Jaguar War God and Venus are directly connected (Chapter 5). In Classic period ceramics, the Jaguar War God's warlike aspect is less pronounced, and he is more closely linked with the ball game and decapitation imagery.

THE JAGUAR PADDLER: THE MOON PAIRED WITH THE SUN

The Jaguar Paddler may represent the moon paired with the sun in scenes that show the two paddling or engaged in similar activities. In some sense, he is a counterpart of the Jaguar War God (Hellmuth 1987: 368, fig. 626; Stuart 1988: 189). Both deities are known only from the Classic period, and they are closely related to the lunar jaguar, Yax Balam, later known as Xbalanque (see below). The jaguar-spotted paddler travels in a canoe with another deity called the Stingray Paddler, characterized by a stingray spine bloodletter piercing his nose (Fig. 4.3a). Schele and Freidel (1990:413) refer to the Paddler Twins as the Old Stingray God of the day and the Old Jaguar God of the night.

Tikal bone MT38a from Burial 116 shows the Jaguar Paddler at the prow of a canoe and the Stingray Paddler at the stern (Fig. 4.3a). The notion of the two traveling in a canoe suggests a trip through the watery underworld. David Freidel et al. (1993, figs. 2: 25, 2:26) propose that the canoe is the Milky Way. In this light, it is worth investigating whether the Milky Way is involved in some way with imagery of the Paddler Twins. As we will see in Chapter 7, the Milky Way may be a divine river in some contexts, and a canoe is required for the crossing. Scholars do not agree on the Long Count equivalent for the Calendar Round date (6 Akbal 11 Zac) recorded on the bone, so it is premature to discuss any possible relationship with astronomical events involving the Milky Way.

Patterns of substitution in glyphic passages indicate that the Paddler Twins are paired in Kin and Akbal texts: the Akbal glyph can substitute for the Jaguar Paddler, and the Kin glyph for the Stingray Paddler (Schele and Miller 1986, fig. 40; Stuart 1984, fig. 9). David Stuart (1988:190, fig. 5.19) notes that their hieroglyphic names can be represented with portrait glyphs and specific suffixes, or the glyphs Kin and Akbal can substitute for the portrait heads. The Jaguar Paddler is named with the Akbal glyph and a *na* suffix, an intriguing combination because Akbal and *na* together approximate the name of the Lacandón Moon Goddess (Akna or Äkna'; Chapter 1). It also should be noted that Kin is paired with Akbal in specific contexts that seem to refer to the moon, as on the Early Classic Tikal Stela 31, where the text at B9-A10 shows the lunar Glyph D followed by Glyph E as a reference to the new moon on 9.0.10.0.7 (Jones 1984:55). An early pairing of Kin and Akbal is seen on the wings of a Late Preclassic bird deity on Kaminaljuyú Altar 10 (Parsons 1988:15, fig. 1.3). And in the Postclassic period, we see Kin paired with Akbal in texts associated with the aging Moon Goddess on Dresden Codex 39b and

67a (discussed below). Akbal can also appear in the center of a lunar-eclipse glyph, as on Dresden Codex 45b (Fig. 6.1a, over third sky beast).

On Ixlu Stela 2, the floating Paddler Twins appear as "cloud riders" (Fig. 4.3b). The associated date is the Katun ending 10.1.0.0.0 5 Ahau 3 Kayab (11/24/849). This Katun ending was marked by a "scattering rite," possibly a blood offering, when Venus was the Evening Star near its maximum altitude (Aveni and Hotaling 1994, table 1; Schele and Freidel 1990:446). The Sun was crossing the Milky Way in Scorpius, and the waxing Moon was positioned at a distance in Aquarius. As we will see, the dates on the Paddlers monuments studied here suggest an association with the dry season (late November to late May), and many can be linked to times when either the Sun or the Moon were positioned in the Milky Way.

Although the Paddlers are not represented as a main theme on Dos Pilas Stela 14 (formerly Stela 25), the text refers to the birth of the Paddler Twins (Houston 1993:111, tables 3-1, 4-1, fig. 3.24; Stuart 1984:14; 1988:192). Their birth is recorded on the Initial Series date 9.14.0.0.0 6 Ahau 13 Muan, a Katun ending (11/29/711). The Sun was in Scorpius, crossing the Milky Way, and the Moon was also in the Milky Way in Taurus. The date coincides with the day of the full Moon, locking the Katun ending to a lunar event. Eight Katuns later the period would end on the new Moon, recorded on Jimbal Stela 1, another monument that bears the Paddlers (Stuart 1984:11, fig. 7a). This interplay of the lunar cycles on a Paddlers monument marking the Katun ending certainly merits study in the future.

Another Paddler text appears on Copán Stela 6 (Fig. 5.8e; Maudslay 1889–1902, pls. 105–107; Schele 1987c; 1989b:32, 93). An Initial Series date of 9.12.10.0.0 9 Ahau 18 Zotz (5/5/682) is followed by 8 Ahau, probably referring to the close of the Katun at 9.13.0.0.0 8 Ahau 8 Uo (3/13/692). The Paddlers are mentioned just following the 8 Ahau date ending the Katun. On this date, the waning Moon was crossing the Milky Way in Scorpius, positioned overhead at dawn, when all five planets could be seen strung out like beads on a chain down to the eastern horizon. The date was only a few days

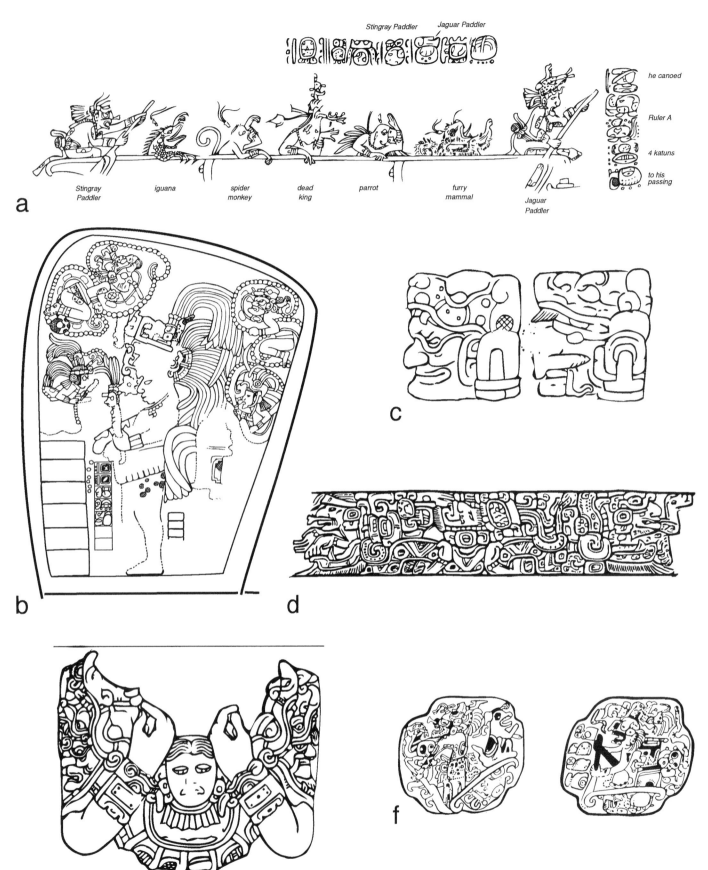

a

Stingray Paddler   Jaguar Paddler

he canoed

Ruler A

4 katuns

to his passing

Stingray
Paddler   iguana   spider
monkey   dead
king   parrot   furry
mammal   Jaguar
Paddler

b

c

d

e

f

before the spring equinox (3/17/692), a seasonal association also seen on Copán Stela P.

The Paddler Twins are positioned in the jaws of a double-headed serpent on Copán Stela P, a monument depicting Butz' Chan, the eleventh ruler of Copán (Fig. 4.3e; Fash 1991:80; Schele 1987c). The Jaguar Paddler on the left has the cruller nose of the Jaguar War God. Stela P bears a Lahuntun ending date of 9.9.10.0.0 2 Ahau 13 Pop (3/16/623), a time when the waxing Moon was in Cancer, just emerging from the Milky Way. The proximity to the spring equinox may also have been of interest.

Stela 7, another Copán monument erected by Butz' Chan, also shows the Paddler Twins in the jaws of the double-headed serpent bar (Schele 1987c, fig. 5a). The text names the Jaguar Paddler and the Stingray Paddler three times. The first text represents the Jaguar Paddler with a jaguar headdress and the Stingray Paddler with a Xoc fish headdress and a Kin cartouche on his forehead (Schele 1987c, fig. 8a). Another mention of the Paddlers occurs at C8-D8, followed by a third text at F2, where the Jaguar is inscribed with Akbal on his cheek as a reference to the night and Kin appears on the cheek of the Stingray Paddler (Fig. 4.3c). The only date is an Initial Series inscription recording the Katun ending 9.9.0.0.0 3 Ahau 3 Zotz (5/7/613), when the waning Moon was in Libra, at the edge of the Milky Way, and the Sun was passing through the Milky Way in Taurus.

One of the earliest known images of the Paddlers is seen on the Tikal ball-court marker dating to A.D. 378 (Schele and Freidel 1990, fig. 4:19). The Sun God is paired with an Akbal-browed figure in a compound that seems to refer to the Paddler Twins. There follows the name of an enigmatic god with his eyes covered by a trident design, not unlike the head in the serpent's jaw on the Hauberg Stela (Fig. 6.4c). Instead of the Katun or Lahuntun ending dates seen on most of the Paddlers monuments discussed above, the ball-court marker bears an Initial Series date of 8.17.1.4.12 11 Eb 15 Mac (1/13/378). The waning Moon was in Sagittarius, crossing the Milky Way, and the Sun was nearby in Capricorn at the edge of the Milky Way (Chapter 7).

Schele (1992b:123–124) suggests that the Paddlers are personifications of night and day at the first moments of creation. She translates a passage on Quiriguá Stela C as "they seated the stone, the Paddler Gods, it happened at House Five-Sky, Jaguar-Throne-Stone." This is part of a larger text that refers to the original creation of the universe on 4 Ahau 8 Cumku. She proposes that the Paddlers are the artists who drew the constellations in the sky, the counterparts for the Shaper and the Modeler in the Popol Vuh, two of the original creator gods (Schele 1992b:140). However, if the Stingray Paddler somehow represents the sun, as proposed here, this scenario seems unlikely. In the creation epics of Mesoamerica, the sun appears relatively late in the narrative sequence dealing with the creation of the universe (Taube 1993).

The Paddler Twins appear only rarely in ceramic arts. A Late Classic vessel from Duke University's collection shows the Paddlers in separate canoes positioned in quatrefoil designs that may represent a cavelike entry to the underworld (Fig. 4.3f; Reents-

---

FIG. 4.3. *a:* Jaguar Paddler at prow and Stingray Paddler at stern, part of assembly of seven gods on incised bones (MT38a) from tomb of HaSawa Chaan K'awil (Burial 116 at Tikal; after Schele and Miller 1986, fig. VII.1).

b: Sun and moon as Paddler Twins amidst clouds on Ixlu Stela 2 (after Schele and Miller 1986, fig. IV.2; Stuart 1984, fig. 6).

c: Paddler Twins glyphs showing pairing of sun and moon, with Akbal on cheek of Jaguar Paddler and Kin on cheek of Stingray Paddler (Copán Stela 7; after Schele 1987c, fig. 8b).

d: Paddler Twins as sun and moon at opposite ends of double-headed serpent held by Maize God (Early Classic cache vessel from Tikal; after Coggins 1980, fig. 4).

e: Paddler Twins emerge from two heads of double-headed serpent bar on Copán Stela P erected by Butz' Chan in seventh century (after Fash 1991, fig. 50).

f: Paddler Twins move in separate canoes through entry to underworld (Late Classic vessel in Duke University Museum collection; after Hellmuth 1987, figs. 626–627).

Budet 1994, fig. 6.47). An Early Classic cache vessel from Tikal shows the Paddler Twins at opposite ends of an undulating double-headed serpent held by the Maize God (Fig. 4.3d). These two heads have been interpreted as the rising and setting Sun, or night and day (Coggins 1980; Schele 1992b:150). I would suggest instead that the image depicts the Sun and the Moon as they are passing through a double-headed serpent that represents the Milky Way (Chapter 7).

We can conclude that the Paddler Twins may represent a conceptual pairing of the sun and the moon, but no specific lunar phase is implicated in the pairing. In Late Classic times, the Paddlers most often are associated with period-ending rites marking Katun endings or Lahuntun endings. Paddlers texts on monuments from Toniná and Piedras Negras (Schele 1987c, 1989b:32) are not analyzed here, but the sample of monuments studied indicates a pattern of dates that fall in the dry season, most often coinciding with times when the Sun or the Moon was crossing the Milky Way. As we will see, the Milky Way seems to be significant in the imagery of the Paddler Twins (Chapter 7).

THE LUNAR TWIN: XBALANQUE

The best-known lunar jaguar is Xbalanque, paired as a twin of the sun in the Popol Vuh, the same way we see the Paddler Twins paired as representations of the sun and the moon in Maya art. In the ancient Quiché tale of the Popol Vuh, Hunahpu and Xbalanque are twin brothers who are blowgun hunters. In one episode they shoot down a bird pretending to be the sun. Subsequently, they take the role of maize farmers using magical farming implements, but they find that farming is not their natural vocation. They become ballplayers, using the equipment of their dead father and uncle. As they are playing ball, the noise annoys the lords of the underworld (Xibalba), and they summon the twins to the land of death. Before the twins go, they plant maize to serve as a sign of their fate in the underworld. Eventually their grandmother sees the corn dry up when they are burned in an oven in Xibalba, but the corn plants grow again when the twins defeat the lords of

Xibalba (D. Tedlock 1985:158–160). Then they rise up to become the sun and the moon. Their ascent seems to be linked to their being burned in an oven, echoing an Aztec legend of how the sun and the moon were created when they rose up from a hearth fire at Teotihuacán (Sahagún 1950–1982, 7:3–7).

The Popol Vuh says the twin boys are transformed into the sun and the moon, but it does not specify which is which (D. Tedlock 1985:160). On the other hand, *El Título de Totonicapán* (7v) states that Xbalanquej is a female ballplayer who is the moon (Carmack and Mondloch 1983:21, 28–29, 174, 213 n. 74). Dennis Tedlock (1985:368–369) notes: "If the name Xbalanque literally means 'Little Jaguar Sun' . . . it could refer specifically to the full moon, which is metaphorically called 'sun' by contemporary Quichés." Karen Bassie-Sweet (1992:190–191) finds Tedlock's interpretation convincing and adds that the jaguar is a good counterpart for the full moon because he emerges from a den at sunset and retreats at dawn, just like the full moon.

The ballplaying Hero Twins decapitate each other in the Popol Vuh (D. Tedlock 1985:150, 153). This type of act suggests eclipse imagery, which would involve the new moon in the case of a solar eclipse and the full moon during a lunar eclipse. Xbalanque decapitating his twin brother would play the role of the new moon covering the sun's light during a solar eclipse. But Hunahpu decapitating Xbalanque suggests a lunar eclipse, indicating the phase would be the full moon. The full moon is a natural "twin" of the sun, similar in both size and shape, and its motions mirror those of the sun, for the full moon rises as the sun sets, and vice versa. The seasonal motions of the full moon are like those of the rising sun, but they take place at the opposite side of the sky in the opposite season.

God CH is the Postclassic counterpart of Xbalanque (Fig. 4.4e–g; Taube 1992b:63). Usually, God CH has a jaguar-spotted mouth like that of Tepeyollotl, the central Mexican jaguar god who is an alter ego of Tezcatlipoca in his lunar aspect (Milbrath 1995a). God CH is sometimes merged with the Tonsured Maize God, evoking Xbalanque's role as a maize farmer (Fig. 4.4e; Taube 1992b:60). Other roles seen in the Popol Vuh are not prominent in the codices. Only one Postclassic image seems to show God CH wearing a ball-game belt (Fig. 4.4g). Only one scene shows him with Hun Ahau, the counterpart of Hunahpu (Fig. 4.4h).

God CH is one of four gods marking the cosmic quarters around a world tree on Dresden Codex 3a (Fig. 4.4h). His name glyph has a jaguar-spotted mouth, but instead of the usual Yax prefix, here his portrait head has a prefix of one (Fig. 4.4b). He is positioned diagonally opposite a partially effaced figure of Hun Ahau, or God S (Coe 1989:179, fig. 28; Taube 1992b:115). God K and the Maize God mark the other two directions. In the center, the world tree grows out of the gaping abdominal wound of a sacrificed individual resting on the earth monster. The astronomical symbolism remains enigmatic but does bear some resemblance to the Codex Fejérváry-Mayer 1, which positions the solar and lunar deities at opposite sides of a cosmic diagram, with the other two directions marked by the Maize God and Tezcatlipoca, the counterpart of God K (Fig. 4.4i).

God CH's Postclassic name usually has a *yax* prefix and a head with a jaguar-spotted mouth, probably signifying *yax balam,* a name retained from the Classic period (Figs. 4.4a, d, e, 4.5d; Coe 1989:168, fig. 8; Schele and Freidel 1990:117). He is the Chicchan God, and he has a Chicchan marking like the day sign Chicchan, associated with a celestial snake (Thompson 1960, table 4). The spoked Chicchan sign crowning his head is usually crosshatched like a net, but occasionally it is marked by three spots (Fig. 4.4b).

Yax Balam is the Classic period counterpart of Xbalanque and God CH of the codices. In calendar records he is the jaguar-spotted god of the number nine (Figs. 4.4d, 4.5a). This link is intriguing because personified numbers may represent an ancient lunar count (Macri 1982:18, 49–54). He can substitute for the Moon Goddess in the Classic period lunar Glyph C (Kelley 1976:92, fig. 32). It is noteworthy that, aside from Yax Balam's role as the number nine, this deity is not well represented in monumental sculpture. Indeed, he is seen primarily in ceramics and cave paintings.

The Hero Twins appear in the deep recesses of the cave at Naj Tunich, the jaguar twin clearly marked by body patches with jaguar spots (Fig. 4.5b; Stone 1995b:149). Both twins have a bound hank of hair and they are seated in a similar fashion. Hunahpu wears a ball-game belt and clusters of three spots on his cheek and body. These seem to be variant forms of the single death spot more often seen on this deity. He touches his lunar twin, whose eyes seem to be closed in death. The death aspect of the lunar deity could indicate the new-moon phase or a lunar eclipse. The Hero Twins together in a cave appear to be fellow travelers to the underworld, bringing to mind modern accounts of the new moon disappearing to a cave in conjunction (Chapter 1). Xbalanque's connection with the night and the underworld is made clear in an account by Antonio de Fuentes y Guzmán, who records that in the Guatemalan highlands the dead were buried at night, when offerings were made to Ixbalanque so that he would accompany the deceased (Ruz 1968:68).

The Hero Twins are known as the Headband Twins in Classic period ceramics (Taube 1992b:60, 63). Hun Ahau, the solar Headband Twin, seems somehow also linked with the Morning Star (Chapter 3). The Headband Twins appear with some frequency in scenes related to maize agriculture. Since the Headband Twins embody the sun and the moon, their association with maize is very appropriate in light of contemporary Maya beliefs about the role the sun and the moon play in maize agriculture (Chapter 1). The Headband Twins hold digging sticks that resemble paddles as their companion, the Maize God, rises out of a bowl that looks curiously like a canoe (Fig. 4.5f; Hellmuth 1987, figs. 444, 446). This suggests some conceptual overlap in the imagery of paddling and planting. In another scene, the Hero Twins pull up the Maize God from a crack in a turtle shell (Fig. 3.11a). A parallel scene on a vessel known as the Resurrection Vase depicts the Headband Twins flanking the Maize God—who apparently is the counterpart of Hun Hunahpu, the father of the Hero Twins in the Popol Vuh—as he sprouts from a turtle shell marked with an Akbal sign signaling darkness (Fig. 3.11b; Coe 1989:177–178). In this scene, the lunar twin pours water on the Maize God, representing the moon's control over the rain that nourishes maize, the moon's role as a water

a   b   c   d

e   f   g

h   i

carrier, and its connection with maize agriculture (Fig. 4.5d). Another vessel depicts the twins holding overturned vases from which issue different kinds of snakes, here reflecting an archetypal metaphor, for the undulating body of a snake suggests a stream of water (Fig. 4.5c; Benson 1997:109).

A court scene depicts the spotted Headband Twin (Hun Ahau), the Maize God, and the lunar twin, his jaguar markings now eroded (Coe 1978b, no. 2). The three gods have come to pay homage to an enthroned male wearing a headdress representing the lily-pad monster, not unlike the glyphic sign for turtle (ak'; Houston 1989:40). This may be one of a number of scenes representing the Sun and the Moon, the cycles of maize cultivation, and the turtle constellation located in the stars of Orion (Chapter 7).

A variety of intriguing scenes hint at other celestial events involving the Headband Twins. On one pot, the twins dance around a water-lily monster with a Kan Cross on its brow, like the deity at the base of the celestial cross in the Temple of the Foliated Cross at Palenque (Fig. 4.5e; Pl. 11). The Hun Ahau twin adopts the pose sometimes used by ballplayers, although in this case he lacks the ball-game belt. Nonetheless, the headband itself may be a sufficient link with the game, for the Popol Vuh specifies that the headband is part of the equipment needed to play ball (D. Tedlock 1985:340).

A polychrome plate depicts the lunar Headband Twin, Yax Balam, seated on a throne formed by two po glyphs (Coe 1989:176, fig. 24; Hellmuth 1987, fig. 435). Coe identifies the double-po throne as a symbol for pop, meaning "mat" or "rulership." The mat connection is reinforced by the twisted element on Yax Balam's back, resembling the mat in the month glyph Pop, signifying "straw mat" in almost all Mayan languages and dialects (Thompson 1960: 107). Another alternative is that the throne may refer to the moon because po is a name for the moon in a number of Mayan languages (Thompson 1960:47). Thrones bearing the po glyph are covered by a jaguar pelt in a number of Maya vase paintings. On the Protoclassic La Mojarra Stela, Martha Macri and Laura Stark (1993:6) identify a hide with po in its center as a lunar symbol. Probably the hide is meant to be a jaguar skin, an apparent allusion to the jaguar aspect of the moon.

A lunar crescent frames the Moon God sitting on a po throne on the Pearlman Trumpet, an incised conch shell trumpet from the Early Classic period (Fig. 4.5g; Schele and Miller 1986:308–309; Taube 1992b:67). Schele and Miller translate his name as "Jaguar Moon Lord" (balam-u-ahau) and suggest that he is the lunar twin of the Popol Vuh. His ballgame belt seems to allude to a role as a ballplayer, comparable to the Hero Twins. He also wears a downturned half-mask characteristic of a number of lunar deities. Mirrorlike markings (T617a) distinguish the Moon God as a bright body, perhaps

---

FIG. 4.4. *a:* Lunar god named Yax Balam is Postclassic Chicchan god known as God CH (Madrid Codex 104b; after Taube 1992b, fig. 28a).

b: Variant name of Postclassic Jaguar-spotted God CH (Dresden Codex 3a; after Taube 1992b, fig. 28b).

c: God CH, Postclassic counterpart of Xbalanque, as head variant of number 19 (Dresden Codex 69; after Taube 1992b, fig. 28c).

d: Yax Balam, head variant of number nine and Classic counterpart of God CH (Olvidado Temple, Palenque; after Taube 1992b, fig. 28d).

e: God CH, wearing headdress of Tonsured Maize God, has jaguar-spotted mouth like his portrait glyph, prefixed by Yax glyph, designating him as Yax Balam (Madrid Codex 28d; after Taube 1992b, fig. 28c).

f: God CH as Postclassic counterpart of lunar twin, Xbalanque (Dresden Codex 7b; after Taube 1992b, fig. 28f).

g: Deity with jaguar patches on face, deer headdress, and heavy belt of ballplayer may be linked with God CH (Paris Codex 10; after Taube 1992b, fig. 28h).

h: God CH (facing bound deer) appears with Maize God, Hun Ahau, and God K positioned around world tree, suggesting four world quarters (Dresden Codex 3a; after Villacorta and Villacorta 1977).

i: Quadripartite division of calendar and associated gods of four world quarters on page 1 of Codex Fejérváry-Mayer from Mixteca-Puebla area (after Krupp 1983:291).

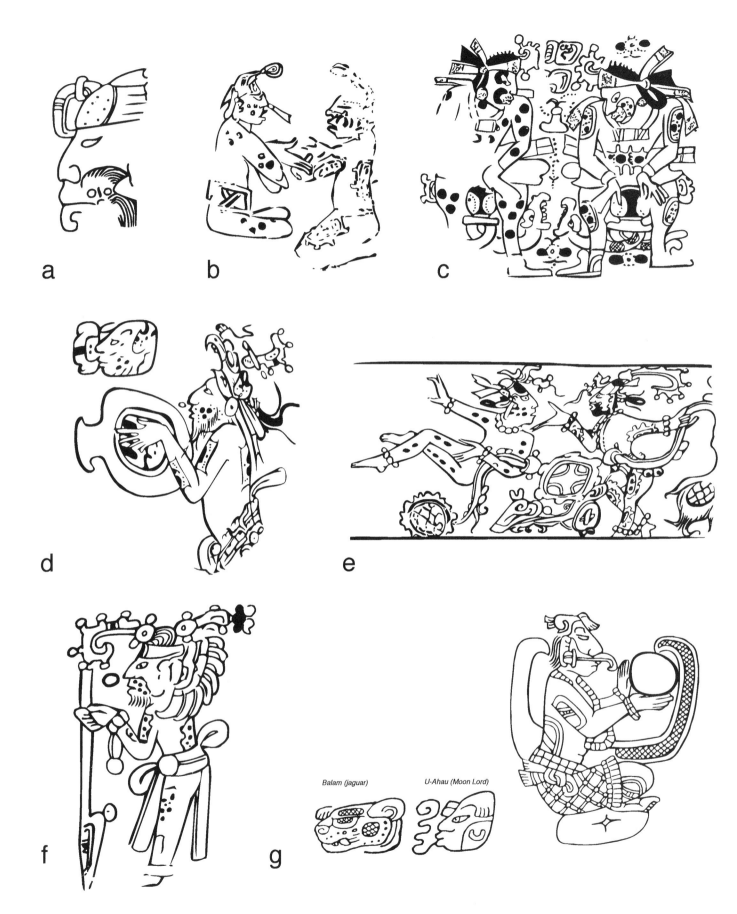

a   b   c

d   e

f   g   Balam (jaguar)   U-Ahau (Moon Lord)

alluding here to the full moon, which has a masculine aspect according to Quiché Maya accounts. Schele and Miller note that the lunar god lacks the breasts characteristic of female figures. Even though he wears a costume typical of Classic Maya women, they point out that this garb is also worn by males involved in bloodletting. The gender ambiguity in the figure's costume is not surprising in light of the female and male variants of Xbalanque in two different versions of the Hero Twins tale discussed above. Indeed, a number of Classic Maya lunar deities seem to be of ambiguous gender, a pattern similar to central Mexican lunar iconography (Milbrath 1995a).

We can conclude that Hun Ahau (Hunahpu) and Yax Balam (Xbalanque) represent the sun and the moon in the underworld, like the Hero Twins in the Popol Vuh. They are most often seen in Classic period ceramic paintings. They wear ball-game equipment, and they appear to be involved in maize agriculture, pointing to a link with the activities of the Hero Twins in the Popol Vuh. Yax Balam may often represent the masculine full moon, which plays an important role in the Quiché maize cycle today (Chapter 1). In the Postclassic period, God CH continues to have Yax Balam's jaguar aspect and lunar nature and is similarly associated with maize. However, he is rarely represented in the codices with Hun Ahau. Apparently, the mythic exploits of the Hero Twins received less emphasis in the codices, probably because these focused on agricultural and weather cycles rather than on mythological events.

The paucity of Postclassic representations of the Hero Twins may also relate to regional differences, reflecting a greater emphasis on female lunar deities in Yucatán, evident at sites like Tulum (see below).

THE CLASSIC PERIOD MOON GOD IN MONUMENTAL ART

The Moon God in Classic period monumental art is relatively rare. The known examples do not exhibit obvious jaguar traits. Perhaps the most intriguing image is seen on Bonampak Altar 2, where a lunar crescent frames the Moon God dressed in a ball-game belt and holding his lunar rabbit (Fig. 4.6a). He has a cruller nose like the Jaguar War God but lacks apparent jaguar traits.

A ball-court marker from Quiriguá known as Monument 18 (Altar R) shows a quatrefoil cave framing the moon symbol and the Moon God, who is wearing a ball-game belt (Fig. 4.6c). This image evokes the new moon in conjunction hiding in a cave. A different phase of the moon is suggested by a figure on Zoomorph P from Quiriguá (Fig. 4.6b). *Zac* (T58) markings on the body of this lunar deity suggest the whiteness of a visible phase of the moon. A masculine gender is indicated by the contorted pose exposing the thighs.

Piedras Negras Stela 19 seems to represent the face of a lunar deity enclosed in a lunar symbol (Fig. 4.6d). Karl Taube (1992b, fig. 30b) groups this deity with images of the Moon Goddess. The figure has a looped hank of hair, a male hairdo seen

---

FIG. 4.5. *a:* Jaguar-spotted god of number nine (Yaxchilán Lintel 48; after Tate 1992, fig. 62).

b: Spotted Hun Ahau with lunar twin, Yax Balam, marked by patches with jaguar spots (cave at Naj Tunich; after Stone 1995b, fig. 6-43).

c: Headband Twins holding overturned vases issuing snakes that symbolize water (Classic Maya vase; after Taube 1992b, fig. 61d).

d: Headband Twin named Yax Balam pours water from Akbal vase (detail of Late Classic Resurrection Vase [see Fig. 3.11b]; after Hellmuth 1987, fig. 439; Stone 1995b, fig. 6-42).

e: Late Classic vessel showing Headband Twins dancing with head of water-lily monster (after Hellmuth 1987, fig. 430).

f: Jaguar-spotted Headband Twin holds digging stick resembling canoe paddle (Late Classic vase dating to Tepeu 1 period; after Taube 1992b, fig. 28g).

g: Lunar crescent frames "Jaguar Moon Lord" (*balam-u-ahau*) sitting on *po* symbol, alongside his lunar name (Early Classic Pearlman Trumpet; after Schele and Miller 1986, pl. 121; Coe 1982, fig. 1).

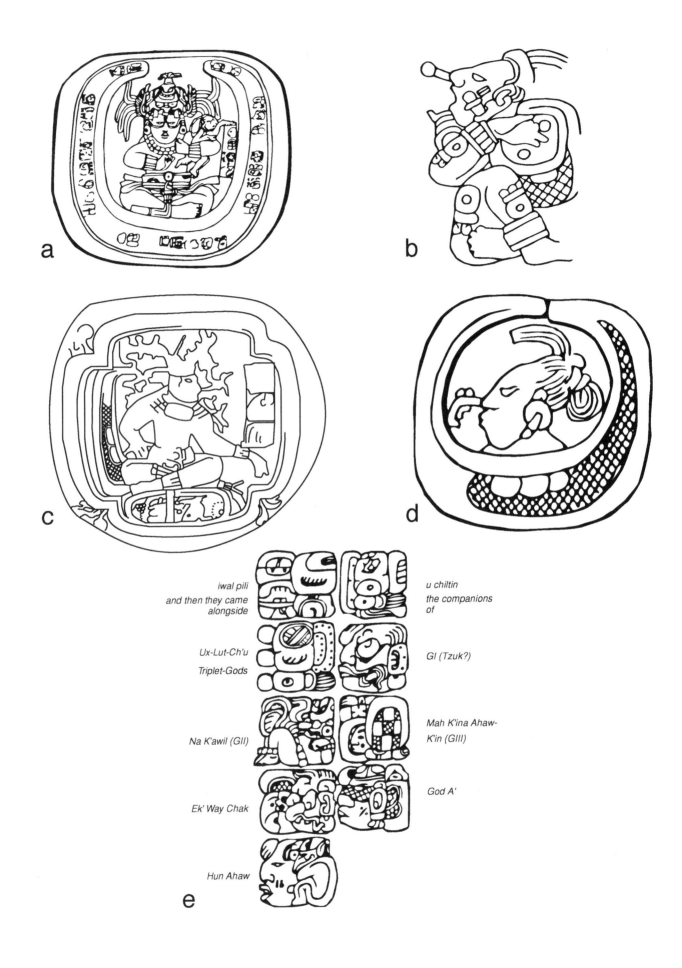

iwal pili
and then they came
alongside

u chiltin
the companions
of

Ux-Lut-Ch'u
Triplet-Gods

GI (Tzuk?)

Na K'awil (GII)

Mah K'ina Ahaw-
K'in (GIII)

Ek' Way Chak

God A'

Hun Ahaw

on images of the Headband Twins (Fig. 4.5b). Occasionally this hairdo is also worn by the Moon Goddess (Fig. 4.10g). The downturned mask is like that worn by the Moon God on the Pearlman Trumpet (Fig. 4.5g). Although the gender is ambiguous, I group the Piedras Negras figure with the Moon God.

One of the finest monumental images of the moon appears on a bench from Las Sepulturas at Copán. The lunar deity in a T683 lunar crescent holds a lunar rabbit (Pl. 19). The deity is probably a male because it has a downturned serpent mask seen on other images of the Moon God (Fig. 4.5g).

On a Copán ball-court marker, Hun Ahau (Hun Ahaw) kneels with the God of Zero, identified by his portrait glyph at the top of the right-hand column of glyphs (Fig. 3.10g; Schele and Miller 1986:251, 257). Schele (1987a) refers to the God of Zero as a death god embodying sacrificial death. However, he may also be connected with the moon, since he holds a handstone representing the lunar rabbit. His death aspect may also be linked with the moon. A Maya vase depicts a female with death attributes and a hand on her chin, as the God of Zero has, (Kerr 1990:229, no. 2286). Possibly she has a death aspect linked with the moon, like the skeletal heads in the lunar Glyph C.

A deity embodying the Classic period version of the Death God, known as God A' in the codices, seems to be linked with the moon in some contexts. In the Temple of the Foliated Cross, a passage naming astronomical gods includes the Palenque Triad (O9-O10), and then names Ek' Way Chak and God A' (Fig. 4.6e; Schele 1992b:170). This death god has a Cimi (death) sign on the cheek, a dark band across the eyes, and a lunar glyph attached to his head. His name appears before Hun Ahaw, suggesting a pairing like that seen on the Copán Ball-court marker.

Another skeletal god clearly is also linked with a lunar crescent on Quiriguá Monument 4 (Stela D). Here Kelley (1977b:61) identifies a moon symbol framing a skeletal face as the symbol for a lunar eclipse, but it could represent the Moon disappearing in conjunction. The Initial Series date on Monument 4 (9.16.15.0.0; 2/13/766) is not even close to the day of a lunar eclipse, but it is one day before the new Moon. Perhaps the Moon in conjunction (in the underworld) is represented in a skeletal form. Another alternative is that the configuration shows Venus as a skeletal Morning Star framed by the Moon, because this date marks the last appearance for both bodies in the morning sky. As we will see, the skeletal Morning Star seems to represent Venus in superior conjunction in other contexts (Chapter 5).

In sum, the most easily recognized aspect of the Moon God is the ballplayer in his lunar crescent. Ball-game belts on two such figures suggest that this aspect of the moon belongs to the masculine realm of the Hero Twins. Scenes involving partial figures in a lunar crescent are more ambiguous in gender, reflecting a trend seen throughout the lunar complex. The God of Zero may represent a death aspect of the moon. Other death aspects of the moon may appear in portrait glyphs that include the lunar crescent and a face bearing the Cimi sign, showing the natural connection between the moon and the realm of the underworld, also noted in modern Maya accounts. The death aspect of the moon may embody

---

FIG. 4.6. *a:* Lunar crescent frames Moon God as ballplayer holding lunar rabbit (Late Classic Bonampak Altar 2; after Schele and Miller 1983:46, fig. 18c).

b: Zac markings on body of lunar deity indicate visible phase of moon (Late Classic Monument 16 [Zoomorph P], at Quiriguá; after Taube 1992b, fig. 31a).

c: Quatrefoil cave frames moon symbol and Moon God wearing ball-game belt, possibly representing new moon (Late Classic Quiriguá Monument 18 [Altar R]; after Stone 1982, fig. 134).

d: Moon God enclosed in lunar symbol (Late Classic Piedras Negras Stela 19; after Taube 1992b, fig. 30b).

e: Passage naming Palenque Triad (Venus, Sun, and Jupiter?) followed by names of Ek' Way Chak (another Venus god?), God A' (Moon?), and Hun Ahaw (underworld Sun and Morning Star?) (Late Classic Temple of Foliated Cross; after Schele 1992b:70).

the moon paired with the underworld sun. Underworld imagery is appropriate to the moon, which spends up to three days each month invisible in the underworld during conjunction.

THE YOUNG MOON GODDESS IN COLONIAL AND POSTCLASSIC TIMES

The moon has multiple aspects in the Popol Vuh. The male ballplayer, Xbalanque, may take the role of the full moon; the youthful Blood Woman may be the waxing moon; and the aged Grandmother (Xmucane) is probably the waning moon (B. Tedlock 1992a:31; 1992b:183–184). After Blood Woman is impregnated by the decapitated head of Hun Hunahpu, the Maize God, she carries a net to collect corn. Her net leaves an imprint in the floor of Xmucane's house, a magical sign that shows she is pregnant with the offspring of Hun Hunahpu (D. Tedlock 1985:118–119; 1991:166). She gives birth to the Hero Twins, one of whom is to become the moon. This apparent anomaly of the mother and son both being identified with the moon can be ex-

plained as a process of transformation: the moon changing from female to male at the full moon. Similarly, the two different females representing the moon can also be explained by changes in lunar phases. Thompson (1960:231) notes that the confusion between the sun's wife and the mother of the sun in contemporary Maya accounts may reflect two different phases of the moon. In a like fashion, he proposes that in the codices a youthful goddess evokes the waxing moon, whereas an aged goddess is identified with the waning moon (Thompson 1960: 83). My own research confirms his findings (Milbrath 1995a, 1996a).

Goddess I of the codices is the young Moon Goddess. In the Dresden Codex, the name for the youthful Goddess I invariably uses the T1026 female portrait head inset with a curled design resembling T171 (Fig. 4.7a; Thompson 1972:47–48, 51). The T171 curl refers to the sound *u* in Landa's syllabary, which also is the word for "moon." Standing alone, T1026 seems to signify "moon lady" (Milbrath 1996a). The T1026 name may be prefixed by T171, which apparently adds emphasis to her lunar quality (Figs. 4.1j,

---

FIG. 4.7. *a:* Postclassic names for young Moon Goddess (Goddess I), *on left* prefixed by T58 symbolizing her whiteness; *on right* prefixed by T171 ("moon") reinforcing her lunar aspect (after Taube 1992b, figs. 29a–b).

b: Young Moon Goddess with headdress representing *zac,* word for "white," probably indicating visible phase of moon (Dresden Codex 18b; after Villacorta and Villacorta 1977).

c: Death spots and closed eyes characterize eclipsed Moon Goddess in eclipse table (Dresden Codex 53b; after Villacorta and Villacorta 1977).

d: Young Moon Goddess (Goddess I) offering symbol for maize (Dresden Codex 22b; after Taube 1992b, fig. 29e).

e: Young Moon Goddess offering fish (Dresden Codex 23b; after Villacorta and Villacorta 1977).

f: Young Moon Goddess in amorous scenes with God N and God A, followed by scene of her carrying children (Dresden Codex 23c; after Villacorta and Villacorta 1977).

g: Young Moon Goddess paired with male consorts has clustered death spots in first scene, and in second she has single death spots and closed eyes, both apparently refer-

ring to lunar eclipse (Dresden Codex 19b; after Villacorta and Villacorta 1977).

h: Young Moon Goddess carrying birds that represent divinely sent disease (Dresden Codex 16c; after Villacorta and Villacorta 1977).

i: Moon Goddess wrapped in lunar crescent pours water from vase decorated with seashell (Dresden Codex 49a; after Taube 1992b, fig. 30c).

j: Old Moon Goddess (named T58:1027 in text) is aged Goddess I wearing coral-snake headdress in her role as beekeeper (Madrid Codex 108c; after Villacorta and Villacorta 1977).

k: Aged Moon Goddess named T58:1027, meaning "old white lunar lady," wears cotton coil headdress as she lays out warp threads (Madrid Codex 102c; after Villacorta and Villacorta 1977).

l: Aged Moon Goddess, bearing name linked with Ix Chel, uses weaving batten to work on weft threads (Madrid Codex 102d; after Villacorta and Villacorta 1977).

m: Old Moon Goddess with hybrid name performs sewing or embroidery with God H (Dresden Codex 2b; after Villacorta and Villacorta 1977).

T 58.1026   T 171.1026.109

a b c d

e f g

h i j

k l m

4.7a, right). When T1026 is prefixed by T58 (*zac* or *sak*), her name becomes "white moon lady" (Fig. 4.7a, left). This name appears with a number of representations of the goddess, including one who wears the symbol for white as a headdress (Fig. 4.7b).

Thompson (1960:83) notes that the young Moon Goddess was the mother goddess and patroness of medicine, weaving, sexual license, the earth, and crops. He identifies virtually all youthful female figures on pages 16–23 of the Maya Dresden Codex as the Moon Goddess (Thompson 1972). Usually she is bare breasted and wears a skirt of varying lengths, sometimes as short as a man's hip cloth. Her skirt is netted in a number of images (Dresden Codex 18c), which is intriguing because legends speak about the moon being lifted up in a net made of fish during the waxing moon (Chapter 1). The net skirt also suggests a connection with the netted bag used to gather maize, an activity sometimes timed by the full moon (Chapter 1).

On Dresden Codex 16–23, Goddess I appears variously in amorous scenes or carrying burdens or making offerings that include maize symbols and fish (Fig. 4.7d–g; Thompson 1972:47). Her burdens show her role as the archetypal mother. Strapped to her back or in her arms, she carries small deities representing her divine children. In one case, she carries two children who may be siblings of different ages (Fig. 4.7f; Thompson 1972:48). Sometimes she carries birds that represent disease (*koch*) that are controlled by the Moon Goddess (Fig. 4.7h; Thompson 1972:51). This calls to mind ethnographic accounts describing how the waxing moon brings illnesses such as infections, tumors, or pustules (Chapter 1).

On Dresden Codex 16–23, Hofling and O'Neil (1992) recognize death aspects of Goddess I, with closed eyes or death spots linked to lunar-eclipse intervals. On page 19b, she has death spots, then 29 days later (one lunar month) she is paired with her lover, a death god covered with death spots (Fig. 4.7g). She has similar death spots and closed eyes like the eclipsed Moon Goddess in the eclipse table (Fig. 4.7c).

Amorous scenes indicate that the Moon Goddess has a roving eye, just as contemporary folktales characterize the Moon Goddess as a deity with many romantic partners (Thompson 1939). In the codices, Goddess I is shown paired with many different male figures (Fig. 4.7f–g). These represent sexual unions that symbolize conjunction. Thompson (1972:57–60) notes that these scenes often have a glyph compound with crossed bands (T552) that refers to her union with another god, indicating conjunction as a form of marriage. This compound may refer to *yatanbil,* a Yucatec word for "wife" (Barrera Vásquez 1980). The Sun God (God G), traditionally named as her husband in Maya legends, is not among her consorts; instead she joins with God N in two scenes, and in other scenes her consorts are death deities and a dog symbolizing Venus, as on Dresden Codex 21b. It seems that the Moon has so many lovers because it moves rapidly through the sky, making frequent encounters with planets as it circles around the sky in only 27⅓ days (Milbrath 1996a).

A voluptuous woman seated on a sky-band throne is the Moon Goddess "par excellence" on Dresden Codex 49a (Fig. 4.7i). A moon symbol wraps around her waist, and she pours water from a vase decorated with a conch shell, suggesting parallels with lunar symbolism in central Mexican cultures (Milbrath 1995a). Thompson (1972:68) identifies her as the youthful Goddess I, and Taube (1992b:64) concurs, although he points out that she has a different name glyph. Her name glyph is a variant with an aged female face infixed with the lunar glyph T181. Andrea Stone (1990) suggests that she is Grandmother Moon, a name common among the contemporary Maya. The goddess on Dresden Codex 49a may be linked to childbirth through imagery of the conch shell, described as a metaphorical womb in an Aztec account discussed earlier. As a lunar deity, she also controls the tides when she pours seawater from her conch shell. In another scene, Goddess I offers fish, her bounty from the sea (Fig. 4.7e).

We can conclude that Goddess I, the youthful Moon Goddess of the codices, is probably the waxing moon. The waxing moon is visualized as a youthful mother goddess associated with young children. She also offers various foods essential to sustenance, such as maize and fish. On the other hand, she has a malevolent side because she brings certain diseases. She is also lascivious, for she has many lovers, apparently because her rapid movement through the sky results in many conjunction events. She may be the wife of the sun, but this role is not clearly represented in the codices. Although the full moon may be male in some contemporary Maya accounts, the codices more often show the youthful Goddess I in a death aspect to represent the eclipsed full moon. The choice of a feminine form for the full moon may be a Postclassic phenomenon, reflecting the popularity of female lunar cults at this time in Yucatán.

THE AGED MOON GODDESS IN COLONIAL AND POSTCLASSIC TIMES

Colonial period accounts indicate that the moon grows old as it wanes, an image that is echoed in modern Maya accounts. In the Popol Vuh, the grandmother of the Hero Twins, Xmucane, has been identified as the waning moon (Girard 1979:52, 167, 287; B. Tedlock 1992b:31). Mary Preuss (1988:8) translates Xmucane's Quiché name as "she who is covered up," an apt name for the waning moon. Xmucane takes the role of an aged midwife and diviner (D. Tedlock 1985:40, 369). This suggests comparison with the Yucatec goddess Ix Chel described in Landa's account, the same name associated with the Lacandón Moon Goddess (Chapter 1).

Landa describes Ix Chel as the goddess of childbirth, medicine, and divination, although he does not specifically identify her as the moon (Tozzer 1941:129). Ix Chel's lunar nature is apparent in a festival held in her honor on the sixth day of Zip involving a dance called *okot uil*, meaning "dance of the moon" (Thompson 1970b:242). Ix Chel was the grandmother of the Bacabs, which makes her an old goddess (Thompson 1939:137). As a goddess of childbirth, Ix Chel takes the role of an old midwife rather than that of the youthful mother giving birth and carrying children (a role reserved for the young Goddess I).

In light of recent glyphic research that links Ix Chel to the Postclassic Goddess O, the identification of Ix Chel with the moon has been questioned by some (Taube 1992b:105) and reaffirmed by others

(Schele and Freidel 1990:366). Taube identifies the aged Goddess O as Landa's Ix Chel, describing her as the goddess of weaving, curing, and divination. He distinguishes her from an aged variant of Goddess I representing the old Moon Goddess (Taube 1992b: 68–69). Nonetheless, Stone (1990) points out that these old goddesses are closely related and can be linked by hybrid names. My research suggests that these aged goddesses are all aspects of the waning moon (Milbrath 1996a). There are three primary variants of the aged Moon Goddess: the aged Goddess I, the aged Goddess O, and an aged goddess with various hybrid names (termed here Goddess I-O). Probably we should abandon the letters designating the aged goddesses, visualizing them instead as aspects of the old Moon Goddess assigned to different roles. Nevertheless, here I retain letter designations to incorporate previous research. All the codical goddesses are linked in a manner similar to the "María system" of the Tzutujil, which represents the Marías as different lunar months (Stone 1990; Tarn and Prechtel 1986:176, 185 n. 7). Future research on the names associated with the various lunar deities in the codices may help to identify different lunar months.

Because the aged Goddess I is usually recognized as an image of the moon, we will begin with study of her character. The name glyph of old Goddess I is an aged lunar face (T1027) with the T171 "moon" infix. Her T1027 name may mean "old lunar lady" or perhaps "Grandmother Moon." The *zac* (white) prefix used in the name of the youthful Goddess I is also sometimes used to name the aged Goddess I (T58.1027; Fig. 4.7j–k; Milbrath 1996a).

The old Goddess I with the T58.1027 name is shown as a beekeeper in the Madrid Codex (Fig. 4.7j). Her beehive is marked by a Caban glyph, signifying a play on the word for "bee" and "honey" (*cab*). John Bolles (1982) records an incantation to protect the beehive that refers to a number of goddesses, including *colel cab* (lady bee). Like the goddesses who guard the beehive in modern Yucatec Maya lore, the old Moon Goddess is the keeper of the beehive. Here she is harvesting the honey, for the beehive is open to reveal its honeycomb, an activity associated with the waning moon, according to ethnographic accounts (Báez-Jorge 1988:247–248).

This provides support for linking the aged goddess with the waning moon.

Thompson (1939:130–132; 1960:83–84) long ago reached the conclusion that a number of goddesses linked to weaving seem to be counterparts of the moon, but he did not explore the iconography of the weaving complex in any detail. He says that the young Moon Goddess is the patroness of weaving, but this does not seem to be the case, because all the scenes related to weaving in the codices involve old women (Ciaramella 1994, fig. 6, table 3; n.d.; Milbrath 1996a). The aged Goddess I and hybrid forms, referred to here as Goddess I-O, are most prominent in activities related to weaving, including warping (attaching the warp threads), weaving, brocading, and sewing or embroidery (Figs. 4.7k–m, 4.9a).

The Moon Goddess is a natural weaver, moving back and forth across the path of the sun (Fig. 2.2a). In a previous study (Milbrath 1996a:379–384, 389), I have discussed the seasonal symbolism of the moon's weaving complex. The moon's weaving activity seems to refer to the motion of the moon during the dry season. According to ethnographic evidence (Earle 1986:160), weaving is a dry-season activity, no doubt based on practical considerations, because weaving is done out-of-doors.

On Madrid Codex 102c, the aged Goddess I wears a headdress with a coil of cotton used in weaving as she lays out the warp threads (Fig. 4.7k; Milbrath 1996a). Her name is prefixed by the color white (*zac*), which is the color of cotton. White may also refer to the white color of the moon or, more specifically, to a visible phase of the moon. Her name (T58.1027) may mean "white old lunar lady."

On Madrid Codex 30a, an unnamed goddess wearing a headdress with a cotton coil and spindles pours water on a Chicchan Serpent (Fig. 4.8a). She has lines around her mouth, suggesting that she is at least middle aged. She wears a net skirt like that of Goddess I, but her activity of pouring water links her with Goddess O. The cotton coil in her headdress could be related to either goddess, but the spindle is more typical of Goddess O and the hybrid goddess I-O.

An aged lunar goddess working with a textile on Dresden 2b and having a *chac* (red) title also may be a hybrid goddess (Fig. 4.7m). Her name combines the *chac* prefix (T109) of Goddess O with the T1027 portrait head of the aged Goddess I with a T145 suffix meaning *che,* a component in the *chel* name used for Goddess O. Thompson (1972:33) refers to her as Goddess O holding a netting implement to indicate her role as Ix Chebel Yax. Mary Ciaramella (n.d.) identifies the goddess as *chac chel* and the activity as sewing, also confirmed by a reading of the associated glyphs by James Fox and John Justeson (1984:66).

Many of the goddesses involved in the weaving complex seem to have hybrid titles linking Goddess I and Goddess O. An aged goddess with a hybrid name on Madrid Codex 102d uses a weaving batten to work on a textile mounted on a wooden frame (Fig. 4.7l). Ciaramella (n.d.) identifies the activity as weaving, the act of moving the weft thread through the warp. Her name glyph incorporates the portrait head of aged Goddess I (T1027) and the T145.612 compound that spells *chel,* a component in the name of the aged Goddess O, a close counterpart of Landa's Ix Chel (Milbrath 1996a:382). Ix is usually translated as "lady" in Colonial period texts (Thompson 1970b:206–207). T1027 can be seen as a logograph for "old lunar lady," and it also may be the glyphic counterpart for Ix. If so, we may have an actual representation of the name Ix Chel on Madrid Codex 102d.

Goddess O is usually named *chel* or *chac chel* (Fig. 4.8b–c; Taube 1992b:105). Although Taube does not recognize a lunar connection, he notes that a phonetic reading links Goddess O to the goddess Ix Chel described by Landa. Goddess O can also be equated with the Lacandón Ix Chel, the Moon Goddess, in her role as goddess of childbirth. As an aged midwife, Goddess O is the goddess of childbirth who prognosticates the future of the newborn. Among the contemporary Quiché, the moon is involved with childbirth because midwives follow a count from full moon to full moon (B. Tedlock 1992a:30).

An old water-pouring goddess on Madrid Codex 10b has the most complete form of Goddess O's name known from the codices (Fig. 4.8b; Milbrath 1996a:386; Taube 1992, fig. 10c). Her name is read as *chac chel,* with the *chel* formed phonetically by T145 (*che*) and T612 (*le*). *Chel* is a Yucatec term for the "arch of heaven" or "rainbow" (Barrera Vásquez 1980). *Chac* can mean either "red" or "great." Here *chac* may refer to a red lunar goddess. The red color evokes Chortí images of the full moon mixed with red as a sign of heavy rains (Fought 1972:387). Alternatively, Goddess O bearing the *chac chel* name could be the "red rainbow moon," also an image of the rainy-season moon (Milbrath 1996a:387–388). Goddess O's name often incorporates the T109 *chac* prefix, as in a scene showing Goddess O wearing a serpent knotted around her head and holding an overturned water jar pouring water (Fig. 4.8c–d). The goddess emptying water from a jar symbolizes rain and the connection between rain and serpents (Garza 1984:211). The Tzutujil say that serpent rainbows surrounding the moon are a sign that there will be rain (Tarn and Prechtel 1986:176). Stone (1990) compares Goddess O's serpent headdress with the ophidian rainbows around Grandmother Moon described by the Tzutujil.

Central Mexican goddesses show specific overlaps with the imagery of Goddess O (Milbrath 1995a; 1996:383; Taube 1992b:103–105). Toci and Tlazolteotl, two closely related lunar goddesses connected with weaving, curing, divining, and childbirth, overlap to some degree with Goddess O (Fig. 4.9c). Goddess O in her role as a water-pourer suggests a direct connection with the Aztec water goddess, Chalchiuhtlicue, who is sometimes shown with weaving implements (Milbrath 1996a:383). Goddess O seems even more closely connected with Cihuacoatl (serpent lady), a warlike goddess who brandishes a weaving batten like a weapon (Fig. 4.9b). Goddess O and Cihuacoatl share an association with serpents, death imagery, and implements associated with weaving. Cihuacoatl, also known as Tonan, is the counterpart of Tonantsi, a contemporary Náhua goddess who represents the moon within the earth, an image of lunar conjunction because the moon seems to disappear into the earth around the time of the new moon (Milbrath 1995a, 1996).

In a previous study (Milbrath 1996a:395–386), I have identified Goddess O on page 74 of the Dresden

Codex as the new moon threatening to eclipse the sun (Figs. 4.8f, 7.4d). Goddess O pours rainwater marked with glyphs referring to an 1,820-day cycle, the same cycle associated with imagery of solar eclipses on Paris Codex 23–24 (Fig. 7.2a; Chapter 7). Goddess O has an especially monstrous quality, with her sharp claws and her skirt with crossed bones. The clawed hands and feet seem to be those of a jaguar. Dresden Codex 74 shows Goddess O with eclipse signs. This makes her a counterpart of the Aztec goddess Cihuacoatl, who takes on a monstrous aspect when she takes the role of an eclipse demon known as a *tzitzimime* threatening to eclipse the sun (Milbrath 1995a, 1997). The Postclassic Maya probably shared the contemporary Lacandón view that eclipses would bring the end of the world, a belief also recorded among the Aztecs (Milbrath 1995b; 1997).

On Dresden 67a, Goddess O has a jaguar-spotted eye and feline claws (Fig. 4.8e). Like Goddess O on Dresden Codex 74, she wears a knotted-serpent headdress and pours water from her vase, and she has other similar monstrous features. The old (jaguar?) Moon Goddess may represent the new moon when the sun and the moon are joined together, a dangerous time for potential solar eclipses. This new-moon aspect of Goddess O can be distinguished from imagery of the waning moon, such as the old Goddess O with human hands and feet seen on Dresden Codex 39b (Fig. 4.8c; Milbrath 1996a:386). The texts on both 39b and 67a show a glyph compound with Kin and Akbal, suggesting the sun and the moon are involved, paired in a manner similar to texts associated with the Paddler Twins.

The serpent headdress found on a number of representations of the old goddess pouring water seems to be linked with the rainy season (Fig. 4.8c–f; Milbrath 1996a). The Madrid Codex (30b, 32b) depicts a related image in the old goddesses with serpent headdresses and streams of water issuing from their bodies (Fig. 4.8g–h). They do not bear the *chac* prefix typical of Goddess O, but they are shown emitting water from their bodies, suggesting a link with Goddess O pouring water during the rainy season. The unnamed Moon Goddess on Madrid Codex 32b wears a serpent belt and a composite headdress with

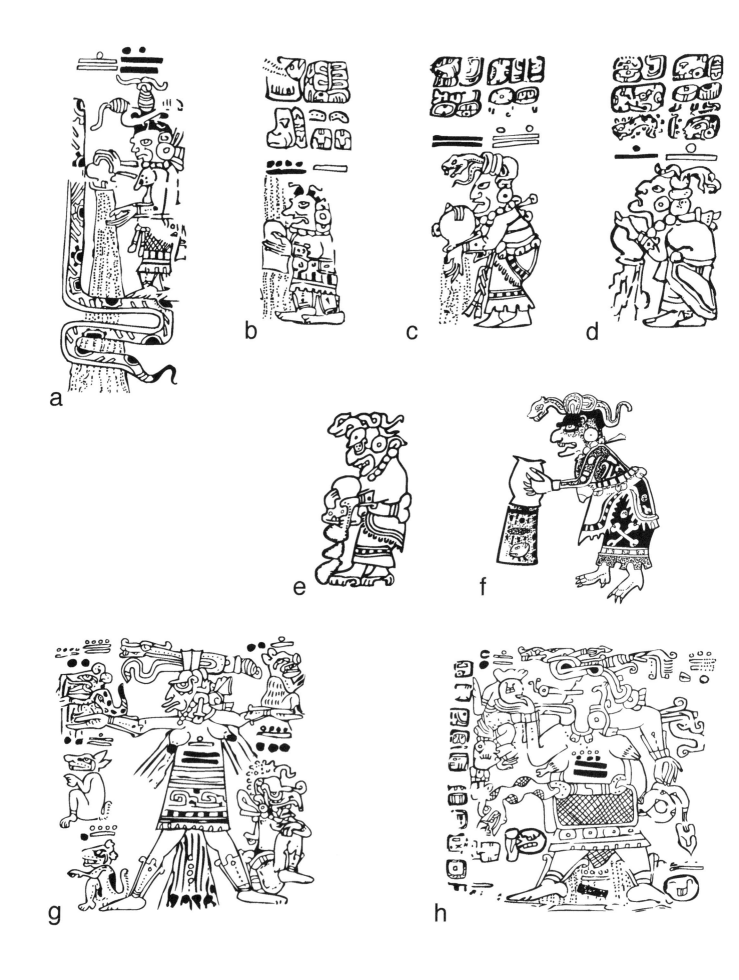

a serpent, a spindle, and a cotton coil (Fig. 4.8h). The serpent and cotton coil in the headdress of the lunar deity are not often seen together. She has human features, but one of her eyes is torn from its socket. This recalls a Maya belief recorded by Thompson (1970b: 235) that the moon is less bright than the sun because the sun plucked out one of her eyes when people complained that they could not sleep at night because of the light. In the blue liquid flowing between her legs, a black bar represents a period of five days and a red coefficient refers to a date with the number nine; and on her chest there is a red date coefficient of four and a black interval of thirteen days. The number thirteen is linked with the moon in a number of contexts (Milbrath 1996a: 382). For example, the *Ritual of the Bacabs* describes thirteen balls of colored thread that belong to Ix Chel (Thompson 1939: 148).

Another old lunar goddess on Madrid Codex 108c wears both a serpent and a cotton coil in her headdress (Fig. 4.7j). She harvests honey, indicating an activity that possibly took place in Tzec (October 14–November 3 N.S.), for Landa notes that owners of the hives gave honey in abundance for this festival (Tozzer 1941: 157). This would indicate the honey harvest took place near the end of the rainy season, correlating with the honey harvest recorded in Pom in a nineteenth-century Tzeltal calendar (Seler 1990–1996, 1: 220). Seasonal transitions may also be implied by her composite headdress. Another goddess wears a cotton coil and spindle in her headdress, a headdress associated with the dry-season weaving complex, but here the lunar goddess pours water (Fig. 4.8a). Another transitional combination is seen in an old goddess, wearing a knotted snake headdress, who brocades on a backstrap loom (Fig. 4.9a; Milbrath 1996a: 382). This headdress is usually associated with goddesses pouring water, but here the image may represent the moon at a time of seasonal change.

Water pouring, a rainy-season activity, is more commonly associated with old lunar ladies wearing a serpent headdress (Fig. 4.8c–f), whereas dry-season activities linked with weaving usually involve the old Moon Goddess wearing a cotton coil headdress (Fig. 4.7k–m). The moon pours water during the rainy season, and the wriggling serpent suggests the undulating path of the moon during the rainy season when snakes are active (Milbrath 1996a). During the dry season the moon weaves across the sky, and the spinning and weaving of cotton thread may describe the undulating path of the moon during the dry season.

The aged Moon Goddess wearing her serpent headdress expresses a connection with the rainy season. In a like fashion, the Tzutujil Maya Moon Goddess wears ophidian rainbows as a sign of rain during the rainy season. The link between a halo (rainbow) around the moon and rainfall in Tzutujil accounts seems to be based on actual observations (Chapter 1). This demonstrates that Maya imagery involves metaphors that encode observations of nature.

FIG. 4.8. *a:* Old Moon Goddess, wearing headdress with cotton coil and spindles, pours water on Chicchan Serpent (Madrid Codex 30a; after Villacorta and Villacorta 1977).

b: Old Moon Goddess pouring rainwater; she bears the name *chac chel* (T109.T145:612) at top of second column (Madrid Codex 10b; after Villacorta and Villacorta 1977).

c: Goddess O, named with *chac* title at top of second column, is aged Moon Goddess who pours rainwater (Dresden Codex 39b; after Villacorta and Villacorta 1977).

d: Old Moon Goddess (Goddess O) pouring rainwater wears typical knotted-serpent headdress (Dresden Codex 43b; after Villacorta and Villacorta 1977).

e: Goddess O as water-pourer has jaguar-spotted eye and feline paws, suggesting monstrous image of new moon (Dresden 67a; after Villacorta and Villacorta 1977).

f: Monstrous Goddess O (new moon?) pours water bearing glyphs that refer to period of 1,820 days (Dresden Codex 74; after Villacorta and Villacorta 1977).

g: Old lunar goddess wearing serpent headdress issues streams of water (Madrid Codex 30b; after Villacorta and Villacorta 1977).

h: Water streams from monstrous lunar goddess with extruded eye, death collar, and composite headdress with serpent, cotton coil, and spindle (Madrid Codex 32b; after Villacorta and Villacorta 1977).

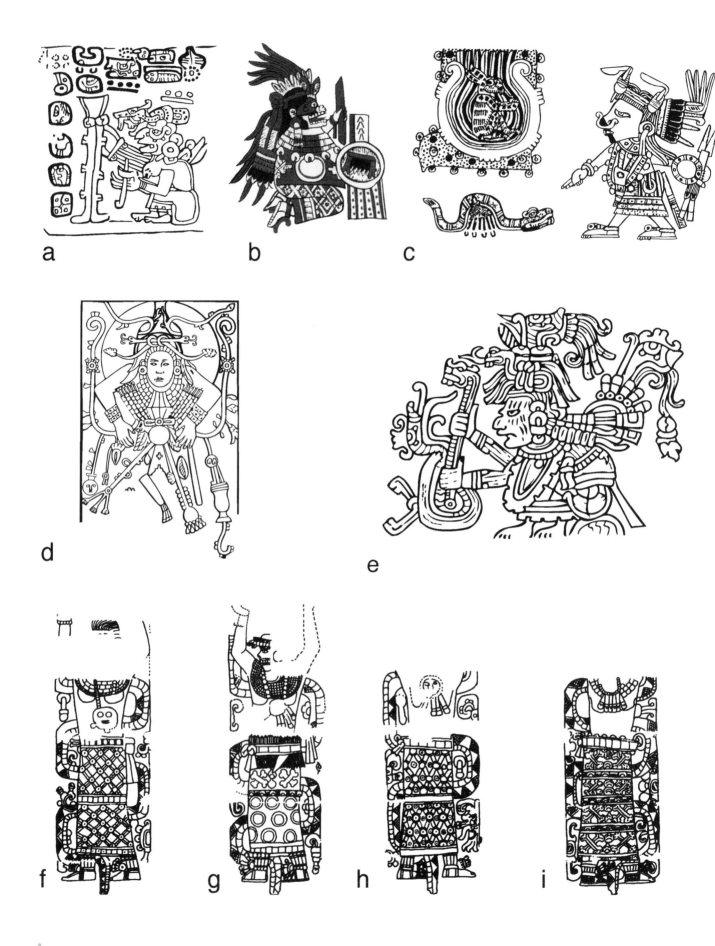

a

b

c

d

e

f

g

h

i

The Moon Goddess wears a serpent in her head-dress in Aztec central Mexico and on the Pacific Slope of Guatemala, indicating a widespread tradition. Coyolxauhqui sometimes wears a coral snake in her headdress, a snake seen in one image of the aged Goddess I (Fig. 4.7j; Milbrath 1997: 188, fig. 1). Coyolxauhqui seems to symbolize the rainy-season moon, and her decapitation is linked to a myth of seasonal transition, for the water dries up on the ball court when she is decapitated (Milbrath 1995a, 1997). A Classic period monument from Guatemala, Bilbao Monument 4, depicts the Moon Goddess wearing a knotted-snake headdress, surrounded by flowering vines as an expression of the moon's association with rainy-season fertility (Fig. 4.9d; Milbrath 1996a: 388). A lunar crescent fits tightly around her body in the manner of a yoke, which could represent a symbolic link with the stone ball-game yokes found in the Bilbao region and in Veracruz.

We can conclude that the aged Goddess I, the old Goddess O, and hybrid variants of the two are all aspects of the moon, most likely associated with the waning moon. A more monstrous form of the old goddess is reserved for images of the new moon, which can threaten the sun with eclipse. There seem to be seasonal differences in the imagery of the aged goddesses associated with the moon. The aged Goddess I and the hybrid Goddess I-O are often associated with activities related to weaving, a dry-season activity. Aged Goddess O, in both human and monstrous aspects, is frequently associated with water-pouring during the rainy season. The imagery of water-pouring goddesses may also indicate that the waning moon and new moon were believed to produce the most rainfall.

THE MOON IN THE POSTCLASSIC MURALS AT TULUM

Mural paintings from Tulum may depict different aspects of the aged Moon Goddess on Structures 5 and 16, dating sometime after A.D. 1400 (Miller 1982: 54, pls. 28, 37). Ix Chel was worshiped in centers all along the east coast of Yucatán, where the waning moon makes an especially dramatic disap-

FIG. 4.9. *a*: Old Moon Goddess with knotted-snake head-dress using bone pick to add brocade designs in textile on backstrap loom (Madrid Codex 79c; after Villacorta and Villacorta 1977).

b: Late Postclassic Aztec goddess Cihuacoatl, with skeletal face and threatening aspect, represented as warrior armed with shield and weaving batten (Codex Magliabecchiano 45r).

c: Postclassic central Mexican goddess Tlazolteotl wears spindle headdress and lunar nose ornament as she stands beside moon symbol with star field surrounding lunar rabbit and water stream (Codex Borgia 55; after Seler 1963).

d: Classic Moon Goddess, framed by flowering vines, wears knotted-snake headdress and lunar symbol around her waist (Bilbao Monument 4 from Pacific Slope of Guatemala; after Tozzer 1957: 488; Parsons 1969, pl. 33c).

e: Aged Moon Goddess (Goddess O) wearing composite headdress with knotted serpent, spindle, and maize symbol (Mural 2, Tulum Structure 16; after Taube 1992b, fig. 51a).

f: Youthful Moon Goddess (Goddess I?) with lattice skirt of jade (east side of north column in Terminal Classic Lower Temple of Jaguars at Chichén Itzá; after Schele and Matthews 1998, fig. 6.11.A3; rubbing by Merle Greene Robertson).

g: Moon Goddess with skeletal features, crossed bones, death eyes, and stars on skirt, counterpart to monstrous aspect of Goddess O (north side of north column in Terminal Classic Lower Temple of Jaguars at Chichén Itzá; after Schele and Matthews 1998, fig. 6.11.A3; Tozzer 1957, fig. 196).

h: Moon Goddess with lattice jade skirt, probably linked with Goddess I (west side of north column in Terminal Classic Lower Temple of Jaguars at Chichén Itzá; after Schele and Matthews 1998, fig. 6.11.A3; rubbing by Merle Greene Robertson).

i: Moon Goddess with pendulous breasts wearing skirt with death eyes between crossed bones, probably counterpart of Goddess O (south side of north column in Terminal Classic Lower Temple of Jaguars at Chichén Itzá; after Schele and Matthews 1998, fig. 6.11.A3; Tozzer 1957, fig. 195).

pearance in conjunction, dipping into the waters of the Caribbean.

Tulum Structure 16, also known as the Temple of the Frescoes, depicts the aged Goddess O wearing a composite spindle and knotted-serpent headdress in the lower band of Mural 2 (Fig. 4.9e; Miller 1982, pls. 37, 38; Taube 1992b:101). The aged goddess carries a serpent staff in her hands and a maize symbol on her back, suggesting an association with agriculture. She seems to be near the end of her life cycle, for she has lines covering her entire face. The aged Tulum goddess is the waning moon as it descends into the waters of the underworld, just prior to conjunction. The complete mural shows that she is about to be devoured by the reptilian jaws of the earth monster, rendered in a style that seems strongly influenced by central Mexico. The earth monster also swallows the sea beneath her. The sea is filled with marine creatures such as a stingray and a fish. According to Miller (1982:91), the goddess is in a liminal state between the world of the living and the world of the dead. Above her, another goddess crowned by lunar rays may be the moon in the waning quarter. This goddess has a line around her mouth, indicating age, but she is not so aged as the goddess floating on the sea. These images suggest a narrative sequence involving the waning moon, which ages as it descends toward the horizon and finally disappears into the sea as it drops into the jaws of the earth monster.

The Temple of the Diving God (Structure 5) depicts a sky band framing a scene with two goddesses seated on sky-band thrones (Fig. 3.3b). The sky band overhead has Venus glyphs alternating with solar rays. Both goddesses wear costumes decorated with shells, and they have earrings with rays that may represent lunar light. The one to the right has a line around her mouth, indicating that she is the more aged of the two. She wears an element around her waist similar to the burden pack of the possums in the New Year pages of the Dresden Codex (25a–28a). Again, a narrative sequence may be implied by the youthful and aged variants of the Moon Goddess.

All the Tulum goddesses described above are seated on twined cords wrapped around star sym-

bols and terminating in serpent heads. Miller (1982: 92, 97) interprets this design as a cosmic umbilical cord like the Kusansum, the marvelous rope or pathway in the sky known from a Maya ethnographic account recorded in Quintana Roo. He notes that the twisted cord in the Tulum murals can simultaneously be an image of the umbilical cord, a twined cord, and intertwined serpents (Miller 1982:95). The cord seems to refer to the path of the sun, the moon, and the planets, like that seen in the codices (Fig. 3.4a–b).

Although nothing in the imagery expressly refers to childbirth, the aged goddesses of Tulum may be linked with a lunar cult dedicated to midwives, who were usually aged women, making them the counterparts of the waning moon. Tulum was part of a pilgrimage route associated with female cults especially connected with childbirth. The Spaniards named the nearby island Isla Mujeres (island of women) because female figurines were so abundant (Miller 1982:85, 96). Just to the south, Ix Chel's principal shrine was located at the island of Cozumel, a pilgrimage site for pregnant woman. The shrine was used in the Late Postclassic period, when the island played a prominent role in long-distance trade networks, but the shrine itself may have originated in Classic period times (Sabloff and Rathje 1975:27).

We can conclude that Tulum was dedicated to a cult of the lunar goddesses, especially the aged aspects of the moon associated with the waning moon descending into the waters of the Caribbean. Mural paintings seem to show the moon's transformation as it descends to the eastern horizon. The waning moon is represented by an aged goddess at Tulum, a patroness of midwives who assisted in childbirth and a counterpart to Goddess O in the codices and Ix Chel in Landa's time. For this reason, the site may have been a center of pilgrimage for pregnant women who sought the assistance of the moon in her aspect as a patroness of midwives.

LUNAR DEITIES AT CHICHÉN ITZÁ

Lunar deities such as Ix Chel may have been worshiped at Chichén Itzá, the most important Yucatec

Maya site in the Terminal Classic and Early Postclassic periods. Andrea Stone (1990) has identified an image of the Moon Goddess framed by a large lunar glyph on Column 39S of the Northwest Colonnade in the Temple of the Warriors (Morris et al. 1931, pl. 105). Other lunar deities seem to be related to the Moon Goddess on Madrid Codex 30a (Fig. 4.8a). Snakes slither up behind four images of the Moon Goddess on the four sides of the north column in the Lower Temple of the Jaguars, part of the ball-court complex dating to the Terminal Classic period (Fig. 4.9f–i). On the north side of the column, the goddess has her arms held aloft in the manner of an Atlantean (Fig. 4.9g). On the other three sides, the upper columns are effaced, but presumably all sides depicted Atlantean figures, because no arms are shown on the lower columns. Despite the similarities, the four goddesses show differences in details of costume and body form that suggest the four lunar phases.

Taube (1992b:101, fig. 51b) identifies the north figure as the aged Goddess O, *chac chel* (Fig. 4.9g). She has a skeletal face and wears a beaded collar; the damaged chest area shows outlines that could be a skeletal rib cage. Her long skirt has three rows of large circles (stars?) beneath crossed bones. This figure evokes a connection with Goddess O on Dresden Codex 74 (Fig. 4.8f). The skeletal Moon Goddess probably represents the monstrous aspect of the new moon. On the south side of the column (Fig. 4.9i), the goddess wears a skirt with death eyes between crossed bones, and she has pendulous breasts, a detail omitted in Tozzer's (1957, fig. 195) drawing. This goddess may represent Goddess O in her more human manifestation as the waning moon of the last quarter.

On the east side of the column, the figure has more rounded and youthful breasts than the figure on the south side (Fig. 4.9f). Her skirt suggests a net pattern made of jade beads. Net skirts are characteristic of youthful and aged aspects of Goddess I and the hybrid Goddess I-O in the codices of a different design. The west figure also wears a skirt with a net pattern (Fig. 4.9h). Perhaps the two different forms of net skirt reflect two different aspects of the moon in the first half of its cycle: from the first quarter to

the full moon. As previously noted, a Mopan Maya legend describes how the moon was lifted up in a fishing net during its waxing phase. On the other hand, a net bag used to gather maize in Quiché accounts implies a connection with the full moon, the ideal time to gather the first ears of maize (Chapter 1).

Four related goddesses representing four lunar phases also may be seen in the four Ix Chels, each associated with different colors and world directions in the *Ritual of the Bacabs* (Roys 1965:14, 28). Another quadripartite division is suggested by four related goddesses worshiped in ancient times at Isla Mujeres who were known as Aixchel, Ix Chelbeliax, Ixhunié, and Ixhunieta (Tozzer 1941:9–10).

The four lunar goddesses have counterparts or mates in the four aspects of God N on the south column of the Lower Temple of the Jaguars. These representations of God N also have their arms raised in an Atlantean pose, and they are similarly positioned in front of undulating serpents (Schele and Mathews 1998, fig. 6.11). The faces are missing on two sides, but the other two show aged features and three show a headdress with a netted cap. On each of the four sides, God N wears a costume representing a different animal: a conch on the east side, a snail on the north side, and a turtle on the south side. The imagery on the west side is more enigmatic, but it may represent a winged insect, based on comparison with the four aspects of God N on the Iglesia facade (Taube 1992b; Tozzer 1957, figs. 266, 615). God N may be an astronomical god with a quadripartite nature. Indeed, a round column from Structure 6E1 at Chichén Itzá depicts four God N figures with star designs (Taube 1992b:94).

A phonetic reading of God N's name spells *patun*, a term that clearly refers to the Pauahtuns described by Landa, each associated with a different color, direction, and year-bearer (Tozzer 1941:137). Some scholars say that the aged Pauahtuns support the earth, whereas youthful Bacabs support the sky. On the other hand, Taube (1992b:92–94, fig. 47a) points out that there are no explicit images showing God N holding up the earth in Maya art, and sometimes he is seen supporting a sky band or the Cosmic Monster representing the sky (Fig. 7.5d; Copán Structure 22).

He sees little reason for distinguishing the Pauahtuns from the Bacabs and suggests that the terms "Mam" and "Bacab" are simply epithets for Pauahtun.

After the great flood, the four Bacabs were placed in four parts of the world to hold up the heavens, and each was associated with a different year-bearer, color, and direction (Tozzer 1941:136–137). The Yucatec Maya worshiped the Bacabs and Pauahtuns in the Uayeb festival, the five-day period marking the end of the old year, honoring a different Bacab and Pauahtun in each of the four years of the year-bearer cycle. Alfred Tozzer (1941:137 n. 638) notes that Colonial period sources designate the Pauahtuns as angels of the winds linked with the Uayeb ceremonies. The Pauahtuns and Bacabs are clearly distinguished from the Uayeb gods represented by clay or wooden idols destroyed at year end (Tozzer 1941: 139 n. 646). The Uayeb god seems to be equivalent to the Mam, a piece of wood dressed and then discarded or buried at year end, according to Cogolludo. God N's name seems to relate him specifically to the Pauahtuns. Nonetheless, Taube (1989b:355) suggests that God N may be linked with the Uayeb possum gods representing the old year at the top of the New Year pages in the Dresden Codex (25–28), for God N sometimes has possum traits. In any case, God N's counterpart took part in the ceremonies during the five-day Uayeb period at the end of the old year.

In his role as a god of the year's end, God N's various guises could relate to symbols connected with the four different directions associated with the year-bearers. His varying attributes could also be linked with four different lunar phases. When viewed over a four-year cycle, the Moon at year end would be at a different point in its 29.5-day cycle each year, because twelve synodic lunar months fall about 11 days short of the 365-day year. Perhaps God N represents a male aspect of the Moon linked with the year end. Other alternatives could explain God N's four different aspects. Two of the planets also are characterized by a quadripartite nature in their four phases. Venus comes to mind first, but the fact that God N appears in the Venus pages of the Dresden Codex positioned above the Morning Star suggests that he does not play the role of Venus (Fig. 5.3c; Chapter 5). Mercury might present a possible counterpart for God N. Perhaps God N is seen holding up the sky because Mercury is always seen close to the horizon. Another alternative is that God N is the aged Sun representing the dying year in a sequence of four years. Future study of God N should involve the mysterious God N events recorded in Classic period texts (Schele 1990a:147–151).

We can conclude that Chichén Itzá features four female aspects of the moon, probably representing four lunar phases, paired with four aged aspects of God N, an astronomical god of uncertain identity connected with the old year. The imagery at Chichén Itzá provides a bridge between the Postclassic and Classic periods, for it carries on a tradition first established in the Classic period. As we will see, images of God N paired with the Moon Goddess and an undulating serpent appear on Late Classic ceramic paintings that suggest a myth referring to the youthful Moon Goddess and her aged lover, a pairing repeated in later times in the codices, although the serpent is no longer present.

THE CLASSIC MAYA MOON GODDESS

The Classic period Moon Goddess often appears with a lunar crescent, and she sometimes has a rabbit companion (Fig. 4.10d₂, g). She often wears a net skirt, and she seems to be a counterpart of the youthful Goddess I of the codices (Taube 1992b:64–69).

The Classic Maya Maize God can substitute for the Moon Goddess in Glyph C of the Lunar Series (Fig. 4.10a; Kelley 1976:92, fig. 32). The two deities take identical roles, marking the same six-month lunar semester in the eighteen-month synodic lunar calendar (Linden 1996, fig. 2l, table 2). Taube (1992b:68) notes that the Moon Goddess often wears the latticed or net skirt of beads, face markings, and the coiffure of the Tonsured Maize God. He suggests that they are merged or conflated in some contexts, pointing out that the moon, the earth, and maize are collectively known as "Our Mother" among the highland Mam. The Yucatec Maya say that the Virgin Mary in her aspect as the Moon Goddess is "beautiful lady, embracer of maize" (Thompson 1954:28). The "ear-of-maize" moon is a term used to refer to both the full moon and the waning moon in various Colonial period Yucatec dictionaries (Lamb 1981:247).

On Copán Stela H, a royal figure wears a long netted skirt, a guise linked with both the Maize God and the Moon Goddess (Baudez 1994, figs. 23–24). Elizabeth Newsome (1991:276–279) interprets the figure as the ruler 18 Rabbit (18 Jog) dressed as the Maize God. On the other hand, Tatiana Proskouriakoff (1993:127) identifies the figure as a woman, most probably the wife of the ruler. Claude-François Baudez (1994:62) says the figure is probably a male dressed as a female, because a loincloth covers the figure's skirt. The stela bears the date 4 Ahau 18 Muan (9.14.19.5.0; 11/29/730), which coincides with the full moon. In my opinion, the royal figure takes the guise of the Moon Goddess merged with the Maize God because the full moon's gender is ambiguous around the full moon, when it transforms to a male, according to contemporary Quiché accounts. A cob of fully developed corn appears in the headdress, suggesting the ripened corn ready for harvest in November. The monument may refer to harvesting practices like those that survive today among the Tzotzil and Quiché Maya, who time the maize harvest by the full moon.

Sometimes the lunar symbol surrounds an ancestor figure visualized as a transformation of the moon, as on Yaxchilán Stela 4 (Fig. 4.10b; Tate 1986: 65; 1992:61). Here the moon symbol has crosshatched design (netting?), a detail characteristic of many lunar symbols. The companion cartouche with a solar ancestor has mirrors. Perhaps the deified ancestors of the ruling family were compared to the sun and the moon as a conjugal couple, a relationship that survives in Maya folklore today.

At Palenque, inscriptions compare the mother of Pacal II to the legendary moon mother, who was the first ruler of Palenque (Robertson 1985b, table III; Schele and Freidel 1990:227, 244–245). Schele and Freidel note that the moon was the mother of the gods at Palenque. She was married to GI' (First Father), who established the order of time and space

just after the fourth world creation on 4 Ahau 8 Cumku. Their children were born 754 years after the beginning of the epoch, but the lunar goddess (First Mother) and her husband were born in the previous epoch or age. First Mother was 760 years old when she gave birth to three divine children over an eighteen-day period. Research suggests that the eldest of the three is Venus (GI), the second born is the Sun God (GIII), and the youngest (GII) is another planet, just as modern Maya legends identify the Moon Goddess as the mother of the Sun and his planetary siblings (Chapters 1, 3, 5). About 35 years later First Mother acceded to the throne of Palenque as the first ruler on a date recorded in the Temple of the Cross (2.1.0.14.2 9 Ik 0 Yax; Lounsbury 1991: 813; Robertson 1985b, table III). This mythological record relates to Thompson's (1960:83) belief that the young Moon Goddess represented the first woman in the world.

Alfonso Arellano (1995) notes that Pacal II inherited the throne from his mother, which was an unusual line of descent; therefore, he probably wanted to legitimize her lineage and his right to the throne by claiming direct descent from the gods through his mother's line. His mother and the founding goddess bear the same name: Sak Bak', or Zac Bak in the Colonial period orthography (Fig. 4.10e). Dennis Tedlock (1992:254) reads this name as Lady Egret (*sak bak' ha'*), referring to the snowy egret. On the other hand, Mathews (1990:96) says that Bak can mean "heron" or "bone." I would suggest her name is "white heron." Arellano (1995) proposes that the name glyph of the goddess was transformed into the emblem glyph of Palenque, making the lords of Palenque the "sacred lords of the lineage of the white heron." The heron apparently substitutes for the lunar rabbit in the Palenque emblem glyph, suggesting a lunar connection. An Aztec account notes that the Moon God wore a heron-feather headdress (Sahagún 1950–1982, 7:5).

Glyphic representations of the Moon Goddess on monumental sculpture from Palenque depict a portrait head glyph with an "IL" sign on the cheek and a lunar crescent (T683) framing the back of the head (Fig. 4.10c). The same face, without the lunar

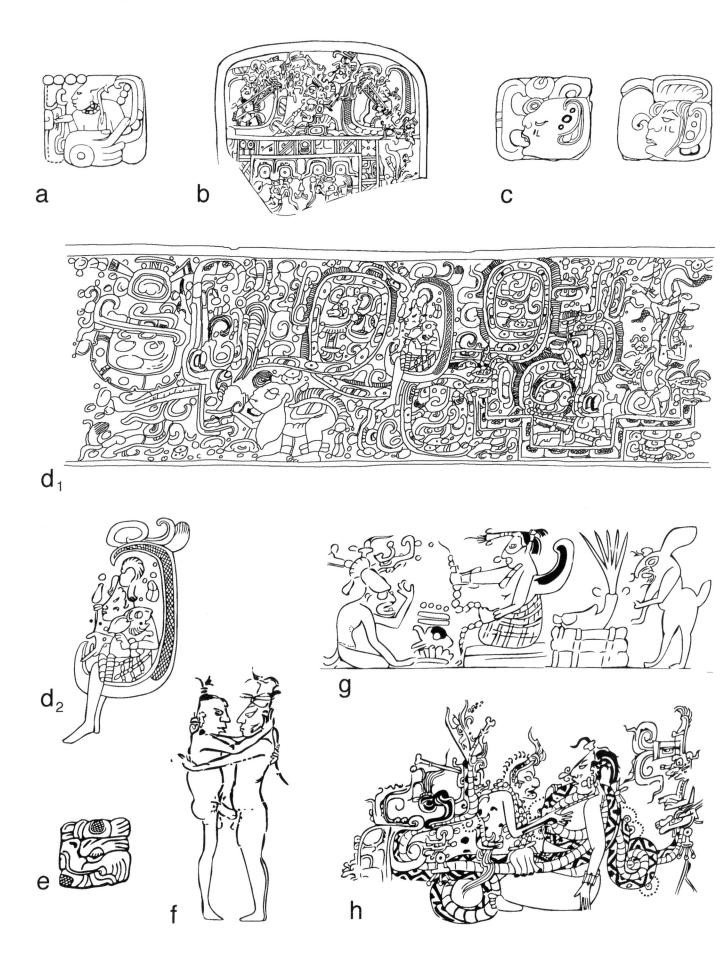

a

b

c

d₁

d₂

e

f

g

h

crescent, is used for the head variant of the number one (T1000). Martha Macri (1982) proposes that different head-variant numbers relate to different lunar phases, the head variant of the number one referring to the first visible crescent.

In the Naj Tunich cave, a Classic period painting depicts a lunar deity copulating with God N (Fig. 4.10f). The figure has hair worn in a long curl, like Goddess I of the codices, but the headdress and body shape seem masculine, making the gender ambiguous. Originally identified as the Moon Goddess, the figure is now believed to be a male impersonating a female as part of a ritual performance (Stone 1995b:143–145). Such impersonations occur in a modern Tzotzil Maya festival in which a Chamula man found guilty of sexual infractions is dressed as a woman when he plays both a clown and the Spanish Lady of Passions representing the moon/Virgin Mary deity (Gossen 1986:233).

Some terra-cotta figurines show the youthful Moon Goddess wrapping her arm around the shoulders of her animal alter ego, variously represented as a rabbit or a feline (Romain 1988, pls. 38, 39, 52). Others show her as the industrious weaver working on her backstrap loom or as a licentious courtesan embracing the old God N (Schele and Miller 1986: 143–144, pls. 51–52). These amorous couples have a counterpart in conjugal pairings of Goddess I with various gods in the codices (Fig. 4.7f–g). It is possible that the scenes involving God N refer either to an astronomical body in conjunction with the moon or to a male alter ego of the moon.

Maya vase paintings depict the young Moon Goddess in amorous scenes with God N (Taylor 1992: 523). Often she appears as a "dragon lady" wrapped in a snake while God N peers from the serpent's jaws and fondles her breasts or makes her an offering (Fig. 4.10h; Kerr 1990:210, no. 2067; Robicsek and Hales 1981, vessels 8–12). Sometimes she kneels in submission to God N cradled in the snake's jaws (Kerr 1990:272, no. 2715). The giant serpent recalls scenes showing the lunar jaguar wrapped in a snake (Pl. 4; Robicsek and Hales 1982, no. 16).

An incised vessel from the American Museum of Natural History shows a mirror-marked snake carrying a lunar crescent that encloses the Moon Goddess (Fig. 4.10d; Schele and Miller 1986:303). This looped snake is discussed in Chapter 7. She wears a short latticed bead skirt and a maize foliation in her headdress, attributes that suggest she is merged with the Maize God (Taube 1992b:68).

In Classic period Maya vase painting, the Moon Goddess may be seated on a sky-band throne with the lunar crescent, or she may have the moon sign tucked under her arm, like the Postclassic Moon Goddess on Dresden Codex 49a (Fig. 4.7i; Coe 1978b, nos. 7, 16; 1982, no. 12). In one such scene, she seems to have traits of the Jaguar War God, including a cruller wrapping around her eyes and

---

FIG. 4.10. *a:* Maize God substituting for Moon Goddess in lunar Glyph C of Lunar Series (after Thompson 1960, fig. 29, no. 17).

b: Lunar symbol used for female ancestor (Yaxchilán Stela 4; after Tate 1992, fig. 86).

c: Glyphic representations of Moon Goddess with "IL" marking on cheek and lunar crescent framing back of head (Palenque Temple XVIII; after Schele and Mathews 1979, nos. 446, 471).

d_1: Mirror-marked snake wrapped around lunar crescent enclosing Moon Goddess and her lunar rabbit, while another lunar rabbit with mirror sign blows trumpet; d_2: detail of Moon Goddess and her lunar rabbit (American Museum of Natural History vase; after Schele and Miller 1986, pl. 120a).

e: Palenque ancestor named White Heron (Zac Bak) may be ancestor with lunar connections (Temple of Cross, Palenque; after Robertson 1991, fig. 9).

f: Late Classic lunar deity copulating with God N (Drawing 18, Naj Tunich, Guatemala; after Stone 1995b, fig. 6.28).

g: Moon Goddess with cruller nose and bound hank of hair seen on Jaguar War God (after Taube 1992b, fig. 43d).

h: Snake wraps around Moon Goddess as "dragon lady" in amorous scene with God N, who emerges from jaws of snake with tail ending in image of God K (after Stone 1995b, fig. 6-30).

bound hank of hair (Fig. 4.10g). Here she wears the traditional netted skirt, and the lunar rabbit is her companion. God L's headdress with the number thirteen is placed before her throne. This is one of a number of scenes that suggest that she or her lunar rabbit has taken God L's regalia (Taube 1992b:85). She holds out beads, seeming to hand them to an aged god (God D?), evoking a connection with Colonial period glosses that say the word for moon (*u*) also means "necklace of glass beads" (Lamb 1981:246).

Ceramic paintings of the Moon Goddess most typically depict a lunar eye crescent, an underarm crescent, and a rabbit (Taylor 1992:519–521). However, Dicey Taylor points out that many lunar figures do not conform to these features. Sometimes the Moon Goddess is named with a female portrait head (T1000) bearing a hair knot above the brow and a T683 lunar crescent (Pl. 5).

A polychrome vase first published by Francis Robicsek and Donald Hales (1982, no. 1) shows a narrative sequence that represents different aspects of the moon (Pl. 5). Taylor (1992:521) interprets this as multiple views of the Moon Goddess, showing her descent into the underworld at dawn, where she joins the aged Moon lord. An interesting detail, not discussed by Taylor, is the ball-game belt she wears as she descends through the sky band. This makes her a female lunar ballplayer, apparently a counterpart for the female aspect of Xbalanque known in one version of the Popol Vuh. Subsequently, she is transformed into a lunar queen overseeing her court. Here the Moon Goddess has a water-lily headdress and a lunar name (T1000 above T683). The sequence may represent the transformation of the moon from a ballplayer to a water-lily goddess, perhaps an image of seasonal change or phase changes. Male companions in the scene include God N figures and an aged Moon Lord with a lunar title, who is seated on a jaguar-skin throne bearing what may be stylized *po* (moon) glyphs. He may be the full moon, sometimes represented as male in contemporary Maya accounts. The sky band represents the place where the ecliptic crosses the Milky Way (Chapter 7).

A codex-style vase shows masculine and feminine aspects of the moon in separate narrative vignettes (Pl. 6). The lunar twin, Yax Balam (Xbalanque), holds up a plate that contains the decapitated head of Hun Nal (Hun Hunahpu), symbolizing his father the Maize God (Coe 1989:178, fig. 27; Taube 1985, fig. 1). In my opinion, this image refers to the maize harvest. Another scene shows the dark-faced Moon Goddess seated before an ipthyphallic Maize God with liquid dripping from his penis. Taylor (1992: 522–523) identifies this scene as the resurrection of maize, with the Maize God perforating his penis in celebration of his rebirth. She notes that the Moon Goddess offers him a Xoc head (a fish?) and a Spondylus shell symbolizing the moon's role in helping in the rebirth of maize. This interpretation can be carried further because blood is equated with semen and seeds. The semen is a symbol for the maize seeds offered to the young Moon Goddess, who holds up a Spondylus shell that may be symbolic of her womb and regeneration. Even though Freidel and Schele (1988) identify the Sun and Venus as the primary icons of sacrifice and regeneration in Maya theology, it seems that the Moon is also important in imagery of cosmic rebirth. The date associated with the phallic scene is 13 Muluc 8 Zip (Schele 1992b:127). This is not a viable date, owing to the structure of the calendar; possibly this date should be 13 Muluc 7 Zip, corresponding to April 21, 626 (N.S.), near when the maize seeds would be planted.

Quiché agricultural practices explain the iconography on this vessel. The annual maize planting is done during the waxing moon, when the moon is female, but the first ears of corn are picked at the full moon, when the moon is male (B. Tedlock 1992b: 183–185). The vase shows that the young Moon Goddess receives the Maize God's seed during the waxing moon, and subsequently the masculine full moon, Yax Balam, picks the harvested maize.

Some Classic period vessels seem to show the Moon Goddess as a water carrier, a role connected with Goddess O in the codices. Coe (1982, no. 12) identifies a female holding a water jar on her shoulder as the young Moon Goddess. Her role as a water carrier is more like codical images of the aged Moon

Goddess. She has a shell painted on her garment, evoking lunar connections, and the dark face painting around the eye may also be a lunar trait.

Taube (1992b:51c) illustrates a rare Classic period image of the aged Goddess O on a painted vessel. Here the old goddess has a jaguar ear like the one symbolizing the day sign Ix and a spotted eye (Thompson 1960:89). She vomits liquid, much like the moon produces menstrual blood and rainwater, according to contemporary Maya accounts. This recalls another scene that shows a Water-lily Jaguar vomiting liquid into a jar (Kerr 1992:405, no. 3312) and Postclassic images of Goddess O issuing liquids from her body (Fig. 4.8g). Given the parallels, the Classic period Goddess O might be the waning moon during the rainy season. In light of the feline traits associated with the she-jaguar, the lunar twin in the *El Título de Totonicapán* (7v), it is certainly intriguing that the aged Goddess O may have jaguar features in the Classic and Postclassic periods.

In sum, the Moon Goddess in Classic Maya art is often accompanied by her lunar crescent, but this element is not necessarily the defining feature in her iconography. Often her lunar traits are more subtle, expressed in costume and coiffure that link her with the lunar complex. Her headdress may include a water lily or maize foliation. Her skirt sometimes has a lattice of jade beads, much like the net skirt worn by the more youthful aspects of the Moon Goddess at Chichén Itzá. She is only rarely represented in monumental sculpture, most commonly in glyphic inscriptions with a lunar infix, such as Glyph C of the Lunar Series. Other aspects of the Moon Goddess are linked with royal ancestors and lineages on monumental sculpture. The lunar lineage seems to be especially important at Palenque, where a layered metaphor refers to the ancestral Moon Goddess as the founder of a dynasty. Maya vase paintings are ideal for study of lunar imagery because they show narrative scenes that sometimes involve multiple images of the moon, apparently referring to changing phases and seasons of the moon. An aged aspect of the Classic Maya Moon Goddess is occasionally represented, but the youthful goddess is much more often represented in this medium.

THE EVER-CHANGING MOON

This chapter shows that we have only begun to unravel the mystery of the moon among the Maya. There is considerable variety in the lunar complex, quite possibly a reflection of images representing different phases and lunar seasons. The metaphor for changing lunar phases is a woman growing up and growing old, best seen in youthful and aged variants of the Moon Goddess in the codices of the Postclassic period. The youthful Goddess I may represent the moon from first visibility to the full moon. The waning moon is represented by an aged aspect of Goddess I, a hybrid variant (I-O), and Goddess O in her more human form. The aged Goddess O as the waning moon lacks monstrous features because the waning moon is not considered particularly malevolent. Only at the new moon does she take on a monstrous form with feline claws.

The two most important Postclassic lunar images are those relating to weaving and serpents, both apparently metaphorical images of lunar motion. During the dry season, the moon weaves like a weaver as it moves back and forth across the ecliptic. The dry-season Moon Goddess, usually represented by aged Goddess I or the hybrid Goddess I-O, weaves through the sky on a cotton cord, her undulating motion connected with the weaving activities of the dry season. The rainy-season Moon Goddess, usually Goddess O or hybrid forms of the goddess (I-O), pours water and wears a snake headdress symbolizing undulating lunar motion.

Metaphorical images in the codices define attributes and roles of the young Moon Goddess. The moon's rapid motion through the sky is seen in images of Goddess I as a licentious lover visiting her many sky lovers. Goddess I's connection with medicine is evident in scenes showing her carrying birds symbolizing various diseases. Her role as a mother goddess is clear in scenes showing her carrying her divine children. Judging from the frequency of deity images in the Postclassic period, the moon was more important than the sun. The reverse seems to be true in the Classic period.

Color symbolism is another element distinguishing the lunar goddesses of the codices. Different colors of the moon may relate to seasonal imagery. White often appears in the name of an old lunar goddess involved in weaving and in the name of a youthful goddess of the waxing moon associated with sexual pleasures, children, or symbols of diseases. The color red is used for aged goddesses linked with water pouring and rainbows.

The eclipsed full moon is sometimes represented by an aged face in Postclassic times, but more commonly it is a youthful female with death attributes. On the other hand, the new moon can take on a monstrous aspect closely linked with the aged Goddess O, especially when the moon threatens the sun with eclipse at the time of the new moon. Imagery of Goddess O is relatively rare in the Classic period but seems to be increasingly important in the Terminal Classic period in monumental images such as those from Chichén Itzá. Classic period images of solar and lunar eclipses are poorly understood. The key to their imagery may lie embedded in the Lunar Series glyphs that track the eclipse cycle.

During the Classic period, changing lunar phases seem to be indicated by different genders. Sometimes the Moon God is merged with the Maize God in imagery that seems to refer to the full moon, apparently reflecting a special link between the full moon and the maize harvest still seen today. The masculine moon, visualized as a jaguar ballplayer who is the twin of the sun, may also symbolize the full moon.

Coe (1989:166) notes that jaguar figures on Classic period ceramics show an "almost protean variability." Such variability may reflect transformations associated with the changing lunar seasons or phases. The Jaguar War God, also known as the Jaguar God of the Underworld, is seemingly connected with the Moon, Venus, and the dry season, the season of warfare. On the other hand, the Water-lily Jaguar is a deity that may embody the rainy-season Moon draped with seasonal vegetation. Other jaguar aspects of the Moon include Yax Balam, the counterpart to Xbalanque and God CH of the codices.

A number of animals are metaphorically linked with the moon. Fish, mollusks, frogs, and toads are connected with the moon's watery nature, for the moon seems to control all bodies of water. The lunar rabbit embodies the moon in a number of ways, and its hopping motion may even be another metaphor expressing rapid motion and the way the moon jumps back and forth across the ecliptic.

Seen in the light of natural history, lunar imagery is transformed from a bewildering array of inconsistencies to a more cohesive picture reflecting the changing aspects of the moon. The moon has remained mysterious because scholars have been looking for *the* moon. In fact, there are many moons. If we consider the four lunar phases and thirteen lunar months, there may be fifty-two different moons!

5

VENUS AND MERCURY: THE BODY DOUBLES

Of all the planets, Venus is clearly the most important in Maya art, cosmology, and calendrics. Like the Moon, Venus has multiple personalities. Different Venus gods embody various phases and seasonal aspects. Some manifestations of Venus seem to be connected with the rainy season and agricultural fertility; others reflect warfare and the dry season. A Venus cult linked with central Mexico emphasizes the feathered serpent. Central Mexican influence also is evident in a Tlaloc cult connected with Venus warfare during the Classic period. Chac, a Yucatec Maya deity merged with Tlaloc in some contexts, is also associated with Venus. Sometimes Venus and the Sun are conflated in imagery that suggests conjunction, as in the case of Hun Ahau, who is linked with both the underworld Sun and Venus.

Except for possible links with owl imagery, we have little information on Mercury, and it is difficult to identify Mercury in Maya art. The reader should be cautioned, however, that some images identified as Venus deities may actually refer to Mercury. And, in this context, we should not ignore the possibility that God N, discussed in Chapter 4, may be linked with Mercury.

This chapter begins with an analysis of the type of Venus observations made by the Maya and follows with a look at Colonial period accounts of Venus. Postclassic Venus images discussed include the Dresden Codex Venus table representing five different deities that show the Morning Star rising at different times of year. The chapter also incorporates a study of central Mexican Venus images and their relationship to Maya Venus images; an examination of Venus connections with dynastic history and the role of warfare in the Venus cult; an analysis of images that may incorporate information about the sidereal position of Venus and images that pair the Moon and Venus. It concludes with a short section on Mercury.

VENUS OBSERVATIONS AMONG THE PRECOLUMBIAN MAYA

The first and last visibility of Venus were certainly of great interest to the Maya, with the first visibility being especially important in the Dresden Codex. In calculating these events, the Dresden Codex uses canonical intervals for the different phases, rather than recording observations of the real intervals. The reappearance of the Morning Star, however, does seem to be keyed to actual observations. The Dresden Codex records the eight-year Venus Almanac, noting 584 days as the average length of an individual Venus cycle, quite close to the true average. The phases of the synodic period are modified to create canonical intervals, and only the 8-day period of inferior conjunction can be considered accurate. The codex records 90 days for superior conjunction, when the true average for this period is around 50 days, and it notes the Morning Star interval as 236 days and the Evening Star period as 250 days, although in reality these phases are approximately the same length, averaging around 263 days. As we will see, the Postclassic Maya chose canonical intervals for Venus phases in order to lock in with the lunar cycles.

The Venus Almanac of the Dresden Codex is like the *octaeteris* of classical antiquity, linking eight solar years, five Venus synodic periods, and ninety-nine lunar months (Aveni 1992b:104). In the discussion that follows, we will see architectural reliefs that incorporate the numbers five and eight as a reference to this Venus Almanac. Ceremonies alluding to the eight-year Venus Almanac are not yet documented, but records may be embedded in Maya texts. A similar interval is evident today in Lacandón rituals performed every eight years (McGee 1990:51). Furthermore, the Venus Almanac is apparent in the Aztec Atamalcualiztli festival, which can be traced back to Classic period Teotihuacán (Milbrath 1995d).

Clearly the Maya observed and recorded the changing horizon positions of Venus in relation to the eight-year Venus Almanac (Aveni 1991). The horizon extremes of Venus correlate with the beginning and end of the rainy season in Mesoamerican latitudes; the greatest northern extreme occurs in late April or early May and the southern extreme in late October or early November (Aveni 1979; 1980:93–94, fig. 37; Sprajc 1987–1988:94). Evidence for such orientations is seen at Uxmal (discussed below). At Chichén Itzá, an oblique line from the inner left to the outer right of Window 1 of the Caracol observatory points to the northern extreme of Venus as the Evening Star at 28°53′ north of west, whereas an oblique line from inner left to outer right in Window 2 points to its southern extreme at 27°49′ south of west (Fig. 3.1b). The lunar standstill alignments illustrated by Sharer (1994:fig. 7.6) are not valid; they are based on fieldwork from the 1930s that has been disproved by Aveni's work (Aveni 1975, 180, fig. 4, table 4; 1980:258–267, figs. 90–91; Aveni et al. 1975).

Since the average period when Venus was visible in the morning and evening sky is close to the length of one Tzolkin (260 days), the Maya may have used subsets of the Tzolkin to record intervals within the period of visibility. The period of ascent as the Morning Star is quite rapid (about 80 days), and the Evening Star phase involves a rapid descent when Venus seems to dive down in only 80 days. Venus is especially bright during the period of descent, but its time of greatest brilliance is when it makes its ascent in the Morning Star phase. Both the phases are represented by specific images in Maya art discussed in later sections.

Scholars have proposed that the Maya observed maximum elongations, that is, when Venus is farthest removed from the Sun (about 47°). Linda Schele and David Freidel (1990:444–446) claim that a significant position is reached when the date in question is within 1° of maximum elongation. On the other hand, Venus remains near maximum elongation for relatively long periods of time. This fact, along with the difficulty of ascertaining the exact time of greatest elongation without modern computer-generated tables, makes the greatest elongation an unlikely candidate for naked-eye observations. Nonetheless, the Maya could have noted that Venus rises three hours before the Sun around the time of maximum elongation and is therefore positioned relatively high in the sky (Aveni 1980:85). And around the spring equinox, the maximum altitude of Venus approximately coincides with its maximum elongation (H. Bricker 1996, fig. 8).

Anthony Aveni and Lorren Hotaling (1994:S31) believe that the Maya observed Venus when it was at its maximum altitude. In their analysis of a set of ninety-eight Classic Maya dates with astronomical "tags" (star glyphs or related iconography), they found that the dates often correlated with times when Venus was high in the sky (Aveni and Hotaling 1994:S34–S35). Furthermore, the astronomical dates more often coincide with Evening Star visibility, with 70 percent of the dates corresponding to that period. The Classic Maya evidently focused on the Evening Star, a conclusion confirmed in studies by Ivan Sprajc (1993a, 1993b).

Floyd Lounsbury (1982:163) notes that the retrograde period of Venus was important in the Classic period. The two stationary points bracket the short period of inferior conjunction, and maximum brilliance as Morning Star follows only a few weeks after the second stationary point, just as the Evening Star is most brilliant a few weeks before the first stationary point.

This summary of observational features associated with Venus serves as a departure point for discussion of Venus imagery. All of these Venus cycles may be evident in Maya dates and images. As will be seen, the greatest emphasis was placed on the Venus Almanac of five Venus cycles in eight solar years. Study of astronomically tagged dates suggests that the Evening Star was of greater importance during the Classic period, but the Dresden Codex shows that the Morning Star received great emphasis in the Postclassic period.

VENUS IN THE POPOL VUH

During the Colonial period, Venus is referred to as the "sun passer" and the "great star" (*nima ch'umil*) in a section of the Popol Vuh dealing with the fourth creation or world age, the historical epoch of the Quiché (Edmonson 1971:159). In previous world ages, Venus seems to have had different names.

Dennis Tedlock (1985:40, 111, 134; 1991) suggests that in a previous world age two brothers known as Hun Hunahpu and Vucub Hunahpu represented the Morning Star playing ball on the eastern horizon. When the lords of death called them to the underworld, they were killed and the Morning Star disappeared. Tedlock interprets Hun Hunahpu's decapitated head, placed in a tree by order of the death gods, as a symbol of the first visibility of the Evening Star above the horizon in the west. Hun Hunahpu's head produces semen that fertilizes the young Moon Goddess, Xquic (Blood Woman), giving birth to Hunahpu and Xbalanque. According to Tedlock, prior to their rebirth as the Sun and the Moon—an event that issues in the fourth world age—the Hero Twins took the role of the Morning Star, replacing their father and uncle (Tedlock 1991:166–168). He rec-

ognizes five episodes involving decapitated heads or balls representing heads and interprets these as five cycles in the Venus Almanac (Tedlock 1991:172–173).

Hun Hunahpu's head on the ball court may be a Venus symbol. The Popol Vuh recounts that when the Hero Twins saw their father (Hun Hunahpu), his head now transformed into a calabash fruit hanging in the fork of a tree in Xibalba, they put him back together and left him at the Place of Ball Game Sacrifice to be worshiped by future generations (D. Tedlock 1985:113, 159). Michael Closs (1989:397) assigns the role of Morning Star to Hun Hunahpu, noting that he stays behind to rule the underworld as the Morning Star when his son Hunahpu is transformed into the Sun.

Citing the fact that Hun Hunahpu's name incorporates 1 Ahau, Michael Coe (1973:93; 1975b:90) identifies Hun Hunahpu as the Morning Star and Vucub Hunahpu as the Evening Star. He notes that 1 Ahau implies heliacal rise, and Vucub Hunahpu's name (equivalent to 7 Ahau) falls 240 days later in the Tzolkin, suggesting a transformation into the Evening Star. Sprajc (1993a:40–41, 53) questions this conclusion, pointing out that the interval from the first of the Morning Star and the first of the Evening Star is 313 days on average (or 326 days in the canonical period of the Dresden Codex). He concludes that both Hun Hunahpu and Vucub Hunahpu represented the Morning Star—until their death, when Hun Hunahpu's severed head became a symbol of the Evening Star with its fertilizing powers. Another possibility is that the period of 240 days approximates the interval between the first and last day of the Morning Star (given as 236 in the Dresden Codex), in which case Hun Hunahpu could represent the first of the Morning Star and Vucub Hunahpu the Morning Star as it disappears.

David Kelley (1980:S26) identifies Hun Hunahpu as the Maize God and the embodiment of Venus, noting that his name means 1 Ahau (Hun Ahau) in Yucatec. Karl Taube (1992b:48) agrees that the Maize God is the counterpart of Hun Hunahpu, but he distinguishes Hun Ahau as a separate entity linked with Hunahpu. Taube (1992b:116) concludes that Hun Ahau in his death aspect is the same as the chief demon of the underworld known as Hun Ahau in Landa's Colonial period account (Tozzer 1941:132 n. 618). The Motul dictionary glosses a similar name (Cumhau) as "Lucifer, prince of the devils." Eric Thompson (1970b:303) points out that Lucifer denotes both devil and the Morning Star. This may also explain why the Morning Star is sometimes linked with the devil in Maya ethnographic accounts (Closs 1989:395). Taube's interpretation finds support in the fact that Hunahpu (Junajpu) is named as the Morning Star by the contemporary Quiché (Chapter 1). If this is the case, the Popol Vuh implies that the Morning Star is transformed into the Sun at the beginning of the fourth world age.

In sum, one or more sets of brothers may play the role of Venus in the Popol Vuh. The situation is not clear because there are conflicting points of view and evidence can be marshaled to support identifying both Hun Hunahpu and Hunahpu with the Morning Star. Whether their brothers were also aspects of Venus remains debatable. Based on evidence presented in Chapter 3, it seems that Hunahpu symbolizes the underworld Sun, closely linked with the Morning Star, which announces the Sun's emergence from the underworld. Perhaps this image also represents Venus in inferior conjunction with the Sun. This would help account for the underworld aspect of Hunahpu. Hun Hunahpu may take the role of Venus in the other underworld phase (superior conjunction) or the Evening Star emerging from the underworld.

COLONIAL AND POSTCLASSIC IMAGES OF VENUS

Some names recorded in the Colonial period refer to different Venus phases. Among the most intriguing is *chac ec,* a reddish wasp that does not sting, used as a reference to the Morning Star in the *Ritual of the Bacabs* (Roys 1965:132, 135). Some dictionary references allude to the Evening Star aspect, such as *ah oczah kin* (he who makes the sun enter [the underworld]) and *hózan ek,* glossed as "the star of the evening," named as the black Bacab of the west (Lamb 1981:235, 242–243). Dictionary entries glossed simply as "Morning Star" or "Evening Star" are usually interpreted as Venus, even though the planet is not always named.

Some terms seem to refer to Venus in both morning and evening skies. Among the recorded names are *noh ek* (big star), *chac ek* (red or great star), *chac noh ek* (red, big star), and *xux ek* (wasp star; Lamb 1981:242–243). All these names appear in contemporary Yucatec dictionaries (Barrera Vásquez 1980). *Noh ich,* meaning "great eye," is a name for Venus that implies a dual nature because *ich* can also mean "twin" (Galindo 1994:81).

Arthur Miller (1982:86) describes sky-band

FIG. 5.1. *a:* Venus as diving god with insect traits (eclipse table on Dresden Codex 58; after Villacorta and Villacorta 1977).

b: Tulum diving god adopts pose similar to images of Maya bees (Structure 25; after Tozzer 1957, fig. 256a).

c: Diving god holding honeycomb, probably representing Venus as Evening Star (Late Postclassic ceramic vessel, Mayapán, Regional Museum of Anthropology, Mérida).

d: Diving-bee god (Madrid Codex 80; after Tozzer 1957, fig. 256b).

e: Postclassic Mixteca-Puebla images of insects with star-tipped wings (Codex Nuttall 19, 38; after Seler 1960–1961, 4:729, figs. 919, 923).

f: Morning Star as Lahun Chan ("10 Sky") with scorpion carapace on torso and stinger terminating in Venus glyph (T510f); maize-foliation headdress may refer to season of ripening maize (Dresden Codex 47b; after Seler 1904a, fig. 101i).

g: Striped star warriors suspended from sky band with Ollin sun and Venus glyphs with rays alternating with lobed designs that represent star-tipped insect wings (Codex Nuttall 21; after Seler 1960–1961, 3:219, fig. 15).

h: Evening Star, Xolotl, faces Sun descending into underworld with skeletal Morning Star disappearing in conjunction (Codex Borbonicus 16; after Séjourné 1976, fig. 26).

i: Nocturnal new-year ceremonies of Ix years with crescent moon and howling dog bearing T559 design on rib cage (T559 also in companion glyphic text), probably refers to Evening Star as Tzul Ahau, or Tsul Ahaw in revised orthography (Madrid Codex 37; after Villacorta and Villacorta 1977).

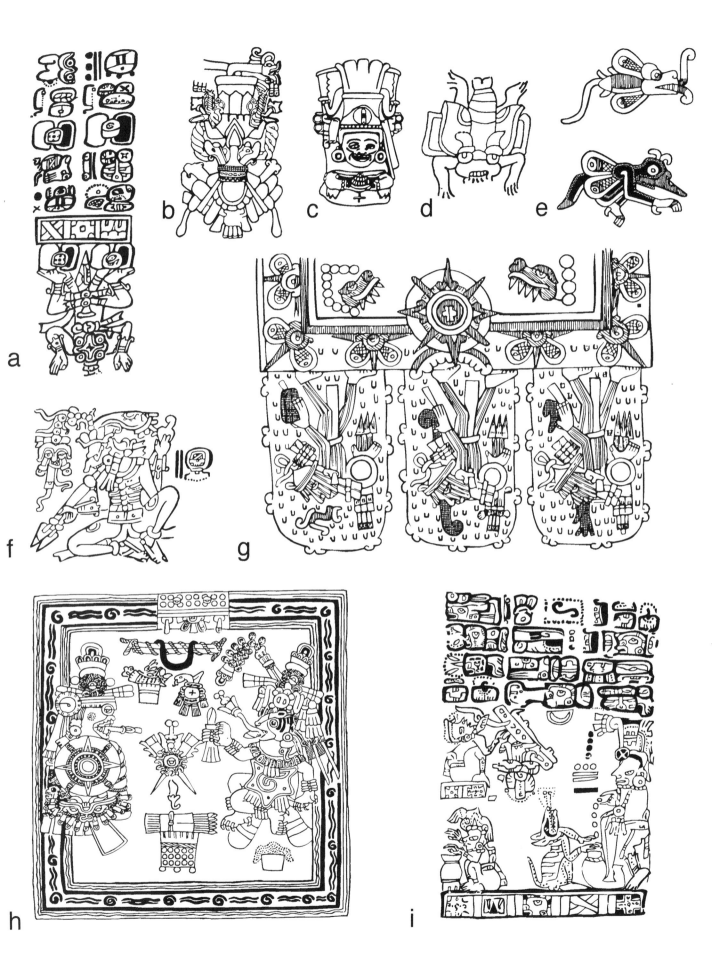

designs on Postclassic murals from Santa Rita and Tulum as stylized images of Venus as the "wasp star" (Fig. 3.3b). Stanislaw Iwaniszewski (1987:211) suggests that a relief on Structure 5 represents Venus as a diving figure (Marquina 1964, pl. 399). Ralph Roys (1967:63 n. 7) identifies the Tulum diving figures as the Maya bee god, Ah Muzencab. Structures 5, 16, and 25 all depict similar figures that resemble Maya images of bees (Fig. 5.1b, d). Indeed, at the Regional Museum of Anthropology in Mérida, a Late Postclassic ceramic vessel depicts a similar diving god holding a honeycomb framed by stacked log hives (Fig. 5.1c). The Mixteca-Puebla Codex Nuttall depicts bees and possibly wasps with pairs of gauzy wings (Fig. 5.1e). The connection between Venus and bees and wasps is evident because the wings are very similar to Venus symbols in sky bands of the same codex. These have a star in the center radiating two gauzy wings that alternate with three red rays (Fig. 5.1g). The Venus glyph seems to represent the insect aspect of Venus. The five radiating elements allude to the "fiveness" of Venus implicit in the Venus Almanac's five synodic periods.

Although Arthur Miller (1982:87, 89–91, 97) links the Tulum diving figures to the cult of the Morning Star, they seem more closely connected with imagery of the Evening Star. The diving pose evokes Venus making its rapid descent over the course of 80 days. These diving gods are positioned on the west face of the temple structures, and the temples themselves have a west-facing entry, a pattern that would seem to be linked with the Evening Star (Sprajc 1993a, 1993b). Maize foliation on the headdress of the diving god at Tulum is appropriate in light of a pattern linking maize and the Evening Star noted by Sprajc (Fig. 5.1b). Cords attached to the diving gods probably symbolize the ecliptical cord linking the sky and Earth, as well as a path of descent for Venus moving into the underworld. This is reminiscent of images of Venus as Ehecatl-Quetzalcoatl descending on a cord in the Codex Vindobonensis (Fig. 5.4f; Milbrath 1988a).

In the Dresden Codex eclipse table (58b), a bee or wasp aspect of Venus is represented by a diving god with a Venus glyph as its head and a knifelike tail that suggests an insect abdomen (Fig. 5.1a; Aveni 1992b:

71). Closs (1989:405–406) suggests that Venus acts as the cause or agent of eclipse in this image.

A Venus god plays the role of a Bacab raising the heavens after the great flood. The Chilam Balam of Chumayel notes that Lahun Chan (10 Sky) went to the west, where the black tree of abundance was located, when the four Bacabs took their position at cardinal points to raise the sky after the great flood. Roys (1967:100–101, 171) suggests that Lahun Chan's placement in the west equates him with the Bacab called Hozanek, a name for the Evening Star in Colonial period sources. Lahun Chan is the same as Lakunchan, an idol with very ugly teeth and claws described by Diego López de Cogolludo (Roys 1967:101 n. 2). From various accounts, Thompson (1960:77, 218) concludes that Lahun Chan had the head of a jaguar and the body of a dog, and he walked like a drunkard. As we will see, Lahun Chan is more closely connected with the Morning Star. The flood account may indicate that the Morning Star was sent to the west in a time of turmoil.

In the Dresden Codex, the glyphic name 10 Sky identifies Lahun Chan, the same name used in Colonial period accounts (Fig. 5.1f). Maize foliation on his headdress leads Closs (1989:397) to compare him to Xolotl, the Aztec god of the Evening Star who brought maize to humankind, according to the *Anales de Cuauhtitlán*. The Codex Borbonicus pairs the canine Xolotl with the Sun descending into the underworld, clearly indicating a role as the Evening Star (Fig. 5.1h). Closs suggests that Lahun Chan is the counterpart of a Maya dog deity named Tsul Ahaw (Tzul Ahau), because of the resemblance of Lahun Chan's rib cage to T559, a glyph interpreted logographically as "dog" (*tsul* or *tzul*). One of the New Year pages in the Madrid Codex clearly shows a dog with a similar T559 rib cage howling at the Moon (Fig. 5.1i). Indeed, the name Tsul Ahaw appears as the last glyph compound on the page, a name apparently linked with the Evening Star (Fig. 5.7r; Closs 1989, fig. 31.5). The Evening Star may be Tsul Ahaw as Closs proposes, but this name, associated with a canine figure and a diving insect in the codices, is not used for Lahun Chan (Fig. 5.1a). Lahun Chan clearly plays the role of the Morning Star in the Dresden Codex, and he has a different glyphic

FIG. 5.2. Introduction to Venus table listing names for Venus in first column (A5–A9); in second column: God N, Moon Goddess, Hun Ahau, Mars Beast?, and Death God as regents (B5–B9); in third column: God L and Lahun Chan as Morning Stars (C4–C8) and God K as first in list of five victims (C8–C12); followed by 9.9.9.16.0 (2/4/623), one day before new Moon on 2/5/623 (Dresden Codex 24; after Villacorta and Villacorta 1977).

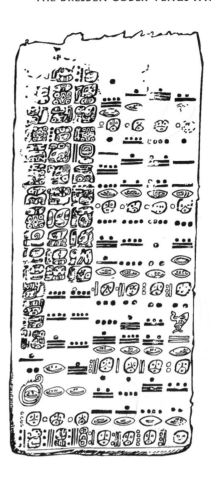

name (10 Sky; Fig. 5.1f). Indeed, Lahun Chan does not even have canine traits. On close inspection we can see that Lahun Chan's torso is the scorpion thorax seen on other Venus gods, such as God L in the Madrid Codex (Fig. 5.11b). This is made clear by the fact that Lahun Chan's headdress has a beaded element representing the scorpion's segmented tail, here terminating with a Venus glyph. The "rib cage" on the dog of the Evening Star is a scorpion thorax (Fig. 5.1i).

In sum, the Colonial period accounts relate to Postclassic imagery of Venus, most notably in the insect aspects of Venus. A diving bee or wasp may be linked with imagery of the Evening Star's rapid descent. Venus is also equated with a sky-bearer or Bacab (Hozanek) associated with the Evening Star. Lahun Chan, named in Colonial period records, has his counterpart in Postclassic representations of Venus as the Morning Star, where he has scorpion traits also

seen on the canine Evening Star. As we will see, the best single source of evidence for imagery of the Postclassic Venus god is found in the Dresden Codex.

THE DRESDEN CODEX VENUS PAGES

The Dresden Codex Venus pages (46–50) depict the most intriguing astronomical images in the Maya codices (Fig. 5.3). This section of the codex has long been recognized as a Venus Almanac, but its relationship to the chronology of the Yucatec Maya has been debated.

John Teeple (1926) showed that the Maya adjusted for the difference between the true length of the synodic period and the canonical Venus Round (VR) of 584 days by including corrections so that the Tzolkin calendar of 260 days and the Venus calendar would synchronize with the rise of the Morning Star on a day 1 Ahau. They accomplished this by

FIG. 5.3. *a:* God L as Morning Star at heliacal rise embodying Venus as dry-season warrior god killing God K (Jupiter?); regent on sky-band throne wears headdress that may represent Mars Beast (Dresden Codex 46; after Villacorta and Villacorta 1977).

b: Lahun Chan as Morning Star rising during season of green corn; his victim below is Water-lily Jaguar representing rainy-season Moon; regent is death god (Dresden Codex 47; after Villacorta and Villacorta 1977).

c: Howler monkey as Morning Star, associated with name linked with Tlahuizcalpantecuhtli, depicts Venus rising at dawn when maize planting season begins; his victim is Maize God; regent is God N (Dresden Codex 48; after Villacorta and Villacorta 1977).

d: Central Mexican Xiuhtecuhtli as Morning Star rising at beginning of dry season; he spears turtle god (Orion) as sign of drought; regent is Moon Goddess pouring seawater from her seashell jar (Dresden Codex 49; after Villacorta and Villacorta 1977).

e: Itztlacoliuhqui, counterpart to central Mexican god of frost, as Morning Star rising on 1 Ahau 13 Mac, just before summer solstice in A.D. 1227; his victim is an enigmatic god possibly associated with fish; regents are Maize God and Hun Ahau (Dresden Codex 50; after Villacorta and Villacorta 1977).

f–j. Layout of Venus cycle on Dresden Codex 46–50 with Calendar Round dates (after Thompson 1972: 66). Line 15, omitted by Thompson, is the "mirror-in-hand" glyph compound, which appears with T181 on all pages except page 46, the first page, and the last column before the Venus god on page 50. Letters A–T (lines 17 and 21) refer to a sequence of deity names.

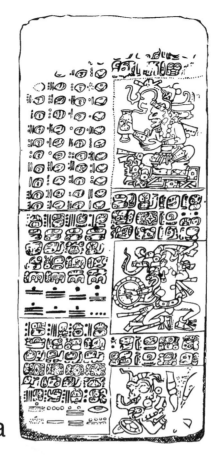

a

b

f

Line	Cib	Cimi	Cib	Kan
1	3	2	5	13
2	11	10	13	8
3	6	5	8	3
4	1	13	3	11
5	9	8	11	6
6	4	3	6	1
7	12	11	1	9
8	7	6	9	4
9	2	1	4	12
10	10	9	12	7
11	5	4	7	2
12	13	12	2	10
13	8	7	10	5
14	4	14	19	7
	Yaxkin	Zac	Zec	Xul
16	N.	W.	S.	E.
17	A	B	C	D
18	Red ½	Red ½	Red ½	Red ½
	Venus	Venus	Venus	Venus
19	236	326	576	584
20	8	18	4	12
	Zac	Muan	Yax	Yax
21	T	A	B	C
22	Winged	Winged	Winged	Winged
	Chuen	Chuen	Chuen	Chuen
23	Red	Red	Red	Red
	Venus	Venus	Venus	Venus
24	E.	N.	W.	S.
25	19	4	14	2
	Kayab	Zotz'	Pax	Kayab
26	236	90	250	8
				Page 46

g

Line	Ahau	Oc	Ahau	Lamat
1	2	1	4	12
2	10	9	12	7
3	5	4	7	2
4	13	12	2	10
5	8	7	10	5
6	3	2	5	13
7	11	10	13	8
8	6	5	8	3
9	1	13	3	11
10	9	8	11	6
11	4	3	6	1
12	12	11	1	9
13	7	6	9	4
14	3	8	18	6
	Cumku	Zotz'	Pax	Kayab
16	N.	W.	S.	E.
17	E	F	G	H
18	Red	Red	Red	1
	Venus	Venus	Venus	Venus
19	820	910	1160	1168
20	3	13	18	6
	Zotz'	Mol	Uo	Zip
21	D	E	F	G
22	..	..	..	
23	Red	Red	Red	Red
	Venus	Venus	Venus	Venus
24	E.	N.	W.	S.
25	13	3	8	16
	Yax	Muan	Ch'en	Ch'en
26	236	90	250	8
				Page 47

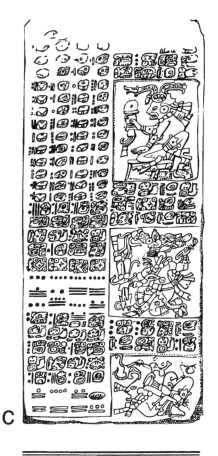

Line	Kan	Ix	Kan	Eb
1	1	13	3	11
2	9	8	11	6
3	4	3	6	1
4	12	11	1	9
5	7	6	9	4
6	2	1	4	12
7	10	9	12	7
8	5	4	7	2
9	13	12	2	10
10	8	7	10	5
11	3	2	5	13
12	11	10	13	8
13	6	5	8	3
14	17	7	12	0
15	Yax	Muan	Ch'en	Yax
16	N.	W.	S.	E.
17	I	J	K	L
18	Red	Red	Red	Red
	Venus	Venus	Venus	Venus
19	1404	1494	1744	1752
20	2	7	17	5
	Muan	Pop	Mac	Kankin
21	Winged	Winged	Winged	Winged
	Chuen	Chuen	Chuen	Chuen
22	H	I	J	K
23	..	..	..	..
24	E.	N.	W.	S.
25	7	17	2	10
	Zip	Yaxkin	Uo	Uo
26	236	90	250	8

Page 48

Line	Lamat	Etz'nab	Lamat	Cib
1	13	12	2	10
2	8	7	10	5
3	3	2	5	13
4	11	10	13	8
5	6	5	8	3
6	1	13	3	11
7	9	8	11	6
8	4	3	6	1
9	12	11	1	9
10	7	6	9	4
11	2	1	4	12
12	10	9	12	7
13	5	4	7	2
14	11	1	6	14
15	Zip	Mol	Uo	Uo
16	N.	W.	S.	E.
17	M	N	O	P
18	Red	Red	Red	Red
	Venus	Venus	Venus	Venus
19	1988	2078	2328	2336
20	16	6	11	19
	Yaxkin	Ceh	Xul	Xul
21	Winged	Winged	Winged	Winged
	Chuen	Chuen	Chuen	Chuen
22	L	M	N	O
23	Red	Red	Red	Red
	Venus	Venus	Venus	Venus
24	E.	N.	W.	S.
25	6	16	1	9
	Kankin	Chuen	Mac	Mac
26	236	90	250	8

Page 49

Line	Eb	Ik	Eb	Ahau
1	12	11	1	9
2	7	6	9	4
3	2	1	4	12
4	10	9	12	7
5	5	4	7	2
6	13	12	2	10
7	8	7	10	5
8	3	2	5	13
9	11	10	13	8
10	6	5	8	3
11	1	13	3	11
12	9	8	11	6
13	4	3	6	1
14	10	0	5	13
15	Kankin	Uayeb	Mac	Mac
16	N.	W.	S.	E.
17	Q	R	S	T
18	Red	Red	Red	Red
	Venus	Venus	Venus	Venus
19	2572	2662	2912	2920
20	15	0	10	18
	Cumku	Zec	Kayab	Kayab
21		Winged	Winged	Winged
	Chuen	Chuen	Chuen	Chuen
22	P	Q	R	S
23	Red	Red	Red	Red
	Venus	Venus	Venus	Venus
24	E.	N.	W.	S.
25	0	10	15	3
	Yaxkin	Cumku		Xul
26	236	90	250	8

Page 50

subtracting four days at the end of sixty-one Venus Rounds (35,624 days or 97.5 years) or by subtracting eight days at the end of fifty-seven Venus Rounds.

Scholars disagree as to whether the table shows a real ephemeris used to predict observable positions of the planet. Closs (1992) argues that the table represents idealized Venusian synodic periods, representing the mean motions of the planets. On the other hand, Lounsbury's (1983) study places the Venus table in the context of Postclassic Maya chronology, correlating the heliacal rise events with specific dates. I favor the latter interpretation and believe that it may be possible to relate the table to observations of Venus at heliacal (dawn) rise as part of a seasonal cycle.

The reference to Long Count dates in the introduction and the Calendar Round dates in the almanac itself present the possibility of placing the images of five Venus gods in the setting of real time, helping to reveal their seasonal associations. The Dresden Codex Venus pages (46–50) represent five different gods of the Morning Star hurling a dart with an atlatl. Eduard Seler (1904b) recognized that the format of five Venus gods spearing victims with atlatls parallels scenes in the Postclassic codices of the Borgia group. Each of the five manifestations is separated from the next by an interval of 584 days, closely approximating the synodic period of Venus. Each subsequent dawn rise occurs about a year and seven months later, and the entire cycle repeats every eight years.

John Justeson (1989:100–101) notes that the use of fixed stations for the Venus cycle in the vague year (365 days) arose because the canonical Venus Round of 584 days does not accommodate well to the 260-day Tzolkin, repeating only after a prohibitively long period of time (104 years), whereas the eight-year intervals provide a relatively short period for repeats. This suggests that the Venus Almanac developed in tandem with the solar calendar.

Ernst Förstemann (1906), a German librarian in Dresden, first recognized that pages 46–50 represent a Venus calendar approximating the average synodic period of Venus (583.92 days). The layout of the pages in Dresden Codex 46–50 presented by Thompson (1960:222; 1972:66) shows that each line running across five pages totals eight years (Fig.

5.3f–j). The dates in the vague year appear on lines 14, 20, and 25. The Tzolkin dates are on lines 1–13, and the subdivisions of the 584-day Venus cycle are on line 26. The Venus cycle incorporates four canonical intervals: 236 days as Morning Star, 90 days of invisibility around superior conjunction, 250 days as Evening Star, and 8 days of invisibility around inferior conjunction, an interval that actually can vary from 0 days up to a few weeks (Aveni and Hotaling 1994:S25). Aveni (1980:184–187) points out that only the 8-day period of inferior conjunction approximates the average interval for the corresponding Venus event. The other intervals used in the table are far off the mark. He notes that the Venus periods in the Dresden Codex are rounded off to conform with lunar intervals (Aveni 1992a; Justeson 1989).

This cycle joins the Sun, the Moon, and Venus in a celestial dance that repeats its sequence every eight years (Aveni 1997:123–124). Aveni (1991:315; 1992a:89–90) notes that the table expresses the occurrence of Venus events in lunar time units, allowing the Moon to be observed in relation to Venus. Teeple (1930) pointed out that the canonical Morning Star interval of 236 days has a lunar significance ($236 = 8 \times 29.5$). Thus the Moon would be in the same phase at the end of this period as it was when Venus rose at dawn. The 90-day interval for superior conjunction is three lunar months plus 1.5 days, a leeway reflecting differences in the length of the lunar month (29.5 days registered as alternating periods of 29 or 30 days). Justeson (1989:94–95) points out that the 90th day is the first date that the Evening Star was visible when the Moon was in the same lunar phase as when Venus rose as the Morning Star. He suggests that the unusual 90-day interval for superior conjunction was a Postclassic invention triggered by a particular eclipse, following Aveni's (1990:315) discovery that the historical base dates of the Venus table are linked to a cycle of eclipses visible in Yucatán. Justeson (1989:95) adds that the number of lunar months incorporated in the table (8 + 3 lunar months and 3 + 8.5 lunar months) are "spans frequently separating, respectively, pairs of visible lunar eclipses and a lunar-solar or solar-lunar eclipse sequence." It is no coincidence that the length of the Venus table equals the length of three eclipse tables plus eight cycles of 260 days, for the Maya related lunar and Venus phenomena (Aveni 1992b:104).

After five Venus Rounds, the seasonal cycle of Venus repeats (5 × 584 = 8 × 365), establishing a pattern linking each Venus Round to different times of year. Over time there would be shift, but the slippage between Venus events and the associated solar dates occurs rather slowly, for the planet appears an average of 5.2 days earlier every two Calendar Rounds (104 years; Lounsbury 1983:4, 9). The Maya adjusted by stopping short of a complete run through the table at an earlier 1 Ahau date that was found to be closer to heliacal rising of the Morning Star. This new date then served as a new base for the table. The original base was 1 Ahau 18 Kayab (Fig. 5.3f–j, lines 13 and 20), and the last time this base was used was in A.D. 1038 (10.10.11.12.0). By this time a 5.2-day error had accumulated from the previous heliacal rise on 1 Ahau 18 Kayab 104 years earlier (65VR) in A.D. 934. By the next pass through the table on the 57th VR (line 12, Fig. 5.3g), the table would call for a heliacal rise on 9 Lamat, but the heliacal rise had slipped back so that it was closer to a 1 Ahau date 8 days earlier. At this point they shifted to 1 Ahau 18 Uo on lines 12 and 20 (10.15.4.2.0; 12/4/1129 O.S.). This replacement base involved an 8-day correction. Around the time the table was actually in use, a new base was introduced involving a 4-day correction that shifted the heliacal rise to 1 Ahau 13 Mac in A.D. 1227 (lines 13 and 14). Subsequently another 4-day correction would realign the Venus Almanac on 1 Ahau 3 Xul in A.D. 1324. These dates are called bases because they are the "day zero" for a specific calendar sequence.

The introduction to the Venus table on pages 46–50 of the Dresden Codex appears on page 24. Although the page numbers imply that the introduction was separated from the table, Thompson (1972:18) notes that the codex was split in two and improperly numbered. He rearranges the pages in his commentary to the codex but retains the earlier page numbers because of long-standing use.

Page 24 opens with glyphic texts referring to a list of Venus names (column A5–A9, Fig. 5.2) paired with the names for regents (column B5–B9), alongside a third column that names victims speared by the Morning Star (last five names in column C). Each column closes with a series of calendric inscriptions (Table 5.1). Using X to mark the place of noncalendric texts, we can diagram the calendar periods to be read from top to bottom (lines 1–27) across columns A–G. Calendar Round dates appear in columns A–C at the bottom, and presumably also at the top, but here they no longer survive except for the date 8 Cumku at C2. Figures in parentheses indicate the total number of days or Venus Rounds.

The numbers begin with 6.2.0 displayed vertically in column A (lines 21–24), followed by 9.9.16.0.0 in column B (lines 14–19), and 9.9.9.16.0 in column C (lines 18–24). The Calendar Round date of 1 Ahau 18 Kayab at the bottom of Column B belongs with a Long Count date, displaced by one column apparently because there was not sufficient space. Columns D through G display multiples of 584 days, except for lines 7–12, which are correction or calculation factors (Table 5.1). The 6.2.0 inscription in Column A is a Ring Number, with a ring around a shell representing zero, indicating it is to be used in addition or subtraction of an interval totaling 2,200 days.

The date 9.9.9.16.0 1 Ahau 18 Kayab corresponds to 2/4/623 (in the 584,283 correlation preferred here; 2/6/623 in Lounsbury 1983). This is the earliest date in the table. It is designated as Base A, the first of a series of fixed dates that mark entry points in the table (Lounsbury 1983, table 3). Base A falls more than two weeks before the heliacal rise of Venus, but Lounsbury (1983:4, fig. 1) considers this an acceptable error because the date was calculated back to a time centuries before the table was recorded. It may be that the Base A date is not an error, but instead refers to a lunar observation made prior to the heliacal rise of Venus. Aveni (1992, table 3.2) notes that the 9.9.9.16.0 date was one of a number of the bases keyed to lunar eclipses. The 9.9.9.16.0 date, one day before the new moon on 2/5/623, represents the last visibility of the Moon in the month following a lunar eclipse on 1/22/623 (Goldstine 1973). The last visible crescent may have begun the lunar month in Classic Maya times (Chapter 4).

The 9.9.16.0.0 inscription in column B is usually interpreted as a Long Reckoning (LR) distance num-

TABLE 5.1. CALENDAR INSCRIPTIONS ON DRESDEN CODEX 24

LINE	A	B	C	D	E	F	G
1	X*	X	X*	1*			
2				1*	15*	10*	5*
3	X	X	8 Cumku	1	16*	10*	5*
4	X	X	X	14	6	16	8
5	X	X	X	0 (260 VR) (151,840 d)	0 (195 VR) (113,220 d)	0 (130 VR) (75,920 d)	0 (65 VR) (37,960 d)
6				1 Ahau	1 Ahau	1 Ahau	1 Ahau
7	X	X	X	1			
8	X	X	X	5	9	4	1
9				14	11	12	5
10	X	X	X	4	7	8	5
11	X	X	X	0 (185,120 d)	0 (68,900 d)	0 (33,280 d)	0 (9,100 d)
12				1 Ahau	1 Ahau	1 Ahau	1 Ahau
13	X	X	X	4	4	4	3
14	X	X	X	17	9	1	13
15	X	X	X	6	4	2	0
16	X	X	X	0 (60 VR) (35,040 d)	0 (55 VR) (32,120 d)	0 (50 VR) (29,200 d)	0 (45 VR) (26,280 d)
17	X			6 Ahau	11 Ahau	3 Ahau	8 Ahau

ber giving the interval from the beginning of the era in 4 Ahau 8 Cumku (Thompson 1972:62). It counts 1,366,560 days since the beginning of the current era, when the chronological "odometer" began again after it reached its maximum at 13.0.0.0.0 4 Ahau 8 Cumku, signaling a new count of 13 Baktuns (on August 11, 3114 B.C., in the Gregorian calendar or September 6, 3114 B.C., in the Julian Calendar). The number 9.9.16.0.0 (1,366,560 days) represents an idealized value for bringing a Venus event back to the same place in the tropical year, and it corresponds to many different calendric cycles (Aveni

1980:192; 1981:S3–S4; Lounsbury 1978; McCluskey 1983:96, 99; Thompson 1960:226). This interval can be divided without remainder by the following cycles: the cycle of Nine Lords of the Night; the 20-day Uinal; the 260-day Tzolkin; the 365-day Haab; the 584-day Venus synodic period; the 780-day Mars synodic period; the 8-year Venus Almanac cycle of 2,920 days; the shorter eclipse cycle of 9,360 days; the Calendar Round of 18,980 days; and the great Venus cycle of 37,960 days (104 years).

The introduction continues to the right in Columns D–G, with four columns divided into five

TABLE 5.1. (*continued*)

LINE	A	B	C	D	E	F	G
18	X	9	9	3	2	2	2
19	X	9	9	4	16	8	0
20	X	16	9	16	14	12	10
21	6			0 (40 VR) (23,360 d)	0 (35 VR) (20,440 d)	0 (30 VR) (17,520 d)	0 (25 VR) (14,600 d)
22	2	0	16	13 Ahau	5 Ahau	10 Ahau	2 Ahau
23				1	1		
24	0	0	0	12	4	16	8
25				5 ***	6	4	2
26	(2,200 d)	(2,340 VR) (1,366,560 d)		0 (20 VR) (11,680 d)	0 (15 VR) (8,760 d)	0 (10 VR) (5,840 d)	0 (5 VR) (2,920 d)
27	4 Ahau 8 Cumku	1 Ahau 18 Kayab	1 Ahau 18 Uo	7 Ahau	12 Ahau	4 Ahau	8 Ahau **

Note: Numbers in parentheses refer to equivalents in numbers of days (d) and Venus Rounds (VR).

* Information missing from table.

** Date written as 8 Ahau should be 9 Ahau to reflect addition of 5 Venus Rounds to 1 Ahau base date.

*** 1.12.5.0 should be 1.12.8.0 for 20 Venus Rounds.

tiers, each ending with an Ahau Tzolkin date. The top tier (lines 1–6) and the bottom three tiers (lines 13–27) show multiples of 584-day Venus Rounds (VR) in decreasing order as you move down and across the page. The inscriptions on lines 7–12 of the second tier have been interpreted as correction factors or calculation factors. All but one of these seem to be intervals that lead from an earlier base to a later one, for they add one or more foreshortened runs of the table to locate a new base on a day 1 Ahau (Lounsbury 1992b:207–208). For example, the 4.12.8.0 inscription (33,280 days) in column F of the second tier is 57 VR minus 8 days or 65 VR (37,960 days) minus 2 × 2,340 days (approximately 4 VR). Lounsbury (1992b) proposes that each of the correction factors involves subtracting a multiple of

2,340 days from a multiple of 65 VR. And each 2,340-day subtraction results in a 4-day correction, while preserving the Tzolkin day 1 Ahau, because 2,340 is divisible by 260 days without remainder, and it is 4 × 584 + 4 days. One of these intervals (1.5.5.0 or 9,100 days; lines 8–11 in column G) had been identified as an error in the table (Thompson 1972: 63). However, Lounsbury (1992b:207–212) has a different explanation for the recorded interval; he proposes that it is another base-shifting mechanism like the other numbers in the second tier, because 1.5.5.0 (16 VR minus 244 days) involves a 244-day correction (236 + 8d), incorporating the canonical intervals of Morning Star and inferior conjunction. Adjustment by subtracting intervals from the Great Venus Round of 37,960 days (65 × 584 days) allowed a foreshortened run through the table, permitting a new base to be located on the date 1 Ahau when the heliacal rise of Venus strayed too far from the canonical 1 Ahau date. On the other hand, both Closs (1977:92) and Justeson (1989:93, 97–98) consider the 1.5.5.0 interval to be a calculation factor referring to 15 Venus Rounds plus 340 days, equivalent to the interval from canonical setting of the Morning Star to the subsequent canonical setting of the Evening Star (15 × 584 + 90 + 250 = 9,100 days). Justeson also notes that this interval is useful in calculating eclipse cycles between base dates (1 Ahau 18 Kayab base to 1 Ahau 13 Mac base = 9.11.7.0 days [column E]; 9.11.7.0 − 1.5.5.0 = 2,025 lunar months). Closs says the calculation factor spans the interval from heliacal rise on 1 Ahau 18 Kayab in 9.9.9.16.0 forward to the heliacal rising of the Evening Star on 1 Ahau 13 Pax, a date not among the recorded bases on page 24, but given in the almanac section on page 47.

The bottom three tiers (lines 13–27, Columns D–G) refer to even multiples of Venus cycles, each associated with an Ahau date that would be reached by adding the given multiple to the 1 Ahau base (Table 5.1). The last tier ends with the inscription 8.2.0, equaling five Venus Rounds and eight years (2,920 days). This inscription leads in to pages 46–50, which represent sets of five Venus Rounds. The Calendar Round dates on pages 46–50 place the five Venus Rounds in relation to eight solar years.

In sum, we can see that the introduction to the table places the Venus events in historical perspective, referring back to a Long Count date of 9.9.9.16.0, the historical base of the table in the seventh century keyed to the last visible crescent just before the heliacal rise of Venus. The introduction also provides the framework for counting forward in time from the early Postclassic period, when the codex was in use at the time of the 1 Ahau 13 Mac base in A.D. 1227.

THE LAYOUT OF PAGES 46–50

In Dresden Codex 46–50, each of the five pages covers 584 days, with a cumulative total across five pages of 2,920 days, equaling five Venus cycles or eight solar years of 365 days (Fig. 5.3a–e). The thirteen rows

of Tzolkin dates at the top indicate that the table was reused thirteen times for a total of 65 (13 × 5) Venus Rounds or 104 vague years (65 d × 584 d = 37,960 d = 104 y = 146 Tzolkins). Thus the table relates the Venus cycle to the solar year and the Great Cycle of two Calendar Rounds (2 × 52 years). The Venus Round interval of 584 days is slightly longer than the true length of the Venus cycle (583.92 days), so an error of approximately 5 days accumulated over 104 years (Lounsbury 1983:9).

Thompson (1960:77, 218, 299; 1972:65) notes that the idealized Venus cycle always ended on the day 1 Ahau, a day that probably named Venus at heliacal rise. Because two columns of Tzolkin dates on page 47 include 1 Ahau dates, a new 1 Ahau base could be adopted when the calendar strayed too far from the real heliacal rise date (Fig. 5.3g). Apparently, the Maya waited to make correction until they were about to complete 65 Venus Rounds in the second run through the table so that they could reuse the 1 Ahau Tzolkin date (Lounsbury 1983:4–11, table 3; Thompson 1972:62–63). With a mean drift of 5.2 days after 65 Venus Rounds (104 years), they could wait until the next cycle on the 57th Venus Round, when the total would be around 8 days, allowing them to recover the 1 Ahau date. They did so by shifting the 1 Ahau day assigned to the last visibility of the Evening Star to the first rise of the Morning Star, taking advantage of the 8-day interval that occurs between those dates on page 47 in the table. This required a shift in the corresponding month as well.

Lounsbury notes that between A.D. 934 and 1129, the table shifted from 1 Ahau 18 Kayab (used in Bases A–D) to 1 Ahau 18 Uo (Base F). Through such calculations a series of base dates have been reconstructed for the table as follows: 9.9.9.16.0 1 Ahau 18 Kayab (Base A), 9.14.15.6.0 1 Ahau 18 Kayab (Base B), 10.0.0.14.0 1 Ahau 18 Kayab (Base C), 10.5.6.4.0 1 Ahau 18 Kayab (Base D), 10.10.11.12.0 1 Ahau 18 Kayab (Base E), 10.15.4.2.0 1 Ahau 18 Uo (Base F), 11.0.3.1.0 1 Ahau 13 Mac (Base G), with the last base on 11.5.2.0.0 1 Ahau 3 Xul falling in the fourteenth century. In the layouts proposed by Lounsbury (1983, table 3) and Aveni (1992, table 4), the base dates fall at the end of a 104-year run through the table, marking the transition from one cycle to another at the time of heliacal rise. Thus in Thompson's layout (Fig. 5.3j), 1 Ahau in line 13 is linked with 13 Mac in line 14 to form the date 11.5.2.0.0, with 18 Kayab in line 20 to form the date 10.0.0.14.0, and with 3 Xul in line 25 to form the date 11.5.2.0.0.

Lounsbury (1983:11) and Justeson (1989:93) agree that the Venus table is contemporary with the 1 Ahau 13 Mac base, which they correlate with the Long Count date of 11.0.3.1.0 in June of A.D. 1227 (Base G). This dating is generally confirmed by the Postclassic style of the codex, ca. 1150/1250–1450 (Paxton 1990). Furthermore, the two central Mexican deities represented in the Venus pages (discussed below) clearly pertain to the Postclassic epoch (Taube 1992b, figs. 56e–g; 67a). Their closest stylistic counterparts are seen in Borgia Group manuscripts, especially Codex Borgia 12–13, and there is no evidence of deities with similar iconographic details in Classic period imagery from central Mexico.

The 13 Mac date is associated with a verb, a flat hand (T713a) and mirror (T24 or T617a) compound on line 15 just above the glyph for "east" on line 16 in the last column before the pictures on page 50 (Figs. 5.3e; 5.7a). In the Venus table, this compound is used to signal times when Venus is visible, including days when Venus first appeared as the Morning Star and canonical dates when it was last visible as the Evening Star. The lower section of each page shows two other sets of month dates (Fig. 5.3f–j, lines 20 and 25). There are no mirror-hand glyphs associated with these dates. The associated base dates suggest that line 20 refers to past events and line 25 to future events.

Lounsbury (1983:11) proposes that 1 Ahau 18 Kayab was reused repeatedly in base dates from A.D. 623 (9.9.9.16.0) through A.D. 1038 (10.10.11.12.0). By 1129, the actual Venus events lagged eight days behind the heliacal rise dates recorded on line 20, so the astronomers were able to shift the heliacal rise event to a date previously used for the last visibility of the Evening Star (1 Ahau 18 Uo; lines 12 and 20; Fig. 5.3g), resulting in a new base by 1129 (10.15.4.2.0 1 Ahau 18 Uo). This base was reused until 1 Ahau 13 Mac became the base in 1227 (11.0.3.1.0). It was recognized that another base shift

would be required in the future, resulting in a new base that would be in use by A.D. 1324 (11.5.2.0.0 1 Ahau 3 Xul). Line 25 predicts the dates when the heliacal rise would take place in the period 1318–1324. In other words, the table contains dates for actual Venus events in the past, present, and future.

Even though Lounsbury (1983:11–16, fig. 1) accepts that 1 Ahau 13 Mac (A.D. 1227) is the end point of the current run of the table, he focuses his analysis on the earlier bases. He notes that the 1 Ahau 18 Uo (12/4/1129) heliacal rise was significant because Venus was in conjunction with Jupiter as it rose, an event that had not been seen since A.D. 244 (Lounsbury 1983:16–17, fig. 3). However, he maintains that the 1 Ahau 18 Kayab base in A.D. 934 is the only one to accurately peg the heliacal rise on 11/20/934 (Lounsbury 1983:8–13, 17, fig. 2). He finds this especially significant because this date also coincides with the heliacal rise of Mars, a pairing that had not occurred since A.D. 6. Despite this intriguing association with planetary conjunctions, the question remains: Why would the table accurately record the heliacal rise in A.D. 934 and not in A.D. 1227 when the table was in use? Dennis Tedlock (1992:268) notes that Lounsbury's reconstruction of the table using the 584,285 correlation would mean that "Mayan astronomers let their Venus calendar run a day or two late, *even in the act of correcting it*" (emphasis in original). He points out that the solution is to apply the 584,283 correlation, which produces not one but two heliacal rises that fall right on target. This correlation gives an unbroken chain of events from the Postclassic into the Early Colonial period, as Thompson (1960:305) recognized when he adopted the GMT2 correlation in his later work. Furthermore, the 584,283 correlation is in accord with the Quiché calendar of today and the Aztec calendar of the sixteenth century, a correspondence recognized by Lounsbury (1992a:199–204).

Aveni (1992, table 3.2) compares the canonical dates with actual heliacal rise dates. Of all the bases, only the dates in A.D. 934 (Base D), A.D. 1129 (Base F), and A.D. 1227 (Base G) place the canonical event in proximity (within two days) to the actual heliacal rise. Using Lounsbury's preferred correlation factor (584,285), he notes that the A.D. 934 base is only one

TABLE 5.2. HELIACAL RISE DATES IN VENUS TABLE OF DRESDEN CODEX COMPARED WITH ACTUAL RISE DATES

PAGE	CALENDAR ROUND	GEORGIAN DATE	JULIAN DATE	ACTUAL RISE DATE
46	5 Kan 7 Xul	1/26/1221	1/19/1221	1/19/1221
47	4 Lamat 6 Kayab	9/2/1222	8/26/1222	8/24/1222
48	3 Eb 0 Yax	4/8/1224	4/1/1224	3/30/1224
49	2 Cib 14 Uo	11/13/1225	11/6/1225	11/4/1225
50	1 Ahau 13 Mac	6/20/1227	6/13/1227	6/13/1227

Source: Based on Aveni 1992a, table 3.2, adjusted for 584,283 correlation.

day off, and the 1 Ahau 18 Uo (A.D. 1129) and 1 Ahau 13 Mac (A.D. 1227) bases are each two days off. But if we shift to the 584,283 correlation, now preferred by Aveni, we find that the last two bases (F and G) are perfect matches with the heliacal rise events on December 4, 1129, and June 13, 1227. This means that the previous run of the table (104 years earlier) and the current run in A.D. 1227 are both precise observations of the event, as would be expected in a record of recent historical events. As noted previously, the base on 1 Ahau 18 Uo in A.D. 1129 is linked to a significant planetary event. When Venus first appeared as Morning Star, it was in conjunction with Jupiter. Furthermore, the Moon was at last quarter, locking in a lunar event. Of all the proposed bases, only the 1 Ahau 13 Mac base on June 13, 1227, places the heliacal rise in proximity to an important solar event. The summer solstice took place on 6/15/1227 in the Julian calendar or 6/22/1227 in the Gregorian calendar (Aveni, personal communication 1995). Since the summer solstice can shift between June 21 and 22 from year to year, the base was probably visualized as falling just before the summer solstice. The 1 Ahau 13 Mac base therefore synchronizes an important Venus event with a significant event in the tropical year. Such a link would be expected because the calendar is laid out to show the relationship between five Venus cycles and eight solar years.

Rather than being a copy of a Classic period table, as has been commonly assumed, the Venus table fo-

cuses on current events in the thirteenth century, incorporating past events as points of reference. The current run of the table is the eight-year Venus-solar cycle that began in 1219 and closed in 1227 with 1 Ahau 13 Mac. In addition to synchronizing the solar and Venus cycles, this run of the table also incorporates a supremely important calendric event. The 10th Baktun (11.0.0.0.0; 5/18/1224) came to a close during the Morning Star period covered by the first column on page 49. At this time, Venus was near its maximum altitude as Morning Star (reached 28 days later; Aveni and Hotaling 1994, table 1).

Laying out the table with the first page correlating with 5 Kan 7 Xul and the last with 1 Ahau 13 Mac gives us five points that record the heliacal rise of Venus on a specific Calendar Round date in the thirteenth century (Table 5.2). Both the first and last Calendar Round dates precisely match with the actual heliacal rise dates of Venus on January 19, 1221, and June 13, 1227 (Aveni 1992, table 3.2). In this layout, the last of the five synodic periods of Venus falls two days before the summer solstice.

In sum, the Calendar Round dates on pages 46–50 refer to current heliacal rise dates, as well as those in the past and future, spanning a period from the tenth through the fourteenth centuries. The lock-in point for the table is 1 Ahau 13 Mac, just before the summer solstice in A.D. 1227. Although the 584,285 correlation provides a close fit with the summer solstice in A.D. 1227, there seems to be greater precision in recording the Venus events if we use the GMT2 correlation, which accurately places the heliacal rise dates in A.D. 1129 (the previous run of the table) and in A.D. 1221 and A.D. 1227. The Dresden Codex Venus pages provide a template for understanding the seasonal aspects of five Venus gods representing the newly emerged Morning Star over the course of an eight-year cycle that was tracked over hundreds of years.

THE SEASONAL ASPECTS OF VENUS

Having established the probable dates for each page, we can turn to the visual imagery to identify the Venus gods and their companions in relation to the seasonal cycle. The five Venus gods represent the Morning Star in different seasonal aspects. All are poised with dart throwers in hand, having just speared their victims below (Fig. 5.3a–e). Seated on sky-band thrones overhead, the regents watch the events from a distance.

On page 46, the first Venus god represents the newly risen Morning Star in the guise of God L (Fig. 5.3a; Schellhas 1904: 34–35). God L's name (T1054) is a black-faced portrait glyph with an Imix prefix, a name paired with a Venus glyph on page 46 (columns E–F). God L's warlike nature may be emphasized in the Dresden Codex, for he is the only one of the five shown holding a war shield. He has an eye volute and a shell beard, attributes that overlap with those of the Jaguar War God, a god specifically associated with war shields in Classic Maya iconography (Chapter 4, Fig. 4.2g). Placing the 1 Ahau 13 Mac date on page 50 just prior to the summer solstice in 1227 indicates that God L on page 46 represents Venus at heliacal rise on 1/19/1221 (Table 5.2). He embodies the first appearance of the Morning Star during the height of the dry season, a time of year for warfare among the Aztecs and the Yucatec Maya (Milbrath 1988b: 63; Torquemada 1943, 2: 299). He may also represent the entire period of the Morning Star's rapid ascent. Taking eighty days as an average for the interval from heliacal rise to maximum western altitude provides an idealized period for ascent ending on 4/9/1221 O.S., still well within the dry season, the epoch of warfare.

Lahun Chan (10 Sky) on page 47 is the second

seasonal manifestation of the Morning Star (Figs. 5.1f, 5.3b; Thompson 1972: 68). The markings on his torso are the segments of a scorpion thorax, and his headdress is a scorpion's tail tipped by a star glyph in place of the stinger, as can be seen by comparing the image of God L representing Venus on Madrid Codex 79a (Fig. 5.11b). Lahun Chan's headdress also has a prominent maize element like that of God E. This seems significant because the heliacal rise date on 8/26/1222 coincides with a time when the maize was ripening. If he also embodies the ascending Morning Star, the eightieth day falls on 11/13/1222 O.S. (11/20/1227 N.S.), coinciding with the first solar nadir at 19°N latitude, a date linked with the maize harvest at the onset of the dry season (Milbrath 1988b: 61–63).

Page 48 shows a monkey as the third seasonal aspect of the Morning Star (Fig. 5.3c). Here the Morning Star has the beard of a male howler and the deer ear seen on a number of howler images in Classic Maya art (Coe 1978a: 345–346). The monkey god wears the vulvate *oyohualli*, an ornament relating him to the central Mexican gods of song and dance (Seler 1960–1961, 2: 167). When howlers awake between 5 and 6 A.M., the troop howls to the rising sun, just as the rising Morning Star announces sunrise. Gordon Whittaker (1986: 57) identifies the glyphic name of the Morning Star god in column E as *tawisikala* (T96: 277: 146.25: 140), linking it with the first syllables in Tlahuizcalpantecuhtli, a name for the central Mexican god of the Morning Star. Venus, as a howler monkey rising at dawn on 4/1/1224, hurls his dart, killing the Maize God at the driest time of year when all the maize has been harvested and the stalks are burned, undergoing a form of death. This death is the preface to the rebirth of maize. The ascent of the Morning Star over the next eighty days parallels the rise of the maize plant out of the ground during the first months of the rainy season.

Karl Taube and Bonnie Bade (1991: 18) were the first to recognize the Morning Star god on Dresden 49 as a representation of Xiuhtecuhtli, the central Mexican Fire God (Fig. 5.3d). Here the god of the Morning Star bears a phonetic name of *chak xiw(i)tei* that resembles the name Xiuhtecuhtli ("turquoise lord" or "year lord"). The Morning Star aspect of Xiuhtecuhtli wears a *xiuhuitzolli* crown with the *xiuhtototl* bird and a medallion that resembles the headpiece of Quetzalcoatl on Dresden Codex page 4a (Taube 1992b:125). Xiuhtecuhtli is primarily a central Mexican deity, but a Postclassic mural from Tulum shows he was also known in the Maya area (Taube 1992b:125, fig. 67d). On page 49, Xiuhtecuhtli shoots the turtle at a time of year coinciding with the beginning of the dry season, for the heliacal rise date corresponds to 11/6/1225 O.S. (11/13/1225 N.S.). Over the next eighty days, as the Morning Star ascended, the rains abruptly ceased. Spearing the turtle victim, a patron of rain, proclaims drought, according to Thompson (1972:69). The association with the onset of the dry season also provides a link with the central Mexican Fire God, who is prominent in dry-season festivals taking place after the maize harvest (Nicholson 1971, table 4).

Thompson (1960:220) proposes that the blindfold worn by the Morning Star god on page 50 of the Dresden Codex refers to the planet moving backward "blindly" in retrograde motion (Fig. 5.3e). Indeed, the heliacal rise of Venus always coincides with retrograde motion. The god on page 50 most closely resembles Tezcatlipoca-Itztlacoliuhqui-Ixquimilli, a central Mexican god who wears a blindfold over his eyes and twin plumes in his headdress on Codex Vaticanus B 39 and on Codex Fejérváry-Mayer 33 (Fig. 5.6a; Taube 1992b:110–112; Thompson 1972:69). Itztlacoliuhqui is the central Mexican god of frost associated with the Venus cult (Sprajc 1993a:32–33; Sullivan 1976:256). In the Codex Fejérváry-Mayer, he wears a rayed corona on the top of his headdress and a smoking mirror on one foot, the insignia of Tezcatlipoca, as he makes an offering to a possum in the temple of the north. We also find Itztlacoliuhqui associated with the temple of the north in the Codex Borgia (50). It seems significant that in the Dresden Codex Itztlacoliuhqui's counterpart represents the Morning Star rising on 1 Ahau 13 Mac (6/13/1227 O.S.), positioned close to the sun at its northern extreme at the summer solstice. Nonetheless, in the Aztec festival calendar, Itztlacoliuhqui played a prominent role as god of frost in the September festival of Ochpaniztli (9/2–9/21 O.S.), which marked the beginning of frosts in central Mexico (Nicholson 1971, table 4; Sahagún 1950–1982, 2:121, 7:19). Frost is not found in lowland Yucatán, where the Dresden Codex was painted, but possibly Itztlacoliuhqui's association with that time of year was retained when his cult was imported from central Mexico. If we view the Venus god on Dresden Codex 50 as ruling a period of eighty days, his reign lasted until the beginning of September, around the time of year his festival began in central Mexico. In Yucatán, this is the time for doubling over the ears of maize (*maíz menudo*).

We can conclude that there are five seasonal aspects of Venus in the Dresden Codex almanac. Perhaps all the Morning Star gods in the Dresden Codex rule not only the day of heliacal rise but also a period of up to eighty days associated with the ascent of the Morning Star. If this is the case, we would have a five-part division of the year, with God L on page 46 ruling from late January through March, a period associated with the season of warfare. The howler monkey on page 48 reigns from April through mid-June, the season of planting. The blindfolded god on page 50 rules from the summer solstice through the end of August, when the crops are maturing. Lahun Chan on page 47 rules from September to early November, when the main harvest began around the end of the rainy season. The central Mexican Fire God on page 49 rules from mid-November through mid-January, a season associated with the beginning of the dry season and Fire God rituals in central Mexico.

REGENTS AND VICTIMS IN THE VENUS PAGES

On each of the five pages of the Venus Almanac, a regent deity looks over the Venus god spearing a victim (Fig. 5.3a–e). Four of the regents clearly have a celestial quality, because they are seated on sky-band thrones. All hold overturned jars, but only some of the jars seem to hold water. The regents are named in the second column of page 24 (B5–B9) in a sequence beginning with a Pauahtun (God N), who is the regent on page 48 (his name prefixed by the number four). The list ends with the Death God regent of page 47 (his name prefixed by a mirror glyph). The same names appear on lines 17, 21, and 22 on pages 46–50 in Thompson's (1972:66) table, which assigns letters of the alphabet to list the names of the gods (these bear no connection with the Postclassic gods identified by letters of the alphabet). The sequence invariably links the regents with the eastern direction (Fig. 5.3f–j; Kelley 1976, fig. 28). One enigmatic aspect in the sequence of names is that each regent's name actually appears in the middle section of the previous page. Thus the Moon Goddess regent on page 49 is named on page 48 in the column associated with the heliacal rise of the Morning Star. The analysis presented links the regents with the events represented on the page they are pictured on, but it is possible that they represent astronomical events 584 days earlier.

Only the Moon Goddess on page 49 has been securely identified, so our analysis should begin with her. She is named in the column associated with the heliacal rise date 4/1/1224 (page 48). On this date, the waxing Moon was located in Leo. On the other hand, if we look at the regent on page 49 as a representation of the Moon on the heliacal rise date recorded on the same page (11/6/1225), we find the waxing Moon above the western sky at dusk in Capricorn on the edge of the Milky Way. In my opinion, the most important feature locating the Moon Goddess in the sky is her sky-band throne. As we will see in Chapter 7, the layout of the Paris Codex zodiac reveals that all the constellations attached to the sky band are located where the ecliptic crosses the Milky Way or at locations framing the crossing point (Capricorn and Libra). Based on this pattern, I have assigned the regent Moon Goddess to the heliacal rise on page 49, rather than 584 days earlier. It would seem that the other regents on sky-band thrones in the Venus pages may also correspond to astronomical gods located on or at the edge of the Milky Way.

The regent on page 46 might be associated in some way with Mars because he wears a headdress very much like the Mars Beast (Dresden 45b). Presuming the image relates to the Morning Star rising on the 5 Kan 7 Xul date recorded on page 46 (1/19/1221), we find a good correspondence because Mars and Venus were rising together in the dawn sky, echoing the conjunction event on 1 Ahau 18 Kayab

in A.D. 934 considered so important by Lounsbury (1983). The Mars regent's sky-band throne may represent the Milky Way. On the heliacal rise date associated with page 46, Mars was in Capricorn at the edge of the Milky Way.

The skeletal regent on page 47 cannot be identified in terms of an astronomical counterpart (Fig. 5.3b). Harvey and Victoria Bricker (1992) have linked a skeletal figure in the Paris Codex with Pisces, but the regent of the Venus pages seems to be different. His closest counterpart is seen on Dresden Codex 12b, where God A wears a similar animal headdress.

In a departure from the pattern seen for other regents, the regent on page 48 is seated on a rooftop, clearly representing a different location than the sky-band throne (Fig. 5.3c). Here a Pauahtun, designated as God N by Schellhas, is seated on a roof decorated with death eyes, which may signal he is close to the horizon or in the underworld. He has a quadripartite nature in other contexts, best seen in his four guises at Chichén Itzá (Schele and Mathews 1998, fig. 6.11; Tozzer 1957, figs. 261–264, 266). As noted in Chapter 4, God N may be linked in some fashion with the four phases of the Moon or the four synodic aspects of the inferior planets (Venus and Mercury). The fact that he appears on the same page with the Morning Star suggests that he must be an entity other than Venus. His identity, however, remains enigmatic.

Page 50 shows two regents associated with the Venus cycle ending 1 Ahau 13 Mac at the time of heliacal rise on 6/13/1227, just before the summer solstice. The Maize God appears with Hun Ahau, a pairing also seen on Dresden Codex 2a (Fig. 4.4h, left). Indeed, Taube (1992b:116) notes that the two appearing together is consistent with Classic Maya imagery of the Popol Vuh, for the Maize God is the Classic period version of Hun Hunahpu, the father of Hunahpu and Xbalanque. Hun Ahau, the Classic period counterpart of Hunahpu, is related to both the Sun and its clarion, the Morning Star (Chapter 3; B. Tedlock 1992a:28; D. Tedlock 1991:160, 342). The sky-band throne is appropriate because both the Sun and Venus were crossing the Milky Way on the date of heliacal rise (the Sun in Gemini, Venus in Orion). The Maize God co-regent may symbolize the maize crop sprouting in the rain-soaked fields of late June, for the glyphs on page 50 refer to an abundance of maize (Thompson 1972:69).

The victims of the five Venus gods are named on page 24 in column C beginning at C8, the victim shown on page 46 (Fig. 5.3a). The list conforms to the sequence of images appearing on the bottom of pages 46–50. The second victim is a feline. The Maize God is the third victim. The turtle is the fourth victim. The fifth victim is identified by Thompson as a fishing god. In the middle of each page (46–50), above the pictures of the Morning Star gods, a set of glyphs pairs the victim's name with the spearing-event glyph (T653). This glyph pair immediately follows glyphs referring to the heliacal rise of the Morning Star. Thus the spearing act is directly related to the rise of the Morning Star. In fact, Venus is the agent of the spearing event.

The turtle victim on page 49 is especially interesting (Fig. 5.3d). Thompson (1972:64, 69–70) links the name (T743[281].227) of the speared victim on page 49 to T227 in the list on page 24 at C11, pointing out that the seated manikin in a "siesta" pose is a dwarf (ac), a homonym for the turtle, which is also called ac, a relationship reinforced by the turtle-head prefix joined with T227 on page 49. Although Closs (1989:406, 411, fig. 31.3) identifies T227 as part of the name for Venus as lord of the underworld, it clearly names the victim in the Dresden Codex. The victim on page 49 seems to be a turtle constellation.

Analysis of the Paris Codex "zodiac" on pages 23–24 indicates that there is a turtle constellation in the region of Orion (H. Bricker and V. Bricker 1992; Love 1994). Although Thompson (1972:67) suggested that the speared victims are constellations in conjunction with the rising Morning Star, the turtle constellation was actually at the opposite side of the sky when Venus rose at dawn on 11/6/1225. Thus the spearing event refers to opposition in the sky rather than conjunction. In the seasonal cycle of Venus, the rise of the Fire God aspect of the Morning Star ushered in the dry season when the turtle constellation died at dawn. The turtle constellation had to die and descend to the underworld in the west so that the dry-season Morning Star could rise in the east.

The last victim in the Venus pages is named with the T1055 glyph at C12 on Dresden 24 and in column E on Dresden 50, where his name has an unusual prefix (T608). Thompson (1972:69) identifies T608 as a fish tail, leading him to conclude that this god is associated with fishing (Figs. 5.3e, 5.7b, lower left). Even though T608 is now more commonly interpreted as a penis (Kurbjuhn 1989), it is interesting to note that the victim may be linked with Sagittarius, which correlates with a fish-snake in the Paris Codex zodiac (H. Bricker and V. Bricker 1992, table 6.5). On 6/13/1227, when Venus rose at dawn, Sagittarius was in opposition to the Morning Star, perhaps symbolized by the victim positioned in opposition to the rising Morning Star on page 50.

Although the victims on pages 49 and 50 may represent constellations, other victims may be planets. The God K victim on page 46 seems to represent Jupiter, which was in opposition to the rising Morning Star and undergoing retrograde motion on 1/19/1221 (Fig. 5.3a). This identification is in accord with my previous research on Classic period images of God K associated with dates when Jupiter was in retrograde motion (Milbrath 1996b; Chapter 6).

The victim on page 47 represents the Moon setting opposite the rising Morning Star (Fig. 5.3b). The Moon sometimes takes the form of a jaguar, especially around the full Moon (Chapter 4). At the time Venus rose heliacally on 8/26/1222, the Moon was three days past full (8/23/1222; Goldstine 1973). The seasonal aspect of the Moon on page 47 may be important. The red feline bears a water-lily headdress and the same name as the Water-lily Jaguar on Dresden 8a (Chac Bolay; Thompson 1972:35, 68, 70). Study of Classic period inscriptions indicates that the Water-lily jaguar may be a rainy-season aspect of the Moon (Chapter 4). Representation of the Moon in the Venus Almanac is not surprising, given the fact that lunar cycles are built in to the calendric structure of the table.

Page 48 represents the Maize God as a victim who dies on 4/1/1224 (Fig. 5.3c). It seems appropriate that the victim is the Maize God at a time of year when the maize seeds are about to be placed in the earth, a form of burial that may be linked with the annual descent of the Maize God into the underworld. Apparently, a specific seasonal aspect of the

Morning Star is responsible for the death of maize, just as certain seasonal positions of the Evening Star were believed to promote maize fertility (Closs et al. 1984; Sprajc 1993a, 1993b). A link between Venus positions and maize agriculture survived into the eighteenth century, as documented in a Quiché codex that describes Venus observations in relation to the agricultural cycle (Tedlock 1994).

In sum, several of the victims in the Dresden Codex Venus pages seem to represent constellations, the Moon, and planets positioned in opposition to the Morning Star. As Venus rose, it hurled its atlatl dart across the sky, killing the astronomical deity at the opposite side of the sky. The regents enthroned on the top of the page may show astronomical bodies positioned at the intersection of the Milky Way and the ecliptic, represented as a sky-band throne. The regents include the Maize God and his co-regent Hunahpu, the Moon Goddess, and a regent possibly connected with Mars, as well as two others whose astronomical identities remain enigmatic. Venus remains the central character in the drama, but the scenes of the victims and regents indicate an interest in the positions of other astronomical bodies as the Morning Star emerged from inferior conjunction.

QUETZALCOATL-KUKULCAN: THE VENUS GOD FROM CENTRAL MEXICO

A Venus cult connected with Quetzalcoatl seems to have been imported from central Mexico to the Maya area at a relatively early time, well before the complex of central Mexican Morning Star gods seen in the Dresden Codex. There is evidence of a cult to Quetzalcoatl-Kukulcan in the Classic period architecture of Uxmal, and Jeff Kowalski (1990:51–53) says that the feathered-serpent symbolism probably spread from Chichén Itzá between A.D. 850 and 900. Just when the cult first arrived in Yucatán is debatable, but the chronicles imply the cult centered on a form of worship linked to a central Mexican ruler named Quetzalcoatl who died in Yucatán. A sixteenth-century source says that Quetzalcoatl led his people from Tollan to Tabasco and then on to Campeche and Yucatán, because he wanted to avoid warfare (Torquemada 1943, 1:255–256). In a sev-

enteenth-century chronicle, Cogolludo (1954:352) identifies Kukulcan of Yucatán as the same individual called Quetzalcoatl in Cholula. According to Landa, the Itzá settlers at Chichén Itzá were ruled by Kukulcan, who came from central Mexico, where he was worshiped as the god Quetzalcoatl (Tozzer 1941:20–23 n. 128). In the year 1 Reed, Quetzalcoatl died and was transformed into the Morning Star in the "land of writing," alluding to the Maya area, according to one central Mexican source (*Anales de Cuauhtitlán;* Seler 1960–1961, 2:740). The white circle in the sky mentioned in the Chilam Balam of Chumayel is a reference to the planet Venus, which is connected with the return of Quetzalcoatl-Kukulcan in the Katun 11 Ahau (Thompson 1960: 219). Quetzalcoatl-Kukulcan is apparently a Toltec ruler who was apotheosized as Venus. His history can also be seen in Mixteca-Puebla codices, where he is similarly identified with Venus (Milbrath 1988a).

A number of early chronicles link round structures to a cult connected with Quetzalcoatl-Kukulcan (Tozzer 1941:25 n. 134). Landa describes a round structure at Mayapán, a city reportedly founded by Kukulcan after he left Chichén Itzá (Tozzer 1941: 23–25). As noted earlier, the most famous round structure, the Caracol at Chichén Itzá, has windows with oblique angles oriented toward the northern and southern horizon extremes of Venus. The stairway to the main platform also has a stylobate niche with one wall aligned to the setting Sun, but the center point from the rear wall faces the northernmost setting point of Venus (Fig. 3.1b). The back of the niche has a pair of columns; one was painted red, the other black. The red and black coloration provides an intriguing link with the cult of Quetzalcoatl, for the Aztecs said that Quetzalcoatl died in the "land of writing" (*tlilan tlapallan*), meaning literally "the land of red and black," the colors used in Maya writing (Seler 1960–1961, 2:740).

Round structures are also connected with Ehecatl-Quetzalcoatl in Guatemala and in central Mexico. Ehecatl-Quetzalcoatl, the central Mexican Wind God characterized by a beaklike mask, appears in the Classic Maya area as early as the 10th Baktun on Seibal Stela 19 (Schlak 1996, fig. 3). Seibal has a round temple dedicated to this deity. It faces west, as do the round temples dedicated to Quetzalcoatl-Kukulcan in Yucatán. Sprajc (1993a:5) points out that this orientation suggests a link with the Evening Star, whereas the central Mexican round temples face east toward the Morning Star. Such a temple is found at Calixtlahuaca, a round temple built in four stages, with the oldest level dating back to Teotihuacán times, which housed a magnificent sculpture of Ehecatl-Quetzalcoatl (Marquina 1964, pl. 91). Perhaps such round structures were symbolically linked to Quetzalcoatl-Kukulcan as a coiled serpent.

Stephen Houston and David Stuart (1984:799–800) identify a coiled serpent on Dresden Codex 36b as Kukulcan (Fig. 5.4c). Although the serpent is not feathered, it bears a five-pointed star, a design that has clear connections with Venus, as we will see in the discussion to follow. The associated sky glyph suggests a link with a "quetzal-sky" compound found on a Uaxactún vessel identified by Houston and Stuart (1984:799–800, figs. 17, 18a) as the only known hieroglyphic reference to Kukulcan during the Classic period.

The anthropomorphic God H seems to be the counterpart of Quetzalcoatl-Kukulcan in the codices. Seler (1960–1961, 1:698–702; 1990–1996, 1:214) noted long ago that a figure that Schellhas identifies as God H on Dresden Codex 4a is probably Quetzalcoatl-Kukulcan with a snail-shell necklace, a quetzal on his back, and a snake in hand (Fig. 5.4a).

Taube (1992b:60, 137) concurs and adds that the figure wears a turquoise headdress disk like that seen on Postclassic images of Quetzalcoatl from central Mexico. This god leads off a series of twenty deities in Almanac 8 of the Dresden Codex (4a–10a) associated with Tzolkin dates that define a period of 5 × 52 days (Hofling 1988). Seler (1960–1961, 1:700, figs. 28–29; 1990–1996, 1:215–216) also recognizes images of Quetzalcoatl-Kukulcan planting maize seeds in the Madrid Codex (26b, 35a). Fertility and plant growth are probably part of God H's domain, for he shares traits with Goddess I and the Maize God. God H is also linked with God D in the codices, as in scenes on Dresden Codex 12c and 15c, where God D appears with God H's flower title (Stone 1995a; Taube 1992b:63).

Taube (1992b:63) links God H with the Water-lily Serpent and with the head variant of the number three, believed to be a wind god because of an association with the Ik glyph. In the Dresden Codex (50), Ik is a day sign associated with the emergence of the Evening Star (Fig. 5.3e). The Ik symbol at Palenque is interpreted as a reference to the Evening Star (Lounsbury 1974:11; Robertson 1985b, fig. 243). Zoomorphs (serpent faces?) from Palenque marked with Ik symbols may be representations of the Evening Star (Fig. 5.7m–n). In the Codex Borgia (9), Ehecatl-Quetzalcoatl is the patron of the day Wind, the counterpart of Ik. This suggests that God H, the

---

FIG. 5.4. *a:* Quetzalcoatl-Kukulcan with snail-shell necklace, quetzal on his back, and snake in hand (Dresden Codex 4a; after Taube 1992b, fig. 27a).

b: Venus God Quetzalcoatl with conical hat, long beak, and beard (Aztec Codex Telleriano-Remensis 9; after Taube 1992b, fig. 27b).

c: Vulture attacks coiled serpent representing Venus as Kukulcan (Dresden Codex 36b; after Villacorta and Villacorta 1977).

d: Ehecatl-Quetzalcoatl, holding implements of priest, watches as skeletal Morning Star descends into underworld carrying implements of war; possibly represents Evening Star rising when Morning Star was no longer visible, hence its skeletal or underworld aspect (Codex Borgia 19; after Seler 1960–1961, 3:256, fig. 48).

e: Twin Venus serpents, holding twin Ehecatl-Quetzal-

coatl figures in their jaws, form center of radiant disk representing planet Venus with red and black rays and star eyes (Codex Borgia 30; after Seler 1963, 2).

f: Ehecatl-Quetzalcoatl descends on celestial cord through fleshy opening in sky band decorated with Venus glyphs, showing Venus passing through Milky Way on ecliptical cord (Codex Vindobonensis 48; after González Torres 1975, fig. 5).

g: Ehecatl-Quetzalcoatl lifts up sky band with water motifs and five Venus glyphs, one of sixteen different transformations of Venus in creation epic of this Mixteca-Puebla codex (Codex Vindobonensis 47b; after Baird 1989, fig. 33).

h: Half-star Venus symbol on Classic feathered rattler (Maltrata, Veracruz; after Baird 1989, fig. 39).

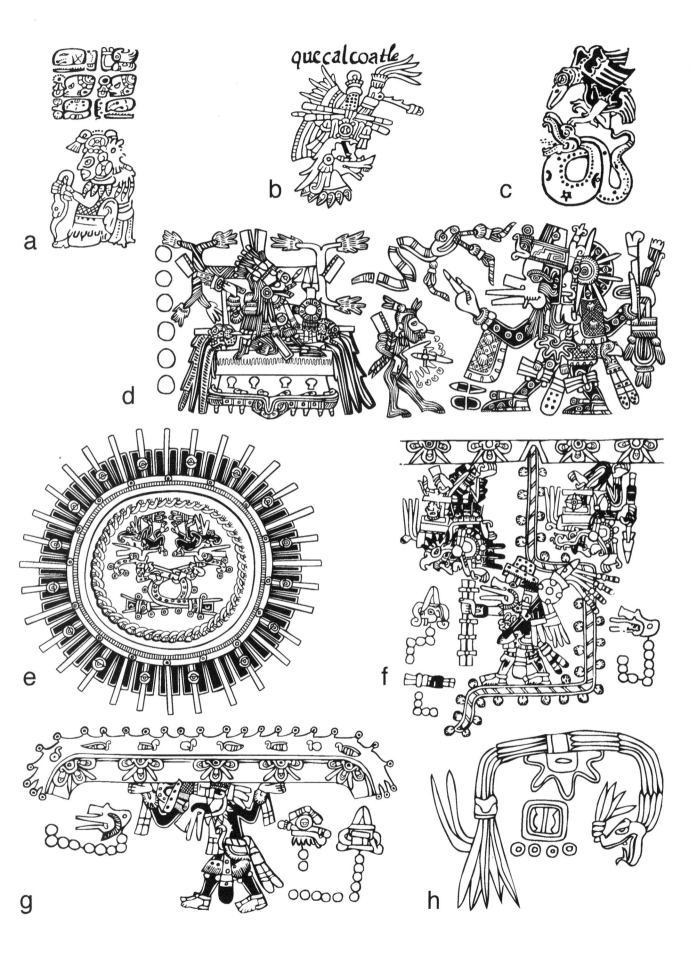

a

b

quecalcoatle

c

d

e

f

g

h

Water-lily Serpent, and Ehecatl-Quetzalcoatl are all related by an association with Venus and the wind. The evidence for associating Ehecatl-Quetzalcoatl with a specific Venus phase, however, remains debatable.

At the dawn of the fifth world age, Quetzalcoatl and Ehecatl faced to the east to await the sunrise, which would suggest a Morning Star association (Sahagún 1950–1982, 4:7, 52). Some texts, however, refer to Quetzalcoatl as Héspero, a name for the Evening Star (Sprajc 1993a:28–29). Aztec legends have Quetzalcoatl traveling to the east, where he is transformed into the Morning Star, at which point he becomes Tlahuizcalpantecuhtli. This suggests perhaps that Quetzalcoatl is a god of the Evening Star who changed identity when he became the Morning Star.

The most comprehensive inventory of Postclassic Venus imagery is found in the Codex Borgia, believed to be from the area of Tlaxcala or Puebla (home to Cholula's cult to Quetzalcoatl). Here we see a great variety of images of Quetzalcoatl. Sometimes he takes the form of Ehecatl, with a long-beaked wind god mask, or he can be a starry Venus serpent wearing the same mask (Fig. 5.4e). Some Codex Borgia images depict Ehecatl-Quetzalcoatl as an anthropomorphic being with a conical hat, a long beak, a shell necklace, and a beard (Fig. 5.4d). Similar images of Ehecatl-Quetzalcoatl are represented in Mixtec and Aztec codices (Fig. 5.4b, f, g).

Codex Borgia 19 may represent contrasting images of Venus as a warrior and a priest (Fig. 5.4d). Ehecatl-Quetzalcoatl watches as the skeletal "lord of dawn" (Tlahuizcalpantecuhtli) descends into the underworld. The imagery suggests that one aspect of Venus is replaced by another. Ehecatl-Quetzalcoatl holds the bloodletting implements of a priest, while the dying Morning Star holds an atlatl and a shield, perhaps indicating a contrast between the Morning Star as a warrior and the Evening Star as a priest. A similar scene in the Codex Borbonicus depicts the Evening Star, Xolotl, watching the Sun carry the mummy bundle of the skeletal Morning Star into the underworld (Fig. 5.1h). Both Venus figures wear very similar headdresses with a star center and stacked knots that may be related to Venus. Bloodletting implements marked with a star are positioned between

them. As Xolotl dances, the skeletal Morning Star, pierced by a dart, descends into the jaws of the earth monster. Perhaps this scene and the one in the Codex Borgia tell us that the Morning Star must descend to the underworld when the Evening Star rises. This is the reverse of the transformation represented in the chronicles, where the priest-ruler Quetzalcoatl dies when the warlike Morning Star rises as Tlahuizcalpantecuhtli (Lord of Dawn), reflecting a transformation from one phase to another.

Throughout the Codex Borgia, there are many Venus transformations representing Quetzalcoatl and Tlahuizcalpantecuhtli (Milbrath 1989). In my opinion, pages 29–46 represent the motions of Venus in a pattern substantially different from that originally proposed by Seler (1963, 2:9–61). My research indicates that this eighteen-page sequence correlates with the eighteen months of the festival calendar, with each page representing a different 20-day period; the Venus cycle is integrated into this calendric sequence (Milbrath 1989, fig. 1).

The first page (29) refers to days 20–40 of the Morning Star phase, when Venus is clearly visible rising above the horizon. The wriggling figures of Ehecatl-Quetzalcoatl emerging from the ashes of a burning bundle apparently symbolize the transformation of Venus as it becomes the Morning Star, recalling an account in the chronicles saying that Quetzalcoatl was burned when he was transformed into the Morning Star.

Page 30 represents days 40–60 of the Morning Star phase, when Venus reaches its maximum brilliance as it rapidly ascends in the dawn sky. The rayed disk on page 30, often referred to as the "night sun," is actually the resplendent planet Venus (Fig. 5.4e; Milbrath 1989). The rayed disk frames intertwined star serpents representing Ehecatl figures in the jaws of the twin Ehecatl serpents, evoking the dual nature of the planet Venus. The Venus disk is a 360-degree version of Ehecatl-Quetzalcoatl's headdress, characterized by a fan of red rays with squared ends on a nocturnal corona of black inlaid with stars (Fig. 5.4d). The red rays alternating with black rays represent the crepuscular light of Venus. In subsequent scenes (pages 39–40), Venus enters the underworld, disappearing into the jaws of the earth monster as Venus becomes invisible in superior conjunction. A similar concept may be found as far back as the Preclassic period, for Izapa Stela 11 depicts a bearded god (Venus?) surrounded by rays positioned in the jaws of the earth monster (Norman 1976, fig. 3.11).

At Chichén Itzá, the cult of the feathered serpent is associated with images of warriors armed with weapons in the Terminal Classic and Early Postclassic periods, spanning the period from A.D. 800 to 1250 (Fig. 5.5c, e). In light of Quetzalcoatl's direct link with Chichén Itzá in the chronicles, it is not surprising that his images are very common at the site (Taube 1992b:136). Taube suggests that feathered-serpent images refer to the Morning Star aspect of Venus, because Quetzalcoatl was transformed into the Morning Star in the chronicles.

Venus glyphs in a non-Maya style appear with images of the feathered serpent in a variety of contexts. A bench in the Mercado depicting a scene of captives and sacrifice has two feathered serpents on the *tablero*, with Venus glyphs grouped in sets of five along the sides of each serpent, suggesting a link with the five Venus cycles in the eight-year Venus Almanac (Fig. 5.5d). Here the Venus glyphs have five rays, a form that also probably symbolizes the five Venus cycles (Carlson 1991). In the Northwest Colonnade, a warrior wearing a Venus symbol as a star belt has the feathered serpent as his alter ego (Fig. 5.5c). A jadeite plaque from the Cenote shows a serpent carrying a warrior with a star belt and an armed dart thrower, an image that may represent the warlike Venus as it rises as the Morning Star (Tozzer 1957, fig. 131). Although this serpent does not have feathers on its body, it does have a design of concentric circles that may represent stars (Chapter 7).

An unusual image on the Venus Platform shows a face in the jaws of a feathered reptile, represented frontally with clawed feet. Seler (1990–1996, 1:211, fig. 14) identifies the reptile as Quetzalcoatl, noting that it appears alongside Venus glyphs on a panel related to the Venus cycle (Fig. 5.5a). Such an image recalls the Ehecatl-Quetzalcoatl serpents with clawed front feet that represent aspects of Venus in the Codex Borgia (Fig. 5.4e). The Chichén Itzá image also evokes comparison with the front head of the Cosmic Monster, which sometimes has clawed front feet and a deity face in its jaws (Fig. 7.5e).

The Upper Temple of the Jaguars, dated between A.D. 800 and 900, has a lintel that depicts a warrior framed by a sun disk and another cradled by a feathered serpent, with a water-lily monster and a Maya star glyph between the two warriors (Fig. 5.5e). In the temple interior, a reclining goddess emits two feathered serpents from her abdomen, alluding to the twin nature of Venus; a similar image is preserved in the North Temple of the Great Ball Court (Fig. 5.5f–g). Her body may represent the Milky Way (Chapter 7; compare Fig. 7.4a).

The feathered serpent warrior is seen repeatedly in murals of the Upper Temple of the Jaguars. The central mural scene opposite the doorway depicts two astronomical warriors (Fig. 5.5h). The solar warrior on the left, representing a local Maya ruler, wears Maya-style costume elements, including a jade nose bar and a jade mask on the front of his headdress, whereas the serpent warrior seems to be a foreigner wearing a gold pectoral (Coggins 1984:160–163, fig. 17). The serpent warrior emanates darts and rays, a non-Maya image suggesting the fiery rays of the Morning Star that may involve a Náhuatl play on words that links darts and rays of light (Taube 1994: 223, fig. 11c). Arthur Miller (1977) identifies the feathered-serpent figure as Captain Serpent, a foreigner leading his troops against Captain Sun Disk, a Maya leader. On the other hand, Charles Lincoln (1988) says the two warriors are Kakupacal (fire shield) and Kukulcan (sprouting serpent), acting as dual rulers of Chichén Itzá. They are linked with two lineages or cults honoring the Sun and Venus (Milbrath 1988c:65–66). The feathered serpent warrior may be the historical Kukulcan-Quetzalcoatl who brought the Venus cult from central Mexico.

The feathered serpent appears with an astronomical warrior in a number of battle scenes in the Upper Temple of the Jaguars (Coggins 1984, figs. 17–20). Often the solar warrior is also represented, but the mural scenes do not show the two in close proximity. A landscape on the east wall depicts warfare taking place in the red hills of the Puuc area; in the scene a Venus god is emerging from the jaws of a serpent (Coggins 1984:159; Wren 1991:55). On the south

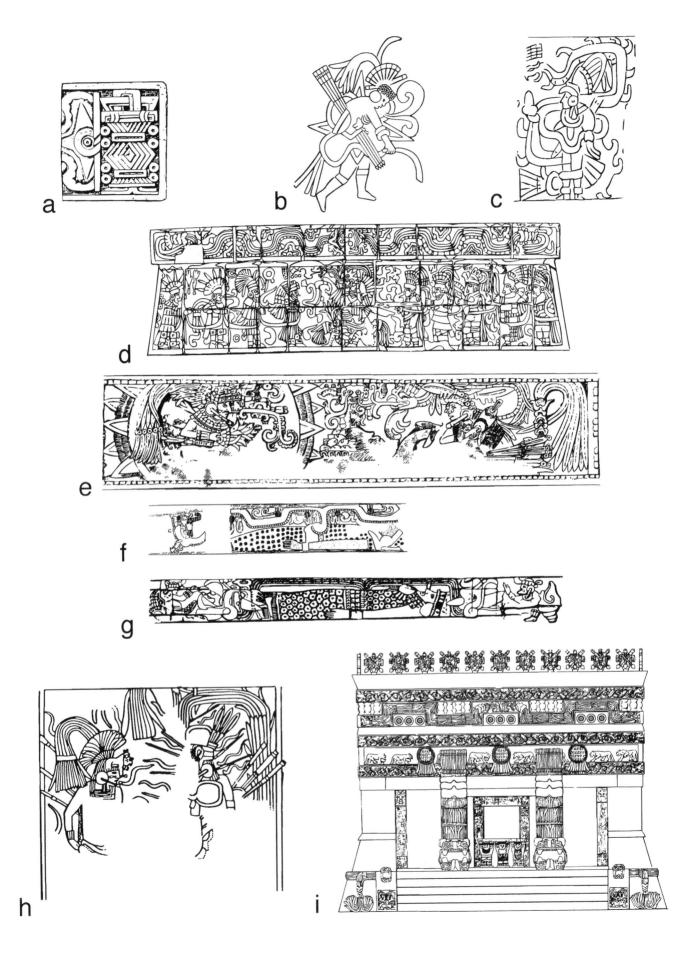

a

b

c

d

e

f

g

h

i

wall, a warrior wrapped in a feathered serpent mounts a scaffold that Linnea Wren (1996) interprets as a siege tower used in warfare (Coggins 1984, fig. 20). Overhead, a solar warrior is accompanied by a star warrior carried by a red-and-yellow serpent. On the west wall, an assault seems to take place near a large body of water, for canoes are prominent in the imagery (Coggins 1984, fig. 19). Once again the solar warrior appears with a star warrior, but this time the serpent seems to be colored yellow.

Clemency Coggins (1984:157–165) relates the sequence of murals to a single synodic period of Venus beginning with heliacal rise on the east wall. She suggests that Venus appears in superior conjunction on the north wall and in inferior conjunction on the south wall, with the four walls giving a quadripartite division of the 584-day Venus cycle. Nonetheless, the format of the mural sequence is better suited to a cycle showing Venus in its different aspects over the course of eight solar years. There is actually an eight-part division of the mural sequence, suggesting an association with the Venus Almanac, with one scene for each solar year. If the campaign of battles shown

in the murals took place over the course of eight years, then each scene may show a different Venus position in the eight-year Venus Almanac. The Maya of Chichén Itzá clearly had knowledge of this cycle, for five Venus cycles is equated to eight solar years in the inscriptions of the Venus Platform (Fig. 5.5a).

Some aspects of Quetzalcoatl and his feathered serpent alter ego are closely linked with origin myths. Quetzalcoatl took part in the original events of creation pictured in the Mixteca-Puebla Codex Vindobonensis. On page 48 of that codex, Ehecatl-Quetzalcoatl descends on a celestial cord through a fleshy opening in a sky band decorated with Venus glyphs in a scene that refers to his rebirth with divine attributes (Fig. 5.4f; Milbrath 1988a). Here Quetzalcoatl descends slowly along a cord, perhaps imitating the slow descent of the Morning Star phase. On Codex Vindobonensis 47b, he lifts up a sky band with water motifs and half-star glyphs representing Venus, a scene that is part of a creation epic involving sixteen different transformations of the deity (Fig. 5.4g; Furst 1978:102–108).

Coggins (1988b:76–77, fig. 8) suggests that Quet-

FIG. 5.5. *a:* Venus Platform at Chichén Itzá depicts predominantly central Mexican images (year bundle, year sign, half star, fleshy opening, and number eight) paired with Maya number five as symbol of Venus Almanac equating ninety-nine lunar months and five Venus cycles with eight solar years (after Seler 1960–1961, 5, fig. 243).

b: Star warrior with Venus belt combining rays and lobes like Mixteca-Puebla Venus glyphs (Terminal Classic mural on southeast wall in Upper Temple of Jaguars, Chichén Itzá; after Miller 1989:294).

c: Venus warrior wearing star belt has feathered serpent as his alter ego (Northwest Colonnade at Chichén Itzá; after Tozzer 1957, fig. 595).

d: Venus glyphs grouped in sets of five along sides of two feathered serpents evoke five Venus cycles in Venus Almanac of eight years (Mercado bench at Chichén Itzá; after Tozzer 1957, fig. 598).

e: Solar warrior (Kakupacal) framed by sun disk and Venus warrior (Quetzalcoatl-Kukulcan) cradled in feathered serpent (Terminal Classic lintel in Upper Temple of Jaguars, Chichén Itzá; after Maudslay 1889–1902, 3, pl. 35).

f: Two feathered serpents, alluding to dual nature of Venus, pass through abdomen of reclining sky goddess (Milky Way?), evoking links with Mixteca-Puebla images that depict Quetzalcoatl emerging from Milky Way (Upper Temple of Jaguars, Chichén Itzá; after Seler 1960–1961, 5:355, fig. 227).

g: On North Temple of Great Ball Court at Chichén Itzá, two Bacabs flank twin Venus serpents emerging from abdomen of reclining sky goddess, whose body may represent Milky Way (after Seler 1960–1961, 5:321, figs. 195–196).

h: Solar warrior (Kakupacal) wearing Maya headdress faces Venus warrior surrounded by feathered serpent (detail from murals of Upper Temple of Jaguars, Chichén Itzá; after Schele and Matthews 1998, fig. 6.30.B7A).

i: Cornice of Upper Temple of Jaguars depicts shields with crescent moons flanked by felines and feathered serpents; entry to temple guarded by two giant feathered rattlesnakes (Great Ball Court complex at Chichén Itzá; after Tozzer 1957, fig. 85).

zalcoatl is part of a Venus cult that links the cosmic sea and rebirth. In the Popol Vuh, the feathered serpent floats in the sea before the first sunrise at the dawn of creation. In a like fashion, representations of the feathered rattler at Teotihuacán float in seawater on the Temple of Quetzalcoatl (Fig. 5.6g). The corona of luminescent quetzal feathers around the serpent's face may symbolize the shining rays of Venus. The placement of the temple complex may incorporate units of measure that allude to the Venus cycle (Sugiyama 1993:114). The deity images were intentionally destroyed, apparently as part of a religious or political conflict (Sugiyama 1989:104). This form of representation predates the quetzal-rattlesnake images associated with blood sacrifice in Teotihuacán Zone 5-A murals, suggesting that the Venus cult changed over time (Fig. 5.6d). Perhaps Quetzalcoatl's role as a creator god was subordinated to a Venus cult connected with warfare and sacrifice in the later periods of Teotihuacán.

Quetzalcoatl is paired with a jawless reptile head bearing reflective mica mirrors in its eyes and twin rings on its brow on the Temple of Quetzalcoatl (Fig. 5.6g). Coggins (1996:24) interprets the twin rings as a reference to the morning and evening phases of Venus. Michael Coe (1981:168) proposes that the reptile is an early form of the starry fire ser-

pent known as Xiuhcoatl among the Aztecs, favoring an identification proposed by Caso and Bernal in the 1950s. He interprets the Temple of Quetzalcoatl as a representation of the initial creation of the universe out of a watery void through the actions of two opposing forces or deities, Quetzalcoatl and the old Fire God. Taube (1992a:54–55, 59–60, fig. 5) identifies the reptile as a headdress representing the War Serpent, a Classic period counterpart of Xiuhcoatl, the serpent of the Fire God. In terms of cosmic symbolism, it is noteworthy that Codex Ríos (folios 6r, 6v), an Aztec codex showing the world destructions, depicts the fire serpent and the feathered serpent as representatives of two sequential world ages. Saburo Sugiyama (1992:207–209, fig. 3) compares the reliefs on the temple to murals in Tepantitla Room 2 depicting a feathered serpent with headdresses along its body (Miller 1973, fig. 173). He does not see dualism in the imagery, and he notes that the feathered serpent swimming in water is the primary image. Nonetheless, other images from the Maya area suggest duality is prominent in related imagery.

A Tikal platform bears Venus glyphs that seem to substitute for the head of Quetzalcoatl on the Temple of Quetzalcoatl at Teotihuacán (Fig. 5.6f). And the paired ring designs on the Tikal platform, possibly representing twin stars, seem to substitute

---

FIG. 5.6. *a:* Tezcatlipoca-Itztlacoliuhqui-Ixquimilli, central Mexican Venus god with blindfolded eyes and headdress of twin plumes, makes offering to opossum at temple of north (Codex Fejérváry-Mayer 33; after Seler 1960–1961, 4:507, fig. 186).

b: Tlahuizcalpantecuhtli's quincunx face painting represents five dots, probably referring to "fiveness" of Venus in Venus Almanac of eight solar years (Codex Borgia 19; after Seler 1960–1961, 3:642, fig. 48).

c: Quincunx face painting characterizes newly risen Morning Star, Tlauhuizcalpantecuhtli, here wearing loincloth with Venus symbol as he spears victim (Codex Vaticanus B 80; after Seler 1960–1961, 1:662, fig. 69).

d: Quetzal-rattlesnake with half stars and rayed lunar disks frames sacrifice scene with priests dressed as owls carrying knives with bloody hearts (Zone 5-A, Portico 19, Mural 1, Teotihuacán; after Baird 1989, fig. 14).

e: Half-star Venus symbol has five points, indicating link with Venus Almanac of five Venus cycles equaling eight solar years (after Carlson 1993, fig. 8.1b).

f: Central Mexican–style Venus glyph with five radiating elements alternating with twin circles probably symbolizing twin stars (Structure 5D-43 at Tikal; after Baird 1989, fig. 20).

g: Quetzalcoatl framed by corona of raylike feathers and feathered body with rattle tail; second jawless head with mosaic or reptile skin has knot in headdress and twin stars on brow (Temple of Quetzalcoatl, Teotihuacán; after Sugiyama 1993, fig. 5).

h: Quincunx face painting decorates Venus heads on sky band above ecliptical cord serving as path for rayed sun disk, Venus glyph, and sky god emerging from cleft in sky band (Palace 4, Church Group, Mitla; after Seler 1960–1961, 3:403, fig. 20).

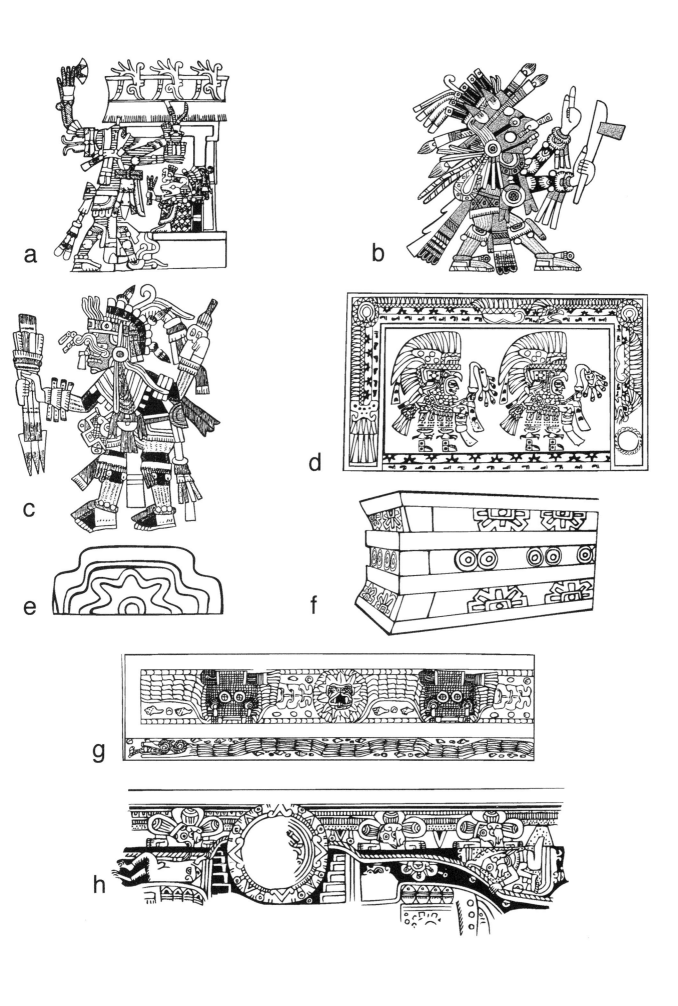

a

b

c

d

e

f

g

h

for the twin circles above the eyes of the Teotihuacán second reptile. The alternating symbols indicate some form of duality that seems related to Venus.

We can conclude that Quetzalcoatl represents the planet Venus, and his imagery does not seem to be confined to a single phase in the Venus cycle. The chronicles and codices provide clear evidence of the connection between Quetzalcoatl-Kukulcan and Venus. The confirmation of his migration legend in chronicles from two different culture areas suggests historical events somehow related to Venus events. In the Maya codices of the Postclassic period, Quetzalcoatl-Kukulcan is represented by the anthropomorphic God H, possibly associated with agriculture. He also is represented as a starry serpent in the codices. At Chichén Itzá, the feathered serpent is associated with Venus glyphs, sometimes represented in groups of five. Venus glyphs also appear on a building with an eight-part mural sequence linked to the eight-year Venus Almanac. Warfare is predominant in this Terminal Classic mural. In late Teotihuacán times, this cult of Venus warfare may have supplanted a cult devoted to Venus as a creator god.

CENTRAL MEXICAN VENUS SYMBOLS IN THE MAYA AREA

John Carlson (1991, 1993) suggests that the half-star symbol is part of a cult of Venus-regulated warfare imported from Teotihuacán to the Maya area. The Teotihuacán half-star symbol of the Classic period usually has five points, indicating a link with the five Venus cycles in the eight-year Venus Almanac (Fig. 5.6d–e; Carlson 1991, 1993). The half-star symbol is often associated with images of death, war, and sacrifice in the later phases of Teotihuacán, after around A.D. 550, according to Ellen Baird (1989:118–119). Late Teotihuacán murals from Zone 5-A depict half stars on a path traveled by priests wearing owl costumes; they carry knives with bloody hearts that indicate human sacrifice (Fig. 5.6d). In the surrounding frame, Quetzalcoatl appears as a rattlesnake with quetzal heads, half stars, and footprints along its body. The half-star symbol is also associated with

the feathered rattler at Maltrata in Veracruz during the Classic period (Fig. 5.4h). Baird notes that the half star at Teotihuacán has its counterpart in the Maya star glyph, and although they are different in form, they have a similar meaning.

The platform at Tikal shows central Mexican–style Venus glyphs with five radiating elements like the five-pointed half stars at Cacaxtla and Teotihuacán (Fig. 5.6d–f; Carlson 1993, figs. 8.1a, 8.9a; Miller 1973, figs. 137, 156, 197; Sugiyama 1993, fig. 6). The Classic period Teotihuacán half stars in turn resemble a cross-sectioned conch with five points in a water band at Cacaxtla (Carlson 1993, fig. 8.11). The conch-star connection is certainly intentional, as can be seen in the five-pointed conch pectoral, worn exclusively by Venus gods such as Quetzalcoatl and Xolotl in the Mixteca-Puebla codices of the Postclassic period (Figs. 5.1h, 5.4d).

The star belt is worn by warriors at both Tula and Chichén Itzá (Fig. 5.5b; Miller 1989, fig. 20.28). At Chichén Itzá, the star belt combines rays and a lobed design that evokes the combination of elements seen in Mixteca-Puebla Venus glyphs that represent star-tipped wings of a bee or wasp (Figs. 5.1e, g, 5.4f–g).

A star belt with five lobes appears on a Venus deity with a scorpion tail at Cacaxtla (Carlson 1993, fig. 8.6b). In the center there is a horseshoe-shaped design framing a star eye, similar to the Venus symbol worn by Tlahuizcalpantecuhtli in the Codex Vaticanus B (Fig. 5.6c). The horseshoe frame around a star may represent Venus glyphs at Maya sites over a wide geographical area (Fig. 5.8k–l).

The Venus Platform at Chichén Itzá combines central Mexican and Maya Venus imagery (Fig. 5.5a). A Mexican-style Venus glyph is tied to a bar symbolizing the number five in Maya glyphic writing. The Venus glyph is framed by a fleshy opening resembling the clefts through which Quetzalcoatl passes in Mixteca-Puebla imagery (Milbrath 1988a). Alongside there is a year sign, a year bundle, and eight dots representing eight years, all rendered in the central Mexican style. The equation is eight years equaling five Venus cycles, if we take into account the Maya-style number five. Carlson (1993:209) says that the year sign embodies the eight-year Venus Almanac.

On the other hand, Seler (1960–1961, 5:366, 375; 1990–1996, 1:211) proposes that a ceremony like the Aztec New Fire Ceremony is represented by the year bundle, signifying a bundle of 52 reeds (one for each year in the Calendar Round), which is to be multiplied by eight to yield 260 Venus Rounds. Clemency Coggins and David Drucker (1988:23) suggest that the Venus Platform commemorates a specific calendar ceremony aligning the Maya and central Mexican calendars, referring to both the New Fire Ceremony and the end of the ninth Maya Baktun falling on the day 7 Ahau (3/9/830), a date that was followed by the end of the 52-year Calendar Round at the heliacal rise of Venus on the day 1 Ahau on the winter solstice.

Another central Mexican–style Venus symbol, quincunx face painting, appears in the Codex Borgia and the Codex Vaticanus B (Fig. 5.6b–c). All five variants of Tlauhuizcalpantecuhtli representing the newly risen Morning Star spearing victims can be seen in the Codex Vaticanus B on pages 80–84. Tlahuizcalpantecuhtli's face painting displays five dots (two on the cheeks, and one each on the nose, brow, and chin), a quincunx design that probably refers to the "fiveness" of Venus in the five Venus cycles of the Venus Almanac. The same face painting is found on heads framed by Venus glyphs at Mitla (Fig. 5.6h; Seler 1960–1961, 3:403). According to Thompson (1960:170–172, fig. 31, nos. 33–40), the Maya quincunx glyph (T585a) may represent a variant of the central Mexican Venus sign. It has considerable antiquity, having been found on an Olmec scorpion sculpture (Monument 43) from San Lorenzo dated before 900 B.C. (Joralemon 1971, fig. 12).

In sum, the half-star glyph in the Maya area seems to be of central Mexican origin, most probably from Teotihuacán. The origin point for the star belt is more difficult to determine, but one of its earliest manifestations is at Cacaxtla, where it is a five-part rayed design evoking a connection with the five Venus cycles in the Venus Almanac. A number of the Venus symbols have five rays or five parts, suggesting the "fiveness" of Venus. The quincunx design, clearly associated with Venus in some contexts, is widespread and quite ancient.

MAYA GLYPHS AND SYMBOLS REPRESENTING VENUS

Central Mexican influence is evident in some forms of Maya Venus imagery, but the Maya Venus glyph has distinctive elements derived from Maya symbolism. Thompson (1960:77, 229) identifies Lamat (T510a), the eighth day in the Maya calendar, as the sign for the planet Venus (Fig. 5.7c). A similar form without the day-sign cartouche is identified as T510b, meaning "star" (*e:k'; Justeson 1984:339). In the Dresden Codex Venus pages, T510b is paired with the T109 glyph in a glyphic compound meaning chac ek (T109.510b), or chak ek' in the revised orthography, a term for Venus as both the Morning and Evening Star (Fig. 5.7a, bottom row). It has a cruciform design surrounded by four doughnut-like circles, often interpreted as symbols for jade or water but here probably connoting the luminescent quality of a star. The fact that there are four circles in a cross-shaped frame naturally suggests the four phases of Venus associated with four different directions. However, the same type of symbol can also refer to bright stars, as in the turtle constellation of Bonampak Room 2 (Fig. 7.1k).

Heinrich Berlin (1977:139–140) notes that a number of Venus intervals recorded in Palenque's Temple of the Inscriptions involve Lamat dates. He points out that the west tablet of the Temple of the Inscriptions records an interval that counts from Pacal II's accession on 5 Lamat 1 Mol forward to another 5 Lamat 1 Mol date, which is separated by an exact Venus interval (80 × 18,980 days) from the accession date. A more general study of Lamat dates should be undertaken to see if there is any Venus patterning. Indeed, Thompson (1960:299–300) notes that prognostications on the day 8 Lamat seem to refer to Venus in the Tizimin manuscript.

The Lamat glyph sometimes represents a half star with a stylized water lily (Imix), resembling a variant of the star glyph known as T510e (Fig. 5.7f; Ringle and Smith-Stark 1996:303). The T510e form appears in the eye of the Cosmic Monster in House E at Palenque, with the water lily serving as an eyelid (Fig. 5.7g).

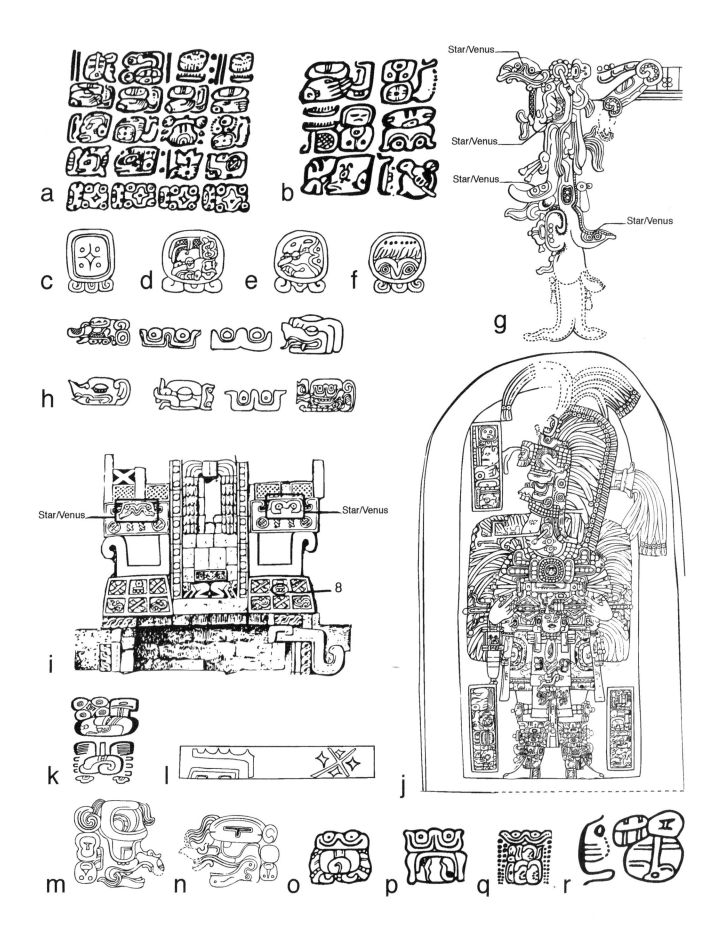

a

b

Star/Venus

Star/Venus

Star/Venus

Star/Venus

g

c

d

e

f

h

Star/Venus   Star/Venus

8

i

k

l

j

m

n

o

p

q

r

A truncated star glyph, sometimes referred to as the half Lamat glyph, has been classified as T510f by William Ringle and Thomas Smith-Stark (1996). Sky bands often incorporate the T510f star glyph or, less commonly, the T510b variant seen in the sky band on page 74 of the Dresden Codex (Fig. 7.4d). Both forms, usually paired with the Chac prefix, are used to refer to Venus in the Dresden Codex Venus pages 46–50 (Fig. 5.3a–e). On page 47 the T510f glyph also appears in the headdress of Lahun Chan (Fig. 5.1f), where the two circles are rendered in a fashion similar to central Mexican star glyphs, like red-lidded circular eyes.

In Classic period Initial Series dates, the T510f star also serves as the introductory glyph for Yax, a month that may be connected with Venus, according to Thompson (1960:111–112). Sometimes a long-snouted "dragon" substitutes instead (Fig. 5.7h). One particularly fine example has a mirror insert in the snout and the T510f star in its eyes (Fig. 5.7h, lower right). Coggins (1988c:101) suggests that this Yax variant is a Venus serpent, but it also seems to resemble the front head of the Cosmic Monster (Fig. 5.7g).

Climbing the stairs of the Tower at Palenque, one cannot help but notice a prominent T510f star glyph painted over the stair passage leading to the second floor (Aveni 1992b, fig. 3.4c). This astronomical glyph has been interpreted as a giant introductory glyph for the month Yax, the rest of which is destroyed (Robertson 1985b:77). The glyph does not necessarily refer to Venus, for similar star glyphs appearing in other architectural contexts at Palenque seem to refer to other planets (Chapter 6). Here its context near a window is intriguing, because it could mark an observation post in the tower.

FIG. 5.7. *a:* On second row from top, verbal compound of flat hand (T713a) and mirror (T617a) signals Venus is visible around beginning and end of Venus phases, as in first visibility of Morning Star on 13 Mac; on bottom row, *chac ek* (T109.510b) refers to Venus in all its phases (Dresden Codex 50; after Villacorta and Villacorta 1977).

b: On bottom row, spearing glyph follows name of victim (T1055) with T608 prefix, variously interpreted as penis or fish tail (Dresden Codex 50; after Villacorta and Villacorta 1977).

c: Lamat (T510a), eighth day in Maya calendar, probably symbolizing planet Venus (after Thompson 1960, fig. 7, no. 58).

d–e: Lamat glyphs depicting Chac's face with elongated upper lip and infixed star glyph, suggesting Chac's link with Venus (after Thompson 1960, fig. 7, nos. 59–60).

f: Lamat glyph evoking Venus as "big eye" with stylized water-lily (Imix) eyelid and star glyph in eye (compare Fig. 5.7g; after Thompson 1960, fig. 7, no. 61).

g: Front head of Cosmic Monster with eye formed by star glyph, deer ear, sky-band body, and water flowing from mouth (House E, Palenque; after Robertson 1985a, fig. 87).

h: Introductory glyphs for month Yax in Classic period Initial Series dates include animal heads and T510f star glyphs, or combinations of both (after Thompson 1960, fig. 22, nos. 50–54, 56–58).

i: Chac mask with star glyphs and number eight evoking Venus-solar cycle (western facade of Chenes temple, House of Magician, Uxmal; after H. Bricker and V. Bricker 1996, fig. 6).

j: Toothy-skull headdress backed by star glyph in scene associated with Katun ending 9.14.0.0.0, when Venus was about to reemerge as Evening Star (Tikal Stela 16; after Jones 1977, fig. 7).

k: Venus glyph (T510b) in murals associated with shell motif signifying underworld or southern direction (south wall of Early Classic Río Azul Tomb 12; after Bricker 1988a, fig. 1).

l: Preclassic cross pattern with star symbols positioned in four quarters, possibly early form of Lamat symbolizing Venus (Olmecoid vessel from Copán; after Schele and Miller 1986:119).

m–n: Two stylized serpent faces may represent Venus as Evening Star marked by Ik; one on left (Pier F) has mirror brow, and one on right (Pier B) has skeletal jaw (House D, Palenque; after Robertson 1985b, fig. 243).

o–q: Star (T510f) over shell glyph, star over earth glyph, and star over place-name for Seibal—all may mark warfare events apparently linked with Venus positions (after Lounsbury 1982, fig. 2).

r: *Tzul ahau* or *tsul ahaw* may be canine name for Evening Star (Dresden Codex 47; after Closs 1989, fig. 31.5).

The T510f star appears as part of an event glyph in a number of Maya texts and is often interpreted as a reference to Venus (Closs 1977; Lounsbury 1982). It appears in a compound known as the "shell star," which is associated with warfare (Fig. 5.7o). After studying twenty-five shell-star dates, Arthur Schlak (1996:186, table 1) concluded that all refer to a time when Venus was moving slowly relative to the Sun, a phenomenon that occurs at specific times in its synodic period (during superior conjunction, during its descent as the Morning Star, and during its ascent as Evening Star). I would add that visual imagery helps support this interpretation, for the shell seems to be that of a mollusk, a slow-moving creature. Furthermore, the shell-star image contrasts with the insect image of Venus, discussed at the beginning of the chapter, which seems to represent Venus when it is moving rapidly as the descending Evening Star.

Among the Maya, the star/Venus glyph appears in a number of contexts, most commonly to indicate a Venus alignment, to note a date when a Venus phenomenon occurred, or as part of general star-war imagery (Miller 1988:180). Less common, but nonetheless intriguing, are sets of Venus symbols that allude to the "fiveness" of Venus, no doubt symbolizing the Venus Almanac of five Venus cycles correlating with eight solar years.

On the north side of the Nunnery at Uxmal, the Venus Temple facade depicts five star glyphs—resembling truncated Lamat glyphs (T510f)—that symbolize Venus (Pl. 22; Kowalski 1990:46, 49–50). Like other buildings in the Nunnery Quadrangle, the Venus Temple is believed to date to around A.D. 900. Although no specific Venus alignment has been documented for the south-facing Venus Temple, the grouping of five Venus symbols confirms an association with the "fiveness" of Venus. Other Puuc-style architectural structures at Uxmal show similar glyphs associated with sets of five Chac masks, as noted below.

The House of the Governor (Governor's Palace) at Uxmal is the best-known example of a building with star/Venus glyphs and an alignment toward a Venus position (Aveni 1980:273–276; 1991:78). It displays Chac masks associated with more than 350 star glyphs, probably indicating a relationship with Venus (Aveni 1991:317; Sprajc 1993a:47). Aveni concludes that the alignment faces Venus when it rises at an azimuth of 118°22′ at its maximum southerly eight-year excursion behind the pyramid of Nohpat 6 km distant. Sprajc (1993a) argues that the alignment is in the opposite direction (azimuth of 288°22′), with the palace serving as the backsight for observing the northern extreme of Venus setting as the Evening Star, as viewed from the top of the principal pyramid at Cehtzuc, located 4.5 km from Uxmal. Aveni (1995:S79; 1997) now recognizes that Cehtzuc marks the alignment, but he stands by his original interpretation that the principal alignment faces east, noting that the House of the Governor faces outward from the predominantly north-south axis of other buildings, and it is skewed by 20° in relation to other buildings.

A sky-band throne on the facade of the Governor's Palace shows constellations, the Sun, the Moon, and Venus in a configuration that may suggest the appearance of the sky in the early tenth century. Harvey and Victoria Bricker's (1996:204, fig. 3) interpretations of the imagery are adapted to fit observations of both the northerly and southerly extremes of Venus. If the Aveni hypothesis is correct, they maintain that the sky band shows a zodiac band replicating the sky at the time Venus rose at its southerly extreme before sunrise in A.D. 912 (4/29/912 O.S.). They note that one of the sky-band glyphs (T510f) most probably alludes to Venus. They suggest that the star glyph has an asymmetrical variant of T109 as a superfix, denoting *chac ek,* a name for Venus. The building facade itself has many Chac masks with T510f star glyphs over the eyes, perhaps forming a kind of rebus for Venus as *chac ek.* On northeast and northwest corners of the fourth platform, these masks have the number eight inscribed in the eyebrow, alluding to the eight-year Venus Almanac and possibly also to the eight-day inferior conjunction period (Aveni 1991:S9, fig. 1; 1992b:197; Aveni and Hartung 1986, fig. 6f; Kowalski 1987, fig. 60; Sprajc 1993b:S47).

The western facade of the Chenes Temple in the Pyramid of the Magician also has a mask with T510f star glyphs and the number eight, evoking the Venus-solar cycle of the Venus Almanac (Fig. 5.7i). An angled sight line (240°13′) from the doorway passes through the center of the ball court to the center of the north plaza in the South Group and the principal door of the West Group toward the maximum southerly extreme of Venus reached every eight years (Sprajc 1995a:45). The temple actually faces sunset on April 12 and August 13 (azimuth 279°17′). Aveni (1991:79–80) notes that this orientation may be part of a count involving the zenith dates at Uxmal, for April 12 is two lunar months before the solar zenith on May 22, and adding three Uinals (60 days) brings you to the second solar zenith on July 22. Observations from the temple probably integrated the Venus cycle, the solar year, and the lunar months as part of the eight-year Venus Almanac.

The East Building of the Nunnery, another building at Uxmal with Chac masks bearing star glyphs, also seems to allude to the eight-year Venus Almanac (Aveni 1991:78; Lamb 1980). The facade has stacked Chac masks flanked by groups of double-headed serpents on a background of X-shaped mosaics. The average number of X-shaped blocks bounded by the five sets of double-headed serpent bars is 584, suggesting an equation with the synodic period of Venus (Lamb 1980). The serpent bars are grouped with eight bars in each set, symbolizing the eight solar years that make up the Venus-solar calendar. On each group of bars there is a mask that may represent an owl (Kowalski 1990:48). As we will see, owls appear in imagery linked with Venus, but the owl itself does not seem to be a Venus god.

Mary Miller (1988:180) suggests that the Venus glyph (T510b) on the Jaguar Stairway at Copán may symbolize the Evening Star, because of its position on the western side of the East Court, although no Venus alignment has been documented to date. The glyph frames the face of the Jaguar War God, linked with both the Moon and Venus (Chapter 4).

Venus glyphs decorate a window in Copán Structure 22 designed to observe Venus during the reign of 18 Rabbit (Aveni 1991:318). The west window was aligned to observe the northerly extremes of Venus as the Evening Star, which invariably occurred in late April or early May in the eighth and ninth centuries (Close et al. 1984:234, table 1). Further

study indicates that the Evening Star's last appearance before inferior conjunction was always preceded by quite a long span of visibility through the window, which included both the maximum brilliancy and the stationary point of the planet (Sprajc 1987–1988:92–94; 1993a:50–53). The window also functioned as a viewing aid to locate the Evening Star at its first visibility after superior conjunction at eight-year intervals, when its appearance in the window served as a sign for the burning of the fields in April.

Analysis of glyphs and dates recorded on Copán Structure 11, built in the reign of Yax Pac, suggests it has a Venus association (Schele and Miller 1986:122–123). David Kelley and Ann Kerr (1973:185–186) point out that this structure has one of the few known Classic period "great star" (*chac ek*) inscriptions that clearly refers to Venus, for it is associated with the same verb seen in the Venus table. The date given (5 Cib 10 Pop) is not a viable calendar date, and it is usually interpreted as 5 Cib 9 Pop (9.15.15.12.16). Linda Schele and Mary Miller (1986:123) point out that the text is partly written in reverse order, and they translate the text as "it shined, the great star," referring to the first appearance of the Evening Star. Lounsbury (1982:154–155) notes that this date probably marks an heir-designation ceremony coinciding with the first visibility of Venus as an Evening Star on 2/11/747. Aveni and Hotaling (1994, table 1) adjust this date to the 584,283 correlation and point out that the Evening Star actually rose five days earlier, but this does not diminish the likelihood that Venus was important in timing the ceremony.

A "smoking" skull on Copán Stela A, another of 18 Rabbit's monuments (Fig. 3.6c; Pl. 20), may represent Venus at the first visibility of the Evening Star. This stela is inscribed with the dedication date of 9.14.19.8.0 12 Ahau 18 Cumku (1/28/731), coinciding with a time when Venus reappeared as the Evening Star, according to my analysis. This was also the day of the full Moon. Another interplay between the Moon and Venus is evident on Stela C, another stela commissioned by 18 Rabbit. The text on this stela mentions Venus in two passages, one that seems to be a mythological antecedent and another that refers to an actual Venus event linked with the Katun ending 9.14.0.0.0 (11/29/711; Lounsbury 1982:156–157; Schele and Matthews 1998:146, fig. 4.16). A toothy-skull glyph appears in a text associated with the Katun end. Although Lounsbury associated it with the first visibility of the Evening Star at the Katun end, Venus actually rose four days later (Aveni and Hotaling 1994, table 1). The toothy-skull glyph may actually refer to Venus in superior conjunction, which would be appropriate because the skeletal form may refer to the underworld. The Katun ending is also the night of the full Moon (6:16 A.M., 11/30/711; Goldstine 1973). Tikal Stela 16, which depicts the ruler wearing a mosaic headdress with a toothy skull backed by a Venus or star glyph, also records the Katun ending 9.14.0.0.0, when the Moon was full and Venus was about to reemerge as Evening Star (Fig. 5.7j). This type of skeletal imagery may relate to Venus when it was still invisible in superior conjunction. Parallel images occur in central Mexico, for the Codex Borgia image discussed earlier shows Xolotl (the Evening Star) watching the skeletal Morning Star disappear into the underworld, indicating that the Morning Star was no longer visible and the Evening Star was ascendant (Fig. 5.4d). In a study of the sequence of Venus images in Codex Borgia 29–46, I concluded that the skeletal Morning Star represents times when Venus was invisible in superior conjunction and times when the Morning Star was not visible because the Evening Star had emerged (Milbrath 1989:112, fig. 1).

A number of Copán monuments with Katun-ending dates may be associated with the first visibility of the Evening Star (Schele 1991a; Schele and Fash 1991). Smoke Imix God K, who came to power in A.D. 628 as the twelfth ruler of Copán, initiated a program of sculpture that focused on the heliacal rise of the Evening Star at the Katun ending 9.11.0.0.0 (10/9/652), recorded on Copán Stelae 2, 3, 10, 13, 19, and 23. Certainly the rise of the Evening Star so close to the Katun ending would have been considered an auspicious beginning for the new Katun, since the Evening Star was associated with agricultural fertility (Šprajc 1993a, 1993b). Lounsbury (1982:156) discovered that the Katun ending 9.11.0.0.0 coincides with the heliacal rise of the Evening Star in the Temple of the Inscriptions at Palenque. Astronomical calculations indicate the Katun ending fell only four days after the heliacal rise of Venus (Aveni and Hotaling 1994, table 1). This Katun ending was a close counterpart to the Katun ending 9.14.0.0.0, which occurred four days before Venus rose as the Evening Star. Indeed, a Venus phenomenon occurring on one date will recur three Katuns later, which may explain the sets of three Katuns recorded at Palenque in the Temple of the Inscriptions (Berlin 1977:123). Lounsbury (1991:817) suggests that the astrological information recorded in the Katun records amounts to astrological "Katun prophecies."

The T510b star glyph represents Venus in murals on the south wall of the Early Classic Río Azul Tomb 12 (Fig. 5.7k). Here it is paired with a shell motif signifying the direction south or the underworld. On the north wall, the Moon glyph is linked with an image of the Maize god, apparently symbolizing the overhead direction, or north (Fig. 3.2b; Chapter 3). Victoria Bricker (1988a) interprets the mural scene as a representation of astronomical events that placed the Moon overhead when Venus was at the opposite side of the sky, close to its nadir.

An early form of the T510b star appears on the La Mojarra Stela, dated to the Protoclassic period, in association with calendar dates representing nine Venus cycles of 584 days (Justeson and Kaufman 1993:1708; Macri and Stark 1993:6). The design has a cruciform center inscribed in a diamond. Different variants show four dots or four rays arranged around the center. The Venus glyph may be traced back to around 800 B.C. at Copán, where an Olmecoid vessel depicts a cross pattern with star symbols positioned in the four quarters, possibly alluding to the four phases of Venus (Fig. 5.7l).

The stucco piers of House D at Palenque may depict two images of Venus as the Evening Star, distinguished by their Ik insignia (Fig. 5.7m–n; Robertson 1985b, fig. 243). The one at the base of Pier B has a skeletal jaw and an Ik glyph at the top of its head; the other, on Pier F, depicts a face with an Ik earring. As noted earlier, Lounsbury (1974:11) links the day sign Ik with the cult of the Evening Star, because this is the canonical day for the rise of the Evening Star in the Dresden Codex Venus table. It is interesting to note that Copán Stela 7 names the Paddler Twins and an Ik god who may be Venus on a date associated with the maximum altitude as Evening Star (9.9.0.0.0; 5/7/613; Aveni and Hotaling 1994, table 1; Schele 1987c). Further testing of the association between Ik and the Evening star is called for.

Venus imagery may appear in a different form on the Palenque Palace Oval Tablet. Pacal II wears an Ik glyph pectoral that may be a Venus reference (Lounsbury 1985:56; Robertson 1985a, fig. 91). The panel was set in a background that has a dancing figure with a star glyph. Venus events coincide with events in Pacal's life in a surprising fashion. His birth date may be linked with the first appearance of Venus as the Evening Star (Dütting 1985:269). His accession date in A.D. 615 (9.9.2.4.8) corresponds to the first appearance of Venus as the Morning Star (Berlin 1977:140). Such coincidences have led scholars to conclude that Pacal manipulated the dates of his life history to correspond to astronomical events (Marcus 1992:346).

In sum, a number of monuments and architectural facades with star glyphs (usually T510b or T510f) are linked with dates or orientations related to Venus events. Groupings of five such glyphs or their association with the number eight suggest the Venus Almanac. Katun endings in the Late Classic period coinciding approximately with the first appearance of the Evening Star are associated with star glyphs and skeletal imagery, possibly an allusion to a specific Venus phase. Not all star glyphs are related to Venus images and events, and not all Venus imagery depicts star glyphs. The Ik symbol and certain star-eye forms may be related to Venus. The star glyph seems to symbolize Venus in the day sign Lamat, in the Initial Series introductory glyph for the month Yax, and in glyphic passages where it is paired with the *chac* prefix. The shell-star compounds may also refer specifically to Venus at times when the planet is moving slowly through the sky.

VENUS WARFARE

Floyd Lounsbury (1982) was the first to associate Venus specifically with warfare. His research demonstrates that warfare or raids are expressed with compounds involving stars, usually T510f over an earth symbol, a shell, or a place-name (Fig. 5.7o–q). His study of the distribution of star-war dates indicates that war imagery is linked with the first visibility of Venus in the morning and evening sky, as well as with the short period of inferior conjunction. The timing of the Venus-war events indicates that they cluster in the dry season, the time of year preferred for warfare, whereas raids could take place during the rainy season (Aveni and Hotaling 1994; Nahm 1994). Apparently, warfare was avoided when Venus was invisible in superior conjunction.

John Justeson (1989, table 8.8) surveyed the star-glyph dates and found that star-war events were uncommon during the canonical period of superior conjunction, an artificially long period of ninety days that overlaps with the last visibility of the Morning Star and the first visibility of the Evening Star. Justeson (1989:123 n. 20) concludes that some territorial wars began at special points in the Venus cycle, but many more were timed by a lunar count beginning with the heliacal rise of Venus. As far back as Protoclassic times, Venus was linked with warfare, for the La Mojarra Stela indicates that battles were timed by Venus and the Venus-star glyph (*matza) was used as a warrior title (Justeson and Kaufman 1993:1705, fig. 7c).

The Venus warfare cult, found at a number of Maya sites with imagery of a goggle-eyed deity later known as Tlaloc, apparently originated in Teotihuacán (Carlson 1991, 1993). Venus warfare can be traced at least as far back as sixth-century Teotihuacán, where the cult is linked with Tlaloc and the atlatl, a spear-thrower common in central Mexico. The Teotihuacán trapeze-and-ray year sign, often associated with this deity in the Maya area, may encode the Venus Almanac, according to Carlson (1993:212).

Monochrome red murals in Teotihuacán's Tepantitla compound depict goggle-eyed warriors emanating flames who are framed by a corona of rays (Fig. 5.8a). Laurette Séjourné (1976:106) identifies these as the warrior aspect of the Morning Star carrying an atlatl. Although these figures do not have Tlaloc's monstrous mouth, they have goggled eyes and may be connected with Venus imagery.

A recently discovered stucco relief in the North

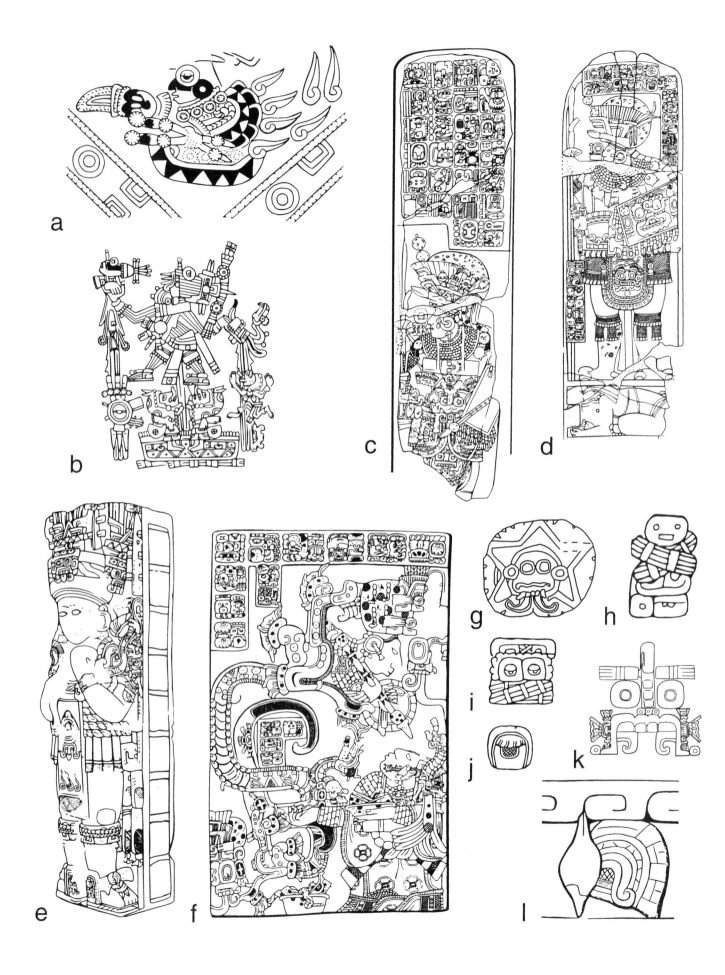

a

b

c

d

e

f

g

h

i

j

k

l

Group at Palenque shows a goggle-eyed figure carrying an atlatl, a counterpart for the storm god of Teotihuacán, indicating a warrior cult linked with Tlaloc at Palenque (Pl. 14). This relief probably represents Venus in a warrior aspect.

Schele (1991a) notes that a complex of symbols borrowed from Teotihuacán accompanies the Maya star-war complex. These include the goggle-eyed war deity called Tlaloc by the Aztecs; a trapeze-and-ray sign symbolizing the Mexican "year sign"; a full-bodied jaguar suit; a spherical "balloon" headdress; a War Serpent mask in a mosaic pattern; owls; and spear-throwers (Fig. 5.8c–d). Linda Schele and David Freidel (1990:444–446, fig. 4:17) propose that the Tlaloc warfare complex on Classic Maya monuments is associated with significant planetary positions of Jupiter, Saturn, and Venus, especially Venus as an Evening Star.

Aveni and Hotaling (1994) provide an excellent synthesis of the star-war dates associated with specific star-glyph compounds (Fig. 5.7o–q), plotting them in terms of their proximity to Venus events, retrograde periods, and eclipses. They also plotted dates associated with the Tlaloc-war complex (Fig. 5.8c–d) and the *tsul ahaw* (*tzul ahau*) glyph (Fig.

5.7r). They use a chi-square statistical model to test whether these "astronomically tagged" dates have a distribution that confirms a relationship with Venus events. Testing ninety-eight dates, they found that 96 percent matched times when Venus was visible, suggesting that the dates are not randomly distributed. The majority of dates (70%) correlate with the Evening Star period. Of these, an unusually high percentage correspond to the first appearances of the Evening Star (84%), if one allows a five-day window on either side of the actual Venus event. Aveni and Hotaling found that when there is not an appropriate Venus event, the dates can often be correlated with the first appearance of Mercury or with retrograde motion of the superior planets.

A convincing connection with Venus events is evident in a star-war date recorded on Dos Pilas Stela 2 (formerly known as Stela 16) and Aguateca Stela 2 (Fig. 5.8c–d). Both monuments bear a "star-over-Seibal" glyph compound that refers to a war event on 9.15.4.6.4 (11/27/735), which corresponds to the first appearance of the Evening Star (Fig. 5.7q; Aveni and Hotaling 1994, table 1; Lounsbury 1982, table 1). Schele and Freidel (1990:445) link these monuments to an astronomical cult related to Tlaloc. The

---

FIG. 5.8. *a:* Warrior aspect of Venus represented by star warrior surrounded by rays (Tepantitla, Patio 9, Mural 3 detail, Teotihuacán; after Séjourné 1976, fig. 23).

b: In group of five Tlalocs on Codex Borgia 27, central one has red striped body paint of star gods and year-sign headdress of Teotihuacán storm god known as Tlaloc A (after Tozzer 1957, fig. 233; Seler 1963).

c–d: Warrior imagery linked with Tlaloc, including Mexican year sign, spherical "balloon" headdress, owl, and spear thrower, on two stelae that record star-war date of 9.15.4.6.4, corresponding to first appearance of Evening Star on 11/27/735 (Dos Pilas Stela 2 and Aguateca Stela 2; after Houston 1993, figs. 3.28, 4.20).

e: Ruler of Copán known as Smoke Imix God K bears Tlaloc images on seventh-century monument recording date coinciding with end of retrograde for planet Venus (Copán Stela 6; after drawing by Barbara Fash in Fash 1991, fig. 60).

f: Double-headed skeletal snake carries Tlaloc-masked ancestor (founder of lineage?) honored in bloodletting

rite; note five-part Venus glyph with heavy-lidded eye on interlaced volute (Yaxchilán Lintel 25; after Tate 1992, fig. 98).

g: Tlaloc on star symbol (Zone 2, Patio of the Jaguars, Portico 1, Mural 1 detail, Teotihuacán; after Miller 1973, fig. 24).

h–i: Lineage glyph known as founder glyph has main sign (T600) formed by two reed bundles symbolizing 104 years in great Venus cycle; goggled eyes on one example evoke founder's guise as Tlaloc (Copán Structure 33; after Schele 1992a, figs. 8d–e).

j: Heavy-lidded eye (T819) may be form of Venus symbol representing Venus as "big eye."

k: Tlaloc mask flanked by rayed "horseshoe" designs that frame heavy-lidded eyes alluding to Venus as "big eye" (Structure 26, Copán; after Fash 1992, fig. 16a).

l: Heavy-lidded eye is framed by rays representing radiant Venus eye (Palace of the Stuccoes, Acancéh; after Miller 1991, fig. 20).

war event coincides with the beginning of the dry season, the epoch of warfare. On both monuments, the ruler wears a Tlaloc mask and a headdress with a Mexican-style year sign, which is associated with a variant of Tlaloc known as Tlaloc A at Teotihuacán (Pasztory 1974). Both rulers wear a goggle-eyed insignia on the torso and an owl pendant as a war insignia. Carlson (1993, fig. 8.2c) calls this bird the War Emblem Owl, noting that it wears a five-pointed Venus symbol on the Dos Pilas stela. Given the link between owl imagery and Mercury discussed at the end of this chapter, it is interesting to note that Mercury had just dipped below the horizon for its last visibility as the Evening Star. Essentially the two planets traded places on 11/27/735.

There is also evidence of Venus warfare in the northern Maya area at Chichén Itzá. The murals of the Upper Temple of the Jaguars show war events that may relate to the Venus Almanac, as noted earlier. Venus may be linked with warfare and the dry season on Lintel 4 of the Temple of Four Lintels. Michel Davoust (1991:156) reads the associated text as *ek' tok' pakal u kaban mah,* translated as "Venus knife shield (war), his land dried."

In Room 2 of Structure 1 at Bonampak, a battle scene is associated with a partial Calendar Round that Lounsbury (1982:149, 164) reconstructs as 9.18.1.15.5 13 Chicchan 13 Yax, the day Venus was in inferior conjunction and the date of the second solar zenith at the site. If we shift to the 584,283 correlation, the date (7/31/792) marks the midpoint of the planet's disappearance interval around inferior conjunction, a few days before the solar zenith (Aveni and Hotaling 1994, table 1). Because the dates are problematical, we must be cautious in interpreting the nature of the Bonampak star-war events (Marcus 1992:426, 431). In any case, the astronomical symbols in the ceiling of Room 2 show that astrology was important in timing the battle (Fig. 7.1i–j). Ultimate victory remained beyond their grasp, for warfare caused Bonampak to be abandoned abruptly before the artists could complete the murals of Structure 1, the last building constructed at the site.

Venus is also implicated in the Calendar Round dates that Lounsbury (1982:146, 158, 163, table 1) reconstructs for Room 1 at Bonampak. One date

(9.18.0.3.4; 12/8/790) records a dynastic ritual that took place at the first stationary point of Venus (12/10/790; Meeus n.d.). A second date (9.18.1.2.0; 11/9/791) corresponds to the first appearance of Venus as the Evening Star and to a ritual designating the heir to the throne. However, there are no clear examples of the star glyph in the Initial Series inscriptions of Room 1 (M. Miller 1986:29).

We can conclude that Venus was closely connected with warfare among the Maya. The patterning of dates suggests that warfare was avoided during times when Venus was invisible in superior conjunction. There was also a seasonal cycle in the warfare, for the star-war dates seem to cluster in the dry season. Although not all of these dates specifically relate to Venus, it seems that Venus was the most prominent planet in events involving warfare. Venus warfare may be closely linked to Tlaloc imagery, and probably was part of a cult imported from Teotihuacán. As we will see, this cult seems to be associated with lineage founders at a number of sites, suggesting that foreigners bringing the cult may also have founded dynasties in the Maya area.

LINEAGE FOUNDERS AND THE VENUS CULT

Venus may be linked with the founders of some Maya lineages. The "founder glyph" appears on Yaxchilán Lintel 25, depicting a double-headed serpent bearing a ruler wearing a Tlaloc mask (Fig. 5.8f). Peter Mathews (1990:91) identifies the masked figure as an ancestral portrait. Tatiana Proskouriakoff (1993:90, 169) refers to the figure as an ancestor of uncertain identity. Schele says the ancestor figure is Yat Balam, the founder of a Yaxchilán lineage or dynasty (Schele 1989a; Schele and Freidel 1990:266–267, fig. 7:3b). The text alongside the serpent ends with a phrase that Carolyn Tate (1992:276) transcribes as "It is recorded, [the] alter ego [in?] [of?] the house of the Founder of the Lineage." The masked figure seems to be a lineage founder connected with a goggle-eyed deity later known as Tlaloc. His warlike stance hurling a spear evokes Venus warfare. Another Tlaloc face appears in the jaws of the second serpent head at the base of the lintel.

The double-headed serpent on Lintel 25 intertwines with a volute bearing a heavy-lidded eye framed by five radiating elements, a form of Venus symbol that may refer to Venus as the "big eye." The Calendar Round date 4 Imix 4 Mac (9.12.9.8.1; 10/18/681) marks a time when Venus was relatively high in the sky as the Evening Star.

Venus seems to be the alter ego, or *way,* of Copán's royal lineage (Andrews and Fash 1992:101). Schele (1992a:141–142) notes that the founder is not actually the first ruler at Copán, but he founded a specific lineage traced back to the early fifth century. The lineage founder at Copán, who bears the name Yax K'uk' Mo', seems to be connected with Tlaloc imagery, for he has goggled eyes on Copán Altar Q. Here he is associated with a founding event on 5 Caban 15 Yaxkin (8.19.10.10.17; 9/3/426), when Venus was approximately at its maximum altitude as the Morning Star (Schele 1989a:2; Schele and Fash 1991). It may also be significant that the full Moon was setting while Mars, Mercury, and Jupiter were all grouped close together on the eastern horizon at dawn on that date.

The upper temple of Structure 16 at Copán has the founder glyph and goggle-eyed lineage founder Yax K'uk' Mo' wearing a headdress with his bird spirit, a quetzal-macaw, as on Altar Q (Schele 1989a: 5; Schele and Fash 1991). The Margarita Building depicts a macaw intertwined with a quetzal, symbolizing the name of the founder, K'inich Yax K'uk' Mo' (Stuart 1997:84–85). This avian image evokes a link with murals from Teotihuacán that show a bird combining attributes of both species (Berrin 1988, pls. 17–19). One of these murals shows a quetzal-macaw holding a dart and a war shield, suggesting a guise of Venus (Miller 1973, fig. 363). The founder may be linked with avian Venus imagery brought from Teotihuacán (Coggins 1988c:98–99).

One example of the founder glyph compound at Copán depicts goggled eyes with pupils that take the same form as central Mexican stars, recalling Tlaloc's star eyes in central Mexican art (Fig. 5.8i; Milbrath 1980a). The main sign (T600) in the founder glyph has been identified as a logograph referring to lineage (Grube, cited in Kurbjuhn 1989:82). Coggins (1993) suggests that the T600 glyph represents

bound bundles like those used in the Aztec New Fire Ceremony, performed every 52 years at the end of a Calendar Round when the "vague year" and divination calendar realigned. In fact, a longer cycle of time is suggested because the bundles in the founder's glyph are in pairs, suggesting instead the Great Cycle of about 104 years that links the Tzolkin, Venus cycles, and solar calendar (Fig. 4.8h–i).

As mentioned earlier, there may be two lineages at Chichén Itzá, one linked with the Sun, the other with Venus. The cycles of these two astronomical bodies are connected in the Venus Almanac of 8 years and the Great Cycle of 104 years. Goggle-eyed figures hold burning year bundles on the Temple of the Warriors, and year bundles appear as part of a calendar inscription on the Platform of Venus (Fig. 5.5a). The Great Cycle is recorded in the Dresden Codex, a manuscript that may have been painted around A.D. 1250 before Chichén Itzá was abandoned.

We can conclude that the founder at two Maya sites is associated with a foreign cult with visual trappings of the Tlaloc complex imported from Teotihuacán, most probably connected with Venus. This complex involves the goggle-eyed deities and deified lineage founders whose attributes suggest central Mexican connections. These founders may be historical figures somehow connected with a Venus cult imported from Teotihuacán, or they may be mythological Venus figures that legitimize the divine ancestry of lineages claiming an affiliation with Teotihuacán.

TLALOC AND THE STORM GOD

Since the founder and Venus imagery are both connected with Tlaloc in the Maya area, we need to better understand the role this storm god plays in central Mexico. The chronicles allude to Tlaloc's astronomical nature. The *Historia de los mexicanos por sus pinturas* (1973:35) notes that Tlaloc is the father of the Moon. In another account, Tlaloc and the Moon rule the lowest heaven, beneath the heaven of the Sun (Codex Ríos, folios 1v–2r). Tlaloc's position in the lowest heaven could allude to an inferior planet; only the Moon and the inferior planets pass in front of the Sun, and in an Earth-centered cosmos, they would seem to be in a layer beneath the Sun. Tlaloc could symbolize either Venus or Mercury, but the evidence seems stronger for linking Tlaloc with Venus.

Cecelia Klein's (1980) extensive study of Tlaloc indicates that he controlled thunder and lightning; he was closely associated with the calendar and time; and he may be especially linked with period endings involving the Sun and Venus. She suggests that the year sign in his headdress alludes to such period endings. Carlson (1993:212) proposes that the trapeze-and-ray year sign, when it appears in Tlaloc's Venus warfare complex, alludes to the Venus Almanac of five Venus cycles in eight solar years. Klein (1980: 178–180) suggests that Tlaloc is the counterpart of the Maya bee Bacab Hobnil, connected with the Evening Star. There are some images that seem to show him with insect attributes (Klein 1980, fig. 9). Evidence presented earlier indicates bees and wasps may be aspects of the Evening Star connected with the period of its rapid descent. Although it seems premature to link Tlaloc with a specific Venus phase, the evidence linking him with Venus seems intriguing.

Klein (1980) identifies Tlaloc's eyes as mirrors, presumably with goggles representing the mirror rim. In the Codex Borgia (25), his eyes are encircled by goggles made of turquoise, the same material used for pendants, collars, and mirror backs. In Aztec art, Tlaloc's eyes are actually stars encircled by goggles (Codex Magliabecchiano, folios 34r, 44r; Milbrath 1980a). Stars and mirrors may overlap in their imagery, for both share a shiny quality, and mirrors symbolize astronomical bodies in a number of different contexts.

Codex Borgia 27 shows five figures of Tlaloc that Esther Pasztory (1974:7–10) identifies as variants of the Teotihuacán storm god known as Tlaloc A, most often characterized by a headdress with knots or a year sign. The Tlaloc figure positioned in the center has a year-sign headdress and the red striped body paint of the star gods (Fig. 5.8b). The four Tlalocs surrounding him appear with year signs marking a sequence of years, each associated with a different cardinal direction and different pests and weather patterns affecting the maize crop. The four dates run counterclockwise around the page at intervals of

thirteen vague years of 365 days beginning with 1 Reed, linked with the day 1 Crocodile. Next we find the year 1 Knife with the day 1 Death, expressing an interval of exactly 13 × 365 days. Then we have the year 1 House followed by the year 1 Rabbit, with day signs appropriate to marking two more intervals of thirteen years. And if we continue the count to the end of the year 1 Rabbit, we have a total of forty years or five Venus Almanacs equaling 5 × 8 years or 5 × 99 lunar months, implying a symbolic link with the five Tlalocs. The year 1 Rabbit may have had special significance because it was the year of the New Fire Ceremony in the epoch of the Codex Borgia, prior to a change made in Aztec times (Milbrath 1989: 117). Presumably the entire fifty-two-year cycle is also represented because the next page (28) brings the count again to 1 Reed, the year that opened the count on page 27.

Page 28 has a similar composition to that seen on page 27, but this time the five Tlalocs are associated with a cycle that runs for about five years. The sequence begins with a date reconstructed as the year 1 Reed, paired with the day 4 Movement, and runs through the year 5 Reed and the day 1 Water, recording a total interval of three synodic cycles of Venus (3 × 584 days), according to Seler (1963, 1:263– 265), who notes that this is just seventy-three days short of five solar years. He concludes that this page reflects an interest in comparing the solar year with the Venus cycle, probably counted from the superior-conjunction phase when Venus and the Sun are joined together. I would add that counting from the end of the year 1 Rabbit on page 27 to the beginning of 5 Reed, the last year on page 28, gives a total of sixteen years, or a double Venus Almanac, again linking the cycles of the Sun, the Moon, and Venus. On page 28, each of the five Tlalocs is associated with a different kind of rain and a different fate for maize. Seler points out that each Tlaloc has different face paint. In the year 1 Reed, symbolizing the eastern direction, Tlaloc wears the face paint of Tezcatlipoca, a god who is sometimes associated with Venus, especially in the cult of Mixcoatl (Nicholson 1971: 426). In the year 2 Knife, representing the north, Tlaloc has the face paint of Tlahuizcalpantecuhtli, the god of the Morning Star. In the year 3 House,

Seler notes that Tlaloc wears the face of the Fire God, although this identification is less convincing. If Seler is correct, there could be an overlap with imagery of Xiuhtecuhtli as the Morning Star on Dresden Codex 49. In the year 4 Rabbit, Tlaloc has the face painting and beard of Quetzalcoatl, another Venus god. In the year 5 Reed, he has the face of Xochipilli, a god who conflates imagery of the Sun and Venus in some contexts (Klein 1976:11).

The Miniature Temple in the Atetelco compound at Teotihuacán has murals depicting feathered serpents framing a panel with multiple images of Tlaloc, represented with goggled eyes, fangs, and a bifurcated serpent tongue (Miller 1973, fig. 346). The layout suggests that there were originally five Tlaloc heads in a panel, implying a connection with the Venus Almanac. Murals from the Patio of the Jaguars in Zone 2 at Teotihuacán depict Tlaloc's face superimposed on a design that is both a cross-section of a conch shell and a five-pointed star symbolizing the "fiveness" of Venus (Fig. 5.8g; Miller 1973, figs. 24, 26, 30).

The Classic period storm god with a headdress bearing a year sign or knots is the Teotihuacán god most often seen in the Maya area (Tlaloc A; Fig. 5.8c–f). Carlson (1993:204, 209) connects the variant of Tlaloc with the year sign with the Venus Almanac, and notes that the central Mexican Tlaloc represents a Venus cult of warfare and sacrifice. This variant of Tlaloc is clearly associated with a date marking the first appearance of the Evening Star on the monuments from Dos Pilas and Aguateca discussed earlier (Fig. 5.8c–d; Schele and Freidel 1990:147, 444–445). Other Maya monuments with Tlaloc A seem to record different patterns in relation to Venus, as noted in the discussion of the lineage founders.

On Copán Stela 6, the ruler Smoke Imix God K wears a jawless Tlaloc headdress with a knot and a year sign (Fig. 5.8e). Jawless Tlaloc A faces, resembling the patron of the Maya month Pax, emerge from either end of a double-headed serpent in the ruler's arms. This monument has Venus associations, according to Schele and Freidel (1990:445), who note that the Initial Series date 9.12.10.0.0 9 Ahau 18 Zotz is related to the retrograde of Venus. Indeed, this date precisely marks the end of the planet's ret-

rograde (5/5/682; Meeus n.d.). Since the planet's maximum brilliance as the Morning Star follows about two weeks after the end of retrograde, the increasing brilliance of the planet would be notable. This date appears with a heavy-lidded eye (T819) that may be a symbol representing Venus as a "big eye," appropriate to the name for Venus recorded in Colonial period texts (Fig. 5.8j).

At Copán, a jawless Tlaloc mask from Structure 26 is flanked by heavy-lidded eyes framed by horseshoe designs with radiating elements representing rays (Fig. 5.8k; Fash 1991, fig. 91). Images of a radiant Venus eye may also be seen at Acancéh, where the horseshoe eye form is similarly surrounded by rays (Fig. 5.8l). Similar forms are seen in a set of five eyes on the Five-story Palace (Structure 5D-52) at Tikal, no doubt related to the "fiveness" of Venus (Pl. 18). This arrangement in turn can be linked to the five Maya-style Venus glyphs on the facade of the Venus Temple at Uxmal (Pl. 22).

We can conclude that the storm god known as Tlaloc in Aztec times is an astronomical deity who moves in the same layer of heaven as the Moon and is the father of the Moon. Both Quetzalcoatl and Tlaloc may represent complementary aspects of Venus. Tlaloc is connected with the Venus Almanac linking the Venus cycles to the cycles of the Sun and Moon, especially when he appears in sets of five. One such set in the Codex Borgia shows Tlaloc conflated with various Venus gods in scenes associated with intervals appropriate to the Venus Almanac. His counterpart in the Maya area may be linked with dates that mark significant positions of Venus. Rays and a "horseshoe" element frame an eye form appearing with Tlaloc imagery on several monuments, apparently a Maya glyph for Venus as the "big eye."

CHAC AND GOD B IN COLONIAL AND POSTCLASSIC YUCATÁN

In the past it has been assumed that Chac and Tlaloc are essentially the same entity in different cultural contexts (Tozzer 1941:138). Today scholars seem reluctant to identify Chac and Tlaloc as the same deity (Kowalski 1987:192; Taube 1992b:22). Is Tlaloc the same as Chac? They control the same realms: rainfall

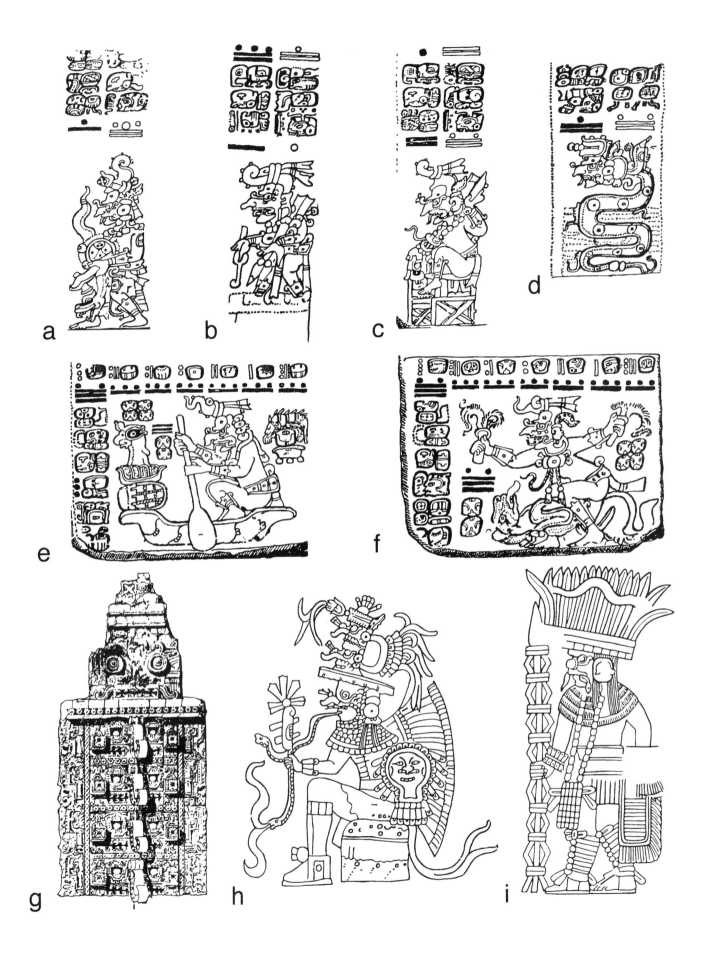

a   b   c   d

e   f

g   h   i

and lightning. Both Tlaloc and Chac (God B) hold a lightning serpent and an axe, possibly symbolizing the sound of thunder (Figs. 5.8b, 5.9a; compare with Codex Vaticanus B 43–48). Page 12 of the Madrid Codex shows Chac wearing a modified year sign like that on Tlaloc A, indicating that the two are merged as a single deity (Fig. 7.3). There are five Chacs on pages 11–18. On the mask towers of the Uxmal Nunnery, the role of the fifth Chac is played by Tlaloc, shown at the top of a stack of four Chac masks (Fig. 5.9g). One tower illustrated by Kowalski (1990:52) depicts Tlaloc with a year sign in his mouth like the headdress of Tlaloc A. Both Chac and Tlaloc are found in similar sets of five. It seems clear they are essentially the same deity, but rendered in different styles.

An axe glyph has been interpreted as the word *ch'ak,* a close counterpart for Chac's name, although Chac's Postclassic name glyph does not actually incorporate an axe. Chac's T668 (*cha*) glyph has a T109 affix that means *chac,* or *chak* in the revised orthography, translated as "red" or "great" in Yucatec (Fig. 5.9b–c, e–f). In the Postclassic Dresden Codex Venus pages, the planet is referred to as *chac ek,* "great star" (Fig. 5.7a, bottom row). This pattern of naming suggests a link between Chac and Venus, for the same term often refers to Venus in contemporary Maya accounts (Chapter 1).

Chac's title among the Maya is "the Chac who makes brilliant the sky," usually interpreted as an image of lightning, but also possibly an image of brilliant light (Thompson 1960:147). This would be an appropriate title for Venus, the brightest planet in the sky. Studies of Venus imagery suggest that "the ultimate power over the rains is held by Venus," and the northerly extreme of Venus coincided with the onset of the rainy season (Closs et al. 1984:230). Sprajc (1993a, 1993b) makes a strong case for linking the Evening Star aspect of Venus with rain-bringing and agricultural fertility. Chac may be linked with Venus in this aspect.

In contemporary Yucatec Maya accounts, Chac's primary association is with weather and rainfall. Informants from Quintana Roo say the Chac of the east is red and sends rain; the Chac of the north is white and sends cold; the Chac of the west is black and sends sickness and death; the Chac of the south is yellow and sends wind, appropriate because the predominant winds in Yucatán come from the southeast (Barrera Marín et al. 1976:483–484). In another Yucatec account, Chac is responsible for bringing rain, and four aspects of the god dwell in the "trunk of heaven" in the eastern sky during the dry season (Redfield and Villa Rojas 1962:116). On June 2 they get their instructions from the archangel Saint Michael and they ride forth on four horses in

---

FIG. 5.9. *a:* Postclassic Chac (God B), decorated with mirror body markings, holds lightning serpent and axe symbolizing sound of thunder (Dresden Codex 66a; after Villacorta and Villacorta 1977).

b: Postclassic Chac, bearing atlatl and darts like gods of Morning Star (Dresden Codex 65b; after Villacorta and Villacorta 1977).

c: Postclassic Chac seated on sky-band throne wearing shell earring topped by owl feather, recalling insignia of other Venus gods (Dresden Codex 66b; after Villacorta and Villacorta 1977).

d: Chac with water-lily headdress and serpent body covered with stars, evoking links with God H (Quetzal-coatl-Kukulcan), and water-lily serpent representing Classic period head variant of number thirteen (Dresden Codex 35b; after Villacorta and Villacorta 1977).

e: Chac paddling his canoe in east, carrying merchant

pack and owl headdress of God L, with an associated prognostication of abundant maize (Dresden Codex 43c; after Villacorta and Villacorta 1977).

f: In west, Chac holds torches and sits astride dead deer, with an associated prognostication of drought and death (Dresden Codex 45c; after Villacorta and Villacorta 1977).

g: Stacked Chac heads with fifth Chac replaced by Tlaloc face (mask tower of north building of Nunnery, Uxmal).

h: Chac figure with war shield, serpent axe, and snake in mouth (mural from Terminal Classic Temple of Chac Mool, Chichén Itzá; after Taube 1992b, fig. 5c).

i: Chac figure with snake in mouth carries spear and war shield (relief from Terminal Classic Lower Temple of Jaguars, Chichén Itzá; after Taube 1992b, fig. 5d).

four different directions. The descriptions suggest that these horses are different-colored clouds associated with different weather phenomena. The archangel may represent the fifth Chac, the one in the center who controls the clouds associated with the four Chacs. They apparently send different kinds of rain, suggesting a link with the five Tlalocs on Codex Borgia pages 27 and 28.

In Yucatec Maya accounts, the rain gods are the Grandfather Chacs (Nucuch Yum Chacob), old bearded gods who are fond of smoking (Tozzer 1941:138 n. 639). They bear a close relationship with the Mams, gods of the mountains and of the rains, each linked with a color and a cardinal direction. Tozzer compares the Chacs to the Lacandón deity Noho Chac Yum, who is one of four brothers associated with different cardinal directions. Their father is Chac Nicte. He may be the fifth Chac, the one at the center.

The god originally identified as God B of the codices is now recognized as the Postclassic Chac. He is the most frequently depicted god in the Dresden Codex, represented 134 times (Thompson 1972:27). Occasionally, Chac's body is marked by mirrors, indicating his shiny aspect (Fig. 5.9a). Chac appears on a road in scenes that Thompson (1972:83) interprets as references to Chac's journey across the sky at the start of the rainy season, carrying the rains to the four corners of the sky. Other scenes show him mounting sky bands and walking through water, suggesting movements through the sky and the watery underworld (Fig. 5.9c). Sometimes he paddles across the water, like the Paddler Twins (Fig. 5.9e).

Five Chacs appear on Dresden Codex pages 29a–30a; four are situated on world trees that Thompson (1972:94) identifies as the four trees of the cardinal points; the fifth scene with Chac in a cave represents the central direction. This imagery evokes the five Chacs known from modern lore and the five Tlalocs in the Codex Borgia. The interval between each of the five scenes in the Dresden Codex is 13 days for a total of 65 days (5 × 13), an interval useful in calculating Venus periods. The dates at the beginning of the almanac indicate four sets of 65 days for a total of 260 days. By running through the 260-day Tzolkin twice and then adding one almanac period of 65 days, one reaches the day beginning the next Venus cycle of 584 days. This means that each scene could refer to Venus events that repeat after 584 days have elapsed. Thus the last picture with Chac in the cave might refer to Venus disappearing in the underworld at the close of a period of visibility—an event that would recur every 584 days, or two Tzolkins plus 65 days. In this case, the four previous pictures of Chac would represent Venus positions prior to the planet's disappearance.

On pages 42c–45c of the Dresden Codex, Chac appears in five guises. Each scene shows black numbers that begin with an interval of 17 days followed by numbers totaling 48 days (6 × 8 days), completing a count of 65 days. Thus the four scenes together total 260 days or one Tzolkin; however, the subdivision into four sets of 65 days suggests an interest in Venus calculations. Each page has a glyph column beginning with a glyph compound referring to one of the four cardinal directions. On page 42c, Chac decapitates the Maize God in the south. On 43c, Chac paddles his canoe in the east, carrying the merchant pack and owl headdress of God L, a god of the Morning Star in the Dresden Codex Venus pages (Fig. 5.9e). Page 44c shows Chac as a fishing god in the north. On the last page of the series (45c), Chac holds torches as he rides a deer in the west, the direction of the Evening Star (Fig. 5.9f). The text seems to refer to drought and death (Thompson 1972:106). The Chac of the west also brings death in modern accounts. Chac wears an owl feather in three scenes, and in the fourth he carries an owl headdress in his boat. As we will see, the owl may be a guise for Mercury, and the Venus god wearing an owl headdress may refer to the close relationship between Venus and Mercury.

Dresden Codex pages 30c–33c cover a period of 2,340 days, equaling four Venus cycles and nine Tzolkin cycles. The scenes show Chac located on a sky band and in trees, and in watery locations. The count begins on 11 Ahau on page 30c; intervals of 13 days associated with each of the nine locations brings the total to 117 days, a period that approximates the synodic period of Mercury. When the run is completed five more times, as indicated by the first column of day signs on page 30c, the total is 585 days.

Three adjacent columns indicate further runs bringing the count to 4 × 585 or 2,340 days (nine Tzolkins, one for each Chac?). Using the slightly larger value of 117 days to approximate the Mercury cycle would have allowed them to equate five Mercury cycles with one Venus cycle (V. Bricker 1988b:84). Jesús Galindo (1994:88) points out that the interval of 117 days may also be integrated with four lunar months. I would add that each column is spaced at an interval of 65 days from the next, which suggests a period useful for Venus calculations, as noted above.

Chac's association with thirteen different locations on Dresden Codex pages 65b–69b is suggestive of thirteen different heavens (Fig. 5.9b–c). Kelley (1976:102, fig. 35) has been able to identify the glyphs of thirteen different localities on these pages. The sequence begins on page 65b with Chac paddling like the Paddler Twins, perhaps indicating a location on or near the Milky Way (Chapter 7). In the adjacent scene, he has an atlatl and darts, like gods of the Morning Star (Fig. 5.9b). In the next scene, he walks on a road carrying a merchant pack. On the next page (66b), he sits on a sky-band throne, just one of many scenes that show him on a sky band (Fig. 5.9c). Victoria and Harvey Bricker (1988; 1992: 51–52) relate this scene to June 21, 950, one day before the summer solstice; however, following interpretations stated in their 1989 publication, this section could relate to the summer solstice of A.D. 1244 (1989:241). Placing this table in the first half of the thirteenth century is in keeping with the date of the codex indicated by the Venus pages. On the summer solstice in A.D. 1244, Venus was the Evening Star exiting the Milky Way near Gemini. As in the Dresden Codex Venus pages, the sky band may refer to the intersection point of the Milky Way and the ecliptic, here serving as a throne for Venus. It should be noted, however, that such interpretations are valid only if we assume that the almanacs without calendar dates can be fixed at a specific point in time, a debatable proposition.

Thompson (1972:83) relates this almanac to the one above on pages 65a–69a because both total 91 days each, referring to one quarter of the computing year of 364 days. One full run through the upper and lower almanacs equals 182 days, and two runs approximate a year of 364 days (V. Bricker and H. Bricker 1989, 1992). The Brickers (1992:51) maintain that the text and pictures on 65a–69a refer to a 182-day period beginning in July of A.D. 949, and the lower table covers a similar span beginning in May of A.D. 950. They note that whereas the upper table correlates the eclipse seasons with the vernal equinox and the Maya New Year, the lower table is concerned with the relationship between the summer solstice and the midpoint of the Haab. The Brickers (1989: 241) align the scene on page 68a showing twin Chacs on a sky-band throne with the vernal equinox on 3/20/950, N.S. (3/15/950 O.S.); the same seasonal position for the almanac is evident in A.D. 1243. Venus was near the maximum altitude as Evening Star and positioned very close to the Pleiades on 3/20/1243 N.S. (3/13/1243 O.S.). During the Classic and Postclassic periods, Venus passed by the Pleiades always between the spring equinox and the summer solstice, predicting or coinciding with the beginning of the rainy season (Milbrath 1988c). Twin Chacs on the sky band may be Venus crossing the Milky Way near the Pleiades. Venus may be represented by the twin Chacs because Venus embodies duality as the "star" of the morning and the evening skies.

On Dresden Codex pages 35b–37b, intervals totaling fifty-two days accompany scenes that show Chac in different aspects. The sequence begins on page 35b, where Chac's head appears on a serpent body (Fig. 5.9d). Chac seems to be shown in a serpent guise that may be the counterpart of the central Mexican feathered serpent. Like the Water-lily Serpent on Classic period ceramics and the serpent on the Early Classic Temple of the Seven Dolls at Dzibilchaltún, Chac on page 35b has a water-lily headdress and a serpent body covered with ring-shaped designs that may represent stars (Chapter 7; Hellmuth 1987, figs. 321–322). Taube (1992b:56–59) links the figure on Dresden 35b to God H, a Postclassic counterpart to the Classic period Water-lily Serpent representing the head variant of the number thirteen. He also suggests a relationship with Quetzalcoatl, who is an aspect of God H on Dresden Codex 4a (Fig. 5.4a). Taube adds that Classic period images link this serpent with the Ik sign. It is also noteworthy that the Ik symbol appears in the eye of

Chac's T668 name glyph. The Water-lily Serpent, in my opinion, is a Venus image linked with a serpent aspect of Chac. Only Chac's head is represented in this imagery. A related image may be seen in a Terminal Classic period relief at Uxmal that depicts a Chac head in the jaws of the feathered serpent (Taube 1992b:138, fig. 76b). Perhaps this complex can be traced back to the Tlaloc heads with feathered serpents at Teotihuacán (Miller 1973, fig. 346).

Chac may also have some connection with the Milky Way, called the "Vía de Santiago" by those Maya people who use traditional Spanish terminology. It should be noted that Santiago is the name for the Morning Star among the Quiché and the Cakchiquel (Cook 1986:149; Sprajc 1993a:39). Among the Chortí, the weather god is Santiago, who rules the Milky Way as a god of thunder and lightning; this makes him the modern-day counterpart of Chac (Girard 1962:251; Milbrath 1980b:455). Schele (1992b:170) suggests a link between Chac and the Milky Way in the context of an inscription in the Temple of the Foliated Cross that pairs Chac's name with the gate to the Milky Way (Ek' Way Chak). Perhaps Chac was Venus as ruler of the Milky Way in the Classic period.

We can conclude that Chac clearly represents an astronomical being associated with storms and rainfall. His glyphic name (T109.668) may be read as *chachac*. There are sections of the Dresden Codex that link Chac with the solar year, suggesting the solar cycle is somehow implicated in Chac's imagery. Perhaps Chac is the Venus god that rules the rainy half of the year. His travels through the sky and into caves suggests that he is one of the celestial wanderers symbolizing a planetary god. His representation in sets of five suggest that he embodies Venus. He is associated with almanacs that can be used to derive intervals that approximate the synodic period of Venus. The subsets of sixty-five days often associated with Chac are useful in calculating Venus periods.

CLASSIC PERIOD IMAGES OF CHAC

Long-nosed mosaic masks dating to the Classic and Terminal Classic periods in Yucatán are traditionally interpreted as Chac masks. Kowalski (1987:202) notes that there is compelling evidence for associating these masks with the long-snouted God B who represents Chac in the codices. These masks, frequently grouped in sets of five, seem to allude to the "fiveness" of Venus, representing five cycles of 584 days that repeat at intervals of eight years (Aveni 1991:315, 317). On the North Building of the Nunnery at Chichén Itzá, there is a group of five Chac masks with T510f star symbols under the eyes. Similarly, at the House of the Governors at Uxmal, there are sets of five Chac masks and masks infixed with star glyphs (Kowalski 1987, figs. 151, 153).

At Chichén Itzá, four or five figures wearing Chac masks appear in murals on the Temple of the Chac Mool (Fig. 5.9h; Morris et al. 1931: Pl. 133). Although only partially preserved, these Chac figures all appear to carry shields and burning serpent axes, the latter a form of lightning axe, according to Taube (1994:220). The Lower Temple of the Jaguars represents another Terminal Classic Chac figure carrying a spear and a shield (Fig. 5.9i). All these Chac figures wear a broad-brimmed hat like that on a ruler of the Terminal Classic period known as Lord Chac, seen on Uxmal Stela 14 (Taube 1992b, fig. 4e). Uxmal Stela 14 depicts this ruler wearing a Chac mask and a headdress with towering tiers of feathers.

Lord Chac is associated with astronomical glyphs on the House of the Governor at Uxmal. His back rack is a stack of sky bands representing eight double-headed serpents, and it bears glyphic texts that refer to the Sun and the Moon as well as a star glyph often linked with Venus (Kowalski 1987:180–181, figs. 113–115). The grouping of eight serpents reflects an overlap with the East Building of the Nunnery, where eight double-headed serpents are arranged in five sets, referring to the eight solar years it takes to complete five Venus cycles (Lamb 1980). As noted earlier, the lattice crosses within these groupings add up to 584, the number of days in one Venus cycle. In a previous section, I also noted that Chac masks carved with the number eight on the fourth platform of the Governor's Palace at Uxmal are related to the Venus cycle, designating the eight-year Venus Almanac and possibly also the inferior conjunction disappearance interval.

In sum, the architectural configurations of Chac masks and Chac figures in groupings of five in Classic period Yucatán are appropriate to Venus imagery. Chac masks, often bearing star glyphs, are associated with the number eight or eight serpents, suggesting a connection with the eight-year Venus Almanac.

CHAC AND GI IN THE CLASSIC PERIOD

GI, so named because he is the first named of the three brothers in the Palenque Triad, shares both physical and thematic traits with the Classic period Chac. Images of Chac and GI sometimes share the same type of ornaments: a shell diadem, Spondylus shell earflares, and a pectoral with trilobe ends (Fig. 5.10b–c; Schele and Miller 1986:275). Chac is sometimes identified as the zoomorphic counterpart of GI, but their relationship is still poorly understood (Taube 1992b:24). The Temple of the Foliated Cross at Palenque names Chac and GI as separate deities (Fig. 4.6e; Schele 1992b:170). Here both portrait heads have a Spondylus shell earflare, but Chac's face is zoomorphic.

Typically, GI has scalloped eyebrows over square eyes, a Roman nose, fish barbels on his cheeks, shell earflares, and a front tooth replaced by a shark's tooth or a tooth filed into a T-shape (Fig. 5.10g; Schele and Miller 1986:48–49). In contrast, the Classic period Chac's face normally has an elongated upper lip, and occasionally a serpent issues from his jaws (Figs. 5.9h–i, 5.10a; Taube 1992b, figs. 5c–d, 6c–e). Some examples of the Lamat glyph depict Chac's face with an infixed star glyph, suggesting links with Venus (Fig. 5.7d–e).

GI is a fish god of some sort. Tom Jones (1991: 249–253, fig. 5) links GI to the old Fish (Stingray) Paddler, the solar deity of the Paddler Twins (Chapter 4). He identifies the fish traits as those of Xoc, a shark monster, suggesting that the fish barbels GI has around his mouth are those of a nurse shark. He notes that the central tooth of GI on the Río Azul mask is a combined form representing both a shark's tooth and a stingray spine, and the same insignia can appear in the quadripartite badge on GI's headdress (Fig. 5.10h). This tooth is also found on the Xoc monster, a creature who also shares the same scroll eyebrows. On the other hand, Taube (1992b:24) identifies GI's face markings as catfish barbels, making him a catfish god instead of a shark.

A number of scholars identify GI of the Palenque Triad as a Classic period Venus god. Kelley (1965; 1976:97) equates GI's birthday on 9 Ik with 9 Wind, the birthday traditionally assigned to Quetzalcoatl, the Venus god of central Mexico. GI clearly belongs to an astronomical family; his mother is the Moon Goddess and one of his brothers is the Sun God (GIII). In establishing a connection between Venus and GI, Lounsbury (1985) points out that Venus is the older brother in Maya folklore, just as GI is the older brother in the Palenque Triad. The elder brother is called Lord Xulab, referring to an ant that is sometimes named as an eclipse monster linked with Venus, or Nohoch Ich (big eye/face), a name often applied to Venus. Following the birth order given in the Classic period inscriptions and the identifications in the Mopan tale, the eldest brother (GI) is Venus, the middle brother (GIII) is the Sun, and the youngest brother (GII) is Mars or Jupiter.

Schele and Miller (1986:306 n. 3) propose that GI is a Venus god with solar associations, linking him with representations of Hun Ahau. Such an identification can be explained in astronomical terms, because there is a close link between Venus and the Sun. The Morning Star is the herald of the rising Sun, and the Evening Star announces sunset.

The connection between Venus and the entry and exit to the underworld may be one reason the deceased ruler was sometimes dressed as GI. This guise is apparent in the jade funerary mask from Río Azul (Fig. 5.10h). Proskouriakoff (1993:58–60) suggests that Copán Stela I depicts a deceased ancestor of the royal house impersonating GI of the Palenque Triad (Fig. 5.10j). This monument, erected in the reign of Smoke Imix God K (A.D. 628–695), bears an Initial Series date of 9.12.3.14.0 (3/17/676), a time when Venus was high in the sky and the Sun was exactly at the vernal equinox (Schlak 1996:182).

Deceased rulers also take the guise of Chac, as on the Dumbarton Oaks Relief Panel 2 (Fig. 5.10d). Schele and Miller (1986:274–276) note that Kan Xul (K'an Hok' Chitam II) dances in Xibalba wearing the costume of Chac Xib Chac. The first date on

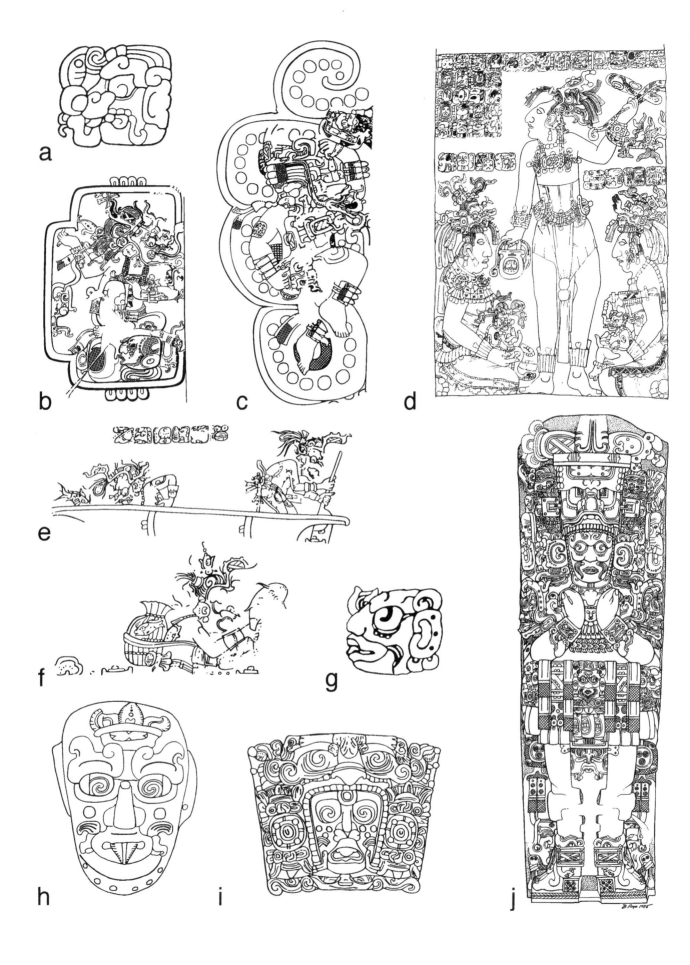

a

b

c

d

e

f

g

h

i

j

the monument (12 Ahau 8 Ceh) corresponds to 9.11.0.0.0 (10/9/652), a Katun ending that coincides with the first visibility of the Evening Star, as noted earlier. On this date, Mars and the first visible crescent Moon were near Venus, just above the western horizon. This fortuitous interlocking of the three astronomical cycles at the end of the Katun 12 Ahau was certainly noteworthy. Another Calendar Round date, 9 Manik 5 Muan (9.14.11.2.7; 11/18/722), seems to be the date of the ruler's apotheosis, when he was transformed in heaven (Lounsbury 1985:55–56). The dead ruler apparently took on the guise of Chac when the Morning Star Venus was about to disappear in conjunction, entering the underworld like the deceased ruler.

Monuments 23 and 24 from Quiriguá depict Chac in images that may also be linked with the ruler's apotheosis (Fig. 5.10c; Baudez 1988, fig. 12). Andrea Stone (1983) shows that the two monuments are closely related, since both depict Chac passing through a Cauac-marked opening. Monument 23 (Altar of Zoomorph O) depicts Chac in profile, and Monument 24 (Altar of Zoomorph P) depicts Chac frontally, with his mouth issuing long bands that end in skeletal zoomorphic heads with Ik eyes. On both monuments, Chac passes through a cleft opening framed by an Ik sign, a glyph some scholars relate to the Evening Star. Venus may be implicated by details in the imagery on Monument 23: Chac's shell beard

and his stacked knot headdress evoke a connection with gods of the Morning Star on Dresden Codex pages 46 and 50 (Figs. 5.3a, e, 5.10c). Taube (1986, fig. 3) identifies the figure on Monument 23 as Chac opening the rock of sustenance with lightning. On the other hand, Baudez (1988:143–144) argues that Monuments 23 and 24 show a dead ruler swallowed by a crack in the earth. It is possible that both monuments show the resurrection or apotheosis of a dead ruler in the guise of Chac, echoing the imagery of the resurrected Maize God emerging from a cleft opening (Fig. 3.11a–b). With so many dates on these two monuments, it is difficult to pinpoint the associated astronomical events. Nonetheless, the Initial Series date on Monument 23, the date of Sky Xul's accession on 9.17.14.16.18 9 Etz'nab 1 Kankin (10/9/785), indicates that astronomy was probably of interest, for on this date Jupiter and Venus were in conjunction in Scorpius, positioned just above the first crescent Moon. The Initial Series date on Monument 24 is a period-ending 9.18.5.0.0 4 Ahau 13 Ceh (9/9/795), when Venus was once again the Evening Star, but now positioned in the adjacent constellation (Libra) in conjunction with Mars.

Naranjo Stela 21 seems to represent the living ruler Smoking Squirrel with deity attributes, including a shell beard and a stacked knot headdress seen on Venus gods (Maler 1908, pl. 35). According to Proskouriakoff (1993:73–74), Smoking Squirrel is

---

FIG. 5.10. *a:* Classic portrait glyph of Chac has elongated upper lip, Spondylus shell ear, and serpent in mouth (after Taube 1992b, fig. 5e).

b: Chac emerges from cavelike opening (Creation Tablet from Palenque; after Robertson 1991, fig. 268).

c: Chac, wearing stacked knot headdress of Venus gods, emerges from Cauac-marked opening in image of apotheosis (Quiriguá Monument 23, Altar of Zoomorph O; after Baudez 1988, fig. 9).

d: Kan Xul's apotheosis in guise of Chac on November 18, 722 (Julian), when Venus was rising at dawn in Scorpius; his ancestors hold deity figures that may refer to planets (Dumbarton Oaks Relief Panel 2; after Schele and Miller 1986, fig. VII.3).

e–f: Chac as paddler and fisherman on inscribed bones (MT 51A, 51B) (Late Classic Burial 116 in Tikal Temple I,

funerary monument of Ruler A; after Hellmuth 1987, fig. 113).

g: Venus, eldest brother of Palenque Triad (GI), has scalloped eyebrows, spiral pupils, Roman nose, fish barbels on his cheeks, and Spondylus shell earflare (Late Classic Palenque Temple XIV, D7; after Lounsbury 1985, fig. 1d).

h: Early Classic greenstone funerary mask representing GI, worn by deceased ruler from Río Azul (after Taube 1992b, fig. 9a).

i: Early Classic Venus god, probably counterpart of GI, wearing Xoc-monster headdress (Tzakol cache vessel; after Hellmuth 1987, fig. 275).

j: Deceased royal ancestor from Copán transformed into GI of Classic Palenque Triad (Copán Stela I; after Proskouriakoff 1993:59).

represented as a warrior at eighteen years of age. The king wears the nose cruller of the Jaguar War God and the shell earflares of Chac or GI, and he holds a Jaguar War God shield (Fig. 4.2h). As noted in Chapter 4, the dates on the monument are appropriate to imagery of the dry-season Moon, but they also signal an interest in Venus. The Initial Series date of 9.13.14.4.2 (3/22/706) marks the time when Venus was the Evening Star in conjunction with Mars, just following the spring equinox. Venus was also in retrograde motion, having reached its first stationary point only five days earlier. A later date, reconstructed as a period-ending 9.13.15.0.0 13 Ahau 18 Pax (12/25/706), relates to the last visibility of Venus as the Morning Star following the winter solstice. Another date, 9.13.1.3.19 5 Cauac 2 Xul (5/23/693), associated with Smoking Squirrel's childhood, also relates to Venus. At this time Venus was especially brilliant as the Evening Star and was approaching its first stationary point (5/30/693; Meeus n.d.). Smoking Squirrel may have had a special connection with Venus, because battle dates on other Naranjo monuments seem to link his exploits in battle to significant positions of Venus (Schele and Freidel 1990: 191–193).

Another ruler with traits of Chac appears at Yaxchilán (Tate 1992, fig. 136). On its rear side facing Structure 40, Stela 11 depicts a Chac-masked ruler standing before kneeling captives. The ruler has been identified as Bird Jaguar IV dressed as Chac Xib Chac (Schele and Miller 1986:215–216, fig. V.5a). Tate (1992:126–128) interprets the masked figure on the back of the monument as Bird Jaguar masquerading as GI to represent the newly emerged Evening Star in a lineage event. The date above the figure is 1 Imix 19 Xul, reconstructed as 9.15.19.1.1 (5/29/750), a time when the Evening Star had been visible for about a month. On the front of the monument, Tate notes that Bird Jaguar and the deceased Shield Jaguar I perform a period-ending event on 9 Ahau 18 Xul (9.15.15.0.0; 5/29/746). This event took place after Shield Jaguar's death on 9.15.10.17.14 6 Ix 12 Yaxkin (6/13/742) and before Bird Jaguar's accession, an event recorded with the Initial Series date 9.16.1.0.0 11 Ahau 8 Zec (4/27/752). Perhaps the Chac-masked figure on the rear face actually represents the deceased Shield Jaguar. If so, he may be apotheosized as Venus in the guise of Chac.

A scene of Chac or GI emerging from water is represented on Copán Structure 11. As noted earlier, a relief on the east door records an heir-designation event associated with a "great star" inscription that is only five days after the first appearance of the Evening Star. The relief on the top step of the south facade represents GI as if he were standing shoulder high in the waters of the underworld with two monkey gods holding rattles, according to Schele and Miller (1986:122–125). This would seem to be an image of the Evening Star just reemerging from the waters of the underworld.

Chac appears as a being with multiple aspects on the Tikal bones (MT 51A, 51B) from Burial 116 in Temple I, the funerary monument of Ruler A (Fig. 5.10e–f). His shell diadem and Spondylus shell earrings are characteristic features. The paired bones each show a water scene with two Chacs in a canoe and one in water. In each scene, one Chac paddles as the other two hold fish. The paddler scenes evoke a link with the Paddler Twins. Chac's activities as a fishing god are also seen in the Postclassic Dresden Codex (44c). Chac appears in this role as far back as the Preclassic period, as seen on Izapa Stela 1 (Coe 1978b:77).

A figure sacrificing a jaguar baby on the Metropolitan Museum vase has been variously identified as GI or Chac Xib Chac, or an anthropomorphic image of Chac (Pl. 8; Schele and Miller 1986:49; Taube 1992b:24). The figure wears the Spondylus shell earflare typical of both GI and Chac. He has an anthropomorphic face like GI, but he carries an axe like Chac. His face ornament could be interpreted as a shell beard or the fish barbels of GI, for it is sometimes difficult to distinguish the two. The two gods could be considered to be aspects of the same deity were it not for the clear separation of Chac and GI in the deity list at Palenque (Fig. 4.6e). The sacrificer on the Metropolitan Museum vase seems ready to decapitate a jaguar god who conflates a solar and lunar deity, suggesting the image of an eclipse (Chapter 4). This places the decapitator in the role of an eclipse monster, a role appropriate to Venus.

A black-background vase may represent one of

the few known ceramic paintings of GI (Fig. 3.3c). He is one of three gods wearing similar costumes that include paper wristlets and ankle bands. All three are positioned on a celestial cord that may represent the ecliptic (Chapter 3). The figures have been compared to the Sun moving through the underworld in three different aspects, one representing GI of the Palenque Triad (Quirarte 1979). The three could instead represent the transformation of Venus as it moves along the ecliptical cord.

Early Classic cache vessels depict GI wearing a headdress that represents either the Xoc monster or the Quadripartite God (Fig. 5.10i). Hellmuth (1987: 351–353, 369) points out that the front tooth of GI is itself a perforator for blood offerings, and GI's cache vessels are often found with stingray spine perforators inside. Perhaps these vessels were buried after blood offerings were made to Venus at important points in the calendar. A number of these cache vessels show GI with face spots like those seen on the Sun God and the Hun Ahau twin.

In sum, both Chac and GI may be related to imagery of Venus, but the relationship between GI and Chac remains puzzling. Whereas Chac is shown fishing, GI seems to embody a fish, a distinction that remains enigmatic. Perhaps they are different aspects of Venus. GI may have a secondary association with the Sun, just as Hunahpu is linked with both the Sun and the Morning Star. Deceased rulers can take the guise of either Chac or GI, transformations that may have to do with the ruler's apotheosis in the sky.

THE SIDEREAL POSITION OF VENUS

The eight-year Venus Almanac, probably in use by the Classic period, indicates that the Maya must also have tracked the sidereal position of Venus. The eight-year period that coordinates the solar year with the synodic period of Venus also refers to the sidereal cycle, because Venus follows a specific pattern of conjunctions with constellations that will repeat every eight years. Even without the Venus Almanac, sidereal positioning was certainly observed. The relatively short sidereal cycle of Venus (an average of 224.7 days) means that the planet can be seen to move through all the star groups of the zodiac, be-

cause the planet's sidereal cycle is shorter than the mean period of its visibility in either the morning or evening sky (263 days).

Dennis Tedlock (1991:172) has found evidence that the position of Venus in the background of stars is important in the Popol Vuh. Cycles of the Venus Almanac are suggested by the five houses where the Hero Twins undergo ordeals in the underworld. These are as follows: the House of Darkness, the House of Cold, the House of the Jaguar, the House of the Bat, and the House of the Knife. Revising an earlier interpretation, Tedlock suggests that the five houses refer to five different sidereal positions of Venus, reflecting the relationship of Venus's synodic periods to eight solar years. In support of this interpretation, I note that at least two of these houses (Bat and Jaguar Houses) coordinate with animal constellations represented in Paris Codex 23–24 (Fig. 7.6; Chapter 7).

Dennis Tedlock (1985:40, 111, 134; 1991) interprets Hun Hunahpu and Vucub Hunahpu positioned at a crossroads in the underworld as Venus crossing the Milky Way near the rift between Scorpius and Sagittarius, the same sidereal position reached when the Hero Twins arrive at the crossroads in the underworld later in the narrative. Since they are not yet transformed into the Sun and the Moon, Tedlock proposes that Hunahpu and Xbalanque replace their father and uncle as gods of the Morning Star, and when they take their trip to the underworld, they represent Venus at the time the planet disappears in superior conjunction. In their descent, they take the black road of Xibalba, indicating the sidereal position of Venus in the rift of the Milky Way near Sagittarius. The rift represents a form of portal into the underworld for Venus as it disappears as the Morning Star, a sidereal position that recurs at this phase approximately every eight years.

The different guises of the Morning Star in the Dresden Codex Venus pages may well relate to different sidereal positions of Venus. Using the seasonal pattern for the Dresden Codex Venus table discussed above, we can see that over the course of eight years (A.D. 1219–1227) the newly risen Morning Star on 1/19/1221 was in Capricorn (page 46); at the next heliacal rise it moved to Leo (page 47), then to

Pisces (page 48), next to Libra (page 49), and on to Taurus (page 50). These Venus positions may influence the attributes of the Venus gods in the Dresden Codex.

At the time of the conquest, the Yucatec Maya observed Venus, Gemini, and the Pleiades to "tell the time of night" (Tozzer 1941:132–133). Thus, we can be sure that they were aware of the periods when Venus was in conjunction with Gemini and the Pleiades. Although I have not made any extensive study of Venus in conjunction with Gemini, such an event would tend to occur during the rainy season. Such a conjunction event might be represented on Lintel 41 from Yaxchilán, which shows Bird Jaguar wearing a Tlaloc headdress represented with a large star-eye with five points, evoking the "fiveness" of Venus (Tate 1992, fig. 148). A "star-over-shell" glyph is noted with a 7 Imix 14 Zec date (9.16.4.1.1; 5/3/755), but there is no Venus station close at hand. The slow motion of the Evening Star at this time may account for the shell-star compound, if we accept Schlak's hypothesis, but the headdress might allude to Venus, now especially prominent in conjunction with Gemini. Perhaps the dual nature of Venus gave it a special connection with Gemini, the brightest twin stars in the sky.

The Yucatec Maya today see a special connection between Venus and the Pleiades, for they say that the Evening Star is the "fire" of the Pleiades (Redfield and Villa Rojas 1962:206). In Precolumbian times, the Maya also placed special emphasis on the times when Venus passed by the Pleiades, called *tzab*, the "rattlesnake's rattle," in Yucatán (Milbrath 1988c). At Teotihuacán and Xochicalco, a feathered rattler appears on Classic period buildings oriented toward the Pleiades setting at dusk, which coincided with the onset of the rains; a similar pattern is apparent at Chichén Itzá during the terminal Classic period (Milbrath 1988c). These structures may express a calendar cycle linking Venus and the Pleiades. A review of the dates during the Late Classic and Postclassic period when Venus passed by the Pleiades (approximate conjunctions) indicates that all fall within a three-month span from the spring equinox (March 21) to the summer solstice (June 21; Mil-

brath 1988c, table 1). For well over a thousand years, Venus passed by the Pleiades (approximate conjunction) only during a three-month window announcing the coming rains or coinciding with the onset of the rains. I believe that this sidereal position came to be seen as a sign of rain, perhaps inspiring images of the feathered serpent (Venus) wearing rattles (the Pleiades) and an association with agricultural fertility.

The Upper Temple of the Jaguars at Chichén Itzá, featuring the feathered serpent with a rattle tail, expresses the relationship between Venus and the Pleiades (Fig. 5.5e; Milbrath 1988c). The doorway is oriented with an azimuth of 285°39′ (Galindo 1994: 127); from the vantage point of the inner temple, the observer could see a view very much like that seen through Window 1 of the Caracol, which has virtually the same azimuth of orientation (285°55′). Around A.D. 900, the Pleiades were framed by the right side of the inner window as they were last seen setting in late April. A similar effect took place in the doorway of the Upper Temple of the Jaguars. The Pleiades setting at dusk during the Late Classic period announced that the time for planting was approaching with the onset of the rains (Milbrath 1988c:69). The doorway probably also incorporates a diagonal axis like that of Window 1 in the Caracol, which has an oblique view oriented to the northern extreme of Venus (Fig. 3.1b; Aveni 1980:263–264, figs. 91–93). The sidereal position of Venus as it set in its northern extreme would repeat at the same time of year at eight-year intervals. The northern extreme of Venus as Evening Star was probably important in predictions about rainfall throughout Mesoamerica because it occurred between April and May during the Late Classic period (Sprajc 1993a, 1993b).

An Early Classic stucco relief at Acancéh in Yucatán represents a rattlesnake with Venus glyphs in what appears to be a zodiac sequence (Fig. 5.11a; Chapter 7). This may be the image of Venus in conjunction with the Pleiades at the onset of the rains. The Venus glyphs are half stars with five rays, like those on the feathered serpents from Teotihuacán and Maltrata, Veracruz (Figs. 5.4h, 5.6d). Virginia Miller (1991:42–43, pl. 4) also notes that the Acancéh star designs bear a resemblance to the Maya completion sign, and Coggins and Drucker (1988: 18) relate the completion sign to the Venus calendar.

Venus passes by the bright red star Antares in Scorpius, located 180° away from the Pleiades, between the fall equinox and the winter solstice, overlapping with the onset of the dry season. Because the Pleiades and Scorpius are at opposite sides of the sky, the seasonal associations are reversed. In some cases, imagery linking Venus with a scorpion may reflect Venus in conjunction with stars in our constellation Scorpius, represented as a scorpion in the Paris Codex zodiac, an unusual case of an overlap with Western astronomy (Fig. 7.7; Chapter 7).

Images connecting Venus and a scorpion are apparent over a long span of time (Baus Czitrom 1990; Carlson 1991, 1993). If we accept the quincunx as an Olmec form of a Venus symbol, one of the earliest examples of the connection between Venus and the scorpion constellation may date back to 900 B.C., as seen on San Lorenzo Monument 43. One of the latest known examples, dating between A.D. 1350 and 1450, is on page 79a of the Madrid Codex, where God L is depicted with a scorpion tail and thorax, possibly a symbol of Venus in conjunction with the scorpion constellation or a seasonal aspect of Venus (Fig. 5.11b).

A Classic period bench from Las Sepulturas at Copán depicts the Venus god with a scorpion tail and his arm laced through a T510f glyph (Pl. 19; Krupp 1997:265). A polychrome plate depicts a T510b glyph with a Venus-scorpion man having attributes of the Maize God (Carlson 1993, fig. 8.6d). This image may be explained by the fact that Venus passes by the heart of the scorpion constellation during the season of the maize harvest.

Analyzing Venus-scorpion imagery, John Carlson sees the scorpion as one of the "faces" of Venus, noting that a scorpion constellation may appear in the Dresden Codex Venus pages, which show a glyphic compound that spells *sinan,* meaning "scorpion" (Fig. 5.11c). The table divides twenty deity names (Fig. 5.3f–j, A–T) among the five synodic periods, with four deities for every cycle, each associated with a different Venus phase. Thompson's (1960:220) lay-

out places the scorpion (B) on line 17 at the end of the canonical period of superior conjunction, when the Evening Star became visible on day 326 of the 584-day cycle. In the layout of the Venus pages described earlier, day 326 fell on 5/25/1220, coinciding with the solar zenith in northern Yucatán and the month when Scorpius was visible for the longest period of time. Here the scorpion may be named because it rose at dusk when the Evening Star was in the west.

In sum, we have only scratched the surface of possible stellar images linked to the seasonal cycle of Venus. Preliminary evidence indicates an interest in the conjunction of Venus with the Pleiades and Scorpius. In addition, Venus probably had five stellar houses associated with constellations that marked important Venus stations in the eight-year almanac. These may appear in the Popol Vuh.

VENUS AND THE MOON

Scholars have noted that the 260-day divination calendar seems to link the length of a human pregnancy with the approximate period Venus is visible in either the morning or evening sky. John Burgess (1991:63) has proposed a more specific correlation between Venus and the Moon. He notes that the interval from the Moon's conjunction with Venus after the planet has emerged from superior conjunction to another such conjunction after inferior conjunction averages 260 days, and he suggests that the Tzolkin may owe its origin to this relationship.

Calendric cycles linking the Sun, the Moon, and Venus are built into the structure of the Dresden Codex Venus table, for the Venus Almanac equates five Venus cycles with ninety-nine lunar months and eight solar years (Aveni 1992b:104). The eclipse cycle could be integrated over the longer run of the table (104 years). Through their lunar-based Venus calendar, Mayan astronomers kept track of lunar eclipses (Aveni 1992b:107–108). Each of the six base dates that served as starting points for the calendar in the Venus table was immediately preceded by a lunar eclipse.

One of the Venus gods in the Dresden Codex Venus pages, God L, appears with the aged Moon

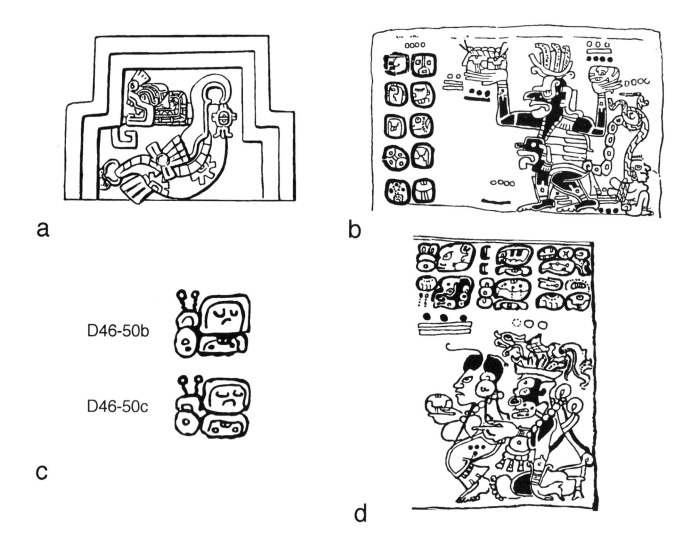

a

b

D46-50b

D46-50c

c

d

e

Goddess in her role as an eclipse monster on Dresden Codex page 74 (Fig. 7.4d; Chapter 4). He is showered by water poured by Goddess O, who may be the new Moon during the rainy season. Although God L represents the dry-season Morning Star in the Venus Almanac, his portrayal on page 74 suggests he is not exclusively a god of the dry season.

God L is involved in imagery that suggests conjunction of the Moon and Venus. On page 14c of the Dresden Codex, God L is paired with the Moon in an amorous scene (Fig. 5.11d). Like God N, he is an aged god lover with only a few remaining teeth. God L holds the young Moon Goddess, who offers the symbol of maize tortillas, represented by the T506 glyph (wah; Justeson 1984:339). This image alludes to the close connection between Venus, the Moon, and maize. His broad-brimmed hat is crowned by an owl with another T506 glyph and maize foliation in place of a tail (compare Taube 1992b, fig. 17f). God L embracing the youthful Moon Goddess probably refers to the waxing Moon joining Venus in its aspect as God L. The link with the waxing Moon would suggest that here God L takes the role of the Evening Star. The maize imagery recalls the connection between the Evening Star and maize noted by Šprajc (1993a, 1993b). As Carlson (1991:24) points out, "Venus and the Moon form a Maya structural pairing within the Maize God complex."

Thompson (1960:228–229) notes that the Maya may have recorded Venus conjunctions with the Moon on Classic Maya monuments. He suggests that a date on the Palenque Tablet of the 96 Glyphs, associated with glyphs for Venus and the Moon, represents their conjunction on this date (9.16.13.0.7 9 Manik 15 Uo; H1-G2). This is a case where the 584,285 correlation seems more compelling, for the date would be 3/4/764 O.S., when the Moon was just above Venus. In this scenario, Venus was being "mooned" as the crescent Moon passed by Venus (Aveni, personal communication 1993). On the other hand, Ringle and Smith-Stark (1996:37, 44) interpret this passage quite differently, and further research is required to confirm possible records of the Moon's conjunction with Venus.

A number of scholars have noted that the Moon and Venus seem to play a role in imagery of resurrection (Ashmore 1991:212; Dütting 1984, 1985). On Yaxchilán Lintel 25, the ancestor figure seems to represent Tlaloc in his aspect as Venus. Lady Xoc may play the role of the first crescent Moon just emerging on the Calendar Round date recorded on the monument (5 Imix 4 Mac; 10/18/681). On this date, the first crescent Moon appeared beneath the Evening Star. Perhaps this spatial relationship is represented by the ruler hovering over Lady Xoc. The ancestor wearing the Tlaloc mask aims his spear at Lady Xoc, who holds up bloodletting equipment and an offering of blood (Schele and Miller 1986:177). The bloodletting act is appropriate as an offering to Venus, for the principal god of penance, sacrifice, and bloodletting among the Aztecs was the Venus god known as Quetzalcoatl (Coe 1988:226).

A painted vase known as Grolier 42 depicts lunar deities with Venus in its aspect as God L (Fig. 5.11e; Coe 1973, no. 42; 1978b, no. 1). Here he sits on a throne with the lunar rabbit acting as his scribe. The owl in his headdress has extremely long tail feathers, reminiscent of a quetzal. He is attended by court ladies, one of whom turns around to watch a scene involving two axe-wielding gods; one is about to de-

---

FIG. 5.11. *a:* Early Classic Venus glyph on Venus serpent with rattle tail representing Pleiades (*tzab*) (Palace of Stuccoes, Acancéh; after Seler 1960–1961, 5, pl. 11).

b: Postclassic God L with torso representing scorpion thorax and tail tipped with stinger (Madrid Codex 79a; after Villacorta and Villacorta 1977).

c: Scorpion glyphs representing one of twenty different deities listed in Dresden Codex Venus pages (Dresden Codex 46; after Kelley 1976, fig. 28).

d: Postclassic God L holds young Moon Goddess in amorous scene; he and Moon Goddess are named in first column of glyphs (Dresden Codex 14c; after Villacorta and Villacorta 1977).

e: God L wearing owl headdress sits with female companions on throne while lunar rabbit acts as his scribe; sacrifice scene involving decapitation takes place in another vignette (Late Classic vase known as Grolier 42; after Coe 1973, no. 42).

capitate a seated deity bearing the same god markings. The Calendar Round date of the sacrifice (8 Caban 5 Ceh) is reconstructed as 9.14.4.15.17 (9/20/716) by Arthur Schlak (1996:197), who proposes that the imagery is linked with the autumn equinox, when Venus had just emerged as the Evening Star. The astronomical new Moon took place about three hours before dusk (Goldstine 1973). Perhaps the sacrificer symbolizes Venus, and the Moon God is about to lose his "head." The scene with God L shows the lunar rabbit, perhaps alluding to a different lunar phase.

A pot known as Regal Rabbit Vase shows God L stripped of his regalia, unclothed and gesturing in submission to a lunar rabbit who holds his owl hat marked with the glyph 13 Sky (Pl. 9, right). The beginning of the sequence, designated by the opening glyph of the Primary Standard Sequence, has a subsidiary set of glyphs that may refer to God L as a Pauahtun (T64:761v:59). This leads Dieter Dütting and Richard Johnson (1993) to conclude that somehow God L is transformed into God N when he loses his regalia. They reconstruct an associated Calendar Round date (13 Oc 18 Uo, far left) as 9.13.8.2.10, when Venus was the Morning Star, and they interpret the lunar imagery based on the 584,285 correlation. Nonetheless, the 584,283 correlation provides a more interesting picture, for the date (3/21/700) correlates with a time when the waning Moon and Venus were in conjunction. This could explain why the lunar rabbit holds God L's regalia, and why the two seem to have changed attributes, for God L has a rabbit paw in place of his left hand, and the rabbit has God L's hand in place of a paw. The two celestial deities may have merged attributes while in conjunction.

A second scene on this vase shows God L kneeling in submission to the Sun God. Dütting and Johnson (1993) link the 7 Akbal date to events thirty-three days later. Here, too, I find an interesting picture by using the 584,283 correlation, for on 4/23/700 the Moon disappeared in conjunction with the Sun (new Moon on 4/24/700; Goldstine 1973). This would explain why the lunar rabbit is now hiding behind the Sun God seated on a jaguar skin throne. At the same time, Venus moved into conjunction with Mars, which might be represented by the deer in front of God L, for Mars seems to have deer traits in Postclassic Maya art (Chapter 6).

We can conclude that a great deal more research is required to fully understand the close relationship between Venus and the Moon in Maya iconography. They form a natural pair in the sky, especially the crescent Moon, which is often seen near Venus. No doubt Maya artists explored this imagery, but we have only begun to understand the nature of this iconography and the calendar cycles implicit in conjunction events involving the two.

MERCURY IN MAYA IMAGERY AND CALENDRICS

Evidence of Mercury cycles is difficult to document in calendar records. Thompson (1960:215) notes that "it is very doubtful that the Maya paid any attention to the synodic revolution of Mercury, which is short and difficult to observe accurately." Nevertheless, they certainly must have been aware of Mercury, because its movements are similar to those of Venus, the most important planet in Maya cosmology. Indeed, it is not inconceivable that some of the ethnographic and Colonial period references to the Morning Star or the Evening Star may actually refer to Mercury.

Mercury is mentioned by its European name in some Colonial period accounts. In the Chilam Balam of Maní, Mercury is connected with illness, death, robbery, debt, and drunkenness, and the planet is said to control the lungs (Craine and Reindorp 1979:49–50). Further study of these attributes in relation to medieval European astrology is required to sort out whether there is any Precolumbian content.

Dennis Tedlock (1985:154, 347, 361) concludes that the Popol Vuh represents Mercury as an owl; there are actually four owls, two of which may be the morning aspect of Mercury and the other two the evening aspect. As the Military Keepers of the Mat for the Lords of Xibalba, Macaw Owl and Shooting Owl have an underworld association appropriate to Mercury. According to Tedlock (1985:154, 347), Macaw Owl (Caquix Tucur) is Mercury as the messenger of Xibalba. The role of Mercury as a messenger to the underworld seems apt, because Mercury spends so much time invisible in conjunction. Tedlock says that Macaw Owl is the Classic Maya Muan bird, which he identifies as an owl with a macaw tail.

Kelley (1976:6) links a table on Dresden Codex 69–73 with Mercury intervals, but he cannot identify a glyph for Mercury. On page 69, a black Chac emerges from the jaws of a feathered serpent. Since Kelley (1980:S20) identifies both Quetzalcoatl-Kukulcan and Chac as Mercury, he presumably would identify these as Mercury images. Nonetheless, the evidence presented in this chapter indicates both are associated with Venus.

In the past, scholars have proposed that intervals of 115 and 117 days are approximations of Mercury's 115.9-day cycle. Beth Collea (1981:216) notes that the 115-day period Ernst Förstemann identified as a Mercury interval has proved invalid. The 117-day interval supported by Yurii Knorozov (1982) and Jesús Galindo (1994:88) seems to be too far from the true length of Mercury's synodical cycle. Nonetheless, over the short term, 117 may be a useful approximation, especially in situations where Mercury is integrated with other calendar cycles. The interval of 117 days is an even multiple of synodic lunar months ($117 = 4 \times 29.25$), and it also approximates one-fifth of the synodical cycle of Venus. As noted earlier, almanacs of 117 days appear in sets of five in the Dresden Codex (30c–33c), for a total of 585 days, an interval that brings the Venus cycle and Mercury into renewed alignment. Chac is the main character on these pages.

Owl imagery may suggest a link with Mercury. On Dresden Codex 43c, Chac carries God L's owl (Mercury?) hat in his canoe (Fig. 5.9e). In other sequences, Chac wears an owl feather, possibly indicating a connection with Mercury, as on pages 45c and 65–69 (Fig. 5.9a, c, f).

On a Classic period vase, God L's owl holds the Jaguar War God's head in his beak, suggesting another image of astronomical conjunction (Coe 1982, no. 15). God L's bird has a celestial aspect, for he is named with a 9 Sky title on the Vase of the Seven Gods (Pl. 7). On the Regal Rabbit Vase, this bird is named 13 Sky, interpreted as a reference to the highest heaven (Pl. 9; Dütting and Johnson 1993:168).

Owls represented in the Dresden Codex (7c, 10a) sometimes also bear the 13 Sky title (Grube and Schele 1994:12). The name 13 Sky is one of the astronomical gods marking the southern direction in the Venus pages of the Dresden Codex (Kelley 1976, fig. 28). A related owl bears the name 13 Muan in a scene where he is carried by the Moon Goddess (Dresden Codex 18b).

Taube (1992b:85) identifies God L's bird as the Moan (Muan) owl, and agrees with Thompson that this bird with a feather crest is a screech owl or a horned owl. Thompson (1960:49, 114–115) identifies the bird with the 13 Sky title as the Muan bird, the main sign for the month Muan (T748:116), a month he associates with rainfall. He notes that the Muan owl must be distinguished from the *cui*, a bird of ill omen representing another species of owl. This is the same one that Grube and Schele (1994:10–12) identify as the *kuy* owl of warfare; they conclude that the Muan bird is a hawk, whereas God L's companion bird is the *kuy* owl, a Ferruginous Pygmy Owl (*Glaucidium brasilianum*). They note that God L's owl was associated with Tlaloc-Venus warfare in the Classic period and generally had an ominous nature. God L's bird, apparently an owl with a negative aspect, may be Mercury, which makes frequent trips to the underworld. This bird may appear as God L's hat, because Venus and Mercury are closely related in their motions. If this is the case, the Muan bird may represent a bird constellation (Chapter 7).

Aveni and Hotaling (1994:S38–S39, table 1) assessed ninety-eight dates that have astronomical tags, including dates associated with the Tlaloc-war complex that involve an owl-like bird that may represent Mercury. Eighteen of the ninety-eight dates showed a correlation with Mercury events. They suggest that sometimes the Mercury event was substituted when Venus was not in the appropriate position. More than half correspond to times when Mercury first appeared in the evening sky simultaneously with the first appearance of Venus as the Evening Star.

Arthur Schlak links the planet Mercury with God K and GII of the Palenque Triad. I disagree with his interpretations and discuss the evidence at length in Chapter 6, where I show God K's affiliation with Jupiter.

In sum, interpretations of the Popol Vuh suggest that Mercury may be a subsidiary figure, possibly a nocturnal bird that is an avian messenger to the underworld. In Postclassic images, Chac sometimes also seems to be associated with an owl, but here is represented more subtly as a feather ornament in his headdress. Mercury may be an owl on God L's headdress, expressing the close relationship between Venus and Mercury that extends back to the Classic period. Mercury also may be an owl represented as a warbird with Tlaloc in Classic period representations.

THE INFERIOR PLANETS IN THE MAYA WORLDVIEW

Except for a possible connection with owl imagery, relatively little is known about Mercury's avatars in Maya art. It may be that one of the gods now thought to represent Venus may in fact refer to Mercury. In future studies, we should bear in mind that Mercury is frequently invisible, so we should expect to find Mercury imagery connected with the underworld.

For Venus, we have almost too much information to condense in a single chapter. Even so, this study has only begun to reveal the multiple personalities of Venus, with its different seasonal aspects, sidereal positions, and phases. Venus is best described as a master of transformation, taking on different guises in its changing relation to the seasons. The Dresden Codex Venus pages provide a template for understanding the seasonal aspects of the Morning Star during the Postclassic period. Here five Venus gods represent the newly emerged Morning Star over an eight-year cycle that was tracked over hundreds of years. The codex seems to show real-time events dating to the mid-thirteenth century, as well as historical references that go back to the seventh century. The historical data are recorded in Long Count inscriptions, whereas the current events are given in Calendar Round dates. The 1 Ahau 13 Mac date on the last page appears to be a date just before the summer solstice in A.D. 1227.

We can recognize five aspects of the Morning Star in the Dresden Codex Venus pages. God L represents the Morning Star during the dry season, the epoch of warfare; however, other sections of the codex indicate that his imagery is not confined to this season and this Venus phase. Itztlacoliuhqui is the aspect of Venus linked with the rainy season around the summer solstice, the time that maize sprouts. Lahun Chan embodies Venus during the rainy-season period in August when the early maize crop matures. A howler monkey represents Venus during the dry-season period in April when the fields are prepared for planting. The central Mexican Fire God depicts Venus at the onset of the dry season in November when the harvest begins. If all the gods of the Morning Star rule the eighty-day period of the planet's rapid ascent, the last two deities can be linked with the season associated with their central Mexican counterparts. As Venus rose it hurled its atlatl dart across the sky, killing the astronomical deity at the opposite side of the sky. The victims at the bottom of each page seem to represent astronomical bodies in opposition to the Morning Star. The turtle probably represents stars in the region of Orion, and a fish god may refer to stars in Sagittarius. God K seems to symbolize Jupiter in retrograde. The Water-lily Jaguar may be a rainy-season aspect of the moon. The enthroned regents may show astronomical gods positioned at the intersection of the Milky Way and the ecliptic depicted by a sky-band throne. Their association with the east derives from their link with the emerging Morning Star.

There seems to be an unbroken chain of imagery from the Classic period through today that makes Venus part of a triad. Birth order makes him the older brother of the Sun. GI, the elder brother in the Palenque Triad, may be identified with Venus. Chac seems closely related to GI. Other elements link Chac and his Postclassic counterpart, God B, to Venus, including an association with sets of five and the number eight, embodying the Venus Almanac of eight years. Chac in turn is linked with Tlaloc, associated with rainfall and the cycle of maize. Tlaloc and Chac also have a warlike aspect in Maya art. Venus is an agent both of warfare and of agricultural fertility, two apparently opposed associations that must be understood in light of the changing nature of Venus. The Dresden Codex shows that the Morning Star had a warlike aspect, and Venus may have an especially warlike nature during the dry season, the epoch of warfare. However, even in the guise of Evening Star, Venus exercises some form of control over maize agriculture. The basic template seems to be the Venus Almanac, and with four phases and five Venus cycles, the possible manifestations of Venus in the almanac number twenty—a very Mesoamerican number.

THE CELESTIAL WANDERERS

To the Chortí, the planets are "stars that travel," evoking a connection with the "wanderers," a name that can be traced back to a Babylonian image of the planets as sheep who had escaped from the fold, which presumably refers to the rest of the stars (Aveni 1997:37). Like players on a stage performing in front of different sets, the planets move through the changing background of stars in different sections of the sky. Given that they are such dynamic actors, we should not be surprised to find them as characters in folktales and visual imagery. Venus, the most brilliant planet, clearly takes the leading part, but the superior planets also play roles in the celestial drama.

Although contemporary tales preserve very little information on planets other than Venus, there are a few that indicate that one of the superior planets plays the role of younger brother of Venus and the Sun. Folktales provide a clue to the identity of the youngest member of the Palenque Triad. As we will see, Jupiter is linked with GII of the Triad, the counterpart of God K in the Postclassic codices. Study of the codices indicates that Mars may be a deer monster. Monkeylike creatures in Classic period Maya art may also represent planets. There are a number of celestial deities that may prove to be linked with the superior planets, but at present they cannot be identified with any certainty due, in part, to a lack of information about the superior planets in the Colonial period sources.

This chapter begins with a discussion of Colonial period information on planets. There follows an analysis of Precolumbian Maya images of Mars, including the well-known Mars Beast. The chapter also explores the role of monkeys in imagery of the planets. God K and his Classic period counterpart are featured in another section that explores links with the planet Jupiter. The chapter closes with sections on Classic Maya calendar inscriptions related to Jupiter and a study of images that depict groups of planetary gods.

COLONIAL PERIOD IMAGES OF THE SUPERIOR PLANETS

Colonial period dictionaries provide relatively little information on the planets. Some names reflect European influence, such as the term *planetob,* combining a European word with the Yucatec plural ending *-ob* (Coe 1975a:19). Others seem to embody native constructs, such as *lacam ek,* meaning "big star" or "great star," glossed as "banner star" and "somersault star" (Lamb 1981:242). The latter suggests the retrograde motion of a planet that seems to "roll over" in the opposite direction before resuming forward motion. Another intriguing Yucatec reference is the "female crocodile star," identified as Saturn (Lamb 1981:242). Another term, *chachac ek,* refers to the seven planets of medieval times, derived from classical antiquity, representing the Sun, the Moon, and five planets visible to the naked eye (Roys 1967:150 n. 4).

The superior planets may appear as characters in the Popol Vuh. Dennis Tedlock (1991) identifies two falcon messengers as Jupiter and Saturn, but this interpretation is based on analysis of their roles rather than on direct identifications made by the Quiché. Tedlock (1985:336, 346) concludes that *uoc* (falcon) may correspond to Jupiter. Laughing Falcon (*uac*), who brings a message to the Hero Twins at one point in the tale, may be Saturn. Tedlock notes that Mars probably is represented by the two monkeys who are the elder half brothers of the Hero Twins in the Popol Vuh (Tedlock 1985:353; 1991:174). This tale recounts that the future Sun and Moon were mistreated by their simian brothers, who gave them almost no food and even tried to kill the twins. The Hero Twins convince the half brothers to climb a tree to get down a bird, and there they turn them into monkeys. As monkeys, they danced and did acrobatics while Hunahpu and Xbalanque played a tune called "Hunahpu Monkey." Tedlock (1985:342) believes that this episode is re-created in Momostenango in the Monkey Dance, in which two men dressed as monkeys with stars on their bodies climb a high pole and do acrobatics on a tightrope.

In sum, the Colonial period Maya sources provide us very few hints about the planets. We only have the most general information on the planets recorded in the early dictionaries. It is possible that falcons and monkeys may play the role of planets in the Popol Vuh, but their identities cannot be confirmed until a more thorough study of Precolumbian Maya imagery is undertaken.

MARS AMONG THE PRECOLUMBIAN MAYA

Fortunately, the Postclassic codices help to identify at least one of the superior planets. Our main source of information on Mars imagery comes from represen-

tations in the Mars table in the Dresden Codex pages 43b–45b (Fig. 6.1a). Robert Willson (1924:22–25) first recognized that the table deals with intervals of 780 days, approximating the mean synodic period of the red planet, and that the almanac section refers to a 78-day period that is very close to the average retrograde period (75 days) of the planet Mars. He notes that the table begins with a Ring Number (17.12, or 352 days) that is close to the interval between the planet's conjunction with the Sun and its first stationary point, or between the second stationary point and conjunction (352 + 76 + 352 = 780 days). His conclusions are now widely accepted (Aveni 1980:195–199; H. Bricker and V. Bricker 1997; Justeson 1989: 110; Knorozov 1982:163). David Kelley (1983:178) supports the association with Mars and points out that a Mars table in the context of a Tzolkin almanac is appropriate because over time the mean synodic period of Mars shifts only slowly from a given Tzolkin date, although the actual conjunctions of Mars with the Sun can vary up to about plus or minus 30 days from the mean.

In his commentary to the Dresden Codex, Eric Thompson (1972:22–23, 107–109) attempts to refute Willson's analysis of the table, arguing that the 780-day intervals refer to three complete Tzolkins (3 × 260) and the content deals primarily with weather. Because the table is not structured like the Venus table, Thompson maintains that it cannot be a planetary table. However, John Justeson (1989: 98–99) points out that the structure of the Venus table is inappropriate for a Mars table, and because the 780-day Mars cycle is inherently related to a triple Tzolkin, the proper format is a divinatory almanac. Victoria and Harvey Bricker (1986b) explore the relationship with Mars in great detail, suggesting additional patterns not noted by Willson. Bruce Love (1995) questions their findings, but they have mounted a spirited defense of their position that deals effectively with many of the issues raised by Love (H. Bricker and V. Bricker 1997). Justeson (1989:98) supports the Brickers in linking the table with Mars. He also agrees with their analysis of the aberrant numbers in the multiplication table, although he differs in the details of how these multiples functioned in relation to heliacal rise dates. He

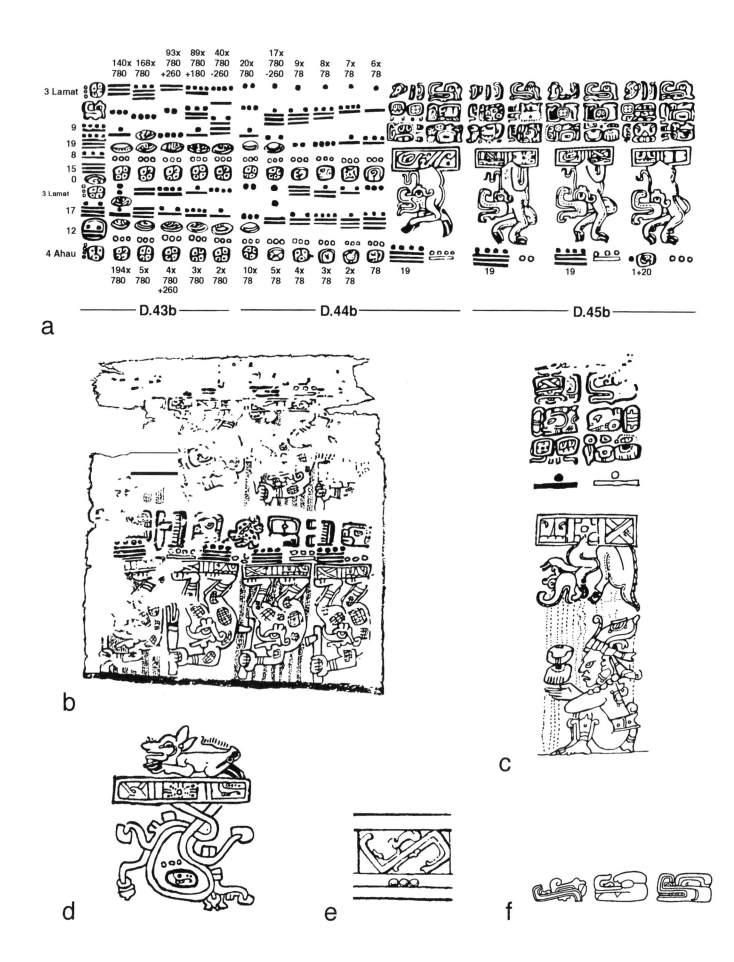

	140x 780	168x 780	93x 780 +260	89x 780 +180	40x 780 -260	20x 780	17x 780 -260	9x 78	8x 78	7x 78	6x 78
3 Lamat											
9											
19											
8											
15											
0											
3 Lamat											
17											
12											
4 Ahau											
	194x 780	5x 780	4x 780 +260	3x 780	2x 780	10x 78	5x 78	4x 78	3x 78	2x 78	78

	19	19	19	1+20

——— D.43b ——— ———D.44b——— ———D.45b———

a

b

c

d

e

f

proposes that the aberrant multiples refer not to the synodic period but rather to multiples of 260 days used to recapture approximate dates of heliacal rise (1989:100). Those that the Brickers identify as multiples involving a 520-day addition (columns six and eight, Fig. 6.1a) Justeson sees as multiples showing subtraction of 260 days. For example, instead of 16 × 780 + 520 on page 44b, Justeson sees 17 × 780 − 260. His model provides a more uniform method of adjustment and seems preferable to the model offered by the Brickers.

The opening inscription is 3 Lamat, followed by the Mars Beast glyph, then an inscription of 9.19.8.15.0, which Thompson (1972:107) interprets as a Long Reckoning giving the interval from the beginning of the era on 13.0.0.0.0 4 Ahau 8 Cumku, although only 4 Ahau is noted at the bottom of the column. This calculation brings the base date of the calendar to 9.19.7.15.8 3 Lamat, correlating with March 24, 818, in the Gregorian calendar (3/20/818 O.S.). Although only the 3 Lamat date is actually noted, scholars generally agree with Thompson that this is the base date for the table.

The retrograde of Mars in the year A.D. 818 began on 5/13/818, when the planet was positioned in the Milky Way in Sagittarius fifty days after the proposed 3 Lamat base of the table. At the end of retrograde, Mars was within one degree of its original position on the base date (3/20/818). Indeed, the entire retrograde period (5/13/818 to 7/7/818) took place while Mars was in Sagittarius. The Mars Beast in all four pictures is suspended from a sky band, conforming to a pattern that links the sky band with the place where the ecliptic crosses the Milky Way (Chapter 7). This suggests that the base date correlates with a time when Mars crossed the Milky Way.

After the introductory column, there follows a series of Tzolkin dates that mark the day reached when adding an interval given in the same column to the day 3 Lamat found at the beginning of the table. Two columns show errors in the intervals recorded, but the Tzolkin dates are correct. All the multiples of 780 days correlate with 3 Lamat dates, including the one that is 1 × 780 or 10 × 78; all other multiples of 78 bear different Tzolkin dates. The multiples of 78 days are apparently to be used with the pictorial almanac that incorporates an interval of 78 days, expressed horizontally with the numbers 19, 19, 19, and 21. The almanac's associated glyphic texts seem to refer to weather events, suggesting the planet's retrograde motion was somehow connected with weather changes. Thompson (1960:258) notes that "there are good grounds for believing that this beast is a symbol of rain or, conceivably, of some planet or constellation regarded as a sender of rain."

Harvey and Victoria Bricker (1997) point out that the Mars almanac is unique in the sequence of intervals expressed, and it is the only one known to add up to 78 days, a close approximation of the average retrograde period of Mars. The almanac could be reused with the ten different Tzolkin dates that accompany the multiples of 78 days in the table to the left

---

FIG. 6.1. *a:* Postclassic Mars table with multiples of 780 days representing synodic period of Mars and 78-day periods approximating retrograde of Mars; Mars Beasts suspended from sky bands may refer to periods when Mars was moving in retrograde motion while crossing Milky Way (Dresden Codex pages 43b–45b; modified after H. Bricker and V. Bricker 1998, fig. 1).

b: Postclassic Mars Beasts carrying torches and axes amid rain during period approximating retrograde of Mars (Madrid Codex 2a; after H. Bricker and V. Bricker 1998, fig. 4).

c: Postclassic Mars Beast, usually represented suspended from sky band, may depict Mars crossing Milky Way (Dresden Codex 68a; after Villacorta and Villacorta 1977).

d: Deer on sky band can be compared to Postclassic Mars Beast (Madrid Codex 47a; after Villacorta and Villacorta 1977).

e: Classic Zip Monster represented in sky bands, as on Palenque Sarcophagus Lid, seems to be counterpart for Postclassic Mars Beast.

f: Classic patron of month Zip evokes link with Postclassic Mars Beast represented by T794 (after Thompson 1960, fig. 22, nos. 11–13).

of the almanac. Justeson (1989:81) says that the almanac of 78 days is re-entered ten times for a total of forty stations spanning 780 days. In this model, the multiples of 78 could be coordinated with the 19- and 21-day intervals in a variety of ways. He proposes that this layout is required in order to accommodate the 78-day almanac to the other stations of the Mars cycle, especially heliacal rise and set, and the two stationary points bracketing retrograde motion.

In analyzing the almanac, Victoria and Harvey Bricker (1986b:59–60) suggest that it refers to specific Mars events in the ninth century, a position that is considered controversial. They maintain that the almanac begins with 3 Cimi (the last date before the almanac begins), which falls 78 days after the 3 Lamat base. The 3 Cimi date fell within a historical retrograde period in A.D. 818, but not at the beginning of retrograde motion. On the other hand, Justeson (1989:124 n. 28) says that 3 Cimi is simply the lowest multiple of 78, and he finds the Brickers' idea that the pictures refer to a specific 78-day span unacceptable. In any case, given that the base date is generally accepted to be in the ninth century, the multiples of 780 could extend the table into the Postclassic period. The highest multiple (194 × 780 days or around 414 years) carries the table forward from A.D. 818 to A.D. 1232, only a few years after the date proposed for the Dresden Codex Venus table.

The almanac probably focuses on events that had the potential of recurring together again. Eclipse glyphs above the third Mars Beast suggest that the almanac represents a solar eclipse followed by a lunar eclipse, both occurring during the retrograde motion of Mars. The historical retrograde in A.D. 818 coincided with a solar eclipse followed fifteen days later by a lunar eclipse, an eclipse pair that occurred near the time of the second stationary point of Mars (V. Bricker and H. Bricker 1986b:55). This may be the historical reference point setting a pattern that was to be significant in the future. Indeed, Kelley (1980:S18–S19, table V) notes that every alternate repetition of the synodic period of Mars will show a similar pattern of eclipses over a long period of time. In my opinion, the Maya were also interested in times when Mars was crossing the Milky

Way during retrograde motion, perhaps because certain weather conditions were expected to occur then. The Mars Beast is represented amid showers of rainfall in the Madrid Codex during a period that approximates the seventy-five-day mean retrograde period of Mars (Fig. 6.1b). Once again the beast is suspended from a sky band, suggesting the retrograde period coincides with Mars crossing the Milky Way. A similar configuration appears on Dresden Codex 68a (Fig. 6.1c). It would seem that Mars crossing the Milky Way may bring rainfall.

Mars crossing the Milky Way may also be linked with Venus events in the Dresden Codex Venus pages. On page 46, a sky band serves as a throne for an aged god wearing a headdress that resembles the Mars Beast (Fig. 5.3a). The Mars Beast glyph (T794) names this deity in the first column of the lower section (T on line 21, Fig. 5.3f). In light of the sky-band association, it is noteworthy that this page correlates with 1/19/1221, when the Morning Star rose with Mars moving in retrograde motion at the edge of the Milky Way. Mercury was also nearby in the Milky Way, and perhaps this is why the sky band has an owl head attached.

The first of the Mars Beasts on Dresden Codex 44b has a star eye that resembles central Mexican star symbols, and all of the beasts have a distinctive fret-nosed snout, like the Mars Beast glyph (T794) named in each of the associated glyph columns (Fig. 6.1a). The cleft hooves have led to the beast being variously identified as a deer, a tapir, or a peccary. Thompson's (1972:57) identification as a deer seems to be correct. The Mars Beast has volutes emerging from its head that could be stylized horns. On Dresden Codex 44b–45b, the Mars Beast has the same style of cleft hooves and stippled underbody seen on the deer on Dresden Codex 45c (Fig. 5.9f). Even the Mars Beast on 68a, which seems to have a back and tail like those of an iguana, has the same stippled underbody (Fig. 6.1c). Like the Mars Beast, deer are often colored white in the Dresden Codex (13c, 60b). And, in a similar fashion, deer can appear on sky bands, as seen on Madrid Codex 40c and 47a (Fig. 6.1d). The celestial deer suggests a connection with an account in the Chilam Balam of Chumayel describing the deer as "that which hooks the sky"

(Roys 1967:127). This hooking action might refer to the retrograde motion of the deer planet.

The Mars Beast glyph (T794) is a fret-nosed animal head resembling the patron of the month Zip (Fig. 6.1f; Kelley 1980:S30). Among the Yucatec Maya of Chan Kom, there is a class of forest spirits called "zip," who are associated with deer hunting (Redfield and Villa Rojas 1962:117–118). The month Zip was the principal festival of the hunters in Landa's time (Tozzer 1941:154–156). The Mars Beast is probably a deer monster related to the patron of the month Zip in Initial Series introductory glyphs (Thompson 1960, fig. 22). The Zip Monster is also represented in Classic period sky bands and in glyphic inscriptions as T1021 (Fig. 6.1e).

The Mars Beast also appears in Classic Maya calendar inscriptions. At Palenque, the Temple of the Inscriptions west panel links Pacal II's accession to Mars (F9-H3; Lounsbury 1991:818 n. 7). Floyd Lounsbury notes that the text refers to Mars (T1021a at G1) because Pacal's accession on 9.9.2.4.8 5 Lamat 1 Mol (7/24/615) was timed by the planet's first stationary point (8/4/615; Meeus n.d.). His accession also coincided with Jupiter's conjunction with the Sun. Other references to Mars appear in the Palenque texts, as in the Temple of the Sun, where the Mars Beast is paired with GIII (D5-D6) in texts referring to the birth of the Sun in the distant past, on 1.18.5.3.6 13 Cimi 19 Ceh in 2697 B.C. The Mars event is part of mythological history, but it would be expected to repeat on 13 Cimi because of the coincidence between one synodic period of Mars and three Tzolkins.

The Mars Beast (T1021a at A10) is named on Lintel 2 of Temple IV at Tikal following a 6 Caban date (Pl. 16). This date falls sixty-five days after the "star-war" (at B8) on 7 Ben 1 Pop (2/2/744), when Jupiter departed from its second stationary point (Lounsbury 1989:255). Although Mars was not in retrograde motion on 6 Caban, it did pass by Jupiter during the sixty-five-day period. Linda Schele and Nikolai Grube (1994, 1995) refer to the Mars Beast as the "Square-nosed Beastie," proposing that the beast names the divine founder of Naranjo. As we have seen, Venus appears as a founder of lineages at a number of sites, and it is possible that Mars plays a role in the lineage of Naranjo.

Justeson (1989:103, table 8.7) points out that the Classic period Maya inscriptions place special importance on a 13-Tun period that equates exactly with six synodic periods of Mars. Analysis of Classic period inscriptions indicates that a high percentage of dates with possible astronomical associations coincide with a time when Mars was visible in the sky, and usually the planet was in a morning or evening period of visibility (Aveni and Hotaling 1994). Further study is required to see whether the Mars Beast is somehow connected with these dates.

In sum, the Mars table displays sets of 780 days that were used to calculate multiples of the synodic period of Mars, and it includes a companion almanac referring to the period of retrograde motion. The 78-day almanac may focus special attention on times when Mars was crossing the Milky Way during retrograde motion. Such recurring cycles apparently were linked with weather predictions. Multiples in the table carry the cycle forward from the historical base date in the ninth century to the Early Postclassic period, contemporary with the Venus table. The Postclassic Mars Beast is a deer monster closely associated with the planet's retrograde motion, but not all images of the beast correspond to times when the planet was in retrograde. The patron of the month Zip associated with hunting seems to be the Classic period counterpart for the Mars Beast, but the details of the connection are poorly understood.

MONKEY DEITIES AND THE PLANETS

Monkeys, our almost-human brothers, seem to play an important part in the astronomical tales of the Maya (Chapter 1). Among the Lacandón, the spider monkey represents the Sun (Bruce 1976:77). On the other hand, the spider monkey is the younger brother of the Sun and Venus and later becomes the Evening Star, according to a Mopan account (Thompson 1970b:361). In another Mopan version of this tale, the youngest brother is a spider monkey (T'up) who becomes Mars or Jupiter (Thompson 1930:120–123). This tale apparently represents a different tradition from the one recounted in the Popol Vuh, which tells how the jealous elder brothers of the Hero Twins were transformed into monkeys.

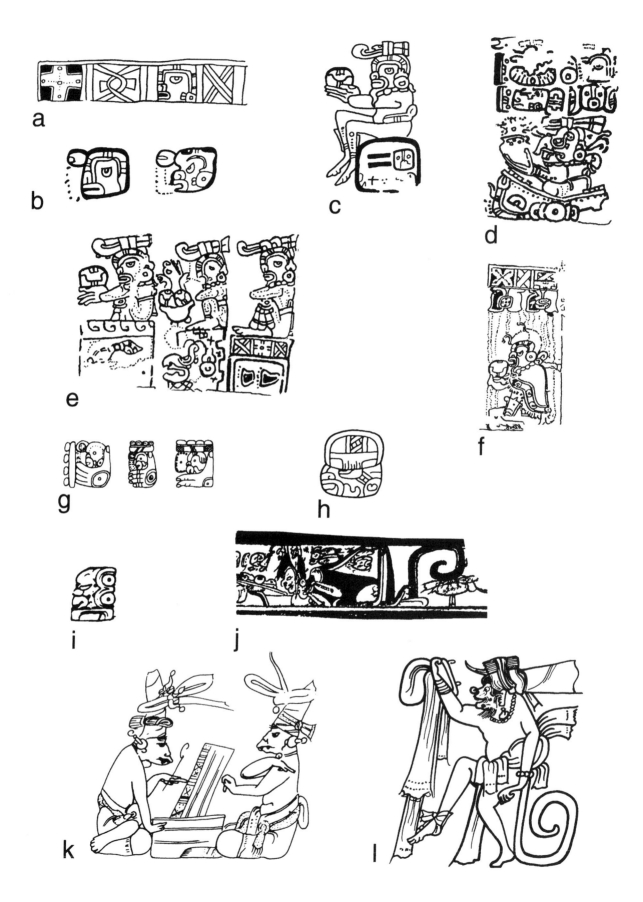

a

b

c

d

e

f

g

h

i

j

k

l

Dennis Tedlock (1985:353) proposes that the Popol Vuh links Mars with the monkey brothers represented by howler monkeys. He notes that *batz* means "howler monkey" in Quiché, and Hun Chouen is "one artisan," but *chouen* means "howler monkey" in archaic Yucatec. Michael Coe (1978a: 328) says that the monkey brothers are both named 1 Howler Monkey, and they are connected with the arts, playing the same role as in central Mexico. On the other hand, Thompson (1970b:360) says that their names refer to two different species of monkeys, with Hun Batz as a howler monkey (*batz*) and Hun Chouen as a spider monkey. He relates Hun Chouen to the Maya calendar day Chuen, the counterpart for Ozomatli in central Mexico, a calendar name referring to a spider monkey (Codex Borgia 13). A magnificent Aztec sculpture in the Musée de l'Homme in Paris depicts a spider monkey (Ozomatli?) wearing the shell ornaments of Quetzalcoatl and Xolotl, indicating a connection with Venus.

The Postclassic God C was originally identified as a simian deity by Paul Schellhas (1904), an identification reaffirmed by some contemporary scholars (Fig. 6.2c; Kelley 1976; Ringle 1988). Although Karl Taube (1992b:27) says that God C does not closely resemble any living creature, one attribute of the god is a small curled nose most often seen on monkeys in Maya art (Fig. 6.2j). Several images of God C are bearded, suggesting a representation of the male howler monkey (Fig. 6.2c, e). An embossed gold and copper disk recovered in the 1961 dredging of the Cenote at Chichén Itzá shows a bearded God C wearing rayed earrings like those worn by celestial deities at Tulum (Dávalos Hurtado 1961:540). The inscribed dates include a 4 Ahau date that seems to refer to the Katun cycle. On Madrid Codex 50c, God C is seated on a series of Ahau thrones that represent dates marking a sequence of Katun endings alternating with Lahuntun endings (Fig. 6.2c).

God C appears in contexts that suggest he is an astronomical deity. God C's face is one of the symbols found on sky bands in Postclassic images (Fig. 6.2a). On Madrid Codex 11c, God C sits on a skyband throne, indicating a clear astronomical connection (Fig. 6.2e). Madrid Codex 53c shows him walking on a road carrying a merchant pack, perhaps indicating he is traveling in a specific section of the sky associated with a sacred road. On Madrid Codex 18a, God B emerges from God C's open jaws, an intriguing image that could show celestial conjunction (Fig. 6.2d). Kelley (1976, fig. 35) notes that on Dresden Codex 68b, God C's glyph marks Chac's position in the tenth heaven. David Kelley and Ann Kerr (1973:201) rather tentatively identified God C with Saturn, although this identification is not repeated in a more recent publication (Kelley 1980).

God C's glyphic name has an affix often referred to as the water group, but it may actually represent blood (Fig. 6.2b; Taube 1992b:30–31). Based on phonetic readings, God C's glyph (T1016) is inter-

FIG. 6.2. *a:* God C's face on Late Postclassic sky band (Madrid Codex 35; after Villacorta and Villacorta 1977).

b: Postclassic God C's glyphic name (T1016) with affix that may represent blood (after Taube 1992b, fig. 10a).

c: Postclassic God C seated on 10 Ahau throne holding maize symbol (T506) (Madrid Codex 50c; after Taube 1992b, fig. 10c).

d: Postclassic God B emerges from God C's open jaws, possibly referring to celestial conjunction (Madrid Codex 18a; after Villacorta and Villacorta 1977).

e: Postclassic God C shown in sea, on Cauac place sign, and on sky band over path marked with footprints (Madrid Codex 11c; after Villacorta and Villacorta 1977).

f: Postclassic God C offers maize symbol (T506 or Kan) amid rain falling from eclipse glyphs suspended from sky band (Dresden Codex 68a; after Villacorta and Villacorta 1977).

g: Classic glyph G1 of "nine lords of night" incorporates God C's face and number nine (after Aveni 1980, fig. 58).

h: Early Classic God C glyph with sky glyph (T561) on brow (Tikal Stela 31; after Taube 1992b, fig. 11c).

i: Simian glyph with star infix and mirror representing monkey star or planet (after Kelley and Kerr 1973:198).

j: Classic spider-monkey face similar to that of God C (after Robicsek and Hales 1981, vessel 48).

k–l: Classic monkey gods wear "rolled-napkin" headdresses like aged God N; one monkey paints codex, another (male howler monkey?) holds up mirror as he dances (after Miller and Taube 1993:135, 138).

preted as the word *ku* or *ch'u,* implying that his name signifies something divine or holy (Houston and Stuart 1996; Ringle 1988). Because of this glyphic reading, Taube (1992b:31) maintains that God C is actually not a deity, but rather an embodiment of godliness. Nonetheless, his conclusion can be questioned, because God C is represented sitting on a sky band and moving through geographical locations, like other astronomical gods. He even offers a Kan symbol symbolizing maize, an action repeated by other astronomical gods (Fig. 6.2f).

Classic period images also suggest God C's astronomical connection. God C appears in Glyph X of the Lunar Series (Fig. 4.1k). On the eaves of House C at Palenque, the simian God C and God K are named in an important passage that seems to refer to four planets, according to Schele (1992b:185). Glyph G1 of the Nine Lords of the Night depicts God C's face in a hand with the number nine as an affix (Fig. 6.2g). Taube (1992b, fig. 11c) notes that God C's glyph has a sky-glyph infix on Tikal Stela 31 (Fig. 6.2h). A God C glyph compound accompanies signs referring to the Sun, the Moon, and Venus in directional imagery of Río Azul Tomb 12 (Fig. 3.2b). Kelley and Kerr (1973:198) link a simian face with a star-glyph infix to God C (Fig. 6.2i). Although this glyph differs from God C in some significant details, it certainly refers to a monkey star or planet.

The Temple of the Foliated Cross at Palenque depicts a maize plant crowned by a bearded monkey with a mirror brow, an image interpreted as God C in the role of the monkey sun or the Sun God himself (Pl. 11; Coggins 1988a:139; Robertson 1991:51; Schele 1976). The face has rectangular eyes with crossed pupils and a T-shaped tooth, like the Sun God, but this tooth form is also seen on Classic period images of God C (Taube 1992b, fig. 11b). The figure has a simian nose and a ruff of fur like a spider monkey, but its beard evokes a link with howler monkeys. A similar face with a "monkey-curl" nose, located at the base of the tree on Pacal's Sarcophagus Lid, has been identified as the God C aspect of the Sun God with a mirror brow (Pl. 10; Stuart 1988: 201). The mirror brows on these two Late Classic Palenque images seem to be related to the sky glyph on the brow of an Early Classic representation of God C, for both are characterized by a vertical band inset with beaded elements (Fig. 6.2h). In my opinion, these simian creatures are not the Sun God, but they may be a planet representing a "false sun" that appears at sunset, the time when the monkey's sun shines, according to contemporary Maya accounts.

On the central panel in the Temple of the Sun at Palenque, a basal band depicts Caban (earth) symbols alternating with a jawless simian face with a mirror brow, crossed eyes, and a monkey-curl nose (Fig. 3.6b). The earth band seems to represent the horizon, and the simian face may represent a planet associated with the horizon and sunrise or sunset.

As noted in Chapter 3, Kin variants represent monkeys of different species. These may refer to a count of days begun at dawn or at dusk, with howler monkeys used for counts beginning at dawn and spider monkeys for those beginning at dusk.

A Classic period vase painting shows a simian face alternating with the Kin glyph in a sky band. Although John Carlson (1988:288, fig. 9.11) interprets the simian face as the sun, the fact that the face alternates with a Kin glyph suggests that it is something other than the sun.

A dusk configuration is suggested by a goggle-eyed spider monkey with an Akbal infix, representing the time or place of sunset on the Pomona Flare (Fig. 3.2c; Hammond 1987:22). Clearly, the creature is something other than the sun. This monkey may be a planet representing a sort of false sun. Perhaps the planet takes the place of the sun after sunset.

One of the Tikal bones (MT38a) from Burial 116 depicts the spider monkey as a passenger in a canoe conveyed by the Paddler Twins, who represent the sun and the moon (Fig. 4.3a). If they are guiding the canoe through waters that lead to the underworld, a sunset configuration is suggested.

Whereas spider monkeys can be linked with sunset imagery, a howler monkey clearly is associated with dawn in the Dresden Codex Venus pages (Fig. 5.3c; Chapter 5). This connection with dawn may come from the fact that the howler's cries announce the rising sun, just as the Morning Star precedes sunrise. The Dresden Codex howler has the same deerlike ear seen on some Classic period monkey artists (Coe 1978a:345). Other monkey artists wear "rolled-napkin" style headdresses, like the aged God N (Fig. 6.2k; Reents-Budet 1994:41–46, figs. 2.5, 2.15, 2.22a–b). The characteristic beard of a male howler monkey is evident on a number of these monkeys, including a dancing monkey looking at his reflection in a mirror (Fig. 6.2l). Classic period howler-monkey artists sometimes appear in pairs (Figs. 3.9e, 6.2k). These allude to a connection with two brothers transformed into howler monkeys in the Popol Vuh.

The monkey artists belong to a larger complex of artist gods named in texts as *its'at,* meaning "artist, sage, man of letters," an epithet also used to name God D and the Paddlers (Reents-Budet 1994:49). The role of the astronomer who studies and records the motions of the heavens certainly was linked with the sage and "man of letters." Indeed, the planetary gods may reveal the key to understanding planetary cycles recorded in the codices.

We can conclude that there was probably more than one monkey planet in Maya cosmology. The howler-monkey aspect of the Morning Star is well known. Tedlock suggests that the howler monkey in the Popol Vuh plays the role of Mars. The spider monkey may also be linked with a planet, perhaps one observed at sunset. God C is a simian character whose astronomical nature is not yet understood. Clearly more research is required to sort out the monkey planets.

GOD K IN THE COLONIAL AND POSTCLASSIC PERIODS

God K can be identified as the sky god called Bolon Dzacab in Colonial period sources. This identification, first proposed by Eduard Seler (1960–1961, 1: 376–477) at the turn of the century, is now widely accepted (Taube 1992b:73). Thompson (1970:281) notes that a passage from the Chilam Balam of Chumayel describes Bolon Dzacab taking the seeds of edible plants to the thirteenth layer of heaven at the time of the great flood. The Motul dictionary glosses Bolon Dzacab as "perpetual thing," meaning "eternal"; however, Thompson (1972:90) translates God K's name as "nine generations." Thompson (1970b:227, 280) proposes that this name may have something to do with the nine lords of the under-

world who ruled over a repeating sequence of nine nights. When combined with other calendar cycles, the nine lords may refer to a long interval of time, such as those used in astronomical calculations involving the planets.

Landa described Bolon Zacab (Bolon Dzacab) as a god worshiped at New Year ceremonies performed annually in the month of July. His counterpart, God K, is involved in some way with the new year. God K may be linked with the year as a representative of Jupiter because the planet is visible in the sky for about one year (mean interval 367 days) during each synodic period.

God K is prominent in ceremonies associated with years named Ben and Etz'nab in the Dresden Codex New Year ceremonies. God K is linked with a column of Ben glyphs marking the year-bearer associated with the eastern direction on Dresden Codex 25b (Fig. 6.3f; Thompson 1972:90–93). His position in the middle register shows that he presides over ceremonies to avert calamity on the first day of Pop, the month beginning the year (Chapter 3). Associated glyphs say that cacao is God K's food. Cacao, the chocolate bean, was the principal currency for Mesoamerica, hence God K is a deity associated with great wealth. This is probably why God K is surrounded by cacao pods on a capstone from Chichén Itzá dating to the Terminal Classic period (Fig. 6.3g).

On page 26c of the Dresden Codex, in the years named Etz'nab, God K offers a beheaded turkey and drops of liquid that are probably turkey blood (Fig. 6.3c). An associated inscription with the number nine recalls God K's association with *bolon,* meaning "nine." God K's position in the lower register indicates that he presides over renewal ceremonies performed during the month of Pop (Chapter 3).

God K's celestial nature is evident in many Maya images. Taube (1992b:69) notes that a winged God K is found in a number of contexts that suggest an association with the sky. A Postclassic mural painting at Tulum, dating after A.D. 1400, depicts a sky band with a winged God K (Fig. 6.3b). A similar association is seen in a winged God K with a sky band arching overhead on a painted capstone from the Temple of the Owls at Chichén Itzá (Fig. 6.3g).

Looking at the alphabetical list of gods, originally

developed by Paul Schellhas (1904) and recently revised by Taube (1992b), suggests that God K is named as one of nineteen or twenty different deities in the Postclassic codices. The Dresden Codex Venus pages also list twenty gods, among which we find the Sun, the Moon, and God K (Kelley 1976, fig. 28). This number evokes the twenty day patrons in the Precolumbian codices of central Mexico, which include gods of the Sun and the Moon as well as Tezcatlipoca, who most likely is a counterpart of God K (Codex Borgia 9–13).

In Postclassic images, God K is characterized by a long snout with branching elements, sometimes inset with a mirror, as on Dresden Codex page 12a (Fig. 6.3e). God K's portrait head glyph also has an elongated snout with a smoking mirror (Fig. 6.3d).

The mirror itself may be an astronomical image, for mirrors are prominent in expressions referring to Venus positions in the Dresden Codex Venus pages (46–50).

Page 46 of the Dresden Codex Venus table shows God K as a victim of the Morning Star god at heliacal rise (Fig. 5.3a; Thompson 1972:66–67). Study of the Venus pages indicates that Venus spearing a victim symbolizes opposition rather than conjunction (Chapter 5; Milbrath 1995c). For this reason, the Venus god kills his victims with an atlatl—a long-distance projectile weapon. On 1/19/1221 (5 Kan 7 Xul), the date recording the heliacal rise on page 46, Jupiter and the emerging Morning Star were at the opposite sides of the sky. This date also coincides with the retrograde period of Jupiter. As we will

---

FIG. 6.3. *a:* Late Postclassic God K bound like prisoner (murals of Mound 1, Santa Rita, Belize; after Taube 1992b, fig. 32f).

b: God K's celestial aspect as winged deity on sky band (Late Postclassic mural from Tulum; after Taube 1992b, fig. 34c).

c: Etz'nab new year with God K offering beheaded turkey and drops of blood (Dresden Codex 26c; after Villacorta and Villacorta 1977).

d: God K's Postclassic portrait head glyph with elongated snout bearing smoking mirror (Paris Codex 24; Madrid Codex 77; after Taube 1992b, fig. 32a–b).

e: Postclassic God K has long snout with branching elements, sometimes inset with mirror, as on Dresden Codex page 12a (after Taube 1992b, fig. 32e).

f: Ben new year with God K in temple of east (Dresden Codex 25b; after Villacorta and Villacorta 1977).

g: Winged God K in jaws of coiled serpent with sky band arching overhead on painted capstone (Terminal Classic Temple of Owls, Structure 5C7, Chichén Itzá; after Tozzer 1957, fig. 384).

h: Terminal Classic relief of God K has both serpent leg and smoking mirror of central Mexican Tezcatlipoca (Structure 4B1, Sayil; after Taube 1992b, fig. 34a).

i–l: Classic images of God K's forehead mirror with burning torch (*left*); smoking cigars and symbols for fire (T563) emanating smoke (*center*); God K's forehead mirror with smoking axe (*right*) (after Schele and Miller 1983, figs. 3k–n).

m: Classic glyph for God K representing smoking mirror (after Schele and Miller 1983, fig. 3i).

n: Palenque Triad god known as GII, shown as full figure in reclining posture, representing counterpart of God K (Temple of Foliated Cross at D2; after Robertson 1991, fig. 153).

o: God K in open jaws of Cosmic Monster arching over ruler's head (detail of Tikal Lintel 3, Temple IV; after Jones 1977, fig. 11).

p: Pacal's apotheosis as God K took place when Jupiter reached its first stationary point in A.D. 683 (detail of Sarcophagus Lid, Temple of Inscriptions at Palenque; after Robertson 1985a, fig. 73).

q: Late Classic God K with smoking axe or mirror emanating from mirror on brow (Pier C, House A at Palenque; after Robertson 1985b, fig. 38).

r: Mirror-browed God K wearing T510f star on torso (West Court of Palace, Palenque; after Robertson 1985b, fig. 358).

s: Mirror-browed God K wearing T510b star on altar (South Palace Substructure, Palenque; after Robertson 1985b, fig. 409a).

t: God K's head emerges from jaws of double-headed serpent flanking portrait of ruler (North Palace Substructure, Palenque; after Robertson 1985b, fig. 339b).

u: Early Classic God K with smoking celt emanating from Akbal mirror brow; note simian quality evident in paw-hands and monkey-curl nose (Tikal Stela 31; after A. Miller 1986, pl. 19).

see, Classic period monuments representing God K bear dates that correlate with Jupiter's position in retrograde.

In Late Postclassic murals of Mound 1 at Santa Rita in Belize, God K is bound like a prisoner or a victim destined for sacrifice, a role similar to that of God K in the Venus pages (Fig. 6.3a). The murals display Maya dates in a sequence that links God K with 1 Ahau (Thompson 1960:198). This is especially interesting in light of a pattern linking Jupiter events to Classic period Katuns ending in 1 Ahau (Thompson 1960: 228). Owing to the structure of the Katun cycle, each of the 13 Katuns is associated with a different Ahau date. The whole Katun series represents approximately 256.25 years (13 × 20 × 360 days).

God K plays a prominent role in Katun ceremonies in the Paris Codex (2–12). His head, presented to different Katun lords seated on sky-band thrones, is the insignia of the Lord of the Katun (Love 1994: 17). Carrying God K's head to the new ruler in the Katun ceremonies may allude to a change in political or religious authority, recalling Classic period accession scenes and dynastic rites involving the presentation of God K (Hellmuth 1987:372, fig. 662–664; Taube 1987).

Each Katun lord ruled a period of 19.71 years (20 × 360 days), very close to the interval between successive Jupiter-Saturn conjunctions. The conjunction of Jupiter and Saturn approximately every 20 years cannot be expected to align with a specific date in the Katun cycle over long periods of time, but those instances when there was a conjunction at a Katun ending certainly would have been notable because the event would repeat at the next Katun end. In the conjunctions between Jupiter and Saturn, Jupiter is the dynamic actor in the scenario, running laps around the slower-moving Saturn. The God K head carried to the enthroned Katun lord in the Paris Codex may symbolize Jupiter transported across the sky to a new encounter with Saturn. The interval of the Katun approximates the period between successive conjunctions of Jupiter and Saturn; and every three Katuns (approximately every 59 years) the conjunction event would be expected to occur in the same part of the sky (Kelley 1985:238).

Many scholars conclude that God K is related to the Postclassic Mexican god Tezcatlipoca of central Mexico, who also wears a smoking mirror and is closely associated with images of rulers. Tezcatlipoca is a god with so many astronomical aspects and associations that he may be the lord of the sky in some sense. One of Tezcatlipoca's aspects is the lunar jaguar known as Tepeyollotl (Milbrath 1995a). Henry Nicholson (1971:412, 426) points out that Tezcatlipoca is also fused with the lunar god Metztli. Among his multiple aspects, we also find one linked with Venus as Mixcoatl and another with the solar god Huitzilopochtli. Nicholson notes that one early account refers to him as "another Jupiter." Others say he was transformed into Ursa Major at the end of the first world age. Among Tezcatlipoca's many guises, the black Tezcatlipoca seems to be closest to God K. The black Tezcatlipoca, linked with the southern direction, is the victim of the Morning Star on Codex Borgia 54 (Seler 1963, 2:121). And it seems significant that the Venus pages of the Dresden Codex name God K as a victim of the Morning Star, also associating him with the southern direction (Kelly 1976, fig. 28).

Tezcatlipoca and God K both share an association with mirrors and serpents. Tezcatlipoca has a smoking mirror on his head and a serpent foot in a Colonial period Aztec codex known as the Codex Ríos (Codex Vaticanus A, folios 3v, 44v). Although a serpent foot is not common in Late Postclassic images of God K, he apparently retains an ophidian aspect in the Madrid Codex (31b). At Chichén Itzá, Terminal Classic and Early Postclassic reliefs depict gods with severed legs or one leg terminating in a serpent that seems to be related to both Tezcatlipoca and God K (Morris et al. 1931, 2, pl. 31; Robertson and Andrews 1992, fig. 21; Tozzer 1957, fig. 138). A Terminal Classic relief of God K at Sayil has both the serpent leg and the smoking mirror of Tezcatlipoca (Fig. 6.3h). These traits seem to appear earlier in the Maya area than in central Mexico, indicating that some aspects of the cult first developed among the Maya.

Taube (1992b:73, 78) points to links between God K and God B, the Postclassic Chac, suggesting that the two share traits and even substitute for one another. Jeff Kowalski (1990:63) notes that God K may also be a rain and storm deity like Chac, and he recognizes possible representations of God K in corner masks of the Great Pyramid at Uxmal dating to the Late Classic period. Perhaps Tlaloc is also involved in the equation, for a rare image from Copán shows Tlaloc with a smoking-mirror headdress (Taube 1992b, fig. 72a). Nevertheless, such conflation of deity traits does not mean direct equation. God K and Chac/Tlaloc may share general traits as planetary gods, but they may be conflated in specific contexts to indicate they are planets seen together in conjunction.

We can conclude that Colonial and Postclassic data suggest a possible relationship between God K and Jupiter. In the Postclassic Katun cycle, God K may represent Jupiter moving around the sky to meet Saturn at intervals of approximately twenty years, the length of one Katun. God K's role in the New Year ceremonies of the annual cycle may relate to Jupiter's year-long period of visibility each synodic period. God K seems to be the counterpart of the black Tezcatlipoca, a central Mexican god who is similarly associated with a smoking mirror and serpent traits.

THE CLASSIC PERIOD GOD K AND GII

There is clear continuity tracing the imagery of God K back through time, but there are stylistic modifications, the most notable of which is that the smoking mirror changes position between the Postclassic and Classic periods (Fig. 6.3h–u). In the Classic period, God K carries a mirror on his brow rather than on his snout. Sometimes a smoking torch emanates from the mirror, its smoke resembling cigar smoke or the smoke from fires (Fig. 6.3h–k). In other images, a smoking celt bearing markings similar to the sky glyph emanates from God K's mirror (Fig. 6.3q–r). God K's nocturnal nature is evident in images from the Palenque Palace that show the mirror-browed God K wearing a star (Fig. 6.3r, s). One of the earliest known images of God K has a smoking sky celt emerging from a nocturnal mirror with Akbal markings (Fig. 6.3u). Here on Tikal Stela 31, God K may have simian traits, with monkey paws and a monkey-curl nose over an elongated upper lip.

God K's Classic period glyph is the head of God K

with a mirrored brow, or sometimes a smoking mirror by itself can name God K (Fig. 6.3m; Taube 1992b, fig. 32c). A number of glyphs show God K's name associated with the number nine, providing a link with the Colonial period Bolon Dzacab (Thompson 1970b, fig. 7). Schele (1984:304) first recognized that "God K's mirror-in-hand" (T1030d:670) is a glyph compound usually denoting the presentation of God K at the time of an heir designation at Palenque. This is just one of many Classic Maya contexts that indicate God K was important as a god of lineage and rulership.

Thompson (1970b:226, 289) emphasizes God K's association with vegetation, and he proposes that the Colonial period God K was known as Kauil, meaning "surplus of our daily bread [maize]." David Stuart's (1987:15) phonetic reading of God K's name as k'awil (kauil) provides support for linking God K with maize (Taube 1992b:78). Copán Stela 11 depicts the ruler Yax Pac in the guise of God K with maize foliation on his brow, suggesting an aspect of God K that may be linked with k'awil (Fash 1991, fig. 108). Nonetheless, more recent interpretations of k'awil suggest that the term refers to stone sculptures, flint, and stone axeheads associated with lightning (Freidel et al. 1994:194–200). K'awil's name is also linked with serpents. Schele (1992b:120) notes that on Copán Stela 11, an 819-day passage refers to the serpent foot as God K's way, or alter ego.

Although K'awil is now more commonly used in translating God K's name, it should be noted that his name has also been read as Tahil, based on linguistic connections with the word for obsidian (tah or toh), suggesting a connection with Tohil, the Quiché god of lightning and storms (Taube 1992b:75–76; Tedlock 1985:365). Tohil was lord of a Quiché lineage at the time of the conquest. Indeed, God K is similarly connected with lineage and lightning. As Taube points out, God K's headdress elements—mirrors, fire, burning axes, torches, and cigars—all may allude to lightning. In my opinion, God K is a planet linked with meteorological phenomena, especially storms and lightning.

God K appears as GII of the Palenque Triad in mythological texts recording the birth of three brothers. The Cross Group records GII's birth date as 1.18.5.4.0 1 Ahau 13 Mac (2697 B.C.). GII glyphs are like those naming God K, but they show the full figure in a reclining posture (Fig. 6.3n). Heinrich Berlin (1963:93) named this god GII because he is the second one listed in texts that name all three brothers of the Triad; however, his mythic birthday makes him the youngest of the brothers in the Triad (Schele 1976:10). In a modern Mopan tale, Mars or Jupiter takes the role of the youngest brother, T'up, transformed into a spider monkey (Chapter 1).

Dennis Tedlock (1992:250–258, 266–267) proposes that Mars is closely linked with GII in the Triad and Hun Hunahpu in the Popol Vuh. He reconstructs Hun Hunahpu's birthday as 8.5.0 before the current Maya epoch, concluding that this god shares GII's 1 Ahau birthday, a date he associates with the heliacal rise of Mars, although he provides no convincing evidence of this association. Tedlock notes that the birth dates of both gods give intervals that are evenly divisible by 780, the mean synodic period of Mars. He also finds a link between Vucub Hunahpu and Jupiter, but here his evidence for that connection is even more tenuous. Furthermore, it should be pointed out that these interpretations contradict his earlier identification of a falcon character as Jupiter and the monkey brothers as Mars (Tedlock 1985). As will be seen, the pattern of Classic period dates provides strong evidence linking GII/God K with Jupiter. Furthermore, God K is specifically named in a cycle known to refer to Jupiter.

God K is featured prominently in an 819-day cycle associated with a high incidence of Jupiter and Saturn events in the Classic period inscriptions (Justeson 1989:103). The 819-day phrases often name God K in the fifth position (Kelley 1976:57–58, fig. 17). A companion glyph (T739) in the fourth position is also used as Glyph Y of the Supplementary Series, where it is governed by a 7-day cycle that may be a "planetary week" (Yasugi and Saito 1991).

There is a clear link between God K and rulership. It is interesting to note that a number of Maya rulers incorporate God K in their personal names or titles. God K is seen in the headdress of Stormy Sky (K'awil Chaan) on Tikal Stela 31, a fifth-century monument that records his accession to the throne (Figs. 3.7b, 6.3u; A. Miller 1986:54, 82). Here God K's torso ap-

pears on a sky glyph as Stormy Sky's personal name worn as a costume accessory (Coggins 1990:84).

On Maya lintels and stelae, God K frequently appears in the jaws of a double-headed serpent that Maya rulers used as a royal insignia (Cohodas 1982: 113; Stuart 1984:19). On architectural reliefs from Palenque, God K's head emerges from the jaws of a double-headed serpent flanking the portrait of a ruler (Fig. 6.3t). Whereas God K's serpent foot often seems to represent a naturalistic snake, the double-headed serpent with an upturned bulbous nose seems to be linked with the front head of the Cosmic Monster discussed in Chapter 7.

Ceramic vessels depict God K with other astronomical deities. God K appears with the Moon Goddess in scenes featuring a large snake (Fig. 4.10h). Typically, God N emerges from the serpent's mouth, the serpent's body wraps around the Moon Goddess, and the tail carries God K. Occasionally the snake is represented as an extension of God K's leg, like God K's serpent foot on the lintel from Sayil (Fig. 6.3h). A number of relief-carved pottery vessels show God K in a specific relationship with God L, a god of the Morning Star in the Dresden Codex (Chapter 5). God L wears God K on his cape on some relief vessels (Robicsek 1978:173, figs. 188–189). Another vessel depicts God L offering the head of God K (Coe 1973:116, no. 56). Small bottles represent God K seated facing God L with an offering between them (Robicsek 1978, fig. 210, pl. 238).

God K has multiple aspects most clearly seen in ceramic representations. A painted pot depicts two aspects of God K, one with the smoking-mirror headdress, the other with a flower positioned on his brow (Coe 1982:47, no. 19). Another pot shows a figure holding a glyph compound referring to Bolon Dzacab and another figure holding a head of God K with a smoking mirror (Coe 1982:118, no. 62). God K is even shown as quadripartite in some representations (Coe 1982:54).

We can conclude that the Classic period representations of God K connect him with lineage, rulership, lightning, and thunder. His imagery often involves celestial associations, including sky monsters, sky glyphs, and stars. His mirror may also be a celestial symbol. He appears in scenes with the

Moon Goddess and the Morning Star, images that may show celestial conjunction. He also is part of the 819-day inscriptions that seem to relate to Jupiter and Saturn events, pointing to a likely association with one of these two planets. As we will see, there is a consistent association between God K and Jupiter events in the Classic period inscriptions.

JUPITER EVENTS AND GOD K ON CLASSIC MAYA MONUMENTS

Late Classic monuments with God K images often bear dates that coincide with Jupiter's retrograde motion. When Jupiter is not in a significant position, a Saturn event may be substituted. Often the dates are associated with dynastic rituals or rituals relating to Katun events. As noted above, the Katun cycle itself reflects the pattern of intervals between successive conjunctions of Jupiter and Saturn.

At Naj Tunich, a God K portrait glyph appears with the date 13 Ahau, referring to the Katun ending 9.17.0.0.0 13 Ahau 18 Cumku (1/18/771; Stone 1995b:142, fig. 6.27). This is especially intriguing because God K's head is represented in the Katun-ending ceremonies of the Postclassic. The 13 Ahau date falls less than three weeks after the first stationary point of Jupiter (1/1/771; Meeus n.d.). Saturn was also in retrograde motion then. As we will see, such correlations led the Maya to focus on observations of these two planets at the Katun end for hundreds of years.

By studying a pattern of dates in the life of Chan Bahlum II, Lounsbury (1989, table 19.1) correlates Palenque monuments with Jupiter's retrograde, although he does not identify specific imagery that refers to Jupiter. At six years of age, the young ruler was designated as heir to the throne on 9 Akbal 6 Xul (9.10.8.9.3; 6/12/641), a date that correlates with Jupiter's departure from its second stationary point and Saturn's approach to its first stationary point (Lounsbury 1989, table 19.1; Meeus n.d.). Some thirty years later, the ruler began his reign under the patronage of Jupiter. At the time of Chan Bahlum's accession on 8 Oc 3 Kayab (1/5/684), Jupiter had just passed its second stationary point and was crossing the meridian at dusk (second stationary point on 12/

23/683; Meeus n.d.). Both his heir designation and accession were timed by Jupiter's departure from the second stationary point (Lounsbury 1989).

The small figure on the central panels of temples in the Cross Group, previously interpreted as Pacal (Schele 1976:13–14), is now recognized as Chan Bahlum at six or seven years of age when he was designated heir to the throne (Robertson 1991:20). The date of the heir-designation event is positioned near the young Chan Bahlum, whereas the accession event is linked with the taller figure representing Chan Bahlum as an adult. All three temples show different aspects of God K, indicating there may be at least three manifestations of God K at Palenque. In the Temple of the Sun, Chan Bahlum holds a God K manikin with a smoking brow at the time of his accession (Fig. 3.6b). The Temple of the Cross depicts the young Chan Bahlum standing on a skeletal head with an elongated snout and the number nine (*bolon*), alluding to the Bolon Dzacab aspect of God K (Pl. 12; compare Thompson 1970b, figs. 9p–q). This image is captioned by the heir-designation event above the smaller figure of Chan Bahlum. The Temple of the Foliated Cross depicts God K emerging from a spiral shell with a maize plant in hand (Pl. 11; Dütting 1984:23; Robicsek 1979:115; Stuart 1978:167). The young Chan Bahlum stands on God K's shell, indicating a direct link with the maize aspect of God K.

Temple XIV at Palenque shows that after his death, Chan Bahlum continued his relationship with God K and the planet Jupiter (Pl. 13). The text opens on the left with a 9 Ik 10 Mol date, followed by a statement that God K was displayed under the auspices of the Moon Goddess; then the date is repeated on the right after an interval of almost 100,000 years (Schele and Miller 1986:272, fig. VII.2). The display of God K is mentioned again, followed by a reference to 9 Ahau 3 Kankin (9.13.13.15.0; 10/31/705), a date that falls about three years and nine months after the death date (3 × 365 days + 260 days). Lounsbury (1989:250, fig. 19.5) links this posthumous date with Jupiter's departure from its second stationary point (second stationary point on 10/21/705; Meeus n.d.). Saturn was in retrograde, and the Moon passed Jupiter a few hours before dusk. The lunar event is especially significant because Chan

Bahlum's deceased mother is compared to the Moon Goddess in the texts. Apparently Lady Ahpo Hel takes the role of the Moon on the panel, for she holds the God K manikin, just as the Moon holds Jupiter in conjunction.

The most important image of apotheosis involving Jupiter is seen on the Sarcophagus Lid of the Temple of the Inscriptions at Palenque, a pyramid that houses the tomb of Chan Bahlum's father, Pacal (Fig. 6.3p; Pl. 10). God K and the Jester God emerge from either end of a bicephalic serpent bar, and Pacal appears in the guise of God K at the base of a cosmic tree (Schele 1976:17; Robertson 1991:18). This scene has an astronomical context, for Pacal is surrounded by a sky band. On the edge of the lid, his death or some other event related to his death is recorded on the Calendar Round 6 Etz'nab 11 Yax (9.12.11.5.18; 8/26/683). David Stuart has deciphered the event glyph as "he entered the road" (och bih; Mathews 1991:161; Schele 1992b:133). Heinrich Berlin (1977:137) notes that this event (T100: 585) refers to the end of a reign, and it may signal death or apotheosis. This expression probably refers to Pacal's apotheosis rather than his death. Coggins (1988b:74–75) suggests that Pacal is shown dancing out of his tomb on the Sarcophagus Lid, suggesting an image of apotheosis. The apotheosis date is only two days short of Jupiter's first stationary point (8/28/683; Meeus n.d.). It is noteworthy that Pacal's son, Chan Bahlum, was not inaugurated as the new ruler until Jupiter had begun to move forward again, four months later.

Jupiter also appears to be involved with the posthumous portrait of Yax Pac of Copán. On Stela 11, Yax Pac appears in a guise of God K, one of only two known portraits of a deceased ruler in this guise (Fash 1991:177, fig. 108). Like Pacal's image of apotheosis as God K, the Copán monument is also associated with the retrograde period of Jupiter. The stela bears the date 8 Ahau, inferred to be that of the Lahuntun ending on 9.19.10.0.0 8 Ahau 8 Xul, marking the halfway point of the Katun cycle. On this date (4/30/820), Jupiter was on the eastern horizon at dusk, approximately at the midpoint of its retrograde motion (from 2/18/820 to 6/21/820; Meeus n.d.). Furthermore, Jupiter was in conjunction with

the full Moon on that night (full Moon 4/31/820; Goldstine 1973).

On Bonampak Stela 1, God K appears on the headdress of an ancestor figure emerging from a cleft in a Cauac (Witz) monster on the base of a monument that marks the first Lahuntun ending of Chaan Muan's reign, recorded in a fragmentary Initial Series date of 9.17.10.0.0 (11/26/780; Mathews 1980:64, fig. 3; Proskouriakoff 1993:163–164). At this time, Jupiter had been in retrograde motion for three weeks (first stationary point on 11/5/780; Meeus n.d.). Jupiter, visible high above the eastern horizon at dawn, was especially brilliant because it was precisely in conjunction with Uranus, a planet that was bright enough at this time to be seen with the naked eye. Meanwhile, Saturn was invisible in conjunction with the Sun.

Lintel 4 from Bonampak Structure 6 depicts a ruler holding a double-headed God K serpent bar (Schele and Grube 1994:109, fig. 180). Both images of God K have mirrored brows with axe inserts, and one has Akbal markings on the mirror, suggesting an opposition of light and dark. The only surviving date on the monument, 7 Chuen 4 Zotz (9.8.9.15.11; 5/11/603), does not correspond to Jupiter's retrograde, but Saturn was in retrograde motion. Saturn may also be significant in the imagery of God K, probably because God K encodes the relationship between Jupiter and Saturn in his role as a Katun god.

Dos Pilas Stela 14 shows a ruler displaying a God K manikin scepter (formerly Stela 25; Houston 1993, tables 3-1, 4-1; fig. 3-24). Two passages have a glyph compound mentioning God K (F2, H4). The stela has an Initial Series date of 9.14.0.0.0 6 Ahau 13 Muan (11/29/711) and a Calendar Round of 8 Ix 2 Cumku (9.14.5.3.14; 1/15/717) associated with a "shell star" compound. As noted in Chapters 4 and 5, the Initial Series date corresponds to the full Moon. It also marks a time when the Evening Star was about to reemerge. Neither date correlates with Jupiter's retrograde, but the Katun-ending date marks a time when Jupiter was overhead at dawn and it coincides precisely with Saturn's first stationary point (11/29/711). The second date also approximates Saturn's first stationary point (1/29/717; Meeus n.d.). Here

Saturn may substitute for Jupiter in the context of monuments depicting God K imagery.

Dos Pilas Stela 15 also shows the display of a God K scepter (Houston 1993, fig. 3.25). One of its three dates is a Calendar Round date of 7 Ahau 3 Kayab (9.14.10.4.0; 12/26/721) that coincides with Jupiter's retrograde motion (first stationary point on 11/15/721; Meeus n.d.). Another date (9.14.9.10.13 1 Ben 16 Tzec; 5/13/721) coincides with Saturn's retrograde motion.

Dates on some Dos Pilas monuments depicting God K cannot be related to the retrograde of either Jupiter or Saturn, but they do record subdivisions of the Katun that could be related to observations of Jupiter and Saturn. Among such examples, we find Dos Pilas Stela 11 (formerly Stela 22) depicting the display of the God K scepter on a Calendar Round date of 12 Ahau 8 Kankin (9.14.5.0.0; 11/2/716; Houston 1993, table 3-1; fig. 3-27).

Monuments from Yaxchilán clearly link God K and Jupiter events. On Stela 1, God K emerges from open jaws of a double-headed serpent represented with a sky-band body and deer attributes (Fig. 3.8d). The Initial Series date on the monument is 9.16.10.0.0 1 Ahau 3 Zip (3/11/761; Proskouriakoff 1993:112). This date coincides with the new Moon falling about two weeks after Jupiter's first stationary point (2/27/761; Meeus n.d.). A fragmentary Calendar Round date, reconstructed as 1 Oc 18 Pop (9.16.8.16.10; 2/14/760), records an 819-day event that is also a little over two weeks after Jupiter's first stationary point (1/27/760; Meeus n.d.). The two dates may be purposefully paired to show Jupiter's retrograde in two sequential synodic cycles.

Yaxchilán Lintel 30 names God K in an 819-day event on 1 Ben 1 Chen (9.13.16.10.13; 7/20/708), a date reached by counting back 397 days from the birth of Bird Jaguar IV recorded on 8 Oc 13 Yax (8/21/709; 9.13.17.12.10; Tate 1992, apps. 2–3, fig. 57). Although neither date pertains to the period of Jupiter's retrograde, the distance number is a close approximation of the synodic period of Jupiter (398.9 days). The 819-day event on 1 Ben 1 Chen refers to the east and red before mentioning God K at A5. At this time, Jupiter and Saturn were in Gemini in the east at dawn, and the waning Moon

was in conjunction with Saturn above the eastern horizon, while Venus was on the eastern horizon in Cancer, about to disappear as the Morning Star. One synodic period later, Jupiter was once again in the east at dawn at the time of Bird Jaguar's birth in A.D. 709. Now Mars was approximately at the midpoint of its retrograde motion, above the eastern horizon in Leo (second stationary point on 9/10/709; Meeus n.d.). At this time, Jupiter and Saturn were precisely in conjunction in Cancer, and Venus was only a few degrees away, now also in Cancer. This massing of three planets above the eastern horizon at dawn may have been considered an auspicious omen for the ruler's birth, and the count backward could relate to a symmetry seen in the previous synodic period with another celestial triad formed by Jupiter, Saturn, and the Moon in Gemini at dawn.

A ruler holding the God K manikin appears on the back of Stela 11 with a 1 Imix 19 Xul date (9.15.19.1.1; 5/29/750) that falls at the midpoint of Jupiter's period of retrograde motion (Tate 1992, fig. 136). Another date (9 Ahau 18 Xul), exactly four years earlier, is positioned in a like fashion just above the ruler on the other side of the stela; this date coincides with the time that the Moon passed by as Jupiter and Mars were precisely in conjunction. On both dates Saturn was in retrograde motion.

Surveying all the dated Yaxchilán monuments provides a test for the link between God K imagery and Jupiter events. At Yaxchilán, eight of the fifteen monuments (53%) that have God K images and legible dates refer to events that coincide with Jupiter's retrograde, allowing a seven-day window on either side of retrograde (Table 6.1). This percentage seems significant in terms of statistical analysis, because even allowing a generous thirty-day window on either end of the period, Jupiter's mean retrograde represents 45 percent of the planet's synodic period (Aveni and Hotaling 1994:S40). And calculating the percentage of Jupiter's mean period of retrograde using a seven-day window indicates it is only 33 percent of its synodic period (120 + 7 + 7 or 134 days out of 399 days total). Thus, in a random sample of dates using a seven-day window, you would expect only around 33 percent of the dates to coincide with retrograde, but the God K monuments at Yax-

TABLE 6.1. YAXCHILÁN GOD K MONUMENTS ASSOCIATED WITH JUPITER RETROGRADE

MONUMENT	IMPLIED DATE ON MONUMENT	JUPITER'S STATIONARY POINTS	
Stela 11	9.15.19.1.1 (5/29/750[a])	1st	3/28/750
		2d	7/28/750[b]
Lintel 42: God K event	9.16.1.2.0 (6/6/752[ac])	1st	6/8/752
Lintels 6 and 43	9.16.1.8.6 (10/10/752[ac])	2d	10/5/752
Lintel 7: God K event	9.16.1.8.8 (10/12/752[c])	2d	10/5/752
Lintel 40	9.16.7.0.0 (3/27/758)	2d	4/29/758
Stela 1: 819-day event	9.16.8.16.10 (2/14/760)	1st	1/27/760
		2d	5/30/760[b]
Stela 1	IS[d] 9.16.10.0.0 (3/11/761)	1st	2/27/761
		2d	6/30/761[b]
Lintel 38	9.16.12.5.14 (6/23/763)	1st	5/7/763
		2d	9/5/763[b]

[a] Date also coincides with Saturn's retrograde period.

[b] When date is very close to one stationary point, only one is given. When date falls closer to midpoint in retrograde, both dates are given to show where it falls relative to the total retrograde period.

[c] Date within seven days of Jupiter's stationary point.

[d] IS means an Initial Series Long Count date; others are Calendar Round dates.

Source: Stationary points from Meeus n.d.; monument dates from Tate 1992.

chilán show a relatively high percentage of such dates. The correlation is strengthened by the fact that the sample is not subject to the problems inherent in selecting the date that works best, because all the Yaxchilán monuments in Table 6.1 bear only a single date, except for Stela 1 with two dates, both of which coincide with Jupiter's retrograde motion. The first date in Table 6.1 accurately pegs the midpoint of Jupiter's retrograde, and the next three precisely pinpoint either the first or second stationary points of Jupiter.

Three other lintels have dates approximating Jupiter's first stationary points (within 21 days). Lintel 39 has a Calendar Round date of 4 Imix 4 Mol (9.15.10.0.1; 6/25/741), one day after the Lahuntun ending, that approximates Jupiter's first stationary point (7/10/741; Meeus n.d.). Lintels 32 and 53 record a Calendar Round date of 6 Ben 16 Mac (9.13.17.15.13; 10/23/709) that Carolyn Tate (1992, app. 2) correlates with the position of Saturn and Jupiter aligned together at stationary points. The fact that Jupiter and Saturn were close together (within 2°) is certainly significant. This date is less than three weeks before Jupiter's first stationary point on 11/10/709, and is even closer to Saturn's first stationary point on 11/2/709 (Meeus n.d.). Since the superior planets slow down as they approach retrograde, it seems that an approximation of the Jupiter event is acceptable.

God K events are noted in texts on four Yaxchilán monuments, all of which depict a ruler holding a God K manikin (Lintels 3, 7, 42, 52; Tate 1992, app. 2). Lintels 7 and 42 bear dates linked with a stationary point of Jupiter, and the date on Lintel 42 relates to a time when Saturn was also at its first stationary point (Table 6.1). The God K event on Lintel 52 coincides with Saturn's second stationary point (2/3/766; Meeus n.d.). Lintel 3 records a Hotun ending (9.16.5.0.0; 4/6/756), and the same Hotun ending appears on Lintel 54, also depicting the ruler holding a God K manikin. Neither Jupiter nor Saturn was in retrograde on the Hotun date recorded on these two monuments, but the date is a subdivision of the Katun that could be used to track the position of Jupiter in relation to Saturn.

In dynastic affairs, Saturn's stationary point may have been considered a suitable substitute if Jupiter was not at the appropriate position for a royal ritual involving God K. Lintel 1, showing Bird Jaguar IV with the God K manikin, has a date that approximates Saturn's first stationary point (4/2/752; Meeus n.d.). The recorded event on this date is his accession on 11 Ahau 8 Zec (9.16.1.0.0; 4/27/752). Mars was in retrograde on this date (second stationary point on 5/5/752; Meeus n.d.).

Allowing a twenty-one-day window on either side of retrograde indicates that thirteen of fifteen monuments with God K imagery have dates relating to the retrograde periods of Jupiter or Saturn. Six correspond to the retrograde periods of both planets (Lintels 6, 32, 42, 43, 53, Stela 11). Five bear dates linked only with the retrograde of Jupiter (Lintels 7, 38, 39, 40, Stela 1), and two other God K monuments relate only to Saturn's retrograde (Lintels 1, 52).

On other Yaxchilán monuments that bear dates coinciding with Jupiter's retrograde, the imagery seems to emphasize events related to the ball game, warfare, and blood offerings, instead of representations of God K. Step VII from Structure 33 relates a ball-game event on 9.15.13.6.9 to Jupiter's stationary point (Tate 1992:96–97, app. 2, fig. 111). A bloodletting event (9.12.9.8.1) on Yaxchilán Lintel 25 coincides with Jupiter's departure from second stationary point and the first stationary point of Mars (Fig. 5.8f). On Stela 18, Shield Jaguar appears with a captive, and the text records a capture event on 3 Eb 14 Mol (9.14.17.15.12; 7/11/729) followed by reference to God K as a sky god (C3) and a bloodletting event at C6 (Tate 1992, apps. 2–3, fig. 145). A capture event (B7) and a fire event are linked with Jupiter's retrograde period in A.D. 808 on Lintel 10 (Tate 1992, fig. 47).

Looking at the entire sample of dates Tate published for Yaxchilán, 27 percent of the total (29 of the 109 dates) fall in Jupiter's retrograde period or within seven days on either side of retrograde. This figure falls below the expected random frequency of 33 percent, using a seven-day window, but when we narrow our focus to those monuments depicting God K, the percentage bearing dates relating to Jupiter's retrograde is relatively high at 53 percent.

Turning to the site of Tikal, we find another set of monuments to test for a possible pattern linking God K images to Jupiter's retrograde period. Although I will not analyze the monuments statistically, a pattern similar to the one at Yaxchilán stands out, especially on monuments that have only one date.

Tikal Stela 20 shows Yaxkin Chaan K'awil (Ruler B) wearing a headdress crowned by God K; his fret-ended mouth mask (possibly a stylized serpent jaw) is decorated with a star glyph (Pl. 17). The inscribed date records the first Katun ending of his reign on 2 Ahau 13 Zec (9.16.0.0.0; 5/3/751; Jones 1977:45). This stela is paired with Altar 8 in Twin-pyramid Complex P (Group 3D-2), one of the many twin-pyramid complexes probably devoted to Katun ceremonies. The Katun ending 9.16.0.0.0 provides a very good correlation with Jupiter's first stationary point (5/2/751; Meeus n.d.). Saturn was also in retrograde motion, and Mars rose at dawn, while Venus was visible near its maximum altitude. This was an auspicious interlocking of astronomical and calendric cycles at the period ending. This Katun ending was surely the focus of major ceremonies involving Jupiter, for the planet stood still to honor the ruler on the first Katun completed in his reign.

A lintel from Structure 5D-52 shows Yaxkin Chaan K'awil holding a God K manikin scepter; an eroded date probably refers to the Lahuntun ending on 3 Ahau 3 Mol (9.15.10.0.0, 6/24/741; Jones 1977: 52, fig. 17). On this period-ending date, Jupiter was about to enter retrograde (first stationary point on 7/10/741; Meeus n.d.). This Lahuntun ending approximates Jupiter's first stationary point, and it marks a halfway point leading up to the exceptional Katun 9.16.0.0.0, when Jupiter reached its first stationary point at the end of the Katun.

The same 3 Ahau 3 Mol Lahuntun date opens the inscription on Lintel 3 of Temple IV, which features God K in the jaws of a Cosmic Monster arching over the ruler's head (Fig. 6.3o, Pl. 15; Jones 1977:36). Of the four Calendar Round dates on Lintel 3, only the Lahuntun ending on 3 Ahau 3 Mol shows a relationship with Jupiter's retrograde, approximating the planet's first stationary point. The lintel depicts God K displaying a mirror glyph in his hand, positioned like the flat-hand mirror compound used to mark Venus positions in the Venus table of the Dresden Codex (Fig. 5.7a).

The Lahuntun ending 3 Ahau 3 Mol, which opens the inscription on Lintel 2 from Temple IV, also coincides with Jupiter's first stationary point. Here Yaxkin Chaan K'awil (Ruler B) holds his God K manikin scepter as a Jaguar War God protector looms over him (Pl. 16; Jones 1977, fig. 12). The latest date on Lintel 2 (9.15.15.14.0 3 Ahau 13 Uo; 3/5/747) falls within retrograde periods of both Jupiter and Saturn. Schele and Grube (1994:187; 1995: 40–46) note that a solar eclipse on 1/19/744 was a prelude to the star-war event recorded on the lintel at B8. According to Lounsbury (1989:255), the star-war event was timed by Jupiter's departure from its second stationary point. This war event dates to 7 Ben 1 Pop (9.15.12.11.13; 2/2/744), coinciding with Saturn's retrograde period and with a time only two weeks after Jupiter's second stationary point (1/17/744; Meeus n.d.). Justeson (1989, table 8.8) points out that a number of war events coincide with the retrograde periods of at least one of the superior planets.

On Lintel 3 of Temple I, a Water-lily Jaguar looms over another Tikal ruler carrying the God K scepter as an insignia of lineage and authority (Fig. 3.6d; Jones 1977, table 1). Originally designated as Ruler A, he is variously called Ah Cacao Caan Chac, Ah Cacau, or, more recently, Hasaw Kan K'awil. A date of 11 Etz'nab 11 Chen (9.13.3.7.18; 8/3/695) at

A3-B3 falls in Saturn's period of retrograde motion. On 12 Etz'nab 11 Zac (9.13.3.9.18; 9/12/695), forty days later, a bloodletting event (C1–D1) coincided approximately with Jupiter's first stationary point and Saturn's second stationary point (Aveni and Hotaling 1994, table 1; Schele and Freidel 1990: 445). It is followed by a reference to the Water-lily Jaguar, which Schele and Grube (1994:180) read as Nu Balam Chaknal, naming the deity on the palanquin. They suggest that the glyph passage names the Water-lily Jaguar as a deity image captured from the vanquished enemy, but it seems more likely that it represents a lunar deity who is the patron of the Tikal ruler.

Stela 5 from Tikal probably also features God K, although here the manikin scepter is almost completely effaced (Jones 1977, table 1, fig. 13). The text begins with a fragmentary Calendar Round date, reconstructed as 9.15.3.6.8 3 Lamat 6 Pax (12/6/734), less than two weeks before Jupiter's first stationary point (12/19/734; Meeus n.d.). The date also coincides with Saturn's retrograde motion, and it approximates the time when Venus was most brilliant as the Evening Star. This date appears with a distance number (9.11.12) that counts forward to 4 Ahau 8 Yaxkin (9.15.13.0.0; 6/8/744), a period ending that is the dedicatory date of the monument. Since 9.11.12 is a lunar interval, the Moon was once again at the last quarter. At this time, Jupiter was in conjunction with the Sun and Saturn was departing from its second stationary point (5/17/744; Meeus n.d.). These two dates seem to correlate with events involving the Moon, Jupiter, and Saturn.

As early as the mid-fifth century, Tikal dynastic monuments link God K with Jupiter's retrograde motion. On the Early Classic Tikal Stela 1, a ruler holds a serpent bar bearing a God K hatchet manikin with a snake leg, the prototype for the serpent-legged God K manikin scepter of the Late Classic period (W. Coe 1970:92; Proskouriakoff 1993:16; Taube 1992b, fig. 37c). Because Chac is probably linked with Venus, it may be significant that Chac appears at the other end of the serpent bar. The monument is believed to date to the reign of Stormy Sky (K'awil Chaan), or shortly thereafter. The fragmentary dates remain debatable, but one reconstruction suggests a date of 9.0.15.11.0 (4/28/451; Freidel et al. 1993:424 n. 58). At this time, Saturn was in retrograde (1/18/451 to 6/7/451) and Jupiter was approaching its second stationary point (5/9/451; Meeus n.d.). Jupiter, Saturn, and Mars were all clustered together in Virgo to the east, while the Evening Star was making its first appearance in Taurus to the west.

Stela 31 from Tikal is one of the first known images associating God K with a living ruler from Tikal (Figs. 3.7b, 6.3u; Coggins 1990:85). The ruler Stormy Sky wears a headdress that includes an image of God K, which, interestingly, also forms part of his personal name. Perhaps Jupiter was Stormy Sky's patron planet in the Early Classic Period, just as Jupiter guided events in the lives of Late Classic rulers, especially at Palenque and Yaxchilán. The Initial Series date recorded on Stela 31 (9.0.10.0.0 7 Ahau 3 Yax; 10/16/445) corresponds to a time when Jupiter was approaching its second stationary point (11/23/445; Meeus n.d.). This date also approximates the heliacal set of Mars. Other coordinating events, discussed in Chapters 3 and 4, include the new Moon and Venus approaching its maximum brilliance as the Morning Star. The ruler himself seems to be compared to Hun Ahau, the underworld Sun linked with the Morning Star, while his father seems to be apotheosized as the Sun God overhead (Chapter 3).

One of the earliest known images of God K appears on the Leyden Plaque, probably from Tikal (Pl. 2). Here the ruler Moon Zero Bird holds a double-headed serpent bearing God K and the Sun God in its jaws (Schele and Miller 1986:121). The recorded date, 8.14.3.1.12 1 Eb 0 Yaxkin (9/14/320 O.S.), corresponds approximately to Jupiter's heliacal rise just prior to the fall equinox. Jupiter's dawn rise so close to the fall equinox links the cycles of the Sun and Jupiter.

Arthur Schlak (1989) correlates dates on monuments depicting God K manikin figures with periods when Mercury was visible, using maximum elongation as a key to determining visibility. His sample is relatively small, and he concentrates on manikin-scepter imagery, excluding many of the God K images discussed here. When these monuments are included, a link with Jupiter events emerges. Among the twenty dates that Schlak correlates with the visi-

bility of Mercury, eight coincide with Jupiter's retrograde motion, allowing a seven-day window. Of those that do not, a significant number come from monuments with multiple dates. If we are free to select another date, we often find one that correlates with Jupiter's retrograde motion. Since Mercury is visible 65 percent of the time (Aveni and Hotaling 1994:S39), a statistical study should be done with a complete corpus of God K monuments from several sites to determine whether there is an unusually high percentage of God K monuments that correspond to times when Mercury was visible.

In a more recent study, Schlak (1996, table 4) takes his original twenty dates and adds another variable to his analysis—altazimuth—which measures Mercury's height above the horizon. He also adds twelve mores dates linked with God K glyphs (Schlak 1996, table 3). Even with this expanded list, Schlak has omitted a number of monuments with God K images that are incorporated in this study. He makes no claim that any of the dates are precisely maximum altitude or maximum elongation, only that they coincide with Mercury's visibility. One-third are within five days of one of Jupiter's stationary points (Dates 3, 9, 10, 12). All but three dates can be linked with times when either Jupiter or Saturn was in retrograde.

Clemency Coggins (1990:84–85, fig. 5.1a) suggests that God K represents Venus as a god of lightning connecting the earth with the sky. She believes that Stormy Sky's personal name is a pun for K'uk' Ka'an (bird-serpent), referring to Kukulcan as Venus. Although a link with lightning seems likely, the connection between God K and the feathered serpent seems tenuous, especially since Coggins makes no attempt to link God K to dates recording significant Venus positions.

In sum, God K seems to embody the planet Jupiter, and the Katun cycle involving Jupiter and Saturn in the Classic period. Jupiter events were apparently important in the lives of Classic Maya rulers, who often appear with the insignia of God K. Jupiter events are implicated in the dates associated with two images of a dead ruler in the guise of God K. At Yaxchilán, Palenque, and Tikal, God K monuments usually bear dates coinciding with Jupiter's retrograde motion. God K might have more than one planetary aspect, for when a Jupiter event is not apparent, Saturn seems to act as a substitute. Between Katun 9.15.10.0.0 and 9.17.0.0.0 there seems to be intense interest in recording dates that coincide with Jupiter's and Saturn's retrograde, probably because the Katun 9.16.0.0.0 links the retrograde periods of both Jupiter and Saturn and precisely marks the first stationary point of Jupiter.

CLASSIC PERIOD CALENDAR RECORDS RELATING TO THE SUPERIOR PLANETS

The Tzolkin calendar has a built-in capacity to measure the synodic periods of planets because three sacred rounds of 260 days equal one synodic period of Mars (780 days), sixteen sacred rounds equal eleven Saturn synodic periods (plus 1 day), and twenty-three sacred rounds are three days less than fifteen Jupiter synodic periods (Justeson 1989:82, tables 8.5, 8.6). Since five sacred rounds are just sixteen hours short of forty-four lunar months, the Moon is also involved. Justeson notes that in less than sixteen years, the 260-day calendar provides the interval that aligns the synodic period of the Moon and of all the visible planets to within 4.31 days.

Justeson (1989:102, table 8.6) points out that it is not possible to structure a table of positions for Mercury, Jupiter, or Saturn in terms of the number of Calendar Rounds (52 vague years) that would be commensurate with any of the average synodic periods. Apparently the Maya used the 360-day civil year (Tun) to correlate the cycles of the superior planets (Justeson 1989:102–103, table 8.7).

Jupiter observations may have been linked to the 360-day Tun, because the mean period it spends as either the Morning or the Evening Star is 367 days. During one complete Tun, Jupiter would be seen in the same sector of the sky at approximately the same time of night. The period of twelve Tuns (4,320 days) is relatively close to the sidereal period of Jupiter (4,332.5 days), separated by about 13 days or one *trecena*.

The Katun cycle of twenty Tuns may have been used in Classic Maya times to track Jupiter and

Saturn. Kelley (1985:238) points out that the interval between successive Jupiter-Saturn conjunctions is between nineteen and twenty years (the approximate length of a Katun), and every sixty Tuns, a conjunction or opposition takes place in the same part of the sky. This may explain why astronomical data are included in the records of Katun-ending rituals. Lounsbury (1991:817) notes that the Katun prophecies are essentially astrological texts.

The Classic Maya tracked the motions of Jupiter and Saturn using the 819-day cycle. This cycle first appears in the middle of the Classic period (Lounsbury 1978:811). The 819-day cycle has a common factor (21) with synodical periods of Jupiter and Saturn, and there seems to be a correlation with Jupiter and Saturn events and the 819-day counts recorded in the inscriptions (Justeson 1989:103). Dennis Tedlock (1992) notes that Palenque records show an idealized 399-day Jupiter cycle that can be divided into 21-day segments, a division that gives the planet a systematic link with the 819-day cycle. The 819-day count is particularly common at Palenque, and it was probably invented there and later spread to other sites (Berlin 1977:78–79). This cycle continued to be recorded as late as 10.2.0.0.0 (Stela 11 at Tikal). Eric Thompson (1960:212–216) first recognized that through the interplay of twenty day signs, colors, and directions, the 819-day cycle breaks down into sets: red-east-Imix; north-white-Ik; west-black-Akbal, and yellow-south-Kan. The relationship of these divisions to planetary cycles remains enigmatic.

A mythological text on the left side of the central panel in Palenque's Temple of the Sun refers to an 819-day station on 1 Ik 10 Tzec (1.6.14.11.2; 8/12/2587 B.C.) that was not to repeat again for more than 3,200 years (63 × 52 vague years; Lounsbury 1989:247–248, fig. 19.2). There is an oblique reference to a sacred Jupiter event associated with the 819-day-count clause in this mythological text, according to Schele (1990:143). Lounsbury points out that the next occurrence of the same 819-day station on 1 Ik 10 Tzec took place sixty-three Calendar Rounds later on a date (9.12.16.2.2; 5/15/688) recorded in the Medallion Series of the Temple of the Inscriptions. At that time, Jupiter and Mars were both just pulling away from conjunction and simultaneously beginning forward motion after retrograde. Although not noted by Lounsbury, Saturn was in retrograde at this time, approaching its second stationary point (6/23/688; Meeus n.d.). This may be significant because the cycles of Jupiter and Saturn are linked through the 819-day count.

A number of monuments seem to record multiples of the synodic intervals of Jupiter and Saturn (Kelley and Kerr 1973, table 2). These may be records of actual observations rather than canonical or predicted cycles (Justeson 1989:82). A Saturn interval of 377.75 days appears on the Temple of the Cross at Palenque and on Caracol Stela 3, Lintel 3 of Tikal Temple I, Tikal Stela 5, Naranjo Stela 12, and Quiriguá Zoomorph G. A Jupiter interval calculated at 398.867 days appears on the Hieroglyphic Stairway of Naranjo, Yaxchilán Lintel 41, Copán Stela I, Caracol Stela 3, and Quiriguá Monument 7 (Zoomorph G). The Caracol Stela 3 date (9.9.18.16.3) also coincides with the first appearance of the Evening Star.

Thompson (1960:227–229) says that even though 1 Ahau and the heliacal rise of Venus are connected in the Dresden Codex, Classic period Katuns ending with 1 Ahau seem to be linked with Jupiter intervals in the Maya inscriptions. He notes that the Hieroglyphic Stairway of Naranjo records a star glyph on a Katun-ending 1 Ahau (9.10.0.0.0), and a distance number (2.5.7.12) separating this date from an earlier one recorded on the stairs (9.7.14.10.8) equals twenty-eight synodic revolutions of Venus and forty-one synodic periods of Jupiter; thus Venus and Jupiter were in the same position in the sky on the two dates. The earlier date may be linked with Jupiter's heliacal rise. Although it was a few days after Jupiter's dawn rise in Aries, it may have been the first day the planet was visible. Venus was the Morning Star in the neighboring constellation (Pisces) and was relatively high in the sky, having dropped about 4° from maximum altitude (Aveni and Hotaling 1994, table 1). On the Lahuntun date, 9.10.0.0.0 1 Ahau 8 Kayab (1/22/633), Jupiter was again visible just above the horizon at dawn, but this time in Capricorn, and Venus was once again high in the sky as the Morning Star in the neighboring constellation

(Sagittarius). On this second date there was a conjunction between Venus, Saturn, and the waning Moon.

Stationary points of Jupiter apparently signaled accession-related rituals at Palenque, and planetary conjunctions also seem to be significant in timing these events (Lounsbury 1989, 1991). As noted earlier, Jupiter's departure from its second stationary point coincided with Chan Bahlum II's heir-designation event at Palenque on 9 Akbal 6 Xul (9.10.8.9.3; 6/12/641). This royal ritual coincides with the third in a series of conjunctions involving Jupiter and Mars. The three conjunctions marked the beat of Jupiter's retrograde period: the first coincided with Jupiter's first stationary point; the second with the opposition of Jupiter and Mars to the Sun; and the third with Jupiter's departure from its second stationary point (Lounsbury 1989:251–252, fig. 19.6). Chan Bahlum's accession ceremony was also timed by Jupiter's departure from its second stationary point. This suggests that dynastic ceremonies at Palenque were considered especially auspicious when Jupiter was resuming its forward motion.

Jupiter observations were also important on the anniversaries of dates associated with Chan Bahlum, who apparently had an obsession with the planet Jupiter (Aveni 1992b:78; Lounsbury 1989). The most common target seems to be those times when Jupiter reached its stationary point and was beginning "forward" motion once again (departure from the second stationary point). Many of the dates studied by Lounsbury also fall on or very near a conjunction of Mars with Jupiter.

Dumbarton Oaks Relief Panel 1, a posthumous portrait of a ruler holding a spear, is associated with the time of retrograde motion for Mars, Jupiter, and Saturn. James Fox and John Justeson (1978:55–56) note that the ruler's date of death on 6 Akbal 11 Pax (9.15.1.6.3; 12/11/732) is a few days from Saturn's second stationary point (12/15/732; Meeus n.d.), and an interval at the end of the inscription counts 378 days (the length of Saturn's synodic period) to 9.15.2.7.1, when Saturn was once again at its second stationary point (12/29/733; Meeus n.d.). More recently, Justeson (1989:109) points out that the death date is also connected with the first stationary point of Mars (12/18/732; Meeus n.d.). It should be noted that the date also coincides approximately with the time of opposition, the midpoint of Jupiter's retrograde motion (10/19/732 to 2/15/733; Meeus n.d.). Fox and Justeson suggest that astrology played a role because astronomical events were of significance when they coincided with historical events. On the other hand, Joyce Marcus (1992:440) maintains that the historical events sometimes were manipulated to fit the astronomical events. In my opinion, the death event may actually refer to the ruler's apotheosis, for such an event could be adjusted to fit the proper astrological conditions.

Tate (1989, table 32.3; 1992:93, 272) points to an interest in stationary points of Jupiter and Saturn and in Jupiter-Saturn conjunctions on Yaxchilán monuments. She refers to a number of dates that coincide with Jupiter-Saturn conjunctions. Tate also notes parallels in the type of events commemorated, for the verbs referring to the ceremonies—bloodletting verbs and a rare God N verb—were used at both Palenque and Yaxchilán (Tate 1989:422–423). Although I have suggested that God N's quadripartite nature could be linked with the Moon or one of the inferior planets, it is also possible that he could be connected with the quadripartite division implied in the four directional aspects of the 819-day cycle known to be connected with Jupiter and Saturn.

As noted earlier, ball-game events seem to be linked with Jupiter's retrograde period. Yaxchilán Step VII from Structure 33 depicts Bird Jaguar's ball game, an event coinciding with Jupiter's retrograde motion (Tate 1992:96–97, app. 2, fig. 111). The game and associated bloodletting event on 3 Muluc 17 Mac (9.15.13.6.9; 10/15/744) is about a week before the first stationary point of Jupiter (10/23/744; Meeus n.d.). A ball-game event on 7/7/881 (10.2.12.1.8 9 Lamat 11 Yax) recorded on Lintel 1 of the Temple of the Four Lintels at Chichén Itzá falls very close to the solar zenith, but in terms of ball-game imagery, it may be more significant that this date coincides with Jupiter's retrograde motion (Chapter 3). Linda Schele and David Freidel (1990:445) note that a ball-game sacrifice and bloodletting

associated with Jupiter's retrograde is also seen on the Chicago Ball-court Panel.

War events recorded at Piedras Negras (Lintels 2 and 4, Stela 35) are also linked with Jupiter's retrograde motion (Schele and Freidel 1990:445). Another war date (9.10.17.2.14, from Tortuguero) involved retrograde of all three planets (Justeson 1989; Tuckerman 1964). Studying star-war dates in the Maya inscriptions, Justeson (1989:109, table 8.8) concludes that warfare events cluster during the dry season, and three-quarters of them occur at significant points in the cycles of Saturn or Jupiter. He points out that the results of his analysis indicate that there are more star-war events involving Saturn or Jupiter than there are associated with Venus events. There is a statistically significant correlation between the clusters of star-war events relating to the retrograde periods of Jupiter, Saturn, and Mars (Justeson 1989:110, 123 n. 20). He notes, however, that Mars events seem to be only rarely recorded in Classic period records (Justeson 1989:109).

Some war events may relate to planetary conjunctions. On the date of a war event recorded on Naranjo Stela 23 (9.13.18.9.15 1 Men 13 Yaxkin; 6/22/710), all five planets visible to the naked eye were clustered in Leo within 6° of each other, and only Jupiter remained beyond a 1° radius (Aveni and Hotaling 1994:S53 n. 56). Indeed, this was the closest clustering of these five planets in five millennia (Olson and White 1997:64).

Conjunction events involving more than two planets are exceedingly rare (Aveni and Hotaling 1994:S42). For example, Mars, Jupiter, and Saturn got together only twice during the entire course of the Classic period: in A.D. 690 and again in A.D. 828. Such conjunctions may involve planets passing one another more than once. In the case of the triple conjunction of A.D. 690, the last of the conjunctions occurred on or near 2 Cib 14 Mol, when Chan Bahlum performed rites to honor the gods, which were recorded on several Palenque monuments (Aveni and Hotaling 1994:S42–S43, S47–S48; Dütting 1982; Lounsbury 1989:248, fig. 19.1). Since the planets were actually closer together ten days after the recorded event, the determining factor for the 2

Cib 14 Mol event has been taken to be the Moon's position passing Jupiter, Saturn, and Mars, all located less that 5° apart in the constellation Scorpius on July 19–20.

Linda Schele (1992b:94, 167–170) interprets the 2 Cib 14 Mol event as First Mother, the goddess of the moon, reuniting with the Palenque Triad representing her three planetary children (see also Schele and Freidel 1990:256, 473–474 n. 41). Nonetheless, the Triad gods are not named together with the 2 Cib 14 Mol date. In the Temple of the Foliated Cross, this date is associated with a god with a shell beard and a jaguar ear (a Venus god or the JGU?) and with GII named at L4-M4 (Pl. 11). The Temple of the Sun at Palenque names only GIII (at O6) in association with this event. The event is not mentioned in the Temple of the Cross. Furthermore, the notion of the Triad being the superior planets is incompatible with Schele's identification of GI as Venus and GIII as the Sun. Finally, it must be noted that the date of the Moon passing by the planets has been determined using the 584,285 correlation, but in the 584,283 correlation, the Moon was still positioned at some distance from the planets on this date (7/18/690). I would argue that the most important factors are Jupiter's and Saturn's departure from the second stationary point, events that are essentially the same in either of the two correlations. Studying the twelve-year anniversary of the event recorded on 1 Cib 14 Mol (7/15/702), Lounsbury (1989:249–250, figs. 19.1, 19.4) points out that both rituals took place at a time when Jupiter was in the same part of its synodic period and was located in the same region of Scorpius. Apparently, Chan Bahlum kept a record of Jupiter's sidereal position.

Chan Bahlum's accession and apotheosis events are within fifteen days of the second stationary point of Jupiter (Lounsbury 1989, table 19.1, fig. 19.3). Jupiter's dawn rise was also of interest. The eight-year anniversary of Chan Bahlum's accession on 5 Eb 5 Kayab (9.12.19.14.12; 1/5/692) coincided with the heliacal rising of Jupiter, when the planet reappeared after more than a month of invisibility (Lounsbury 1989:252). The anniversary may also reflect an interest in Venus, for that planet was near

its maximum altitude (Aveni and Hotaling 1994).

Marcus (1992:440) believes that political propaganda played a role in the dates selected to document the important points in the lives of rulers. In some cases, events in a ruler's life were forced into a pattern to fit the astronomical events. As noted earlier, Dumbarton Oaks Relief Panel 1 records the apotheosis of a ruler (9.15.1.6.3) in a context that seems to be timed by astrology, for the date (12/11/732) can be linked with the retrograde motion of all three superior planets. Similarly, there are instances in which Venus events seem to guide the choice of dates marking historical events (Chapter 5). Anthony Aveni and Lorren Hotaling (1994:S22) note that if astronomical reference points prove to be so important in the lives of rulers, perhaps the conclusions about the nature of Maya inscriptions reached by an earlier generation of scholars are not so far off the mark. In other words, in some cases history seems to be subordinate to the astronomical cycles, and historical events were being "adjusted" to fit the skies.

Aveni and Hotaling's (1994:S40) chi-square statistical test of ninety-eight Maya dates with astronomical "tags" indicates that 38 percent of the dates fall during a retrograde period of two of the superior planets (usually Jupiter and Saturn); this is statistically significant because the anticipated random percentage would be 24 percent, using a generous thirty-day window. Moreover, twenty-nine dates that do not correspond to one of the four Venus stations fall very close to the appearance or disappearance of one of the other planets. Since the study grouped a number of different types of dated events, further research is needed in the future to sort out patterns that may distinguish events involving the superior planets from those referring to Venus.

In sum, a number of Classic period calendar cycles lend themselves to records involving the superior planets, including the 260-day sacred round or Tzolkin, the Katun cycle, and the 819-day count. Jupiter and Saturn intervals are recorded in a number of Classic Maya inscriptions, suggesting that the Maya observed these planets in tandem. Indeed, the

Katun itself relates to the interval between successive conjunctions of Jupiter and Saturn. Jupiter may be linked with the Tun because the planet's period of visibility is relatively close to one Tun. At Palenque, Chan Bahlum's accession and apotheosis events were timed by Jupiter's departure from its second stationary point. Observations of Jupiter and Saturn may be connected with ball games, bloodletting ceremonies, star wars, and accession anniversaries at a number of Maya sites. In some cases, the dates of Classic Maya history were manipulated to fall into alignment with astronomical events, placing the lives of rulers in the context of mythic history.

ASSEMBLY OF THE GODS

We can only identify a small percentage of planetary gods with any degree of certainty. If we see any of these among a group of deities, we could be looking at an image showing an assembly of planets. Their astronomical nature is sometimes shown by shared insignia, such as a pendant with trilobe ends or a headband.

The Las Sepulturas bench from Copán represents an assembly of astronomical gods (Pl. 19). Venus appears as a scorpion-man (Chapter 5). The cross-eyed Sun God and the Moon deity with the lunar crescent and rabbit are easy to pick out. An anthropomorphic deity with a deer ear may represent Mars as the deer planet. Two heads, resembling the Principal Bird Deity, may represent a King Vulture (Benson 1997: 91). The Principal Bird Deity is the avian counterpart of God D, a deity whose astronomical identity remains uncertain.

Copán's Structure 22 depicts seven different dei-

ties positioned in cloud symbols along the Cosmic Monster's back (Fig. 7.5d, bottom). One wears a trilobed pendant like GI's, and another represents Chac (Venus?) wielding an axe. A third deity has a serpent foot that links him with God K (Jupiter). A skeletal god with a death collar may be a lunar deity. The others are difficult to identify, but the total of seven suggests a grouping of the Sun, the Moon, and the five planets visible to the naked eye (Chapter 7).

Chac is one of six deities on the limbs of the Cauac Monster on Quiriguá Monument 16, also known as Zoomorph P (Fig. 6.4a). The assembly includes two variants of Chac, the Sun God with a mirror brow and the Moon God with white markings (Fig. 4.6b). One deity is effaced and another is difficult to identify. The ruler in the jaws of the Cauac Monster holds a God K scepter, perhaps completing the quorum of the seven "planets" of classical antiquity.

The central panel of Palenque's Temple of the Sun has an intriguing group of deities (Fig. 3.6b). As noted in previous chapters, we see a Jaguar War God shield (the dry-season moon), a crouching Sun God with a mirror brow, and God K (Jupiter) as a manikin held by Chan Bahlum at the time of his accession on 1/5/684. Another crouching figure on the right bears body markings representing God C, who may be linked with a monkey planet, as noted earlier. God L, who represents the dry-season Morning Star in the Dresden Codex, here supports a double-headed bar portraying a zoomorph; an enigmatic figure who shares many of God L's attributes supports the other end of the bar. Although we cannot specifically identify all of these gods as astronomical deities, it is noteworthy that the accession date shows a number of interesting planetary positions. In addition to a correlation with Jupiter's departure from

---

FIG. 6.4. *a:* Assembly of six deities on body of Late Classic Cauac Monster includes Sun, Moon, Chac in two aspects, and two other unknown deities (Quiriguá Zoomorph P; after Maudslay 1889–1902, 2, pl. 64).

b: Early Classic list of nine gods that includes sky god (God C), earth deity, Paddler Twins, Ik God (T1082), God D variant, solar god, and aged Bacab (Tikal Stela 31; after A. Miller 1986, fig. 19).

c: Protoclassic assembly of gods, including four "climbers," led by deity wearing zoomorphic headdress with star glyph; snake climbers include deity with Xoc monster headdress and Chac on snake's tail; three dismembered gods dive to their deaths along stream of liquid that may depict underworld side of Milky Way (Hauberg Stela; after Schele 1985, fig. 1).

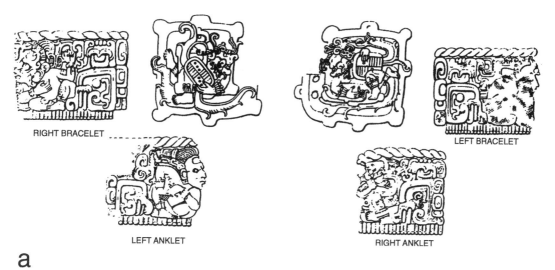

RIGHT BRACELET

LEFT BRACELET

LEFT ANKLET

RIGHT ANKLET

a

b

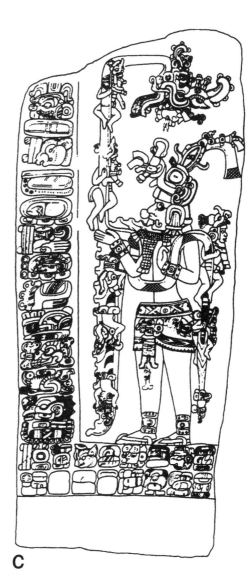

c

its second stationary point, noted previously, Mars was in retrograde motion (second stationary point on 2/8/684; Meeus n.d.), Mercury was just visible in the dawn sky, and Venus was approaching its maximum altitude as Morning Star (reached twenty days later).

Lists of astronomical gods are known from Palenque. In addition to the group of four deities on the eaves of House C, discussed earlier in relation to God C, there is a list of six gods in the Temple of the Foliated Cross at Palenque (Fig. 4.6e). One of the six is a vulture paired with the personified number one; because the vulture lacks a day-sign cartouche, the reference is to a deity name rather than to the vulture variant of the day sign Ahau seen in other inscriptions (Thompson 1960, fig. 11, nos. 30, 31). The vulture might be a planet, because he takes an active role in the affairs of the Moon Goddess, being the Moon Goddess's lover in folktales and in the codices (Dresden Codex 19a). Schele (1992b:170) takes the 2 Cib 14 Mol event to be the key to the imagery of the six gods, but this date is not directly associated with the list. The six gods are named directly following a distance number of 6.11.6 linked to the Calendar Round 8 Oc 3 Kayab (9.12.11.12.10; 1/5/684), the date of Chan Bahlum's accession, when Jupiter had just departed from its second stationary point and Mars was in retrograde motion. The distance number (6.11.6) prefixed by T126 calls for subtraction, alluding to an earlier date of 9.12.5.1.4 1 Kan 7 Yaxkin (6/24/677) not recorded in the text. The most interesting thing about this interval is that it counts back precisely to the first stationary point of Mars (Meeus n.d.). Despite the Mars connection, the Mars Beast is not among the gods named. The list includes the Triad and a lunar deity discussed in Chapter 4, as well as Chac and the vulture god called Hun Ahaw. It is puzzling that the list includes the names of both GI and Chac, who seem to be linked with Venus in some manner.

A list of gods on the Early Classic Tikal Stela 31 could refer to an assembly of gods (Fig. 6.4b). The earth god, his head marked by a Cab (earth) symbol, is paired with God C, who has a sky glyph infixed on his head (for greater detail, see Fig. 6.2h). The names for the Paddler Twins follow just below

(Schele 1989b). Next we find an Ik God (T1082), the counterpart of the personified number three, paired with a long-nosed god, possibly an early form of God D. There follows a god with attributes of the Sun God, but lacking the Kin infix, and an aged Bacab with raised hands who seems to emerge from a star glyph. A jawless head seems to be a variant of the Uinal sign (T521) prefixed by the number one. The passage ends with a compound incorporating the number nine, which is exactly the number of gods named.

On the Protoclassic Hauberg Stela, a group of small deities may be one of the earliest known Maya representations of the Sun, the Moon, and the planets (Fig. 6.4c). The astronomical context of this imagery is clear, because the uppermost figure climbing the celestial serpent wears a star headdress. Chac, the lowest of four climbers, carries an axe in his hand, much like God B, the Postclassic god of rain and storms (Stuart 1988, fig. 5.48; Taube 1992b, fig. 7b). The serpent is a representation of the ecliptic, according to Schele (1992b:143–144), who identifies the climbing figures as constellations. It seems more likely that they are planetary gods, but their headdresses could refer to specific constellations. Three climbers wear headbands, evoking the Headband Twins. There are seven figures in total if we add the group of descending figures led by the figure wearing a Kin headdress. The descending gods are dead, their severed torsos spewing blood. Linda Schele and Mary Miller (1986:191, pl. 66) reconstruct the date as 3 Ahau 13 Xul (10/8/199; the month Xul has an erroneous coefficient of twelve), one of two dates originally proposed by Schele (1985). There is nothing particularly notable about this date in terms of astronomy, except perhaps that the first visible crescent probably corresponds to this date. Schlak (1996:182, fig. 1) proposes that the ruler on this stela impersonates Venus as GI, although here he lacks the characteristic shell earrings. Schlak relates the image to a time when Venus was relatively high as the Morning Star on 8.8.0.7.0 3 Ahau 13 Xul.

Painted vases depicting the Holmul Dancer theme may show an assembly of astronomical gods at the time of an accession ceremony or Katun event. The vase known as Princeton 14 shows three dancing figures with backracks holding deities that carry inverted heads of God K (Coe 1978b:94, no. 14). As noted earlier, these scenes show the sky-band backracks framing God K's head, suggesting parallels with the transfer of power at the end of the Katun represented on Paris Codex pages 2–12. Dorie Reents-Budet (1991:220–221, fig. 7) points out that three different deities are represented in the backracks, each identified by glyphic names. Ix Balam is the Water-lily Jaguar linked with the Moon in Chapter 4. The monkey deity, 10 Chuen, could be a monkey planet. A furry animal called 6 Sky evokes the god named 6 Sky, listed among the five gods of the west in the Dresden Codex Venus table (Kelley 1976, fig. 28).

The Vase of the Seven Gods shows an assembly of seven gods associated with the creation date 4 Ahau 8 Cumku (Pl. 7; Coe 1973:107–108, no. 49). God L appears as the ruler of a court of gods who gesture in submission. He smokes a cigar, like his counterpart in the relief panel on the right side of the Temple of the Cross at Palenque (Schele 1977, fig. 4.2). This aspect of God L is different from his guise as a merchant with a merchant pack and a staff (Taube 1922b, fig. 40). The Jaguar War God heads the top row of gods but is named last in the glyph column. The Sun God brings up the rear on the bottom row (Chapter 3). Most of the gods are named with glyphs introduced by God C's glyph compound accompanied by the water/blood group prefix, here designating their sacred status. The only name without such a title is the jawless God of T1058 (the patron of Pax?), whose name stands alone before the Calendar Round date. Other names include Bolonyocte (IX.765:87), who appears as one of the planetary gods on the eaves of House C at Palenque and was especially revered at Palenque (Berlin 1977:150; Schele 1992b:185).

The date 4 Ahau 8 Cumku on the vessel is usually interpreted as a reference to the beginning of time in the Maya calendar (13.0.0.0.0; Closs 1979:151; Coe 1973:108; Dütting 1981:221). Another alternative is that the vase shows a commemoration of an anniversary event when the Calendar Round date repeated during the Late Classic period. All 4 Ahau 8 Cumku dates in the Late Classic period fall in the dry season,

which seems appropriate for the imagery of the Jaguar War God symbolizing the dry-season. Half of the dates also coordinate with the periods when Venus was the Morning Star. The vessel has been dated between A.D. 750 and 800 on stylistic grounds (Fields 1994:319). This would make the 4 Ahau 8 Cumku anniversary date of 1/4/785 the most likely, coinciding with when Venus was the Morning Star. This seems appropriate because God L represents the dry-season Morning Star in the Dresden Codex, an association also seen in Classic period times in Palenque's Temple of the Sun.

We can conclude that the assembly of gods is an important theme represented in a variety of media. Several images depict sets of seven gods, presumably indicating the seven planets of classical antiquity. Such groups suggest iconic imagery alluding to all the major powers of the sky rather than to specific observations of the planets in sky positions. Nonetheless, we should not ignore the possibility that some planetary data are conveyed in such images. Such groupings provide another key to identifying the more enigmatic planetary gods.

THE CELESTIAL WANDERERS AS PLANETARY GODS

Some twenty-five years ago, Thompson (1974:88) said: "We know neither names nor glyphs of any planet other than Venus." The situation has improved somewhat, because we can now definitively identify the Mars Beast, and there seems to be strong evidence associating God K with Jupiter. Perhaps the best approach for solving the problem of planetary identities is to look for patterning in dates and calendar periods associated with specific deities. Such an approach has helped to reveal the planetary identity of God K.

God K imagery correlates with dates coinciding with the retrograde period of Jupiter at a number of major Maya sites, such as at Palenque, Tikal, and Yaxchilán. Two posthumous portraits of rulers incorporate God K images and dates that coincide with Jupiter's retrograde motion, suggesting that Jupiter's position was significant in the dates chosen for the apotheosis of Maya rulers. God K is also prominent on monuments recording subdivisions of the Katun, a time period that may have been used to track Jupiter and Saturn. Postclassic evidence also points to a link between God K and Jupiter, especially apparent in God K's role in the Katun cycle. The Jupiter association is bolstered by God K's role as a victim of the Morning Star in the Dresden Codex at a time when Jupiter was in retrograde motion disappearing below the horizon as the Morning Star rose.

God K is also a god of thunder and lightning, sharing the same role that Jupiter had in ancient Greece and Italy. Perhaps this notion has an explanation in nature, one that is connected with folklore linking Jupiter to storms. God K's role as the god of Maya rulers also presents an overlap with ancient European traditions identifying Jupiter as the planet of kings. There is a natural basis for the association with kings, since Jupiter seems to dominate the night sky and is second only to Venus in brilliance. Jupiter is rarely absent from the sky (mean disappearance interval = 32 days). Steady, strong, and ever-present, Jupiter makes a perfect celestial ruler, the counterpart to the good ruler on Earth.

Groupings of six or seven different gods on Classic period monuments usually include the Sun and the Moon and planetary companions, suggesting an iconic grouping like that of classical antiquity. A triad of brothers represents Venus, Jupiter, and the Sun, similar to a pattern seen in modern Maya folklore. When the Moon is not in evidence, these are the three brightest astronomical bodies in the sky.

The anthropomorphic deity representing Mars may have deer ears on one Copán monument. The planet's animal counterpart is a deer monster known as the Mars Beast. Another aspect of Mars may be simian, possibly connected with the spider monkey. A closely related being is God C, a monkey deity who may be connected with a planet, but his astronomical nature is poorly understood. A howler monkey seems to be connected with the Morning Star, and it is possible that a number of the planets may have monkey alter egos.

Unfortunately, there is still insufficient evidence to identify the god representing Saturn. Saturn's slow movement could be represented by an aged being, but as yet no clear candidate has emerged. There is still a great deal to do in terms of identifying the planets and their various alter egos. Although animals may play a role in the imagery of planets, we would expect anthropomorphic deities, including our simian relatives, to predominate. Indeed, since the creatures of the zodiac are mostly animals (Chapter 7), the planets may be distinguished by their anthropomorphic guises.

7 STARS, THE MILKY WAY, COMETS, AND METEORS

This chapter explores Precolumbian Maya imagery of temporary celestial phenomena, stars, constellations, and the Milky Way. We have surprisingly little information on comets, meteors, and supernovas. Comets and meteors seem to be of secondary importance, appearing not as gods themselves, but as their cigars. Metaphorical images allude to the multitude of stars as jaguar spots, flowers, fireflies, and the "eyes of the night." Topographical features such as sacred trees represent cross constellations that serve as signposts in the celestial landscape. More often the constellations are starry animals appearing as companions to the Sun, the Moon, and the planets. A Postclassic "zodiac" from Yucatán helps to identify thirteen constellations, including bird constellations, a jaguar or ocelot, two snakes, a peccary, a turtle, and various other creatures. Some of these Precolumbian Maya constellations have at least one first-magnitude star that could be tracked even in bright moonlight. Individual stars were also named, but we are able to identify only a few from Colonial period sources. Architectural orientations help to identify which constellations were important to the Classic Maya.

Constellations located at the intersection points of the Milky Way and the ecliptic seem to be especially important in Precolumbian Maya cosmology. The Pleiades are represented by the rattlesnake's rattle in Yucatán, an image that is also found in central Mexico. Orion's Belt represents a turtle constellation, but other stars in Orion may be linked with the Hearthstones of Creation. Scorpius is a scorpion in the northern Maya area, but to the south it may be a skeletal serpent known as the White-Bone-Snake. There is a fish-snake constellation in the region of Sagittarius, a star group associated with the Quadripartite God forming the rear head of the Cosmic Monster. The Cosmic Monster itself seems to embody the Milky Way, and the two areas where it intersects the ecliptic represent opposite seasons. Itzamna, described extensively in Colonial period accounts, may symbolize the entire sky, his four bodies formed by the two sides of the Milky Way and the two sides of the ecliptic. A similar configuration is suggested by the four roads of the Popol Vuh.

The relationship of the stars to the seasons has shifted slightly due to precession, but the starry sky we see today is not too different from that of Classic and Postclassic Maya times. Although we look for precise events, such as a star's heliacal rise date, most probably the Maya looked for a more general association with the seasons. I should note that the Precolumbian constellations are not configured with the same stars as our Western constellations. Even though I use the European designations for convenience, the reader should be cautioned that I refer only to stars in the region of these constellations rather than a star group conforming to the European definition. For example, the constellation we know as Sagittarius was probably divided into two constellations in Precolumbian times.

This chapter begins with a discussion of temporary sky phenomena, including comets, meteors, and supernovas. Subsequent sections focus on imagery of the stars, the Maya zodiac, and individual constellations, most often connected with animals. Cross constellations are described in relation to specific temple orientations and rituals at Palenque. The following sections focus on the imagery of the Milky Way, including discussion of the Cosmic Monster and Itzamna. The closing section places Maya astronomy in the context of world astronomy.

COMETS, METEORS, AND SUPERNOVAS

Supernovas are considered quite spectacular by astronomers using modern telescopes, but they are very transitory events that apparently were not commonly recorded in the inscriptions. Only one known Classic Maya date coincides with a historically documented supernova (A.D. 393; Justeson 1989:104, 115). Aveni (1980:97) notes that the Crab Nebula Supernova seen in early July of A.D. 1054 was exceptionally bright; however, it occurred after the Long Count ceased to be recorded on monuments. No record of it can be documented in the codices.

Comets and meteors were no doubt important to the ancient Maya, and they may have distinguished the two because of their different patterning. The cycles of comets involve relatively long periods of time, varying according to the comet involved. For example, Halley's comet reappears approximately every seventy-six years. Meteor showers, also known as shooting stars, recur in the same constellation at the same time of year. As annual events, they are more predictable and therefore less ominous than the return of comets.

Since meteor showers emanate from the constellation for which they are named, images of them may be combined with the imagery of their "parent" constellation. The Maya may also have linked shooting stars with different colors. For example, the Perseids have a marked yellow cast. Viewed over long periods of time, meteors undergo changes in intensity that can be connected with comets, such as the Leonid shower that has a period of intensity related to the 33.17-year period of the comet Tempel-Tuttle from which it derives (Trenary 1987–1988:110, fig. 7).

Some contemporary Maya accounts say that obsidian is the excrement dropped from shooting stars, but more commonly the meteors themselves are described as excrement of the stars, paralleling accounts recorded in recent Mixtec and Náhuatl texts (Chapter 1; Trenary 1987–1988, table 1). The ancient heritage of this image is evident in graphic scenes of star excrement in Mixteca-Puebla codices (Codex Borgia 26; Trenary 1987–1988, fig. 2). Parallel scenes involving star excrement in the Maya codices are not apparent; however, Maya images involving obsidian, cigars, and torches should be studied for a possible relationship with seasonal meteor showers. Contemporary Maya people say that meteors are connected with discarded celestial cigars and cigarettes, torches, and ancient arrowheads made of obsidian (Chapter 1).

A number of contemporary Maya terms do not distinguish between comets and meteors (Tedlock 1992b:181). This may also have been true in earlier times. The Colonial period term *chamal dzutan* (cigar of the devil) is interpreted as a comet, but Jesús Galindo (1994:111) suggests that when these cigars are discarded, they are transformed into meteors. The Colonial period Maya dictionaries do not contain an entry for meteors, but Ulrich Köhler (1989: 295) notes that there are a few entries under *cometa* that seem to refer to meteors. Among these he includes *u halal dzutan* (arrow of the devil), which is glossed as "ignited comet" (Lamb 1981:245–246). Other terms for comets noted by Weldon Lamb include *halal ek* (arrow star), referring to a "comet that runs"; *kak tamay,* glossed as "carbuncle"; and *kak noh ek* (fire big star), glossed as "big comet."

In the Colonial period, the Yucatec Maya associated comets with bad omens (Tedlock 1992b:180). The contemporary Maya link comets to fire and arrows (Chapter 1). Although the last appearance of Halley's comet in 1986 was rather disappointing, there have been spectacular displays of the comet in the past, such as the 1910 passage still remembered by older residents of communities in the Mayan and central Mexican area. Köhler (1989:292) points out that since the Mexican Revolution followed shortly after this comet, the historical events confirmed the ancient fears of calamities following comets. Similar notions probably existed in Precolumbian times. Comets, called *citlalinpopoca* (star that smokes) in the Aztec chronicles, are often linked with the death of a noble or ruler (Aveni 1980:27).

The Aztec Codex Telleriano-Remensis represents Venus as a smoking star in A.D. 1533, linking Venus to imagery of comets (Aveni 1980:27). A Maya text in the Songs of Dzitbalche seems to identify Venus as a smoking star (Edmonson 1982a:183). There may be a natural connection between Venus and comets. Carlos Trenary (1987–1988:110) points out that comets are usually first noticed as they approach or recede from the Sun, which positions them close to Venus. He notes that this may explain why an ancient Chinese source states that comets originate from Venus.

Several unpublished studies have linked the image of God L smoking a cigar in the Temple of the Cross at Palenque with the passage of Halley's comet in A.D. 684 (Robertson 1991, fig. 43). Although God L is clearly a Venus god, his cigar could represent a comet. The Hero Twins in the Popol Vuh smoke cigars, possibly alluding to a connection with comets. Since the cigar smoking takes place in Xibalba, identified as a southern section of the Milky Way where the rift is located, Barbara Tedlock's (1992b:181) interpretation of the cigars as meteors seems unlikely because this is not an area of the sky characterized by meteor showers.

Comets appear in historical records in Asian and European sources that date well before the time of Christ (Hasegawa 1980, table 1). It seems reasonable to assume that comets would also have been important in the historical records of the Maya; however, few published studies include interpretations of comets in Classic period times. Justin Shrove and Alan Fletcher (1984, app. B) compiled a list of comets recorded in written records dating from A.D. 1 to 1000 that could be useful in further studies of the role of comets in Classic Maya iconography and calendrics.

David Kelley (1976:42, 133, fig. 9) notes that a star glyph prefixed by a man's head with a tubular pipe in his mouth (at B10) on Tikal Stela 5 may be read as *budz ek* (smoking star), a Yucatec term for a comet. The glyph compound is apparently unique, and Kelley was not able to confirm an association with a known comet. In the Colonial period, the term *budz ek* was glossed as "maned comet like the one that appeared in the year 1577" (Lamb 1981:245).

In sum, temporary celestial events such as comets and meteors clearly need further study. A rare Maya text referring to a smoking star evokes connections with Aztec descriptions of comets. Comets may be cigars smoked by Maya gods; but a discarded cigar could refer to a meteor, more commonly known as a shooting star. Meteor showers are seasonal events, an association that may help to define their iconography. Since meteor showers are visualized as arrowheads and torches, however, it may be difficult to distinguish shooting-star images from imagery related to warfare and fire.

IMAGES OF STARS

The Yucatec dictionaries contain a number of metaphorical terms for stars. *Ek* (*ek'*) can refer to a star or the spots on a jaguar and a deer (Lamb 1981:234, 241). Indeed, a jaguar skin was the symbol of the starry sky (Thompson 1972:64 n. 1). The Chilam Balam of Chumayel describes a star as *u lol akab,* "the flower of the night," and refers to the night sky as *nicen(hal) caan,* meaning "flowering sky" (Roys 1967:27, 94). Early dictionaries compare a rising star to a plant sprouting (*hokol ek;* Lamb 1981:241).

The "queen of the stars" is a firefly (*cocay*), according to one Colonial Yucatec source, and fireflies are said to carry "lights from the stars" (Lamb n.d.a). "Firefly" is also a ritual term used to refer to a cigar or smoking tube in the Chilam Balam of Chumayel (Roys 1967:30, 97). As we have seen, comets are also compared to cigars.

Stars are the "eyes of the night" in a Postclassic scene from the Madrid Codex (34) interpreted as an astronomer looking out at the night sky (Fig.

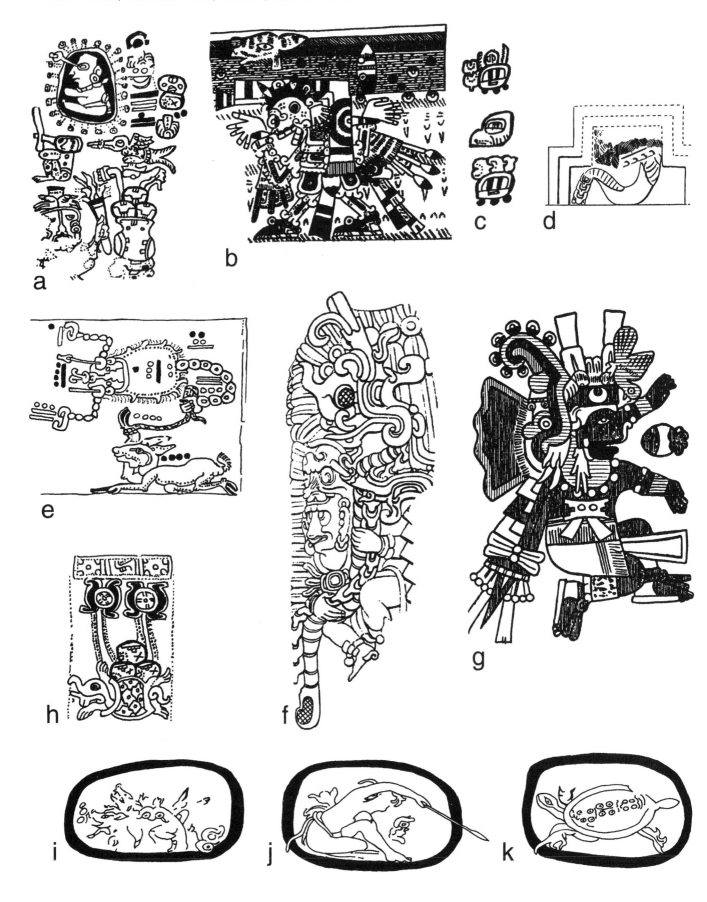

7.1a; Aveni 1980, fig. 1). The astronomer's eyeball stretched from its socket resembles a "death eye." He sits in a nocturnal circle surrounded by death eyes representing stars. In the Classic period, disembodied eyes and crossed bones represent the night sky and the starry underworld on the Vase of the Seven Gods (Pl. 7). Michael Coe (1973:83) points out that the deities of the underworld and the luminaries of the night sky may actually be the same. In this light, "death collars" formed by a circle of disembodied eyes probably represent stars, indicating an association with both the night sky and the underworld. These death eyes evoke central Mexican images of stars, represented as a stylized eye bisected by a red lid, as seen in the Death God holding up the night sky on Codex Borgia 51 (Fig. 7.1b). He wears a crown of stars and his eyes are actually stars.

Concentric rings can be used as signifiers for water or stars, depending on the context. Designs of small circles or rings may be star symbols (Coe 1973:83, no 37; 1982:32, no. 10). The same forms appear in the star glyph (T510f), which resembles the letter W or M framing two rings (Ringle and Smith-Stark 1996:303). This form is used as a star glyph in texts and as a symbolic element in images representing bright stars and planets. The T510f glyph sometimes shows the starry aspect of an ani-

mal constellation (Fig. 7.1i). Venus and other planets are depicted by a cruciform design framing four rings (T510b). Occasionally this glyph is used for bright stars, as in the turtle constellation at Bonampak (Fig. 7.1k).

Individual stars may be represented by birds. Today the Yucatec Maya say that Theta Taurus is *chamukuy,* the name of a small bird (Sosa 1985:341). The *Ritual of the Bacabs* speaks of the Ix Ko-ti-tzab located in the fifth layer of the sky, which is the "*ko*-bird-in-the-rattles constellation," interpreted as a bird star in the Pleiades (Roys 1965:7, 42, 136, 155). The Lacandón say that Rigel and Sirius are woodpeckers (Bruce et al. 1971:15), and woodpeckers do appear in starry contexts in Maya art, most notably in imagery of sky bands (Coe 1982:32, no. 10; Houston et al. 1992:502; Kerr 1992:498, no. 4464).

In sum, the imagery of stars in Precolumbian Maya art is still poorly understood. Many designs conventionally interpreted as death eyes may actually represent stars. Birds can also symbolize stars, but their celestial nature is not easily recognized, except when they are placed on sky bands. Flowers, fireflies, and even jaguar spots may represent stars, but once again, they are difficult to recognize as such unless the context clarifies an astronomical nature.

FIG. 7.1. *a:* Stars as "eyes of night" observed by astronomer, whose eye is stretched from its socket (Late Postclassic Madrid Codex 34; after Villacorta and Villacorta 1977).

b: Central Mexican images of stars represented as stylized eyes on sky band, here associated with death god bearing stars (Codex Borgia 51; after Seler 1960–1961, 5, fig. 289).

c: Katun and Tun glyphs joined with T207 glyph representing Pleiades (Dresden Codex 70; after Villacorta and Villacorta 1977).

d: Rattlesnake symbolizing Pleiades in zodiac-like sequence (north facade of Late Classic Palace of Stuccoes, Acancéh, Yucatán; after Seler 1960–1961, 5, pl. 11).

e: Deer attached to scorpion by rope, possibly representing deer planet in conjunction with Scorpius (Madrid Codex 44b; after Villacorta and Villacorta 1977).

f: Segmented snake with skeletal snout and scorpion stinger, probably representing Scorpius (Late Classic Copán Stela A; after Maudslay 1889–1902, 1, pl. 26).

g: Aztec Xiuhcoatl representing star-snouted serpent that may be linked with Scorpius (Codex Borbonicus 20; after Beyer 1965, fig. 230).

h: Turtle carries Cauac signs representing three hearthstone stars that symbolize three bright stars in Orion (Madrid Codex 71a; after Villacorta and Villacorta 1977).

i: Two stellar peccaries probably represent Leo with T510f star glyphs (vault of Room 2 in Structure 1, Bonampak; after Miller 1982, pl. 16). Note that adjacent cartouche is not shown.

j–k: Venus as warrior (Morning Star?) hurling spear at starry turtle representing Orion, here marked with three T510b star glyphs depicting Orion's Belt (Room 2 of Structure 1, Bonampak; after Miller 1982, pl. 19).

THE MAYA ZODIAC

Our best evidence of formal constellations among the Maya comes from a sequence of celestial figures in the Postclassic Paris Codex (23–24), long recognized as a form of zodiac representing thirteen star groups (Fig. 7.2a; Gates 1910:31). These same celestial animals also appear in the Madrid Codex, although not in a formal zodiac sequence (Knorozov 1982).

The Paris Codex table shows five rows of Tzolkin dates with red numerals spaced at intervals of 28 days (Fig. 7.2a; Appendix 3). The reading order is right to left, as indicated by the "mirror writing" with the glyphs facing opposite to the normal direction, a pattern first noted by Eduard Seler (1904b: 21). With thirteen dates per row (some now effaced), each row completes a period of 13×28 days totaling 364 days, a computing year which falls 6.282 days short of five sidereal years (H. Bricker and V. Bricker 1992:152). Five rows constitute five computing years, equal to 1,820 days or seven complete Tzolkins (7×260), bringing the computing year and the Tzolkin into renewed alignment.

In the upper row, between each zodiac figure, black numbers record intervals of 8.8 in Long Round notation (168 days), representing six "months" (6×28 days). A similar set was probably recorded below, although there are some perplexing variations in the notations, including three that seem to record only the number eight (H. Bricker and V. Bricker 1992: 158). Alongside the intervals of 168 days, blue-green numbers record correction factors that serve to realign the Tzolkin calendar dates with the solar year and the position of the constellations. Seler (1904b: 21) recognized these as factors used to add 20 days to the Tzolkin dates. Love (1994:99–102) notes that

they were added some time after the original codex was painted. He explains that slippage in the positions of constellations occurs because the table is based on multiples of 364 days, while the constellations reappeared in the same position relative to the horizon at sunset every 365.25 days. It was necessary to move the Tzolkin days forward 20 days to bring them into alignment with the constellations. The Maya did so by changing the bar-and-dot coefficient. For example, by adding 20 days, 3 Kan would become 10 Kan (Appendix 3). Thus the observation time would shift to 20 days later, by which time the constellation would have reached the appropriate position on the horizon.

Kelley (1976:45–50) proposes that the Paris Codex animals represent constellations spaced at 168-day intervals, because the number 8.8 appears between the animals. Given the apparent solar motion in the background of stars of about 1° a day, after an interval of 168 days the Sun is almost halfway around the sky, and the next interval of 168 days brings it back to a position only 29 days short of the solar year. This would place the constellations that are next to one another in the codex at opposite sides of the sky. Kelley's proposed zodiac, however, departs from the long-standing association between the Pleiades and the rattlesnake among the Maya of Yucatán. He also suggests that the animals biting the eclipse signs refer to eclipse events. The 168-day interval is very close to the "eclipse half-year" (173.25 days), indicating that the table was probably used for eclipse prediction. It also should be noted that the table could chart the position of the Moon, because the 168-day interval is halfway between the eclipse half-year and six draconic months ($6 \times 27.21 = 163.26$ days $+ 4.74 = 168$ days). Furthermore, the average between the synodic lunar month and the

---

FIG. 7.2. *a:* Late Postclassic zodiac with animal constellations suspended from sky band in upper row, here representing stars on or near where ecliptic crosses Milky Way; lower row represents star groups located along other points of ecliptic (Paris Codex 23–24; after Villacorta and Villacorta 1977).

b: Zodiac-like sequence showing crossed bands alternating with signs representing Moon, various constellations, and star signs that might show Venus positions (Nunnery, Chichén Itzá; after Seler 1960–1961, 5, fig. 42).

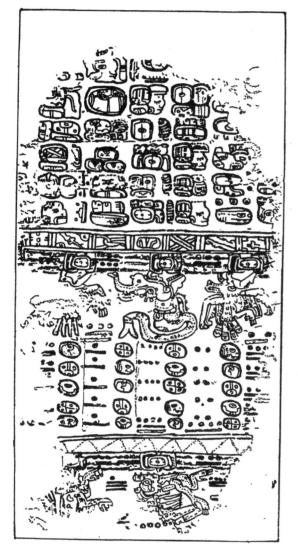
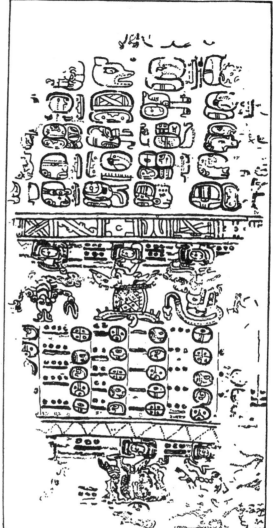

a

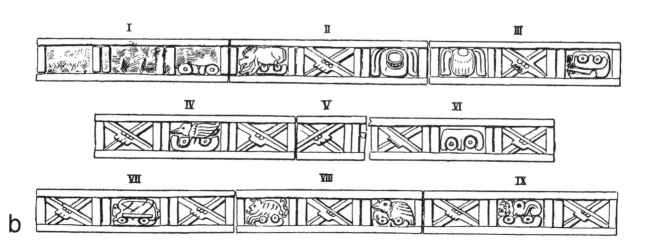

b

TABLE 7.1. LAYOUT OF THE ZODIAC OF THE POSTCLASSIC PARIS CODEX 23–24

Capricorn	Sagittarius	Gemini	Scorpius	Orion	Pleiades	Libra
(bird 3)	(fish-snake)	(bird 2)	(scorpion)	(turtle)	(rattlesnake)	(bird 1)
Aries	Pisces	Virgo	Leo	Aquarius	Cancer*	
(ocelot)	(skeleton)	(?)	(peccary?)	(bat)	(frog)	

Source: Based on H. Bricker and V. Bricker 1992, 1996.
*Western Leo in the Brickers' zodiac is replaced by Cancer in my revised layout.

TABLE 7.2. PAIRINGS OF CONSTELLATIONS, A.D. 755–756

	DAWN SET AND LONGEST VISIBILITY	DAWN RISE AND FIRST VISIBILITY AFTER CONJUNCTION
November 10	Pleiades (rattlesnake) sets dawn	Libra (bird 1) rises dawn
December 8	Orion (turtle) sets dawn	Scorpius (scorpion) rises dawn
January 5	Gemini (bird 2) sets dawn	Sagittarius (fish-snake) rises dawn
February 2	Cancer (frog*) sets dawn	Capricorn (bird 3) rises dawn
March 1	Leo (peccary?) sets dawn	Aquarius (bat) rises dawn
March 29	Virgo (?) sets dawn	Pisces (skeleton) rises dawn
April 26	Libra (bird 1) and Virgo (?) set dawn	Aries (ocelot) rises dawn
May 24	Scorpius (scorpion) sets dawn	Pleiades (rattlesnake) rises dawn
June 21	Sagittarius (fish-snake) sets dawn	Orion (turtle) rises dawn
July 19	Capricorn (bird 3) sets dawn	Gemini (bird 2) rises dawn
August 16	Aquarius (bat) sets dawn	Cancer (frog*) rises dawn
September 13	Pisces (skeleton) sets dawn	Leo (peccary?) rises dawn
October 11	Aries (ocelot) sets dawn	Virgo (?) rises dawn

Source: Based on H. Bricker and V. Bricker 1992.
* The frog as Western Leo is replaced by Cancer in my revised layout.

sidereal lunar month is 28.426 days, approximating the 28-day interval recorded in the table.

Gregory Severin (1981) proposes that the zodiac represents constellations that are next to each other in the sky, an arrangement originally proposed by Herbert Spinden. Some of the constellations Severin identifies are in accord with Colonial period sources. For example, the rattlesnake is linked to the Pleiades in Taurus, and the turtle to Orion or Gemini. Like

other scholars, he relates the constellations to thirteen zodiacal months of 28 days forming a 364-day computing year with a full round of 1,820 days after five passes through the Tzolkin table (Severin 1981: 13). However, other aspects of his interpretation differ markedly from those of other scholars. He says that the winged Kin glyphs are signs of the Sun at the vernal equinox, and he believes that the whole sequence represents the change in the vernal equinox through the 26,000-year cycle of precession of the equinox. Another interpretation that has not found a following among scholars is Severin's (1981:20, 23) notion that the blue-green numbers are modifying coefficients that refer to the Katun cycle.

Bruce Love (1994:89–102) notes that, given the division of the stars into thirteen constellations, arranging the dates in thirteen sets of 28 days makes sense because the average time for one constellation to replace another relative to the horizon is 28 days forming a sidereal "month" (13 × 28 = 365 days). Like Severin, Love links the turtle with Orion and the rattlesnake with the Pleiades, and he also proposes that the animal constellations represent adjacent star groups. He maintains, however, that the Paris Codex does not represent a true zodiac because some of the constellations are beyond the relatively narrow band of the ecliptic (about 18° wide). Love compares the layout to the Quiché constellations, and he points out that half of the constellations observed by the Quiché are not on the ecliptic. The Quiché star groups serve as "signs of the night" during the period of longest visibility, as opposed to our European zodiac that identifies constellations with the month of solar conjunction.

Harvey and Victoria Bricker (1992) provide an intriguing solution to the layout of constellations in the Paris Codex. The Brickers note that some paired constellations represent adjacent constellations, following the principle of a 28-day sidereal month, but others represent constellations at opposite sides of the sky in accord with the 168-day intervals of six sidereal months, as suggested by Kelley. Tables 7.1 and 7.2 reconstruct the associated constellations and the dates of their positions at both dawn rise and dawn set. The star groups paired from November through April in Table 7.2 reproduce the zodiac sequence. Like Kelley, the Brickers note that the separation of solar-eclipse glyphs by 168-day (8.8) intervals reflects a period close to the eclipse half-year. Nonetheless, the eclipse signs do not show eclipses in those specific constellations (Harvey Bricker, personal communication 1996).

Another form of zodiac is seen in the facade of the Nunnery (Las Monjas) at Chichén Itzá. In addition to a series of animals, some with T510f glyphs, there

is a lunar glyph (T683), an Imix glyph, and a T510f glyph standing alone (Fig. 7.2b). Seler 1960–1961, 5:228–231) proposes that the Nunnery shows Venus represented in a sequence of positions amid the background of stars. The order of the constellations shows that only some overlap with the Paris Codex (Kelley 1976, fig. 14). The Brickers (1992:166) note that the blocks may be out of order, but even rearranging them, they could find no extensive correspondence with the Paris Codex zodiac. There are a total of twenty-five different elements in the sky band, twelve of which are variants of the sky glyph and seven correspond to figures in the Paris Codex, including a turtle, a scorpion, a peccary, two birds, a snake, and a skeletal figure (H. Bricker and V. Bricker 1992, table 6.3). The skeletal figure is associated with Pisces in the Paris Codex. Pisces marked the spring equinox in the Classic and Postclassic periods, an intriguing correlation, given the abundance of skeletal images in Maya art.

A zodiac-like sequence is represented on the north facade of the Palace of the Stuccoes at Acancéh, Yucatán, dating to A.D. 600–700 (Miller 1991:15, pls. 3–6; Seler 1960–1961, 5, pl. 11). Animals noted for their nocturnal activities, such as the frog, the bat, the feline, and the gopher, wear eye rings (Miller 1991: 35). Some of the same animals—the bat, the owl, and the rattlesnake—are seen in the Paris Codex (Fig. 7.1d). A spider monkey evokes the monkey planet. A howler monkey might be related to the Morning Star in the Dresden Codex. A blue figure may be the Classic period counterpart of Hunahpu (Miller 1991:45). The facade has twenty-one figures, suggesting thirteen constellations grouped with the Sun, the Moon, and the planets, possibly with two different gods representing the dual aspects of Venus.

In sum, there is strong evidence for a zodiac in Classic and Postclassic Yucatán. The Paris Codex zodiac suggests dawn observations made during the dry season. All the constellations are on the ecliptic or nearby. The zodiac may refer to the moon's position crossing the node, indicating a potential for eclipses at intervals spaced approximately six months apart. Some of the Postclassic constellations can be traced back as far as A.D. 600. As we will see, some may even date back to Preclassic times.

TABLE 7.3. MAYA CONSTELLATIONS LINKED WITH WESTERN ZODIAC

MAYA CONSTELLATION	WESTERN CONSTELLATION	SOLAR CONJUNCTION (A.D. 0)
Bird 1	Libra	October
Scorpion	Scorpius	November
Fish-snake	Sagittarius	December
Bird 3	Capricorn	January
Bat	Aquarius	February
Skeleton	Pisces	March
Ocelot	Aries	April
Rattlesnake	Pleiades in Taurus	April–mid-May
Turtle	Orion added in Maya system	May–mid-June
Bird 2	Gemini	June
Frog	Cancer	July
Peccary?	Leo	August
(?)	Virgo	September

THE PLEIADES

The Pleiades are a sign for planting today, just as they were some two thousand years ago. The Pleiades rose at dawn in mid-May in the Protoclassic Maya period, just prior to planting at the onset of the rains; by the end of the Postclassic, they were seen rising in late May, a shift of only about two weeks (Table 7.4). By this time, their rise coincided with the planting season. Today, they disappear in early May, just prior to the planting.

The disappearance of the Pleiades around planting time may be the subject of a legend in the Popol Vuh. The Pleiades are the four hundred boys who trick Zipacna (a crocodile) into digging a hole for a giant post in their house. The boys try to kill Zipacna by burying him beneath the post; he gains revenge by pulling the house down on them and killing them, after which they are transformed into stars called *motz* (the group), the same name used for the Pleiades today (Edmonson 1971:48; Girard 1979:77). Dennis Tedlock (1991:171) suggests that Zipacna represents the earth monster who devours the

Pleiades when they disappear in conjunction at the beginning of the planting season (Tables 7.3, 7.4).

Quite a different image appears in Yucatán, where the Pleiades are the *tzab,* the "rattlesnake's rattle," a name known from sixteenth-century sources and one that still survives today (Lamb 1981:244; Tozzer 1941:133). Landa notes that the Yucatec Maya observed the Pleiades (*tzab*) to tell the time of night (Tozzer 1941:133, 220). The *tzab* were special insignia of the priests, who carried a short stick with rattlesnakes' tails attached to it (Tozzer 1941:105). Representations of God D from the codices and in the murals of Santa Rita show him holding a staff shaped like a rattlesnake (Taube 1992b, fig. 14). The Paris Codex confirms the association between the Pleiades and the rattlesnake in Postclassic times (Fig. 7.2a).

The *Ritual of the Bacabs* describes the red Sun with the snake-rattles constellation, clearly an image of their celestial conjunction in May (Roys 1965:147, 159). Other names such as Ix Hom-ti-tzab (she who sinks into the rattlesnake constellation) and "lady in the rattles constellation" may refer to the Moon in

TABLE 7.4. DISAPPEARANCE INTERVAL OF PLEIADES OVER TIME AT 21° N LATITUDE (DZIBILCHALTÚN, YUCATÁN)

YEAR	DISAPPEARANCE INTERVAL	PLEIADES DAWN RISE
500 B.C.	March 30–May 6	May 7
0 B.C.	April 6–May 12	May 13
A.D. 500	April 13–May 18	May 19
A.D. 1000	April 20–May 23	May 24
A.D. 1500	April 27–May 28	May 29

Source: Aveni 1980, table 10 (dates N.S.).

)65:37, 52, 1e Moon is there may ip between

ttlesnakes' still poorly points out lex 61 are ;lyph, fol- 000 Tuns. ; a Katun .1c). Eric e column le inter- nt num- of more ... ...:e a connection with the precession of the equinox (26,000 years).

My study of Madrid Codex pages 12–18 shows that the 260-day calendar on these pages coordinates with a stellar cycle marked by the changing position of the Pleiades, which is represented by a rattlesnake that changes its form and position (Fig. 7.3; Milbrath 1980b, 1981). On page 12b, the sequence opens with the serpent emerging from the sky band. As we will see in subsequent discussions, the sky band marks the intersection point of the Milky Way and the ecliptic, a crossroads where the Pleiades are located. The sky band is featured because this intersection point is positioned on the eastern horizon around the winter solstice. Indeed, the sky band appears only on pages that correspond to times when the crossroads of the Milky Way and the ecliptic is on the horizon at dusk. Page 12b marks the beginning of the astronomical year, when the Pleiades were seen in the east at dusk around the winter solstice. The next six pages represent a fixed 260-day agricultural calendar running from February to late October. The calendar overlies a sequence of serpents that show the movement of the Pleiades over the course of the planting cycle in the fifteenth century, the epoch of the Madrid Codex. For discussion of the solar dates and agricultural events, see Chapter 3.

The layout indicates that the agricultural calendar begins in early February on page 13b with the Pleiades overhead at dusk at the beginning of the fixed 260-day agricultural cycle. By the March equinox, the Pleiades are past the meridian at dusk, beginning their descent, as seen on page 14b. The sequence continues on page 15b, where the Chicchan serpent loses its rattles as a sign that the Pleiades have become invisible at dusk at the onset of the rainy season in May. The intersection point of the Milky Way and the ecliptic touches the western horizon, and this is why the sky band is represented prominently on page 15. And when the crossroads of the ecliptic and the Milky Way begins to emerge above the eastern horizon in late August, the sky band reappears on page 17. As the calendar comes to a close in late October on page 18, the serpent reemerges from the

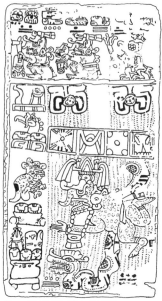

Page 12 Introduction 13 days

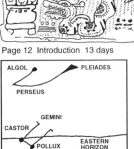

December 22 dusk Winter Solstice

Page 13 32 days beginning February 8

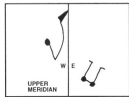

February 8 Pleiades at Zenith

Page 14 36 days beginning March 12

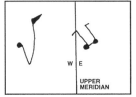

March 21 dusk Spring Equinox

Page 15 40 days beginning April 17

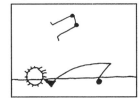

May 20 dusk, First Solar Zenith
20° latitude; Pleiades sets

Page 16 40 days beginning May 27

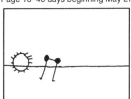

June 21 Summer Solstice
Gemini sets

Page 17 40 days beginning July 6

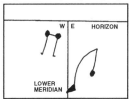

July 24 dusk, Second Solar Zenith;
Pleiades crosses lower meridian

Page 18 38 days? beginning August 15

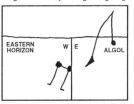

September 20 dusk, Autumn Equinox
Algol in Perseus rising

Missing Page?

36 days complete 260 days?

underworld without its rattles, just prior to the dusk rise of the Pleiades.

The Pleiades glyph (T207) appears on Madrid Codex 16a (upper left) above a sequence of Chicchan serpents, some bearing rattle tails identical to those on the Pleiades glyph (Fig. 7.3). The Chicchan serpents bear serpent markings like the day sign Chicchan, implying a link with Maya horoscopes that give the prognostication (*mut*) for the days Kan and Chicchan as *ah tzab ti can,* meaning "the rattlesnake rattle in the sky" (Lamb n.d.a).

The Chicchan serpent, a rain serpent associated with agricultural fertility in contemporary Maya accounts, may be linked with the Madrid Codex serpent, which has a feathered crest and a rattle tail. It is possible that the Pleiades represented as the rattlesnake's rattle can be traced back to Olmec times. As early as 900–400 B.C., we see Olmec images of the rattler with a feathered crest, as on La Venta Monument 19 (Milbrath 1979, table II, fig. 70).

The Chicchan serpent is linked with the day sign Chicchan and the Pleiades, and it is possible that Venus is also part of the image. The serpent's rattle tail may show that the Pleiades are closely related with Venus in its manifestation as a feathered serpent. Karl Taube (1992b:140, fig. 76e) suggests that the Chicchan serpents in the Madrid Codex are one of a group of "crested" serpents that may be linked with Quetzalcoatl, noting that the serpent aspect of Quetzalcoatl has a strong connection with water and fertility. The rattles certainly represent the Pleiades, but the serpent might be the counterpart of Quetzalcoatl as the planet Venus. Venus observations may also have been coordinated with a 260-day cycle representing the fixed agricultural calendar. Indeed, Daniel Flores (1989) finds a direct connection between the 260-day interval and Venus observations. For example, he notes that counting the average interval from the first appearance of Venus as Evening Star to the last day of visibility gives an average of 259.87 days. A link with Venus is also suggested because the

Madrid Codex displays the 260-day calendar in four rows of 65 days, an arrangement convenient for calculating Venus events such as heliacal rise dates (Milbrath 1981:277).

As noted in Chapter 5, Venus passing by the Pleiades is a sign associated with rain, for this occurs invariably from mid-March through mid-June. Rain appears as a background in the Madrid Codex serpent sequence because the calendar relates to weather patterns presented in relation to observations of the Pleiades and possibly also of Venus. The Chicchan serpents in the Madrid Codex seem to be the counterparts of the Chortí Maya Chicchan serpents, especially the northern Chicchan that is the chief who directs the Chicchans in their rainmaking activities (Wisdom 1940:393–396). Ivan Sprajc (1993a:27) suggests that the northern Chicchan reflects the observed coincidence of Venus in northerly extremes with the onset of the rains. The northern extreme of Venus may have been linked with the Pleiades, because they are relatively far north on the ecliptic. Furthermore, if we consider Perseus to be part of the serpent constellation, as I proposed in my original study, the constellation extends quite far north.

The Chicchan serpent takes a peculiar form in the Madrid Codex, resembling a hook (Fig. 7.3). This form led me to study stars in the vicinity of the Pleiades to see if the serpent's body could be a nearby star group. Plotting the movements of Perseus and the Pleiades shows a good correspondence with the changing positions of the Chicchan serpent in the Madrid Codex. The Pleiades and Perseus are a natural pair, forming a sort of bent serpent like that in the Madrid Codex (Aveni 1980, fig. 70; Milbrath 1980b, 1981). Yucatec lore describes the Pleiades as the rattler's tail, but the Paris Codex zodiac shows the complete serpent, indicating a larger constellation. This star group probably included the neighboring stars of Perseus, a constellation to the north of the ecliptic with a bright binary star, Algol.

FIG. 7.3. Chicchan serpent with *tzab* tail ("rattlesnake's rattle") in sequence showing changing position of Pleiades in relation to 260-day agricultural calendar and Tzolkin at 20° latitude ca. A.D. 1450. All dates Gregorian (N.S.). (Madrid Codex 12–18; modified after Milbrath 1981, fig. 23.2a)

The Chortí Chicchans are responsible for most of the sky phenomena, and they are closely associated with the "Working Men," who bear lightning axes. These men would seem to be counterparts of the Chacs, a pairing like that on Madrid Codex 13b, where Chac rides the Chicchan serpent when he is pouring rain from his jar. Chac mounts the Chicchan serpent in the same way that the five Chacs ride horses representing different kinds of clouds and weather in modern Yucatec Maya lore (Chapter 5). Indeed, there are five Chacs on pages 12b–18b.

In my original study of the Madrid Codex, I suggested that Chac may be connected with Gemini, marking the Sun's position at the onset of heavy rains in June (Milbrath 1980b, 1981). Subsequent research points toward Chac having a planetary identity; nonetheless, Chac's planet could have a stellar "home" in Gemini (Chapter 5). Indeed, all the planets probably had astrological "homes" in different constellations (Kelley 1985:236). Landa reports that Venus, the Pleiades, and Gemini were the most important bodies observed by the Maya. On page 12b, Chac has the year-sign headdress of Tlaloc A, suggesting that he is involved in the eight-year Venus Almanac, an idealized cycle that brings a Venus event into alignment with specific solar, lunar, and stellar events. Venus passes by Gemini during the rainy season, an association similar to that seen with the Pleiades. When the Sun enters the Pleiades, it is the time of the solar zenith when the rains begin in Yucatán; and when the Sun enters Gemini, the rains are at their maximum intensity and the Sun is at its northern extreme. Conversely, when Gemini is in opposition to the Sun, visible for the longest period of time, it is the time of the winter solstice. The Pleiades are in opposition to the Sun around the beginning of the dry season in November, the time of the solar nadir in Yucatán. It seems clear that by watching the Sun, Venus, the Pleiades, and Gemini, a very reliable Venus Almanac could be constructed.

The Pleiades may be represented by the serpent rattles on a bag held by the ruler on Bonampak Stelae 2 and 3 (Mathews 1980:60–64, figs. 2, 4). This bag could be the counterpart for the rattle staff carried in Postclassic times. Stela 3 bears a date (9.17.15.0.0; 10/31/785) that correlates approximately with the midnight zenith of the Pleiades. The accession date of Chaan Muan (9.17.5.8.9; 6/9/776) on Stela 2 is around three weeks after the dawn rise of the Pleiades (Table 7.4). The accession event was probably guided by other astronomical events, most notably the first stationary point of Jupiter (6/18/776), the second stationary point of Saturn (6/19/776), and the conjunction of Mars and Venus, when the Evening Star was near its maximum elongation and its maximum altitude (Aveni and Hotaling 1994, table 1; Lounsbury 1982:159; Meeus n.d.; Schele and Freidel 1990:446).

The Pleiades bag is also represented on Yaxchilán Stela 18, which has one of the few representations of the *tzab* glyph (T207) in the central Maya area during the Classic period. The apparent reference to a Yucatec word for the Pleiades is interesting in light of the fact that Yaxchilán is a bilingual site where Yucatec was probably spoken along with Chol (Mathews 1990, fig. 2). The text on Stela 18 begins with Shield Jaguar capturing Chuen of Bonampak on a Long Count date reconstructed as 9.14.17.15.11, based on a Calendar Round date, 3 Eb 14 Mol, with a one-day error in the Tzolkin notation (Tate 1992:244, app. 2). The Long Count corresponds to a date in early July (7/8/729) when the Pleiades were overhead at dawn and Jupiter and Saturn were nearby undergoing retrograde motion in Pisces. Jupiter and Saturn moved in tandem, reaching their second stationary points together in late October, by which time the Pleiades were overhead at midnight. A glyph for "sky center" appears with the Pleiades glyph preceding a Katun 5 Ahau expression associated with a fire event (D1-E2; Tate 1992, fig. 145, app. 3). The Katun 5 Ahau could refer to the next 5 Ahau Katun ending, 10.1.0.0.0 (11/24/849), when Jupiter and Saturn would once again be in proximity as they approached their second stationary points at a time when the Pleiades once again passed overhead at midnight.

Inscriptions on Yaxchilán Lintel 31 include a house dedication phrase with the *tzab* glyph and a fire glyph (Schele 1990a:149, fig. 9.6). Carolyn Tate (1992:163–165, 277, fig. 57) transcribes the text as: "2 Ahau 8 Uo (B2-A4), fire is drilled to dedicate Mah K'ina Itzam Na . . . its holy name, the temple

(B4-C1) [of Bird Jaguar] (D1)." This Calendar Round date, reconstructed as 9.16.13.0.0 (2/24/764), marks a fire event associated with the dedication of Bird Jaguar's temple. At this time, the Pleiades were overhead at dusk; more significant, Saturn was in conjunction with the Pleiades, an event that would recur approximately every twenty-nine years (one and a half Katuns).

Yaxchilán Lintel 10 has a *tzab* reference associated with an 18 Zotz inscription (D8) tentatively reconstructed as 9.18.17.13.10 5 Oc 18 Zotz (4/3/808; Tate 1992, app. 2). This date coincides approximately with the dusk set of the Pleiades at the latitude of Yaxchilán if we presume a slightly raised horizon. At this time, Jupiter was undergoing retrograde motion, and possibly this was also noteworthy in the inscriptions.

The Pleiades were also recognized as far west as Palenque, for an inscription on Temple XIV records a variant of T207 (Pl. 13; Ringle and Smith-Stark 1996:292). This glyph is interpreted as a reference to the apotheosis of Chan Bahlum on 9 Ahau 3 Kankin (9.13.13.15.0; Schele and Miller 1986:272). His apotheosis on 10/31/705 coincided with events involving Jupiter, Saturn, and the Moon (Chapter 6). It is noteworthy that Saturn, having just passed its first stationary point, was undergoing retrograde near the Pleiades.

The Yucatec rattlesnake constellation may also have been represented in the Petén during the Early Classic at Tikal (Stela 1; Coe 1970:92). Tikal Stela 1 depicts Stormy Sky framed by feathered standards, with a rattlesnake and a feline climbing the standard on the left, and a fish-snake and a fragmentary figure climbing on the right. The two standards may represent two sides of the sky, with the Pleiades on one side and Sagittarius on the other side.

In the central and southern Maya area, we would expect to find images linking the Pleiades with sandals, the Chol name for the Pleiades (Chapter 1). Such imagery is much more difficult to pinpoint, because sandals often appear on royal figures, and no glyphic expression for the word *sandals* is recognized to date. Arthur Schlak (1989) concludes that jaguar-pelt sandals appear on rulers represented on monuments bearing dates related to significant Pleiades positions. However, since he links any number of jaguar costume elements with the Pleiades, the analysis is not sufficiently refined to determine whether jaguar sandals are depicted at a specific time in the cycle of the Pleiades. Also, his sample of figures with jaguar sandals is by no means sufficient to conclude that there is a connection with the Pleiades.

Observations of the Pleiades in relation to the Sun and Venus are documented in orientations at Chichén Itzá. A stairway niche in the Caracol shows an alignment (paralleling Window 1) to the northern extreme of Venus and another to the zenith sunset (Fig. 3.1b). And Window 1 was used to view the Pleiades in late April as they set heliacally at dusk, before the onset of the rains at the time of the first solar zenith in late May (Aveni 1980:266, fig. 93). The window has a broad enough opening so that the Pleiades could be seen setting prior to the zenith sunset over a relatively long period of time, despite the shift in their setting position from 288° azimuth in A.D. 500 to 290° in A.D. 1000 (Aveni 1980, table 9). A similar orientation is seen in the doorway of the inner temple in the Upper Temple of the Jaguars (Milbrath 1988b, 1988c). As noted in Chapter 5, the feathered-serpent columns in the portico of this temple represent Venus in conjunction with the Pleiades, an event that invariably occurs between March 21 and June 21. This calendric image is reinforced by the orientation of the temple, which faces sunset on April 29, midway between the spring equinox and the summer solstice (Chapter 3). The orientation underscores a connection between the Venus serpent, the Pleiades, and a time of year associated with the rains to come. The feathered-serpent columns with rattle tails also frame the entrance to the Temple of the Warriors, a structure oriented precisely to the setting Pleiades in A.D. 1000 (290°). Another Pleiades image may appear in the rattlesnake accompanying a warrior on the north jamb of the west doorway of the Castillo (Cohodas 1978, fig. 68). The west face is oriented precisely to the position of the zenith sunset (291°) marking the onset of the rains (Milbrath 1988c).

In sum, the most easily identifiable image of the Pleiades is the rattlesnake's rattle, especially common in Yucatán. The Pleiades were clearly important calendar stars at the time of the conquest. The Postclassic Madrid Codex shows a Pleiades calendar corresponding to the agricultural season. Other codices show that longer cycles of time are linked with the Pleiades. Both dawn and dusk observations of the Pleiades were important in certain Classic Maya inscriptions and architectural orientations.

THE SCORPION AND SKELETAL SNAKE CONSTELLATIONS

As noted in Chapter 1, ethnographic accounts give varying identifications for the scorpion constellation: Ursa Major (Tojolabal area in Chiapas), Scorpius (Tzotzil area in Chiapas and Yucatec area in Quintana Roo), a large constellation running from Gemini to Sirius (Yucatec area southeast of Valladolid), and a constellation running from Orion to Sirius (Yalcobá in Yucatán). This gives us perhaps too many options to work with when interpreting Maya images of celestial scorpions.

The Colonial period dictionaries from Yucatán identify *zinaan ek* (scorpion stars) as the sign of Scorpio (Justeson 1989:116; Lamb 1981:244; Roys 1972:96). The Chilam Balam books also list the "black scorpion" (*ek chuuah*) among the stellar deities involved in Katun prophecies (Kelley 1976:103; Roys 1967:151 n. 3). A centipede labeled *ch'apat*, another form of stinging insect, represents the zodiacal sign of Scorpio in the Chilam Balam of Kaua (Lamb n.d.a).

The layout of the Paris Codex indicates that Scorpius represents a scorpion constellation in Postclassic Yucatán. Although Scorpius appears next to a turtle on the sky band, it is actually at the other side of the sky, meaning that its seasonal associations are opposite (Fig. 7.2a). At Chichén Itzá, the lintel of the eastern doorway of the Nunnery depicts a text that shows a celestial scorpion, and the Nunnery at Uxmal represents the scorpion constellation on a sky band (Fig. 7.2b; V. Bricker and H. Bricker 1995:98, figs. 1–2).

We also find a stellar scorpion in the Madrid Codex on pages 44 and 48. A series of images show a scorpion holding a rope tied to a deer, suggesting possibly celestial conjunction with a deer planet or perhaps proximity to a deer star or deer constellation

(Fig. 7.1e). A scene on Madrid Codex 11a shows the old Moon Goddess wearing a scorpion tail, perhaps an image of the Moon in conjunction with Scorpius. Madrid Codex 79a depicts the Venus God L with a scorpion body, suggesting another image of celestial conjunction (Fig. 5.11b).

John Carlson (1991) notes that one of the twenty directional aspects of Venus in the Dresden Codex Venus pages may refer to a scorpion constellation. As noted in Chapter 5, the scorpion constellation is named in columns B and C on page 46 of the Dresden Codex Venus pages (Figs. 5.3a, 5.11c). The scorpion constellation (B) is linked with day 326 and the west, referring to the canonical day the Evening Star would reemerge. In the Postclassic layout described in Chapter 5, day 326 fell on 5/7/1220, and in Postclassic northern Yucatán this was the month when Scorpius was visible for the longest period of time, making it the "sign of the night" (Table 7.2). The list of twenty deities also names the Sun, God K (Jupiter), and the five regent gods, including the Moon Goddess and God N. It may well be that the total number comprises thirteen different constellations, five planets, and the Sun and the Moon.

In the Classic Period, the scorpion may be portrayed as a segmented snake with a skeletal snout, only very rarely showing a scorpion stinger, as on Copán Stela A (Fig. 7.1f). The segmented body recalls representations of the Aztec Xiuhcoatl, a star-snouted serpent apparently linked with Scorpius (Fig. 7.1g; Milbrath 1980a, 1995b, 1997). The date on Stela A (9.14.19.8.0; 1/28/731) corresponds to a time when Scorpius was overhead at dawn. Perhaps this is why the Sun God holds the snake over his head.

On the west face of Copán Structure 10L-29, skeletal snake heads appear in sets of four, framing cartouches that may originally have held solar symbols (Andrews and Fash 1992, fig. 10). The diving figures at the bases of the cartouches recall imagery of the Evening Star. The skeletal serpent, which Linda Schele (1992b) calls the White-Bone-Snake (formerly the snaggletoothed dragon), may be an image of Scorpius, located at the intersection of the Milky Way and the ecliptic. A background of S-shaped scrolls evoke the cloudy aspect of the Milky Way (see below).

At Palenque, there are a number of representations of the skeletal snake. Four skeletal snakes frame Kin symbols on the thirteen ancestor cartouches of House A (Fig. 3.4k; Robertson 1985b, figs. 112–138). Their arrangement radiating from the Sun symbol is like that of Xiuhcoatl's framing the Sun disks at Chichén Itzá (Fig. 3.5i). Such images may show the Sun in conjunction with Scorpius, reflecting the Sun's position in November at the beginning of the dry season. The Sun God is conceptually linked with the White-Bone-Snake in Classic Maya ancestor cartouches, evoking comparison with the image of Xiuhcoatl framing the Sun God at Chichén Itzá and that of Xiuhcoatl held by the Aztec solar god Huitzilopochtli (Fig. 3.5i; Milbrath 1980a).

The central panel of the Temple of the Sun depicts skeletal snake heads on crossed spears, indicating a connection with warfare (Fig. 3.6b). The date (1/5/684) directly above corresponds to a time when Scorpius was high above the eastern horizon at dawn with the morning star (Table 7.2).

On Pacal's Sarcophagus Lid, the skeletal snake is a portal to the otherworld in the Milky Way (Pl. 10; Freidel et al. 1993:269–270, fig. 6:11b). Schele (1992b:133, 137) notes that the jaws correspond to the glyph for "hole" in the codices and the glyph for the five-day Uayeb, and she interprets the creature as the White-Bone-Snake representing a place of transformation and an entry to the underworld in the rift branch of the Milky Way. I would add that the skeletal snake represents Scorpius in the underworld section of the Milky Way. The date (8/26/683) of Pacal's apotheosis recorded on the Sarcophagus corresponds to a time when Scorpius was seen high above the western sky at dusk, marking the portal to the underworld in the rift of the Milky Way (Fig. 7.8c).

Yaxchilán Lintel 25 also depicts the skeletal snake with hooked teeth at the end of the snout and a segmented body, as on Copán Stela A, but a second head replaces the scorpion's tail (Fig. 5.8f). Here the tail is visualized as a form of jaw, just as the scorpion stinger around the eclipse glyph in the Paris Codex zodiac substitutes for the animal jaws biting the eclipse glyphs seen in the other constellations (Fig. 7.2a). Schele and Miller (1986:187–188, pl. 63) originally designated this snake as a Vision Serpent, but more recently Taube (1992a:59–68) suggests that it is a War Serpent linked with a mosaic serpent headdress seen on the Temple of Quetzalcoatl at Teotihuacán and worn by warriors in Maya art (Fig. 5.6g, Pl. 15). The Yaxchilán snake has a skeletal jaw, suggesting links with the White-Bone-Snake on Pacal's Sarcophagus and on the spears in Palenque's Temple of the Sun. The ringed designs on the snake's body may represent the stars of Scorpius marking the rift branch of the Milky Way, the underworld road of xibalba be (Chapter 1). This section of the Milky Way may be the place where dead ancestors enter the underworld, and this may be why Lintel 25 shows the serpent jaws holding an ancestor with the attributes of Tlaloc, a god who may be linked with Venus. Tlaloc in the serpent's jaws may represent Venus in Scorpius. On the date carved on Lintel 25 (10/18/681), Venus was visible as the Evening Star passing by Antares, the brightest star in Scorpius. Such a conjunction event during the Classic period took place from September through December, overlapping with the onset of the season of warfare. This may account for the warlike imagery in the scene.

Other Yaxchilán images involve what may be symbolic pairings rather than actual images of celestial conjunction with Scorpius. On Yaxchilán Lintel 39, for example, a skeletal snake with a segmented body bears God K (Jupiter) in its jaws, but this pairing does not seem to represent conjunction. On the recorded date (9.15.10.0.1; 6/25/741), Jupiter rose after midnight and was about to enter retrograde, while Scorpius was at the opposite side of the sky above the western horizon. Yaxchilán Stela 1 depicts the Sun God holding a skeletal snake forming a serpent bar (Fig. 3.8d). The dates on Stela 1 (2/14/760 and 3/11/761) do not refer to the Sun in conjunction with Scorpius, but the image embodies a link between the dry-season Sun and Scorpius.

On Tikal Stela 22, Ruler C at the time of his accession wears a backrack with a cartouche framed by skeletal snakes, resembling the ancestor cartouches of Yaxchilán and Palenque (Jones 1977: 36, fig. 3; Tate 1992, fig. 23). The Calendar Round date 13 Ahau 18 Cumku refers to the Katun ending 9.17.0.0.0, when Jupiter and Saturn were in retrograde motion. The ruler holds a latticed staff and drops seeds or liquid (blood?) from his right hand. Bloodletting is the last event named in the inscriptions, just following the date of 11 Kan 12 Kayab (9.16.17.16.4; 12/23/768). This date is one month after Antares emerged from solar conjunction. At this time Venus was in Scorpius, an interesting overlap with the planet's sidereal positioning on the date recorded on Yaxchilán Lintel 25, another monument featuring a bloodletting event (Fig. 5.8f).

In Maya vase painting, Scorpius may be represented by a naturalistic scorpion in some contexts. The Blowgunner's Pot shows Hunahpu shooting a bird in a tree with a scorpion at its base (Fig. 3.10k). On the opposite side of the pot, a rattlesnake appears with a "Cauac cluster" on his tail. Some scholars identify the scorpion as Scorpius and the rattlesnake as Sagittarius (Freidel et al. 1993:102, figs. 2:7c, 3:33; Schele 1992b:131). They identify the tree as the Milky Way. I, on the other hand, link the tree with stars in Sagittarius that form a sort of celestial cross alongside Scorpius (see below). The Pleiades are the rattlesnake's Cauac tail. The scorpion is Scorpius positioned at the opposite side of the sky. The Calendar Round date on the vessel is 1 Ahau 3 Kankin (Coe 1989:170). On every repetition of this date during the Late Classic period, Scorpius was visible near the eastern horizon around dusk, and by dawn it had moved to the western horizon. Thus the scorpion represents Scorpius on the horizon.

We can conclude that there is strong evidence that Scorpius was visualized as a scorpion in the Postclassic period. In earlier times, scorpion traits may be seen on a skeletal snake representing Scorpius. Sometimes the snake has a segmented body like a scorpion. The skeletal serpent may be equated with the War Serpent and the White-Bone-Snake. Certain dates on Classic Maya monuments with the skeletal serpent indicate an interest in significant positions of Scorpius or times when the planets pass through Scorpius. Other images seem to be symbolic representations, showing the Sun or a solar deity associated with the skeletal snake, perhaps indicating a special association between the Sun and Scorpius not unlike that seen later in Aztec art.

ORION AND GEMINI

Gemini has the brightest twin stars in the sky, Castor and Pollux, marking the northern extreme of the Sun at the summer solstice. For over one thousand years Castor and Pollux remained in conjunction with the Sun on the summer solstice (Aveni 1980, table 10). Gemini is next to Orion, so they share similar seasonal associations. Orion's Belt has the brightest group of three stars in the sky. Orion is positioned overhead when it crosses the meridian in the latitudes of Mesoamerica. The three stars are very close to the celestial equator, dividing the sky in two halves. The belt rotates in an interesting fashion, positioned roughly east to west when rising and north to south when setting.

The importance of Orion in Quiché cosmology is attested to by a number of temples oriented toward the setting points of stars in Orion at Utatlán, a Postclassic Quiché site (Freidel et al. 1993:103). In this area of Mesoamerica, the stars of Orion are seen in a true zenith position. This may be why they express the notion of centrality among the Quiché Maya, who associate Orion with a deity known as Heart of Sky. Juan de León (1945:44–45) notes that in ancient times the Quiché linked Orion with Jun Rakán (Huracán or Hunracán) of the Popol Vuh, an identification supported by Carmack (1981:356). Huracán is another way of referring to Hurricane, one of the three aspects of Heart of Sky, who appears with the plumed serpent in the creation epic (D. Tedlock 1985:72–75, 341, 343, 365). His aspect as a one-legged god can be deduced from the name Hurricane, which means "1 Leg" (hu[n]rakan; Edmonson 1971:11–12). Hurricanes are also associated with specific positions of the Big Dipper (see below).

The idea of centrality may be seen in the hearthstones of the home fire in the Popol Vuh, which symbolize a triangular group of stars in Orion (Alnitak, Saiph, and Rigel) that form the three celestial hearthstones still recognized by the Quiché (D. Tedlock 1985:261). The three stones seem to be mentioned in the creation mythology of the Chilam Balam of Chumayel, which speaks of "the three-cornered precious stone of creation" (Looper 1995:24; Roys 1967:

107). On page 71a of the Madrid Codex, a turtle representing stars in Orion carries three Cauac signs (Fig. 7.1h). These are the "three stones of creation," known as the "three-stone place" in Classic period inscriptions at Palenque and Quiriguá (Freidel et al. 1993:82–83, fig. 2.16; Tedlock 1995:119–120).

A constellation known as the fire drill, suggesting a connection with the seat of the fire in the three hearthstones of creation, seems to be linked with Orion or Gemini. The Colonial period Motul dictionary glosses *mehem ek* (semen star) as "the *astillejos*, a constellation in the sky"; *astillejos* (fire drill) is a Spanish term referring to Orion in the Nebrija dictionary of the Colonial period (Lamb 1981:236, 344). Thompson (1972:68) says that this fire-drill constellation refers specifically to Orion's Belt. He equates it with the Aztec fire-drill constellation (*mamalhuaztli*), but this is identified as Castor and Pollux of Gemini by Arthur Anderson and Charles Dibble (Sahagún 1950–1982, 7:60). Alfred Tozzer (1941:133 n. 623) says that the *astillejos* are Gemini. Similarly, modern Spanish dictionaries link the term *fire drill* with Castor and Pollux (Lamb 1981:237). We must conclude that the fire drill could be located in Orion or Gemini. Since they are adjacent in the sky, there could have been some confusion among the chroniclers between the astrological "sign" and the constellation itself. Floyd Lounsbury (1982:166) points out that the zodiacal sign of Gemini actually included the stars of Orion and much of Taurus in the sixteenth century, for the signs remained fixed while the stars shifted with precession. This also may account for different identifications made for the turtle constellation.

Landa identifies *ac ek* (the turtle star) as one of the two most important constellations in the Maya calendar (Tozzer 1941:132–133). Tozzer and other scholars link Landa's turtle constellation with Gemini (Knorozov 1982:204). The Motul dictionary says that *ac ek* is a constellation formed by three stars in the sign of Gemini that, with others, make a turtle (Lounsbury 1982:166–167). The Lacandón and the Yucatec Maya of Chan Kom also identify the turtle as Gemini (Chapter 1). On the other hand, Thompson (1960:111, 116) notes that a Yuca-

tec Maya informant described the square of Orion that includes Rigel and Betelgeuse as a turtle constellation (*ac*). Furthermore, the Paris Codex layout links Orion with a turtle and Gemini with a bird (Table 7.1). As noted below, this bird is probably an owl.

As discussed in Chapter 5, the turtle victim on Dresden Codex 49 seems to represent Orion setting in opposition to the rising Morning Star in November of 1225 (Fig. 5.3d). Equating the Dresden Codex turtle with a tortoise, Thompson notes that the Yucatec Maya say that the tortoise weeps for rain. They recount that when the woods are wet and the earth moist, the tortoise is not seen, whereas when the land is thirsty, the tortoise walks about (Redfield and Villa Rojas 1962:207). Apparently, the tortoise is seen on land when the celestial turtle is prominent at the time of the dry season. Orion has its longest visibility in December during the dry season (Table 7.2). The speared victim on Dresden Codex 49 bears a title with a seated manikin (T227) that may represent a dwarf (*ac*) (Thompson 1972:64, 69–70). It is paired with a turtle-head glyph referring to the turtle constellation. This turtle head is essentially the same glyph used for the month Kayab, and both show a Kan Cross in the turtle's eye, which can be seen in the first glyph at the bottom of page 46 noting 19 Kayab (Fig. 5.3a). The glyph for Kayab incorporates a turtle head that may be linked with the turtle constellation (Thompson 1960:116).

The turtle constellation could also be represented by a turtle head with a water-lily headband. This turtle is a logograph for *ac* (*ak*) in Maya glyphic writing (Houston 1989:40). Ralph Roys (1965:xxii–xxiii) notes that *ac* is a homonym with five different meanings in Yucatec, including a certain grass, a turtle, a boar peccary, a dwarf, and stars in Gemini.

Star-marked dwarfs on the Yaxchilán Hieroglyphic Step VII of Structure 33 bring to mind the wordplay between *dwarf* and the *ac* stars in Gemini (Tate 1992, fig. 111). The dwarfs watch Bird Jaguar playing with a ball formed by the body of a bound victim. The last Calendar Round inscription on the monument is the date of Bird Jaguar's ball game (Schele and Miller 1986:249, fig. VI.7). Tate (1992:273) links this 3

Muluc 17 Mac date (9.15.13.6.9; 10/15/744) with Jupiter's first stationary point (10/23/744; Meeus n.d.). At this time, Jupiter passed by Castor and Pollux, which may be represented by the two star dwarfs next to the ballplayer.

Other representations of the turtle constellation appear in Classic Maya imagery. A celestial turtle appears in the sky band on the Nunnery facade at Chichén Itzá (Fig. 7.2b). The Bonampak murals depict a stellar turtle with three bright stars on its back, calling to mind Orion's Belt (Fig. 7.1k; H. Bricker and V. Bricker 1992: 177; Freidel et al. 1993: 80, fig. 2: 15).

The painted pot known as the Resurrection Vase depicts the Hero Twins (the Sun and the Moon) pouring water on the Maize God as he sprouts from a turtle shell (Fig. 3.11b). Although this turtle is often interpreted as a representation of the earth (Benson 1997: 97; Coe 1989), Schele proposes that it represents stars in Orion and that the Maize God is the Milky Way represented in the form of a tree (Freidel et al. 1993: 82, fig. 2: 17). Although I disagree with identifying the Maize God with the Milky Way, there is a strong link between the turtle constellation in Orion and the cycle of maize. For thousands of years, the period that Orion (the turtle) was invisible in conjunction with the Sun coincided with the time of maize planting, and its reemergence in June correlated with the sprouting maize (Tables 7.2, 7.3). In Mesoamerican latitudes, Orion's Belt disappeared from the sky from April 29 to June 17 around A.D. 0; by A.D. 1000 the disappearance interval had shifted only slightly, running from May 11 to June 28 in the Gregorian calendar (Aveni 1980, table 10). Perhaps the birthplace of maize is in the turtle constellation, for the Chilam Balam of Chumayel tells us that the tender green maize shoot was born in heaven (Roys 1967: 112).

We can conclude that both the Classic and Postclassic Maya linked the turtle and the celestial hearthstones with stars in Orion. A long-standing association between the period of Orion's conjunction and maize planting can be seen in Classic Maya imagery that shows maize sprouting from the celestial turtle associated with Orion. Castor and Pollux may be linked with twin dwarfs in one Classic Maya representation. Stars in Gemini seem to be an owl in the

Paris Codex, but it is not clear whether this association extends back through time. Gemini and Orion, two neighboring constellations, sometimes bear the same name in Colonial period dictionaries, probably reflecting a confusion between the European constellation and the astrological sign.

THE PECCARY CONSTELLATION

We do not have direct evidence for the peccary constellation in Colonial period accounts, but the Lacandón speak of a peccary formed by bright stars in Orion, with nearby stars as the piglets (Chapter 1). The name *ac* in early dictionaries has caused confusion because it is applied to a peccary and a turtle, as well as star groups in both Gemini and Orion, as noted in the previous discussion. Such confusion may be why David Freidel, Linda Schele, and Joy Parker (1993: 85, figs. 2: 15, 2: 19, 2: 33) identify Gemini as both a peccary and a turtle, and at another point they say that Orion is also linked with a peccary.

It is noteworthy that modern Maya accounts say that two collared peccaries convey the Sun on the long, slow days around the summer solstice (Thompson 1967: 38). This suggests a connection with Gemini, marking the summer solstice, or possibly another nearby star group. One possible candidate is Leo, based on the layout of the Paris Codex zodiac (Table 7.3). Leo's brightest star (Regulus) disappears in conjunction with the Sun a few weeks after the summer solstice.

The Paris Codex zodiac has a partially effaced figure that may be a peccary constellation linked with Leo (H. Bricker and V. Bricker 1992: 171–172, 178). Although the Brickers originally proposed that Leo was divided into two constellations, it seems more likely that the frog constellation they identify as western Leo actually refers to stars in Cancer (Tables 7.1, 7.2; Milbrath 1996a).

Two stellar peccaries are painted in the vault of Room 2 in Structure 1 at Bonampak (Fig. 7.1i). Following the patterning from the Paris Codex zodiac, Harvey and Victoria Bricker (1992: 178, fig. 6.11) link the Bonampak peccaries with Leo. Although Lounsbury (1982: 166–167, table 3) does not identify the star peccaries, he reconstructs a battle date inscribed in Room 2 as 9.18.1.15.5, noting that the date marks the time when Venus was in inferior conjunction. Using the Gregorian date and the 584,285 correlation, Freidel, Schele, and Parker propose that the scene on the vault with the peccaries and three other starry cartouches represents four celestial deities seen close together on the night of August 6, 792 (Freidel et al. 1993:80–82, fig. 2:15). They refer to the copulating peccaries as Gemini, and the turtle as Orion's Belt. Two other anthropomorphic figures in between are identified as Mars and Saturn positioned between these two constellations. On the other hand, if the peccaries represent Leo, the vault could show the underworld sky on the battle date. Using the 584,283 correlation, the date (7/31/792) is precisely the day Venus was in inferior conjunction, four days before Venus would rise at dawn (Aveni and Hotaling 1994, table 1). At this time, Venus and the Sun were positioned in Leo. The star deity aiming a spear at the celestial turtle could be Venus, who must kill the Orion turtle in order to rise at dawn four days later.

We have a great number of peccary images that could be identified with the peccary constellation. A celestial peccary appears in the sky band on the Nunnery facade at Chichén Itzá (Fig. 7.2b). The West Court at Palenque depicts two celestial peccaries framing the aged Sun God, evoking the long days of summer when the Sun moves with the celestial peccaries (Fig. 3.7h). Similar images in portable art show a peccary with a Kin symbol (Freidel et al. 1993, fig. 2:19; Hellmuth 1987, fig. 593). One such vase illustrated by Coe (1973, no. 66) has a peccary and a deer on opposite sides, suggesting that the two sides symbolize opposite seasons; unlike the slow-moving peccaries, the deer carries the Sun quickly across the sky during the winter (Chapter 1). The deer constellation remains enigmatic, but it might be the Hyades, a V-shaped configuration in Taurus that resembles deer horns.

On a peccary skull from Tomb 1 at Copán, celestial ballplayers seated in a cavelike opening appear with three peccaries that may represent a constellation (Fash 1991, fig. 24). Two ballplayers in the center of the composition are Venus twins, according to Clemency Coggins (1986; 1988c:106, fig. 7). The

peccaries are arranged at one corner of the composition; at another we see a spider monkey wearing a headband (a monkey planet?). The spotted feline alongside could be the jaguar moon. A vulture below could be a planet or a bird constellation. A deer standing on the baseline next to a skeletal ballplayer with deer features evokes imagery of a celestial deer (a constellation or the deer planet?). The skull bears a 1 Ahau 8 Chen Calendar Round date, but the corresponding date is not certain, so it is not possible to accurately reconstruct the astronomical events.

Discussing the Vase of the Seven Gods (Pl. 7), Coe (1973:107) suggests that the peccary with a death collar is a constellation. (But see Taube 1992b, fig. 39b.) The 4 Ahau 8 Cumku date may be an anniversary of the creation date. This date invariably falls in the dry season during the Late Classic period. As noted in Chapter 6, the Calendar Round anniversary of 4 Ahau 8 Cumku in December 785 is suggested on stylistic grounds. At this time, Leo was above the Morning Star in the dawn sky, mirroring the position of the animal over God L's head on the vase.

We can conclude that the peccary constellation probably represents Leo in the Postclassic period, and possibly also in Classic period times. Another alternative is that the peccary relates to Gemini. There are many peccary images in Maya art that may depict stellar imagery. In any case, the peccary seems to be a constellation marking the position of the Sun during the summer.

BIRD CONSTELLATIONS

Birds, the paramount rulers of the sky, represent planets, constellations, and individual stars in Maya cosmology—but it is difficult to sort out which is which. Our best evidence for bird constellations comes from the Paris Codex zodiac, where Harvey and Victoria Bricker (1992:171, table 6.5) identify three different bird constellations. Bird 3, a fragmentary bird to the left on the upper row, probably depicts Capricorn (Fig. 7.2a; Table 7.1). Gemini is represented by Bird 2, a form of owl in the upper band. Bird 1, all but effaced on the far right in the upper row, is linked with Libra.

One of the partially preserved birds in the zodiac

could be a vulture, which appears prominently in astronomical contexts. On Dresden Codex page 36b, a vulture perches on a starry snake that may depict Venus, perhaps representing the planet in conjunction with a vulture constellation (Fig. 5.4b). Similarly, a vulture perches on a star or Venus symbol in the Nunnery sky band at Chichén Itzá (Fig. 7.2b).

In the Paris Codex zodiac, Bird 2 representing Gemini is an important constellation because it is the "sign of the night" in December, the month of the winter solstice, and at the summer solstice it is in conjunction with the Sun. It is also the only zodiac bird sufficiently well preserved in the Paris Codex to discuss in terms of iconography. The Brickers follow Seler (1960–1961, 4:642) in describing the bird as the *cox* bird, a black pheasant in the Motul dictionary (Tozzer 1941:202 n. 1115), but Bird 2 is clearly an owl. Its mottled feathers and tuft of head feathers are traits of owls found in Mexico, such as *Bubo virginianus* or *Otus asio*. Stars on the tail identify Bird 2 as a nocturnal creature. The brightest twin stars in the sky, Castor and Pollux in Gemini, probably evoked the owl's eyes. Love (1994, fig. 10.7) identifies the Paris Codex owl as the Maya Muan bird, named after the bird representing the month Muan. Thompson (1960:114–115) says that the Muan bird is a Yucatecan horned owl or a screech owl, both characterized by tufts of feathers on the head. He notes that the Muan bird often is represented on or above the celestial dragon. The Paris Codex (10) also depicts a similar bird, a symbol of Katun 12 Ahau, identified by Taube (1987) as the Muan bird representing a screech owl or a horned owl, a companion of God L ("Moan owl" in Taube 1992b:85). On the other hand, Nikolai Grube and Linda Schele (1994:10–12) identify the Muan bird as a hawk and God L's companion bird as the *kuy* owl, a Ferruginous Pygmy Owl (*Glaucidium brasilianum*) associated with warfare in the Classic period. Chapter 5 presents evidence linking God L's owl to Mercury.

In sum, there are multiple birds represented in the Paris Codex zodiac, and clearly we have a wealth of possible bird constellations. Bird 2 is an owl associated with Gemini. The relationship of this bird to the bird representing the month Muan and to God L's owl is not yet clear. A vulture may be linked with one of the two other zodiac birds that represent Libra and Capricorn.

CROSS CONSTELLATIONS AND STELLAR TREES

Birds naturally bring us to trees and their celestial counterparts—stellar crosses. Cosmic crosses and celestial trees representing cross constellations appear in ethnographic accounts (Chapter 1). Among the Lacandón, the Southern Cross is a ceiba tree, the place where souls of the dead ascend to heaven (Bruce 1979:155). Colonial period records tell us that the Yucatec Maya believed that the ceiba shaded the souls of the dead in a land of milk and honey (Thompson 1970b:301). Among the Yucatec Maya, the ceiba is represented by a wooden cross painted green (Sosa 1989:137). Although not explicitly described as astronomical, these crosses may be associated with stellar crosses imbued with Christian imagery. The Yucatec Maya say that the Southern Cross is *cruz ek* (cross star), representing the cross of Jerusalem at the southern edge of the world (Redfield and Villa Rojas 1962:206; Villa Rojas 1945:150, 156). A location in Jerusalem is implied by the description of the Quiché cross constellations, because as "thieves' crosses" they flank Christ's cross at Calvary.

The Quiché of Momostenango, in the department of Totonicapán, identify two thieves' crosses; one is the Southern Cross and the other is in Sagittarius (Tedlock 1992a:29). These two stellar crosses are in the Milky Way in the southern sky. Because the Southern Cross is visible exclusively during the rainy season, it is called the rainy-season thieves' cross (B. Tedlock 1985:83). The dry-season thieves' cross is a seven-star asterism in Sagittarius. Judith Remington (1977:85–87) collected data on three cross constellations found among the Quiché in the department of Quetzaltenango and among the Cakchiquel in the department of Guatemala. One is the Southern Cross; the second is a star cross centered on the delta star in Sagittarius—two identifications that apparently overlap with the two Quiché constellations recorded in Momostenango—and a third cross was recorded by Remington but remains unidentified. Although the Northern Cross is not mentioned in ethnographic accounts, its cross configuration is easily seen in the sky (Fig. 7.8b, northwest). It is clearly important in the orientation of a temple at Palenque.

In light of the imagery of cross constellations in the Quiché area, it is noteworthy that a Protoclassic sculpture from Santa Cruz de Quiché in Guatemala (now in the National Museum of the American Indian [9/6718]) depicts a crosslike form with circular designs that probably represent stars. On the cross we see a zoomorphic head with a mirror brow, a long front tooth, and scroll eyebrows; the head rests on a bound bundle with trilobe ends, not unlike the pendant worn by astronomical gods.

Seventh-century Classic Maya monuments from Palenque also seem to represent cross constellations. Two magnificent tree-crosses are found in the Cross Group at Palenque (Pls. 11–12). These images seem to represent stellar crosses. The orientations of the Temple of the Cross and the Temple of the Foliated Cross help reveal the nature of these celestial crosses. The alignment of the temples indicates an interest in celestial crosses located at northern and southern sections of the Milky Way. The Temple of the Cross is oriented toward the southwest to an azimuth of 211°45′ (Aveni and Hartung 1979, table 1, fig. 1). With a mountainous horizon like that on the south side of Palenque, Beta Crucis in the Southern Cross could be seen setting through the doorway of the inner sanctuary (with a horizon elevation of 3°, Beta Crucis set at 211°07′ circa A.D. 500; Aveni 1980, table 9). The Temple of the Foliated Cross has a 312°30′ azimuth facing toward the northwest, where the horizon is relatively flat, but the sight line passes over the Temple of the Sun, artificially raising the horizon. Thus the temple is aligned toward the setting point of Deneb, the brightest star in the Northern Cross (with a horizon elevation of 3°, Deneb set at 312°48′ circa A.D. 500; Aveni 1980, table 9). Given these associations and the importance of cross constellations today, we can conclude that the Temple of the Foliated Cross is a temple dedicated to the Northern Cross, and the Temple of the Cross is dedicated to the Southern Cross.

The principal themes of the panels in the Temple of the Cross and the Temple of the Foliated Cross are heir designation and accession. Both temples depict the heir apparent, young Chan Bahlum, in his bloodletting costume (Pls. 11–12). Although events in Chan Bahlum's life seem to be linked with Jupiter's retrograde motion, as noted in Chapter 6, star positions also seem to be significant in the dates selected for these events. Schlak (1996) notes that the heir designation on 6/12/641 (9.10.8.9.3) coincided with the sunset rise of Deneb (Alpha Cygnus), the brightest star in the Northern Cross. And the accession date (1/5/684; 9.12.11.12.10) can be linked with Deneb's rise at dawn. Although not noted by Schlak, the Southern Cross also shows a relationship with the heir-designation and accession dates. The Southern Cross was crossing the meridian above the mountainous southern horizon at dusk on the heir-designation date in A.D. 641. And some forty years later, the Southern Cross was again positioned above the southern horizon at dawn at the time of Chan Bahlum's accession in A.D. 684.

The tree-cross in the Temple of the Foliated Cross, actually a maize plant, seems to be linked to the Northern Cross, whereas the one in the Temple of the Cross symbolizes the Southern Cross. In the Temple of the Cross, Chan Bahlum's heir-designation date (9 Akbal 6 Xul) is inscribed above the young ruler, who faces a celestial tree representing the Southern Cross. His temple is aligned so that the Southern Cross was seen from the inner sanctuary around dusk when Chan Bahlum was designated heir on 6/12/641 (Pl. 12). The Temple of the Foliated Cross faces the setting position of the Northern Cross when Chan Bahlum was crowned king on 1/5/684 (Deneb set at dusk on 1/25/500 N.S., at 21°N latitude; Aveni 1980, table 10). In this temple, the accession date associated with the mature Chan Bahlum is clearly the main focus, because the heir-designation date is not even represented with the young Chan Bahlum (Pl. 11). At the time of his accession, King Chan Bahlum faces a celestial cross representing the Northern Cross as a maize plant.

At age forty-nine, the newly crowned Chan Bahlum is metaphorically compared to a mature maize plant, for the foliated cross is a maize plant with its ears doubled over in preparation for harvest. The maize is ripe and ready to serve as food for the people, just as the ruler is mature and ready to serve the people. The metaphor extends into the sky, bringing the stars into play. At the time of Chan Bahlum's accession in January of 684, the Northern Cross stood erect over the horizon to the northwest at dusk, and its light streamed into the inner chamber of the Temple of the Foliated Cross. Thus the Northern Cross is the embodiment of the mature maize drying on the stalk in January. Indeed, the Northern Cross itself has bent arms, just like the bent maize ears on a dried stalk ready for harvest. The foliated cross reflects the image of the Northern Cross on the horizon, just as the cross in the Temple of the Cross mirrors the Southern Cross as it makes its brief transit across the sky. The two structures present a perfect harmony between temple orientation, iconography, and dated events signaling two of the most important ceremonies in the reign of Chan Bahlum.

Connecting royal rituals to the position of a constellation may seem to be fanciful to some people, but here again we have to turn to the modern Maya for instruction. The Cakchiquel of Chinautla still send young boys out when they turn six or seven to fight for the stars of a cross constellation called the Thieves' Dagger so that they will gain the proper skills to become an adult (Remington 1977:87). It seems more than coincidence that at six years of age, the young Chan Bahlum is shown with a cross constellation in a ceremony to make him ready to assume his proper role as the future king.

A third structure in the Cross Group at Palenque signals a relationship with a cross constellation. In the Temple of the Sun, Chan Bahlum's accession date is the focus of the imagery because it is placed in the center of the composition (Fig. 3.6b). His accession date was timed by Jupiter's departure from its second stationary point, and Jupiter may be represented by the God K manikin held by the ruler on the right (Chapter 6). As in the case of the other temples of the Cross Group, the iconography of the Temple of the Sun bears a relationship to the temple's alignment. The accession date tells us the day of observation, and the orientation tells us where to look on the horizon. The time of observation is most prob-ably dawn, given the temple's alignment toward the winter solstice sunrise, an event occurring around two weeks before the ruler's accession (Chapter 3). The temple orientation aligns with Sagittarius rising in early January. The cosmic power of this constellation streamed into the inner temple just before sunrise on the January accession date. Stars in Sagittarius form a cross constellation described in contemporary Maya accounts as centered on delta Sagittarius, equivalent to the bow in the Sagittarius archer's hand (Fig. 7.8a, lower center).

In the Temple of the Sun, a celestial cross is suggested by the crossed spears (Fig. 3.6b). As noted earlier, the spears bear skeletal snakes that may symbolize Scorpius, a constellation adjacent to Sagittarius. Since only part of Sagittarius is seen as a celestial cross today, it seems that the constellation may have been divided into two different asterisms in times past. The rest of Sagittarius may be represented by a fish-snake serpent bar below, the counterpart of the fish-snake in the Paris Codex (Fig. 7.2a). The Temple of the Sun depicts God L supporting a zoomorphic bar that bears two heads of a shark monster known as Xoc, one at either end. As Andrea Stone (1992) points out, zoomorphic bars are often referred to as thrones because people sit on them, but they actually represent supernatural locales. In this case, the Xoc zoomorph evokes the fish-snake in Sagittarius located adjacent to the celestial cross in Sagittarius, probably represented by the crossed spears.

Stellar imagery is also prominent in an important image of apotheosis in the Temple of the Inscriptions at Palenque, a pyramid that houses the tomb of Chan Bahlum's father, Pacal II. As noted in Chapter 6, Pacal's apotheosis as God K coincided with Jupiter's first stationary point (8/28/683). Instead of describing a death event, the text says "he entered the road," referring to an astrologically timed apotheosis. As noted earlier, the giant maw framing God K and his celestial tree is none other than the skeletal snake embodying Scorpius, the entry to the Milky Way—the *xibalba be* in the southern sky (Pl. 10). The cosmic tree on the Sarcophagus Lid shows a context for Pacal's apotheosis. The tree has similar attributes to the one in the Temple of the Cross, also depicting the Quadripartite God at the base. As we will see, the skeletal Quadripartite God may represent the place where the ecliptic crosses the Milky Way at its southern extreme. The imagery suggests the tree is the Southern Cross located in the southern sky on the southern part of the Milky Way, where the souls of the dead ascend. Among the Lacandón, the Southern Cross is a stellar ceiba, which the dead climb to reach heaven. In light of contemporary Maya beliefs that the souls of the dead become stars (Thompson 1960:85), it may be that the stars of the Milky Way were seen as the spirits of the dead traveling along the soul's road.

In sum, cross constellations seem especially important in the imagery of seventh-century rulers at Palenque. Study of the Sarcophagus Lid suggests that the deceased Pacal entered the Milky Way near Scorpius and ascended to heaven on the Southern Cross to reach his planet Jupiter. The imagery, dates, and orientations of Chan Bahlum's temples indicate specific associations with cross constellations representing world trees located in the Milky Way. Chan Bahlum stands in the Temple of the Foliated Cross alongside an image of the Northern Cross, a giant maize plant representing a cosmic tree that bestowed a blessing on his reign at his accession in January of A.D. 684. In a like fashion, at his heir designation when he was six years old, he appears with the Southern Cross, another cosmic tree, but this one in the Temple of the Cross. This temple focuses on the heir-designation date in June, and it is oriented to the Southern Cross setting at this time, whereas the Temple of the Foliated Cross focuses on the accession date in early January when the Northern Cross could be seen setting from the temple interior. The accession event is also featured prominently in the Temple of the Sun, but here the temple is oriented to a third celestial cross in Sagittarius that rose at dawn in January. Like the other two temples, the central image here can be related to a cross constellation in the Milky Way.

THE NORTH STAR AND THE "DIPPERS"

Precession brought Polaris to the position of a true Pole Star for the Northern Hemisphere in medieval times. Today it still remains the pivot of the sky fixing the north point. Its elevation above the horizon can be used to determine latitude. At 15° latitude, Polaris is approximately 15° above the horizon. It is so low on the horizon in tropical latitudes of Mesoamerica that in mountainous regions it would barely be visible. The best place for observing the Pole Star in the Maya area is northern Yucatán, where the flat horizon gives optimum visibility. Indeed, it may be that some rare north-facing structures in this area were used for such observations, the most notable being Structures 1 and 2 in the Northwest Quadrangle at Uxmal (Aveni 1980, app. A; Aveni and Hartung 1986, table 1).

Some Yucatec dictionaries of the Colonial period name *xaman ek* as "star of the north" and "guide of the merchants," referring to the North Star (Polaris) in Ursa Minor; others use this term to refer to the whole constellation, glossing it as "guards of the north" (Lamb 1981:243). *Chimal ek* (shield star) is the "star of the north" (Polaris) in Yucatec dictionaries, but this name sometimes also applies to Ursa Minor and neighboring stars (D. Tedlock 1985:330).

Paul Schellhas (1904:20) originally identified God C of the codices as the North Star, and this interpretation is still repeated today (Coggins 1988a:140; Galindo 1994:100; Sharer 1994:535). Schellhas points out that the glyph for north has a face that resembles God C, but he also notes that on Dresden Codex pages 29c–30c, all four directions are associated with the God C head (Schellhas 1904:21). Similarly, on the Río Azul tomb, God C appears associated with all four directions (Fig. 3.2b). Taube (1992b:27) points out that God C never serves as the main sign for north in the Dresden Codex, the most carefully painted of the Maya manuscripts. Kelley (1976:630) notes that God C's role as a representative of the North Star seems highly questionable. In Chapter 6, God C is identified as a monkey planet. Perhaps he is also lord of the four directions.

Schele (1990:151–152, fig. 9.7) also proposes that Polaris is mentioned in Classic period mythological texts in the Temple of the Cross at Palenque (Pl. 12). She identifies the date 13 Ik 0 Chen as a creation event in 3112 B.C. linked to a Long Count set at the beginning of the epoch (1.9.2). She suggests that an expression she translates as "entering or becoming the sky" (*och ta chaan*) is paired with the establishment of a house named "raised up sky of the north" (*wakah chaan xaman*), translating *wak* as "something raised on high"; however, *wak* more commonly refers to the number six. She proposes that this image refers to lifting up the sky from the sea, with *xaman* referring to the sky pivoting around Polaris. This interpretation remains highly speculative, and the text may alternatively be translated as "six sky in the north."

Linda Schele and Mary Miller (1986:277) suggest that the clustering of burial sites to the north of Tikal and the north-facing burials at Palenque indicate that the ancestral dead rose to occupy the north sky. Be that as it may, it seems clear that the dead entered the sky to the south, in the *xibalba be* section of the Milky Way (see below).

Surprisingly, terms for the Big Dipper or Ursa Major do not appear in Colonial period Yucatec dictionaries, except for an erroneous reference to *chimal ek* as Ursa Major. Lamb (1981:243, 245) proposes that Ursa Major is linked with the starry ball-court constellation called *ekel ek* (darkness stars), glossed as "game of ball." Modern Yucatec references to the Big Dipper or Ursa Major as the "seventh sacrament" seem to link the Big Dipper to the Catholic last rites performed just before death (Redfield and Villa Rojas 1962:206). Another Yucatec term for Ursa Major, *noria ek* (water wheel star), also clearly refers to Postconquest imagery, naming a European invention.

Quiché Maya dictionaries identify Ursa Major as Vucub Caquix, meaning "seven macaw" (Alvarado 1975:73; *gucup cakix* in León 1954:33). Dennis Tedlock (1985:36, 91, 330, 360) says that Vucub Caquix is the Big Dipper, a seven-star configuration in Ursa Major. In the Popol Vuh, Vucub Caquix moves up in a tree to proclaim himself as the Sun, but Hunahpu shoots him down, ending his reign as the false Sun. His wife is Chimalmat, a Nahua-derived name that Tedlock notes is linked with *chimal ek,* a name for Ursa Minor, a constellation close to the Big Dipper. A calendar regulated by positions of the Big Dipper may be implied in the ascent and descent of Vucub Caquix, for Tedlock (1991) notes that the Big Dip-

per's descent in the dusk sky marks the beginning of the hurricane season, just as its rise marks the onset of the dry season.

In terms of astronomy, it is noteworthy that the Big Dipper has been linked with Principal Bird Deity, an alter ego of God D named Itzam-Yeh (Freidel et al. 1993:79, 89, 112, 449, fig. 2:13; D. Tedlock 1985:90–91). Tedlock interprets a Classic period scene showing the Hun Ahau twin killing the Principal Bird Deity as the death of Vucub Caquix (Fig. 3.10k). Elizabeth Benson (1997:91–92) tentatively identifies the Principal Bird Deity as a King Vulture. She notes that Vucub Caquix is the ancestor of the scarlet macaws, but his representation in the Classic period is complex and partly vulturine. Vucub Caquix loses a tooth in the Popol Vuh, which suggests a connection with a modern Maya account that describes how King Vulture was forced to give up the Moon when the Sun caused him to have a toothache (Benson 1996:311–312). On the other hand, Nicholas Hellmuth (1987:365) reaches the conclusion that the Principal Bird Deity is not Vucub Caquix, but is instead a hawk mentioned in a second shooting incident of the Popol Vuh.

We can conclude that the identification of northern stars and constellations in Precolumbian Maya art remains elusive. The Colonial period Yucatec sources provide some evidence to suggest that the Little Dipper or Polaris was visualized as a shield, but no direct connection with Precolumbian Maya imagery has been demonstrated to date. The often-repeated notion that God C represents the North Star is untenable. Identifications of the Big Dipper among the Precolumbian Maya are by no means conclusive, despite recent research linking this star group to Vucub Caquix and to the Principal Bird Deity.

CENTRAL MEXICAN IMAGES OF THE MILKY WAY

The Aztecs of central Mexico visualized the Milky Way as a white road created when Tezcatlipoca and Quetzalcoatl walked across the sky (*Historia de los mexicanos por sus pinturas* 1973:32). The *Historia de México* (1973:105) says that Tezcatlipoca and

Ehecatl made the heavens by entering the earth goddess (Tlalteutl) and joining together to form a low heaven, which the other gods helped them raise up. The next year, the stars were created, including the Milky Way, represented as a male and female pair known as Citlaltonac (where the stars shine) and Citlalicue (star skirt). In both accounts, the world was restored after a great flood, and the sky had to be raised before the Milky Way was created in the world age of the Aztecs. This was the epoch of the fifth sun, for the destruction of the world had been repeated four times. In another account, however, the Milky Way creation sequence is reversed, for Quetzalcoatl and Tezcatlipoca are among the many divine children of Citlalicue (González Torres 1975: 130). The gods were born when Citlalicue gave birth to a stone knife that she threw to earth. Although the Milky Way has a male and female aspect, Citlalicue is most often named by herself in legends and invocations referring to the Milky Way (González Torres 1975:129–133).

On Codex Vindobonensis 47b, Ehecatl-Quetzalcoatl holds up a band of celestial water on a sky band with Venus glyphs, possibly alluding to the Milky Way as a celestial river (Fig. 5.4g). And Codex Vindobonensis 48 shows Quetzalcoatl emerging through a cleft opening in a sky band with Venus glyphs in a scene representing his rebirth in the heavens (Fig. 5.4f; Milbrath 1988a:158–159). The image of Quetzalcoatl emerging through a cleft sky band parallels scenes in the Codex Borgia (29–46) that show Quetzalcoatl passing through a sky band forming the body of a figure that Karl Nowotny (1976) describes as a sky goddess (Fig. 7.4a–b). I have identified this goddess as the Milky Way, noting that she is probably the counterpart of the Milky Way goddess known as "star skirt" (Citlalicue) in Aztec mythology (Milbrath 1988a:160–164; 1989). The goddess bears stars and Venus signs, much like the sky bands in Mixtec codices. The cleft in her body marks the place where the ecliptic crosses the Milky Way, which is also the place where the Venus deity, Quetzalcoatl, is reborn (Milbrath 1988a; 1989). A similar construct appears in the imagery of Chichén Itzá (Fig. 5.5f–g). Here the feathered serpent emerges from the abdomen of an elongated goddess. Taube (1992b:129–131) links these Chichén Itzá murals with a myth in the *Historia de México* (1973:108) that describes how Tezcatlipoca and Quetzalcoatl tore apart the earth goddess by transforming themselves into two great serpents and squeezing the earth in the middle. The myth states that her lower body rose up to the sky—hence the celestial associations of this goddess are quite appropriate. In the murals, her body is covered with blue-green jade disks, implying a shiny quality, for jade sparkles like water. In central Mexican imagery, jade symbols appear in representations of water, but they may also allude to stars in some contexts.

We can conclude that in some Aztec accounts, Quetzalcoatl and Tezcatlipoca are responsible for creating the Milky Way, variously described as a celestial road, a divine star couple, or, more specifically, a star skirt. In others, the goddess of the Milky Way gives birth to Quetzalcoatl, Tezcatlipoca, and a multitude of other gods. Central Mexican and Mixtec codices show Venus-Quetzalcoatl positioned at the intersection of the ecliptic and the Milky Way. Quetzalcoatl emerges from the abdomen of a star-skirted goddess of the Milky Way in the Codex Borgia, suggesting a form of celestial rebirth. At Chichén Itzá, central Mexican influence is evident in images that show the feathered serpent emerging from the elongated body of a sky goddess who may represent the Milky Way. Mixtec scenes show the rebirth of Quetzalcoatl as he emerges from a cleft in a sky band that probably shows where the ecliptic crosses the Milky Way. In other scenes, the Venus deity holds up sky waters that may be the Milky Way.

THE COSMIC MONSTER AND THE MILKY WAY

A zoomorph that Andrea Stone (1985) dubbed the Cosmic Monster sometimes has an elongated sky-band body that evokes a link with the central Mexican goddess of the Milky Way (Fig. 7.4a–b). On Paris Codex 22, the ecliptical cord crosses over the sky-band body of the Cosmic Monster, serving as a sky rope connecting six deities, among which we find two death gods and four gods representing different aspects of God N (Fig. 7.4c). Another

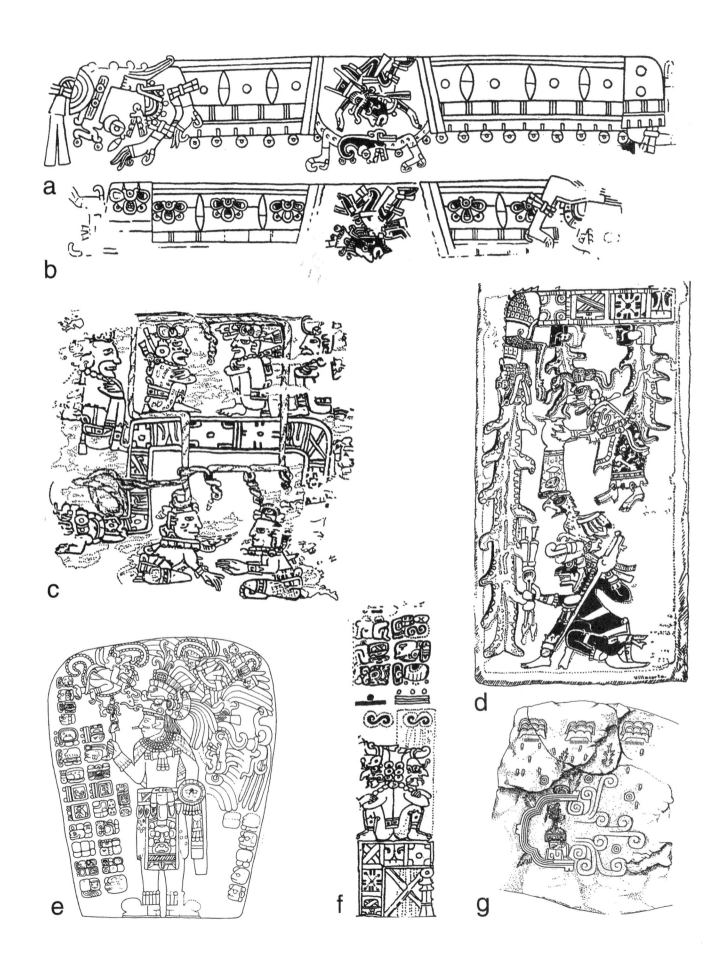

a

b

c

d

e

f

g

Postclassic image from the Dresden Codex shows the Cosmic Monster with reptile skin, a sky-band body, and deer feet (Fig. 7.4d). The monster is positioned at the top of the composition, like sky bands in Classic Maya art. In Classic period representations, Freidel, Schele, and Parker interpret the Cosmic Monster as the Milky Way monster, but they identify the sky band as the ecliptic bearing symbols of planets and constellations (Freidel et al. 1993:67, 422 n. 34). On the other hand, a number of scholars have suggested that the sky band is the Milky Way (Galindo 1994:103; Robertson 1985a:27). Both interpretations have an element of truth because the sky band refers to the place where the ecliptic crosses the Milky Way.

My study of the Paris Codex zodiac layout indicates that all the constellations suspended from the sky band are either on the Milky Way or at the edge of the Milky Way (Figs. 7.2a, 7.6; Table 7.1). The second group of constellations, suspended from a white band with zigzag lines (the ecliptical cord?), consists of constellations on the ecliptic that are not near the Milky Way. The image of the sky band as the place where the ecliptic crosses the Milky Way is confirmed by independent analysis of the Dresden Codex Venus pages, where the Sun, the Moon, and planets crossing the Milky Way are represented as gods on sky-band thrones (Chapter 5).

The Cosmic Monster with a sky-band body appears at the top of various stelae at Yaxchilán (Stelae 1, 4, 10; Figs. 3.8c, 4.2i; Tate 1992, fig. 130). Stela 1 represents the Cosmic Monster with the same head at either end of a sky-band body. Serpent bars held by Classic Maya rulers take a similar form. David Stuart (1984:15) suggests that these double-headed serpent bars may be images of the Milky Way. The Milky Way is clearly related to serpent imagery in contemporary Maya accounts (Chapter 1; Girard 1949:458). The Cosmic Monster incorporates serpent imagery, but it also seems to include other animals.

The Cosmic Monster has a variety of body forms, most often covered with reptile skin bearing a sky band or scrolls (cloud symbols), or more rarely net markings (Fig. 7.5a–e; Stone 1983:171–173). The net design could be stylized reptile skin or it may refer to an actual net, recalling a Maya myth that alludes to a net of fish transformed into the Milky Way (Chapter 1). If a watery context is implied, the allusion may be to the Milky Way as a celestial river or ocean, as seen in the Codex Vindobonensis (Fig. 5.4g). The Cosmic Monster overlaps in some sense with the Cauac Monster (Stone 1983:186). Cauac markings, like an inverted pyramid of beads, have been variously interpreted as a symbol of rain or storm (Thompson 1960:89), but more recent interpretations of the Cauac Monster suggest that he is the Witz Monster symbolizing the mountains (Stuart, cited in Fash 1992:92, figs. 4–5).

The Cosmic Monster on Copán Structure 22 is covered with cloud symbols, which are related to the cloudy aspect of the Milky Way (Fig. 7.5d). Two aged figures of the Pauahtuns (God N) hold the Cosmic Monster aloft. Its front head has a face with reptilian

---

FIGS. 7.4. *a–b:* Late Postclassic sky goddesses representing Milky Way with cleft opening for passage of central Mexican Venus god known as Quetzalcoatl (Codex Borgia 46; after Seler 1963).

c: Cosmic Monster sky-band body wrapped in sky rope representing ecliptical cord, with four aspects of God N seated above (Paris Codex 22; after Villacorta and Villacorta 1977).

d: Aged Moon Goddess and Venus as God L showered by water from front end of Cosmic Monster, symbolizing rainy season section of Milky Way (Dresden Codex 74; after Villacorta and Villacorta 1977).

e: Terminal Classic monument depicting ruler surrounded by "cloud-rider" deities passing through Milky Way at Katun ending 10.2.0.0.0 (8/11/869), when four planets were positioned in Milky Way (Jimbal Stela 1; after Schele and Freidel 1990, fig. 10.8a).

f: Twin Chacs sit back to back on sky-band throne beneath cloudlike scrolls probably symbolizing Milky Way (Dresden Codex 68a; after Villacorta and Villacorta 1977).

g: Preclassic ruler in cave opening holds ceremonial bar with S-shaped scroll that may symbolize Milky Way, while tiered cloud symbols above issue rain (Chalcatzingo Relief 1; after Coe 1968:93).

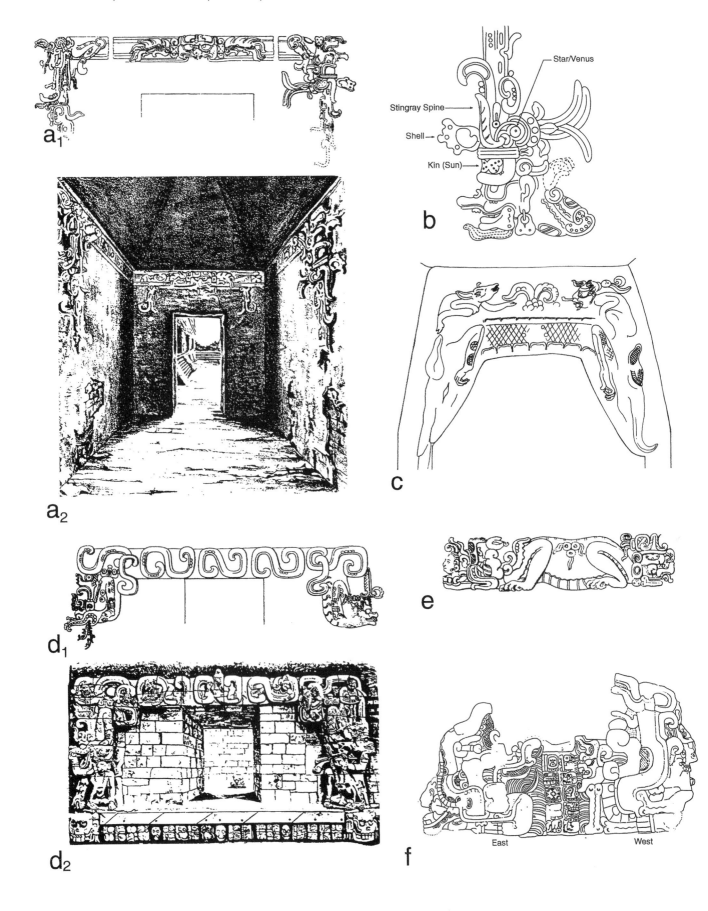

traits and may also have deer attributes, whereas the rear head depicts the Quadripartite God, including the Kin brow and a bloodletter (Stuart 1988, fig. 5.32). Seven supernatural figures along the body probably represent the Sun, the Moon, and five planets (Chapter 6). Such figures are described as "cloud-riders" by Proskouriakoff (1993:98, 185–187, 192). These S-shaped scrolls are usually described as clouds or smoke (Andrews and Fash 1992: 74; Reilly 1996). The scrolls have also been interpreted as blood (Stuart 1988). In my opinion they represent a cloudy aspect of the Milky Way. Star symbols interlace with two of the scrolls covering the body of the Cosmic Monster on Copán Structure 22.

Although an S-shaped scroll in a beaded frame (T632) has commonly been interpreted as a cloud, based on an image in the Dresden Codex that shows it as a source of rainfall (Fig. 7.4f), we cannot be sure that this is the only meaning for this symbol. The Cosmic Monster embodying an aspect of the Milky Way also seems to be a source of rainfall or celestial water (Figs. 5.7g, 7.5a). Furthermore, an Olmec petroglyph from the Preclassic epoch suggests that rain clouds and the S-shaped scroll were distinguished at an early time, for Chalcatzingo Relief 1 depicts a ruler holding a ceremonial bar bearing an S-shaped scroll, also on his throne, but the clouds issuing rain above are quite different in form (Fig. 7.4g). Here the ruler's ceremonial bar can be compared with the serpent bar that invokes Milky Way imagery in later times.

David Stuart and Stephen Houston (1994:44) identify T632 as the symbol for clouds (*muyal*), and they note that *muyal* often appears in celestial contexts. On the other hand, Stone (1992; 1996) identifies the *muyal* compound as a supernatural locale. The *muyal* place may be located on the Milky Way, and *muyal* itself seems to refer to the cloudiness of the Milky Way or to a cloudy place on the Milky Way.

In a broad study of Precolumbian imagery, Terence Grieder (1982:100–104, 126–128) links the S-shaped scroll to Scorpius. Another possibility is that it represents an S-shaped dark cloud in the Milky Way that runs from Canis Major to the Southern Cross, identified by the Quechua as the snake Machacuay (Urton 1981, fig. 33). This is the area of Canopus, an especially bright star that certainly would have attracted some attention (Aveni 1980: 108). The association with rainfall seen in the Dresden Codex can be explained by the fact that this dark cloud would be prominent at dusk at the onset of the rainy season. On the other hand, if the S-shaped design alludes to Scorpius, it could be associated with clouds and rainfall, because this star group is seen in the evening sky during the rainy season. Alternatively, the T632 scroll may be a more general reference to the cloudy aspect of the Milky Way.

Variations in body forms of the Cosmic Monster may allude to different parts of the Milky Way. Indeed, there may be an underworld-upperworld dichotomy in the imagery of the Cosmic Monster's body. Reptile body markings predominate on the

---

FIG. 7.5. a_1: Late Classic Cosmic Monster with sky-band body terminating in two heads that represent seasonal duality; a_2: monster frames doorway, giving view of northern sky (House E, Palace, Palenque; after Maudslay 1889–1902, 4, pl. 43).

b: Upside-down rear head of Cosmic Monster (here shown upright) with skeletal jaw, Kin brow, and headdress with shell, bloodletter, star symbol, and stream of blood; also known as Quadripartite Monster, this deity may allude to Sun crossing rift (underworld) section of Milky Way at winter solstice during dry season (House E, Palenque; after Robertson 1985a, fig. 89).

c: Reptile variant of Cosmic Monster frames east sub-

terranean doorway in House E (Palace, Palenque; after Robertson 1985a, fig. 115).

d_1: Cosmic Monster covered with cloud symbols; d_2: Cosmic Monster, supported by two aged figures of God N, carries seven deities in cloud volutes (Late Classic Structure 22, Copán; after Maudslay 1889–1902, 1, pl. 12).

e: Late Classic double-headed Cosmic Monster with skin and feet like crocodile (Altar 41 at Copán; after Maudslay 1889–1902, 1, pl. 114).

f: Double-headed Cosmic Monster with rear head in form of skeletal snake (Late Classic Altar G1 at Copán; after Schele 1987b).

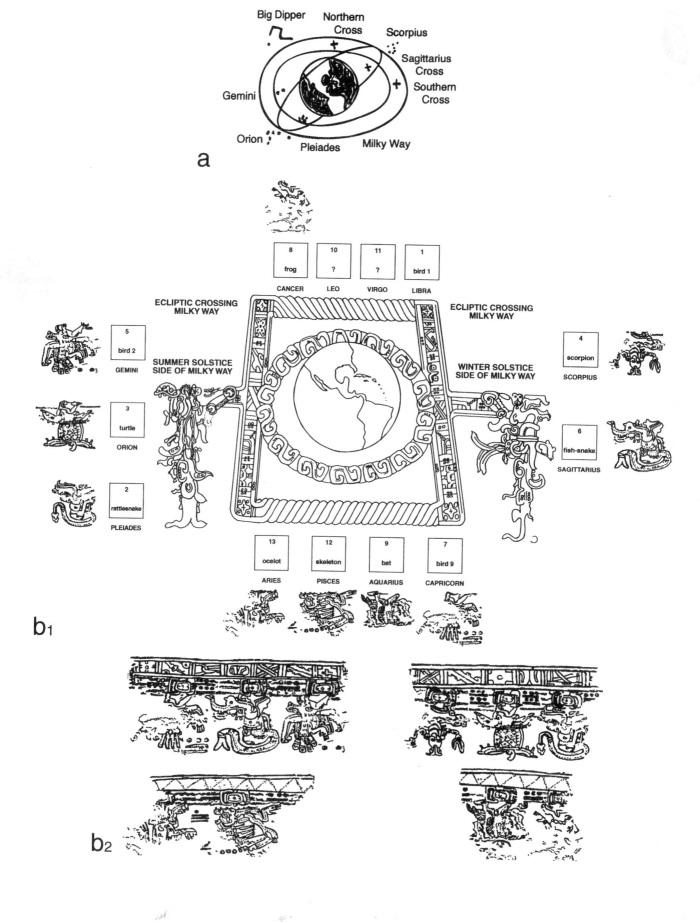

a

ECLIPTIC CROSSING MILKY WAY

ECLIPTIC CROSSING MILKY WAY

SUMMER SOLSTICE SIDE OF MILKY WAY

WINTER SOLSTICE SIDE OF MILKY WAY

8	10	11	1
frog	?	?	bird 1
CANCER	LEO	VIRGO	LIBRA

5
bird 2
GEMINI

3
turtle
ORION

2
rattlesnake
PLEIADES

4
scorpion
SCORPIUS

6
fish-snake
SAGITTARIUS

13	12	9	7
ocelot	skeleton	bat	bird 9
ARIES	PISCES	AQUARIUS	CAPRICORN

b₁

b₂

Cosmic Monsters framing the entries to subterranean passages of House E at Palenque (Fig. 7.5c; Robertson 1985a, fig. 109; Stone 1985:48). On the other hand, a Cosmic Monster with a sky-band body on House E frames a doorway that gives a clear view of the sky (Fig. 7.5a).

A deer ear on one head of the Cosmic Monster on House E is typical of the deer features associated with the front head (Fig. 5.7g). Such attributes may allude to a deer constellation (Hyades?) located on the Milky Way. The front head in House E has a heavy-lidded eye inset with the T510f star, evoking a link with "big eye," a Maya name for Venus (Chapter 5). Indeed, some scholars link the front head of the Cosmic Monster to Venus (Miller 1988:179–180; Schele and Miller 1986:45).

The sky-band body on House E wraps around to connect with an upside-down rear head marked with a Kin glyph (Fig. 7.5a–b). The front and rear heads seem to represent an opposition of sorts. There may also be a dichotomy in the liquids associated with the two heads on House E. In Merle Greene Robertson's reconstruction of the colors in a replica made for the Florida Museum of Natural History, the rear head issues a liquid from the brow that is predominantly red, whereas the front head disgorges a liquid that is predominantly blue, like the water flowing from the Cosmic Monster's mouth on Dresden Codex page 74 (Fig. 7.4d). As noted in Chapter 4, page 74 seems to show rainy-season imagery of the Moon, and the rain comes from the front head of the Cosmic Monster. The water flow may indicate that the front head is linked with the rainy-season side of the Milky Way.

The rear head of the Cosmic Monster represents the Quadripartite God, a skeletal god who carries a quadripartite badge: a shell, a bloodletter, a Kin symbol, and a fourth element usually including a tri-lobed design reminiscent of the pendants worn by GI and other planetary gods (Fig. 7.5b). The skeletal imagery of the rear head refers to the death and the resurrection of the Sun (Stone 1983:204). This is in accord with Schele's (1976:17) suggestion that the rear head may be linked with the Sun at the winter solstice. The monster has a death aspect seen in its skeletal jaw and in the Cimi sign associated with death that sometimes replaces the Kin sign. The Kin symbol may be the glyphic counterpart of T546, a Kin bowl that is sometimes interpreted as lak'in, the symbol of east (Chapter 3). The bloodletter in the headdress, a stingray spine, is sometimes replaced by a shark's tooth also used in bloodletting (Jones 1991). This symbol may allude to the shark-like Xoc monster evoking Sagittarius as a fish-snake in the zodiac of the Paris Codex. In my opinion, the Quadripartite God with its skeletal face and prominent solar glyph probably depicts the Sun in Sagittarius. The rear head seems to represent the place where the ecliptic crosses the Milky Way in the southern sky at the winter solstice. And here the Sun is reborn at dawn on the winter solstice, following the longest night of the year, when the Sun passes through the xibalba be section of the Milky Way. Perhaps this is why the quadripartite monster's Kin symbol apparently symbolizes the east.

Sometimes the rear head is replaced by a skeletal snake, as on Altar G1 at Copán (Fig. 7.5f; Schele 1987b). This serpent (Schele's White-Bone-Snake) represents Scorpius marking the Sun's position at the onset of the dry season in November, as noted earlier. Thus the rear head of the Cosmic Monster may be associated with Scorpius and Sagittarius, constellations that track the Sun's position from the beginning of the dry season through the winter solstice, when the Sun dies and is reborn after the longest night of the year (Fig. 7.6). Conversely, the constel-

FIG. 7.6. *a:* Ecliptic visualized as giant celestial ring crossing Milky Way at two places, creating two crossroads, probably linked with two crossroads in Popol Vuh.
b₁: Rear head of Cosmic Monster with Scorpius and Sagittarius, constellations that track Sun's position from beginning of dry season through winter solstice; front head with Pleiades, Orion, and Gemini, marking Sun's position at onset of rainy season through summer solstice; other constellations on or near ecliptic probably associated with imagery of ecliptical cord (drawing by Stacey Breheny); *b₂:* inset of actual arrangement of constellations in Paris Codex 23–24 (after Villacorta and Villacorta 1977).

lations associated with the position of the front head are the Pleiades and Orion, star groups that mark the Sun's position at the onset of the rainy season, and Gemini, which designates the Sun's northernmost position at the summer solstice. Venus may also be linked with the front head of the monster because that planet passing by the Pleiades is a sign of rain, and the northern extreme of Venus (reached only when it is in the northern section of the ecliptic) is associated with the onset of the rains (Chapter 5).

Lamanai Stela 9 depicts an Early Classic image of the Cosmic Monster's front head, here with deer antlers and a T510f star symbol on the creature's deer ear and another in its heavy-lidded eye (Stone 1983:198–200, fig. 128b). This is in accord with other images of the front head showing deer attributes and heavy-lidded eyes. The deer attributes call to mind the horned serpent in a Tzotzil account, apparently related to the Chicchan Serpent of the Chortí (Chapter 1). As noted earlier, the Chicchan Serpent of Yucatán may be linked with Venus, especially when it is in the northern sky crossing the Milky Way.

We can conclude that the Cosmic Monster is one of the main images of the Milky Way in both Classic and Postclassic times. During the Classic period, its two heads represent a form of opposition that seems to reflect seasonal duality. The reptilian front head probably represents the place where the Sun moves to the northern sky, crossing the Milky Way at the onset of the rains in May through June. The front head is closely associated with the northern Chicchan Serpent (a deer-serpent?), who brings rain perhaps associated with Venus in the northern sector of the Milky Way. The rear head, with its skeletal aspect, represents the Sun crossing the southern part of the Milky Way, when it passes through Scorpius at the beginning of the dry season and Sagittarius at the winter solstice. Here death imagery is appropriate because the vegetation dries up and the Sun descends to the underworld at the winter solstice, the longest night of the year. The rear head is usually represented by the Quadripartite God wearing a headdress that includes a bloodletter, sometimes a symbol of the Xoc monster that may embody Sagittarius as a fish-snake. Occasionally the rear head is accompanied by, or even replaced by, a skeletal snake, also known as the White-Bone-Snake. This figure seems to represent stars in Scorpius, marking the Sun's position at the onset of the dry season.

SERPENT FORMS OF THE MILKY WAY

Colonial period dictionaries of Yucatán may help to identify the serpent associated with the Cosmic Monster. One of the serpent names for the Milky Way, *tamacaz,* refers to the fer-de-lance, an extremely deadly pit viper (Coe 1975:27; Lamb 1981:245). Because of its yellow chin, the fer-de-lance is called *barba amarilla* (yellow beard) in Latin America. It is noteworthy that the Cosmic Monster sometimes has a beard, which suggests a link with the fer-de-lance (Figs. 5.7g, 7.5a–b).

The species of fer-de-lance still found in Quintana Roo, *Bothrops atrox,* is characterized by lattice markings on its body formed by a design of diamonds of dark against light. A relief-carved vessel from the National Museum of the American Indian depicts bearded serpents with fer-de-lance body markings (Pl. 21). Schele and Miller (1986:193–194, pls. 73, 73a) describe them as Vision Serpents invoked by hallucinations during a bloodletting rite, an interpretation that has been questioned because blood loss does not cause hallucinations (Stross and Kerr 1990). As I noted in the *Star Gods of the Ancient Americas* exhibit (1982), these serpents seem to be images of the Milky Way held by the Sun God (Pl. 21, far right). He wears a skeletal snake headdress that indicates his position in Scorpius, where the ecliptic crosses the underworld branch of the Milky Way known as *xibalba be* among the contemporary Quiché. One of the serpents has a skeletal zoomorph kneeling in front of a decapitated head (to far left, Pl. 21). The serpent's front head has a skeletal death god riding on its snout (Schele and Miller 1986, pl. 73a). The death associations of this serpent are appropriate to the underworld branch of the Milky Way in the southern sky, the left hand of the Sun in modern Maya cosmology. The other serpent, in the Sun's right hand, symbolizes the *saki be* or rainy-season half of the Milky Way. With this serpent, we see a turtle depicting stars in Orion.

Ceramic vessels also show other variations in imagery of the Cosmic Monster. A tripod plate depicts the Cosmic Monster wrapping around the edge, with the rear head bearing the insignia of the Quadripartite God (Schele and Miller 1986:312, pl. 122c). Here the Cosmic Monster arches over a serpent emerging from a cosmic plant sprouting from Chac's head. Perhaps this is the serpent aspect of Venus.

A scene on a painted vase depicts the bearded serpent rising out of a canoe infixed with the Kin glyph on the head of a long-lipped god (Coe 1982:91, no. 46). This long-lipped deity apparently is the rear head of the Cosmic Monster in a free-form style reserved for pottery painting. It conforms to Schele and Miller's (1986:44) description of the rear head of the Cosmic Monster as the "half-skeletal zoomorph with a sun-bowl on its forehead." The bearded serpent takes the place of the front head of the Cosmic Monster.

An incised vessel from the American Museum of Natural History depicts a serpent emerging above the front head of the Cosmic Monster, positioned in a stepped cleft opening (Fig. 4.10d₁). The Cosmic Monster has a crocodilian aspect and deer feet, but its eye form is similar to the serpent emerging from its jaws, which has eyes with half-closed lids and long lashes (deer eyes?). Ring-shaped designs on the serpent's body, interpreted as jade disks by Schele and Miller (1986:308), may in fact be stars, their luminous quality enhanced by shiny mirrors alongside. The serpent twines around the Moon Goddess, making her a "dragon lady," a scene frequently repeated in painted pottery (Chapter 4). A monkey planet and other planetary deities ride along the serpent's coiled body. The stepped cleft with Akbal zoomorphs is an opening to the underworld. Here we see the Sun God and two other gods climbing a tree. This tree may depict Sagittarius as a cross constellation at the intersection of the Milky Way and the ecliptic, marking the place where the Sun ascends at sunrise after the longest night of the year.

On the Protoclassic Hauberg Stela, probably dating to A.D. 199, a deified ruler or a god (GI?) appears with four climbers and three divers who trail blood from their severed bodies (Fig. 6.4c). The total of seven figures, among which we find the Sun and

Chac (Venus?), evokes the classical planets of antiquity, as noted in Chapter 6. A Wak Chan (6 Sky) title on the eyebrows of the serpent arching overhead names the sky serpent with a play on words, for Chan can mean both "sky" and "serpent." Schele (1992b:143) says the snake is the ecliptic, whereas she identifies the form framing the ruler as a tree representing the Milky Way. This element seems more like a stream of liquid, as we can see by comparing it with images such as the one on Dresden Codex 74 (Fig. 7.4d). As such it may embody the Milky Way as a stream of blood flowing from the severed bodies, recalling the blood stream associated with the rear head of the Cosmic Monster on Palenque's House E. The snake overhead may refer to the Milky Way in its serpent aspect, apparently closely linked with the front head of the Cosmic Monster. It is noteworthy that the snake is bearded, once again evoking the fer-de-lance aspect of the Milky Way. Its tail may carry an early form of the upside-down rear head of the Cosmic Monster.

In sum, contemporary and Colonial period Maya accounts refer to the Milky Way as a serpent, establishing a connection with the serpent imagery most often seen in the front head of the Cosmic Monster, but early forms of the monster may associate the serpent's tail with the rear head of the Cosmic Monster. The Cosmic Monster is characterized by a beard that seems to link him with imagery of the fer-de-lance—known as "yellow beard" in Mesoamerica—a serpent equated with the Milky Way.

FOUR ROADS IN THE SKY AND FOUR ITZAMNAS

The snake is not the only image of the Milky Way known from Colonial period accounts. The Popol Vuh describes the Milky Way as a road, recalling Aztec accounts. When the Hero Twins reached a crossroads in the underworld and chose the black road of Xibalba, they went along the *xibalba be*, or "underworld road," a branch of the Milky Way with a rift or cleft (from the Northern Cross south to Sagittarius); at the opposite side of the Milky Way we find the "white road" (*saki be*; Chapter 1). Dennis Tedlock (1985:111, 134, 334; 1991:172) points out that the crossroads is the point where the ecliptic crosses the rift or cleft in the Milky Way. Since there are actually two crossroads at different points in the narrative, I would suggest that a second crossroads is located at the opposite side of the sky (Fig. 7.6a). The two crossroads form four paths that intersect at opposite sides of the sky. The Popol Vuh says the roads are four different colors, providing a key to their nature. The white and black roads, actually two sides of the Milky Way, form a giant ring in the sky encircling the earth. The ecliptic is another giant celestial ring that crosses the Milky Way at two places, creating two crossroads. The red road is probably the Sun's path during the dry season, the epoch of warfare and bloodshed. The fourth road is green at one crossroads and yellow at the other. This seems to be the Sun's path during the rainy season. The green road symbolizes the road of newly green vegetation, whereas the yellow road is that of mature maize.

Just as there are four different colored roads, the creator god, Itzamna, has four aspects assigned to world colors and directions in the *Ritual of the Bacabs:* the red to the east, the white to the north, the black to the west, and the yellow to the south (Roys 1965:23 n. 23; Thompson 1970b:212). In my opinion, Itzamna's four bodies are equated with the four celestial roads of the Quiché coming together in the sky to enclose our world. The two crossroads mark the two heads of Itzamna, the intersection points of the Milky Way and the ecliptic. His white body probably refers to the rainy-season side of the Milky Way, just as his black body evokes the underworld side of the Milky Way linked with *xibalba be.*

Itzamna is translated as "iguana house" in the Vienna dictionary, but other Yucatec dictionaries suggest different translations. Alfredo Barrera Vásquez (1975:205) suggests that Itzamna means the "magician who has the knowledge of creative power," whereas Itzam-cab-aín means "magician who gives birth to life on earth." He translates *itzam* as "wizard of the water." The chronicler Lizana notes that Itzamna (Itzamat Ul) describes himself as the dew and the sustenance of the sky and clouds (cited in Thompson 1970b:211). Contemporary Yucatec accounts say that *itz* refers to liquids excreted drop by drop, such as resin, tears, milk, semen, and candle

wax (Sosa 1985:435). Apparently, the essence of Itzamna (*itz*) was visualized as liquid drops or dew in the sky—an image completely appropriate to the Milky Way. This notion is preserved among the Jacalteca Maya, who call the Milky Way the "dew road" (La Farge and Byers 1931:130).

Yucatec Maya lore also describes a white road that may be an image of the rainy-season side of the Milky Way. According to the Kusansum legend, in a previous world age the *sacbe* (white road) was a cord filled with blood that stretched across the sky from Tulum and Cobá to Chichén Itzá and Uxmal. Arthur Miller (1982:92–95) links this mythical cord to the imagery of a twined cord in the murals at Tulum (Fig. 3.3b). Chapter 3 demonstrated that twined cords represent the ecliptic. The serpent heads on the Tulum cords add another dimension, for they form double-headed serpents with twined-cord bodies, not unlike those on a black-background vase of the Classic period (Fig. 3.3c). These evoke the intertwined paths of the Sun, the Moon, and the planets. The serpent-cords wrap around the composition, enclosing the celestial figures in sacred space. The same notion of enclosure is evident in the imagery of the god Itzamna.

Piedras Negras accession monuments show the Cosmic Monster with its sky-band body wrapping around the enthroned ruler, who is positioned near the top of the monument. These niche-figure stelae refer to world creation and the agricultural and astronomical cycles (Stone 1989:155; Taube 1988b). The footprint path below the ruler suggests a possible link with the Milky Way as a road or path in the sky.

Many scholars link the Classic period double-headed serpent with Itzamna. According to Michael Coe (1978b:28; 1982:91), the Bearded Dragon is the serpent guise of Itzamna, who takes a double-headed form when represented as the ceremonial bar held by Maya rulers. Sharer (1994:530) notes that the Milky Way is depicted as a two-headed serpent that is probably another manifestation of Itzamna, whose body represents the Milky Way or the sky. In many contexts, the double-headed serpent represents the front head of the Cosmic Monster in duplicate form.

Thompson (1970b:212–214, fig. 4; 1973:58–59) proposes that the Cosmic Monster is the Classic period counterpart of Itzamna. He interprets Itzamna as a double-headed creature representing a section drawing of the monster, whose body had four sides forming Itzamna. He notes that Itzamna is a being with four bodies, each occupying a quarter of the sky. He suggests that by joining two of the four Itzamnas together rear to rear, Maya artists developed the two-headed monster now generally referred to as the Cosmic Monster. I would add that the two heads of the Classic Maya Cosmic Monster are the crossroads in the sky where the ecliptic crosses the Milky Way (Fig. 7.6b).

According to Thompson (1970b:209–233), Itzamna was the creator and the chief god in Yucatán, and he came close to incorporating most of the other major gods in his various aspects. His main roles are reflected in his many names, among which we find Itzamna Kinich Ahau (a solar aspect) and Itzamna Cab (an earth aspect). Thompson proposes that Bolon Dzacab, a name for God K, is a manifestation of the vegetal aspect of Itzamna associated with images of sprouting maize, whereas God D is Itzamna in his role as a creator god. Schele (1992b:125) sees Itzamna's divine dew manifested in God D. Taube (1989a:9) identifies Itzamna as an earth caiman (Itzam Cab Ain in the chronicles) and a manifestation of God D, without resolving the problem of how this identification relates to God D's zoological alter ego—the Principal Bird Deity. The face of the Principal Bird Deity is represented on the sky band forming the back of the Cosmic Monster over the doorway in House E at Palenque (Fig. 7.5a). In Postclassic codices, God D appears in the jaws of the Cosmic Monster, as on Dresden Codex 4b–5b (Thompson 1970b:228–229, fig. 4b). But God D is only one of a number of deities associated with Itzamna. I would suggest that God D, the Sun God, and God K become aspects of Itzamna when they are located in the Milky Way. The Cosmic Monster–Itzamna carries celestial gods in his mouth because he is carrying the Sun, the Moon, and the planets as they cross the Milky Way.

The earth aspect of Itzamna may relate to the position of the Milky Way below the horizon or, more specifically, to the region of the Milky Way linked with the celestial hearthstones. The *Ritual of the Bacabs* gives an incantation for opening the hearth (*pib*), telling Itzam Cab to open his mouth as the earth is removed for the fire (Roys 1965:49–50). The text says that Itzam Cab has the hearthstones as his head, a blazing fire as his tongue, and the firewood as his thighs, and he stands erect over the hearth fire of the house (Thompson 1970:230). This may be explained by the fact that the hearthstone stars of Orion are located on the head of Itzamna, associated with the front head of the Cosmic Monster in Classic times. He stands erect over the hearth fire because the stars of Orion are positioned close to the zenith in the Maya area.

Other stellar references link Itzamna to constellations on the Milky Way. The Chilam Balam of Chumayel mentions Itzam Tzab, an image that links the Pleiades with Itzamna. The text notes that Itzam Tzab is Itzamna's face during the Katun 13 Ahau, a time of hunger due to locusts (Roys 1967:134).

We can conclude that the Itzamna of the chronicles has a quadripartite body. The four colored bodies of Itzamna relate to the four celestial roads in Quiché accounts. The image of four roads in the Popol Vuh reveals a cosmic diagram describing the intersecting paths of the ecliptic and the Milky Way. In Maya art, this translates into zoomorphic imagery, with a double-headed Cosmic Monster being the counterpart of Itzamna. Itzamna's celestial dew is the substance of clouds that are the essence of the Milky Way. Different aspects of Itzamna in the chronicles seem to reflect a relationship with the Sun, the Moon, and the planets, perhaps symbolizing when these bodies were seen in the Milky Way. Important star groups located where the ecliptic crosses the Milky Way are also mentioned in relation to Itzamna.

CLASSIC PERIOD MONUMENTS WITH IMAGES OF THE MILKY WAY

We can now turn to Classic Maya monuments that depict celestial ancestors and deities passing through the Milky Way. The images of gods in the jaws of the Cosmic Monster are so common that they would require a separate study to see if they do in fact bear dates that signal an astronomical body passing through the Milky Way. Setting these aside at this time, we turn to the cloud riders, an image that may refer to positioning in the Milky Way. In some cases, it is difficult to distinguish deities amid the clouds from apotheosized ancestors. Patricia McAnany (1995b:44–46) describes images of ancestors wreathed in clouds from Ucanal and Jimbal, but these cloud riders are identified as deities by David Stuart (1984:11). In any case, we should bear in mind that clouds and the substance of the Milky Way may be interchangeable in some contexts, especially in the imagery of rulers ascending to the heavens to take on attributes of the gods.

On Jimbal Stela 1, two cloud riders appear amidst scrolls with beaded borders (Fig. 7.4e). Although Stuart (1984:11–12; 1988:203) refers to these as the Jaguar God and the Fish God, the details of their facial features are by no means clear. Even though the Sun and Moon were not passing through the Milky Way, on the Katun ending recorded on this monument (10.2.0.0.0; 8/11/869), all the planets were crossing the Milky Way except for Mercury, which was invisible in conjunction with the Sun and the Moon in Leo. Thus we have no shortage of planetary gods in the Milky Way. Furthermore, Jupiter and Saturn were in conjunction in Sagittarius, and both planets were in retrograde motion, with Jupiter precisely at its second stationary point (8/10/869; Meeus n.d.).

The Paddler Twins, mentioned as celebrants of the new cycle at the creation some five thousand years ago on Ixlu Stela 2, are represented floating amid S-shaped scrolls (Fig. 4.3b; Stuart 1984:11–13). This monument bears a Katun-ending date (10.1.0.0.0; 11/24/849) that correlates with a number of astronomical events, including Jupiter and Saturn both approaching their second stationary points, the Evening Star near its maximum altitude, and the Pleiades crossing overhead at midnight. David Stuart (1988) describes the solar deity as the Fish God. It is noteworthy that on this date the Sun was in the Milky Way entering Sagittarius, the constellation that would later mark the position of the Sun at the winter solstice, when it reached its southernmost position crossing the Milky Way. Perhaps

the Fish God wears a fish-bone bloodletter because he is linked with a fish-snake constellation (shark?) in Sagittarius, known as Xoc among the Classic Maya. As noted in Chapter 4, the Jaguar God and the Fish God appear as the Paddler Twins on monuments bearing dates that coincide with times when either the Sun or the Moon was crossing the Milky Way. In the imagery of the Paddlers, the Milky Way is a celestial river that carries the Paddlers across the sky.

Schele (1992b:153) suggests that the number six attached to an S-shaped scroll (T632) recorded in Tomb 12 at Río Azul refers to the ruler's burial place at "six-raised-up-cloudy-sky." Stuart and Houston (1994:44) interpret the inscription wak kaan muyal nal as the terrestrial location of Tomb 12. Stone (1992) describes it as a celestial locale. In my opinion, it refers to the Milky Way or, more specifically, to a location in the xibalba be section of the Milky Way. In any case, its context in a burial is interesting in light of imagery discussed above that suggests that deceased rulers travel through the Milky Way.

Quiriguá Monument 7 (Zoomorph G) may represent the deceased ruler's connection with the Milky Way. Claude-François Baudez (1988:140) identifies the imagery as the accession of Sky Xul on 9.17.14.16.18, one of the latest dates recorded on the monument. On the other hand, Stone (1983:90) identifies both sides of the zoomorph as posthumous portraits of Cauac Sky, carved after his death on 9.17.14.13.0, a date also on the monument. Another date records an Initial Series date of 9.17.15.0.0 (10/31/785), and Stone (1992) points out that the Paddler Twins celebrated this period ending at a celestial place called wak muyal (6 cloud), a supernatural locale associated with deceased rulers at both Quiriguá and Río Azul. The wak muyal compound may appear in the funerary text as a reference to the Milky Way, the place where the dead king ascended after death. It is noteworthy that the Sun reached the rift of the Milky Way, entering Scorpius, at the time the Paddler Twins celebrated the period-ending rites. Jupiter was visible at dusk in Scorpius, and Venus was near its maximum altitude in Sagittarius.

On Quiriguá Monument 23, Chac dances amid beaded scrolls beside a T-shaped Cauac opening that evokes a connection with the cleft passages through the Milky Way in central Mexican codices (Fig. 5.10c). The beaded scrolls suggest a correspondence with the cloud riders. A similar image appears on Quiriguá Monument 24 (Baudez 1988, fig. 12). If Chac is Venus, as suggested in Chapter 5, it is significant that each of the two monuments records an Initial Series date that corresponds to a time when Venus was crossing the Milky Way, if we consider Libra as the edge of the Milky Way. Baudez (1988:143–144) says that Monuments 23 and 24 show a dead ruler, and it is possible that both monuments show the resurrection or apotheosis of a dead ruler here in the guise of Chac as Venus crossing the Milky Way.

Kan Xul's apotheosis event on the Dumbarton Oaks Relief Panel 2, dated to 9 Manik 5 Muan (9.14.11.2.7; 11/18/722), corresponds to a time when Venus was just above the eastern horizon in Scorpius (Fig. 5.10d; Chapter 5). Apparently, the dead ruler in the guise of Chac represented Venus about to disappear in superior conjunction. His planet Venus was located in Scorpius, a constellation associated with the underworld branch of the Milky Way. The ruler's shell diadem could represent the curve of stars in Scorpius.

On the Sarcophagus Lid, the jaws framing Pacal embody stars in Scorpius, and the tree represents the Southern Cross, both star groups in the southern section of the Milky Way, the *xibalba be* (Pl. 10). The Southern Cross tree grows from the rear head of the Cosmic Monster (the Quadripartite God), marking the southernmost point of the ecliptic crossing the Milky Way. At the time of his apotheosis on 8/26/683, Pacal seems to have taken a trip on the Milky Way. The phrase "he entered the road," associated with Pacal's apotheosis, evokes his travel along the underworld road of the Milky Way road to reach Jupiter at its first stationary point (Chapter 6). Pacal's journey to apotheosis may be reconstructed as follows: When the Milky Way rift opened like a maw into the underworld at dusk, he passed to the rear head of the Cosmic Monster and on through the jaws of the Scorpius serpent. From here he moved to ascend the Southern Cross. Then, as the Southern Cross disappeared below the horizon, the *saki be*, or

"white road," of the Milky Way rose overhead at dawn. Apparently, Pacal traveled along the underworld branch of the Milky Way to reach the other side of the sky, where he joined his planet Jupiter at its first stationary point, located precisely in conjunction with the Pleiades overhead at dawn.

Milky Way imagery that appears on Copán Stela I depicts the apotheosized ruler in the guise of GI, with the skeletal rear head of the Cosmic Monster as a headdress (Fig. 5.10j; Baudez 1985:37; Proskouriakoff 1993:58–59). An inscription with 10 Ahau is partially destroyed, but it is worth noting that Venus was in the Milky Way or on its edge on both 10 Ahau dates proposed by Proskouriakoff (8/22/627 and 9/3/659). If the second date is correct, the monument could refer to the apotheosized ruler as Venus-GI in the Milky Way. On the second date, Venus and Saturn were in conjunction in Libra on the edge of the underworld section of the Milky Way. The Quadripartite God headdress suggests that Venus was positioned in the underworld section of the Milky Way. Perhaps the ruler took the form of Venus when it crossed the Milky Way in the region known as *xibalba be*.

As noted in Chapter 4, Copán Stela H portrays a royal person who seems to embody the full Moon of the maize harvest, either a royal woman or the ruler 18 Rabbit (Baudez 1994, figs. 22–24). The ruler may embody the Moon deity merged with the Maize God wearing a netted skirt. An inscription referring to the date 4 Ahau 18 Muan (9.14.19.5.0; 11/29/730) marks a time when the full Moon was crossing the Milky Way in Orion. Although the imagery does not seem to represent apotheosis, unless perhaps the ruler's mother is represented, the figure is at the center of the cosmos, surrounded by images of the Cosmic Monster. The individual holds a serpent bar with skeletal snake heads, representing Scorpius at the southern side of the Milky Way. The royal backrack has a skeletal face with a Kin sign on the brow and a stingray-spine bloodletter, elements referring to the Quadripartite God, symbolizing the southernmost intersection point of the Milky Way and the ecliptic. The date on the monument marks the time when the Sun was entering Sagittarius, located in the underworld branch of the Milky Way. The Principal Bird Deity (God D's bird) perching on the bloodletter may also be an astronomical deity. Preliminary study indicates that Venus may be represented by this bird deity, essentially a bird with snake attributes, just as Quetzalcoatl is a snake with bird attributes. The Venus association is reinforced by the fact that Venus was crossing the Milky Way in Sagittarius on the recorded date.

On Tikal Stela 5, the ruler's backrack has a skeletal face in a Kin cartouche that may represent the Sun in the month of the winter solstice (Jones 1977, fig. 13). The fragmentary Calendar Round date, reconstructed as 3 Lamat 6 Pax (9.15.3.6.8; 12/6/734), refers to a time when the Sun was in Sagittarius. The skeletal face is a symbol associated with the Sun's position at the winter solstice, when it descends to the underworld in Sagittarius on the longest night of the year. Skeletal snakes surrounding the Kin cartouche probably represent Scorpius, the star group adjacent to Sagittarius in the southern sector of the Milky Way.

We can conclude that a number of Classic period monuments record dates that place the Sun, the Moon, and the planets in the Milky Way. The cloud riders may allude to any of these celestial bodies crossing in the Milky Way. A favored time for the apotheosis of dead rulers was when one of the planets was positioned on the Milky Way. This type of imagery is most often linked with the southern extreme of the ecliptic where it crosses the Milky Way in the region of Sagittarius and Scorpius. The living ruler may also appear with imagery of the Milky Way, placing the ruler at the center of the cosmos.

ROTATING THE MILKY WAY

When the Sun enters the Milky Way, the seasons change; and when the Sun starts to move out of the Milky Way, the solstices occur. The Sun reaches the Milky Way in May at the beginning of the Mesoamerican rainy season. At this point, the Sun is in zenith position around the time it moves into conjunction with the Pleiades in Taurus. Then the Sun passes to the next constellation, where Gemini marks the Sun's position at the summer solstice in June, and the Sun reaches its northern extreme on the ecliptic. At this time the Sun exits the Milky Way and travels around to the opposite side of the sky, where the ecliptic again crosses the Milky Way. Now the Sun is in conjunction with Scorpius at the onset of the dry season in November. Passing through the Milky Way, the Sun reaches Sagittarius at the winter solstice in December at the southern extreme of the ecliptic.

In interpreting the relationship of Maya images to these seasonal configurations of the Milky Way, we must bear in mind that the observation time is important in defining the configuration, for the Milky Way can rotate dramatically during the course of one night. On the other hand, The Milky Way gradually changes position when observed at the same time of night over the course of the year.

In terms of the Mesoamerican seasons, there seem to be four important seasonal orientations. The Milky Way arches overhead running southeast to northwest at dusk in March, around the spring equinox (Fig. 7.7a). This type of configuration, placing the hearthstone stars of Orion overhead, can be seen at different times of night from October through April, making it a sign of the dry season. Around the summer solstice in June, the Milky Way surrounds the horizon like a cosmic ocean at dusk (Fig. 7.7b). Such a configuration can be seen at different times of night from mid-January through mid-June, bridging the transition into the rainy season. Around the fall equinox, the Milky Way arches overhead from northeast to southwest at dusk, with the dark rift in the Milky Way running overhead and down to the

---

FIG. 7.7. *A:* Night sky seen from latitudes 30°, 20°, and 10° N; dry-season aspect of Milky Way at dusk near spring equinox arches overhead from southeast to northwest; same position seen at different times of night from October to April (after Rey 1976:100).

B: Night sky seen from latitudes 30°, 20°, and 10° N; Milky Way surrounds horizon like cosmic ocean at dusk near summer solstice in June; same position seen at different times of night from January to June, moving from dry season to rainy season (after Rey 1976:100).

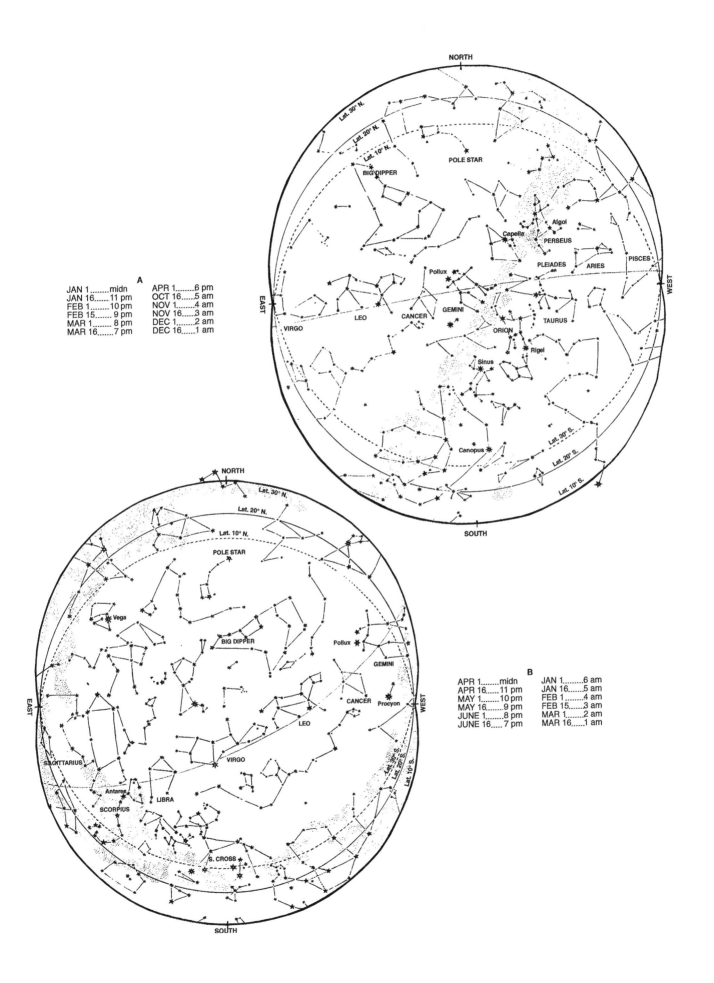

A

JAN 1 ....midn	APR 1 ....6 pm
JAN 16 ......11 pm	OCT 16 ......5 am
FEB 1 ....10 pm	NOV 1 ....4 am
FEB 15 ......9 pm	NOV 16 ......3 am
MAR 1 ....8 pm	DEC 1 ....2 am
MAR 16 ......7 pm	DEC 16 ......1 am

B

APR 1 ....midn	JAN 1 ....6 am
APR 16 ......11 pm	JAN 16 ......5 am
MAY 1 ....10 pm	FEB 1 ....4 am
MAY 16 ......9 pm	FEB 15 ......3 am
JUNE 1 ....8 pm	MAR 1 ....2 am
JUNE 16 ......7 pm	MAR 16 ......1 am

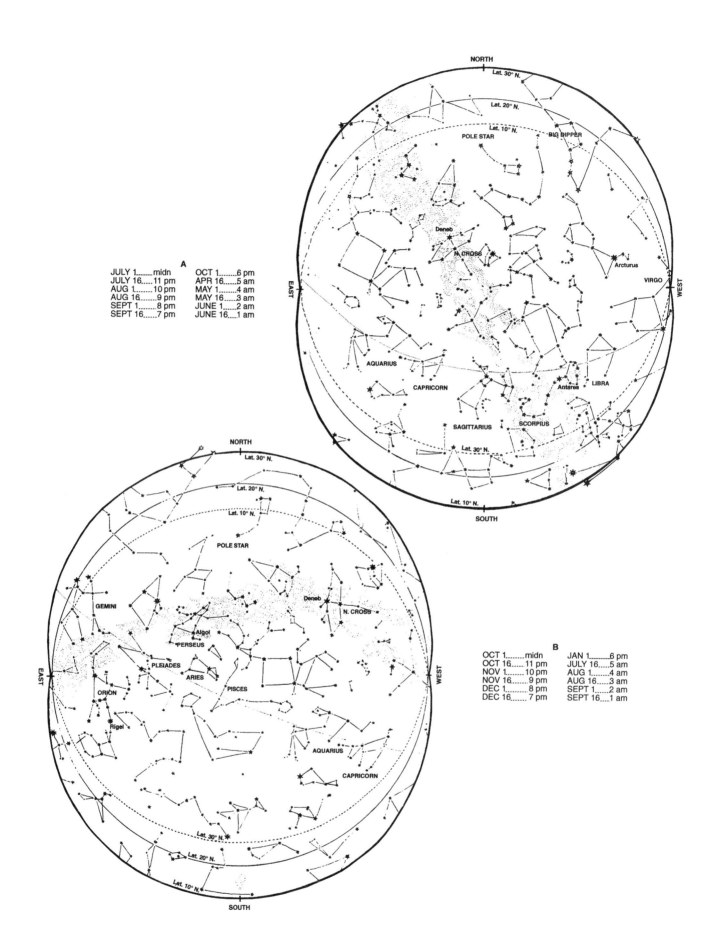

NORTH

Lat. 30° N.

Lat. 20° N.

Lat. 10° N.

POLE STAR

BIG DIPPER

A

JULY 1........midn	OCT 1........6 pm
JULY 16.....11 pm	APR 16.....5 am
AUG 1........10 pm	MAY 1........4 am
AUG 16.......9 pm	MAY 16.......3 am
SEPT 1.......8 pm	JUNE 1.......2 am
SEPT 16......7 pm	JUNE 16.....1 am

Deneb

N. CROSS

Arcturus

EAST

VIRGO

WEST

AQUARIUS

CAPRICORN

Antares

LIBRA

SAGITTARIUS

SCORPIUS

Lat. 30° N.

Lat. 10° N.

SOUTH

NORTH

Lat. 30° N.

Lat. 20° N.

Lat. 10° N.

POLE STAR

GEMINI

Deneb

N. CROSS

Algol

PERSEUS

PLEIADES

ARIES

PISCES

B

OCT 1.........midn	JAN 1.........6 pm
OCT 16......11 pm	JULY 16.....5 am
NOV 1.......10 pm	AUG 1........4 am
NOV 16.......9 pm	AUG 16.......3 am
DEC 1.........8 pm	SEPT 1.......2 am
DEC 16........7 pm	SEPT 16.....1 am

EAST

WEST

ORION

Rigel

AQUARIUS

CAPRICORN

Lat. 30° N.

Lat. 20° N.

Lat. 10° N.

SOUTH

southern horizon (Fig. 7.8a). This type of sky is seen at different times of night from April to October, coinciding with the rainy season. Several months later, around the winter solstice, the Milky Way arches over the sky in an east-west configuration at dusk, and the rift has moved from the overhead position to the western horizon (Fig. 7.8b). This type of sky can be seen at different times of night from July to January, bridging the transition from wet to dry.

Schele (1992b:135–136) says that we see the Cosmic Monster aspect of the Milky Way (east-west) at dusk during winter, a conclusion that is supported by the analysis presented here. Imagery associated with the east-west position of the Milky Way at dusk on the winter solstice may be linked with the death of the Sun, seen especially in representations of the Cosmic Monster's rear head marking the rift in the underworld branch of the Milky Way (Fig. 7.8b Pl. 10). The gap in the Milky Way makes it look almost like a monster with a mouth positioned to the west. The Sun passes through the rift on the longest night of the year. On the following day at dawn, when the Sun reappears, the Milky Way has changed position dramatically, resembling a cosmic ocean surrounding the horizon, an image of renewal. Now the rift opening is to the east (Fig. 7.7b).

Schele (1992b:131–132) hypothesizes that the southeast-to-northwest configuration of the Milky Way represents a tree associated with the image of the Milky Way at sunset around the summer solstice. This idea was probably inspired by Eva Hunt's (1977:205) notion that the Milky Way is an *axis mundi* that can be compared with tree trunks, umbilical lines, rivers, and roads. More recently, Freidel and Schele (1995:134) document a Lacandón account that says that the roots of the tree are in the Milky Way south of Scorpius. I would add that this is the area where we find a celestial tree incorporat-

ing stars in Sagittarius, and further to the south we see another tree in the Southern Cross, described as a sacred ceiba by the Lacandón. Clearly there are celestial trees with their roots on the Milky Way, but Schele's notion that the Milky Way itself is a tree seems untenable. The tree stands "up" only if you consider it in relation to modern sky maps that show north as up, and the top of the tree is actually quite low on the horizon (Tedlock 1995:119). The celestial trees on the Milky Way may hold up the sky, but trees were not responsible for raising the Milky Way, nor do we find trees representing the Milky Way in accounts describing the creation of the Milky Way in central Mexican sources discussed earlier.

In sum, the rotation of the Milky Way was clearly important in Maya iconography. Different seasonal configurations were certainly recognized, but we have yet to determine what observation time was used, a detail that is crucial to such interpretations. The Cosmic Monster is best seen in the east-west position of the Milky Way seen at dusk, when the rift-mouth of the monster is on the western horizon as the Sun sets into the underworld on the winter solstice. Future research may help to define images of the Milky Way as a cosmic ocean, a position that makes the Milky Way seem to surround the horizon. If dusk was the observation time, this could allude to the rainy season, when the Milky Way and its liquid descend to the earth. The association, however, would be with the dry season if the observation time was at dawn.

THE MAYA IN THE HISTORY OF WORLD ASTRONOMY

Maya images of the Milky Way as a celestial river and a sky serpent may reflect ancient archetypes, for

FIG. 7.8. *A:* Night sky seen from latitudes 30°, 20°, and 10° N; Milky Way arches overhead from northeast to southwest at dusk near fall equinox, with dark rift in Milky Way running overhead and down to southern horizon; same position visible at different times of night from April to October during rainy season (after Rey 1976:101).

B: Night sky seen from latitudes 30°, 20°, and 10° N; Milky Way arches over sky in east-west configuration at dusk on winter solstice, with rift above western horizon; same position seen at different times of night from July to January, bridging transition from wet to dry (after Rey 1976:101).

such images are quite widespread across the world. Among the Quechua of South America, such images are particularly well developed; there the Milky Way is a celestial river that circulates the waters of the cosmos (Urton 1981). The association of the Milky Way with the dead is also common. Edward Krupp (1993) notes that among the Lapps, the Milky Way is the road for the dead leaving earth, and similar images are found in the transformational notions in Siberia, where the Milky Way is a path of migrating birds whose departure is compared to the soul's departure from Earth. Indeed, the link between the Milky Way and the realm of death is so widespread that it may have been part of the traditions brought over during the Pleistocene migrations.

Like the people of classical Greece and early Renaissance Europe, the Maya visualized an earth-centered universe with celestial heroes traveling from the sky to the underworld. The Popol Vuh is an astronomical legend like the classical Greek myths that account for the location of constellations and relate the adventures of astronomical gods representing the Sun, the Moon, and the planets. In a curious overlap, the planet Jupiter is a god linked with rulers and the weather in both cultures. Jupiter is the planet of kings in both cultures; however, among the Maya, Jupiter was not king of the sky but rather one of three brothers who formed a celestial triad with the Sun and the Morning Star. And although the Maya pictured God K with an axe that may symbolize thunder, rainfall was apparently controlled by Chac, a god who may represent Venus.

Other similarities in the ancient astronomies are due to independent invention resulting from observing similar patterns in the sky. The Maya discovered the *octaeteris,* an eight-year period of Venus events meshed with ninety-nine lunar months, a cycle also known in classical Greece and Mesopotamia. And like the Greeks of classical times, the Maya apparently also recognized the metonic cycle, which indicates that these cycles were developed independently in the New World as a result of direct observation (Krupp 1995:72). Like the Old World astronomers, Maya starwatchers studied positional astronomy to track the position of the Sun, the Moon, and the planets in the background of stars. They also prac-

ticed horizon astronomy, tracking the horizon extremes of these celestial bodies, a form of observation that requires fixed observation points, usually involving monumental architecture.

The scholars of earlier generations noted that the Classic Maya were fascinated by calendrics and astronomy. We now know that they were recording the histories of lineages and rulers, but history seems to be integrated with observation of astronomical events. This is not surprising because astronomy and political events are inextricably linked in many ancient civilizations, especially those of Mesopotamia and China. Indeed, recent research suggests that changes in dynasties in ancient China were timed by planetary conjunctions (Pankenier 1997).

David Kelley (1960; 1972; 1974:136–342; 1976: 92) sees a resemblance between the Mesoamerican and Eurasian concepts of time and astronomy. He links the Mesoamerican cycle of the Lords of the Night to the Hindu planetary week of nine days that refers to five planets, the Sun, the Moon, and two invisible planets believed to cause eclipses. Other parallels include the organization of time into four world ages associated with different colors, and the idea of cyclical destructions of the world. Kelley also notes a link between the Mesoamerican calendar and the Hindu lunar mansions that track the position of the Moon amid the stars. Transpacific contacts are one way of explaining such similarities. More likely, a similar worldview developed because both cultures are located in tropical latitudes, where there is a marked contrast between the rainy and dry seasons, and the seasons are similarly linked to the positions of certain stars.

The seasonal associations of specific constellations could have been maintained for almost two thousand years by shifting from an observation of dawn rise in Preclassic times to a dusk-set observation in the Postclassic period. There is evidence for both dawn-rise and dusk-set observations in the Postclassic period. A constellation's position in opposition was also important, rising at dusk and setting at dawn, as seen in the Aztec New Fire Ceremony, which focuses on the longest visibility of the Pleiades, a ritual that may also be represented among the Maya of Yucatán during the Terminal Classic period.

The system is in place today among the Quiché, who identify individual constellations as "signs of the night" when they are visible for the longest period during the dry season. Constellations in opposition to the Sun also mark the location of the full Moon, which suggests comparison with the lunar mansions of Asia. The Paris Codex zodiac seems to be based on both dawn rise and dawn set observations.

Although there are few demonstrable overlaps in terms of star terminology of the Chinese lunar mansions, the most intriguing is the twentieth lunar mansion (*tsui*), which is a turtle star in Orion (Needham 1959, table 24). Indeed, worship of certain constellations may be so ancient that they date back to the time of Asian migrations to the New World. Grieder (1982:100–104, 126–128) argues that worship of Scorpius in the Americas and in Asia pertains to a very ancient stratum of beliefs apparent in the Shang Dynasty dating as far back as 3100 B.C. The Pleiades and Scorpius may be among the first star groups to be used in calendars of the New World. Their roles as seasonal markers in Mesoamerica are mirrored in the central Andes, but the seasonal associations are reversed (Dearborn and White 1982: 252; Urton 1981).

Given the imagery of quadripartite space in Mesoamerican cosmology, it is interesting to note that the Chinese also divided the sky into quarters. They distributed the lunar mansions among four star animals ranging all the way around the equatorial circle:

the blue dragon of the east (including Spica in Virgo and stars of Scorpius), the vermilion bird of the south, the white tiger of the west (including Taurus and Orion), and the black tortoise of the north, which includes stars in Capricorn (Needham 1959: 242). The blue dragon represents spring, when the stars in Scorpius and Virgo were visible for the longest period of time. The ancient association of the dragon with spring continues today in the Chinese New Year celebration, when the dragon is paraded through the streets. This colorful pageant probably originated as a dramatization of events involving stars of the Spring Dragon, spanning one quarter of the heavens. In Han times, the full Moon rose in between the two horns of the Spring Dragon during the festivities for the new year, hence the oft-repeated image of the dragon and its pearl—the Moon (Needham 1959:252, fig. 95, table 24).

We are only beginning to understand the role of astronomy in Maya imagery. Through iconographic studies focusing on astronomy, decipherment of Maya hieroglyphs, and study of traditions preserved by the Maya today, it may be possible to recognize a wealth of seasonal images and rituals dating back to the Classic Maya period. Such studies will add a missing piece of the puzzle in world history, allowing us to compare images of the universe across the globe, and someday we will recognize Maya images every bit as colorful as the Chinese Spring Dragon and its lunar pearl.

APPENDIX 1

GUIDE TO ASTRONOMICAL IDENTITIES

Cosmic Monster: Milky Way with heads at crossing points of ecliptic

God A': Male Moon?

God B (Chac): Venus?

God C: Monkey planet

God CH: Male Moon

God E: Maize God linked with Moon and possibly also Venus

God G: Sun

God H: Counterpart to central Mexican Venus god Quetzalcoatl

God K: Jupiter

God L: Venus (especially in dry season?)

God S (1 Ahau): Solar god linked with Morning Star; also called Hun Ahau

Goddess I: Waxing Moon and full Moon

Goddess O with human features: Waning Moon

Goddess O with monstrous features: New Moon

Headband Twins: Solar and lunar pair represented with headbands

Hero Twins: Hunahpu and Xbalanque, who became the Sun and the Moon in the Popol Vuh

Howler Monkey: Venus as Morning Star (especially in dry season?)

Itzamna: Sky surrounding Earth, featuring four paths formed by Milky Way and ecliptic

Jaguar War God: God of Number Seven, also known as Jaguar God of the Underworld, associated with dry-season Moon and Venus

Junajpu: Morning Star among modern Quiché (counterpart of Hunahpu)

Lahun Chan: Venus as Morning Star (especially in rainy season?)

Mars Beast: Mars as a deer monster

Muan bird: Stars in Gemini

Palenque Triad: GI is Venus, GII is Jupiter, GIII is underworld Sun

Quadripartite God: Southern point where ecliptic crosses Milky Way

Rattlesnake: Pleiades and possibly also Perseus

Skeletal snake (White-Bone-Snake): Stars in Scorpius

Three Hearthstones: Three stars in Orion

Turtle: Orion's Belt

Water-lily Jaguar: Rainy-season Moon

Xoc or Fish-snake: Stars in Sagittarius

Xbalanque: Lunar twin in Popol Vuh

Yax Balam: Precolumbian counterpart to Xbalanque representing lunar twin

APPENDIX 2

TABLE OF CLASSIC PERIOD DATES, MONUMENTS, AND ASSOCIATED ASTRONOMICAL EVENTS

LONG COUNT	IS	JULIAN DATE	GREGORIAN DATE	JULIAN DAY NUMBER	SITE
1.6.14.11.2 1 Ik 10 Tzec		8/12/2587 B.C.	7/22/2587 B.C.	776745	Palenque
8.17.1.4.12 11 Eb 15 Mac	IS	1/13/378	1/14/378	1859135	Tikal
8.19.10.10.17 5 Caban 15 Yaxkin		9/3/426	9/4/426	1876900	Copán
9.0.10.0.0 7 Ahau 3 Yax	IS	10/16/445	10/17/445	1883883	Tikal
9.0.15.11.0 12 Ahau 13 Pop ?		4/28/451	4/29/451	1885903	Tikal
9.7.17.12.14 11 Ix 14 Zotz	IS	5/17/591	5/19/591	1937057	La Esperanza
9.8.9.15.11 7 Chuen 4 Zotz		5/11/603	5/14/603	1941434	Bonampak
9.9.0.0.0 3 Ahau 3 Zotz	IS	5/7/613	5/10/613	1945083	Copán
9.9.10.0.0 2 Ahau 13 Pop		3/16/623	3/19/623	1948683	Copán
9.9.18.16.3 7 Akbal 16 Muan		12/22/631	12/25/631	1951886	Caracol
9.10.8.9.3 9 Akbal 6 Xul		6/12/641	6/15/641	1955346	Palenque
9.11.0.0.0 12 Ahau 8 Ceh		10/9/652	10/12/652	1959483	Dumbarton Oaks
9.11.0.0.0 12 Ahau 8 Ceh		10/9/652	10/12/652	1959483	Palenque
9.12.3.14.0 5 Ahau 8 Uo	IS	3/17/676	3/20/676	1968043	Copán
9.12.9.8.1 5 Imix 4 Mac		10/18/681	10/21/681	1970084	Yaxchilán
9.12.10.0.0 9 Ahau 18 Zotz	IS	5/5/682	5/8/682	1970283	Copán

MONUMENT	TARGET EVENTS
Temple of the Sun	819-day station
Ball-court marker	Moon in Sagittarius crossing Milky Way; Sun in Capricorn
Altar Q	Maximum altitude of Morning Star; full Moon setting in west; heliacal rise of Mars in Virgo; Mercury and Jupiter near Mars
Stela 31	Jupiter in retrograde; new Moon; Venus as Morning Star near maximum brilliance; heliacal set of Mars
Stela 1	Jupiter, Saturn, and Mars in Virgo in east; Venus as Evening Star making first appearance in Taurus in west; Saturn in retrograde; Jupiter approaching second stationary point
Ballplayer Relief	End of the dry season; date linked with seasonal transition
Lintel 4, Structure 6	Saturn in retrograde
Stela 7	Venus at maximum altitude as Evening Star; Moon in Libra; Sun in Taurus crossing Milky Way
Stela P	Waxing Moon in Cancer close to Milky Way; Morning Star in Aquarius
Stela 3	First appearance of the Evening Star
Cross Group: Heir-Designation Date	Saturn within two weeks of first stationary point; Mars and Jupiter in conjunction; Jupiter's departure from second stationary point; sunset rise of Deneb in Northern Cross
Relief Panel 2	Five days after appearance of Venus as Evening Star; first visible crescent Moon; Mars just above western horizon
Temple of the Inscriptions	Five days after appearance of Venus as Evening Star; first visible crescent Moon; Mars above western horizon
Stela I	Venus high in sky as Morning Star; Sun at vernal equinox
Lintel 25	Jupiter's second stationary point; first crescent Moon; Venus high in sky as Evening Star passing Antares in Scorpius; Mars at first stationary point
Stela 6	Venus ends retrograde as Morning Star

LONG COUNT	IS	JULIAN DATE	GREGORIAN DATE	JULIAN DAY NUMBER	SITE
9.12.11.5.18 6 Etz'nab 11 Yax		8/26/683	8/29/683	1970761	Palenque
9.12.11.12.10 8 Oc 3 Kayab		1/5/684	1/8/684	1970893	Palenque
9.12.16.2.2 1 Ik 10 Tzec		5/15/688	6/18/688	1972485	Palenque
9.12.18.5.16 2 Cib 14 Mol		7/18/690	7/21/690	1973279	Palenque
9.12.19.12.9 1 Muluc 2 Muan		11/23/691	11/26/691	1973772	Tikal
9.12.19.14.12 5 Eb 5 Kayab		1/5/692	1/8/692	1973815	Palenque
9.13.0.0.0 8 Ahau 8 Uo		3/13/692	3/16/692	1973883	Copán
9.13.3.7.18 11 Etz'nab 11 Chen		8/3/695	8/6/695	1975121	Tikal
9.13.3.9.18 12 Etz'nab 11 Zac		9/12/695	9/15/695	1975161	Tikal
9.13.10.8.16 1 Cib 14 Mol		7/15/702	7/19/702	1977659	Palenque
9.13.13.15.0 9 Ahau 3 Kankin		10/31/705	11/4/705	1978863	Palenque
9.13.14.4.2 8 Ik 0 Zip	IS	3/22/706	3/26/706	1979005	Naranjo
9.13.15.0.0 13 Ahau 18 Pax ?		12/25/706	12/29/706	1979283	Naranjo
9.13.16.10.13 1 Ben 1 Chen		7/20/708	7/24/708	1979856	Yaxchilán
9.13.17.12.10 8 Oc 13 Yax		8/21/709	8/25/709	1980253	Yaxchilán
9.13.17.15.12 5 Eb 15 Mac		10/22/709	10/26/709	1980315	Yaxchilán
9.13.17.15.13 6 Ben 16 Mac		10/23/709	10/27/709	1980316	Yaxchilán
9.13.17.15.13 6 Ben 16 Mac		10/23/709	10/27/709	1980316	Yaxchilán
9.14.0.0.0 6 Ahau 13 Muan		11/29/711	12/3/711	1981083	Copán
9.14.0.0.0 6 Ahau 13 Muan		11/29/711	12/3/711	1981083	Tikal
9.14.0.0.0 6 Ahau 13 Muan		11/29/711	12/3/711	1981083	Dos Pilas
9.14.5.3.14 8 Ix 2 Cumku		1/15/717	1/19/717	1982957	Dos Pilas
9.14.9.10.13 1 Ben 16 Tzec		5/13/721	5/17/721	1984536	Dos Pilas
9.14.10.4.0 7 Ahau 3 Kayab		12/26/721	12/30/721	1984763	Dos Pilas

MONUMENT	TARGET EVENTS
Temple of the Inscriptions, Sarcophagus Lid	Jupiter at first stationary point, in conjunction with Pleiades
Cross Group: Accession Date	Jupiter departs from second stationary point, close to Pleiades; Mars in retrograde; dawn rise of Mercury; Venus near maximum altitude as Morning Star in Scorpius; dawn rise of Deneb
Temple of the Inscriptions	819-day station; Jupiter and Mars pulling away from conjunction and moving forward after retrogrades; Saturn in retrograde
Cross group	Jupiter and Saturn aligned at second stationary point
Altar 5	Last visible crescent Moon joins the Morning Star at the onset of the dry season
Cross Group	Heliacal rise of Jupiter; Venus near maximum altitude as Morning Star
Stela 6	Moon in Scorpius crossing Milky Way; all five naked-eye planets visible; proximity to spring equinox
Temple I, Lintel 3	Saturn in retrograde
Temple I, Lintel 3	Jupiter at first stationary point; Saturn at second stationary point
Temple of the Inscriptions	Jupiter at second stationary point
Temple XIV	Moon passing Jupiter departing from second stationary point; Saturn in retrograde near Pleiades; Venus in Sagittarius crossing Milky Way
Stela 21	Venus in retrograde; waxing crescent Moon and Saturn in conjunction; Evening Star and Mars in conjunction
Stela 21	Last visibility of Morning Star following winter solstice; one day after full Moon
Lintel 30	819-day station spaced 397 days from 9.13.17.12.10, a close approximation of Jupiter's synodic cycle; Jupiter in Gemini; Moon passing Saturn in Gemini; Venus about to disappear as Morning Star
Lintel 30	Venus, Jupiter, and Saturn in conjunction in Cancer; Mars at midpoint of retrograde
Lintel 24	Jupiter and Saturn in conjunction; both approximately at first stationary points
Lintel 32	Jupiter and Saturn in conjunction; both approximately at first stationary points
Lintel 53	Jupiter and Saturn in conjunction; both approximately at first stationary points
Stela C	Four days before appearance of Venus as Evening Star in Sagittarius; full Moon in Taurus crossing Milky Way; Saturn at first stationary point; Sun in Scorpius crossing Milky Way
Stela 16	Four days before appearance of Venus as Evening Star in Sagittarius; full Moon in Taurus crossing Milky Way; Saturn at first stationary point; Sun in Scorpius crossing Milky Way
Stela 14	Four days before appearance of Venus as Evening Star in Sagittarius; full Moon in Taurus crossing Milky Way; Saturn at first stationary point; Sun in Scorpius crossing Milky Way
Stela 14	Proximity to first stationary point of Saturn
Stela 15	Saturn in retrograde
Stela 15	Jupiter in retrograde

LONG COUNT	IS	JULIAN DATE	GREGORIAN DATE	JULIAN DAY NUMBER	SITE
9.14.11.2.7 9 Manik 5 Muan		11/18/722	11/22/722	1985090	Dumbarton Oaks
9.14.14.13.16 5 Cib 14 Yaxkin ?	IS	6/19/726	6/23/726	1986399	Yaxchilán
9.14.17.15.11 2 Chuen 14 Mol ?		7/8/729	7/12/729	1987514	Yaxchilán
9.14.17.15.11 2 Chuen 14 Mol		7/8/729	7/12/729	1987514	Yaxchilán
9.14.19.5.0 4 Ahau 18 Muan		11/29/730	12/3/730	1988023	Copán
9.14.19.5.0 4 Ahau 18 Muan		11/29/730	12/3/730	1988023	Copán
9.14.19.8.0 12 Ahau 18 Cumku	IS	1/28/731	2/1/731	1988083	Copán
9.15.1.6.3 6 Akbal 11 Pax		12/11/732	12/15/732	1988766	Dumbarton Oaks
9.15.2.7.1 7 Imix 4 Kayab		12/24/733	12/28/733	1989144	Dumbarton Oaks
9.15.3.6.8 3 Lamat 6 Pax ?		12/6/734	12/10/734	1989491	Tikal
9.15.4.6.4 8 Kan 17 Muan		11/27/735	12/1/735	1989847	Aguateca
9.15.10.0.0 3 Ahau 3 Mol		6/24/741	6/28/741	1991883	Tikal
9.15.10.0.0 3 Ahau 3 Mol		6/24/741	6/28/741	1991883	Tikal
9.15.10.0.1 4 Imix 4 Mol		6/25/741	6/29/741	1991884	Yaxchilán
9.15.12.2.2 11 Ik 15 Chen		7/26/743	7/30/743	1992645	Tikal
9.15.12.2.3 12 Akbal 16 Chen		7/27/743	7/31/743	1992646	Tikal
9.15.12.11.13 7 Ben 1 Pop		2/2/744	2/6/744	1992836	Tikal
9.15.13.0.0 4 Ahau 8 Yaxkin ?		6/8/744	6/12/744	1992963	Tikal
9.15.13.6.9 3 Muluc 17 Mac		10/15/744	10/19/744	1993092	Yaxchilán
9.15.15.0.0 9 Ahau 18 Xul		5/29/746	6/2/746	1993683	Yaxchilán
9.15.15.2.3 13 Akbal 1 Chen		7/11/746	7/15/746	1993726	Tikal
9.15.15.12.16 5 Cib 9 Pop ?		2/9/747	2/13/747	1993939	Copán
9.15.15.14.0 3 Ahau 13 Uo		3/5/747	3/9/747	1993963	Tikal
9.15.19.1.1 1 Imix 19 Xul		5/29/750	6/2/750	1995144	Yaxchilán
9.16.0.0.0 2 Ahau 13 Tzec		5/3/751	5/7/751	1995483	Tikal
9.16.1.0.0 11 Ahau 8 Tzec	IS	4/27/752	5/1/752	1995843	Yaxchilán

MONUMENT	TARGET EVENTS
Relief Panel 2	Venus as Morning Star (in Scorpius) about to disappear in conjunction
Lintel 26, front edge	Rainy-season Moon; lunar eclipse
Stela 18	Jupiter and Saturn aligned; both at first stationary points; Pleiades overhead at dawn
Structure 44, Step I	Jupiter and Saturn aligned; both at first stationary points; Pleiades overhead at dawn
Stela H	Sun entering Sagittarius in Milky Way; last day of visibility of Venus as Morning Star; full Moon crossing Milky Way in Orion
Stela A	Sun entering Sagittarius in Milky Way; last day of visibility of Venus as Morning Star; full Moon crossing Milky Way in Orion
Stela A	Venus reappears as Evening Star; Scorpius overhead at dawn; full Moon
Panel 1	Saturn at second stationary point; Mars just past first stationary point; midpoint of Jupiter's retrograde
Panel 1	378 days later, Saturn at second stationary point again
Stela 5	Saturn in retrograde; Venus at greatest brilliance as Evening Star; approximates first stationary point of Jupiter; last quarter Moon; Sun crossing Milky Way in Sagittarius
Stela 2	Heliacal rise of Venus as Evening Star; onset of dry season; first quarter Moon
Temple IV, Lintel 2	Approximates first stationary point of Jupiter
Temple IV, Lintel 3	Approximates first stationary point of Jupiter
Lintel 39	Approximates first stationary point of Jupiter
Temple IV, Lintel 3	Jupiter in Taurus crossing Milky Way; Mercury at maximum elongation; may be associated with solar eclipse one day previous
Temple IV, Lintel 3	Jupiter in Taurus crossing Milky Way; may be associated with solar eclipse two days previous
Temple IV, Lintel 2	Saturn in retrograde; approximates full Moon; approximates second stationary point of Jupiter; Jupiter in Taurus crossing Milky Way; Mars and Jupiter in proximity
Stela 5	Jupiter in conjunction with Sun; last quarter Moon; Saturn departs from second stationary point
Structure 33, Step VII	Approximates first stationary point of Jupiter; Jupiter in Gemini
Stela 11, front	First stationary point of Jupiter; Moon passing; Jupiter and Mars in conjunction; Saturn in retrograde
Temple IV, Lintel 3	Jupiter in Taurus crossing Milky Way
Structure 11, East Door	Five days after first appearance of Venus as Evening Star
Temple IV, Lintel 2	Jupiter and Saturn in retrograde
Stela 11, rear side, facing Structure 40	Venus as Evening Star in Gemini crossing Milky Way; Saturn in retrograde; Jupiter at midpoint of retrograde
Stela 20	First stationary point of Jupiter; Saturn in retrograde; Venus as Morning Star near maximum altitude; a few days after heliacal rise of Mars
Lintel 1	Approximates first stationary point of Jupiter; Mars in retrograde

LONG COUNT	IS	JULIAN DATE	GREGORIAN DATE	JULIAN DAY NUMBER	SITE
9.16.1.0.0 11 Ahau 8 Tzec	IS	4/27/752	5/1/752	1995843	Yaxchilán
9.16.8.16.10 1 Oc 18 Pop ?		2/14/760	2/19/760	1998693	Yaxchilán
9.16.10.0.0 1 Ahau 3 Zip	IS	3/11/761	3/15/761	1999083	Yaxchilán
9.16.13.0.0 2 Ahau 8 Uo		2/24/764	2/28/764	2000163	Yaxchilán
9.16.15.0.0 7 Ahau 18 Pop	IS	2/13/766	2/17/766	2000883	Quiriguá
9.16.15.0.0 7 Ahau 18 Pop		2/13/766	2/17/766	2000883	Yaxchilán
9.16.15.0.0 7 Ahau 18 Pop ?		2/13/766	2/17/766	2000883	Yaxchilán
9.16.17.16.4 11 Kan 12 Kayab		12/23/768	12/27/768	2001927	Tikal
9.17.0.0.0 13 Ahau 18 Cumku		1/18/771	1/22/771	2002683	Tikal
9.17.0.0.0 13 Ahau 18 Cumku	IS	1/18/771	1/22/771	2002683	Quiriguá
9.17.0.0.0 13 Ahau 18 Cumku		1/18/771	1/22/771	2002683	Naj Tunich
9.17.5.0.0 6 Ahau 13 Kayab		12/23/775	12/27/775	2004483	Yaxchilán
9.17.5.8.9 6 Muluc 17 Yaxkin		6/9/776	6/13/776	2004652	Bonampak
9.17.10.0.0 12 Ahau 8 Pax ?	IS	11/26/780	11/30/780	2006283	Bonampak
9.17.14.16.18 9 Etz'nab 1 Kankin	IS	10/9/785	10/13/785	2008061	Quiriguá
9.17.15.0.0 5 Ahau 3 Muan		10/31/785	11/4/785	2008083	Quiriguá
9.17.15.0.0 5 Ahau 3 Muan		10/31/785	11/4/785	2008083	Bonampak
9.17.15.0.0 5 Ahau 3 Muan		10/31/785	11/4/785	2008083	Quiriguá
9.17.19.13.16 5 Cib 14 Chen		7/13/790	7/17/790	2009799	Santa Elena Poco Uinic
9.18.0.3.4 10 Kan 2 Kayab		12/8/790	12/12/790	2009947	Bonampak
9.18.1.2.0 8 Ahau 13 Muan		11/9/791	11/13/791	2010283	Bonampak
9.18.1.15.5 13 Chicchan 13 Yax ?		7/31/792	8/4/792	2010548	Bonampak
9.18.5.0.0 4 Ahau 13 Ceh	IS	9/9/795	9/13/795	2011683	Quiriguá
9.18.17.13.10 5 Oc 18 Zotz ?		4/3/808	4/7/808	2016273	Yaxchilán
9.19.10.0.0 8 Ahau 8 Xul		4/30/820	5/4/820	2020683	Copán

MONUMENT	TARGET EVENTS
Stela 11	Approximates first stationary point of Jupiter; Mars in retrograde
Stela 1	819-day station; two weeks after Jupiter's first stationary point; last quarter Moon
Stela 1	Dry-season new Moon; two weeks after first stationary point of Jupiter
Lintel 31	Saturn in conjunction with Pleiades overhead at dusk
Monument 4 (Stela D)	Disappearance of Moon and Morning Star in conjunction; approximates second stationary point of Jupiter
Lintel 52	Disappearance of Moon and Morning Star in conjunction; approximates second stationary point of Jupiter
Stela 10	Disappearance of Moon and Morning Star in conjunction; approximates second stationary point of Jupiter
Stela 22	Venus in Scorpius
Stela 22	Jupiter and Saturn in retrograde
Monument 5 (Stela E)	Jupiter and Saturn in retrograde; possible record of solar eclipse if 584,285 correlation used
Cave Painting	Jupiter and Saturn in retrograde
Stela 4	Waning dry-season Moon; Venus newly emerged as Evening Star
Stela 2	Mars and Venus in conjunction; maximum altitude of Venus as Evening Star; first stationary point of Jupiter; second stationary point of Saturn; approximates dawn rise of Pleiades
Stela 1	Jupiter in retrograde; Saturn in conjunction with Sun
Monument 23 (Altar of Zoomorph O)	Second stationary point of Saturn; first crescent Moon; Jupiter and Venus in conjunction in Scorpius
Monument 23 (Altar of Zoomorph O)	Approximate midnight zenith of Pleiades; Venus near maximum altitude in Sagittarius crossing Milky Way at dusk; Sun in Scorpius; Jupiter crossing Milky Way
Stela 3	Approximate midnight zenith of Pleiades; Venus near maximum altitude in Sagittarius crossing Milky Way at dusk; Sun in Scorpius; Jupiter crossing Milky Way
Monument 7 (Zoomorph G)	Approximate midnight zenith of Pleiades; Venus near maximum altitude in Sagittarius crossing Milky Way at dusk; Sun in Scorpius; Jupiter crossing Milky Way
Stela 3	Coincides with total eclipse (7/16/790), but only if 584,286 correlation used
Room 1 (Structure 1)	First stationary point of Venus as Evening Star
Room 1 (Structure 1)	First appearance of Venus as Evening Star
Room 2 (Structure 1)	Venus in inferior conjunction; close to second solar zenith at Bonampak
Monument 24 (Altar of Zoomorph P)	Venus as Evening Star in conjunction with Mars in Libra at edge of Milky Way
Lintel 10	Approximate last visibility at dusk of Pleiades; Jupiter in retrograde
Stela 11	Jupiter at approximate midpoint of retrograde, in conjunction with full Moon

LONG COUNT	IS	JULIAN DATE	GREGORIAN DATE	JULIAN DAY NUMBER	SITE
10.1.0.0.0 5 Ahau 3 Kayab		11/24/849	11/28/849	2031483	Ixlu
10.1.0.0.0 5 Ahau 3 Kayab ?		11/24/849	11/28/849	2031483	Yaxchilán
10.2.0.0.0 3 Ahau 3 Ceh		8/11/869	8/15/869	2038683	Jimbal
10.2.12.1.8 9 Lamat 11 Yax		7/7/881	7/11/881	2043031	Chichén Itzá

MONUMENT	TARGET EVENTS
Stela 2	Sun crossing Milky Way in Scorpius; waxing Moon in Aquarius; Venus as Evening Star near maximum altitude; Pleiades overhead at midnight; Jupiter and Saturn approaching second stationary points
Stela 18	Sun crossing Milky Way in Scorpius; waxing Moon in Aquarius; Venus as Evening Star near maximum altitude; Pleiades overhead at midnight; Jupiter and Saturn approaching second stationary points
Stela 1	New Moon; Saturn in retrograde; Jupiter at second stationary point; all planets in Milky Way except Mercury; Mercury in conjunction with Sun and Moon in Leo
Temple of the Four Lintels	Ball game held nine days before the second solar zenith; Jupiter in retrograde; Mars in conjunction; waxing quarter Moon

APPENDIX 3

TABLE FOR CALCULATING THE TZOLKIN INTERVALS

DAY #	1	2	3	4	5	6
BASE #						
1	Imix	Ik	Akbal	Kan	Chicchan	Cimi
14	Ix	Men	Cib	Caban	Etznab	Cauac
27	Manik	Lamat	Muluc	Oc	Chuen	Eb
40	Ahau	Imix	Ik	Akbal	Kan	Chicchan
53	Ben	Ix	Men	Cib	Caban	Etznab
66	Cimi	Manik	Lamat	Muluc	Oc	Chuen
79	Cauac	Ahau	Imix	Ik	Akbal	Kan
92	Eb	Ben	Ix	Men	Cib	Caban
105	Chicchan	Cimi	Manik	Lamat	Muluc	Oc
118	Etznab	Cauac	Ahau	Imix	Ik	Akbal
131	Chuen	Eb	Ben	Ix	Men	Cib
144	Kan	Chicchan	Cimi	Manik	Lamat	Muluc
157	Caban	Etznab	Cauac	Ahau	Imix	Ik
170	Oc	Chuen	Eb	Ben	Ix	Men
183	Akbal	Kan	Chicchan	Cimi	Manik	Lamat
196	Cib	Caban	Etznab	Cauac	Ahau	Imix
209	Muluc	Oc	Chuen	Eb	Ben	Ix
222	Ik	Akbal	Kan	Chicchan	Cimi	Manik
235	Men	Cib	Caban	Etznab	Cauac	Ahau
248	Lamat	Muluc	Oc	Chuen	Eb	Ben

Instructions:

To find the number of the day, add the row number to the column base number.

> For example, 4 Manik is day number 144 + 4 = 148.

To get the interval between two days, subtract the earlier day from the later one.

> For example, the number of days separating 6 Men (day #176) from 4 Manik is 176 − 148 = 28 days.

If the later day has a lower number than the earlier one, then the result will be negative. In this case, add 260 to the negative result to get the interval.

> For example, there are 148 − 176 + 260 = 232 days from 6 Men to 4 Manik.

7	8	9	10	11	12	13
Manik	Lamat	Muluc	Oc	Chuen	Eb	Ben
Ahau	Imix	Ik	Akbal	Kan	Chicchan	Cimi
Ben	Ix	Men	Cib	Caban	Etznab	Cauac
Cimi	Manik	Lamat	Muluc	Oc	Chuen	Eb
Cauac	Ahau	Imix	Ik	Akbal	Kan	Chicchan
Eb	Ben	Ix	Men	Cib	Caban	Etznab
Chicchan	Cimi	Manik	Lamat	Muluc	Oc	Chuen
Etznab	Cauac	Ahau	Imix	Ik	Akbal	Kan
Chuen	Eb	Ben	Ix	Men	Cib	Caban
Kan	Chicchan	Cimi	Manik	Lamat	Muluc	Oc
Caban	Etznab	Cauac	Ahau	Imix	Ik	Akbal
Oc	Chuen	Eb	Ben	Ix	Men	Cib
Akbal	Kan	Chicchan	Cimi	Manik	Lamat	Muluc
Cib	Caban	Etznab	Cauac	Ahau	Imix	Ik
Muluc	Oc	Chuen	Eb	Ben	Ix	Men
Ik	Akbal	Kan	Chicchan	Cimi	Manik	Lamat
Men	Cib	Caban	Etznab	Cauac	Ahau	Imix
Lamat	Muluc	Oc	Chuen	Eb	Ben	Ix
Imix	Ik	Akbal	Kan	Chicchan	Cimi	Manik
Ix	Men	Cib	Caban	Etznab	Cauac	Ahau

GLOSSARY

(Based on Aveni 1980:98–100, Ortiz 1997, and other sources)

Annular eclipse: Eclipse of the sun in which a ring of sunlight is visible around the new moon, because the moon is too distant from the earth to completely cover the sun.

Azimuth: Angular distance measured from a zero point at true north moving in an easterly direction for 360° along the horizon, measured to a specific horizon position of the sun, the moon, or a planet or to the base of a star's vertical circle.

Celestial equator: Great circle in the sky that is located 90° from both the north and south celestial poles. This circle is the celestial counterpart of the terrestrial equator.

Celestial longitude: Position of the sun, moon, or an individual planet when measured along the ecliptic in degrees counting from a zero point at the vernal equinox.

Conjunction: Position of two or more celestial bodies close to one another (usually within 2° of celestial longitude). When the Sun is involved in a conjunction event, the other celestial body cannot be seen. The Moon disappears for up to 3 days when in conjunction with the Sun. For the superior planets, the mean disappearance intervals are 25 days for Saturn, 32 days for Jupiter, and 120 days for Mars. On the other hand, the inferior planets exhibit two periods of conjunction (inferior and superior conjunction). The exact midpoint of the disappearance interval is conjunction, but the term is often used more generally to refer to the entire period of invisibility.

Declination: Angular distance measured from the celestial equator to a star along the star's hour circle, measured in positive degrees to the north of the equator and negative to the south, like latitude on a terrestrial map.

Draconic month: Interval between successive passages of the moon by a given node in its orbit; 27.21222 days.

Eclipse year: Interval between successive passages of the sun by the same node of the lunar orbit (346.62 days), also known as the draconitic year. One-half of the eclipse year (173.31 days) is the eclipse half-year, the time it takes for the sun to move from one node to another (ascending node to descending node or vice versa; see Fig. 2.2a).

Ecliptic: Apparent seasonal path of the sun through the background of stars along a plane angled at 23½° relative to the celestial equator. This angle has changed very slightly from about 22° to a little over 24° over the course of a cycle that repeats every 41,000 years. Currently the angle is diminishing, and it is expected to begin increasing in about 15,000 years.

Elongation: Angular distance between the sun and the moon or the sun and a planet.

Ephemeris: Table that lists the position of a celestial body at different times.

Equinox: Point on the celestial sphere at which the sun crosses the celestial equator in its apparent annual motion. The spring or vernal equinox is when the sun crosses the equator moving north around March 21; the autumnal equinox is when it moves from north to south around September 21. Actual date varies by a day or two depending on the leap year cycle.

Heliacal rise: Day a planet or star reappears after a period of invisibility in conjunction with the sun, usually at dawn.

Heliacal set: Day a planet or star is last visible before conjunction with the sun, usually at dusk.

Hour circles: Great circles passing through the celestial poles, dividing up the sky into sections like an orange.

Inferior conjunction: Configuration of a planet in which it is obscured by passage in front of the Sun. This only occurs for inferior planets, which circle between the Sun and Earth in their orbits. Mean inferior conjunction intervals for the two inferior planets are three days for Mercury and eight days for Venus.

Lunar standstill: See Regression of nodes.

Lunation: One full synodic period of the moon, comprising one lunar month of 29.530588 days.

Maximum elongation: Greatest angular distance of a planet or the moon from the sun, most often of interest in reference to the position of an inferior planet.

Meridian: Great circle that passes through the zenith and the north and south celestial poles.

Metonic cycle: Period of 6939.6 days (about nineteen years) that returns the full moon to the same date in the calendar year.

Nadir: See Zenith.

Nodes: Points of intersection of the plane of the moon's orbit around the earth and the 23½° plane of the earth's orbit around the sun, known as the plane of the ecliptic (see Fig. 2.1b).

Occultation: Eclipse of a star or planet by the moon or another planet.

Opposition: Configuration of a body when it is opposite the sun, at 180° elongation, so that it rises at dusk and is seen overhead at midnight, when the earth is positioned between that body and the sun.

Precession: Slow conical motion of the earth's axis of rotation about the poles of the ecliptic, resulting in a motion of the celestial poles among the stars in a cycle of approximately 26,000 years.

Regression of nodes: Westward (backward) movement of the nodes (of the lunar orbit) along the ecliptic, one cycle being completed in 18.61 years. Lunar standstills, most noticeable in regions beyond the Tropics, reflect this 18.61-year cycle by marking the extreme positions in the north-south movement of the moon along the horizon at rising or setting. *See also* Nodes.

Retrograde motion: Apparent westward motion of a planet in the sky relative to the stars. Mean retrograde interval for Venus is 42 days; Mars, 75 days; Jupiter, 120 days; and Saturn, 140 days.

Right ascenscion: Position of a star in the equatorial system of celestial coordinates (similar to longitude in the system of terrestrial coordinates), used with declination to locate a star's position on the celestial sphere, which is fixed regardless of the observer's location. Right ascension (R.A.) is measured eastward from the zero point at the vernal equinox and given in hours, minutes, and seconds with 24 hours corresponding to 360°.

Saros cycle: Cycle of similar eclipses that recurs after a period of about 18.03 years or 223 lunations (6,585.32 days).

Sidereal cycle or period: Time it takes for a celestial body to return to the same part of the sky when observed from Earth against the background of stars. Sidereal period for the Moon is 27.32166 days; Mercury, 88.0 days; Venus, 224.7 days; Mars, 687.1 days; Jupiter, 4,332.5 days; and Saturn, 10,758.9 days.

Stationary point: When a planet stops its eastward motion through the background of stars at the first stationary point and then moves backward until it reaches the second stationary point, after which it resumes forward motion.

Summer solstice: Point on the celestial sphere where the sun reaches its greatest distance north of the celestial equator (23½°N) about June 21, but viewed from the Southern Hemisphere, this date marks the winter solstice. Around the solstices the sun seems to move very slowly along the horizon when compared to its rapid motion around the equinoxes.

Superior conjunction: Point at which a planet is invisible as it passes behind the Sun relative to the observer on Earth. The term is generally reserved for the inferior planets that have two disappearance intervals, the longer disappearance interval being superior conjunction.

Synodic period: The period of time it takes a planet to return to the same position relative to Earth's orbit around the Sun, as determined by observing successive heliacal risings of the planet. Synodic period for Mercury is 115.9 days; Venus, 583.9 days; Mars, 780.0 days; Jupiter, 398.9 days; Saturn, 378.1 days.

Tropic of Cancer: Position on Earth parallel to 23½° north, the northern extreme of the Sun's apparent motion in the annual cycle.

Tropic of Capricorn: Position on Earth parallel to 23½° south, the southern extreme of the Sun's apparent motion in the annual cycle.

Tropical year: Period of revolution of the earth around the sun with respect to the vernal equinox (365.24220 days), which looks like the sun moving around the earth from our geocentric perspective.

Vertical circles: Great circles passing through the zenith and nadir, perpendicular to the horizon.

Winter solstice: Point on the celestial sphere where the sun reaches its greatest distance south of the celestial equator (23½°S) about December 22, but in the Southern Hemisphere, this date marks the summer solstice.

Zenith: Point directly overhead of the observer. The nadir is the point underfoot, opposite the zenith.

BIBLIOGRAPHY

Aguilera, Carmen

1989 Templo Mayor: Dual Symbol of the Passing of Time. In *The Imagination of Matter: Religion and Ecology in Mesoamerican Traditions,* edited by Davíd Carrasco, pp. 129–135. Oxford: BAR International Series 515.

Agurcia Fasquelle, Ricardo, and Juan Antonio Valdés

1994 *Secretos de dos ciudades mayas/Secrets of Two Maya Cities: Copán and Tikal.* San José, Costa Rica: Credomatic.

Alvarado López, Miguel

1975 *Léxico médico Quiché-Español.* Guatemala: Instituto Indigenista Nacional.

Anderson, Neal S., and Moisés Morales

1981 Solstitial Alignments of the Temple of the Inscriptions at Palenque. *Archaeoastronomy: The Bulletin for the Center for Archaeoastronomy* 4(3):30–33.

Anderson, Neal S., Moisés Morales, and Alfonso Morales

1981 A Solar Alignment of the Palace Tower at Palenque. *Archaeoastronomy: The Bulletin for the Center for Archaeoastronomy* 4(3):34–36.

Andrews, E. Wyllys, and Barbara W. Fash

1992 Continuity and Change in a Royal Maya Residential Complex at Copán. *Ancient Mesoamerica* 3(1):63–89.

Arellano Hernández, Alfonso

1995 Una diosa madre para Palenque. Paper presented at the Seventeenth International Congress of the History of Religions, Mexico City.

Armador Naranjo, Ascensión

1995 La desaparición del sol en Yucatán. In *Religión y sociedad en el área maya,* edited by Carmen Varela Torrecilla, Juan Luis Bonor Villarejo, and Yolanda Fernández Marquínez, pp. 311–318. Sociedad Española de Estudios Mayas, pub. 3. Madrid: Instituto de Cooperación Iberoamericana.

Ashmore, Wendy

1991 Site-Planning Principles and Concepts of Directionality among the Ancient Maya. *Latin American Antiquity* 2(3):199–226.

Aulie, H. Wilbur, and Evelyn W. de Aulie, comps.

1978 *Diccionario Ch'ol-Español; Español-Ch'ol.* Serie de Vocabularios y Diccionarios Indígenas, no. 21. Mexico City: Instituto Lingüístico de Verano.

Aveni, Anthony F.

1975 Possible Astronomical Orientations in Ancient Mesoamerica. In *Archaeoastronomy in Pre-Columbian America,* edited by Anthony F. Aveni, pp. 163–190. Austin: University of Texas Press.

1979 Venus and the Maya. *American Scientist* 67:274–285.

1980 *Skywatchers of Ancient Mexico.* Austin: University of Texas Press.

1981 Archaeoastronomy in the Maya Region: A Review of the Past Decade. *Journal of the History of Astronomy* 11(3):S1–S13.

1989 *Empires of Time: Calendars, Clocks, and Cultures.* New York: Basic Books.

1991 The Real Venus-Kukulcan in the Maya Inscriptions and Alignments. In *Sixth Palenque Round Table, 1986,* edited by Merle Greene Robertson and Virginia M. Fields, pp. 309–321. Norman: University of Oklahoma Press.

1992a The Moon and the Venus Table: An Example of the Commensuration in the Maya Calendar. In *The Sky and Mayan Literature,* edited by Anthony F. Aveni, pp. 87–101. Oxford: Oxford University Press.

1992b *Conversing with the Planets.* New York: Times Books.
1995 Frombork 1992: Where Worlds and Disciplines Collide. *Archaeoastronomy* 20:S74–S79.
1997 *Stairway to the Stars.* New York: John Wiley & Sons.

Aveni, Anthony F., Sharon L. Gibbs, and Horst Hartung

1975 The Caracol Tower at Chichen Itza: An Ancient Astronomical Observatory? *Science* 188(4192): 977–985.

Aveni, Anthony F., and Horst Hartung

1979 Some Suggestions about the Arrangement of Buildings at Palenque. In *Proceedings of the Tercera Mesa Redonda de Palenque,* vol. 4, edited by Merle Greene Robertson and Donna Call Jeffers, pp. 173–177. San Francisco: Pre-Columbian Art Research Center.
1986 Maya City Planning and the Calendar. In *Transactions of the American Philosophical Society,* vol. 76, no. 7, pp. 1–84. Philadelphia: The American Philosophical Society.
1988 Astronomy and Dynastic History at Tikal. In *New Directions in American Archaeoastronomy,* edited by Anthony F. Aveni, pp. 1–16. Proceedings of the 46th International Congress of Americanists. Oxford: BAR International Series 454.
1989 Uaxactun, Guatemala, Group E and Similar Assemblages: An Archaeoastronomical Reconsideration. In *World Archaeoastronomy: Selected Papers from the Second Oxford International Conference on Archaeoastronomy,* edited by Anthony F. Aveni, pp. 441–461. Cambridge: Cambridge University Press.
1991 Archaeoastronomy and the Puuc Sites. In *Arqueoastronomía y etnoastronomía en Mesoamérica,* edited by Johanna Broda, Stanislaw Iwaniszewski, and Lucrecia Maupomé, pp. 65–96. Mexico City: Universidad Nacional Autónoma de México.

Aveni, Anthony F., and Lorren D. Hotaling

1994 Monumental Inscriptions and the Observational Basis of Maya Planetary Astronomy. *Archaeoastronomy* (Supplement to *Journal for the History of Astronomy*) 19:S21–S54.
1996 Monumental Inscriptions and the Observational Basis of Mayan Planetary Astronomy. In *Eighth Palenque Round Table, 1993,* edited by Martha J. Macri and Jan McHargue; Merle Greene Robertson, general editor; pp. 357–368. San Francisco: Pre-Columbian Art Research Institute.

Aveni, Anthony F., Steen J. Morandi, and Polly A. Peterson

1995 The Maya Number of Time: Intervalic Time Reckoning in the Maya Codices, Part I. *Archaeoastronomy* (Supplement to *Journal for the History of Astronomy*) 20:S1–S28.

Baer, Phillip, and Mary Baer

n.d. Notes on Lacandon Mythology and Beliefs. Chiapas, Mexico: Summer Institute of Linguistics.

Baer, Phillip, and William R. Merrifield

1972 *Los Lacandones de México: Dos estudios.* Mexico City: Instituto Nacional Indigenista, Secretaría de Educación Pública.

Báez-Jorge, Félix

1983 La cosmovisión de los zoques de Chiapas. In *Antropología e historia de los mixe-zoques y mayas,* edited by Lorenzo Ochoa and Thomas A. Lee, Jr., pp. 383–411. Mexico City: Universidad Nacional Autónoma México–Brigham Young University.
1988 *Los oficios de las diosas.* Xalapa: Universidad Veracruzana.

Baird, Ellen T.

1989 Stars and War at Cacaxtla. In *Mesoamerica after the Decline of Teotihuacan, A.D. 700–900,* edited by Richard A. Diehl and Janet Catherine Berlo, pp. 105–122. Washington, D.C.: Dumbarton Oaks.

Baker, Mary

1992 Capuchin Monkeys (*Cebus capucinus*) and the Ancient Maya. *Ancient Mesoamerica* 3:219–228.

Barrera Marín, Alfredo, Alfredo Barrera Vásquez, and Rosa María López Franco

1976 *Nomenclatura etnobotánica maya: Una interpretación taxonómica.* Mexico City: Instituto Nacional de Antropología e Historia, Colección Científica no. 36.

Barrera Vásquez, Alfredo

1975 La ceiba-cocodrilo. *Anales del Instituto Nacional de Antropología e Historia* (época 7a) 5:187–208.
1980 *Diccionario Maya Cordemex: Maya-Español, Español-Maya.* Mérida, Yucatán, Mex.: Ediciones Cordemex.

Basseta, Domingo

1698 Vocabulario de la lengua Quiché. Manuscript in the Bibliothèque Nationale, Paris.

Bassie-Sweet, Karen

1991 *From the Mouth of the Dark Cave: Commemorative Sculpture of the Late Classic Maya.* Norman: University of Oklahoma Press.

Baudez, Claude-François

1985 The Sun Kings at Copán and Quiriguá. In *Fifth Palenque Round Table, 1983,* vol. 7, edited by Merle Greene Robertson and Virginia M. Fields, pp. 29–38. San Francisco: Pre-Columbian Art Research Institute.

1986 Iconography and History at Copán. In *The Southeastern Maya Periphery,* edited by Patricia Urban and Edward Schortman, pp. 17–26. Austin: University of Texas Press.

1988 Solar Cycle and Dynastic Succession in the Southeast Maya Zone. In *The Southeast Classic Maya Zone,* edited by Elizabeth H. Boone and Gordon Willey, pp. 125–147. Washington, D.C.: Dumbarton Oaks Library and Research Collection.

1994 *Maya Sculpture of Copán: The Iconography.* Norman: University of Oklahoma Press.

Baus Czitrom, Carolyn

1990 El culto de Venus en Cacaxtla. *La época clásica: Nuevos hallazgos, nuevas ideas,* coordinated by Amalia Cardos de Méndez, pp. 351–370. Mexico City: Museo Nacional de Antropología and Instituto Nacional de Antropología e Historia.

Benavides, Antonio

1996 Edzná, Campeche. *Arqueología Mexicana* 3(18): 26–31.

Benson, Elizabeth P.

1989 In Love and War: Hummingbird Lore. In *In Love and War: Hummingbird Lore and Other Selected Papers from LAILA/ALILA's 1988 Symposium,* edited by Mary H. Preuss, pp. 3–8. Culver City, Calif.: Labyrinthos.

1996 The Vulture: The Earth and the Sky. In *Eighth Palenque Round Table, 1993,* edited by Martha J. Macri and Jan McHargue; Merle Greene Robertson, general editor; pp. 309–320. San Francisco: Pre-Columbian Art Research Institute.

1997 *Birds and Beasts of Ancient Latin America.* Gainesville: University Press of Florida.

Berlin, Heinrich

1963 The Palenque Triad. *Journale de la Société des Américanistes* 52:91–99.

1967 The Calendar of the Tzotzil Indians. In *The Civilizations of Ancient America: Selected Papers of the 29th International Congress of Americanists,* edited by Sol Tax, pp. 155–164. New York: Cooper Square Publishers.

1977 *Signos y significados en las inscripciones mayas.* Guatemala City: Instituto Nacional del Patrimonio Cultural de Guatemala.

Berlo, Janet C.

1984 *Teotihuacan Art Abroad: A Study of Metropolitan Style and Provincial Transformation in Incensario Workshops.* 2 vols. Oxford: BAR International Series 199.

Berrin, Kathleen, ed.

1988 *Feathered Serpents and Flowering Trees: Reconstructing the Murals of Teotihuacan.* San Francisco: The Fine Arts Museum of San Francisco.

Beyer, Hermann

1965 El llamado "Calendario Azteca": Descripción e interpretación del Cuauhxicalle de la "Casa de las Aguilas." *El México Antiguo* 10:134–256.

Blair, Robert, and Refugio Vermont-Salas

1965 *Spoken Yucatec Maya I.* Chicago: University of Chicago Library.

Blom, Frans, and Oliver La Farge

1926–1927 *Tribes and Temples.* 2 vols. Tulane University, Middle American Research Institute, pub. 1.

Bolles, John S.

1977 *Las Monjas: A Major Pre-Mexican Architectural Complex at Chichen Itza.* Norman: University of Oklahoma Press.

1982 Two Yucatecan Maya Ritual Chants. *Mexicon* 4: 65–68.

Braakhuis, H. E. M.

1987 Sun's Voyage to the City of the Vultures: A Classic Mayan Funerary Theme. *Zeitschrift für Ethnologie* 112(2):237–259.

Bradley, Donald A., Max A. Woodbury, and Glenn W. Brier

1962 Lunar Synodical Period and Widespread Precipitation. *Science* 237:748–749.

Bricker, Harvey M.

1996 Nightly Variation in the Characteristics of Venus near Times of Greatest Eastern Elongation. In

Eighth Palenque Round Table, 1993, edited by Martha J. Macri and Jan McHargue; Merle Greene Robertson, general editor; pp. 369–378. San Francisco: Pre-Columbian Art Research Institute.

Bricker, Harvey M., and Victoria R. Bricker

1983 Classic Maya Prediction of Solar Eclipses. *Current Anthropology* 24:1–23.

1992 Zodiacal References in the Maya Codices. In *The Sky and Mayan Literature,* edited by Anthony F. Aveni, pp. 148–183. Oxford: Oxford University Press.

1996 Astronomical References in the Throne Inscription of the Palace of the Governor at Uxmal. *Cambridge Archaeological Journal* 6(2):191–229.

1997 More on the Mars Table in the Dresden Codex. *Latin American Antiquity* 8(4):384–397.

Bricker, Harvey M., Victoria R. Bricker, and Bettina Wulfing.

1997 Determining the Historicity of Three Astronomical Almanacs in the Madrid Codex. *Archaeoastronomy* (Supplement to *Journal for the History of Astronomy*) 22:S17–S36.

Bricker, Victoria R.

1981 *The Indian Christ, the Indian King: Historical Substate of Maya Myth and Ritual.* Austin: University of Texas Press.

1983 Directional Glyphs in Maya Inscriptions and Codices. *American Antiquity* 48:347–353.

1988a A Phonetic Glyph for Zenith: Reply to Closs. *American Antiquity* 53(2):394–400.

1988b The Relationship between the Venus Table and an Almanac in the Dresden Codex. In *New Directions in American Archaeoastronomy,* edited by Anthony F. Aveni, pp. 81–104. Proceedings of the 46th International Congress of Americanists. Oxford: BAR International Series 454.

Bricker, Victoria R., and Harvey M. Bricker

1986a Archaeoastronomical Implications of an Agricultural Almanac in the Dresden Codex. *Mexicon* 8(2):29–35.

1986b The Mars Table in the Dresden Codex. *Research and Reflections in Archaeology and History: Essays in Honor of Doris Stone,* edited by E. Wyllys Andrews V, pp. 51–79. Middle American Research Institute, pub. 47. New Orleans: Tulane University.

1988 The Seasonal Table in the Dresden Codex and Related Almanacs. *Archaeoastronomy* (Supplement to *Journal for the History of Astronomy*) 12:S1–S62.

1989 Astronomical References in the Table on Pages 61–69 of the Dresden Codex. In *World Archaeoastronomy: Selected Papers from the Second Oxford International Conference on Archaeoastronomy,* edited by Anthony F. Aveni, pp. 232–245. Cambridge: Cambridge University Press.

1992 A Method for Cross-Dating Almanacs with Tables in the Dresden Codex. In *The Sky and Mayan Literature,* edited by Anthony F. Aveni, pp. 43–86. Oxford: Oxford University Press.

1995 An Astronomical Text from Chichen Itza. *Human Mosaic: A Journal of the Social Sciences* 28(2):91–105.

Broda, Johanna

1982 Astronomy, *Cosmovisión,* and Ideology in Pre-Hispanic Mesoamerica. In *Ethnoastronomy and Archaeoastronomy in the American Tropics,* edited by Anthony F. Aveni and Gary Urton, pp. 81–110. New York: New York Academy of Sciences.

1989 Geography, Climate, and Observation of Nature in Pre-Hispanic Mesoamerica. In *The Imagination of Matter: Religion and Ecology in Mesoamerican Traditions,* edited by David Carrasco, pp. 139–153. Oxford: BAR International Series 515.

Bruce, Robert D.

1976 *Textos y dibujos lacandones de Naja.* Colección Científica 45. Mexico City: Instituto Nacional de Antropología e Historia.

1979 *Lacandon Dream Symbolism.* Mexico City: Ediciones Euroamericanas.

Bruce, Robert D., Carlos Robles U., and Enriqueta Ramos Chao

1971 *Los Lacandones: Cosmovisión maya.* Departamento de Investigaciones Antropológicas, pub. 26. Mexico City: Instituto Nacional de Antropología e Historia.

Burgess, John W.

1991 Some Astronomical Correlations to the Mesoamerican Calendar System Involving the Sun, Venus, Moon, and Mars. In *Past Present, and Future: Selected Papers on Latin American Indian Literatures,* edited by Mary H. Preuss, pp. 63–72. Culver City, Calif.: Labyrinthos.

Burns, Allan F.

1983 *An Epoch of Miracles: Oral Literature of the Yucatec Maya.* Austin: University of Texas Press.

Carlson, John

1976 Astronomical Investigations and Site Orientation Influences at Palenque. In *Segunda Mesa Redonda de Palenque,* part III, edited by Merle Greene Robertson, pp. 107–115. Pebble Beach, Calif.: Robert Louis Stevenson School.

1988 Sky Band Representations in Classic Maya Vase Painting. In *Maya Iconography,* edited by Elizabeth P. Benson and Gillett G. Griffin, pp. 277–293. Princeton: Princeton University Press.

1991 *Venus-regulated Warfare and Ritual Sacrifice in Mesoamerica: Teotihuacan and the Cacaxtla "Star Wars" Connection.* College Park, Md.: Center for Archaeoastronomy Technical Publication no. 7.

1993 Venus-regulated Warfare and Ritual Sacrifice in Mesoamerica. In *Astronomies and Cultures,* edited by Clive L. N. Ruggles and Nicholas J. Saunders, pp. 202–252. Boulder: University of Colorado Press.

Carlson, John, and Linda C. Landis

1985 Bands, Bicephalic Dragons, and Other Beasts: The Sky Band in Maya Art and Iconography. In *Fourth Palenque Round Table, 1980,* vol. 6, edited by Merle Greene Robertson and Elizabeth P. Benson, pp. 115–140. San Francisco: Pre-Columbian Research Institute.

Carmack, Robert M.

1981 *The Quiché Maya of Utatlán: The Evolution of a Highland Guatemala Kingdom.* Norman: University of Oklahoma Press.

Carmack, Robert M., and James L. Mondloch

1983 *El Título de Totonicapán.* Fuentes para el Estudio Maya, no. 3. Mexico City: Universidad Autónoma de México.

Carrasco, Pedro

1969 Central Mexican Highlands: Introduction. In *Ethnology,* part 2, edited by Evon Vogt, pp. 579–601. *Handbook of Middle American Indians,* vol. 8, Robert Wauchope, general editor. Austin: University of Texas Press.

Carrasco, Ramón

1985 La señora de la familia de la luna en las inscripciones tardías de Yaxchilán y Bonampak. In *Fifth Palenque Round Table, 1983,* edited by Virginia M. Fields, pp. 85–95. San Francisco: Pre-Columbian Art Research Institute.

Caso, Alfonso

1971 Calendric Systems of Central Mexico. In *Archaeology of Northern Mesoamerica,* part 1, edited by Gordon Ekholm and Ignacio Bernal, pp. 333–348. *Handbook of Middle American Indians,* vol. 10,

Robert Wauchope, general editor. Austin: University of Texas Press.

Chiu, Bella C., and Phillip Morrison

1980 Astronomical Origin of the Offset Street Grid at Teotihuacan. *Archaeoastronomy* (Supplement to *Journal for the History of Astronomy*) 2:S55–S64.

Ciaramella, Mary A.

1994 The Lady with the Snake Headdress. In *Seventh Palenque Round Table, 1989,* edited by Virginia M. Fields; Merle Greene Robertson, general editor; pp. 202–209. San Francisco: Pre-Columbian Art Research Institute.

n.d. The Weavers in the Codices. Ms.

Cleere, Gail S.

1994 Celestial Events: Moonstruck. *Natural History* 4/94:94–97.

Closs, Michael P.

1977 The Date-Reaching Mechanism in the Venus Table of the Dresden Codex. In *Native American Astronomy,* edited by Anthony F. Aveni, pp. 89–99. Austin: University of Texas Press.

1979 Venus in the Maya World: Glyphs, Gods, and Associated Astronomical Phenomena. In *Tercera Mesa Redonda de Palenque,* vol. 4, edited by Merle Greene Robertson and Donna Call Jeffers, pp. 147–165. Palenque, Chiapas, Mex.: Pre-Columbian Art Research Center.

1989 Cognitive Aspects of Ancient Maya Eclipse Theory. In *World Archaeoastronomy: Selected Papers from the Second Oxford International Conference on Archaeoastronomy,* edited by Anthony F. Aveni, pp. 389–415. Cambridge: Cambridge University Press.

1992 Some Parallels in the Astronomical Events Recorded in the Maya Codices and Inscriptions. In *The Sky and Mayan Literature,* edited by Anthony F. Aveni, pp. 133–147. Oxford: Oxford University Press.

Closs, Michael P., Anthony F. Aveni, and Bruce Crowley

1984 The Planet Venus and Temple 22 at Copán. *Indiana* 9:221–247.

Codex Telleriano-Remensis. *See* Quiñones Keber, Eloise.

Coe, Michael D.

1968 *America's First Civilization.* New York: American Heritage Publishing Co.

1973 *The Maya Scribe and His World.* New York: Grolier Club.

1975a Native Astronomy in Mesoamerica. In *Archaeoastronomy in Pre-Columbian America,* edited by Anthony F. Aveni, pp. 3–31. Austin: University of Texas Press.

1975b Death and the Ancient Maya. In *Death and the Afterlife in Pre-Columbian America,* edited by Elizabeth P. Benson, pp. 87–104. Washington, D.C.: Dumbarton Oaks.

1978a Supernatural Patrons of Maya Scribes and Artists. In *Social Process in Maya Prehistory,* edited by Norman Hammond, pp. 327–347. London: Academic Press.

1978b *Lords of the Underworld.* Princeton: The Art Museum, Princeton University.

1981 Religion and the Rise of Mesoamerican States. In *The Transition to Statehood in the New World,* edited by Grant D. Jones and Robert R. Kautz, pp. 157–171. Cambridge: Cambridge University Press.

1982 *Old Gods and Young Heroes: The Pearlman Collection of Maya Ceramics.* Jerusalem: The Israel Museum.

1988 Ideology of the Maya Tomb. In *Maya Iconography,* edited by Elizabeth P. Benson and Gillett G. Griffin, pp. 222–235. Princeton: Princeton University Press.

1989 The Hero Twins: Myth and Image. In *The Maya Vase Book,* vol. 1, edited by Justin Kerr, pp. 161–184. New York: Kerr Associates.

1992 *Breaking the Maya Code.* New York: Thames and Hudson.

1999 *The Maya.* Rev. ed. New York: Thames and Hudson.

Coe, William

1970 *Tikal: A Handbook of the Ancient Maya Ruins.* Philadelphia: The University Museum, University of Pennsylvania.

Coggins, Clemency C.

1975 *Painting and Drawing Styles at Tikal: An Historical and Iconographic Reconstruction.* Ph.D. diss., Harvard University. Ann Arbor: University Microfilms.

1980 The Shape of Time: Some Political Implications of the Four-Part Figure. *American Antiquity* 45: 727–739.

1983 *The Stucco Decoration and Architectural Assemblage of Structure 1-sub, Dzibilchaltun, Yucatan, Mexico.* Middle American Research Institute, pub. 49. New Orleans: Tulane University.

1984 *Cenote of Sacrifice: Maya Treasures from the Sacred Well at Chichén Itzá.* Austin: University of Texas Press.

1986 The Name of Tikal. *Primer Simposio Mundial sobre Epigrafía Maya,* pp. 23–46. Guatemala: Instituto Nacional de Antropología e Historia de Guatemala.

1988a The Manikin Scepter: Emblem of Lineage. *Estudios de Cultura Maya* 17:123–148.

1988b Classic Maya Metaphors of Death and Life. *RES: Anthropology and Aesthetics* 16:66–84.

1988c On the Historical Significance of Decorated Ceramics at Copán and Quiriguá and Related Classic Maya Sites. In *The Southeast Classic Maya Zone,* edited by Elizabeth H. Boone and Gordon Willey, pp. 95–124. Washington, D.C.: Dumbarton Oaks.

1990 The Birth of the Baktun at Tikal and Seibal. In *Vision and Revision in Maya Studies,* edited by Flora S. Clancy and Peter D. Harrison, pp. 79–97. Albuquerque: University of New Mexico Press.

1993 The Age of Teotihuacan and Its Mission Abroad. In *Teotihuacan: Art from the City of the Gods,* edited by Kathleen Berrin and Esther Pasztory, pp. 140–155. New York: Thames and Hudson.

1996 Creation Religion and the Numbers at Teotihuacan and Izapa. *RES: Anthropology and Aesthetics* 29/30: 16–38.

Coggins, Clemency Chase, and R. David Drucker.

1988 The Observatory at Dzibilchaltun. In *New Directions in American Archaeoastronomy,* edited by Anthony F. Aveni, pp. 17–56. Proceedings of the 46th International Congress of Americanists. Oxford: BAR International Series 454.

Cogolludo, Diego López de

1954 *Historia de Yucatán.* Campeche: Comisión de Historia.

Cohodas, Marvin

1978 *The Great Ball Court at Chichen Itza, Yucatan, Mexico.* New York and London: Garland Publishing.

1982 The Bicephalic Monster in Classic Maya Sculpture. *Antropológica* 24:105–146.

Colby, Benjamin N., and Lore M. Colby

1981 *The Daykeeper: The Life and Discourse of an Ixil Diviner.* Cambridge: Harvard University Press.

Collea, Beth

1981 The Celestial Bands in Maya Hieroglyphic Writing. In *Archaeoastronomy in the Americas,* edited by Ray A. Williamson, pp. 215–232. College Park, Md.: Center for Archaeoastronomy.

1982 A General Consideration of the Maya Correlation Question. In *Ethnoastronomy and Archaeoastron-*

omy in the American Tropics, edited by Anthony F. Aveni and Gary Urton, pp. 124–134. Annals of the New York Academy of Sciences, vol. 385. New York: New York Academy of Sciences.

Cook, Garrett

1986 Quichean Folk Theology and Southern Maya Supernaturalism. In *Symbol and Meaning beyond the Closed Community: Essays in Mesoamerican Ideas,* edited by Gary H. Gossen, pp. 139–154. Studies in Culture and Society, vol. 1. Albany: Institute for Mesoamerican Studies, State University of New York at Albany.

Craine, Eugene R., and Reginald D. Reindorp

1979 *The Codex Pérez and the Book of Chilam Balam of Maní.* Norman: University of Oklahoma Press.

Cruz Guzmán, Aucensio

1994 T'an Lak Ch'uhul Na': Cuento de la Luna (Our Holy Mother the Moon), Chol text with Spanish translation. In *T'an to Wajali: Cuentos Choles Antiguos* (Chol tales of long ago), edited by J. Kathryn Josserand and Nicholas A. Hopkins, pp. 11–39. In Nicholas A. Hopkins and J. Kathryn Josserand, *Chol Texts, Vocabulary, and Grammar, Final Technical Report to the National Science Foundation, Grant BNS-8308506,* Part III, Chol Texts.

Dávalos Hurtado, Eusebio

1961 Into the Well of Sacrifice. *National Geographic* 120(4):540–561.

Davoust, Michel

1991 Nuevas lecturas de los textos mayas de Chichén Itzá. *Anuario Cei 3 (1989–1990).* San Cristóbal, Chiapas, Mex.: Centro de Estudios Indígenas, Universidad Autónoma de Chiapas.

Dearborn, David S., and Ray E. White

1982 Archaeoastronomy at Machu Picchu. In *Ethnoastronomy and Archaeoastronomy in the American Tropics,* edited by Anthony F. Aveni and Gary Urton, pp. 249–260. Annals of the New York Academy of Sciences, vol. 385. New York: New York Academy of Sciences.

1989 Inca Observatories: Their Relation to the Calendar and Ritual. In *World Archaeoastronomy: Selected Papers from the Second Oxford International Conference on Archaeoastronomy,* edited by Anthony F. Aveni, pp. 462–469. Cambridge: Cambridge University Press.

Demarest, Arthur A.

1997 The Vanderbilt Petexbatun Regional Archaeology Project 1989–1994: Overview, History, and Major Results of a Multidisciplinary Study of the Classic Maya Collapse. *Ancient Mesoamerica* 8:209–227.

Duby, Gertrude, and Frans Blom

1969 The Lacandon. In *Ethnology,* part 1, edited by Evon Vogt, pp. 276–297. *Handbook of Middle American Indians,* vol. 7, Robert Wauchope, general editor. Austin: University of Texas Press.

Durán, Fray Diego

1971 *Book of the Gods and Rites and the Ancient Calendar.* Translated and edited by Fernando Horcasitas and Doris Heyden. Norman: University of Oklahoma Press.

Dütting, Dieter

1981 Life and Death in Mayan Hieroglyphic Inscriptions. *Zeitschrift für Ethnologie* 106:7–73.

1982 The 2 Cib 14 Mol Event in the Palenque Inscriptions. *Zeitschrift für Ethnologie* 107:233–258.

1984 Venus, the Moon, and the Gods of the Palenque Triad. *Zeitschrift für Ethnologie* 109:7–74.

1985 On the Astronomical Background of Mayan Historical Events. In *Fifth Palenque Round Table, 1983,* vol. 7, edited by Merle Greene Robertson and Virginia M. Fields, pp. 261–274. San Francisco: Pre-Columbian Art Research Institute.

Dütting, Dieter, and Richard E. Johnson

1993 The Regal Rabbit, the Night-Sun and God L: An Analysis of Iconography and Texts on a Classic Maya Vase. *Baessler-Archiv* 41:167–195.

Earle, Duncan M.

1986 The Metaphor of the Day in Quiché: Notes on the Nature of Everyday Life. In *Symbol and Meaning Beyond the Closed Community: Essays in Mesoamerican Ideas,* edited by Gary H. Gossen, pp. 173–184. Studies in Culture and Society, vol. 1. Albany: Institute for Mesoamerican Studies, State University of New York at Albany.

Earle, Duncan Maclean, and Dean R. Snow

1985 The Origin of the 260-Day Calendar: The Gestation Hypothesis Reconsidered in Light of Its Use among the Quiche-Maya. In *Fifth Palenque Round Table, 1983,* edited by Merle Greene Robertson and Virginia M. Fields, pp. 241–244. San Francisco: Pre-Columbian Art Research Institute.

Edmonson, Munro S.

1971 *The Book of Counsel: The Popol Vuh of the Quiche Maya of Guatemala.* Middle American Research Institute, pub. 35. New Orleans: Tulane University.

1982a The Songs of Dzitbalche: A Literary Commentary. *Tlalocan* 9:173–208.

1982b *The Ancient Future of the Itza: The Book of Chilam Balam of Tizimin.* University of Texas Press, Austin.

1988 *The Book of the Year: Middle American Calendrical Systems.* Salt Lake City: University of Utah Press.

Fash, Barbara W.

1992 Late Classic Architectural Sculpture Themes in Copán. *Ancient Mesoamerica* 3(1):89–104.

Fash, William F.

1991 *Scribes, Warriors, and Kings.* London: Thames and Hudson.

Ferrández Martín, Francisco

1990 El interior del laberinto. *Oxkintok* 3. Madrid: Misión Arqueológica de España en México, Proyecto Oxkintok, Ministerio de Cultura.

Fialko C., Vilma

1988a El marcador de juego de pelota de Tikal: Nuevas referencias epigráficas para el período clásico temprano. *Mesoamerica* 15 (June):117–136.

1988b Mundo perdido, Tikal: Un ejemplo de complejos de comunicación astronómica. *Mayab* 4:13–21.

Fields, Virginia M.

1994 Catalogue of the Exhibition. In *Painting the Maya Universe: Royal Ceramics of the Classic Period.* Durham, N.C.: Duke University Press and Duke University Museum of Art.

Flores Gutiérrez, Daniel

1989 260: Un período astronómico. *Memorias del Segundo Coloquio Internacional de Mayistas,* vol. 1. Mexico City: Universidad Nacional Autónoma de México.

1995 En el problema del inicio del año y el origen del calendario mesoamericano: Un punto de vista astronómico. *Coloquio Cantos de Mesoamérica: Metodologías científicas en la búsqueda del conocimiento prehispánico,* edited by Daniel Flores, pp. 119–132. Mexico City: Instituto de Astronomía, Facultad de Ciencias, Universidad Nacional Autónoma de México.

Folan, William J., Joyce Marcus, Sophia Pincement, María del Rosario Domingues Carrasco, Larain Fletcher, and Abel Morales López

1995 Calakmul: New Date from an Ancient Maya Capital in Campeche, Mexico. *Latin American Antiquity* 6(4):310–334.

Förstemann, Ernst Wilhelm

1906 Commentary on the Maya Manuscript in the Royal Public Library at Dresden. *Papers of the Peabody Museum of Archaeology and Ethnology, Harvard University,* vol. 4, no. 2. Cambridge: The Peabody Museum.

Fought, John G.

1972 *Chorti Maya Texts.* Philadelphia: University of Pennsylvania Press.

Fox, James A., and John S. Justeson

1978 A Mayan Planetary Observation. *Contributions of the University of California Archaeological Research Facility* 36:55–60.

1984 Polyvalence in Maya Hieroglyphic Writing. In *Phoneticism in Mayan Hieroglyphic Writing,* edited by John S. Justeson and Lyle Campbell, pp. 17–76. Institute for Mesoamerican Studies, pub. 9. Albany: State University of New York at Albany.

Freidel, David

1975 The Ix Chel Shrine and Other Temples of Talking Idols. In *A Study of Changing Pre-Columbian Commercial Systems,* edited by Jeremy A. Sabloff and William L. Rathje, pp. 107–113. Cambridge: Peabody Museum of Archaeology and Ethnology, Harvard University.

1990 The Jester God: The Beginning and End of a Maya Royal Symbol. In *Vision and Revision in Maya Studies,* edited by F. S. Clancy and P. D. Harrison, pp. 67–76. Albuquerque: University of New Mexico Press.

Freidel, David, and Linda Schele

1988 History of a Maya Cosmogram. In *Maya Iconography,* edited by Elizabeth P. Benson and Gillett G. Griffin, pp. 44–93. Princeton: Princeton University Press.

1995 Some Last Words. Review Feature of *Maya Cosmos: Three Thousand Years on the Shaman's Path. Cambridge Archaeological Journal* 5(1):133–137.

Freidel, David, Linda Schele, and Joy Parker

1993 *Maya Cosmos: Three Thousand Years on the Shaman's Path.* New York: William Morrow and Company.

Furst, Jill

1978 *Codex Vindobonensis Mexicanus I: A Commentary.* Institute for Mesoamerican Studies, pub. 4. Albany: State University of New York at Albany.

Furst, Peter T.

1986 Human Biology and the Origin of the 260-Day Sacred Almanac: The Contributions of Leonhard Schultze Jena (1872–1955). In *Symbol and Meaning beyond the Closed Community: Essays in Mesoamerican Ideas,* edited by Gary H. Gossen, pp. 69–76. Studies in Culture and Society, vol. 1. Albany: Institute for Mesoamerican Studies, State University of New York at Albany.

Galindo Trejo, Jesús

1994 *Arqueoastronomía en la América Antigua.* Madrid: Editorial Equipo Sirius.

Garza, Mercedes de la

1984 *El universo sagrado de la serpiente entre los Mayas.* Mexico City: Universidad Nacional Autónoma de México.

Gates, William F.

1910 Commentary upon the Maya-Tzental Perez Codex. *Papers of the Peabody Museum of Archaeology and Ethnology, Harvard University,* vol. 4, no. 2. Cambridge: The Peabody Museum.

Gillespie, Susan D.

1991 Ballgames and Boundaries. In *The Mesoamerican Ballgame,* edited by Vernon Scarborough and David Wilson, pp. 317–345. Tucson: The University of Arizona Press.

Girard, Raphael

1948 El calendario maya-mexica: Origen, función, desarrollo y lugar de procedencia. Mexico City: Editorial Stylo.
1949 *Los chortis ante el problema maya,* vol. 2. Mexico City: Colección Cultura Precolumbiana.
1962 *Los maya eternos.* Mexico City: Libro Mex Editores.
1979 *Esotericism of the Popol Vuh.* Pasadena: Theosophical University Press.

Goldstine, Herman H.

1973 *New and Full Moons: 1001 B.C. to A.D. 1651.* Philadelphia: American Philosophical Society.

González Torres, Yólotl

1975 *El culto a los astros entre los mexicas.* Mexico City: SEP/SETENTAS, 217.

Gossen, Gary H.

1974a A Chamula Calendar Board from Chiapas, Mexico. In *Mesoamerican Archaeology: New Approaches,* edited by Norman Hammond, pp. 217–254. Austin: University of Texas Press.
1974b *Chamulas in the World of the Sun.* Cambridge: Harvard University Press.
1980 Two Creation Texts from Chamula, Chiapas. *Tlalocan* 8:131–165.
1982 Review of *The Transformation of the Hummingbird* by Eva Hunt. *Archaeoastronomy: The Bulletin for the Center for Archaeoastronomy* 5(3):26–32.
1986 The Chamula Festival of Games: Native Macroanalysis and Social Commentary in a Maya Carnival. In *Symbol and Meaning beyond the Closed Community: Essays in Mesoamerican Ideas,* edited by Gary H. Gossen, pp. 173–184. Studies in Culture and Society, vol. 1. Albany: Institute for Mesoamerican Studies, State University of New York at Albany.

Graham, John, Robert Heizer, and Edwin Shook

1978 Abaj Takalik 1976: Exploratory Investigations. *Contributions of the University of California Archaeological Research Facility* 36:85–110.

Grieder, Terence

1982 *The Origins of Pre-Columbian Art.* Austin: University of Texas Press.

Grube, Nikolai

1992 Classic Maya Dance: Evidence from Hieroglyphs and Iconography. *Ancient Mesoamerica* 3:201–218.

Grube, Nikolai, and Linda Schele

1994 Kuy, the Owl of Omen and War. *Mexicon* 16(1): 10–17.

Guiteras Holmes, Calixta

1961 *Perils of the Soul: The World View of a Tzotzil Indian.* New York: Free Press of Glencoe.

Hammond, Norman

1985 The Sun Is Hid: Classic Depictions in Maya Myth. In *Fourth Palenque Round Table, 1980,* vol. 6, edited by Merle Greene Robertson and Elizabeth P. Benson, pp. 167–174. San Francisco: Pre-Columbian Research Institute.

1987   The Sun Also Rises: Iconographic Syntax of the Pomona Flare. *Research Reports on Ancient Maya Writing,* no. 7. Washington, D.C.: Center for Maya Research.

Harris, John F., and Stephen K. Stearns

1997   *Understanding Maya Inscriptions: A Hieroglyphic Handbook.* Philadelphia: The University of Pennsylvania Museum of Archaeology and Anthropology.

Hasegawa, Ichiro

1980   Catalogue of Ancient and Naked-Eye Comets. *Vistas in Astronomy* 24:59–102.

Hazen, Henry Allen

1900   The Origin and Value of Weather Lore. *Journal of American Folk-Lore* 13:191–198.

Hellmuth, Nicholas M.

1987   *Monster und Menschen in der Maya-Kunst.* Graz: Akademische Druck u. Verlagsanstalt.

1988   Early Maya Iconography on an Incised Cylindrical Tripod. In *Maya Iconography,* edited by Elizabeth P. Benson and Gillett G. Griffin, pp. 152–174. Princeton: Princeton University Press.

Heyden, Doris

1985   *Mitología y simbolismo de la flora en el México Prehispánico.* Mexico City: Universidad Nacional Autónoma de México.

Historia de los mexicanos por sus pinturas

1973   In *Teogonía e historia de los mexicanos,* edited by Angel M. Garibay K., pp. 21–90. Mexico City: Editorial Porrúa.

Historia de México (Histoire du Mechique)

1973   In *Teogonía e historia de los mexicanos,* edited by Angel M. Garibay K., pp. 90–120. Mexico City: Editorial Porrúa.

Hodell, David A., Jason H. Curtis, and Mark Brenner

1995   Possible Role of Climate in the Collapse of Classic Maya Civilization. *Nature* 375(6530):391–394.

Hofling, Charles A.

1988   Venus and the Miscellaneous Almanacs in the Dresden Codex. *Journal of Mayan Linguistics* 6:79–102.

Hofling, Charles A., and Thomas O'Neil

1992   Eclipse Cycles in the Moon Goddess Almanacs in the Dresden Codex. In *The Sky and Mayan Literature,* edited by Anthony F. Aveni, pp. 102–132. Oxford: Oxford University Press.

Holland, William

1964   Conceptos cosmológicos tzotziles como una base para interpretar la civilización maya prehispánica. *América Indígena* 24:11–28.

Hotaling, Lorren

1995   A Reply to Werner Nahm: Maya Warfare and the Venus Year. *Mexicon* 7(2):32–37.

Houston, Stephen D.

1989   *Maya Glyphs.* Berkeley and Los Angeles: University of California Press, and London: British Museum.

1993   *Hieroglyphs and History at Dos Pilas: Dynastic Politics of the Classic Maya.* Austin: University of Texas Press.

1997   The Shifting Now: Aspect, Deixis, and Narrative in Classic Maya Texts. *American Anthropologist* 99 (2):291–305.

Houston, Stephen D., and David Stuart

1984   An Example of Homophony in Maya Script. *American Antiquity* 49(4):790–805.

1989   The Way Glyph: Evidence for "Co-essences" among the Classic Maya. *Research Reports on Ancient Maya Writing,* no. 30. Washington, D.C.: Center for Maya Research.

1996   Of Gods, Glyphs and Kings: Divinity and Rulership among the Classic Maya. *Antiquity* 70:289–312.

Hunn, Eugene S.

1977   *Tzeltal Folk Zoology.* New York: Academic Press.

Hunt, Eva

1977   *The Transformation of the Hummingbird: Cultural Roots of a Zinacantecan Mythical Poem.* Ithaca: Cornell University Press.

Ilía Nájera Coronado, Martha

1995   El temor a los eclipses entre comunidades mayas contemporáneas. In *Religión y sociedad en el área maya,* edited by Carmen Varela Torrecilla, Juan Luis Bonor Villarejo, and Yolanda Fernández Marquínez, pp. 319–327. Sociedad Española de Estudios Mayas, pub. 3. Madrid: Instituto de Cooperación Iberoamericana.

Isbell, Billie Jean

1982   Culture Confronts Nature in the Dialectical World of the Tropics. In *Ethnoastronomy and Archaeoastronomy in the American Tropics,* edited by

Anthony F. Aveni and Gary Urton, pp. 353–364. Annals of the New York Academy of Sciences, vol. 385. New York: New York Academy of Sciences.

Iwaniszewski, Stanislaw

1987 El templo del dios descendiente en Tulum: Enfoque arqueoastronómico. In *Memorias del Primer Coloquio Internacional de Mayistas,* pp. 209–217. Mexico City: Universidad Nacional Autónoma de México.

1992 On Some Maya Chol Astronomical Concepts and Practices. In *Readings in Archaeoastronomy, Papers Presented at the International Conference: Current Problems and Future of Archaeoastronomy,* edited by Stanislaw Iwaniszewski, pp. 131–134. Warsaw: State Archaeological Museum, Warsaw University.

Jones, Christopher

1977 Inauguration Dates of Three Late Classic Maya Rulers of Tikal, Guatemala. *American Antiquity* 42(1):28–60.

1984 *Deciphering Maya Hieroglyphs.* 2d ed. Philadelphia: The University Museum, University of Pennsylvania.

Jones, Christopher, and Linton Satterthwaite

1982 The Monuments and Inscriptions of Tikal: The Carved Monuments. *Tikal Report No. 33, Part A.* Philadelphia: The University Museum, University of Pennsylvania.

Jones, Tom

1991 Jaws II: Return of the Xoc. In *Sixth Palenque Round Table, 1986,* edited by Merle Greene Robertson and Virginia M. Fields, pp. 246–254. Norman: University of Oklahoma Press.

Joralemon, Peter David

1971 *A Study of Olmec Iconography.* Studies in Pre-Columbian Art and Archaeology 7. Washington, D.C.: Dumbarton Oaks.

Josserand, J. Kathryn

1995 Participant Tracking in Maya Hieroglyphic Texts: Who Was That Masked Man? *Journal of Linguistic Anthropology* 5(1):65–89.

Josserand, J. Kathryn, and Nicholas A. Hopkins

1993 *Maya Hieroglyphic Writing: Workbook for a Short Course on Maya Hieroglyphic Writing.* Tallahassee: Jaguar Tours.

Justeson, John S.

1984 Appendix B: Interpretations of Mayan Hieroglyphs. In *Phoneticism in Mayan Hieroglyphic Writing,* edited by John S. Justeson and Lyle Campbell, pp. 315–362. Institute for Mesoamerican Studies, pub. 9. Albany: State University of New York at Albany.

1988 The Non-Maya Calendars of Southern Veracruz-Tabasco and the Antiquity of the Civil and Agricultural Years. *Journal of Mayan Linguistics* 6:1–22.

1989 The Ancient Maya Ethnoastronomy: An Overview of Hieroglyphic Sources. In *World Archaeoastronomy: Selected Papers from the Second Oxford International Conference on Archaeoastronomy,* edited by Anthony F. Aveni, pp. 76–129. Cambridge: Cambridge University Press.

Justeson, John S., and Terrence Kaufman

1993 A Decipherment of Epi-Olmec Hieroglyphic Writing. *Science* 259:1703–1711.

Kelley, David H.

1960 Calendar Animals and Deities. *Southwestern Journal of Anthropology* 16(3):317–337.

1965 The Birth of the Gods at Palenque. *Estudios de Cultura Maya* 5:93–134.

1972 The Nine Lords of the Night. *Contributions of the University of California Archaeological Research Facility* 5(16):53–68.

1974 Eurasian Evidence and the Mayan Calendar Correlations Problem. In *Mesoamerican Archaeology: New Approaches,* edited by Norman Hammond, pp. 405–408. Austin: University of Texas Press.

1975 Planetary Data on Caracol Stela 3. In *Archaeoastronomy in Pre-Columbian America,* edited by Anthony F. Aveni, pp. 257–262. Austin: University of Texas Press.

1976 *Deciphering the Maya Script.* Austin: University of Texas Press.

1977a A Possible Maya Eclipse Record. In *Social Process in Maya Prehistory: Studies in Honour of Sir Eric Thompson,* edited by Norman Hammond, pp. 405–408. London, New York, and San Francisco: Academic Press.

1977b Maya Astronomical Tables and Inscriptions. In *Native American Astronomy,* edited by Anthony F. Aveni, pp. 57–74. Austin: University of Texas Press.

1980 Astronomical Identities of Mesoamerican Gods. *Archaeoastronomy* (Supplement to *Journal for the History of Astronomy*) 2:S1–S54.

1983 The Maya Correlation Problem. In *Civilization in the Ancient Americas: Essays in Honor of Gordon R.*

Willey, edited by Richard Leventhal and Alan Kolata, pp. 157–208. Cambridge: Peabody Museum of Archaeology and Ethnology, Harvard University.

1985 The Lords of Palenque and the Lords of Heaven. In *Fifth Palenque Round Table, 1983*, vol. 7, edited by Merle Greene Robertson and Virginia M. Fields, pp. 235–240. San Francisco: Pre-Columbian Art Research Institute.

1989 Mesoamerican Astronomy and the Maya Calendar Correlation Problem. In *Memorias II Coloquio Internacional de Mayistas*, pp. 65–96. Mexico City: Universidad Nacional Autónoma de México.

Kelley, David H., and K. Ann Kerr

1973 Mayan Astronomy and Astronomical Glyphs. In *Mesoamerican Writing Systems*, edited by Elizabeth P. Benson, pp. 179–216. Washington, D.C.: Dumbarton Oaks.

Kerr, Justin

1994 Where Do You Keep Your Paint Pot? Supplement to *The Maya Vase Book*, vol. 4, edited by Justin Kerr. New York: Kerr Associates.

Kerr, Justin, ed.

1990 *The Maya Vase Book*. Vol. 2. New York: Kerr Associates.

1992 *The Maya Vase Book*. Vol. 3. New York: Kerr Associates.

Klein, Cecelia F.

1976 The Identity of the Central Deity on the Aztec Calendar Stone. *Art Bulletin* 56(1):1–12.

1980 Who Was Tlaloc? *Journal of Latin American Lore* 6(2):155–204.

Knorozov, Yurii

1982 *Maya Hieroglyphic Codices*. Translated by Sophie D. Coe. Institute for Mesoamerican Studies, pub. 8. Albany: State University of New York at Albany.

Köhler, Ulrich

1980 Cosmovisión indígena e interpretación europea en estudios mesoamericanistas. In *La antropología americanista en la actualidad: Homenaje a Raphael Girard*, vol. 1, pp. 583–596. Mexico City: Editores Mexicanos Unidos.

1989 Comets and Falling Stars in the Perception of Mesoamerican Indians. In *World Archaeoastronomy: Selected Papers from the Second Oxford International Conference on Archaeoastronomy*, edited by Anthony F. Aveni, pp. 289–299. Cambridge: Cambridge University Press.

1991a Review of *The Great Tzotzil Dictionary of Santo Domingo Zinacantán*. *Ethnohistory* 38(3):318–321.

1991b Conceptos acerca del ciclo lunar y su impacto en la vida diaria de indígenas mesoamericanos. In *Arqueoastronomía y etnoastronomía en Mesoamérica*, edited by Johanna Broda, Stanislaw Iwaniszewski, and Lucrecia Maupomé, pp. 235–248. Mexico City: Universidad Nacional Autónoma de México.

1991c Conocimientos astronómicos de indígenas contemporáneos y su contribución para identificar constelaciones aztecas. In *Arqueoastronomía y etnoastronomía en Mesoamérica*, edited by Johanna Broda, Stanislaw Iwaniszewski, and Lucrecia Maupomé, pp. 249–265. Mexico City: Universidad Nacional Autónoma de México.

Kowalski, Jeff K.

1987 *The House of the Governor: A Maya Palace at Uxmal, Yucatan, Mexico*. Norman: University of Oklahoma Press.

1989 Mythological Identity of the Figure on the La Esperanza ("Chinkultic") Ball Court Marker. *Research Reports on Ancient Maya Writing*, no. 27. Washington, D.C.: Center for Maya Research.

1990 *Guide to Uxmal and the Puuc Region: Kabah, Sayil, and Labná*. Mérida, Yucatán, Mex.: Editorial Dante.

Kowalski, Jeff K., and William L. Fash

1991 Symbolism of the Maya Ball Game at Copán: Synthesis and New Aspects. In *Sixth Palenque Round Table, 1986*, edited by Merle Greene Robertson and Virginia M. Fields, pp. 59–67. Norman: University of Oklahoma Press.

Krochock, Ruth J.

1988 *The Hieroglyphic Inscriptions and Iconography of Temple of the Four Lintels and Related Monuments, Chichén Itzá, Yucatán, Mexico*. Master's thesis, University of Texas at Austin.

1989 Hieroglyphic Inscriptions at Chichén Itzá, Yucatán, México: The Temples of the Initial Series, the One Lintel, the Three Lintels, and the Four Lintels. *Research Reports on Ancient Maya Writing*, no. 23, pp. 7–14. Washington, D.C.: Center for Maya Research.

Krupp, Edward C.

1982 The "Binding of the Years," The Pleiades, and the Nadir Sun. *Archaeoastronomy: The Bulletin for the Center for Archaeoastronomy* 5(1):9–13.

1983 *Echoes of the Ancient Skies: The Astronomy of Lost Civilizations.* New York: Harper and Row.

1991 *Beyond the Blue Horizon: Myths and Legends of the Sun, Moon, Stars, and Planets.* New York and Oxford: Oxford University Press.

1993 The Winter Hexagon. *Sky and Telescope* (December):66–67.

1995 New Year, No Moon. *Sky and Telescope* (January): 72–73.

1997 *Skywatchers, Shamans, and Kings.* New York: John Wiley & Sons.

Kurbjuhn, Kornelia

1989 *Maya: The Complete Catalogue of Glyph Readings.* Kassel, Germany: Schneider & Weber.

La Farge, Oliver, and Douglas Byers

1931 *The Yearbearer's People.* Middle American Research Series, pub. 3. New Orleans: Tulane University.

Lamb, Weldon W.

1980 The Sun, Moon, and Venus at Uxmal. *American Antiquity* 45(1):79–86.

1981 Star Lore in the Yucatec Maya Dictionaries. In *Archaeoastronomy in the Americas,* edited by Ray A. Williamson, pp. 233–248. Los Altos, Calif.: Ballena Press.

1995 Tzotzil Maya Cosmology. *Tribus* 44:268–279.

n.d.a Yucatecan Maya Astronomy since the Conquest. Ms.

n.d.b Tzotzil Starlore. Ms.

Laughlin, Robert M.

1969 The Tzotzil. In *Ethnology,* part 1, edited by Evon Z. Vogt, pp. 152–194. *Handbook of Middle American Indians,* vol. 7, Robert Wauchope, general editor. Austin: University of Texas Press.

1975 *The Great Tzotzil Dictionary of San Lorenzo Zinacantán.* Smithsonian Contributions to Anthropology, no. 19. Washington, D.C.: Smithsonian Institution Press.

1977 *Of Cabbages and Kings: Tales from Zinacantán.* Smithsonian Contributions to Anthropology, no. 23. Washington, D.C.: Smithsonian Institution Press.

1988 *The Great Tzotzil Dictionary of Santo Domingo Zinacantán.* Vol. 1, *Tzotzil-English.* Smithsonian Contributions to Anthropology, no. 31. Washington, D.C.: Smithsonian Institution Press.

Laughlin, Robert M., and Carol Karasik

1988 *The People of the Bat.* Washington, D.C.: Smithsonian Institution Press.

Lebeuf, Arnold

1995 Astronomía en Xochicalco. In *La Acrópolis de Xochicalco.* Mexico City: Instituto de Cultura de Morelos.

León, Juan de

1945 *Mundo Quiché.* Guatemala City: Miscelánea.

1954 *Diccionario Quiché-Español.* Guatemala City: Editorial Landirzar.

León-Portilla, Miguel

1988 *Time and Reality in the Thought of the Maya.* Norman: University of Oklahoma Press.

Lincoln, Charles

1988 Dual Kingship at Chichén Itzá, Yucatán. Paper presented at the Fifty-third Annual Meeting of the Society for American Archaeology, Phoenix, Arizona.

Lincoln, Jackson S.

1942 *The Maya Calendar of the Ixil Indians of the Guatemalan Highlands.* Carnegie Institute of Washington, pub. 528, Contributions to American Anthropology and History, no. 38. Washington, D.C.: Carnegie Institution of Washington.

Linden, John H.

1986 Glyph X of the Maya Lunar Series: An Eighteen-Month Lunar Synodic Calendar. *American Antiquity* 51(1):122–136.

1996 The Deity Head Variants of Glyph C. In *Eighth Palenque Round Table, 1993,* edited by Martha J. Macri and Jan McHargue; Merle Greene Robertson, general editor; pp. 343–356. San Francisco: Pre-Columbian Art Research Institute.

Looper, Matthew G.

1995 The Three Stones of Maya Creation Mythology at Quiriguá. *Mexicon* 17(2):24–30.

López-Austin, Alfredo

1994 *Tamoanchan y Tlalocan.* Mexico City: Fondo de Cultura Económica.

Lounsbury, Floyd G.

1973 On the Derivation and Reading of the "Ben-Ich" Prefix. In *Mesoamerican Writing Systems,* edited by Elizabeth P. Benson, pp. 99–144. Washington, D.C.: Dumbarton Oaks.

1974 The Inscription of the Sarcophagus Lid at Palenque. In *Primera Mesa Redonda de Palenque,* part 2, edited by Merle Greene Robertson, pp. 5–21. Pebble Beach, Calif.: Robert Louis Stevenson School.

1978 Maya Numeration, Computation, and Calendrical Astronomy. *Dictionary of Scientific Biography*, vol. 15, suppl. 1, edited by Charles Coulston-Gillispie, pp. 757–818. New York: Charles Scribner's Sons.

1982 Astronomical Knowledge and Its Uses at Bonampak. In *Archaeoastronomy in the New World*, edited by Anthony F. Aveni, pp. 143–168. Cambridge: Cambridge University Press.

1983 The Base of the Venus Tables of the Dresden Codex, and Its Significance for the Calendar-Correlation Problem. In *Calendars in Mesoamerica and Peru: Native American Computations of Time*, edited by Anthony F. Aveni and Gordon Brotherston, pp. 1–26. Oxford: BAR International Series 174.

1985 The Identities of the Mythological Figures in the Cross Group Inscriptions of Palenque. *Fourth Palenque Round Table, 1980*, vol. 6, edited by Merle Greene Robertson and Elizabeth P. Benson, pp. 45–58. San Francisco: Pre-Columbian Art Research Institute.

1989 A Palenque King and the Planet Jupiter. In *World Archaeoastronomy: Selected Papers from the Second Oxford International Conference on Archaeoastronomy*, edited by Anthony F. Aveni, pp. 246–259. Cambridge: Cambridge University Press.

1991 Distinguished Lecture: Recent Work in the Decipherment of Palenque's Hieroglyphic Inscriptions. *American Anthropologist* 93:809–824.

1992a A Derivation of the Mayan-to-Julian Calendar Correlation from the Dresden Codex Venus Chronology. In *The Sky and Mayan Literature*, edited by Anthony F. Aveni, pp. 184–206. Oxford: Oxford University Press.

1992b A Solution for the Number 1.5.5.0 of the Mayan Venus Table. In *The Sky and Mayan Literature*, edited by Anthony F. Aveni, pp. 206–215. Oxford: Oxford University Press.

Love, Bruce

1994 *The Paris Codex: Handbook for a Maya Priest.* Austin: University of Texas Press.

1995 A Dresden Codex Mars Table? *Latin American Antiquity* 6 (4):350–361.

MacKie, Ewan

1985 *Excavations at Xunantunich and Pomona, Belize.* Oxford: BAR International Series 251.

MacPherson, H. G.

1987 The Maya Lunar Season. *Antiquity* 61:440–449.

Macri, Martha J.

1982 *Phoneticism in Maya Head Variant Numerals.* Master's thesis, University of California, Berkeley.

Macri, Martha J., and D. Beattie

1996 The Lunar Cycle and the Mesoamerican Counts of Twenty, Thirteen, Nine, and Seven. Paper presented at the Oxford Fifth Conference on Archaeoastronomy, Santa Fe.

Macri, Martha J., and Laura M. Stark

1993 *A Sign Catalog of the La Mojarra Script.* San Francisco: Pre-Columbian Art Research Institute Monograph 5.

Maler, Theobert

1908 *Explorations in the Department of Petén, Guatemala, and Adjacent Region: Topoxte, Yaxha, Benque Viejo, Naranjo.* Memoirs of the Peabody Museum of Archaeology and Ethnology, vol. 4, no. 2. Cambridge: Harvard University.

Malmström, Vincent

1991 Edzna: Earliest Astronomical Center of the Maya. In *Arqueoastronomía y etnoastronomía en Mesoamérica*, edited by Johanna Broda, Stanislaw Iwaniszewski, and Lucrecia Maupomé, pp. 37–47. Mexico City: Universidad Nacional Autónoma de México.

1997 *Cycles of the Sun, Mysteries of the Moon.* Austin: University of Texas Press.

Marcus, Joyce

1992 *Mesoamerican Writing Systems: Propaganda, Myth, and History in Four Ancient Civilizations.* Princeton: Princeton University Press.

Marquina, Ignacio

1964 *Arquitectura prehispánica.* Memorias del I.N.A.H. Mexico City: Instituto Nacional de Antropología e Historia.

Martin, Frederick

1993 A Dresden Codex Eclipse Sequence: Projections for the Years 1970–1992. *Latin American Antiquity* 4(1):74–93.

Mathews, Peter

1980 Notes on the Dynastic Sequence of Bonampak, Part I. In *Third Palenque Round Table, 1978*, part II, edited by Merle Greene Robertson, pp. 60–73. Austin: University of Texas Press.

1990 *The Proceedings of the Maya Hieroglyphic Weekend, October 27–28, 1990, Cleveland State University.* Transcribed and edited by Phil Wanyerka. Photocopy.

1991 *The Proceedings of the Maya Hieroglyphic Weekend, October 26–27, 1991, Cleveland State University.* Transcribed and edited by Phil Wanyerka. Photocopy.

Maudslay, A. P.

1889–1902 *Biologia Centrali-Americana.* Vols. 1–4. London: R. H. Porter and Dulau.

Mayers, Marvin

1958 *Pocomchí Texts with Grammatical Notes.* Summer Institute of Linguistics, pub. 2. Norman: University of Oklahoma.

McAnany, Patricia

1995a Ancestors and the Classic Maya Built Environment. Paper presented at the Dumbarton Oaks Fall Symposium: "Function and Meaning in Classic Maya Architecture," Washington, D.C.

1995b *Living with the Ancestors: Kinship and Kingship in Ancient Maya Society.* Austin: University of Texas Press.

McCluskey, Stephen C.

1983 Maya Observations of Very Long Periods of Venus. *Journal for the History of Astronomy* 14:92–101.

McGee, R. Jon

1990 *Life, Ritual, and Religion among the Lacandón Maya.* Belmont, Calif.: Wadsworth Publishing Company.

McVicker, Donald

1985 The "Mayanized" Mexicans. *American Antiquity* 50(1):82–101.

Meeus, Jean

n.d. Stations of Jupiter, Saturn, Venus, and Mars. Ms. in possession of the author.

Milbrath, Susan

1979 *A Study of Olmec Sculptural Chronology.* Studies in Pre-Columbian Art and Archaeology 23. Washington, D.C.: Dumbarton Oaks.

1980a Star Gods and Astronomy of the Aztecs. In *La antropología americanista en la actualidad: Homenaje a Raphael Girard,* vol. 1, pp. 289–303. Mexico City: Editores Mexicanos Unidos.

1980b A Star Calendar in the Codex Madrid. In *La antropología americanista en la actualidad: Homenaje a Raphael Girard,* vol. 1, pp. 445–464. Mexico City: Editores Mexicanos Unidos.

1981 Astronomical Imagery in the Serpent Sequence of the Madrid Codex. *Archaeoastronomy in the Americas,* edited by Ray A. Williamson, pp. 263–283. College Park, Md.: Center for Archaeoastronomy.

1982 *Star Gods of the Ancient Americas: Exhibition Script.* New York: Museum of the American Indian.

1988a Birth Images in Mixteca-Puebla Art. In *The Role of Gender in Pre-Columbian Art and Architecture,* edited by Virginia E. Miller, pp. 153–178. Lanham: University Press of America.

1988b Representación y orientación astronómica en la arquitectura de Chichén Itzá. *Boletín de la Escuela de Ciencias Antropológicas de la Universidad de Yucatán* 15:25–40.

1988c Astronomical Images and Orientations in the Architecture of Chichen Itza. In *New Directions in American Archaeoastronomy,* edited by Anthony F. Aveni, pp. 57–79. Proceedings of the Forty-sixth International Congress of Americanists. Oxford: BAR International Series 454.

1989 A Seasonal Calendar with Venus Periods in Borgia 29–46. In *The Imagination of Matter: Religion and Ecology in Mesoamerican Traditions,* edited by David Carrasco, pp. 103–127. Oxford: BAR International Series 515.

1995a Gender and Roles of Lunar Deities in Postclassic Central Mexico and Their Correlations with the Maya Area. *Estudios de Cultura Nahuatl* 25:45–93.

1995b Eclipse Imagery in Mexica Sculpture of Central Mexico. *Vistas in Astronomy* 39:479–502.

1995c A New Interpretation of the Dresden Codex Venus Pages. In *Cantos de Mesoamérica: Metodologías científicas en la búsqueda del conocimiento prehispánico,* edited by Daniel Flores, pp. 257–292. Mexico City: Instituto de Astronomía, Facultad de Ciencias, Universidad Nacional Autónoma de México.

1995d Xochiquetzal as a Lunar Deity in the Codex Borgia. Paper presented at the Seventeenth International Congress of the History of Religions, Mexico City.

1996a Postclassic Maya Metaphors for Lunar Motion. In *Eighth Palenque Round Table, 1993,* edited by Martha J. Macri and Jan McHargue; Merle Greene Robertson, general editor; pp. 379–392. San Francisco: Pre-Columbian Art Research Institute.

1996b Jupiter in Classic and Postclassic Maya Art. Paper presented at the Fifth Oxford International Conference on Archaeoastronomy, Santa Fe, New Mexico.

1997 Decapitated Lunar Goddesses in Aztec Art, Myth, and Ritual. *Ancient Mesoamerica* 8(2):185–206.

Miles, Suzanne W.

1965 Sculpture of the Guatemala-Chiapas Highlands and Pacific Slopes, and Associated Hieroglyphs. In *Archaeology of Southern Mesoamerica,* part 1, edited by Gordon R. Willey, pp. 237–275. In *Handbook of Middle American Indians,* vol. 2, Robert Wauchope, general editor. Austin: University of Texas Press.

Miller, Arthur G.

1973 *Mural Painting of Teotihuacán.* Washington, D.C.: Dumbarton Oaks.

1977 Captains of the Itza: Unpublished Mural Evidence from Chichen Itza. In *Social Process in Maya Prehistory: Studies in Honour of Sir Eric Thompson,* edited by Norman Hammond, pp. 197–225. New York: Academic Press.

1982 *On the Edge of the Sea: Mural Painting at Tancah-Tulum, Quintana Roo.* Washington, D.C.: Dumbarton Oaks.

1986 *Maya Rulers of Time: A Study of Architectural Sculpture at Tikal, Guatemala.* Philadelphia: The University Museum, University of Pennsylvania.

Miller, Mary E.

1975 *Jaina Figurines* (with an appendix by David Joralemon). Princeton: The Art Museum, Princeton University.

1986 *The Murals of Bonampak.* Princeton: Princeton University Press.

1988 The Meaning and Function of the Main Acropolis, Copán. In *The Southeast Classic Maya Zone,* edited by Elizabeth H. Boone and Gordon Willey, pp. 149–194. Washington, D.C.: Dumbarton Oaks Library and Research Collection

Miller, Mary E., and Karl Taube

1993 *The Gods and Symbols of Ancient Mexico and the Maya: An Illustrated Dictionary of Mesoamerican Religion.* London: Thames and Hudson.

Miller, Virginia E.

1989 Star Warriors at Chichén Itzá. In *Word and Image in Maya Culture,* edited by William F. Hanks and Don S. Rice, pp. 287–305. Salt Lake City: University of Utah Press.

1991 *The Frieze of the Palace of the Stuccoes, Acanceh, Yucatan, Mexico.* Studies in Pre-Columbian Art and Archaeology 31. Washington, D.C.: Dumbarton Oaks.

Morante López, Rubén B.

1995 Los observatorios subterráneos. *La palabra y el hombre. Revista de la Universidad Veracruzana* 94: 35–71.

Morales Valderrama, Carmen

1990 Hallazgos arqueoastronómicos del 89. *I'INAJ* 1(1): 29–34.

Morley, Sylvanus

1915 An Introduction to the Study of Maya Hieroglyphs. *Bureau of American Ethnology Bulletin,* no. 57. Washington, D.C.: Smithsonian Institution.

Morris, Earl H., Jean Charlot, and Ann Axtell Morris

1931 *The Temple of the Warriors at Chichen Itza, Yucatan.* Carnegie Institution of Washington, pub. 406. Washington, D.C.: Carnegie Institution of Washington.

Morris, Walter F., Jr.

1986 Maya Time Warps. *Archaeology* 39:52–59.

Morris, Walter F., and Jeffrey J. Foxx

1987 *Living Maya.* New York: Harry N. Abrams.

Nahm, Werner

1994 Maya Warfare and the Venus Year. *Mexicon* 16(1): 6–10.

Nash, June

1970 *In the Eyes of the Ancestors: Belief and Behavior in a Maya Community.* New Haven: Yale University Press.

Needham, Joseph

1959 *Science and Civilization in China.* Vol. 3. Cambridge: Cambridge University Press.

Neuenswander, Helen

1981 Vestiges of Early Maya Time Concepts in Contemporary Maya (Cubulco Achi) Community: Implications for Community. *Estudios de Cultura Maya* 13:125–163.

Newsome, Elizabeth Ann

1991 *The Trees of Paradise and the Pillars of the World: Vision Quest and Creation in the Stelae Cycle of 18-Rabbit-God K, Copán, Honduras.* Ph.D. diss., University of Texas, Austin. Ann Arbor: University Microfilms International.

Nicholson, Henry B.

1971   Religion in Pre-Hispanic Central Mexico. In *Archaeology of Northern Mesoamerica*, part 1, edited by Gordon F. Ekholm and Ignacio Bernal, pp. 395–446. *Handbook of Middle American Indians*, vol. 10, Robert Wauchope, general editor. Austin: University of Texas Press.

Norman, V. Garth

1976   *Izapa Sculpture*, part 2. Papers of the New World Archaeological Foundation, no. 30. Provo: Brigham Young University.

Nowotny, Karl Anton

1976   *Codex Borgia.* Codices Selecti. Graz: Akademische Druck u. Verlagsanstalt.

Olson, Donald W., and Brian D. White

1997   A Planetary Grouping in Maya Times. *Sky and Telescope* (August): 63–64.

Oppolzer, Theodor Ritter von

1962   *Canon of Eclipses.* Translated by Owen Gingerich. New York: Dover Publications.

Orellana, Sandra

1977   Aboriginal Medicine in Highland Guatemala. *Medical Anthropology* 1(1):113–156.

Ortiz García, Elena

1997   La astronomía como fuente: El universo meso-americano. *Anales del Museo de América* 5:17–42.

Ottewell, Guy

1990   *Astronomical Calendar, 1990.* Greenville, S.C.: Department of Physics, Furman University.

Pankenier, David W.

1997   The Mandate of Heaven. *Archaeology* (March/April):26–33.

Parsons, Lee Allen

1969   *Bilbao, Guatemala: An Archaeological Study of the Pacific Coast Cotzumalhuapa Region.* 2 vols. Publications in Anthropology 12. Milwaukee: Milwaukee Public Museum.

1988   Proto-Maya Aspects of Miraflores-Arenal Monumental Stone Sculpture from Kaminaljuyu and the Southern Pacific Coast. In *Maya Iconography*, edited by Elizabeth P. Benson and Gillett G. Grif-

fin, pp. 6–43. Princeton: Princeton University Press.

Pasztory, Esther

1974   *The Iconography of the Teotihuacan Tlaloc.* Studies in Pre-Columbian Art and Archaeology 15. Washington, D.C.: Dumbarton Oaks.

Paxton, Meredith

1990   Codex Dresden: Late Postclassic Ceramic Depictions and Problems of Provenience and Date of Painting. In *Sixth Palenque Round Table, 1986*, edited by Merle Greene Robertson and Virginia M. Fields, pp. 303–308. Norman: University of Oklahoma Press.

Perera, Victor, and Robert D. Bruce

1982   *The Lacandon Mayas of the Mexican Rain Forest.* Boston and Toronto: Little Brown and Company.

Pérez Toro, Augusto

1942   *La milpa.* Mérida, Yucatán, Mex.: Publicaciones del Gobierno de Yucatán.

1945   El clima. In *Enciclopedia Yucatanense*, vol. 1, edited by Carlos A. Echánove Trujillo, pp. 81–108. Mexico City: Edición oficial del Gobierno de México.

1946   La agricultura milpera de los mayas de Yucatán. In *Enciclopedia Yucatanense*, vol. 6, edited by Carlos A. Echánove Trujillo, pp. 173–204. Mexico City: Edición oficial del Gobierno de México.

Pieper, Jeanne

1988   *Guatemalan Masks: The Pieper Collection.* Los Angeles: Craft and Folk Art Museum.

Prechtel, Martin, and Robert S. Carlsen

1988   Weaving and Cosmos amongst the Tzutujil Maya of Guatemala. *RES: Anthropology and Aesthetics* 15:123–132.

Preuss, Mary H.

1988   *Gods of the Popol Vuh.* Culver City, Calif.: Labyrinthos.

1995   A Love Story between the Sun and Moon. *Institute of Maya Studies Journal* 1(2):31–38.

Proskouriakoff, Tatiana

1950   *A Study of Classic Maya Sculpture.* Carnegie Institution of Washington, pub. 593. Washington, D.C.: Carnegie Institution of Washington.

1960   Historical Implications of a Pattern of Dates at Piedras Negras, Guatemala. *American Antiquity* 25:454–475.

1978 Olmec Gods and Maya God-Glyphs. In *Codex Wauchope: A Tribute Roll,* edited by M. Giardino, B. Edmonson, and W. Crenier, pp. 113–117. *Human Mosaic,* vol. 12. New Orleans: Tulane University.

1993 *Maya History.* Edited by Rosemary A. Joyce. Austin: University of Texas Press.

Quiñones Keber, Eloise. *Codex Telleriano-Remensis: Ritual, Divination, and History in a Pictorial Aztec Manuscript.* Austin: University of Texas Press.

Quirarte, Jacinto

1979 The Representation of Place, Location, and Direction on a Classic Maya Vase. In *Tercera Mesa Redonda de Palenque,* vol. 4, edited by Merle Greene Robertson and Donna Call Jeffers, pp. 99–110. Palenque, Chiapas, Mex.: Pre-Columbian Art Research Center.

1982 The Santa Rita Murals: A Review. *Middle American Research Institute Occasional Paper,* no. 4., pp. 43–58. New Orleans: Tulane University.

Rands, Robert

1965 Jades of the Maya Lowlands. In *Archaeology of Southern Mesoamerica,* part 2, edited by Gordon Willey, pp. 561–580. *Handbook of Middle American Indians,* vol. 3, Robert Wauchope, general editor. Austin: University of Texas Press.

Rätsch, Christian

1985 *Bilder aus der unsichtbaren Welt.* Munich: Kindler Verlag.

Rätsch, Christian, and K'ayum Ma'ax

1984 *Ein Kosmos im Regenwald.* Cologne: Eugen Diederichs Verlag.

Redfield, Robert, and Alfonso Villa Rojas

1962 *Chan Kom: A Maya Village.* Chicago: University of Chicago Press.

Reed, Nelson

1964 *The Caste War of Yucatan.* Stanford: Stanford University Press.

Reents-Budet, Dorie

1991 The "Holmul Dancer" Theme in Maya Art. In *Sixth Palenque Round Table, 1986,* edited by Merle Greene Robertson and Virginia M. Fields, pp. 217–222. Norman: University of Oklahoma Press.

1994 *Painting the Maya Universe: Royal Ceramics in the Classic Period.* Durham, N.C.: Duke University Press and Duke University of Art.

Reilly, F. Kent

1996 The Lazy S: A Formative Period Iconographic Loan to Maya Hieroglyphic Writing. In *Eighth Palenque Round Table, 1993,* edited by Martha J. Macri and Jan McHargue; Merle Greene Robertson, general editor; pp. 413–424. San Francisco: Pre-Columbian Art Research Institute.

Remington, Judith

1977 Current Astronomical Practices among the Maya. In *Native American Astronomy,* edited by Anthony F. Aveni, pp. 75–88. Austin: University of Texas Press.

Rey, H. A.

1976 *The Stars: A New Way to See Them.* Boston: Houghton Mifflin.

Ringle, William M.

1988 Of Mice and Monkeys: The Value and Meaning of T1016, the God C Hieroglyph. *Research Reports on Ancient Maya Writing,* no. 18. Washington, D.C.: Center for Maya Research.

Ringle, William M., and Thomas C. Smith-Stark

1996 *A Concordance to the Inscriptions of Palenque, Chiapas, Mexico.* Middle American Research Institute, pub. 62. New Orleans: Tulane University.

Robertson, Merle Greene

1985a *The Sculpture of Palenque: Volume 2, The Early Buildings of the Palace.* Princeton: Princeton University Press.

1985b *The Sculpture of Palenque: Volume 3, The Late Buildings of the Palace.* Princeton: Princeton University Press.

1991 *The Sculpture of Palenque: Volume 4, The Cross Group, the North Group, the Olvidado, and Other Pieces.* Princeton: Princeton University Press.

Robertson, Merle Greene, and Margaret Andrews

1992 Una reevaluación del arte del Templo del Chac Mool y de la Columnata Noroeste en Chichén Itzá: Coexistencia y conflicto interior. *Mayab* 8:54–87.

Robicsek, Francis

1978 *The Smoking Gods: Tobacco in Maya Art, History, and Religion.* Norman: University of Oklahoma Press.

1979 The Mythical Identity of God K. In *Tercera Mesa Redonda de Palenque,* vol. 4, edited by Merle Greene Robertson and Donna Call Jeffers, pp. 111–128. Palenque, Chiapas, Mex.: Pre-Columbian Art Research Center.

Robicsek, Francis, and Donald M. Hales

1981 *The Maya Book of the Dead: The Ceramic Codex.* Charlotte: University of North Carolina.

1982 *Maya Ceramic Vases from the Classic Period.* Charlotte: University of North Carolina.

Romain, Marianne

1988 Die Mondgöttin der Maya und ihre darstellung in der figurinenkunst. *Baessler-Archiv,* Neue Folge, 36:281–353.

Roth, Gunter

1970 *Handbook for Planet Observers.* London: Forbes and Forbes.

Roys, Ralph L.

1967 *The Book of Chilam Balam of Chumayel.* Norman: University of Oklahoma Press.

1972 *The Indian Background of Colonial Yucatan.* Norman: University of Oklahoma Press.

Roys, Ralph L., trans. and ed.

1965 *Ritual of the Bacabs.* Norman: University of Oklahoma Press.

Ruz Lhuillier, Alberto

1968 *Costumbres funerarias de los antiguos mayas.* Mexico City: Seminario de Cultura Maya, Universidad Nacional Autónoma de México.

Sabloff, Jeremy A., and William L. Rathje.

1975 *A Study of Changing Pre-Columbian Commercial Systems.* Cambridge: Peabody Museum of Archaeology and Ethnology, Harvard University.

Sahagún, Fray Bernardino de

1950–1982 *Florentine Codex: General History of the Things of New Spain.* 12 vols. (2d ed. of Book 1 [1981] and Book 2 [1970]), translated by Arthur J. O. Anderson and Charles E. Dibble. Salt Lake City: School of American Research and University of Utah Press.

Salvador, Ricardo J.

1998 Broken Maize Stalks. *Institute of Maya Studies Newsletter* 27(3):3–4.

Satterthwaite, Linton

1965 Calendrics of the Maya Lowlands. In *Archaeology of Southern Mesoamerica,* part 2, edited by Gordon Willey, pp. 603–631. *Handbook of Middle American Indians,* vol. 3, Robert Wauchope, general editor. Austin: University of Texas Press.

1967 Moon Ages of the Maya Inscriptions: The Problem of Their Seven-Day Range of Deviation from Calculated Mean Ages. In *The Civilizations of Ancient America: Selected Papers of the Twenty-ninth International Congress of Americanists,* edited by Sol Tax, pp. 142–154. New York: Cooper Square Publishers.

Saville, Marshall

1919 A Sculptured Vase from Guatemala. *Leaflets of the Museum of the American Indian Heye Foundation,* no. 1. New York: Museum of the American Indian.

Schaefer, Bradley E.

1987 Heliacal Rise Phenomena. *Archaeoastronomy* (Supplement to *Journal for the History of Astronomy*) 11:S19–S33.

Schackt, Jon

1986 *One God—Two Temples.* Oslo Occasional Papers in Social Anthropology, no. 13. Oslo: Department of Social Anthropology, Universitetsbokhandelen.

Schele, Linda

1974 Observations on the Cross Motif at Palenque. In *Primera Mesa Redonda de Palenque,* part I, edited by Merle Greene Robertson, pp. 41–62. Pebble Beach, Calif.: Robert Louis Stevenson School.

1976 Accession Iconography of Chan-Bahlum in the Group of the Cross at Palenque. The Art, Iconography, and Dynastic History of Palenque, part 3, pp. 9–34. *Proceedings of the Segunda Mesa Redonda of Palenque,* edited by Merle Greene Robertson. Pebble Beach, Calif.: Robert Louis Stevenson School.

1977 Palenque: The House of the Dying Sun. In *Native American Astronomy,* edited by Anthony F. Aveni, pp. 42–56. Austin: University of Texas Press.

1984 Some Suggested Readings of the Event and Office of Heir-Designate at Palenque. In *Phoneticism in Mayan Hieroglyphic Writing,* edited by John S. Justeson and Lyle Campbell, pp. 287–306. Institute for Mesoamerican Studies, pub. 9. Albany: State University of New York at Albany.

1985 The Hauberg Stela: Bloodletting and the Mythos of Maya Rulership. In *Fifth Palenque Round Table, 1983,* edited by Virginia M. Fields, pp. 135–150. San Francisco: Pre-Columbian Art Research Institute.

1986 Paraphrase of the Text of Altar U. *Copán Note 5.* Austin: Kinkos.

1987a The Figures on the Central Marker of the Ballcourt AIIb at Copán. *Copán Note 13.* Austin: Kinkos.

1987b Two Altar Names at Copán. *Copán Note* 36. Austin: Kinkos.

1987c New Data on the Paddlers from Butz'-Chan of Copán. *Copán Note* 29. Austin: Kinkos.

1989a A Brief Commentary on the Top of Altar Q. *Copán Note* 66. Austin: Kinkos.

1989b *Notebook of the Thirteenth Maya Hieroglyphic Workshop at Texas, March 11–12, 1989.* Austin: Art Department, University of Texas.

1990a House Names and Dedication Rituals at Palenque. In *Vision and Revision in Maya Studies,* edited by Flora S. Clancy and Peter D. Harrison, pp. 143–158. Albuquerque: University of New Mexico Press.

1990b *Proceedings of the Maya Hieroglyphic Workshop, March 10–11, 1990.* Transcribed and edited by Phil Wanyerka. Austin: University of Texas.

1991a Venus and the Monuments of Smoke-Imix-God K and Others in the Great Plaza. *Copán Note* 101. Austin: Kinkos.

1991b The Demotion of Chac-Zutz': Lineage Compounds and Subsidiary Lords at Palenque. In *Sixth Palenque Round Table, 1986,* edited by Merle Greene Robertson and Virginia M. Fields, pp. 6–11. Norman: University of Oklahoma Press.

1992a The Founders of Maya Lineages at Copán and Other Maya Sites. *Ancient Mesoamerica* 3(1): 135–144.

1992b *Workbook for the Sixteenth Maya Hieroglyphic Workshop at Texas.* Austin: Department of Art History and the Institute of Latin American Studies, University of Texas.

Schele, Linda, and Barbara Fash

1991 Venus and the Reign of Smoke-Monkey. *Copán Note* 100. Austin: Kinkos.

Schele, Linda, and David Freidel

1990 *A Forest of Kings: The Untold Story of the Ancient Maya.* New York: William Morrow.

Schele, Linda, and Nikolai Grube

1994 *The Proceedings of the Maya Hieroglyphic Workshop: Tlaloc-Venus Warfare, March 12–13, 1994.* Transcribed and edited by Phil Wanyerka. Austin: University of Texas.

1995 *The Proceedings of the Maya Hieroglyphic Workshop: Late Classic and Terminal Classic Warfare, March 11–12, 1995.* Transcribed and edited by Phil Wanyerka. Austin: University of Texas.

Schele, Linda, and Rudi Larios

1991 Some Venus Dates on the Hieroglyphic Stair of Copán. *Copán Note* 99. Austin: Kinkos.

Schele, Linda, and Matthew Looper

1994 The 9.17.0.0.0 Eclipse at Quiriguá and Copán. *Copán Note* 115. Austin: Kinkos.

Schele, Linda, and Peter Mathews

1979 *The Bodega of Palenque, Chiapas, Mexico.* Washington, D.C.: Dumbarton Oaks.

1998 *The Code of Kings: The Language of Seven Sacred Maya Temples and Tombs.* New York: Scribner.

Schele, Linda, and Jeffrey H. Miller

1983 *The Mirror, the Rabbit, and the Bundle: "Accession" Expressions from the Classic Maya Inscriptions.* Studies in Pre-Columbian Art and Archaeology 25. Washington, D.C.: Dumbarton Oaks.

Schele, Linda, and Mary Miller

1986 *The Blood of Kings: Dynasty and Ritual in Maya Art.* Fort Worth: Kimbell Art Museum.

Schellhas, Paul

1904 Representation of Deities of the Maya Manuscripts. *Papers of the Peabody Museum of Archaeology and Ethnology, Harvard University,* vol. 4, no. 1. Cambridge: The Peabody Museum.

Schlak, Arthur

1989 Jaguar and Serpent Foot: Iconography as Astronomy. In *Word and Image in Maya Culture,* edited by William F. Hanks and Don S. Rice, pp. 260–271. Salt Lake City: University of Utah Press.

1996 Venus, Mercury, and the Sun: GI, GII, GIII of the Palenque Triad. *RES: Anthropology and Aesthetics* 29/30: 181–202.

Sedat, Guillermo

1955 *Nuevo Diccionario de las lenguas K'ekchi' y Española.* Chamelco, Alta Verapaz, Guatemala: Instituto Indigenista Nacional.

Séjourné, Laurette

1976 *Burning Water: Thought and Religion in Ancient Mexico.* Berkeley: Shambala Publications.

Seler, Eduard

1904a Venus Period in the Picture Writings of the Borgian Codex Group. *Bureau of American Ethnology Bulletin,* no. 28, pp. 353–392. Washington, D.C.: Smithsonian Institution.

1904b Mexican Chronology. *Bureau of American Ethnology Bulletin,* no. 28, pp. 11–56. Washington, D.C.: Smithsonian Institution.

1960–1961 *Gesammelte Abhandlungen zur Amerikanischen Sprach und Altertumskunde.* 5 vols. Graz: Akademische Druck u. Verlagsanstalt. (Reprinted from the 1902–1903 edition, Berlin)

1963 *Comentarios al Códice Borgia.* 2 vols. and facsimile. Mexico City: Fondo de Cultura Económica.

1990–1996 *Collected Works in Mesoamerican Linguistics and Archaeology,* translation under the supervision of Charles P. Bowditch. Vols. 1–5, Frank E. Comparato, general editor. Lancaster, Calif.: Labyrinthos.

Severin, Gregory M.

1981 The Paris Codex: Decoding an Astronomical Ephemeris. In *Transactions of the American Philosophical Society,* vol. 71, part 5. Philadelphia: The American Philosophical Society.

Sharer, Robert J.

1994 *The Ancient Maya.* 5th ed. Stanford: Stanford University Press.

Shrove, D. Justin, and Alan Fletcher

1984 *Chronology of Eclipses and Comets: A.D. 1–1000.* Suffolk, England: Boydell Press.

Slocum, Marianna C.

1965a The Origin of Corn and Other Tzeltal Myths. *Tlalocan* 5(1):1–45.

1965b *Vocabulario Tzeltal de Bachajón.* Mexico: Instituto Lingüístico de Verano.

Sosa, John R.

1985 *The Maya Sky, the Maya World: A Symbolic Analysis of Yucatec Maya Cosmology.* Ph.D. diss., State University of New York. Ann Arbor: University Microfilms.

1986 Maya Concepts of Astronomical Order. In *Symbol and Meaning beyond the Closed Community: Essays in Mesoamerican Ideas,* edited by Gary H. Gossen, pp. 185–196. Studies in Culture and Society, vol. 1. Albany: Institute for Mesoamerican Studies, State University of New York at Albany.

1989 Cosmological, Symbolic, and Cultural Complexity among the Contemporary Maya of Yucatan. In *World Archaeoastronomy: Selected Papers from the Second Oxford International Conference on Archaeoastronomy,* edited by Anthony F. Aveni, pp. 130–142. Cambridge: Cambridge University Press.

Spinden, Herbert

1916 The Question of the Zodiac in America. *American Anthropologist* 18(1):53–80.

Sprajc, Ivan

1987–1988 Venus and Temple 22 at Copán: Revisited. *Archaeoastronomy: The Bulletin of the Center for Archaeoastronomy* 10:88–97.

1993a The Venus-Rain-Maize Complex in the Mesoamerican World View: Part I. *Journal of the History of Astronomy* 17:17–70.

1993b The Venus-Rain-Maize Complex in the Mesoamerican World View: Part II. *Archaeoastronomy* (Supplement to the *Journal of the History of Astronomy*) 18:S27–S53.

Stone, Andrea

1982 Recent Discoveries from Naj Tunich. *Mexicon* 4:93–99.

1983 The Zoomorphs of Quiriguá, Guatemala. Ph.D. diss., University of Texas at Austin. Ann Arbor: University Microfilms.

1985 Variety and Transformation in the Cosmic Monster Theme at Quiriguá, Guatemala. In *Fifth Palenque Round Table, 1983,* vol. 7, edited by Merle Greene Robertson and Virginia M. Fields, pp. 171–181. San Francisco: Pre-Columbian Art Research Institute.

1989 Disconnection, Foreign Insignia, and Political Expansion: Teotihuacan and the Warrior Stelae of Piedras Negras. In *Mesoamerica after the Decline of Teotihuacan A.D. 700–900,* edited by Richard A. Diehl and Janet C. Berlo, pp. 153–172. Washington, D.C.: Dumbarton Oaks.

1990 A Case of Dual Identity: The Grandmother and the Unfaithful Wife as a Paradigm in Maya Art. Paper presented at the Symposium on Gender in Pre-Columbian Mesoamerica, Eighty-ninth annual meeting of the American Anthropological Association, New Orleans.

1992 Zoomorph G from Quiriguá as the Jaguar Throne of Stone. Paper presented at the Ninety-first annual meeting of the American Anthropological Association, Chicago.

1995a The *Nik* Name of the Codical God H. Paper presented at the Ninety-fourth annual meeting of the American Anthropological Association, Washington, D.C.

1995b *Images from the Underworld: Naj Tunich and the Tradition of Maya Cave Painting.* Austin: University of Texas Press.

1996 The Cleveland Plaque: Cloudy Places of the Maya Realm. In *Eighth Palenque Round Table, 1993,* edited by Martha J. Macri and Jan McHargue; Merle Greene Robertson, general editor; pp. 403–412. San Francisco: Pre-Columbian Art Research Institute.

Stross, Brian, and Justin Kerr

1990   Notes on the Maya Vision Quest through Enema. In *The Maya Vase Book,* vol. 2, edited by Justin Kerr, pp. 348–361. New York: Kerr Associates.

Stuart, David

1978   Some Thoughts on Certain Occurrences of the T565 Glyph Element at Palenque. In *Tercera Mesa Redonda de Palenque,* vol. 4, edited by Merle Greene Robertson and Donna Call Jeffers, pp. 167–172. San Francisco: Pre-Columbian Art Research Institute.

1984   Royal Auto-sacrifice among the Maya. *RES: Anthropology and Aesthetics* 7/8:7–20.

1986   The Hieroglyphic Name of Altar U. *Copán Note* 4. Austin: Kinkos.

1987   Ten Phonetic Syllables. *Research Reports on Ancient Maya Writing,* no. 14. Washington, D.C.: Center for Maya Research.

1988   Blood Symbolism in Maya Iconography. In *Maya Iconography,* edited by Elizabeth P. Benson and Gillett G. Griffin, pp. 175–221. Princeton: Princeton University Press.

1992   Hieroglyphs and Archaeology at Copán. *Ancient Mesoamerica* 3(1):169–184.

Stuart, David, and Stephen Houston

1994   *Classic Maya Place-Names.* Studies in Pre-Columbian Art and Archaeology 33. Washington, D.C.: Dumbarton Oaks.

Stuart, George

1989   Introduction: The Hieroglyphic Record of Chichén Itzá and Its Neighbors. *Research Reports on Ancient Maya Writing,* no. 23. Washington, D.C.: Center for Maya Research.

1997   The Royal Crypts of Copán. *National Geographic* 192(6):68–93.

Sugiyama, Saburo

1989   Burials Dedicated to the Old Temple of Quetzalcoatl at Teotihuacan. *American Antiquity* 54(1):85–106.

1992   Rulership, Warfare, and Human Sacrifice at the Ciudadela: An Iconographic Study of Feathered Serpent Representations. In *Art, Ideology, and the City of Teotihuacan,* edited by Janet Catherine Berlo, pp. 205–230. Washington, D.C.: Dumbarton Oaks.

1993   Worldview Materialized in Teotihuacán, Mexico. *Latin American Antiquity* 4(2):103–129.

Sullivan, Thelma D.

1976   The Mask of Itztlacoliuhqui. *Actas del XLI Congreso Internacional de Americanistas,* vol. 2, pp. 252–262. Mexico City: Instituto Nacional de Antropología e Historia.

Tarn, Nathaniel, and Martin Prechtel

1986   Constant Inconstancy: The Feminine Principle in Atiteco Mythology. In *Symbol and Meaning beyond the Closed Community: Essays in Mesoamerican Ideas,* edited by Gary H. Gossen, pp. 173–184. Studies in Culture and Society, vol. 1. Albany: Institute for Mesoamerican Studies, State University of New York at Albany.

Tate, Carolyn E.

1986   *The Language of Symbols in the Ritual Environment of Yaxchilan, Chiapas, Mexico.* Ph.D. diss., University of Texas at Austin. Ann Arbor: University Microfilms International.

1989   The Use of Astronomy in Political Statements at Yaxchilan, Mexico. In *World Archaeoastronomy: Selected Papers from the Second Oxford International Conference on Archaeoastronomy,* edited by Anthony F. Aveni, pp. 416–429. Cambridge: Cambridge University Press.

1992   *Yaxchilan: The Design of a Maya Ceremonial City.* Austin: University of Texas Press.

Taube, Karl A.

1985   The Classic Maya Maize God: A Reappraisal. *Fifth Palenque Round Table, 1983,* vol. 7, edited by Merle Greene Robertson and Virginia M. Fields, pp. 171–181. San Francisco: Pre-Columbian Art Research Institute.

1986   The Teotihuacan Cave of Origin. *RES: Anthropology and Aesthetics* 12:51–82.

1987   A Representation of the Principal Bird Deity in the Paris Codex. *Research Reports on Ancient Maya Writing,* no. 6. Washington, D.C.: Center for Maya Research

1988a   A Prehispanic Maya Katun Wheel. *Journal of Anthropological Research* 44:183–203.

1988b   A Study of Classic Maya Scaffold Sacrifice. In *Maya Iconography,* edited by Elizabeth P. Benson and Gillett G. Griffin, pp. 331–351. Princeton: Princeton University Press.

1989a   Itzam Cab Ain: Caimans, Cosmology, and Calendrics in Postclassic Yucatan. *Research Reports on Ancient Maya Writing,* no. 26. Washington, D.C.: Center for Maya Research.

1989b Ritual Humor. In *Word and Image in Maya Culture,* edited by William F. Hanks and Don S. Rice, pp. 351–382. Salt Lake City: University of Utah Press.

1992a The Temple of Quetzalcoatl and the Cult of Sacred War at Teotihuacan. *RES: Anthropology and Aesthetics* 21:54–87.

1992b *The Major Gods of Ancient Yucatan.* Studies in Pre-Columbian Art and Archaeology 32. Washington, D.C.: Dumbarton Oaks.

1993 *Aztec and Maya Myths.* Austin: University of Texas Press.

1994 The Iconography of Toltec Period Chichén Itzá. *Hidden among the Hills: Maya Archaeology of the Northwest Yucatan Peninsula,* edited by Hanns J. Prem, pp. 213–246. Möckmül, Germany: Verlag Von Flemming.

Taube, Karl A., and Bonnie L. Bade

1991 An Appearance of Xiuhtecuhtli in the Dresden Venus Pages. *Research Reports on Ancient Maya Writing,* no. 35. Washington, D.C.: Center for Maya Research.

Taylor, Dicey

1992 Painted Ladies: Costumes for Women on Tepeu Ceramics. *The Maya Vase Book,* vol. 3, edited by Justin Kerr, pp. 513–525. New York: Kerr Associates.

Tedlock, Barbara

1983 Quichean Time Philosophy. In *Calendars in Mesoamerica and Peru: Native American Computations of Time,* edited by Anthony F. Aveni and Gordon Brotherston, pp. 59–72. Oxford: BAR International Series 174.

1985 Hawks, Meteorology, and Astronomy in Quiché-Maya Agriculture. *Archaeoastronomy: The Bulletin of the Center for Archaeoastronomy* 8:80–89.

1991 La dialéctica de la agronomía y astronomía maya-quiché. In *Arqueoastronomía y etnoastronomía en Mesoamérica,* edited by Johanna Broda, Stanislaw Iwaniszewski, and Lucrecia Maupomé, pp. 179–192. Mexico City: Universidad Nacional Autónoma de México.

1992a The Road of Light: Theory and Practice of Mayan Skywatching. In *The Sky and Mayan Literature,* edited by Anthony F. Aveni, pp. 18–43. Oxford: Oxford University Press.

1992b *Time and the Highland Maya.* Rev. ed. Albuquerque: University of New Mexico Press.

1994 Divinatory Narratives in a Quiché Codex. Paper presented at the Forty-third annual conference of the Center for Latin American Studies, University of Florida, Gainesville.

Tedlock, Dennis

1985 *Popol Vuh.* New York: Simon and Schuster.

1991 La siembra y el amanecer de todo el cielo-tierra: Astronomía en el *Popol Vuh.* In *Arqueoastronomía y etnoastronomía en Mesoamérica,* edited by Johanna Broda, Stanislaw Iwaniszewski, and Lucrecia Maupomé, pp. 168–178. Mexico City: Universidad Nacional Autónoma de México.

1992 Myth, Math, and the Problem of Correlation in Mayan Books. In *The Sky and Mayan Literature,* edited by Anthony F. Aveni, pp. 247–273. Oxford: Oxford University Press.

1995 Visions of the Maya Sky. Review Feature of *Maya Cosmos: Three Thousand Years on the Shaman's Path. Cambridge Archaeological Journal* 5(1): 118–120.

Teeple, John E.

1926 Maya Inscriptions: The Venus Calendar and Another Correlation. *American Anthropologist* 28:402–408.

1930 *Maya Astronomy.* Carnegie Institution of Washington pub. 403, Contributions to American Archaeology no. 2. Washington, D.C.: Carnegie Institution of Washington.

Tena, Rafael

1987 *El calendario mexica y la cronografía.* Mexico City: Instituto Nacional de Antropología e Historia, Serie Historia.

Thompson, Donald

1954 *Maya Paganism and Christianity: A History of the Fusion of Two Religions.* Middle American Research Institute pub. 19, pp. 1–36. New Orleans: Tulane University.

Thompson, J. Eric S.

1930 *Ethnology of the Mayas of Southern and Central British Honduras.* Anthropological Series 2. Chicago: Field Museum of Natural History.

1934 *Sky Bearers, Colors, and Directions in Maya and Mexican Religion.* Carnegie Institute of Washington pub. 436, Contributions to American Archaeology no. 10. Washington, D.C.: Carnegie Institution.

1939 *The Moon Goddess in Middle America.* Carnegie Institution of Washington pub. 509, Contributions to American Anthropology and History no. 29. Washington, D.C.: Carnegie Institution.

1960 *Maya Hieroglyphic Writing: An Introduction.* 3d ed. Norman: University of Oklahoma Press.

1962 *A Catalog of Maya Hieroglyphs.* Norman: University of Oklahoma Press.

1965 Maya Hieroglyphic Writing. In *Archaeology of Southern Mesoamerica,* part 2, edited by Gordon Willey, pp. 632–658. *Handbook of Middle American Indians,* vol. 3, Robert Wauchope, general editor. Austin: University of Texas Press.

1967 Maya Creation Myths (Part 2). *Estudios de Cultura Maya* 6:15–44.

1970a The Bacabs: Their Portraits and Glyphs. *Papers of the Peabody Museum of Archaeology and Ethnology, Harvard University,* vol. 61, part 5, no. 3. Cambridge: The Peabody Museum.

1970b *Maya History and Religion.* Norman: University of Oklahoma Press.

1972 *A Commentary on the Dresden Codex: A Maya Hieroglyphic Book.* Philadelphia: The American Philosophical Society.

1973 Maya Rulers of the Classic Period and the Divine Right of Kings. In *The Iconography of Middle American Sculpture,* pp. 52–71. New York: Metropolitan Museum of Art.

1974 Maya Astronomy. *Philosophical Transactions of the Royal Society of London, Annual* 276:83–98.

Torquemada, Fray Juan de

1943 *Monarquía Indiana.* 3 vols. 3d ed. Mexico City: Editorial Chávez Hayhoe.

Tozzer, Alfred M.

1941 Landa's "Relación de las Cosas de Yucatán": A Translation. *Papers of the Peabody Museum of Archaeology and Ethnology, Harvard University,* vol. 18. Cambridge: The Peabody Museum.

1957 *Chichén Itzá and Its Cenote of Sacrifice.* Memoirs of the Peabody Museum, Harvard University, vols. 11, 12. Cambridge: The Peabody Museum.

Tozzer, Alfred M., and Glover M. Allen

1910 Animal Figures in the Maya Codices. *Papers of the Peabody Museum of American Archaeology and Ethnology, Harvard University,* vol. 4, no. 3. Cambridge: The Peabody Museum.

Trenary, Carlos

1987–1988 Universal Meteor Metaphors and Their Occurrence in Mesoamerican Astronomy. *Archaeoastronomy: The Bulletin of the Center for Archaeoastronomy* 10:9–11.

Tuckerman, Bryant

1964 *Planetary, Lunar, and Solar Positions A.D. 2 to A.D. 1649.* Memoirs of the American Philosophical Society 59. Philadelphia: The American Philosophical Society.

Upton, Edward K. L.

1977 The Leonids Were Dead, They Said. *Griffith Observer* (May):2–9.

Urton, Gary

1981 *At the Crossroads of the Earth and Sky: An Andean Cosmology.* Austin: University of Texas Press.

Valdés, Juan Antonio, Federico Fahsen, and Héctor Escobedo

1994 *Obras maestras del Museo de Tikal.* Guatemala City: Instituto de Antropología e Historia de Guatemala.

Villacorta, J. Antonio, and Carlos A. Villacorta

1977 *Códices mayas.* 2d ed. Guatemala City: Tipografía Nacional.

Villa Rojas, Alfonso

1945 *The Maya of East Central Quintana Roo.* Carnegie Institution of Washington, pub. 559. Washington, D.C.: Carnegie Institution of Washington.

1969 The Mayas of Yucatan. In *Ethnology,* part 1, edited by Evon Z. Vogt, pp. 244–275. *Handbook of Middle American Indians,* vol. 7, Robert Wauchope, general editor. Austin: University of Texas Press.

1988 The Concepts of Space and Time among the Contemporary Maya. In *Time and Reality in the Thought of the Maya,* Appendix A, pp. 113–159. Norman: University of Oklahoma Press.

1990 *Etnografía Tzeltal de Chiapas: Modalidades de una cosmovisión prehispánica.* Mexico City: Gobierno del Estado de Chiapas and Miguel Angel Porrúa.

Vivó Escoto, Jorge A.

1964 Weather and Climate of Mexico and Central America. In *Natural Environments and Early Cultures,* edited by Robert C. West, pp. 187–216. *Handbook of Middle American Indians,* vol. 1, Robert Wauchope, general editor. Austin: University of Texas Press.

Vogt, Evon

1964 Ancient Maya and Contemporary Tzotzil Cosmology: A Comment on Some Methodological Problems. *American Antiquity* 30:192–195.

1969 *Zinacantán: A Maya Community in the Highlands of Chiapas.* Cambridge: Harvard University Press.

1976 *Tortillas for the Gods: A Symbolic Analysis of Zinacanteco Rituals.* Cambridge: Harvard University Press.

1990 *The Zinacantecos of Mexico: A Modern Maya Way of Life.* 2d ed. Orlando: Holt, Rinehart and Winston.

1997 Zinacanteco Astronomy. *Mexicon* 19(6):110–116.

Vogt, Evon, and Catherine C. Vogt

1980 Pre-Columbian Mayan and Mexican Symbols in Zinacanteco Ritual. In *La antropología americanista en la actualidad: Homenaje a Raphael Girard,* vol. 1, pp. 499–524. Mexico City: Editores Mexicanos Unidos.

Watanabe, John M.

1983 In the World of the Sun: A Cognitive Model of Mayan Cosmology. *Man* 18:710–728.

1992 *Maya Saints and Souls in a Changing World.* Austin: University of Texas Press.

Whittaker, Arabelle, and Viola Warkentin

1965 *Chol Texts on the Supernatural.* Summer Institute of Linguistics Publications in Linguistics and Related Fields, no. 13. Norman: University of Oklahoma.

Whittaker, Gordon

1986 The Mexican Names of Three Venus Gods in the Dresden Codex. *Mexicon* 8(3):56–59.

Willson, Robert W.

1924 Astronomical Notes in the Maya Codices. *Papers of the Peabody Museum of American Archaeology and Ethnology, Harvard University,* vol. 6, no 3. Cambridge: The Peabody Museum.

Wisdom, Charles

1940 *The Chorti Indians of Guatemala.* Chicago: University of Chicago Press.

Wren, Linnea H.

1991 The Great Ball Court Stone from Chichén Itzá. In *Sixth Palenque Round Table, 1986,* edited by Merle Greene Robertson and Virginia M. Fields, pp. 51–58. Norman: University of Oklahoma Press.

1996 Ball Game Imagery at Chichén Itzá. Paper presented at Fourth Annual Maya Symposium, Brevard Community College, Cocoa, Florida.

Yasugi, Yoshiho, and Kenji Saito

1991 Glyph Y of the Maya Supplemental Series. *Research Reports on Ancient Maya Writing,* no. 34. Washington, D.C.: Center for Maya Research.

INDEX

PLATES

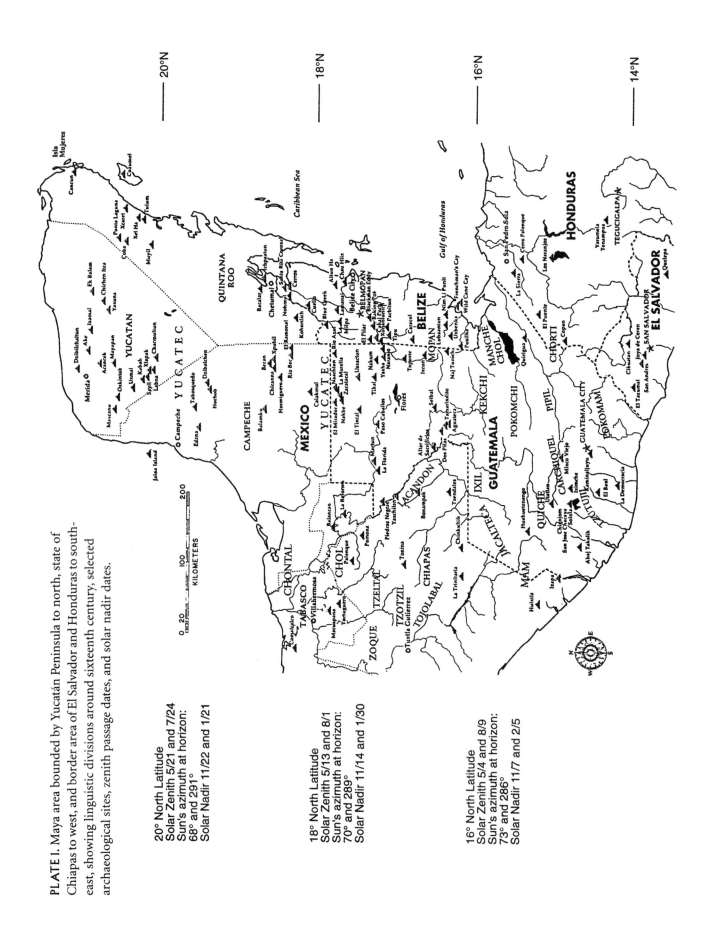

PLATE 1. Maya area bounded by Yucatán Peninsula to north, state of Chiapas to west, and border area of El Salvador and Honduras to south-east, showing linguistic divisions around sixteenth century, selected archaeological sites, zenith passage dates, and solar nadir dates.

20° North Latitude
Solar Zenith 5/21 and 7/24
Sun's azimuth at horizon:
68° and 291°
Solar Nadir 11/22 and 1/21

18° North Latitude
Solar Zenith 5/13 and 8/1
Sun's azimuth at horizon:
70° and 289°
Solar Nadir 11/14 and 1/30

16° North Latitude
Solar Zenith 5/4 and 8/9
Sun's azimuth at horizon:
73° and 286°
Solar Nadir 11/7 and 2/5

PLATE 2. Jadeite celt known as Leyden Plaque (originally from Tikal) depicts ruler known as Moon Zero Bird, who stands on bound prisoner and holds serpent bar bearing God K and Sun God; Initial Series date of 8.14.3.1.12 1 Eb 0 Yaxkin dates to September 14, 320, in Julian calendar (Rands 1965, fig. 46).

PLATE 3 A-B. Postclassic Dresden Codex eclipse table depicting solar-eclipse symbols (52b, 54b), solar-eclipse symbols with aged Sun God (55a, 56a), lunar eclipse with dead Moon Goddess (53b), Venus serpent devouring Sun (56b, 57b), skeletal Venus god (53a), and Venus as eclipse monster (58b); only last interval and cumulative total before picture noted in diagram; brackets indicate correction to recorded number, and parentheses signal an effaced number that has been reconstructed (Dresden Codex 51–58; after Villacorta and Villacorta 1977).

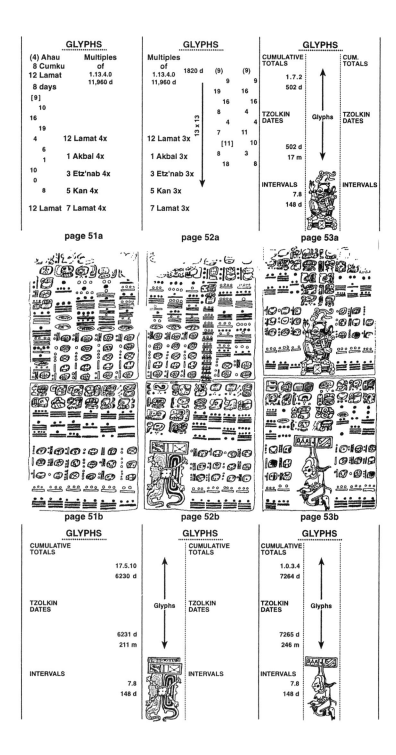

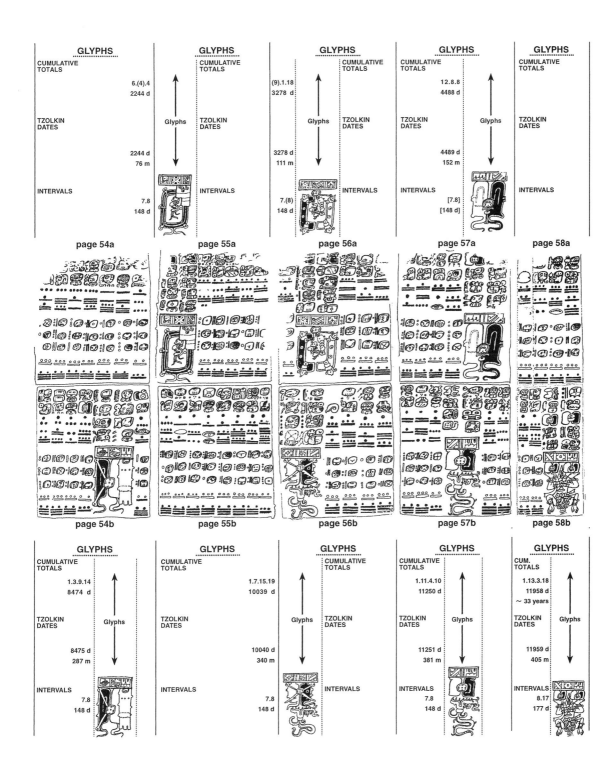

GLYPHS

CUMULATIVE TOTALS

6.(4).4
2244 d

TZOLKIN DATES

2244 d
76 m

INTERVALS

7.8
148 d

page 54a

GLYPHS

CUMULATIVE TOTALS

Glyphs

TZOLKIN DATES

INTERVALS

page 55a

GLYPHS

CUMULATIVE TOTALS

(9).1.18
3278 d

Glyphs

TZOLKIN DATES

3278 d
111 m

INTERVALS

7.(8)
148 d

page 56a

GLYPHS

CUMULATIVE TOTALS

12.8.8
4488 d

TZOLKIN DATES

Glyphs

4489 d
152 m

INTERVALS

[7.8]
[148 d]

page 57a

GLYPHS

CUMULATIVE TOTALS

TZOLKIN DATES

Glyphs

INTERVALS

page 58a

page 54b

page 55b

page 56b

page 57b

page 58b

GLYPHS

CUMULATIVE TOTALS

1.3.9.14
8474 d

TZOLKIN DATES

Glyphs

8475 d
287 m

INTERVALS

7.8
148 d

GLYPHS

CUMULATIVE TOTALS

1.7.15.19
10039 d

Glyphs

TZOLKIN DATES

10040 d
340 m

INTERVALS

7.8
148 d

GLYPHS

CUMULATIVE TOTALS

1.11.4.10
11250 d

TZOLKIN DATES

Glyphs

11251 d
381 m

INTERVALS

7.8
148 d

GLYPHS

CUM. TOTALS

1.13.3.18
11958 d
~ 33 years

TZOLKIN DATES

Glyphs

11959 d
405 m

INTERVALS

8.17
177 d

PLATE 4. Water-lily Jaguar faces death god who is decapitating himself (Late Classic codex-style vase; photo © Justin Kerr 1980, K1230).

PLATE 7. Late Classic assembly of seven gods, with God L as Morning Star facing lunar Jaguar War God with planetary gods; Sun God with skeletal snake headdress brings up rear; note restoration has obliterated Kin glyph visible in Coe 1973, no. 49 (Vase of Seven Gods; photo © Justin Kerr 1985, K2796).

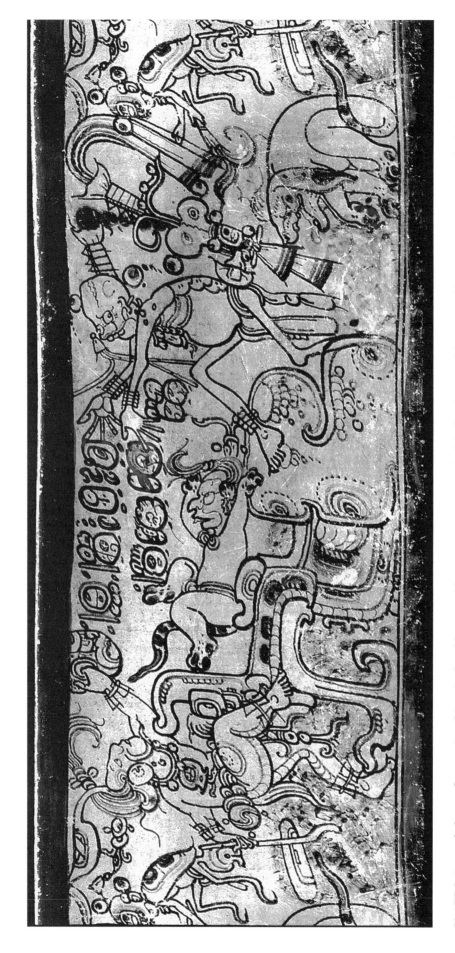

PLATE 8. Jaguar baby conflates traits of Sun God and lunar god known as Jaguar War God, indicating possible image of lunar conjunction; inscribed date of 12 Kan 12 Kayab may refer to new Moon on January 23, 627, in Julian Calendar (Late Classic codex-style vase from Metropolitan Museum; photo © Justin Kerr 1973, K521).

PLATE 9. *Left:* God L kneels in submission to enthroned Sun God with lunar rabbit hiding behind Sun God's knee, possibly referring to lunar conjunction on March 21, 700 (Julian). *Right:* God L stripped of his regalia, unclothed and gesturing in submission to lunar rabbit, who holds owl hat marked with glyph 13 Sky (Regal Rabbit Vase; photo © Justin Kerr 1980, K1398).

PLATE 10. Pacal's apotheosis as God K when Jupiter was at its first stationary point in August 683; he "entered the road" near stellar tree or cross in region of skeletal snake (Scorpius); Quadripartite God located at base of star cross in Sagittarius marks southernmost point on ecliptic in winter branch of Milky Way (Sarcophagus Lid, Temple of Inscriptions at Palenque; Robertson 1985a, fig. 73; copyright Merle Greene Robertson, 1976).

PLATE II. *On right*: At time of his heir designation, youthful Chan Bahlum stands on shell housing God K, who holds sprouting maize that embodies young ruler; *on left*: subsequently Chan Bahlum appears fully mature at time of accession, facing mature maize plant that symbolizes Northern Cross aligned with doorway of Temple of Foliated Cross at time of accession in January A.D. 684 (Palenque; Robertson 1991, fig. 153; copyright Merle Greene Robertson, 1976).

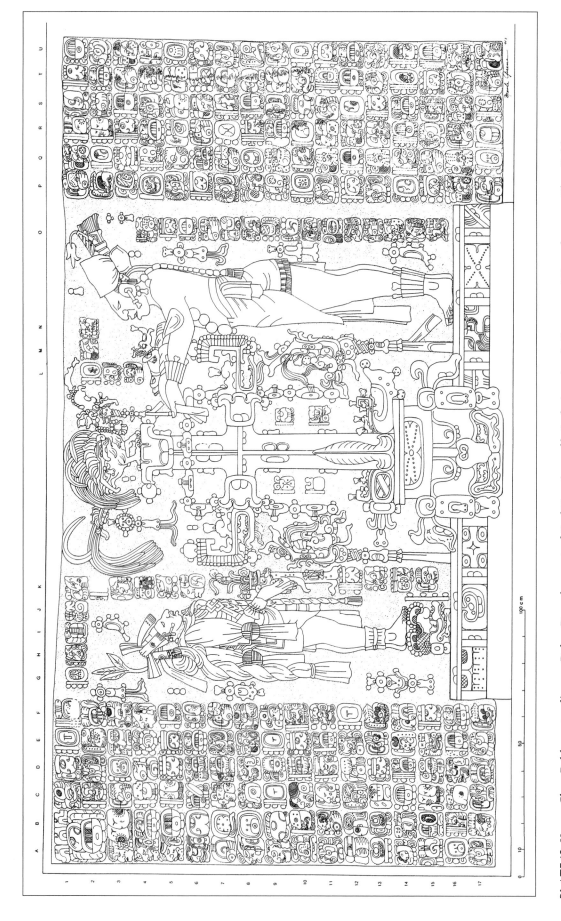

PLATE 12. Young Chan Bahlum standing on Bolon Dzacab aspect of God K at time of heir designation in June A.D. 641, and mature Chan Bahlum appears at forty years of age at time of accession in A.D. 684; they face Southern Cross aligned with doorway of Temple of Cross at time of heir designation (Palenque; Robertson 1991, fig. 9; copyright Merle Greene Robertson, 1976).

PLATE 13. Apotheosis of Chan Bahlum on October 31, 705 (Julian), correlates with time when Jupiter departed from its second stationary point; Lady Ahpo Hel holds manikin of God K, probably symbolizing Moon and Jupiter in conjunction on that date (Temple XIV, Palenque; Robertson 1991, fig. 176; copyright Merle Greene Robertson, 1976).

PLATE 14. Teotihuacán-style Tlaloc carrying atlatl, probably representing warrior cult linked with Venus (North Group, Palenque; photo by author, courtesy of I.N.A.H.).

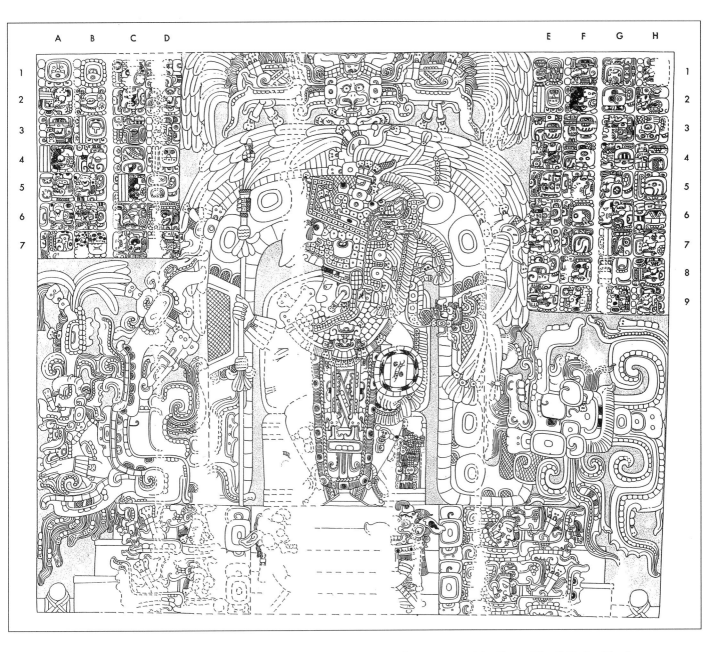

PLATE 15. God K carried in jaws of front head of Cosmic Monster arching over Yaxkin Chaan K'awil (Ruler B) of Tikal; rear head bears an image of God C; inscription opens with Lahuntun ending date (9.15.10.0.0 3 Ahau 3 Mol) in A.D. 741 that approximates Jupiter's first stationary point, when Jupiter (God K) was approaching summer branch of Milky Way symbolized by front head of Cosmic Monster (Lintel 3, Temple IV, Tikal; Jones 1977, fig. 11; reproduced by permission of the University of Pennsylvania Museum).

PLATE 16. Yaxkin Chaan K'awil (Ruler B), with his God K manikin scepter and Jaguar War God protector, on relief that bears dates coinciding with retrograde periods of both Jupiter and Saturn and star-war event timed by Jupiter's departure from its second stationary point (Lintel 2, Temple IV, Tikal; Jones 1977, fig. 12; reproduced by permission of the University of Pennsylvania Museum).

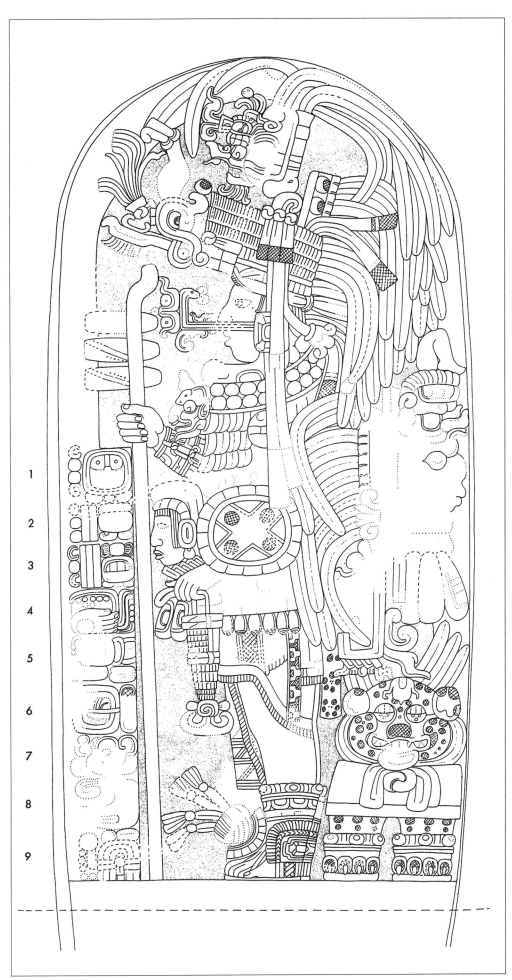

PLATE 17. Yaxkin Chaan K'awil (Ruler B) in stellar aspect, wearing headdress crowned by God K at time of Jupiter's first stationary point on May 3, A.D. 751 (Tikal Stela 20; Jones 1977, fig. 15; reproduced by permission of the University of Pennsylvania Museum).

PLATE 18*a*–*b*. Five symbols of Venus as "big eye" and detail of same symbolize fiveness of Venus, from Five-Story Palace designated as Structure 5D-52 at Tikal (photos by author, courtesy of I.D.A.E.).

PLATE 19. Classic period bench representing assembly of gods that include: *top*, moon deity with lunar crescent and rabbit, anthropomorphic deity with deer ear (Mars?); *bottom*, Venus as scorpion-man, cross-eyed Sun God (Las Sepulturas bench excavated by Pennsylvania State University Project at Copán; photos by E. C. Krupp, Griffith Observatory).

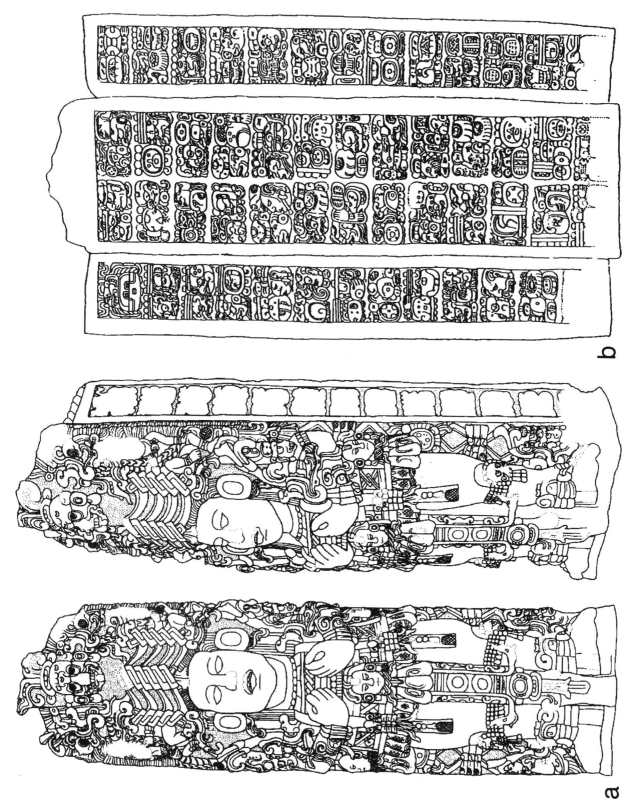

PLATE 20. Late Classic Copán Stela A showing ruler with Sun God emerging from serpent heads at his feet and from double-headed serpent bar in his arms. Dates to A.D. 1/30/731 with Initial Period inscription of 9.19.19.8.0 7 Ahau 18 Cumku (after drawings by Anne S. Dowd, courtesy of the Instituto Hondureño de Antropología e Historia, and Linda Schele).

PLATE 21. Bearded serpents with fer-de-lance body markings seem to be Milky Way serpents held by Sun God who wears skeletal snake headdress alluding to Scorpius and Sun's position at onset of dry season; turtle figure alludes to Orion at opposite side of Milky Way (relief-carved vessel from National Museum of American Indian; photo © Justin Kerr 1985, K2776).

PLATE 22. Venus temple showing five Venus glyphs expressing "fiveness" of Venus (Nunnery, Uxmal; photo by author).